Lecture Notes in Computer Science 8128

Commenced Publication in 1973
Founding and Former Series Editors:
Gerhard Goos, Juris Hartmanis, and Jan van Leeuwen

Alfredo Cuzzocrea   Christian Kittl
Dimitris E. Simos   Edgar Weippl   Lida Xu (Eds.)

Security Engineering and Intelligence Informatics

CD-ARES 2013 Workshops: MoCrySEn and SeCIHD
Regensburg, Germany, September 2-6, 2013
Proceedings

 Springer

Volume Editors

Alfredo Cuzzocrea
ICAR-CNR
and University of Calabria
Rende Cosenza, Italy
E-mail: cuzzocrea@si.deis.unical.it

Christian Kittl
Evolaris Next Level
Graz, Austria
E-mail: christian.kittl@evolaris.net

Dimitris E. Simos
SBA Research
Vienna, Austria
E-mail: dsimos@sba-research.org

Edgar Weippl
Vienna University of Technology
and SBA Research
Vienna, Austria
E-mail: edgar.weippl@tuwien.ac.at

Lida Xu
Old Dominion University
Norfolk, VA, USA
E-mail: lxu@odu.edu

ISSN 0302-9743
ISBN 978-3-642-40587-7
DOI 10.1007/978-3-642-40588-4
Springer Heidelberg New York Dordrecht London

e-ISSN 1611-3349
e-ISBN 978-3-642-40588-4

Library of Congress Control Number: 2013946088

CR Subject Classification (1998): C.2, H.2-4, I.2, K.4.4, K.6.5, D.4.6

LNCS Sublibrary: SL 3 – Information Systems and Application, incl. Internet/Web and HCI

Typesetting: Camera-ready by author, data conversion by Scientific Publishing Services, Chennai, India

Printed on acid-free paper

Springer is part of Springer Science+Business Media (www.springer.com)

Preface

The Cross-Domain Conference and Workshop CD-ARES is focused on the holistic and scientific view of applications in the domain of information systems.

The idea of organizing cross-domain scientific events originated from a concept presented by the IFIP President Leon Strous at the IFIP 2010 World Computer Congress in Brisbane, which was seconded by many IFIP delegates in further discussions. Therefore CD-ARES concentrates on the many aspects of information systems in bridging the gap between the research results in computer science and the many application fields.

This effort leads us to the consideration of the various important issues of massive information sharing and data integration, which will (in our opinion) dominate scientific work and discussions in the area of information systems in the second decade of this century.

The organizers of this event who are engaged within IFIP in the area of Enterprise Information Systems (WG 8.9), Business Information Systems (WG 8.4) and Information Technology Applications (TC 5) very much welcome the typical cross-domain aspect of this event.

The collocation with the SeCIHD 2013 Workshop was another possibility to discuss the most essential application factors. Special thanks to Professor Ilsun You for all his efforts in this special track, which was held this year for the third time.

Also, we are proud to announce the Special Session Human–Computer Interaction and Knowledge Discovery (HCI-KDD), which is organized in the context of CD-ARES 2013. The ultimate goal of the task force HCI-KDD is to combine the best of two worlds: human–computer interaction (HCI), with emphasis on human intelligence, and knowledge discovery from data (KDD), dealing with computational intelligence. The cross-domain integration and appraisal of different fields provide an atmosphere in which to foster different perspectives and opinions. Special thanks to Dr. Andreas Holzinger, who made it possible to bring together researchers from diverse areas in a highly inter-disciplinary manner, to stimulate fresh ideas and encourage multi-disciplinary work.

Today, e-business depends heavily on the major cryptographic breakthroughs of almost 40 years ago. Without asymmetric cryptography, hardly any form of business transaction would be as easy to secure as it is today. We are thus very happy to have an excellent section on applied cryptography in this book.

The special track on modern cryptography and security engineering (MoCrySEn) attracted 30 submissions of which the Program Committee selected 16 for publication in the workshop proceedings. The accepted papers dealt with symmetric-key cryptography, public-key cryptography, algorithmic cryptanalysis, software and hardware implementation of cryptographic algorithms, database encryption and interaction between cryptographic theory and implementation issues.

The papers presented at this conference were selected after extensive reviews by the Program Committee with the essential help of associated reviewers.

We would like to thank all the Program Committee members and the reviewers who made great effort contributing their time, knowledge, and expertise and foremost the authors for their contributions.

September 2013

Alfredo Cuzzocrea
Christian Kittl
Dimitris E. Simos
Edgar Weippl
Lida Xu

Organization

Second International Workshop on Modern Cryptography and Security Engineering (MoCrySEn 2013)

Program Chair

Dimitris E. Simos   SBA Research, Austria

Program Co-chairs

Nicolas Sendrier   INRIA, France
Edgar Weippl   SBA Research, Austria

Program Committee

Athanasios Angelakis	Leiden University, The Netherlands, Universite Bordeaux 1, France
Paulo Barreto	Universidade de Sao Paulo, Brazil
Christina Boura	Technical University of Denmark, Denmark
Pierre-Louis Cayrel	Université Jean Monnet, France
Matthieu Finiasz	CryptoExperts, France
Stefan Heyse	Ruhr-Universitat Bochum, Germany
Aleksandar Hudic	SBA Research, Austria
Peter Kieseberg	SBA Research, Austria
Christos Koukouvinos	National Technical University of Athens, Greece
Spyros Magliveras	Florida Atlantic University, USA
Ayoub Otmani	University of Rouen, France
Christiane Peters	Technical University of Denmark, Denmark
Ludovic Perret	Université Pierre et Marie Curie 06 / INRIA, France
Maria Naya-Plasencia	INRIA, France
Jean-Pierre Tillich	INRIA, France
Zlatko Varbanov	Veliko Tarnovo University, Bulgaria
Amr Youssef	Concordia Institute for Information System Engineering, Canada

External Reviewers

Adrian Dabrowski   SBA Research, Austria
Gregory Landais   INRIA, France

Georg Merzdovnik   SBA Research, Austria
Rafael Misoczki   INRIA, France
Maciej Piec   SBA Research, Austria
Sebastian Schrittwieser   SBA Research, Austria

Third International Workshop on Security and Cognitive Informatics for Homeland Defense (SeCIHD 2013)

General Chairs

Ilsun You   Korean Bible University, Republic of Korea
Fang-Yie Leu   Tunghai University, Taiwan

General Vice-Chairs

Francesco Palmieri   Second University of Naples, Italy
Ugo Fiore   University of Naples "Federico II", Italy

Program Co-chairs

Aniello Castiglione   University of Salerno, Italy
Marek Ogiela   AGH University of Science and Technology,
                                 Poland

Program Committee

Giovanni Acampora   TU/e, Eindhoven University of Technology,
                                 The Netherlands
Christina Alcaraz   University of Malaga, Spain
Joonsang Baek   Khalifa University of Science, Technology &
                                 Research, UAE
Francesca Bosco   United Nations Interregional Crime and Justice
                                 Research Institute, Italy
Antonio Colella   Italian Army, Italy
Gabriele Costa   University of Genoa, Italy
Christian Czosseck   Estonian Business School, Estonia
Bonaventura D'Alessio   Carabinieri Specialist Mobile Unit Command,
                                 Italy
Massimo Ficco   Second University of Naples, Italy
Alessandro Gigante   European Space Agency, ESRIN Health, Safety
                                 and Security Officer, Italy
Tomasz Hachaj   Pedagogical University in Krakow, Poland
Leonardo Impagliazzo   Engineering Signalling Busines Unit,
                                 AnsaldoSTS, Italy

Shinsaku Kiyomoto	KDDI R&D Laboratories Inc., Japan
Giovanni Motta	Google Inc., USA
Jordi Nin	Universitat Politènica de Catalunya, Barcelona, Spain
Kyung-Hyune Rhee	Pukyong National University, Republic of Korea
Sergio Ricciardi	Universitat Politènica de Catalunya, Barcelona, Spain
Alessandra Sala	Bell Labs, Ireland
Germán Santos-Boada	Universitat Politècnica de Catalunya, Barcelona, Spain
Athanasios V. Vasilakos	University of Western Macedonia, Greece
Shuichiro Yamamoto	Nagoya University, Japan
Toshihiro Yamauchi	Okayama University, Japan
Siu Ming Yiu	The University of Hong Kong, SAR China
Wei Yu	Towson University, USA

Table of Contents

Security Engineering

Software and Hardware Implementation of Cryptographic Algorithms

Database Encryption

Interaction between Cryptographic Theory and Implementation Issues

3rd International Workshop on Security and Cognitive Informatics for Homeland Defense (SeCIHD 2013)

Cyber Security and Dependability

Network Security and Privacy

Multimedia Technology for Homeland Defense

Differential Cryptanalysis and Boomerang Cryptanalysis of LBlock

Jiageng Chen and Atsuko Miyaji*

School of Information Science,
Japan Advanced Institute of Science and Technology,
1-1 Asahidai, Nomi, Ishikawa 923-1292, Japan
{jg-chen,miyaji}@jaist.ac.jp

Abstract. LBlock is a lightweight block cipher proposed in ACNS 2011. It has a 64-bit block size and 80-bit key size which is the typical parameter setting accepted by most of the recent proposed lightweight block ciphers. It has fast hardware implementation efficiency and it still remains rather secure considering the recent results and the security margin it provides. In this paper, we investigate the differential behavior of the cipher in detail and propose (multiple) differential attack and boomerang attack against it. We are able to construct 15-round multiple differential paths which can lead to 17-round attack with complexity as low as $2^{67.52}$. Also 16-round boomerang distinguisher can be build which leads us to 18-round boomerang (rectangle) attack with complexity $2^{70.8473}$. These are the best differential attacks for LBlock in the single key scenario, which helps us understanding the differential behavior of the cipher.

Keywords: LBlock, ultra lightweight block cipher, multiple differential cryptanalysis, boomerang attack, ladder switch.

1 Introduction

Lightweight block ciphers have attracted much of the research attention due to the cheap computational cost in both hardware and software implementation which is suitable for resource-restricted devices such as RFID tag and so on. The security margin they provide, although reduced compared with the traditional block ciphers, is considered to be reasonable given the cost of information being protected. Generally speaking, key size is usually chosen to be 80 bits, while the popular versions of block size are 32, 48 and 64 bits. The first famous block cipher that was widely considered to be lightweight is PRESENT [4]. After that, many lightweight block ciphers have been proposed such as KATAN/KTANTAN family [5], TWINE [11], PRINTcipher [7], LBlock [13] and so on. Compared with AES which was selected through competitions, lightweight block ciphers get started only recently, and the lack of enough cryptanalysis will prevent those ciphers from being adopted by the industrial world. In this paper, we target

* This study is partly supported by Grant-in-Aid for Scientific Research (A) (21240001).

one of the recent proposed cipher LBlock, which being as a recent cipher, still needs a lot of security analysis to be performed on it before we are able to have confidence in its security.

In ACNS2011, LBlock [13] was proposed as a lightweight block which targets fast hardware and software implementation. It is designed using a 32-round Feistel structure with a 64-bit block size and 80-bit key size. In the original paper, the authors gave several attacks against LBlock, among which the impossible differential attack is the best one that can attack 20 rounds. This record was later improved by [8] and [6] to 21 and 22 rounds using the same impossible differential technique. For differential related attack, the original paper only mentioned the active S-Boxes from which it drew the conclusion that no useful differential path is available for more than 15 rounds. Later in [9], the authors first analyze the differential behavior in detail and proposed 12 and 13 rounds attack which improved the bound in the original paper.

In this paper, we further investigate the differential behavior of LBlock and proposed two attacks in single key scenario. The first one is differential attack by using single differential and multiple differentials. We take advantage of the multiple differential statistic model [3] to evaluate the success probability and the time complexity. 15-round single differential path with probability $2^{-61.2351}$ is found and 17-round attack can be performed based on it. $2^{74.23}$ is the best cost we can achieve by using one single path. We then take advantage of the fact that there exists a set of such efficient differential paths, which can be used to further reduce the time complexity and the data complexity in multiple differential statistic model. As a result, we can break 17-round cipher with best time complexity of $2^{67.5211}$. Secondly, we apply the boomerang attack to further investigate the short differential behavior of LBlock instead of a long one. We are able to build a 16-round boomerang distinguisher including an eight-round upper trail and an eight-round lower trail. This cannot be achieved without applying the ladder switch technique in the middle of the switching point, which can help us to escape three active S-Boxes. The key recovery phase follows the rectangle procedure which can as a result break 18 rounds of the cipher with complexity $2^{70.8437}$. The results are summarized in Table 1.

This paper is organized as follows. Section 2 describes the specification of LBlock. In Section 3, we describe the differnetial and multiple differential attack against 17-round LBlock. Section 4 demonstrates the boomerang attack against

Table 1. Single key scenario attacks against LBlock

# Round	Methods	Time Complexity	Data Complexity	Source
18	Integral Attack	$2^{62.3}$	$2^{62.3}$	[13]
22	Impossible Differential Attack	$2^{79.28}$	2^{58}	[6]
20	Impossible Differential Attack	2^{63}	$2^{72.7}$	[13]
21	Impossible Differential Attack	$2^{62.5}$	$2^{73.7}$	[8]
13	Differential Attack	$2^{42.08}$	$2^{42.08}$	[9]
17	Differential Attack	$2^{67.52}$	$2^{59.75}$	This paper
18	Boomerang Attack	$2^{70.84}$	$2^{63.27}$	This paper

18-round LBlock with path searching and ladder switch techniques included. Finally Section 5 concludes the paper.

2   LBlock

LBlock consists of a 32-round variant Feistel network with 64-bit block size and 80-bit key size. The encryption algorithm works as follows:

1. For $i = 2, 3, ..., 33$, do $X_i = F(X_{i-1}, K_{i-1}) \oplus (X_{i-2} <<< 8)$
2. Ciphertext is $C = X_{32}||X_{33}$

Here round function F contains a S-Box layer and a diffusion layer which are denoted as S and P.

$$F : \{0,1\}^{32} \times \{0,1\}^{32} \to \{0,1\}^{32}, (X, K_i) \to P(S(X \oplus K_i))$$

There are eight 4-bit S-Boxes for each of the nibbles. Suppose the input and output of the S-boxes are Y and Z. The S layer can be denoted as

$$Y = Y_7||Y_6||Y_5||Y_4||Y_3||Y_2||Y_1||Y_0 \to Z = Z_7||Z_6||Z_5||Z_4||Z_3||Z_2||Z_1||Z_0$$

$$Z_7 = s_7(Y_7), Z_6 = s_6(Y_6), Z_5 = s_5(Y_5), Z_4 = s_4(Y_4)$$

$$Z_3 = s_3(Y_3), Z_2 = s_2(Y_2), Z_1 = s_1(Y_1), Z_0 = s_0(Y_0)$$

For diffusion layer with the input and output of the layer being Z and U, it can be denoted as:

$$U_7 = Z_6, U_6 = Z_4, U_5 = Z_7, U_4 = Z_5, U_3 = Z_2, U_2 = Z_0, U_1 = Z_3, U_0 = Z_1$$

All the above details are concluded in Figure 1. Key schedule part is not used during the analysis so we omit the description here. Please refer to [13] for the details.

3   (Multiple) Differential Attack against 17-round LBlock

3.1   Statistical Framework of Multiple Differential Attack

[10] addressed the success probability of linear and differential attack, and this result has been used since then widely. However, the normal distribution approximation for the differential attack is not accurate, which is later improved by [12] with a hybrid distribution. When dealing with multiple differentials with different probabilities, the counter itself does no longer follows a binomial distribution, so a new formula should be used to address the success probability in this scenario. A solution is given in [3], which proposed a general framework by expressing the distribution of counters in terms of a hybrid distribution which include Kullback-Leibler divergence and a Poisson distribution. Please refer to the Appendix for the success probability of the multiple-differential cryptanalysis.

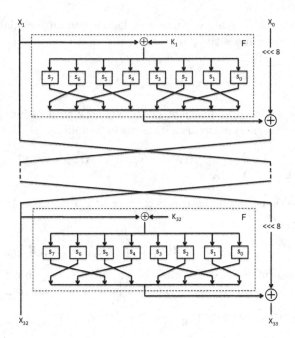

Fig. 1. LBlock

We will evaluate the complexity based on this statistical model for the multiple differential attack in this paper.

The differential set described in [3] gives a direct way to connect with the statistical model they proposed. While it is very obvious to understand from the statistical model's point of view, the restriction of the differential set is too strong which limits the practical attack. Actually, the typical way of doing differential cryptanalysis by using a hash table can easily avoid this restriction as described in [12]. In [3], only differential sets satisfied specific conditions can be used. In [12], many to one differential paths are used. Actually, by using following algorithm, we can avoid double counting which gives us a wide number of options, and the only concern is how to optimize the result by using these multiple differential paths. In this paper, due to the property of differential paths, we found out that one to many differential paths can be used to achieve a relatively good result, which is exactly the opposite to the pattern in [12].

3.2   Notations and Configurations for the (Multiple)Differential Cryptanalysis

The key recovery algorithm was pretty well summarized by [12], and we summarize it in the Appendix. By applying the algorithm, differential path will not be double counted and statistical model of [3] can still be used. Related notations and configurations that are required for the further reading are described as follows.

- m: the block size of the block cipher.
- k: the key size of the block cipher.
- $|\Delta_0|$: the number of differentials.
- p_i: the probability of the differential with input difference Δ_0^i.
- N_p: the number of plain texts bits involved in the active S-boxes in the first round for all differentials.
- N_c: the number of cipher texts bits involved in the non-active S-boxes in the last round deriving from Δ_r.
- N_s: the number of samples pairs required of the cryptanalysis.
- β: the filtering probability for the ciphertext pairs.
- p_f : the filtering probability for the ciphertext pairs according to active S-boxes, $p_f = \beta \cdot 2^{N_C}$.
- l: the size of the candidate key list is 2^l.
- n_k: the number of guessed sub key bits in the last $R - r$ rounds.
- N: Data complexity is 2^N.
- $2^{N_{st}}$ structures are constructed.

3.3   Strategies for Finding Differentials for LBlock

Iterative differential paths are widely used in differential cryptanalysis such as DES and PRESENT, etc. However, we found that iterative differential path will not lead to better result here for LBlock. We search the iterative differential path and found that due to the 4-bit block permutation, the iterative path is rather well controlled, this could be seen from Table 2, which shows the active S-Boxes in each round.

Table 2. AS for Iterative Differential Paths

	2R	3R	4R	5R	6R	7R	8R
AS	9	10	16	20	18	20	18

Thus we switch to non-iterative differential path. Due to the property that the internal bits will be permutated only between the S-boxes, we could consider first to run a truncated differential search which treats all the input to the 4-bit S-box as 0 or 1 for r round characteristic. By running the truncated differential search, first we confirm the result of smallest active S-Boxes in each round of [13], especially, for round 14 and 15 we are interested in, the number of the smallest active S-boxes is 30 and 32. Given the smallest differential probability is 2^{-2} for each S-Box, 15 rounds seems to be the maximum bound for differential attack. Then for each of the structure candidate which has achieved the best number of active S-boxes, we derive the specific differentials by using branch and bound algorithm. All the differential paths with probability greater than 2^{-72} are considered, which is mostly decided based on the experimental experience. It shows that further smaller probability paths will not make any improvements on the total probability any more. We list the truncated differential path with

Table 3. Best 15-round Differential Paths

Truncated Diff	Best Diff	$log_2(Prob)$	#Diff with $Prob < 2^{-64}$
0000000011010000 ↓ 0001111000100100	0000000011030000, 0003222000200100 0000000011030000, 0003422000200900 0000000011030000, 0003522000200900 0000000011030000, 0003622000200100 0000000011030000, 000b222000200100 0000000011030000, 000b422000200900 0000000011030000, 000b522000200900 0000000011030000, 000b622000200100	-61.2351	1290

the largest probability along with the corresponding concrete differential paths we found in Table 3.

We can derive from Table 3 that for the truncated form (0000000011010000 → 00011110001001000), differential paths with the largest probability $2^{-61.2351}$ can be found. All the other truncated forms we found have a smaller probability than this one and we omit the description here. We also list the number of specific differential paths with probability larger than the average value 2^{-64}, which forms a structure that we can take advantage in multiple differential cryptanalysis.

3.4 Key Recovery Attack on 17-round LBlock Using Single Differential Path

For reaching 16 and 17 rounds, given the output truncated differential $\Delta_{15} = (00011110, 00100100)$, we can get $(00011110, 00100100) \to (11011011, 00011110) \to (1\star\star11111, 11011011)$, where $\star$ denotes the differential status that can not be decided. In round 17, except the nibble for S-Boxes S_2 and S_5, differentials are involved for other S-Boxes, and thus we target $6 \times 4 = 24$ bits of k_{17}. In round 16, active S-boxes involve S_1, S_2, S_3 and S_4, thus we target $4 \times 4 = 16$ bits of k_{16}. In total, $n_k = 40$ bits. $N_p = 4 \times 3 = 12$ bits according to the truncated input differential. Assuming the data complexity is 2^N, then the number of structure can be derived as $N_{st} = N - 12$, and each structure contains 2^{12} plaintexts. At the beginning, we have in total $2^{N-12} \cdot 2^{2 \times 12 - 1} = 2^{N+11}$ pairs to consider. Inserting the ciphertexts into the hash table according to the nibble e_{17}^2 and e_{17}^5 will take complexity 2^N and also the same amount of memory cost. For each structure, we have 2^{23} pairs to consider at the beginning, and after inserting into the hash table, we have left $2^{23-8} = 2^{15}$ pairs. By studying the propagation of the differentials in the last two rounds, we can further filter out the pairs whose differentials are definitely impossible. Since $e_{17}^0 = e_{16}^0 = e_{15}^{10}, e_{17}^3 = e_{16}^3 = e_{15}^{13}, e_{17}^{11} = e_{16}^{13} = e_{15}^5, e_{17}^{12} = e_{16}^{14} = e_{15}^6$, we have another 16-bit filter which leaves us with $2^{15-16} = 2^{-1}$ pairs. Also we have $e_{17}^1 = e_{16}^1 = S_4(e_{15}^3)$, $e_{17}^4 = e_{16}^4 = S_2(e_{15}^5)$, $e_{17}^6 = e_{16}^6 = S_3(e_{15}^4)$, $e_{17}^7 = e_{16}^7 = S_1(e_{15}^6)$, $e_{17}^9 = e_{15}^3 \oplus S_4(e_{15}^{13})$ and $e_{17}^{10} = e_{15}^4 \oplus S_7(e_{15}^{10})$. Thus for the nibbles $1, 4, 6, 7, 9, 10$ in the ciphertexts, some of the differentials are not possible according to the differential tables. We compute the average probability that an output difference can be achieved given an input difference for $S_0, ..., S_7$, and we find that $P_{S_0} \approx \cdots \approx P_{S_7} \approx 0.4267$. Thus after this filtering, there remains $2^{-1} \cdot (0.4267)^6 = 2^{-8.37}$ pairs for each structure and $2^{N-12-8.37} = 2^{N-20.37}$ pairs in total. For each of these pairs, we check whether the corresponding input differences are legal or not. This step will take computational cost $2^{N-20.37}$ and $2^{N-20.37-12} = 2^{N-32.37}$ pairs remain. Then for each of these pairs, we guess the 40-bit subkey in round 16 and 17 to decrypt the ciphertext pairs to see if it will result in the corresponding Δ_{15}. This step takes time $2^{N-32.37} \times 2^{40} = 2^{N+7.63}$. Given the size of the key candidate list 2^l, searching the candidate key list will take time 2^{40+l}. As a result, the total complexity is $2^N + 2^{N-20.37} + 2^{N+7.63} + 2^{40+l}$.

Now we have two parameters involved in the computational complexity, namely, data complexity 2^N and the size of key candidate list 2^l. Here we want the success probability to be as high as 90%. This standard can be measured by the following formula which can be derived from the framework described in Section 3.1, and also involves only the above two parameters while others are fixed.

$$2^N = -4 \cdot \frac{ln(2\sqrt{\pi}2^l2^{-n_k})}{|\Delta_0|D(p_*||p)}$$

According to Table 3, we choose the best probability path with $p_* = 2^{-61.2351}$. Then we can derive the relations between l, N and the computational complexity as shown in Table 4.

Table 4. Size of the key candidate list, data complexity and computational cost with success probability 90%

l	34	35	36	37	38
N	63.8294	63.4343	62.8884	61.9996	59.2471
$log(Time)$	74.2300	75.0917	76.0321	77.0087	78.0007

From Table 4, we can see that if data complexity is the bottleneck, then we can choose $l = 38, N = 59.2471$ which gives the complexity cost 2^{78}. On the other hand, if the computational cost is the bottleneck, we can set $l = 34, N = 63.8294$ which gives the computational cost $2^{74.23}$. Both cases can lead to the break of the 17-round LBlock.

3.5   Key Recovery Attack Using Multiple Differential Paths

Let's investigate the situation where multiple differential paths are used. Table 3 demonstrates the best probability differential paths along with the largest amount of differential paths. So we investigate this truncated differential category to search of the best multiple differential path. Through the experiment, we found that the best computational complexity and the best data complexity can be both derived by using the 188 best differential paths. If we choose $l = 38$, the data complexity can be as small as $N = 53.4064$ while the computational cost is $2^{78.0}$. If we decrease the size of the key candidate list to $l = 24$, the computational complexity can be reduced $2^{67.5211}$ and the corresponding data complexity will increase to $N = 59.7523$. Of course, balance can always be achieved in between. As a result, we can see that multiple differential paths are effective for LBlock cipher. Due to the space limit, we omit these 188 paths here.

4 Boomerang Attack against 18-round LBlock

The great idea of boomerang attack is to use two short efficient differentials instead of one long differential, hope to do better than the traditional differential attack. The boomerang distinguisher is usually denoted by a cascade cipher $E = E_1 \cdot E_0$, where E_0 has a differential $\alpha \to \beta$ with probability p and E_1 has a differential $\gamma \to \delta$ with probability q. Basic boomerang attack is an adaptive chosen ciphertext attack, and later it was extended to rectangle attack which is a non-adaptive chosen plaintext attack. The attacker encrypts many plaintext pairs with input difference α, and collects quartets which satisfy $P_1 \oplus P_2 = P_3 \oplus P_4 = \alpha$ and $C_1 \oplus C_3 = C_2 \oplus C_4 = \delta$. Three conditions should be satisfied in this scenario, namely, $E_0(P_1) \oplus E_0(P_2) = E_0(P_3) \oplus E_0(P_4) = \beta$, $E_0(P_1) \oplus E_0(P_3) = \gamma$ and $C_1 \oplus C_3 = C_2 \oplus C_4 = \delta$. Figure 2 shows the boomerang structure with E_0, E_1, plaintext quartets, ciphertext quartets and the corresponding differentials. It was noted that the probability of p and q can be increased by exploiting multiple differentials as $\hat{p} = \sqrt{\sum_\beta Pr^2[\alpha \to \beta]}$ and $\hat{q} = \sqrt{\sum_\gamma Pr^2[\gamma \to \delta]}$. It is well known that if $\hat{p}\hat{q} > 2^{-n/2}$, cipher can be distinguished from a random permutation. The number of right quartets can be computed by $N^2 \cdot 2^{-n}\hat{p}^2\hat{q}^2$ given N number of plaintext pairs. In this paper, the boomerang attack used is indeed the rectangle

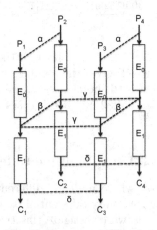

Fig. 2. Boomerang Structure

attack but we keep the name boomerang attack for simplicity. For the details of the boomerang attack and related rectangle attack, please refer to paper [1].

4.1 Differential Path

We search the differential path of E_0 using the similar strategies with the multiple differential analysis. First we find the best truncated differential path, and then search the concrete path using the branch-and-bound algorithm. The best truncated E_0 trail is shown in Table 5. Each line of L and R represents the differential states after the current round. Round 0 denotes the initial value before the first round.

Table 5. 8-round E_0 Differential Path   Table 6. 8-round E_1 Differential Path

Round	AS	L	R
0	0	00001010	11100000
1	2	10000000	00001010
2	3	00001000	10000000
3	4	00000000	00001000
4	4	00100000	00000000
5	5	00010000	00100000
6	6	11000000	00010000
7	8	11100000	11000000
8	11	10110011	11100000

Round	AS	L	R
0	0	00011100	10111010
1	3	10100000	00011100
2	5	01000000	10100000
3	6	00000010	01000000
4	7	00000000	00000010
5	7	00001000	00000000
6	8	00000010	00001000
7	9	00100001	00000010
8	11	00011100	00100001

After searching all the concrete paths, it gives 128 paths with probability 2^{-22}, 1312 paths with probability 2^{-23}, 4672 paths with probability 2^{-24}, 7040 paths with probability 2^{-25} and 3840 paths with probability 2^{-26}. As a result, we can compute $\hat{p}$ as follows:

$$\hat{p} = \sqrt{128 \cdot 2^{-22} + 1312 \cdot 2^{-23} + 4672 \cdot 2^{-24} + 7040 \cdot 2^{-25} + 3840 \cdot 2^{-26}} = 2^{-17.1151}$$

For the lower trail E_1, obviously we need to do better than $2^{-17.1151}$ in order to launch an effective attack. We investigate the concrete paths within the same truncated structure first, and then try to gather paths with multiple input differences which will generate the same output difference. After evaluate the total probabilities, we generate several candidates with the best probability close to each other. We pick the 8-round trail in Table 6 for the attack use. The reason that we choose this trail is related to the ladder switch technique descirbed in the following section.

E_1 truncated structure gives us the best probability:

$$\hat{q} = \sqrt{16 \cdot 2^{-22} + 96 \cdot 2^{-23} + 192 \cdot 2^{-24}} = 2^{-19.1498}$$

4.2   Ladder Switch

Unfortunately, the probability of $\hat{p}$ and $\hat{q}$ is still too small for us to build an effective boomerang distinguisher, which requires $\hat{p}\hat{q} > 2^{-32}$. Here we consider to apply ladder switch to increase the path probability, which was first proposed in [2] to attack the full-round AES in the related-key model. The basic idea of ladder switch is that instead of dividing the cipher into separate rounds, we can go further to divide based on concrete operations as long as they are parallel independent with each other. If the final round of E_0 or the first round of E_1 has many active S-boxes, we can consider to switch the active S-boxes to the upper or lower trail where the S-Boxes are non-active, so that we don't need to pay the corresponding probabilities. Figure 3 shows the switch given the last

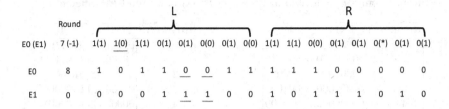

Fig. 3. Ladder switch

round of E_0 and the first round of E_1. If no switch is performed, we would pay for three active S-Boxes in the last round for E_0, and also three active S-Boxes for the first round of E_1. For nibble 10 and 11 which are active in E_1, we can set the switching point after the S-Box operation, since this two nibbles in the last round of E_0 are not active which can help us save two active S-Boxes. Due to the property of Feistel structure, we can go back one round and derive the differential path of L for E_1. The 14th nibble in round 8 of E_0 is active while it is not active for round -1 of E_1. Thus we can set the switching point of this nibble right after the S-Box operation in round 8 of E_0 instead of the last nibble after round 8. For the differential of R in round -1 of E_1, there is one $*$ which we can not determine, but that does not affect other differential value since they all can be computed independently. In total this helps us saving three S-Boxes, one from E_0 and two from E_1. Thus the boomerang distinguisher probability is now increased to:

$$\hat{p}\hat{q} = 2^{-15.1151-15.1498} = 2^{-30.2149} > 2^{-32}$$

Namely, we are able to observe one right quartet in $2^{62.2649}$ plaintext pairs.

4.3   Key Recovery Procedure

We target to attack 18 rounds LBlock using 16 rounds boomerang distinguisher. Before E_0 we add one round E_b and after E_1 we add another rounds E_f.

Thus the structure of the cipher can be described as $E = E_f \cdot E_1 \cdot E_0 \cdot E_b$. The structure of the chosen plaintexts is organized as $2^{31.2649}$ structures with 2^{32} plaintexts each. In each structure, we can form 2^{31} pairs that follow the input difference α. In total, we have $2^{62.2649}$ pairs which gives us $2^{124.5298}$ quartets. The number of right quartets can be computed by $(2^{31} \cdot 2^{31.2649})^2 \cdot 2^{-64} \cdot (\hat{p}\hat{q})^2 = 1$. The key recovery algorithm works as follows:

1. Generate $2^{31.2649}$ structures of 2^{32} plaintexts each. Ask for the encryption of these plaintexts and get the corresponding ciphertexts. $2^{63.2649}$ data complexity is required and $2^{63.2649}$ time complexity is required for 18-round LBlock encryption.
2. Generate $2^{12+12} = 2^{24}$ counters for the 24-bit subkeys in E_b and E_f. This costs time complexity 2^{24} memory access.
3. Insert all the $2^{63.2649}$ ciphertexts into a hash table indexed by 32 bit of non active bits of the output truncated differential $0001110000100001(\delta) \rightarrow$ 0001110011001110. This gives us 2^{32} entries with $2^{31.2649}$ ciphertexts in each of the entries. There are total $2^{61.5298}$ pairs for each of the entry. Some of them can be filtered according to the differential pattern. There are 5 nibbles where the differentials are fixed according to the differential δ which can be filtered with probability $2^{-5 \times 4}$. There are another 3 nibbles pass through S-boxes, and thus the filter probability become $(0.4267)^3$ considering the average probabilities. So in total there remains $2^{61.5298} \cdot 2^{-5 \times 4} \cdot (0.4267)^3 = 2^{37.8437}$ pairs. Note that we don't need to search all the $2^{61.5298}$ pairs to generate the remaining $2^{37.8437}$ pairs. We can apply the meet in the middle approach to first sort the ciphertexts in each of the entry, and then for every ciphertexts in the entry, add the corresponding differential and check if it equals the ciphertext in the sorted table or not. The cost for each of the entry is slightly more than $2^{31.2649}$ which is not the dominant cost. In order to check if the ciphertext difference is the expected difference, we need to do $2^{32} \cdot 2^{37.8437} = 2^{69.8437}$ memory access.
4. For each of the remaining ciphertext pairs, we try to test the plaintext pairs (P_1, P_2) and (P_3, P_4) to see if they can form a quartet candidate. According to the pattern in E_b, we have $1110000010101110 \rightarrow 0000101011100000(\alpha)$. Thus, 5 nibbles should be exact the same as the input difference α, and 3 nibbles go through S-Boxes. This provides filtering probability $2^{-5 \times 4} \times 2^{-2.678 \times 3}$. Also the proper plaintext pairs should be in the same structure, which takes probability 2^{-32}. As a result, the number of quartet candidates is $2^{69.8437} \times 2^{69.8437} \times 2^{-32 \times 2} \times (2^{-5 \times 4})^2 \times 0.4267^{3 \times 2} = 2^{28.3152}$. By using the same meet in the middle approach as in step 3, we can perform the check ((P_1, P_2) and (P_3, P_4)) with $2^{70.8437}$ memory accesses.
5. For each of the candidate quartets, we encrypt E_b and decrypt E_f using the 24-bit subkey, if the differential matches with the characteristic, add one to the corresponding subkey counter. This step takes time complexity $2^{28.3152} \times 2^{24} = 2^{52.3152}$.

Given the average probability for the each S-Box $\frac{1}{16 \times 0.4267} = 2^{-2.77}$, the probability for the wrong key to be suggested by a quartet is $\left(2^{-2.77 \times 3} \times 2^{-2.77 \times 3}\right)^2 =$

$2^{-33.24}$. Then the number of subkeys suggested by one quartet is $2^{24} \times 2^{-33.24} = 2^{-9.24}$. Thus all candidate quartets suggest $2^{28.3152} \times 2^{-9.24} = 2^{19.0751}$, which means the expected number of times a wrong key gets suggested is $2^{-4.93}$. This will guarantee us to eliminate almost all the wrong keys. It is clear that step 4 dominants the time complexity which requires $2^{70.8437}$ memory access, and the data complexity is $2^{63.2649}$.

5   Conclusion

In this paper, we take a deep investigation of the differential behavior of lightweight block cipher LBlock, which was proposed recently. We are able to build 15-round non-iterative differential path based on which 17-round (multiple) differential attack is available with complexity $2^{67.52}$. Then we investigate the security of the cipher against boomerang attack. Firstly based on the optimized searching and ladder switch technique, we build a 16 rounds boomerang distinguisher which contains two 8 sub trails E_0 and E_1. Then 18-round attack is successfully applied with complexity $2^{70.8437}$. Our result doesn't pose any threat to the full round LBlock, but help us understanding the differential behavior and its strength under differential attack and boomerang attack.

References

1. Biham, E., Dunkelman, O., Keller, N.: The Rectangle Attack - Rectangling the Serpent. In: Pfitzmann, B. (ed.) EUROCRYPT 2001. LNCS, vol. 2045, pp. 340–357. Springer, Heidelberg (2001)
2. Biryukov, A., Khovratovich, D.: Related-key cryptanalysis of the full AES-192 and AES-256. In: Matsui, M. (ed.) ASIACRYPT 2009. LNCS, vol. 5912, pp. 1–18. Springer, Heidelberg (2009)
3. Blondeau, C., Gérard, B.: Multiple differential cryptanalysis: Theory and practice. In: Joux, A. (ed.) FSE 2011. LNCS, vol. 6733, pp. 35–54. Springer, Heidelberg (2011)
4. Bogdanov, A., Knudsen, L.R., Leander, G., Paar, C., Poschmann, A., Robshaw, M.J.B., Seurin, Y., Vikkelsoe, C.: PRESENT: An Ultra-Lightweight Block Cipher. In: Paillier, P., Verbauwhede, I. (eds.) CHES 2007. LNCS, vol. 4727, pp. 450–466. Springer, Heidelberg (2007)
5. De Cannière, C., Dunkelman, O., Knežević, M.: KATAN and KTANTAN — A Family of Small and Efficient Hardware-Oriented Block Ciphers. In: Clavier, C., Gaj, K. (eds.) CHES 2009. LNCS, vol. 5747, pp. 272–288. Springer, Heidelberg (2009)
6. Karakoç, F., Demirci, H., Harmancı, A.E.: Impossible differential cryptanalysis of reduced-round LBlock. In: Askoxylakis, I., Pöhls, H.C., Posegga, J. (eds.) WISTP 2012. LNCS, vol. 7322, pp. 179–188. Springer, Heidelberg (2012)
7. Knudsen, L., Leander, G., Poschmann, A., Robshaw, M.J.B.: PRINTCIPHER: A Block Cipher for IC-Printing. In: Mangard, S., Standaert, F.-X. (eds.) CHES 2010. LNCS, vol. 6225, pp. 16–32. Springer, Heidelberg (2010)

8. Liu, Y., Gu, D., Liu, Z., Li, W.: Impossible differential attacks on reduced-round LBlock. In: Ryan, M.D., Smyth, B., Wang, G. (eds.) ISPEC 2012. LNCS, vol. 7232, pp. 97–108. Springer, Heidelberg (2012)
9. Minier, M., Naya-Plasencia, M.: Some preliminary studies on the differential behavior of te lightweight block cipher LBlock. In: ECRYPT Workshop on Lightweight Cryptography, pp. 35–48 (2011)
10. Selçuk, A.A., Biçak, A.: On probability of success in linear and differential cryptanalysis. In: Cimato, S., Galdi, C., Persiano, G. (eds.) SCN 2002. LNCS, vol. 2576, pp. 174–185. Springer, Heidelberg (2003)
11. Suzaki, T., Minematsu, K., Morioka, S., Kobayashi, E.: TWINE: A lightweight block cipher for multiple platforms. In: Knudsen, L.R., Wu, H. (eds.) SAC 2012. LNCS, vol. 7707, pp. 339–354. Springer, Heidelberg (2013)
12. Wang, M., Sun, Y., Tischhauser, E., Preneel, B.: A model for structure attacks, with applications to present and serpent. In: Canteaut, A. (ed.) FSE 2012. LNCS, vol. 7549, pp. 49–68. Springer, Heidelberg (2012)
13. Wu, W., Zhang, L.: LBlock: A lightweight block cipher. In: Lopez, J., Tsudik, G. (eds.) ACNS 2011. LNCS, vol. 6715, pp. 327–344. Springer, Heidelberg (2011)

Appendix

Probability Evaluation for (Multiple)Differential Cryptanalysis

The success probability of the multiple-differential attack can be derived as follows [3]. First let $p_* = \frac{\sum_{i,j} p_*^{(i,j)}}{|\Delta_0|}$ and $p = \frac{|\Delta|}{2^m|\Delta_0|}$. p_* denotes the average probability of the multiple differentials and p denote average probability for the wrong key case. Define $G_*(\tau) = G(\tau, p_*), G(\tau) = G(\tau, p)$, which is defined as follows:

$$G(\tau, q) = \begin{cases} G_-(\tau, q), & \text{if } \tau < q - 3\sqrt{q/N_s} \\ 1 - G_+(\tau, q), & \text{if } \tau > q + 3\sqrt{q/N_s} \\ G_p(\tau, q), & \text{otherwise} \end{cases}$$

$$G_- = e^{-N_s D(\tau||q)} \cdot \left[\frac{q\sqrt{1-\tau}}{(q-\tau)\sqrt{2\pi\tau N_s}} + \frac{1}{\sqrt{8\pi\tau N_s}}\right]$$

$$G_+ = e^{-N_s D(\tau||q)} \cdot \left[\frac{(1-q)\sqrt{\tau}}{(\tau-q)\sqrt{2\pi N_s(1-\tau)}} + \frac{1}{\sqrt{8\pi\tau N_s}}\right]$$

$$D(\tau||q) = \tau ln(\frac{\tau}{q}) + (1-\tau)ln(\frac{1-\tau}{1-q}) \text{ (Kullback-Leibler divergence)}$$

And the success probability is defined as follows:

$$P_S \approx 1 - G_*[G^{-1}(1 - \frac{l-1}{2^{n_k} - 2}) - 1/N_s], \ G^{-1}(y) = min\{x|G(x) \geq y\}$$

Note that the above formula is also effective in the case of single differential path where $|\Delta| = |\Delta_0| = |\Delta_r| = 1$.

Table 7. Key recovery attack in the (multiple)differential cryptanalysis scenario

---

Input: 2^N plaintexts and corresponding ciphertexts.

Output: Master secret key K.

1: For each structure $2^{N_{st}}$, do

  1-1. Insert all the ciphertexts into a hash table indexed by N_c bits of the non-active S-boxes in the last round.

  1-2. For each entry with the same N_c bit values, check if the input difference is any one of the total $|\Delta_0|$ possible input differences. If a pair satisfies one input difference, then go to the next step.

  1-3. For the pairs in each entry, check whether the output differences of active S -boxes in the last round can be caused by the input difference of the previous rounds according to the differential distribution table. Go to the next step if passes.

  1-4. Guess n_k bits sub keys to decrypt the ciphertext pairs to round r and check if the obtained output difference at round r is equal to Δ_r. If so, add one to the corresponding counter. 2: Choose the list of l best key candidates from the counters.

3: For each key candidate in the list, do:

  3-1. Test if the corresponding key is the correct master key or not.

Key Recovery Procedure for (Multiple)Differential Cryptanalysis

Key recovery procedure is summarized in Table 7.

Complexity

Denote by $T_{1-1}, T_{1-2}, T_{1-3}, T_{1-4}$ and T_3 the time complexity for step 1-1, 1-2, 1-3, 1-4 and step 3. We ignore step 2 since it is negligible compared with other steps. At beginning, we have in total $2^{N_{st}+2N_p-1}$ pairs to consider. In step 1-1, we store all the ciphertext in the memory, so we need $2^{N_{st}+N_p}$ memory accesses, as well as the same amount of memory storage. After 1-1, we filter out some pairs and we are left with $2^{N_{st}} \cdot 2^{2N_p-1} \cdot 2^{-N_c}$ pairs. The rest of the process is summarized in the following Table 8.

For step 3, the complexity can be simply computed as $T_3 = 2^l \cdot 2^{k-n_k}$. And $T_{1-1} + T_{1-2} + T_{1-3} + T_{1-4} + T_3$ will be the total complexity.

Table 8. Complexity evaluation for step 1

-	complexity	remaining pairs after the step
Beginning	-	$2^{N_{st}} \cdot 2^{2N_p - 1}$
1-1	$T_a = 2^{N_{st} + N_p}$	$2^{N_{st}} \cdot 2^{2N_p - N_c - 1}$
1-2	$T_b = 2^{N_{st} + 2N_p - N_c - 1}$	$|\Delta_0| \cdot 2^{N_{st} + N_p - N_c - 1}$
1-3	$T_c = |\Delta_0| \cdot 2^{N_{st} + N_p - N_c - 1}$	$|\Delta_0| \cdot 2^{N_{st} + N_p - N_c - 1} \cdot p_f$
1-4	$T_d = |\Delta_0| \cdot 2^{N_{st} + N_p - N_c - 1} \cdot p_f \cdot 2^{n_k}$	-

Information-Theoretically Secure Aggregate Authentication Code:
Model, Bounds, and Constructions

Asato Kubai, Junji Shikata, and Yohei Watanabe

Graduate School of Environment and Information Sciences,
Yokohama National University, Japan
{shikata,watanabe-yohei-xs}@ynu.ac.jp

Abstract. In authentication schemes where many users send authenticated messages to a receiver, it is desirable to aggregate them into a single short authenticated message in order to reduce communication complexity. In this paper, in order to realize such a mechanism in information-theoretic security setting, we first propose aggregate authentication codes. Specifically, we newly propose a model and a security definition for aggregate authentication codes. We also show tight lower bounds on sizes of entities' secret-keys and (aggregated) tags. Furthermore, we present optimal (i.e., most efficient) constructions for aggregate authentication codes.

1 Introduction

1.1 Background

The security of most of present cryptographic systems is based on the assumption of difficulty of computationally hard problems such as the integer factoring problem or the discrete logarithm problem in finite fields or elliptic curves. However, taking into account recent rapid development of algorithms and computer technologies, such a system based on the assumption of difficulty of computationally hard problems might not maintain sufficient long-term security. In fact, it is known that quantum computers can easily solve the factoring and discrete logarithm problems. From these aspects, it is necessary and interesting to consider cryptographic techniques whose security does not depend on any computationally hard problems, especially for the long-term security.

Authentication is one of the fundamental and important functionalities in cryptography. Many papers in modern cryptography focus on constructing secure authentication schemes so that they are as efficient as possible, especially, in terms of communication complexity (e.g., size of authentication data including a MAC (message authentication code) or a digital signature sent via a public channel) and storage space (i.e., memory-size of users to keep secret-key data) in addition to time complexity (i.e., running time required for executing algorithms in the schemes). In authentication schemes where many users send authenticated

A. Cuzzocrea et al. (Eds.): CD-ARES 2013 Workshops, LNCS 8128, pp. 16–28, 2013.

messages to a receiver (e.g., see the *multisender authentication code* [4],[9]), it is desirable to aggregate them into a single short authenticated message, since communication complexity required can be reduced. In particular, this mechanism is useful in the applications in which data-size per transmission in a channel is restricted (e.g., wireless communication). To solve this problem, Boneh et al. [2] proposed the first *aggregate signature* scheme. Unlike *multi-signatures* (e.g., [10]) in which a set of users all sign the same message and the result is a single signature, this is a scheme for combining various signatures from different signers on different messages into a single short signature. Since Boneh et al. gave a formal definition of aggregate signatures in [2], various research on aggregate signatures has been done based on computational security: for instance, sequential aggregate signatures (e.g., [8],[7]) for certificate chains and certificateless aggregate signatures (e.g., [3]). We note that the first aggregate signature scheme [2] is restricted in the sense that only aggregation of distinct messages is allowed. For lifting the restriction, Bellare et al. [1] proposed *unrestricted aggregate signatures*. On the other hand, as these protocols mentioned above are specific to the public-key setting, Katz et al. [6] proposed the *aggregate message authentication code* (aggregate MAC for short) which is specific to the shared-key (secret-key) setting. The aggregate MAC is a useful tool for the problem of authenticated communication in a mobile ad-hoc network where communication is considered as a highly expensive resource.

To the best of our knowledge, there is no paper which reports on the study of information-theoretically secure aggregate authentication schemes. Therefore, in this paper we newly introduce and realize *aggregate authentication codes* (aggregate A-codes for short) with information-theoretic security.

1.2   Our Contribution

The authentication code (A-code for short) (e.g., see [12]) is one of the fundamental cryptographic primitives with information-theoretic security. In the model of the traditional A-code, a single sender transmits an authenticated message to a single receiver. In the scenario where there are many entities and they communicate each other, it is not practical to use the A-code for every possible pair of entities. In particular, in authentication schemes where many users send authenticated messages to a receiver, it is desirable to aggregate them into a single short authenticated message in order to reduce communication complexity. Therefore, we study information-theoretically secure aggregate A-codes. Specifically, our contribution is as follows.

- We propose a model and formalization of security for aggregate A-codes in information-theoretic security setting. In our model, aggregation of not only distinct messages but also same messages is possible, and in this sense our scheme is unrestricted;
- We also derive tight lower bounds on entities' memory-sizes and (aggregated) tags required for aggregate A-codes; and
- We present two kinds of constructions, generic and direct ones. Our generic construction of aggregate A-codes is very simple: aggregate A-codes can be

constructed from only traditional A-codes. Since the generic construction does not lead to an optimal construction of aggregate A-codes, we also propose a direct construction which is optimal (i.e., most efficient).

The rest of our paper is organized as follows. In Section 2, we propose a formal model and formalization of security for aggregate A-codes with information-theoretic security. In Section 3, we derive tight lower bounds on entities' memory-sizes and (aggregated) tags required for aggregate A-codes. Section 4 is devoted to present generic and direct constructions. Finally, in Section 5 we give concluding remarks of the paper.

Throughout this paper, we use the following notation. For any finite set $\mathcal{Z}$, let $\mathcal{P}(\mathcal{Z}) := \{Z \subset \mathcal{Z}\}$ be the family of all subsets of $\mathcal{Z}$. Also, for any finite set $\mathcal{Z}$ and any non-negative integer z, let $\mathcal{P}(\mathcal{Z}, z) := \{Z \subset \mathcal{Z} \mid |Z| \leq z\}$ be the family of all subsets of $\mathcal{Z}$ whose cardinality is less than or equal to z.

2   The Model and Security Definition

In this section, we introduce a model and a security definition of aggregate A-codes, based on those of aggregate MACs with computational security and those of traditional A-codes with information-theoretic security.

2.1   The Model

We show a model of aggregate A-codes. For simplicity, we assume that there is a trusted authority whose role is to generate and to distribute secret-keys of entities. We call this model the *trusted initializer model* as in [11]. In aggregate A-codes, there are $n + 2$ entities, n senders $T_1, T_2, \ldots, T_n$, a receiver R and a trusted initializer TI, where n is a positive integer. In this paper, we assume that the identity of each sender T_i is also denoted by T_i, and the receiver is honest in the model. Our model of aggregate A-codes is almost the same as that of aggregate MACs [6] except for considering the trusted initializer in our model. For simplicity, we consider a *one-time model* of aggregate A-codes, in which each sender is allowed to generate an authenticated message and aggregation is allowed to be executed at most only once.

Informally, an aggregate A-code is executed as follows. In the initial phase, TI generates secret-keys on behalf of T_i ($1 \leq i \leq n$) and the receiver R. After distributing these keys via secure channels, TI deletes them in his memory. Any set of senders participate in the protocol, and in this paper we call them *active senders* for convenience. Each active sender generates a tag (or an authenticator) by using his secret-key. These tags can be aggregated into a single short tag, which we call an *aggregated tag*, without any secret-key. After the aggregated tag is transmitted, the receiver can check the validity of the aggregated tag by using his verification-key.

Formally, we give a definition of aggregate A-codes as follows.

Definition 1 (Aggregate A-code). An *aggregate authentication code* (*aggregate A-code* for short) Π involves $n + 2$ entities, TI, $T_1, T_2, \ldots, T_n$ and R, and consists of a four-tuple of algorithms (*KGen, Auth$_i$, Agg, Vrfy*) with five spaces, $\mathcal{M}, \mathcal{A}, \mathcal{A}^*, \mathcal{E}_T$, and $\mathcal{E}_R$, where all of the above algorithms except *KGen* are deterministic and all of the above spaces are finite. In addition, Π is executed with four phases as follows.

0. **Notation.**
   - *Entities*: TI is a trusted initializer, T_i ($1 \leq i \leq n$) is a sender and R is a receiver. Let $\mathcal{T} := \{T_1, T_2, \ldots, T_n\}$ be the set of all senders, and let $\mathcal{S} := \{T_{i_1}, \ldots, T_{i_j}\} \in \mathcal{P}(\mathcal{T})$ be a set of active senders with $|\mathcal{S}| \geq 1$.
   - *Spaces*: $\mathcal{M}$ is a set of possible messages, $\mathcal{A}$ is a set of possible tags (or authenticators) generated by each $T_i \in \mathcal{S}$. For any $\mathcal{S} \in \mathcal{P}(\mathcal{T})$ with $l = |\mathcal{S}|$, let $\mathcal{M}^{(l)} := \bigcup_{j=1}^{l}(\mathcal{M} \times \mathcal{S})^j$ and $\mathcal{A}^{(l)} := \bigcup_{j=1}^{l}\mathcal{A}^j$. $\mathcal{A}^*$ is a set of possible aggregated tags. Also, $\mathcal{E}_i$ is a set of possible T_i's secret-keys and $\mathcal{E}_R$ is a set of possible verification-keys. For simplicity, we assume $\mathcal{E}_1 = \mathcal{E}_2 = \cdots = \mathcal{E}_n$.
   - Algorithms: *KGen* is a key generation algorithm which on input a security parameter 1^k, outputs each sender's secret-key and a receiver's verification-key. *Auth$_i$*: $\mathcal{M} \times \mathcal{E}_i \to \mathcal{A}$ is T_i's authentication algorithm. For every $1 \leq l \leq n$, *Agg$_l$*: $\mathcal{A}^{(l)} \to \mathcal{A}^*$ is an aggregation algorithm which compresses l tags into a single tag, and *Vrfy$_l$*: $\mathcal{M}^{(l)} \times \mathcal{A}^* \times \mathcal{E}_R \to \{true, false\}$ is a verification algorithm for l messages. In the following, we will briefly write *Agg* and *Vrfy* for *Agg$_l$* and *Vrfy$_l$*, respectively, if l is clear from the context.

1. **Key Generation and Distribution.** In the initial phase, by using *KGen* TI generates a secret-key $e_i \in \mathcal{E}_i$ for T_i ($i = 1, 2, \ldots, n$) and a verification-key $e_v \in \mathcal{E}_R$ for R. These keys are distributed to corresponding entities via secure channels. After distributing these keys, TI deletes them from his memory. And, T_i and R keep their keys secret, respectively.

2. **Authentication.** For a message $m_i \in \mathcal{M}$, each $T_i \in \mathcal{S}$ can compute a tag $tag_i = Auth_i(m_i, e_i) \in \mathcal{A}$ by using his secret-key e_i.

3. **Aggregation.** Let $M := ((m_{i_1}, T_{i_1}), \ldots, (m_{i_j}, T_{i_j}))$. Any user can compute an aggregated tag $tag = Agg(tag_{i_1}, \ldots, tag_{i_j})$ by using only tags. [1] Then, the user transmits (M, tag) to R via an insecure channel.

4. **Verification.** Suppose that R has received (M, tag) via an insecure channel. R checks the validity of tag by a verification-key e_v: if $Vrfy(M, tag, e_v) = true$, then R accepts (M, tag) as valid, and rejects it otherwise.

In the model of aggregate A-codes, the following correctness condition is required to hold: for all possible $m_i \in \mathcal{M}$, $e_i \in \mathcal{E}_i$ ($1 \leq i \leq n$), and $e_v \in \mathcal{E}_R$, if $tag_i = Auth_i(m_i, e_i)$ for each $T_i \in \mathcal{S}$ and $tag = Agg(tag_{i_1}, \ldots, tag_{i_j})$, it holds that

$$Vrfy(M, tag, e_v) = true.$$

---

[1] Not only any sender, but also anyone who does not have a secret-key can compute an aggregated tag, since this algorithm is executed without any secret-key. And also, in this model we represent multiple messages and tags as sequences for convenience, however, unlike [7], [8], our scheme is not sequential one (i.e., the order of messages and tags is not important).

The above requirement implies that any legal aggregated tag can be accepted without any error if entities correctly follow the specification of aggregate A-codes.

In addition, we formally define an *aggregation rate* which measures efficiency of compression for aggregated tags.

Definition 2 (Aggregation rate). Let Π be an aggregate A-code. An aggregation rate in Π is defined by

$$\gamma := \frac{\log |\mathcal{A}^*|}{\log |\mathcal{A}|}.$$

Note that it is natural to assume $|\mathcal{A}^*| \geq |\mathcal{A}|$, which implies $\gamma \geq 1$. On the other hand, considering the trivial aggregate A-code where the algorithm Agg_l is the identity mapping (i.e., an aggregated tag consists of concatenation of l multiple-tags) for any $1 \leq l \leq n$, we have $\gamma \leq l(\leq n)$. Therefore, for any $\mathcal{S} \in \mathcal{P}(\mathcal{T})$, it holds that

$$1 \leq \gamma \leq |\mathcal{S}| \ (\leq n).$$

An interesting case is $\gamma \ll |\mathcal{S}|$ even for large $\mathcal{S}$, and it is ideal when $\gamma \approx 1$ not depending on the size $|\mathcal{S}|$. In this paper, we will actually propose construction of aggregate A-codes which satisfies $\gamma = 1$ with having enough security (a formal security definition is given in the next subsection).

2.2   Security Definition

We formalize a security definition for aggregate A-codes. Let ω $(< n)$ be the maximum number of possible corrupted senders. For a set of corrupted senders (i.e., a colluding group) $W = \{T_{l_1}, T_{l_2}, \ldots, T_{l_j}\} \in \mathcal{P}(\mathcal{T}, \omega)$, $\mathcal{E}_W := \mathcal{E}_{l_1} \times \mathcal{E}_{l_2} \times \cdots \times \mathcal{E}_{l_j}$ denotes the set of possible secret-keys held by W.

In aggregate A-codes, we consider *impersonation attacks* and *substitution attacks*. The formalization of security notions for the above two kinds of attacks is given as follows.

Definition 3 (Security). Let Π be an aggregate A-code with an aggregation rate γ. For any set of active senders $\mathcal{S} \in \mathcal{P}(\mathcal{T})$ and any set of colluding groups $W \in \mathcal{P}(\mathcal{T}, \omega)$ such that $\mathcal{S} - W \neq \emptyset$, Π is said to be $(n, \omega, \epsilon, \gamma)$-*one-time secure*, if $\max(P_I, P_S) \leq \epsilon$, where P_I and P_S are defined as follows.

a) *Impersonation attacks.* The adversary who corrupts at most ω senders tries to generate a fraudulent pair of messages and aggregated tags (M, tag) such that (M, tag) is accepted by the receiver R. The success probability of this attack denoted by P_I is defined as follows: We define $P_I(\mathcal{S}, W)$ by

$$P_I(\mathcal{S}, W) = \max_{e_W \in \mathcal{E}_W} \max_{(M, tag)} \Pr(\mathit{Vrfy}(M, tag, e_v) = \mathit{true} \mid e_W).$$

The probability P_I is defined as $P_I := \max_{\mathcal{S}, W} P_I(\mathcal{S}, W)$.

b) *Substitution attacks.* Let $\mathcal{S} = \{T_{i_1}, \ldots, T_{i_j}\}$. The adversary corrupts at most ω senders, and after observing valid pairs of messages and tags generated by $\mathcal{S}$, $((m_{i_1}, tag_{i_1}), \ldots, (m_{i_j}, tag_{i_j}))$, the adversary tries to generate a fraudulent pair of messages and aggregated tags, (M', tag'), that has not been legally generated by $\mathcal{S}$ but will be accepted by the receiver R such that $(M, tag) \neq (M', tag')$, where $M = ((m_{i_1}, T_{i_1}), \ldots, (m_{i_j}, T_{i_j}))$ and tag is an aggregated tag of M. The success probability of this attack denoted by P_S is defined as follows: We define $P_S(\mathcal{S}, W)$ by

$$P_S(\mathcal{S}, W) = \max_{e_W \in \mathcal{E}_W} \max_{((m_{i_1}, T_{i_1}), \ldots, (m_{i_j}, T_{i_j}))} \max_{(M', tag') \neq (M, tag)}$$

$$\Pr(\mathit{Vrfy}(M', tag', e_v) = true \mid e_W, ((m_{i_1}, T_{i_1}, tag_{i_1}), \ldots, (m_{i_j}, T_{i_j}, tag_{i_j}))).$$

The probability P_S is defined as $P_S := \max_{\mathcal{S}, W} P_S(\mathcal{S}, W)$.

3 Lower Bounds

In this section, we derive lower bounds on success probabilities of attacks and memory-sizes required for $(n, \omega, \epsilon, \gamma)$-one-time secure aggregate A-codes. Let $\mathcal{MA}_i := \{(m_i, tag_i) \in \mathcal{M} \times \mathcal{A} \mid \mathit{Auth}_i(m_i, e_i) = tag_i \text{ for some } e_i \in \mathcal{E}_i\}$ be a set of possible pairs of messages and tags such that each element of the set can be generated by the sender T_i. And let $\mathcal{MA}^* := \{(m_{i_1}, \ldots, m_{i_j}, tag) \in \mathcal{M}^j \times \mathcal{A}^* \mid \mathit{Agg}(tag_{i_1}, \ldots, tag_{i_j}) = tag \wedge \mathit{Auth}_i(m_i, e_i) = tag_i \text{ for some } e_i \in \mathcal{E}_i (1 \leq i \leq j)\}$ be a set of possible pairs of messages and aggregated tags such that each element of the set can be generated by the senders $\mathcal{S} = \{T_{i_1}, T_{i_2}, \ldots, T_{i_j}\}$. Furthermore, let MA_i, MA^*, E_i, E_v, and E_W be random variables which take values in $\mathcal{MA}_i$, $\mathcal{MA}^*$, $\mathcal{E}_i$, $\mathcal{E}_R$, and $\mathcal{E}_W$, respectively. And also, let $(MA^*, \tilde{M}\tilde{A}^*)$ be a joint random variable which takes values in the set $\mathcal{MA}^* \times \mathcal{MA}^*$ such that $MA^* \neq \tilde{M}\tilde{A}^*$.

We assume that there exists the following mapping in the model of aggregate A-codes:

$$\pi : \mathcal{E}_R \to \mathcal{E}_1 \times \cdots \times \mathcal{E}_n.$$

Note that this assumption is not so strong, since we will actually see this mapping in our simple construction in Section 4.2. Then, we can derive lower bounds on success probabilities of attacks as follows.

Theorem 1. For any $i \in \{1, 2, \ldots, n\}$, any set of active senders $\mathcal{S} = \{T_{i_1}, \ldots, T_{i_j}\} \in \mathcal{P}(\mathcal{T})$ and any set of colluding groups $W \in \mathcal{P}(\mathcal{T}, \omega)$ such that $\mathcal{S} - W \neq \emptyset$, it holds that

    1. $\log P_I(\mathcal{S}, W) \geq -I(MA^*; E_v \mid E_W)$,
    2. $\log P_S(\mathcal{S}, W) \geq -I(\tilde{M}\tilde{A}^*; E_v \mid E_W, MA_{i_1}, \ldots, MA_{i_j})$.

Proof Sketch. The proof can be shown in a way similar to that of Theorem 1 in [5]. Here, we show an outline of a proof of the first inequality.

We define a characteristic function $\mathcal{X}_I$ as follows.

$$\mathcal{X}_I((M, tag), e_v, e_W) = \begin{cases} 1 \text{ if } Vrfy(M, tag, e_v) = true \\ \quad \wedge \Pr((M, tag), e_v, e_W) \neq 0, \\ 0 \text{ } otherwise. \end{cases}$$

Then, from Definition 3, we can express $P_I(\mathcal{S}, W)$ as

$$P_I(\mathcal{S}, W) = \max_{(M, tag)} \max_{e_W} \sum_{e_v} \mathcal{X}_I((M, tag), e_v, e_W) \Pr(e_v \mid e_W).$$

By a way similar to the proof of Theorem 1 in [5], we have $P_I(\mathcal{S}, W) \geq 2^{-I(MA^*; E_v \mid E_W)}$. Similarly, the second inequality can also be proved. $\square$

We next show lower bounds on memory-sizes of entities in aggregate A-codes.

Theorem 2. Let Π be an $(n, \omega, \epsilon, \gamma)$-one-time secure aggregate A-code. Let $q := \epsilon^{-1}$. Then, for any $i \in \{1, 2, \ldots, n\}$, we have

$$(i) \ |\mathcal{E}_i| \geq q^2, \quad (ii) \ |\mathcal{E}_R| \geq q^{2(\omega+1)}, \quad (iii) \ |\mathcal{A}| \geq q, \quad (iv) \ |\mathcal{A}^*| \geq q.$$

Proof. In order to complete the proof of Theorem 2, we show the following lemmas.

Lemma 1. For arbitrary $i \in \{1, 2, \ldots, n\}$, let $\mathcal{S}_i = \{T_{i_1}, \ldots, T_{i_j}\} \in \mathcal{P}(\mathcal{T})$ and $W \in \mathcal{P}(\mathcal{T}, \omega)$ such that $\mathcal{S}_i - W = \{T_i\}$. Then, we have

$$\log P_I(\mathcal{S}_i, W) \geq -I(MA^*; E_i \mid E_W),$$
$$\log P_S(\mathcal{S}_i, W) \geq -H(E_i \mid E_W, MA_{i_1}, \ldots, MA_{i_j}).$$

Proof. For the first inequality, we get

$$\begin{aligned} I(MA^*; E_v \mid E_W) &= H(MA^* \mid E_W) - H(MA^* \mid E_v, E_W) \\ &= H(MA^* \mid E_W) - H(MA^* \mid E_i, E_W) \quad (1) \\ &= I(MA^*; E_i \mid E_W), \end{aligned}$$

where (1) follows from the following equality: from the mapping π,

$$H(A^* \mid E_v, E_W, M) = H(A^* \mid E_i, E_W, M) = 0.$$

Hence, by Theorem 1, we have $\log P_I(\mathcal{S}_i, W) \geq -I(MA^*; E_i \mid E_W)$.
For the second inequality, we derive

$$\begin{aligned} I(\tilde{M}\tilde{A}^*; E_v \mid & E_W, MA_{i_1}, \ldots, MA_{i_j}) \\ &= H(\tilde{M}\tilde{A}^* \mid E_W, MA_{i_1}, \ldots, MA_{i_j}) \\ &\quad - H(\tilde{M}\tilde{A}^* \mid E_v, E_W, MA_{i_1}, \ldots, MA_{i_j}) \\ &= H(\tilde{M}\tilde{A}^* \mid E_W, MA_{i_1}, \ldots, MA_{i_j}) \\ &\quad - H(\tilde{M}\tilde{A}^* \mid E_i, E_W, MA_{i_1}, \ldots, MA_{i_j}) \quad (2) \\ &= I(\tilde{M}\tilde{A}^*; E_i \mid E_W, MA_{i_1}, \ldots, MA_{i_j}) \\ &\leq H(E_i \mid E_W, MA_{i_1}, \ldots, MA_{i_j}). \end{aligned}$$

where (2) follows from the following equality: from the mapping π,

$$H(\tilde{A}^*|E_v, E_W, MA_{i_1}, \ldots, MA_{i_j}, \tilde{M})$$
$$= H(\tilde{A}^*|E_i, E_W, MA_{i_1}, \ldots, MA_{i_j}, \tilde{M}) = 0.$$

Hence, by Theorem 1, we have $\log P_S(\mathcal{S}_i, W) \geq -H(E_i \mid E_W, MA_{i_1}, \ldots, MA_{i_j})$. $\square$

Lemma 2. $|\mathcal{E}_i| \geq q^2$ for any $i \in \{1, 2, \ldots, n\}$.

Proof. For arbitrary $i \in \{1, 2, \ldots, n\}$, let $W \in \mathcal{P}(\mathcal{T}, \omega)$ and $\mathcal{S}_i = \{T_{i_1}, \ldots, T_{i_j}\} \in \mathcal{P}(\mathcal{T})$ such that $\mathcal{S}_i - W = \{T_i\}$. Then, we have

$$\left(\frac{1}{q}\right)^2 \geq P_I(\mathcal{S}_i, W)P_S(\mathcal{S}_i, W)$$
$$\geq 2^{-I(MA^*;E_i|E_W)-H(E_i|E_W, MA_{i_1}, \ldots, MA_{i_j})} \tag{3}$$
$$= 2^{-H(E_i|E_W)+H(E_i|E_W, MA^*)-H(E_i|E_W, MA_{i_1}, \ldots, MA_{i_j})}$$
$$\geq 2^{-H(E_i|E_W)} \tag{4}$$
$$\geq 2^{-H(E_i)}$$
$$\geq 2^{-\log|\mathcal{E}_i|} = \frac{1}{|\mathcal{E}_i|},$$

where (3) follows from Lemma 1 and (4) follows from the deterministic algorithm $Agg: \mathcal{A}^{(l)} \to \mathcal{A}^*$: since it follows that $H(MA_{i_1}, \ldots, MA_{i_j}) \geq H(MA^*)$, we have $H(E_i|E_W, MA^*) - H(E_i|E_W, MA_{i_1}, \ldots, MA_{i_j}) \geq 0$. $\square$

Lemma 3. $|\mathcal{E}_R| \geq q^{2(\omega+1)}$.

Proof. Without loss of generality, we assume that the best situation for the adversary is when he corrupts all active senders except for the only one of them since the adversary can get $|\mathcal{S}| - 1$ active senders' secret keys. Therefore, we consider the situation in this proof. For arbitrary $i \in \{1, 2, \ldots, n\}$, let $W_i := \{T_1, \ldots, T_{i-1}, T_{i+1}, \ldots, T_{i_{\omega+1}}\}$ and $\mathcal{S}_i \in \mathcal{P}(\mathcal{T})$ such that $\mathcal{S}_i - W_i = \{T_i\}$. Then, we have

$$\left(\frac{1}{q}\right)^{2(\omega+1)} \geq \prod_{j=1}^{\omega+1} P_I(\mathcal{S}_i, W_i)P_S(\mathcal{S}_i, W_i)$$
$$\geq 2^{-\sum_{i=1}^{\omega+1} H(E_i|E_{W_i})} \tag{5}$$
$$\geq 2^{-\sum_{i=1}^{\omega+1} H(E_i|E_1, \ldots, E_{i-1})}$$
$$= 2^{-H(E_1, \ldots, E_{\omega+1})}$$
$$\geq 2^{-H(E_v)} \tag{6}$$
$$\geq 2^{-\log|\mathcal{E}_R|} = \frac{1}{|\mathcal{E}_R|},$$

where (5) follows from the same way as (4), and (6) follows from the mapping π. $\square$

Lemma 4. $|\mathcal{A}| \geq q$.

Proof. In this lemma, for any $\mathcal{S} = \{T_{i_1}, \ldots, T_{i_j}\} \in \mathcal{P}(\mathcal{T})$, M_i and A_i denotes random variables which take values in $\mathcal{M}$ and $\mathcal{A}$, respectively, to be sent from $T_i \in \mathcal{S}$. We note that each M_i may differ from each other, and also that each M_i is independent of each other.

For arbitrary $i \in \{1, 2, \ldots, n\}$, let W and $\mathcal{S}_i = \{T_{i_1}, \ldots, T_{i_j}\}$ such that $\mathcal{S}_i - W = \{T_i\}$. Then, we have

$$
\begin{aligned}
\frac{1}{q} &\geq P_I(\mathcal{S}_i, W) \\
&= 2^{-H(MA^*|E_W)} \tag{7} \\
&\geq 2^{-H(MA_{i_1}, \ldots, MA_{i_j}|E_W)} \tag{8} \\
&= 2^{-H(MA_i|E_W)} \\
&= 2^{-I(MA_i; E_v|E_W)} \\
&= 2^{-I(M_i; E_v|E_W) - I(A_i; E_v|E_W, M_i)} \\
&\geq 2^{-H(A_i)} \geq \frac{1}{|\mathcal{A}|},
\end{aligned}
$$

where (7) follows from Theorem 1 and (8) follows from the deterministic algorithm $Agg: \mathcal{A}^{(i_j)} \rightarrow \mathcal{A}^*$. $\qquad\square$

Lemma 5. $|\mathcal{A}^*| \geq q$.

Proof. By the assumption $|\mathcal{A}^*| \geq |\mathcal{A}|$ (or equivalently, $\gamma \geq 1$) and Lemma 4, it is clear that $|\mathcal{A}^*| \geq q$. $\qquad\square$

As we will see in Section 4.2, the above lower bounds are all tight since our direct construction will meet all the above inequalities with equalities. Therefore, we define optimality of constructions of aggregate A-codes as follows.

Definition 4. A construction of aggregate A-codes is said to be *optimal*, if it is $(n, \omega, \epsilon, 1)$-one-time secure (i.e., $\gamma = 1$) and it meets equality in every inequality of (i)-(iv) in Theorem 2.

Remark 1. It should be noted that, in the case of $|\mathcal{S}| = 1$, $W = \emptyset$, and the algorithm Agg being the identity mapping, the lower bounds of aggregate A-codes in Theorem 2 are the same as those of traditional A-codes [12]. Namely, our results on aggregate A-codes are regarded as extension of those of A-codes.

4   Constructions

In this section, we propose two kinds of constructions of $(n, \omega, \epsilon, \gamma)$-one-time secure aggregate A-codes.

4.1 Simple Generic Construction

We introduce a simple generic construction of $(n, \omega, \epsilon, \gamma)$-one-time secure aggregate A-codes starting from only traditional A-codes (e.g., see [12]). First, we briefly explain the traditional A-codes as follows.[2]

A-code. We consider a scenario where there are three entities, a sender S, a receiver R and an adversary A. The A-code Θ consists of a three-tuple of algorithms $(AGen, Tag, Ver)$ with three spaces, $\tilde{\mathcal{M}}$, $\tilde{\mathcal{A}}$ and $\tilde{\mathcal{E}}$, where $\tilde{\mathcal{M}}$ is a finite set of possible messages, $\tilde{\mathcal{A}}$ is a finite set of possible tags (or authenticators) and $\tilde{\mathcal{E}}$ is a finite set of possible secret-keys, respectively. $AGen$ is a key generation algorithm, which takes a security parameter on input and outputs a secret-key e. Tag is a deterministic algorithm for generating a tag. Tag takes a message $m \in \tilde{\mathcal{M}}$ and a secret-key $e \in \tilde{\mathcal{E}}$ on input and outputs a tag $\alpha \in \tilde{\mathcal{A}}$, and we write $\alpha = Tag(m, e)$ for it. On receiving α, a receiver R can check the validity of it by using Ver. Ver takes a message m, a tag α and a secret-key e on input, and outputs *true* or *false*, and we write *true* $= Ver(m, \alpha, e)$ or *false* $= Ver(m, \alpha, e)$ for it. In A-codes, there are two kind of attacks: *impersonation attacks* and *substitution attacks*. Here, Θ is said to be ϵ-*secure* if each of success probabilities of these attacks is at most ϵ.

The detail of our generic construction of aggregate A-codes $\Pi = (KGen, Auth_i, Agg, Vrfy)$ by using A-codes $\Theta = (AGen, Tag, Ver)$ is given as follows.

1. **KGen**. For a security parameter 1^k, $KGen$ outputs matching secret-keys e_i and e_v for T_i $(1 \le i \le n)$ and R, respectively, as follows. $KGen$ calls $AGen$ with input 1^k n times, and suppose its output is $(e^{(1)}, e^{(2)}, \ldots, e^{(n)})$, where $e^{(i)}$ is the i-th output by $AGen$. Then, $KGen$ outputs secret-keys $e_i := e^{(i)}$, and $e_v := (e^{(1)}, \ldots, e^{(n)})$ for T_i $(1 \le i \le n)$ and R, respectively.
2. **Auth$_i$**. For a message m_i which T_i wants to authenticate and a secret-key $e_i = e^{(i)}$, $Auth_i$ calls Tag, and it computes a tag $\alpha^{(i)} = Tag(m_i, e^{(i)})$. Finally, $Auth_i$ outputs $tag_i := \alpha^{(i)}$.
3. **Agg**. For tags $(tag_{i_1}, \ldots, tag_{i_j}) = (\alpha^{(i_1)}, \ldots, \alpha^{(i_j)})$, Agg computes an aggregated tag tag by XORing all tags: $tag := \bigoplus_{k=1}^{j} \alpha^{(i_k)}$. Then, Agg outputs it.
4. **Vrfy**. For $M := ((m_{i_1}, T_{i_1}), \ldots, (m_{i_j}, T_{i_j}))$, an aggregated tag tag, and a verification-key $e_v = (e^{(1)}, \ldots, e^{(n)})$, $Vrfy$ calls Tag with inputting them, and suppose $\alpha^{(i_k)} = Tag(m_{i_k}, e^{(i_k)})$ for all $1 \le k \le j$ such that $T_{i_k} \in \mathcal{S}$. Then, $Vrfy$ outputs *true* if and only if $tag = \bigoplus_{k=1}^{j} \alpha^{(i_k)}$.

The security of the above construction is shown as follows.

Theorem 3. *Given an ϵ-secure A-code Θ, then the aggregate A-code Π formed by the above construction based on Θ is $(n, \omega, \epsilon, \gamma)$-one-time secure, where $\omega = n - 1$ and $\gamma = 1$. Furthermore, memory-sizes of tags and secret-keys required in the above construction are given by*

$$|\mathcal{E}_i| = |\tilde{\mathcal{E}}|, \ |\mathcal{E}_R| = |\tilde{\mathcal{E}}|^n, \ |\mathcal{A}^*| = |\mathcal{A}| = |\tilde{\mathcal{A}}|.$$

---

[2] More precisely, we explain *Cartesian A-codes without splitting* in this paper.

Proof Sketch. The proof can be easily shown by the security of the underlying A-code, and the estimation of memory-sizes is straightforward. Here, we only describe the outline of the proof of $P_S \leq \epsilon$, since $P_I \leq \epsilon$ can be shown by a similar idea.

Without loss of generality, we suppose that $S = \mathcal{T}$ and $W = \mathcal{T} - \{T_n\}$. The adversary can know $n-1$ secret-keys from corrupted senders and n valid pairs of messages and tags, however, he cannot know T_n's secret-key $e^{(n)}$. Thus, since the underlying A-code is ϵ-secure, success probability of substitution attacks is at most ϵ. Hence, the adversary cannot guess the aggregated tag $tag := \bigoplus_{i=1}^{n} \alpha^{(i)}$ with probability larger than ϵ. Therefore, we have $P_S \leq \epsilon$. In manner similar to this, we can prove $P_I \leq \epsilon$. Hence, we have $\max(P_I, P_S) \leq \epsilon$. □

Remark 2. This generic construction is very simple. However, even if we apply optimal constructions of A-codes in the above generic construction, we cannot obtain an optimal construction of aggregate A-codes for any ω except $\omega = n - 1$. Therefore, in the next subsection we will show that there exists a direct construction (i.e., a construction from scratch) which satisfies Definition 4 for any $\omega(< n)$.

4.2   Optimal Direct Construction

We propose a direct construction of $(n, \omega, \epsilon, \gamma)$-one-time secure aggregate A-codes. In addition, it is shown that the construction is optimal. The detail of our construction of aggregate A-codes, $\Pi=(KGen, Auth_i, Agg, Vrfy)$, is given as follows.

1. **KGen.** For a security parameter 1^k, *KGen* outputs matching secret-keys e_i and e_v for T_i $(1 \leq i \leq n)$ and R, respectively, as follows. *KGen* picks a k-bit prime power q, where $q > n$, and constructs the finite field $\mathbb{F}_q$ with q elements. We assume that the identity of each user T_i is encoded as $T_i \in \mathbb{F}_q \backslash \{0\}$. And, *KGen* chooses uniformly at random $f(x) := \sum_{i=0}^{\omega} a_i x^i$ and $g(x) := \sum_{i=0}^{\omega} b_i x^i$ over $\mathbb{F}_q$ with a variable x in which a degree of x is at most ω. *KGen* also computes $e_i := (f(T_i), g(T_i))$ $(1 \leq i \leq n)$. Then, *AGen* outputs secret-keys e_i $(1 \leq i \leq n)$ and $e_v := (f(x), g(x))$ for T_i $(1 \leq i \leq n)$ and R, respectively.
2. **Auth$_i$.** For a message $m_i \in \mathbb{F}_q$ which T_i wants to authenticate and a secret-key e_i, *Auth$_i$* generates a tag, $tag_i := f(T_i)m_i + g(T_i)$, and outputs it.
3. **Agg.** For tags $(tag_{i_1}, \ldots, tag_{i_j})$, *Agg* computes an aggregated tag, $tag := \sum_{k=1}^{j} tag_{i_k}$. Then, *Agg* outputs it.
4. **Vrfy.** For $M = ((m_{i_1}, T_{i_1}), \ldots, (m_{i_j}, T_{i_j}))$, an aggregated tag tag, and a verification-key e_v, *Vrfy* outputs *true* if $tag = \sum_{k=1}^{j} f(T_{i_k})m_{i_k} + g(T_{i_k})$ holds, and otherwise outputs *false*.

The security and optimality of the above construction is stated as follows.

Theorem 4. *The resulting aggregate A-code Π by the above construction is $(n, \omega, \frac{1}{q}, 1)$-one-time secure and optimal.*

Proof Sketch. Here, we only describe the outline of the proof of $P_S \leq \frac{1}{q}$, since $P_I \leq \frac{1}{q}$ can be shown by a similar idea.

Without loss of generality, we suppose that $W = \{T_1, \ldots, T_\omega\}$, $T_n \in \mathcal{S}$, and $T_n \notin W$. To succeed in the substitution attack by an adversary who corrupts the colluding group W, the adversary will generate fraudulent messages and an fraudulent aggregated tag (M', tag') under the following conditions: the adversary can obtain ω secret-keys from corrupted senders, and $|\mathcal{S}|$ valid pairs of messages and tags, one of the pairs is generated by T_n. However, each degree of $f(x)$ and $g(x)$ with respect to x is at most ω, the adversary cannot guess at least one coefficient of $f(x)$ and $g(x)$ with probability larger than $1/q$. Therefore, we have $P_S \leq 1/q$. In a manner similar to this, we can prove that $P_I \leq 1/q$. Thus, we have $\max(P_I, P_S) \leq 1/q$.

Finally, it is straightforward to see that the construction satisfies all the equalities of lower bounds in Theorem 2. □

5   Concluding Remarks

In this paper, we studied aggregate authentication codes (aggregate A-codes) with information-theoretic security. Specifically, we first proposed a formal model and formalization of security for aggregate A-codes. We also derived tight lower bounds on memory-sizes required for aggregate A-codes. Furthermore, we presented a simple generic construction and an optimal direct construction of aggregate A-codes.

Acknowledgments. The authors would like to thank the referees for their helpful comments. The third author is supported by JSPS Research Fellowships for Young Scientists.

References

1. Bellare, M., Namprempre, C., Neven, G.: Unrestricted Aggregate Signatures. In: Arge, L., Cachin, C., Jurdziński, T., Tarlecki, A. (eds.) ICALP 2007. LNCS, vol. 4596, pp. 411–422. Springer, Heidelberg (2007)
2. Boneh, D., Gentry, C., Lynn, B., Shacham, H.: Aggregate and Verifiably Encrypted Signatures from Bilinear Maps. In: Biham, E. (ed.) EUROCRYPT 2003. LNCS, vol. 2656, pp. 416–432. Springer, Heidelberg (2003)
3. Castro, R., Dahab, R.: Efficient Certificateless Signatures Suitable for Aggregation. In: Cryptology ePrint Archive: Report 2007/454 (2007), http://eprint.iacr.org/2007/454
4. Desmedt, Y., Frankel, Y., Yung, M.: Multi-receiver/Multi-sender network security: efficient authenticated multicast/feedback. In: IEEE Infocom 1992, pp. 2045–2054 (1992)
5. Johansson, T.: Lower Bounds on the Probability of Deception in Authentication with Arbitration. IEEE Trans. on Information Theory 40(5), 1573–1585 (1994)
6. Katz, J., Lindell, A.Y.: Aggregate Message Authentication Codes. In: Malkin, T. (ed.) CT-RSA 2008. LNCS, vol. 4964, pp. 155–169. Springer, Heidelberg (2008)

7. Lu, S., Ostrovsky, R., Sahai, A., Shacham, H., Waters, B.: Sequential Aggregate Signatures and Multisignatures Without Random Oracles. In: Vaudenay, S. (ed.) EUROCRYPT 2006. LNCS, vol. 4004, pp. 465–485. Springer, Heidelberg (2006)
8. Lysyanskaya, A., Micali, S., Reyzin, L., Shacham, H.: Sequential Aggregate Signatures from Trapdoor Permutations. In: Cachin, C., Camenisch, J.L. (eds.) EUROCRYPT 2004. LNCS, vol. 3027, pp. 74–90. Springer, Heidelberg (2004)
9. Martin, K., Safavi-Naini, R.: Multisender Authentication Systems with Unconditional Security. In: Han, Y., Quing, S. (eds.) ICICS 1997. LNCS, vol. 1334, pp. 130–143. Springer, Heidelberg (1997)
10. Okamoto, T.: A Digital Multisignatures Scheme Using Bijective Public-key Cryptosystems. ACM Trans., Computer Systems 6(4), 432–441 (1988)
11. Rivest, R.: Unconditionally Secure Commitment and Oblivious Transfer Schemes Using Private Channels and a Trusted Initializer. Manuscript (1999), http://people.csail.mit.edu/rivest/Rivest-commitment.pdf
12. Simmons, G.J.: Authentication Theory/Coding Theory. In: Blakely, G.R., Chaum, D. (eds.) CRYPTO 1984. LNCS, vol. 196, pp. 411–431. Springer, Heidelberg (1985)

On Constructions of MDS Matrices from Companion Matrices for Lightweight Cryptography

Kishan Chand Gupta and Indranil Ghosh Ray

Applied Statistics Unit, Indian Statistical Institute,
203, B. T. Road, Kolkata 700108, India
{kishan,indranil_r}@isical.ac.in

Abstract. Maximum distance separable (MDS) matrices have applications not only in coding theory but also are of great importance in the design of block ciphers and hash functions. It is highly nontrivial to find MDS matrices which could be used in lightweight cryptography. In a crypto 2011 paper, Guo et. al. proposed a new MDS matrix $Serial(1, 2, 1, 4)^4$ over $\mathbb{F}_{2^8}$. This representation has a compact hardware implementation of the AES MixColumn operation. No general study of MDS properties of this newly introduced construction of the form $Serial(z_0, \ldots, z_{d-1})^d$ over $\mathbb{F}_{2^n}$ for arbitrary d and n is available in the literature. In this paper we study some properties of MDS matrices and provide an insight of why $Serial(z_0, \ldots, z_{d-1})^d$ leads to an MDS matrix. For efficient hardware implementation, we aim to restrict the values of z_i's in $\{1, \alpha, \alpha^2, \alpha + 1\}$, such that $Serial(z_0, \ldots, z_{d-1})^d$ is MDS for $d = 4$ and 5, where α is the root of the constructing polynomial of $\mathbb{F}_{2^n}$. We also propose more generic constructions of MDS matrices e.g. we construct lightweight 4×4 and 5×5 MDS matrices over $\mathbb{F}_{2^n}$ for all $n \geq 4$. An algorithm is presented to check if a given matrix is MDS. The algorithm follows from the basic properties of MDS matrix and is easy to implement.

Keywords: Diffusion, Companion matrix, MDS matrix, MixColumn operation, minimal polynomial.

1 Introduction

Claude Shannon, in his paper "Communication Theory of Secrecy Systems" [21], defined *confusion* and *diffusion* as two properties, required for the design of block ciphers. In [8–10], Heys and Tavares showed that the replacement of the permutation layer of Substitution Permutation Networks (SPNs) with a diffusive linear transformation improves the avalanche characteristics of the block cipher which increases the cipher's resistance to differential and linear cryptanalysis. Thus the main application of *MDS matrix* in cryptography is in designing block ciphers and hash functions that provide security against differential and linear cryptanalysis. MDS matrices offer diffusion properties and is one of the vital constituents of modern age ciphers like Advanced Encryption Standard (AES) [3],

A. Cuzzocrea et al. (Eds.): CD-ARES 2013 Workshops, LNCS 8128, pp. 29–43, 2013.
© IFIP International Federation for Information Processing 2013

Twofish [19, 20], SHARK [16] and Square [2]. MDS matrices are also used in the design of hash functions. Hash functions like Maelstrom [4], Grøstl [5] and PHOTON family light weight hash functions [6] use MDS matrices as main part of their diffusion layers.

Nearly all ciphers use predefined MDS matrices for incorporating diffusion property. Although in some ciphers the possibility of random selection of MDS matrices with some constraint is provided [23]. In this context we would like to mention that in papers [6,7,12,13,17,23], new constructions of MDS matrices are provided. In [6], authors construct lightweight MDS matrices from *companion* matrices by exhaustive search. In [7], authors construct new involutory MDS matrices using properties of Cauchy matrices over additive subgroup of $\mathbb{F}_{2^n}$ and have shown its equivalence with Vandermonde matrices based construction under some constraints. In [12], authors construct efficient 4×4 and 8×8 matrices to be used in block ciphers. In [13, 17], authors constructed involutory MDS matrices using Vandermonde matrices. In [23], authors construct new involutory MDS matrices using properties of Cauchy matrices.

Authors of [6] defined $Serial(z_0, \ldots, z_{d-1})$, which is the companion matrix of $z_0 + z_1 x + z_2 x^2 + \ldots + z_{d-1} x^{d-1} + x^d$. Their objective was to find suitable candidates so that $Serial(z_0, \ldots, z_{d-1})^d$ is an MDS matrix. In [6], authors proposed an MDS matrix $Serial(1, 2, 1, 4)^4$ over $\mathbb{F}_{2^8}$ for AES *MixColumn operation* which has compact and improved hardware footprint [6]. It is to be noted that in $Serial(1, 2, 1, 4)$, $z_0 = z_2 = 1$, $z_1 = 2 = \alpha$ and $z_3 = 4 = \alpha^2$, where α is the root of the irreducible polynomial $x^8 + x^4 + x^3 + x + 1$. The proper choice of z_0, z_1, z_2 and z_3 (preferably of low Hamming weight) improves the hardware implementation of AES MixColumn transformation. It may be noted that MixColumn operation in [6] is composed of d ($d = 4$ for AES) applications of the matrix $Serial(z_0, \ldots, z_{d-1})$ to the input column vector. More formally, let $X = (x_0, \ldots, x_{d-1})^T$ be the input column vector of MixColumn and $Y = (y_0, \ldots, y_{d-1})^T$ be the corresponding output. Then we have $Y = A^d \times X = \underbrace{(A \times (A \times (A \times \ldots \times (A \times X))))\ldots)}_{d \text{ times}}$, where $A = Serial(z_0, \ldots, z_{d-1})$.

So the hardware circuitry will depend on companion matrix A and not on the MDS matrix A^d. Note that authors of [6] used MAGMA [1] to test all possible values of z_0, z_1, z_2 and z_3 and found $Serial(1, 2, 1, 4)$ to be the right candidate, which raised to the power 4 gives an MDS matrix. Authors of [18, 22] proposed new diffusion layers ($d \times d$ MDS matrices) based on companion matrices for smaller values of d. In this paper we provide some sufficient conditions for such constructions but our approach is different from [18, 22]. We also propose new and more generic constructions of $d \times d$ MDS matrices for $d = 4$ and 5.

For efficient implementation, we aim to restrict the values of z_i's in the set $\{1, \alpha, \alpha^2, \alpha + 1\}$, such that $Serial(z_0, \ldots, z_{d-1})^d$ is MDS, where α is the root of the constructing polynomial of $\mathbb{F}_{2^n}$. It may be noted that multiplication by 1, which is the unit element of $\mathbb{F}_{2^n}$, is trivial. When α is the root of the constructing polynomial of $\mathbb{F}_{2^n}$, the multiplication by α can be implemented by a shift by one bit to the left and a conditional XOR with a constant when a carry bit is set (multiplication by α is often denoted as xtime). Multiplication by $\alpha + 1$ is done by a multiplication by α and one XOR operation. Multiplication by α^2 is done by two successive multiplication by α. We also explore some properties of MDS matrices and based on that we provide an algorithm to check whether the matrix is MDS. This algorithm is easy to implement. We implemented the algorithm and ran it for upto 8×8 matrices over $\mathbb{F}_{2^{24}}$.

In general we also study the cases where we restrict the values of z_i's in the set $\{1, \beta, \beta^2, \beta + 1\}$ for any non zero $\beta \in \mathbb{F}_{2^n}$, such that $Serial(z_0, \ldots, z_{d-1})^d$ is MDS.

The paper is organized as follows: In Section 2 we provide definitions and preliminaries. In Section 3, we discuss a few relevant properties of MDS matrices and provide an algorithm to check if a given square matrix is MDS. In Section 4 and Subsections therein, we study $Serial(z_0, z_1, z_2, z_3)^4$. In Appendix F we study few more MDS matrices of the form $Serial(z_0, z_1, z_2, z_3)^4$. In Appendix G, we study MDS properties of $Serial(z_0, z_1, z_2, z_3, z_4)^5$ and propose new constructions of 5×5 MDS matrices. We conclude the paper in Section 5.

2   Definition and Preliminaries

Let $\mathbb{F}_2 = \{0, 1\}$ be the finite field with two elements and $\mathbb{F}_{2^n}$ be the finite field with 2^n elements. We will often denote a matrix by $((a_{i,j}))$, where $a_{i,j}$ is the (i, j)-th element of the matrix. The *Hamming weight* of an integer i is the number of non zero coefficients in the binary representation of i and is denoted by $H(i)$. For example $H(5) = 2, H(8) = 1$.

A *cyclotomic coset* C_s modulo $(2^n - 1)$ is defined as [14, page 104]

$$C_s = \{s, s \cdot 2, \cdots, s \cdot 2^{n_s - 1}\}$$

where n_s is the smallest positive integer such that $s \equiv s2^{n_s} \pmod{2^n - 1}$. The subscript s is the smallest integer in C_s and is called the *coset leader* of C_s. Note that n_s is the size of the coset C_s which will also be denoted by $|C_s|$. When $n_s = n$, we call it a full length coset and when $n_s < n$, we call it a smaller coset. The set of all coset leaders modulo $(2^n - 1)$ is denoted by $\Upsilon(n)$. The computations in cosets are performed in $\mathbb{Z}_{2^n - 1}$, the ring of integers modulo $(2^n - 1)$. For $n = 4$ the cyclotomic cosets modulo $2^4 - 1 = 15$ are: $C_0 = \{0\}, C_1 = \{1, 2, 4, 8\}, C_3 = \{3, 6, 12, 9\}, C_5 = \{5, 10\}, C_7 = \{7, 14, 13, 11\}$. Note $|C_5| = 2$, $|C_1| = 4$ and $\Upsilon(4) = \{0, 1, 3, 5, 7\}$.

Let $\beta \in \mathbb{F}_{p^n}$, p being a prime number. The *minimal polynomial* [14, page 99] over $\mathbb{F}_p$ of β is the lowest degree monic polynomial, say $M(x)$, with coefficients from $\mathbb{F}_p$ such that $M(\beta) = 0$. It is easy to check that the minimal polynomial is irreducible [14, page 99]. If $f(x)$ is any polynomial over $\mathbb{F}_p$ such that $f(\beta) = 0$, then $M(x)|f(x)$ [14, page 99].

Using the notation of [6], we define $Serial(z_0, \ldots, z_{d-1})$ as follows.

$$Serial(z_0, \ldots, z_{d-1}) = \begin{pmatrix} 0 & 1 & 0 & 0 & \ldots & 0 \\ 0 & 0 & 1 & 0 & \ldots & 0 \\ \vdots & \vdots & \vdots & \vdots & & \vdots \\ 0 & 0 & 0 & 0 & \ldots & 1 \\ z_0 & z_1 & \ldots & \ldots & \ldots & z_{d-1} \end{pmatrix},$$

where $z_0, z_1, z_2, \ldots, z_{d-1} \in \mathbb{F}_{2^n}$ for some n. Note that this matrix is a companion matrix of the polynomial $z_0 + z_1 x + z_2 x^2 + \ldots + z_{d-1} x^{d-1} + x^d$.

We note that,

$$Serial(z_0, \ldots, z_{d-1})^{-1} = \begin{pmatrix} \frac{z_1}{z_0} & \frac{z_2}{z_0} & \cdots\cdots\cdots & \frac{1}{z_0} \\ 1 & 0 & 0 & 0 & \ldots & 0 \\ 0 & 1 & 0 & 0 & \ldots & 0 \\ \vdots & \vdots & \vdots & \vdots & & \vdots \\ 0 & 0 & 0 & \ldots & 1 & 0 \end{pmatrix}. \tag{1}$$

It is to be noted that like encryption, decryption can also be implemented by repeated use (d times) of $Serial(z_0, \ldots, z_{d-1})^{-1}$, and also whenever $z_0 = 1$, the hardware footprint for decryption is as good as that of encryption circuitry.

Definition 1. *Let $\mathbb{F}$ be a finite field and p and q be two integers. Let $x \rightarrow M \times x$ be a mapping from $\mathbb{F}^p$ to $\mathbb{F}^q$ defined by the $q \times p$ matrix M. We say that it is an MDS matrix if the set of all pairs $(x, M \times x)$ is an MDS code, i.e. a linear code of dimension p, length $p + q$ and minimal distance $q + 1$.*

An MDS matrix provides diffusion properties that have useful applications in cryptography. The idea comes from coding theory, in particular from maximum distance separable codes (MDS codes). In this context we state two important theorems of Coding Theory.

Theorem 1. *[14, page 33] If C is an $[n, k, d]$ code, then $n - k \geq d - 1$.*

Codes with $n - k = d - 1$ are called maximum distance separable codes, or MDS codes for short.

Theorem 2. *[14, page 321] An $[n, k, d]$ code C with generator matrix $G = [I|A]$, where A is a $k \times (n-k)$ matrix, is MDS if and only if every square submatrix (formed from any i rows and any i columns, for any $i = 1, 2, \ldots, \min\{k, n-k\}$) of A is nonsingular.*

The following fact is another way to characterize an MDS matrix.

Fact: 1 *A square matrix A is an MDS matrix if and only if every square submatrices of A are nonsingular.*

Fact: 2 *All entries of an MDS matrix are non zero.*

3 Few Properties of MDS Matrices

In this Section we develop some tools for studying $Serial(z_0, z_1, \ldots, z_{d-1})^d$, $z_i \in \mathbb{F}_{2^n}$ for $d = 4, 5$. We also use these tools to provide an algorithm (Algorithm 1) at the end of this Section to check whether a matrix is MDS. It may be noted that from the entries of the inverse of a $d \times d$ nonsingular matrix, it can be checked whether all its $(d-1) \times (d-1)$ submatrics are nonsingular or not. In this direction we state the following Lemma which will be used in Algorithm 1.

Lemma 1. *All entries of inverse of MDS matrix are non zero.*

Proof. Let $\mathbb{M} = ((m_{i,j}))$ be a $d \times d$ MDS matrix. We know that $M^{-1} = Adj(\mathbb{M})/det(\mathbb{M})$, where $Adj(\mathbb{M}) = ((M_{i,j}))$ and $M_{i,j}$ is co-factor of $m_{j,i}$ in $\mathbb{M}$ which is the determinant of $(d-1) \times (d-1)$ submatrix obtained by omitting j'th row and i'th column of $\mathbb{M}$. Since $\mathbb{M}$ is an MDS matrix, all its $(d-1) \times (d-1)$ submatrices are nonsingular. Thus all $M_{i,j}$ values are non zero. $\qquad\square$

Corollary 1. *Any 2×2 matrix over $\mathbb{F}_{2^n}$ is MDS matrix if and only if it is a full rank matrix and all entries of its inverse is non zero.*

Proof. Proof is given in the Appendix A.

Fact: 3 *It may be noted that if all the entries of the inverse of a $d \times d$ nonsingular matrix are non zero, then all its $(d-1) \times (d-1)$ submatrics are nonsingular.*

Corollary 2. *Any 3×3 matrix over $\mathbb{F}_{2^n}$ with all non zero entries is an MDS matrix if and only if it is a full rank matrix and all entries of its inverse are non zero.*

Proof. Proof is given in the Appendix B.

In the next Proposition we study the necessary and sufficient condition for any 4×4 matrix to be MDS. This Proposition will be referred to at many places throughout the paper.

Proposition 1. *Any 4×4 matrix over $\mathbb{F}_{2^n}$ with all entries non zero is an MDS matrix if and only if it is a full rank matrix with the inverse matrix having all entries non zero and all of its 2×2 submatrices are full rank.*

Proof. Let $\mathbb{M} = ((m_{i,j}))$ be a 4×4 matrix satisfying the conditions of this proposition. Since its inverse matrix has all non zero entries, therefore by Fact 3, all $(4-1) \times (4-1)$ i.e. 3×3 submatrices of $\mathbb{M}$ are full rank matrices. Also inverse matrices of all 2×2 submatrices are full rank. Therefore all square submatrices of $((m_{i,j}))$ are full rank. Thus the matrix is MDS. The other direction of the proof is immediate. $\qquad\square$

We close this Section by providing an algorithm to check if a $d \times d$ matrix is MDS. The algorithm directly follows from Lemma 1, Fact 1, Fact 2 and Fact 3. We implemented the algorithm and ran it for up to 8×8 matrices over $\mathbb{F}_{2^{24}}$.

One approach of checking if a $d \times d$ matrix M is an MDS is to use $[I|M]$ as a generator matrix and check if the code produced is MDS code. Note, if the underlying field is $\mathbb{F}_{2^n}$, the number of code words will be 2nd and finding the minimum weight non zero code word is NP-complete.

For testing if a matrix is MDS, a naive approach may be to check for non singularity of all its square submatrices. The number of computations in this case will be $n^2 \sum_{i=1}^{d} \binom{d}{i}^2 i^3$. It is easy to check that the number of computations of our algorithm is $n^2 \sum_{i=1}^{d/2} \binom{d}{2i}^2 (2i)^3$ for d even and $n^2 \sum_{i=1}^{d/2} \binom{d}{2i+1}^2 (2i+1)^3$ for d odd.

Algorithm 1. Checking if a $d \times d$ matrix $((a_{i,j}))$ over $\mathbb{F}_{2^n}$ is an MDS matrix

---

Input $n > 1$, irreducible polynomial $\pi(x)$ of degree n, the $d \times d$ matrix $((a_{i,j}))$ over $\mathbb{F}_{2^n}$.

Output Outputs a boolean variable b_mds which is true if $((a_{i,j}))$ is an MDS matrix, else is false.

1: $b\_mds = true$.
2: Compute inverse of $((a_{i,j}))$ in $((b_{i,j}))$; If inverse does not exist, set $b\_mds = false$ and goto 13;
3: check if all d^2 entries of $((a_{i,j}))$ and $((b_{i,j}))$ are non zero. If not, set $b\_mds = false$;

4: **if** $(d = 3)$: Go to 13;
5: $t \leftarrow d - 2$;
6: **while** $(t > 1 \ \& \ b\_mds = true)$ **do**
7:    List all $\binom{d}{t}^2$ submatrices of dimension $t \times t$ in a list $list\_submatrices$;
8:    **for** $(e = 0 \ ; \ e < \binom{d}{t}^2 \ ; \ e = e + 1)$ **do**
9:       Find inverse of $list\_submatrices[e]$ in $((inv\_Matrix_{i,j}))$;
10:       **if** $(((inv\_Matrix_{i,j}))$ does not exist or any entry of $((inv\_Matrix_{i,j}))$ is zero) : $b\_mds = false$;
11:       **if** $(b\_mds = false)$: break the loop and go to 13;
12:    $t \leftarrow t - 2$;
13: Set b_mds as output;

For example, when $n = 8$ and $d = 4$, number of computations by the naive method is $2^6 \times 800$. In the same context, our algorithm takes only $2^6 \times 352$ computations. So the ratio of number of computations required by the naive method with number of computations required by our method is approximately 2. Note that this ratio is independent of n. When $n = 20$ and $d = 8$, number of computations by the naive method is $20^2 \times 988416$ and that by our method is $20^2 \times 489728$ and the ratio is approximately 2.

4   MDS Properties of $Serial(z_0, z_1, z_2, z_3)^4$

In this Section we consider low Hamming weight candidates $z_0, z_1, z_2, z_3 \in \mathbb{F}_{2^n}$ for arbitrary n, such that $Serial(z_0, z_1, z_2, z_3)^4$ is MDS. Low Hamming weight coefficients are desirable for better hardware implementation. So we restrict the values of z_i's to $1, \alpha, \alpha^2, 1+\alpha$ and also try to maximize the occurrence of 1', where α is the root of constructing polynomial of $\mathbb{F}_{2^n}$. Now we provide cases (from Lemma 2 to Lemma 7) for which matrices of the form $Serial(z_0, z_1, z_2, z_3)^4$ are non MDS except for one special case of Lemma 6 (see Remark 4). In Subsection 4.1, Subsection 4.2 and Appendix F, we will construct lightweight 4×4 MDS matrices and in Appendix G we will construct lightweight 5×5 MDS matrices of the form $Serial(z_0, z_1, z_2, z_3, z_4)^5$.

Lemma 2. $Serial(z_0, z_1, z_2, z_3)^4$ is never an MDS matrix when any three or all of z_0, z_1, z_2 and z_3 are 1.

Proof. Proof is given in Appendix C.

Remark 1. If 1 is allowed in any three or more places of z_0, z_1, z_2, and z_3, then the matrix $Serial(z_0, z_1, z_2, z_3)^4$ is not MDS (from Lemma 2). We next study the possibility of having MDS matrices which are of the form $Serial(z_1, z_2, z_3, z_4)^4$ when any two out of z_0, z_1, z_2, and z_3 are 1 and restrict the other two values to be from the set $\{\alpha, \alpha^2, \alpha + 1\}$ for efficient implementation. Note that there are 6 such cases. It is easy to check that out of these 6 cases, $Serial(z_0, z_1, 1, 1)^4$ and $Serial(z_0, 1, z_2, 1)^4$ will never be MDS. So we concentrate on remaining four cases, i.e. $Serial(1, 1, z_2, z_3)^4$, $Serial(1, z_1, z_2, 1)^4$, $Serial(1, z_1, 1, z_3)^4$ and $Serial(z_0, 1, 1, z_3)^4$.

Lemma 3. *Let* $S = Serial(1, 1, z_2, z_3)$ *and* $z_2, z_3 \in \{\alpha, \alpha^2\}$ *or* $z_2, z_3 \in \{\alpha, \alpha + 1\}$, *which are defined over* $\mathbb{F}_{2^n}$, *where* α *is the root of constructing polynomial of* $\mathbb{F}_{2^n}$. *Then* S^4 *is non MDS matrix.*

Lemma 4. *Let* $S = Serial(1, z_1, z_2, 1)$ *and and* $z_1, z_2 \in \{\alpha, \alpha^2\}$ *or* $z_1, z_2 \in \{\alpha, \alpha + 1\}$, *which are defined over* $\mathbb{F}_{2^n}$, *where* α *is the root of constructing polynomial of* $\mathbb{F}_{2^n}$. *Then* S^4 *is non MDS matrix.*

Remark 2. Note that $Serial(1, 1, z_2, z_3)^4$ and $Serial(1, z_1, z_2, 1)^4$ over $\mathbb{F}_{2^n}$ become MDS if elements other than 1 are distinct and are from the set $\{\alpha + 1, \alpha^2\}$, for higher values of n (See in Appendix F).

Lemma 5. *Let* $A = Serial(1, \alpha, 1, \alpha^2)$ *and* $A' = Serial(1, \alpha^2, 1, \alpha)$ *which are defined over* $\mathbb{F}_{2^n}$, *where* $1 \leq n \leq 4$ *and* α *is the root of constructing polynomial of* $\mathbb{F}_{2^n}$. *Then* A^4 *and* A'^4 *are non MDS matrix.*

Proof.

$$A^4 = \begin{pmatrix} 1 & \alpha & 1 & \alpha^2 \\ \alpha^2 & \alpha^3 + 1 & \alpha^2 + \alpha & \alpha^4 + 1 \\ \alpha^4 + 1 & \alpha^5 + \alpha^2 + \alpha & \alpha^4 + \alpha^3 & \alpha^6 + \alpha \\ \alpha^6 + \alpha & \alpha^7 + \alpha^4 + \alpha^2 + 1 & \alpha^6 + \alpha^5 + \alpha^2 & \alpha^8 + \alpha^4 \end{pmatrix} \quad (2)$$

and

$$A^{-4} = \begin{pmatrix} \alpha^4 + \alpha^2 & \alpha^4 + \alpha^3 + \alpha & \alpha^5 + \alpha^4 + \alpha^2 + 1 & \alpha^3 + \alpha^2 \\ \alpha^3 + \alpha^2 & \alpha^3 + \alpha^2 & \alpha^4 + \alpha^2 + \alpha & \alpha^2 + 1 \\ \alpha^2 + 1 & \alpha^2 + \alpha & \alpha^3 + 1 & \alpha \\ \alpha & 1 & \alpha^2 & 1 \end{pmatrix} \quad (3)$$

Note that three irreducible polynomials of degree 4 are $x^4 + x + 1$, $x^4 + x^3 + 1$ and $x^4 + x^3 + x^2 + x + 1$. It is easy to observe that $A^4[2][1] = \alpha^5 + \alpha^2 + \alpha = \alpha(\alpha^4 + \alpha + 1)$, $A^4[3][2] = \alpha^6 + \alpha^5 + \alpha^2 = \alpha^2(\alpha^4 + \alpha^3 + 1)$ and $A^4[3][0] = \alpha^6 + \alpha = \alpha(\alpha^5 + 1) = \alpha(\alpha + 1)(\alpha^4 + \alpha^3 + \alpha^2 + \alpha + 1)$. So, when the minimal polynomial of α is $x^4 + x + 1$ or $x^4 + x^3 + 1$ or $x^4 + x^3 + x^2 + x + 1$, $A^4[2][1]$ or $A^4[3][2]$ or $A^4[3][0]$ will be 0 respectively. Thus A^4 is a non MDS matrix for $n = 4$.

Similarly, $A^{-4}[0][1] = \alpha^4 + \alpha^3 + \alpha = \alpha(\alpha^3 + \alpha^2 + 1)$ and $A^{-4}[1][2] = \alpha^4 + \alpha^2 + \alpha = \alpha(\alpha^3 + \alpha + 1)$. So, when the minimal polynomial of α is $x^3 + x^2 + 1$ or

$x^3 + x + 1$, $A^{-4}[0][1]$ or $A^4[1][2]$ will be zero respectively. Thus A^4 is a non MDS matrix for $n = 3$.

Again $A^4[1][1] = \alpha^3 + 1 = \alpha(\alpha^2 + \alpha + 1)$ which is zero when the minimal polynomial of α is $x^2 + x + 1$. Thus A^4 is a non MDS matrix for $n = 2$.

Lastly, when $n = 1$, α is 1, making $A = Serial(1, 1, 1, 1)$ and from Lemma 2, A^4 will be a non MDS matrix.

Similarly it can be proved that A'^4 is non MDS matrix.   □

Remark 3. $Serial(1, \alpha, 1, \alpha + 1)^4$, defined over $\mathbb{F}_{2^n}$, is non MDS for $1 \leq n \leq 3$. The proof is similar to Lemma 5. In Proposition 4 of Section 4, we will show that $Serial(1, \alpha, 1, \alpha + 1)^4$ is MDS for all $n \geq 4$.

Lemma 6. *Let* $B = Serial(\alpha, 1, 1, \alpha^2)$ *and* $B' = Serial(\alpha^2, 1, 1, \alpha)$ *which are defined over* $\mathbb{F}_{2^n}$, *where* $1 \leq n \leq 4$ *and* α *is the root of the constructing polynomial of* $\mathbb{F}_{2^n}$. *Then* B^4 *is non MDS for all* n *such that* $1 \leq n \leq 4$ *except when* $n = 4$ *and* α *is a root of* $x^4 + x + 1$. *Also* B'^4 *is non MDS for all* n *such that* $1 \leq n \leq 4$.

Proof. Proof is given in Appendix D.

Remark 4. Note for $n = 4$, if the Galois field $\mathbb{F}_{2^4}$ is constructed by $x^4 + x + 1$ then we can construct an MDS matrix $Serial(\alpha, 1, 1, \alpha^2)^4$ where α is the root of $x^4 + x + 1$.

Lemma 7. *Let* $A = Serial(\alpha, 1, 1, \alpha + 1)$ *and* $A' = Serial(\alpha + 1, 1, 1, \alpha)$ *which are defined over* $\mathbb{F}_{2^n}$, *where* α *is the root of the constructing polynomial of* $\mathbb{F}_{2^n}$. *Then* A^4 *and* A'^4 *are non MDS matrices.*

Proof. The proof technique is similar to that used in the proof of Lemma 5.   □

So far we have mainly considered the cases for which the constructed matrices are non MDS. Now we consider the cases for which the matrices are MDS.

4.1   Lightweight MDS Matrix of the Form $Serial(1, z_1, 1, z_3)^4$

In this Subsection, we study the MDS property of the matrices of the form $Serial(1, z_1, 1, z_3)^4$. We concentrate on $z_1, z_3 \in \{\alpha, \alpha^2, \alpha + 1\}$ for better hardware implementation, where α is the root of constructing polynomial of $\mathbb{F}_{2^n}$ for different n. Here $z_0 = 1$. $Serial(1, z_1, 1, z_3)^{-1}$ is as defined in equation 1 with $d = 4$. So the hardware footprint for decryption is as good as that of encryption circuit in Substitution Permutation Networks (SPNs). In this Subsection we will construct MDS matrices for better hardware footprint by letting $z_1, z_3 \in \{\alpha, \alpha^2\}$ or $z_1, z_3 \in \{\alpha, \alpha + 1\}$ and ignore the case when $z_0, z_3 \in \{\alpha^2, \alpha + 1\}$.

Proposition 2. *Let* $A = Serial(1, \alpha, 1, \alpha^2)$ *be a* 4×4 *matrix over the finite field* $\mathbb{F}_{2^n}$ *and* α *is the root of the constructing polynomial of* $\mathbb{F}_{2^n}$. *Then,* A^4 *is MDS for all* $n \geq 5$ *except when* $n = 6$ *and* α *is the root of* $x^6 + x^5 + x^4 + x + 1 = 0$.

Proof. Proof is given in Appendix E.

Remark 5. It is easy to check that when $n = 8$ and α is the root of irreducible polynomial $x^8 + x^4 + x^3 + x + 1$, we get the MDS matrix $Serial(1, \alpha, 1, \alpha^2)^4$, which is proposed in [6].

Now we study $Serial(1, \beta, 1, \beta^2)^4$ for any non zero $\beta \in \mathbb{F}_{2^n}$ in Proposition 3. So far, we restricted β to be the root of the constructing polynomial of $\mathbb{F}_{2^n}$. It is easy to note that $\beta = \gamma^i$ for some integer i, where γ is any primitive element in $\mathbb{F}_{2^n}$. These propositions resembles the earlier propositions of this Subsection and proof techniques are also similar.

Proposition 3. *Let $A = Serial(1, \beta, 1, \beta^2)$ be a 4×4 matrix over the finite field $\mathbb{F}_{2^n}$. Also let γ be any primitive element of $\mathbb{F}_{2^n}$ and $\beta = \gamma^i$ such that $i \in C_s$. Then if $|C_s| \geq 5$ then A^4 is always an MDS matrix except when $|C_s| = 6$ and the minimal polynomial of β is $x^6 + x^5 + x^4 + x + 1$.*

Remark 6. Note, Proposition 2 is a particular case of Proposition 3 by taking $\beta = \alpha$, where α is the root of the constructing polynomial of $\mathbb{F}_{2^n}$. In canonical representation of $\mathbb{F}_{2^n}$, MDS matrix construction from Proposition 2 is more efficient.

Now we study $Serial(1, \beta, 1, \beta + 1)^4$ for any non zero $\beta \in \mathbb{F}_{2^n}$.

Proposition 4. *Let $A = Serial(1, \beta, 1, \beta + 1)$ be a 4×4 matrix over the finite field $\mathbb{F}_{2^n}$. Also let γ be any primitive element of $\mathbb{F}_{2^n}$ and $\beta = \gamma^i$ such that $i \in C_s$. Then if $|C_s| \geq 4$ then A^4 is always an MDS matrix.*

Remark 7. Similar to Remark 6, if we take $\beta = \alpha$ in Proposition 4, where α is the root of the constructing polynomial of $\mathbb{F}_{2^n}$, we get another *efficient* MDS matrix $Serial(1, \alpha, 1, \alpha + 1)^4$ in canonical representation of $\mathbb{F}_{2^n}$.

We observe that if $Serial(1, \beta, 1, \beta^2)^4$ is an MDS matrix, then the matrices $Serial(1, \beta, 1, \beta^2)^{-4}$ and $Serial(1, \beta^2, 1, \beta)^4$ are also MDS. We record this in Lemma 8 and Lemma 9

Lemma 8. *If $Serial(1, \beta, 1, \beta^2)^4$ is an MDS matrix for some $\beta \in \mathbb{F}_{2^n}$, then so is the matrix $Serial(1, \beta, 1, \beta^2)^{-4}$.*

Lemma 9. *If $Serial(1, \beta, 1, \beta^2)^4$ is an MDS matrix for some $\beta \in \mathbb{F}_{2^n}$, then so is the matrix $Serial(1, \beta^2, 1, \beta)^4$.*

4.2   Lightweight MDS Matrix of the Form $Serial(z_0, 1, 1, z_3)^4$

In the Subsection 4.1, we study the MDS property of the matrices of the form given by $Serial(1, z_1, 1, z_3)^4$ for z_i's in $\{\alpha, \alpha^2, \alpha + 1\}$, where α is the root of constructing polynomial of $\mathbb{F}_{2^n}$ for arbitrary n. In this Subsection we study matrices of the form $Serial(z_0, 1, 1, z_3)^4$ over $\mathbb{F}_{2^n}$ for arbitrary n, where $z_0, z_3 \in \{\alpha, \alpha^2\}$. Note that if $z_0, z_3 \in \{\alpha, \alpha + 1\}$, then the matrices will be non MDS (see Lemma 7). Also for better hardware footprint we omit the case when $z_0, z_3 \in \{\alpha^2, \alpha + 1\}$. We observe that no MDS matrix exits of the form $Serial(\alpha, 1, 1, \alpha^2)^4$ over $\mathbb{F}_{2^n}$, where $1 \leq n \leq 3$. In the next Proposition we consider matrices of the form $Serial(\beta, 1, 1, \beta^2)^4$ for any non zero $\beta \in \mathbb{F}_{2^n}$.

Proposition 5. *Let* $B = Serial(\beta, 1, 1, \beta^2)$ *be defined over* $\mathbb{F}_{2^n}$. *Also let* γ *be the primitive element of* $\mathbb{F}_{2^n}$ *and* $\beta = \gamma^i$ *such that* $i \in C_s$. *Then if* $|C_s| \geq 4$ *then* B^4 *is always an MDS matrix except when* $|C_s| = 4$ *and the minimal polynomial of* β *is* $x^4 + x^3 + x^2 + x + 1$ *or* $x^4 + x^3 + 1$ *and also when* $|C_s| = 7$ *and the minimal polynomial of* β *is* $x^7 + x^6 + x^5 + x^4 + 1$.

Remark 8. Similar to Remark 6, if we take $\beta = \alpha$ in Proposition 5, where α is the root of the constructing polynomial of $\mathbb{F}_{2^n}$, we get another *efficient* MDS matrix $Serial(\alpha, 1, 1, \alpha^2)^4$ in canonical representation of $\mathbb{F}_{2^n}$.

Remark 9. Note if $Serial(\beta, 1, 1, \beta^2)^4$ is an MDS matrix, then not necessarily $Serial(\beta, 1, 1, \beta^2)^{-4}$ and $Serial(\beta^2, 1, 1, \beta)^4$ are MDS (See Lemma 8 and Lemma 9).

In this Section we found values of $z \in \mathbb{F}_{2^n}$ which are of low hamming weight, such that $Serial(1, z, 1, z^2)^4$ and $Serial(1, z^2, 1, z)^4$ are MDS matrices for all $n \geq 5$ and $Serial(z, 1, 1, z^2)^4$ is MDS matrix for all $n \geq 4$. It may be checked that for $n = 3$ no $Serial(z_0, z_1, z_2, z_3)^4$ is an MDS having two of its entries as one; though for $n = 3$, many such MDS matrices of the form $Serial(z_0, z_1, z_2, z_3)^4$ exist where exactly one of its entries is one. Take for example $Serial(1, \alpha, \alpha^5, \alpha)^4$, where α is the root of $x^3 + x^2 + 1$. For $n = 2$ and 1, no MDS matrix of the form $Serial(z_0, z_1, z_2, z_3)^4$ exists.

5   Conclusion

In this paper, we developed techniques to test if a given $d \times d$ matrix over $\mathbb{F}_{2^n}$ is an MDS matrix. We propose a simple algorithm (Algorithm 1) based on some basic properties of MDS matrix. We run the algorithm for up to $n = 24$ and $d = 8$. It might be of interest to explore how further properties related to MDS matrix can be used to develop more efficient algorithm for checking whether a given matrix is MDS.

We developed theories to justify why matrices of the form given by $Serial(z_0, z_1, z_2, z_3)^4$ and $Serial(z_0, z_1, z_2, z_3, z_4)^5$ over $\mathbb{F}_{2^n}$ are MDS for different values n for low Hamming weight choices of values of z_i's, preferably within the set $\{1, \alpha, \alpha^2, \alpha + 1\}$. This leads to new constructions of 4×4 MDS matrices over $\mathbb{F}_{2^n}$ for all $n \geq 4$ and and 5×5 MDS matrices over $\mathbb{F}_{2^n}$ for all $n \geq 8$. We tried to generalize such results for $Serial(z_0, \ldots, z_{d-1})$ so that $Serial(z_0, \ldots, z_{d-1})^d$ is $d \times d$ MDS matrix for $d > 5$. In doing so, we tried to explore the properties of a companion matrix and its corresponding characteristic polynomial. We use the property that eigen values of a matrix A (in our case $A = Serial(z_0, \ldots, z_{d-1})$) are precisely the roots of the characteristic polynomial (in our case it is $z_0 + z_1 x + z_2 x^2 + \ldots + z_{d-1} x^{d-1} + x^d$); Together with the property that if λ is an eigen value of A, then $f(\lambda)$ is the eigen value of $f(A)$ (in our case $f(x) = x^d$) [15]. But with this simple technique, finding sufficient conditions seem difficult for arbitrary d. It may be interesting to carry out more research to construct $d \times d$ MDS matrix $Serial(z_0, \ldots, z_{d-1})^k$ for arbitrary d and $k \geq d$.

Acknowledgements. We wish to thank Professor Palash Sarkar who motivated the problem. We also wish to thank Subhabrata Samajder, Sumit Kumar Pandey and anonymous reviewers for providing several useful and valuable suggestions.

References

1. Bosma, W., Cannon, J., Playoust, C.: The Magma Algebra System I: The User Language. J. Symbolic Comput. 24(3-4), 235–265 (1997); Computational algebra and number theory, London (1993)
2. Daemen, J., Knudsen, L.R., Rijmen, V.: The block cipher SQUARE. In: Biham, E. (ed.) FSE 1997. LNCS, vol. 1267, pp. 149–165. Springer, Heidelberg (1997)
3. Daemen, J., Rijmen, V.: The Design of Rijndael: AES - The Advanced Encryption Standard. Springer (2002)
4. Filho, G.D., Barreto, P., Rijmen, V.: The Maelstrom-0 Hash Function. In: Proceedings of the 6th Brazilian Symposium on Information and Computer Systems Security (2006)
5. Gauravaram, P., Knudsen, L.R., Matusiewicz, K., Mendel, F., Rechberger, C., Schlaffer, M., Thomsen, S.: Grøstl a SHA-3 Candidate, Submission to NIST (2008), http://www.groestl.info
6. Guo, J., Peyrin, T., Poschmann, A.: The P*HOTON* Family of Lightweight Hash Functions. In: Rogaway, P. (ed.) CRYPTO 2011. LNCS, vol. 6841, pp. 222–239. Springer, Heidelberg (2011)
7. Chand Gupta, K., Ghosh Ray, I.: On Constructions of Involutory MDS Matrices. In: Youssef, A., Nitaj, A., Hassanien, A.E. (eds.) AFRICACRYPT 2013. LNCS, vol. 7918, pp. 43–60. Springer, Heidelberg (2013)
8. Heys, H.M., Tavares, S.E.: The Design of Substitution-Permutation Networks Resistant to Differential and Linear Cryptanalysis. In: Proceedings of 2nd ACM Conference on Computer and Communications Security, Fairfax, Virginia, pp. 148–155 (1994)
9. Heys, H.M., Tavares, S.E.: The Design of Product Ciphers Resistant to Differential and Linear Cryptanalysis. Journal of Cryptography 9(1), 1–19 (1996)
10. Heys, H.M., Tavares, S.E.: Avalanche Characteristics of Substitution-Permutation Encryption Networks. IEEE Trans. Comp. 44, 1131–1139 (1995)
11. Nakahara Jr., J., Abrahao, E.: A New Involutory MDS Matrix for the AES. International Journal of Network Security 9(2), 109–116 (2009)
12. Junod, P., Vaudenay, S.: Perfect Diffusion Primitives for Block Ciphers Building Efficient MDS Matrices. In: Handschuh, H., Hasan, A. (eds.) SAC 2004. LNCS, vol. 3357, pp. 84–99. Springer, Heidelberg (2004)
13. Lacan, J., Fimes, J.: Systematic MDS erasure codes based on vandermonde matrices. IEEE Trans. Commun. Lett. 8(9), 570–572 (2004) CrossRef
14. MacWilliams, F.J., Sloane, N.J.A.: The Theory of Error Correcting Codes. North Holland (1986)
15. Rao, A.R., Bhimasankaram, P.: Linear Algebra, 2nd edn. Hindustan Book Agency
16. Rijmen, V., Daemen, J., Preneel, B., Bosselaers, A., Win, E.D.: The cipher SHARK. In: Gollmann, D. (ed.) FSE 1996. LNCS, vol. 1039, pp. 99–112. Springer, Heidelberg (1996)
17. Sajadieh, M., Dakhilalian, M., Mala, H., Omoomi, B.: On construction of involutory MDS matrices from Vandermonde Matrices in $GF(2^q)$. Designs, Codes and Cryptography 2012, 1–22 (2012)

18. Sajadieh, M., Dakhilalian, M., Mala, H., Sepehrdad, P.: Recursive Diffusion Layers for Block Ciphers and Hash Functions. In: Canteaut, A. (ed.) FSE 2012. LNCS, vol. 7549, pp. 385–401. Springer, Heidelberg (2012)
19. Schneier, B., Kelsey, J., Whiting, D., Wagner, D., Hall, C., Ferguson, N.: Twofish: A 128-bit block cipher. In: The First AES Candidate Conference, National Institute for Standards and Technology (1998)
20. Schneier, B., Kelsey, J., Whiting, D., Wagner, D., Hall, C., Ferguson, N.: The Twofish encryption algorithm. Wiley (1999)
21. Shannon, C.E.: Communication Theory of Secrecy Systems. Bell Syst. Technical J. 28, 656–715 (1949)
22. Wu, S., Wang, M., Wu, W.: Recursive Diffusion Layers for (Lightweight) Block Ciphers and Hash Functions. In: Knudsen, L.R., Wu, H. (eds.) SAC 2012. LNCS, vol. 7707, pp. 355–371. Springer, Heidelberg (2013)
23. Youssef, A.M., Mister, S., Tavares, S.E.: On the Design of Linear Transformations for Substitution Permutation Encryption Networks. In: Workshop on Selected Areas in Cryptography, SAC 1997, pp. 40–48 (1997)

A   Proof of Corollary 1

Proof. Let $((a_{i,j}))$ be a 2×2 full rank matrix and let all entries of its inverse be non zero. Let its inverse matrix be $\frac{((b_{i,j}))}{det(A)}$. It is easy to check that $b_{0,0} = a_{1,1}$, $b_{1,1} = a_{0,0}, b_{0,1} = -a_{0,1}$ and $b_{1,0} = -a_{1,0}$. Since all entries of $((b_{i,j}))$ are non zero, all entries of $((a_{i,j}))$ are also non zero. So $((a_{i,j}))$ is MDS. The other direction of the proof is immediate. □

B   Proof of Corollary 2

Proof. Let $\mathbb{M} = ((m_{i,j}))$ be a 3×3 full rank matrix with all non zero entries, such that its inverse matrix also has got all non zero entries. So, all 2×2 submatrices of $\mathbb{M}$ are nonsingular. Note that all 1×1 submatrices, which are nothing but the elements $m_{i,j}$'s, are also non zero. Thus the matrix is MDS matrix. The other direction of the proof is immediate. □

C   Proof of Lemma 2

Proof. It is easy to check that,

$$Serial(1,1,1,1)^4 = \begin{pmatrix} 1 & 1 & 1 & 1 \\ 1 & 0 & 0 & 0 \\ 0 & 1 & 0 & 0 \\ 0 & 0 & 1 & 0 \end{pmatrix}.$$

Since some entries of $Serial(1,1,1,1)^4$ are zero, so from Fact 2, clearly $Serial(1,1,1,1)^4$ is not an MDS matrix. Similarly it can be shown that when any three of z_0, z_1, z_2 and z_3 are 1, some entries of the matrix $Serial(z_0, z_1, z_2, z_3)^4$ are zero. Hence the result. □

D Proof of Lemma 6

Proof.

$$
B^4 = \begin{pmatrix}
\alpha & 1 & 1 & \alpha^2 \\
\alpha^3 & \alpha^2 + \alpha & \alpha^2 + 1 & \alpha^4 + 1 \\
\alpha^5 + \alpha & \alpha^4 + \alpha^3 + 1 & \alpha^4 + \alpha^2 + \alpha + 1 & \alpha^6 + 1 \\
\alpha^7 + \alpha & \alpha^6 + \alpha^5 + \alpha + 1 & \alpha^6 + \alpha^4 + \alpha^3 & \alpha^8 + \alpha^4 + \alpha + 1
\end{pmatrix} \tag{4}
$$

also

$$
B^{-4} = \frac{1}{\alpha^4} \begin{pmatrix}
\alpha^3 + \alpha^2 + \alpha + 1 & \alpha^3 + \alpha^2 + 1 & \alpha^6 + \alpha & \alpha^4 + 1 \\
\alpha^5 + \alpha & \alpha^4 + \alpha^3 + \alpha^2 + \alpha & \alpha^4 + \alpha^3 + \alpha^2 & \alpha^2 + \alpha \\
\alpha^3 + \alpha^2 & \alpha^5 + \alpha^2 & \alpha^4 + \alpha^3 & \alpha^2 \\
\alpha^3 & \alpha^3 & \alpha^5 & \alpha^3
\end{pmatrix}
$$

$$\tag{5}$$

The list of determinants of all 36, 2×2 submatrices of B^4 are

α^2, α, α, $\alpha + 1$, $\alpha^3 + 1$, $\alpha^2 + 1$, α^4, $\alpha^3 + \alpha^2$, $\alpha^3 + \alpha$, $\alpha^3 + \alpha^2 + \alpha$, $\alpha^5 + \alpha^2 + 1$, $\alpha^4 + \alpha^3 + \alpha^2 + 1$, $\alpha^6 + \alpha^2$, $\alpha^5 + \alpha^4 + \alpha$, $\alpha^5 + \alpha^3 + \alpha^2 + \alpha$, $\alpha^5 + \alpha^4 + \alpha^3 + \alpha + 1$, $\alpha^7 + \alpha^4 + \alpha^3 + \alpha^2 + \alpha + 1$, $\alpha^6 + \alpha^5 + \alpha^4 + \alpha + 1$, α^2, $\alpha^4 + \alpha$, $\alpha^3 + \alpha$, $\alpha^3 + \alpha^2 + \alpha + 1$, $\alpha^3 + \alpha^2 + \alpha + 1$, $\alpha^5 + \alpha$, $\alpha^4 + \alpha^2$, $\alpha^6 + \alpha^3 + \alpha$, $\alpha^5 + \alpha^4 + \alpha^3 + \alpha$, $\alpha^5 + \alpha^4 + \alpha^3 + \alpha^2 + \alpha + 1$, $\alpha^5 + \alpha^4 + \alpha^3 + 1$, $\alpha^7 + \alpha^2 + \alpha + 1$, $\alpha^4 + \alpha^2$, $\alpha^4 + \alpha^3 + \alpha^2 + \alpha$, $\alpha^6 + \alpha^2$, 1, $\alpha^4 + \alpha^3$, $\alpha^4 + 1$.

There are three irreducible polynomials with coefficients from $\mathbb{F}_2$ and degree 4, namely $x^4 + x + 1$, $x^4 + x^3 + 1$ and $x^4 + x^3 + x^2 + x + 1$. It is easy to observe that $B^4[2][1] = \alpha^4 + \alpha^3 + 1$ and $B^4[3][1] = \alpha^6 + \alpha^5 + \alpha + 1 = (\alpha + 1)^2(\alpha^4 + \alpha^3 + \alpha^2 + \alpha + 1)$. Thus, when the minimal polynomial of α is $x^4 + x^3 + 1$ or $x^4 + x^3 + x^2 + x + 1$, $B^4[2][1]$ or $B^4[3][1]$ will be 0 respectively. Also note that no polynomial in the above list or in the entries of B^4 or its inverse is a multiple of $\alpha^4 + \alpha + 1$. Thus B^4 is a non MDS matrix for $n = 4$ except when the minimal polynomial of α is $x^4 + x + 1$,

It is easy to observe that $B^4[3][2] = \alpha^6 + \alpha^4 + \alpha^3 = \alpha^3(\alpha^3 + \alpha + 1)$ and $B^4[2][2] = \alpha^4 + \alpha^2 + \alpha + 1 = (\alpha + 1)(\alpha^3 + \alpha^2 + 1)$. So, when the minimal polynomial of α is $x^3 + x + 1$ or $x^3 + x^2 + 1$, $B^4[3][2]$ or $B^4[2][2]$ will be zero respectively. Thus B^4 is a non MDS matrix for $n = 3$.

Again $B^4[2][3] = \alpha^6 + 1 = (\alpha + 1)^2(\alpha^2 + \alpha + 1)^2$ which is zero when the minimal polynomial of α is $x^2 + x + 1$. Thus B^4 is a non MDS matrix for $n = 2$.

Lastly, when $n = 1$, α is 1, making $B = Serial(1, 1, 1, 1)$ and from Lemma 2, B^4 will be non MDS matrix.

Similarly it can be proved that B'^4 is non MDS matrix. $\qquad\square$

E Proof of Proposition 2

Proof. The minimal polynomial of α must be of degree $n \geq 5$. From equation 2 and equation 3, we get A^4 and A^{-4}. It is easy to check that $A^4[2][1] = \alpha^5 + \alpha^2 + \alpha = \alpha(\alpha^4 + \alpha + 1) \neq 0$, $A^4[2][3] = A^4[3][0] = \alpha^6 + \alpha = \alpha(\alpha + 1)(\alpha^4 + \alpha^3 + \alpha^2 + $

$\alpha + 1) \neq 0$, $A^4[3][2] = \alpha^6 + \alpha^5 + \alpha^2 = \alpha^2(\alpha^4 + \alpha^3 + 1) \neq 0$, $A^4[3][3] = \alpha^8 + \alpha^4 = \alpha^4(\alpha + 1)^4 \neq 0$, $A^{-4}[0][2] = \alpha^5 + \alpha^4 + \alpha^2 + 1 = (\alpha + 1)(\alpha^4 + \alpha + 1) \neq 0$.

Out of all polynomials in α that are occurring in the entries of A^4 and its inverse, the above polynomials are of degree more than 5 and rest of the entries are of degree less than 5 except $A^4[3][2] = \alpha^7 + \alpha^4 + \alpha^2 + 1 = (\alpha + 1)(\alpha^6 + \alpha^5 + \alpha^4 + \alpha + 1)$. So $A^4[3][2] = 0$ if $n = 6$ and α is the root of $x^6 + x^5 + x^4 + x + 1 = 0$. Thus all entries of A^4 and its inverse are non zero for $n \geq 5$ except when $n = 6$ and α is root of $x^6 + x^5 + x^4 + x + 1 = 0$.

It is easy to check that the number of 2×2 submatrices of A^4 is 36. Determinants of all these 2×2 submatrices of A^4 are

1, α, 1, $\alpha^2 + 1$, $\alpha^2 + \alpha$, $\alpha^3 + 1$, α^2, $\alpha^3 + 1$, $\alpha^2 + \alpha$, $\alpha^4 + \alpha^2 + \alpha$, $\alpha^4 + \alpha^3 + \alpha^2$, $\alpha^5 + \alpha$, $\alpha^4 + 1$, $\alpha^5 + \alpha^2 + \alpha$, $\alpha^4 + \alpha^3$, $\alpha^6 + \alpha^4 + \alpha^3 + \alpha^2 + 1$, $\alpha^6 + \alpha^5 + \alpha^4 + \alpha^2$, α^7, 1, $\alpha^2 + \alpha$, $\alpha^3 + 1$, $\alpha^3 + \alpha^2$, $\alpha^4 + \alpha^2$, $\alpha^4 + \alpha^2$, $\alpha^2 + \alpha$, $\alpha^4 + \alpha^3 + \alpha^2$, $\alpha^5 + \alpha$, $\alpha^5 + \alpha^4 + \alpha^3 + \alpha$, $\alpha^6 + \alpha^4 + \alpha^2 + 1$, $\alpha^6 + \alpha^2$, $\alpha^3 + 1$, $\alpha^4 + \alpha^2$, $\alpha^4 + \alpha^2$, α^5, $\alpha^3 + \alpha$, $\alpha^6 + \alpha^3$.

It is evident that these polynomials in this list which are of degree less than 5 are non zero. Rest of the polynomials in the list having degree ≥ 5 are

$\alpha^5 + \alpha, \alpha^5 + \alpha^2 + \alpha, \alpha^6 + \alpha^4 + \alpha^3 + \alpha^2 + 1, \alpha^6 + \alpha^5 + \alpha^4 + \alpha^2, \alpha^7, \alpha^5 + \alpha, \alpha^5 + \alpha^4 + \alpha^3 + \alpha, \alpha^6 + \alpha^4 + \alpha^2 + 1, \alpha^6 + \alpha^2, \alpha^5, \alpha^6 + \alpha^3$.

It is easy to check that these values are all non zero as all can be factored into polynomials of degree less than 5. Thus from Proposition 1, A^4 is an MDS matrix.   □

F   Few More Lightweight 4×4 MDS Matrices

Here we provide few more 4×4 MDS matrices which are of the form $Serial(1, 1, z_2, z_3)^4$ and $Serial(1, z_1, z_2, 1)^4$.

– $Serial(1, 1, \alpha + 1, \alpha^2)^4$ is MDS for all $n \geq 5$ except for the case when $n = 5$ and the minimal polynomial of α is $x^5 + x^3 + 1$ or $x^5 + x^4 + x^3 + x + 1$.
– $Serial(1, 1, \alpha^2, \alpha + 1)^4$ is MDS for all $n \geq 4$ except for the case when $n = 5$ and the minimal polynomial of α is $x^5 + x^2 + 1$ or $x^5 + x^4 + x^3 + x + 1$ or when $n = 4$ and the minimal polynomial of α is $x^4 + x^3 + 1$ or $x^4 + x + 1$.
– $Serial(1, \alpha^2, \alpha + 1, 1)^4$ is MDS for all $n \geq 5$ except for the case when $n = 5$ and the minimal polynomial of α is $x^5 + x^3 + 1$ or $x^5 + x^4 + x^3 + x + 1$.
– $Serial(1, \alpha + 1, \alpha^2, 1)^4$ is MDS for all $n \geq 4$ except for the case when $n = 5$ and the minimal polynomial of α is $x^5 + x^2 + 1$ or $x^5 + x^4 + x^3 + x + 1$ or when $n = 4$ and the minimal polynomial of α is $x^4 + x^3 + 1$ or $x^4 + x + 1$.

G   Lightweight 5×5 MDS Matrix of the Form $Serial(1, z_1, 1, 1, z_4)^5$

In this Subsection we study $Serial(z_0, z_1, z_2, z_3, z_4)^5$, where the elements $z_0, z_1, z_2, z_3, z_4 \in \mathbb{F}_{2^n}$. As mentioned in Remark 1, we restrict values of z_i's to $1, \alpha, \alpha^2, \alpha + 1$ and try to maximize the occurrence of 1's in the matrix $Serial(z_0, z_1, z_2, z_3, z_4)$ for better hardware implementation. If 1 is allowed in all four or more places of z_0, z_1, z_2, z_3 and z_4, the matrix $Serial(z_0, z_1, z_2, z_3, z_4)^5$ is not MDS (similar to Lemma 2). We next study the possibility of having MDS matrices of the form $Serial(z_0, z_1, z_2, z_3, z_4)^5$ when any three out of z_0, z_1, z_2, z_3 and z_4 are 1. Note that there are 10 such cases. We have the following propositions similar to Proposition 2.

Proposition 6. *Let $A = Serial(1, \alpha, 1, 1, \alpha^2)$ which is defined over $\mathbb{F}_{2^n}$, where α is the root of the constructing polynomial of $\mathbb{F}_{2^n}$. Then A^5 is MDS for all $n \geq 7$ except when $n = 8$ and α is the root of $x^8 + x^7 + x^6 + x^4 + x^3 + x^2 + 1 = 0$ or $n = 7$ and α is the root of $x^7 + x^3 + x^2 + x + 1$ or $x^7 + x^6 + x^5 + x^2 + 1$ or $x^7 + x^6 + x^5 + x^4 + 1$ or $x^7 + x^6 + x^5 + x^4 + x^3 + x^2 + 1$.*

Remark 10. $Serial(1, \alpha, 1, 1, \alpha^2)^5$ of Proposition 6 is MDS when $n = 6$ and minimal polynomial of α is $x^6 + x^5 + 1$ or $x^6 + x^4 + x^3 + x + 1$

Proposition 7. *Let $A' = Serial(1, \alpha^2, 1, 1, \alpha)$ which is defined over $\mathbb{F}_{2^n}$, where α is the root of the constructing polynomial of $\mathbb{F}_{2^n}$. Then A'^5 is MDS for all $n \geq 8$ except when $n = 8$ and α is the root of $x^8 + x^7 + x^6 + x^4 + x^3 + x^2 + 1 = 0$.*

Remark 11. We observe that $Serial(z_0, z_1, z_2, z_3, z_4)^5$ does not give MDS matrices when any three of z_0, z_1, z_2, z_3 and z_4 are set as 1 and rest two are restricted in $\{\alpha, \alpha^2, \alpha + 1\}$ except the cases mentioned in Proposition 6 and Proposition 7.

Code-Based Public-Key Encryption Resistant to Key Leakage*

Edoardo Persichetti

University of Warsaw

Abstract. Side-channel attacks are a major issue for implementation of secure cryptographic schemes. Among these, key-leakage attacks describe a scenario in which an adversary is allowed to learn arbitrary information about the private key, the only constraint being the number of bits learned. In this work, we study key-leakage resilience according to the model presented by Akavia, Goldwasser and Vaikuntanathan at TCC '09. As our main contribution, we present a code-based hash proof system; we obtain our construction by relaxing some of the requirements from the original definition of Cramer and Shoup. We then propose a leakage-resilient public-key encryption scheme that makes use of this hash proof system. To do so, we adapt a framework featured in a previous work by Alwen et al. regarding identity-based encryption (EUROCRYPT '10). Our construction features error-correcting codes as a technical tool, and, as opposed to previous work, does not require the use of a randomness extractor.

1   Introduction

Traditionally, the security of cryptographic schemes is analyzed with respect to an idealized, abstract adversarial model [14]. Unfortunately, in the real world, implementations of cryptographic schemes are often vulnerable to an additional kind of threat, of a more physical nature. These are the so-called *side-channel* attacks, which are based on the observation of phenomena directly connected with the implementation, such as power or timing measurements, detection of internal faults and leakage of some private information. It is therefore important to build schemes whose security can be argued even in presence of such attacks.

In this work, we focus on one particular type of attacks, known as "cold boot" or memory attacks, first introduced by Halderman et al. [16] in 2008. The authors show how it is possible to recover private information stored in the device's memory after the device is turned off; this is because typical DRAM memories only lose their content during a gradual period of time. In particular, a significant fraction of the cryptographic key stored in the memory can be easily recovered, leading to potentially devastating attacks. We therefore speak about *key-leakage* attacks. A general framework that models key-leakage attacks was

---

* European Research Council has provided financial support under the European Community's Seventh Framework Programme (FP7/2007-2013) / ERC grant agreement no CNTM-207908.

A. Cuzzocrea et al. (Eds.): CD-ARES 2013 Workshops, LNCS 8128, pp. 44–54, 2013.

introduced by Akavia, Goldwasser and Vaikuntanathan [1]. In this model, the adversary is allowed the knowledge of arbitrarily chosen functions of the private key, with the restriction that the total output of these functions doesn't exceed a certain bound λ. Attacks can be performed, as usual, both in an adaptive or non-adaptive fashion. The authors then show that the lattice-based public-key encryption scheme of Regev [23] and the identity-based encryption scheme of Gentry, Peikert and Vaikuntanathan [13] are resistant to such leakage. The framework was subsequently revisited by Naor and Segev [21] and further generalized by Alwen, Dodis and Wichs [3], who provide the first public-key primitives in the *Bounded Retrieval Model (BRM)*. This model had been previously introduced by Dziembowski and Di Crescenzo in independent works [10,7] for symmetric encryption schemes.

To date, many cryptographic primitives have been shown to be resilient to key-leakage attacks, based on a variety of assumptions such as DDH or d-Linear, quadratic residuosity, composite residuosity and LWE; however, there is no known construction based on coding theory assumptions. Code-based cryptography is one of the candidates for "post-quantum" cryptography; compared to LWE-based schemes, code-based schemes have the advantage of a simpler structure (for example, they usually work over the binary field) thus allowing for more practical implementations.

Our contribution. In this paper, we propose a protocol based solely on coding theory assumptions, that achieves semantic security against key-leakage attacks. The first step is to build a *Hash Proof System (HPS)*. This primitive, essentially a special kind of non-interactive zero-knowledge proof system for a language, was first introduced by Cramer and Shoup in [6] as a theoretical tool to construct efficient public-key encryption schemes. It was later shown by Kiltz et al. [20] that it is possible to view a HPS as a key encapsulation mechanism (KEM) with special properties, and that it is possible to obtain secure hybrid encryption schemes by using randomness extractors. The work of Naor and Segev [21] builds on this method, and the authors present a general framework to design leakage-resilient encryption schemes using any HPS together with a randomness extractor. This is also the basis for a recent paper by Alwen et al. [2] in which the framework is extended to the identity-based setting. Our construction works as follows. The private key has a high min-entropy that is guaranteed by analyzing the volume of spheres centered on codewords of a randomly generated code. This induces an error in the decapsulation procedure; however, we manage to bound the size of the error term by carefully choosing the scheme's parameters. This allows us to deal with the possible decryption error by using error-correcting codes in our encryption scheme. Finally, we achieve ciphertext indistinguishability thanks to the pseudorandomness of the syndrome construction (Fischer and Stern [11]) for low-weight error vectors. To the best of our knowledge, this is the first construction of a hash proof system from coding theory assumptions.

The paper is structured as follows: in Section 2 we give some preliminary definitions necessary for the remainder of the paper. Next, we describe hash proof systems (Section 3) and leakage-resilient public-key encryption (Section 4).

Our construction of a code-based hash proof system is presented in Section 5, and the encryption scheme based on it in Section 6. We conclude in Section 7.

2   Preliminaries

We start by providing some probability notions that are relevant for the paper. The notation $x \leftarrow \chi_\rho$ means sampling an element x from the Bernoulli distribution with parameter ρ: this extends naturally to vectors and matrices with notation, respectively, χ_ρ^n and $\chi_\rho^{m \times n}$. The *statistical distance* between two random variables X and Y with values in Ω is defined as $\Delta(X, Y) = \frac{1}{2} \sum_{\omega \in \Omega} \left| \Pr[X = \omega] - \Pr[Y = \omega] \right|$. The *min-entropy* of a random variable X is $H_\infty(X) = -\log(\max_{\omega \in \Omega} \Pr[X = \omega])$. We also present the notion of *average min-entropy*, which is useful to describe the unpredictability of a random variable X conditioned on the value of another random variable Y, as $\tilde{H}_\infty(X|Y) = -\log \left(\mathbb{E}_{y \overset{\$}{\leftarrow} Y} \left[2^{-H_\infty(X|Y=y)} \right] \right)$.

Next, we present a few basic coding theory notions. Throughout the paper, we will treat all vectors as column vectors, and denote them by a boldface letter. An $[n, k]$ linear code over the finite field $\mathbb{F}_q$ is a vector subspace $\mathcal{C}$ of $\mathbb{F}_q^n$ of dimension k. A *generator matrix* for $\mathcal{C}$ is a matrix whose rows form a basis for the subspace. A *parity-check matrix* for $\mathcal{C}$ is an $(n - k) \times n$ matrix H such that $H\boldsymbol{x} = \boldsymbol{0}$ for all codewords $\boldsymbol{x}$. For every vector $\boldsymbol{x} \in \mathbb{F}_q^n$ the *Hamming weight* $\mathsf{wt}(\boldsymbol{x})$ is the number of its non-zero positions; $\mathsf{d}(\boldsymbol{x}, \boldsymbol{y}) = \mathsf{wt}(\boldsymbol{x} - \boldsymbol{y})$ is the *Hamming distance* between the two words $\boldsymbol{x}$ and $\boldsymbol{y}$. The *minimum distance* of a code $\mathcal{C}$ is simply the minimum between the distance of all codewords of $\mathcal{C}$. The following is a very important bound on the minimum distance of linear codes.

Definition 1 (GV Bound). *Let $\mathcal{C}$ be an $[n, k]$ linear code over $\mathbb{F}_q$. The* Gilbert-Varshamov (GV) Distance *is the largest integer d_0 such that*

$$|\mathcal{B}(\boldsymbol{0}, d_0 - 1)| \leq q^{n-k} \tag{1}$$

where $\mathcal{B}(\boldsymbol{x}, r) = \{\boldsymbol{y} \in \mathbb{F}_q^n | d(\boldsymbol{x}, \boldsymbol{y}) \leq r\}$ is the n-dimensional ball of radius r centered in $\boldsymbol{x}$.

For an integer w below the GV bound, the following problem is hard (Berlekamp, McEliece and van Tilborg [4]).

Definition 2 (Syndrome Decoding Problem). *Given an $(n - k) \times n$ parity-check matrix H for an $[n, k]$ linear code $\mathcal{C}$ over $\mathbb{F}_q$, a vector $\boldsymbol{s} \in \mathbb{F}_q^{n-k}$ and an integer $w \in \mathbb{N}^+$, find $\boldsymbol{e} \in \mathbb{F}_q^n$ such that $\boldsymbol{s} = H\boldsymbol{e}$ and $\mathsf{wt}(\boldsymbol{e}) \leq w$.*

3   Hash Proof Systems

Like in the majority of previous work, we use a HPS for our construction. To describe our HPS, we adapt the "simplified" definition of [2] to public-key encryption schemes.

Table 1. Hash Proof System

Setup	The setup algorithm takes as input a security parameter θ and returns the public parameters of the scheme. The algorithm also defines the set K of encapsulated keys.
KeyGen	The key generation algorithm takes as input the public parameters and outputs a public key pk and a private key sk.
Encap	The *valid* encapsulation algorithm receives as input the public key pk and returns a ciphertext/key pair (ψ_0, K).
Encap*	The *invalid* encapsulation algorithm receives as input the public key pk and samples an invalid ciphertext ψ_0.
Decap	The decapsulation algorithm takes as input a private key sk and a ciphertext ψ_0 and outputs a key K'.

Note that all of the above algorithms are probabilistic, except Decap, which is deterministic. There are two important requirements on the output of Decap. If ψ_0 is a valid ciphertext (i.e. produced by Encap) we require *correctness*.

Definition 3 (Correctness of decapsulation). *Fix any values of pk and sk, as output by KeyGen, and let* $(\psi_0, K) = Encap(pk)$ *and* $K' = Decap(sk, \psi_0)$. *Then:*

$$Pr[K \neq K'] = negl(\theta). \tag{2}$$

For our scheme, a relaxation of the above requirement will suffice, called *approximate correctness*. This notion was introduced by Katz and Vaikuntanathan in [19], and asks that the output of Decap is "close" (in Hamming sense) to the actual encapsulated key.

Definition 4 (*t*-Approximate Correctness). *Fix any values of pk and sk, as output by KeyGen, and let* $(\psi_0, K) = Encap(pk)$ *and* $K' = Decap(sk, \psi_0)$. *Then:*

$$Pr[d(K, K') > t] = negl(\theta). \tag{3}$$

For invalid ciphertexts (i.e. produced by Encap*), instead, we want Decap to return strings that are almost uniformly distributed. Following [2], we present three distinct notions in this regard.

Definition 5 (Universality). *Let SK and PK be random variables representing, respectively, sk and pk. We say that an HPS is (η, ν)-universal if* $\tilde{H}_\infty(SK|PK) \geq \eta$ *and, for any fixed values pk and sk $\neq$ sk', it holds:*

$$Pr[Decap(sk, \psi_0) = Decap(sk', \psi_0)] \leq \nu \tag{4}$$

where $\psi_0 = Encap^*(pk)$.

Definition 6 (Smoothness). *For any fixed pk and sk $\neq$ sk', let* $\psi_0 = Encap^*(pk)$, $K = Decap(sk, \psi_0)$. *Then we say that an HPS is smooth if:*

$$\Delta((\psi_0, K), (\psi_0, K')) = negl(\theta) \tag{5}$$

where $\psi_0 = Encap^*(pk)$, $K = Decap(sk, \psi_0)$ and K' is chosen uniformly at random.

Definition 7 (Leakage Smoothness). *We say that an HPS is λ-leakage smooth if, for any (possibly randomized) function f with output size bounded by λ, it holds:*

$$\Delta((\psi_0, f(sk), K), (\psi_0, f(sk), K')) = negl(\theta) \qquad (6)$$

for ψ_0, K and K' sampled as in Definition 6.

Finally, an HPS requires an indistinguishability property for ciphertexts, that is, a random valid ciphertext should be computationally indistinguishable from an invalid one. The definition is the following.

Definition 8 (Ciphertext Indistinguishability). *We define the following attack game between a challenger and an adversary $\mathcal{A}$:*

1. *Fix system parameters.*
2. *The adversary $\mathcal{A}$ makes a sequence of queries to the challenger, getting back public key/private key pairs (pk, sk).*
3. *The challenger fixes a target public key pk^*, then chooses a random bit b. If $b = 0$, it computes $(\psi_0, K) = Encap(pk^*)$, otherwise computes $\psi_0 = Encap^*(pk^*)$. It then gives ψ_0 to $\mathcal{A}$.*
4. *$\mathcal{A}$ keeps performing queries as above. No restrictions apply, hence $\mathcal{A}$ can even get sk^*.*
5. *Finally, $\mathcal{A}$ outputs $b^* \in \{0,1\}$.*

The adversary succeeds if $b^* = b$. More precisely, we define the advantage *of $\mathcal{A}$ against HPS as*

$$Adv_{HPS}(\mathcal{A}, \theta) = \left| Pr[b^* = b] - \frac{1}{2} \right|. \qquad (7)$$

We say that an HPS satisfies the ciphertext indistinguishability *property if the advantage Adv_{HPS} of any polynomial-time adversary $\mathcal{A}$ in the above adaptive attack model is negligible.*

Remark 1. In the original definition for an identity-based protocol, the adversary would perform queries adaptively submitting a certain identity and getting back the corresponding private key. Adapting this to the public-key setting just means that the adversary is allowed to see public key/private key pairs, including the "target" one. In both cases, this is a very strong requirement, meaning that ciphertexts have to be computationally indistinguishable even if the whole private key is revealed.

4 Leakage-Resilient Public-Key Encryption

We define here the notion of security for public-key encryption schemes under key-leakage attacks. An adversary in this setting is allowed to (adaptively) query a *leakage oracle*, submitting any function f and receiving $f(sk)$, with the only restriction that the total length of the output is not greater than a certain threshold λ. As pointed out by Akavia et al. [1], this is equivalent to querying the leakage oracle on a single function f whose total output doesn't exceed λ bits. The definition is given below.

Definition 9. *An adversary $\mathcal{A}$ for key-leakage security is a polynomial-time algorithm that plays the following attack game:*

1. *Query a key generation oracle to obtain a public key* pk.
2. *Submit a query f to the leakage oracle. The oracle will reply with $f(sk)$ provided that the output is less or equal to λ bits.*
3. *Choose $\phi_0, \phi_1 \in P$ and submit them to an encryption oracle. The oracle will choose a random $b \in \{0,1\}$ and reply with the "challenge" ciphertext $\psi^* = \text{Enc}(pk, \phi_b)$.*
4. *Output $b^* \in \{0,1\}$.*

We define the advantage of $\mathcal{A}$ against PKE as

$$Adv(\mathcal{A}, \theta) = \left| Pr[b^* = b] - \frac{1}{2} \right|. \tag{8}$$

We say that a PKE scheme is semantically secure against λ-key-leakage attacks *if the advantage of any adversary $\mathcal{A}$ in the above attack model is negligible.*

As usual, the above notion can be extended to the chosen-ciphertext attack model, allowing for decryption queries before (CCA1) or after (CCA2) the generation of the challenge ciphertext. In this case we speak about resistance to, respectively, *a priori* and *a posteriori* chosen-ciphertext key-leakage attacks.

5   The Construction

The choice of parameters here is important to guarantee that the construction satisfies the requirements presented in the previous section. In particular, we will need the rate $R = k/n$ to be high enough for ρ to be less than $1/\sqrt{n}$. We now analyze the three properties one at a time:

t-**Approximate Correctness.** As in Definition 4, let $(\psi_0, K) = \text{Encap}(pk)$ and $K' = \text{Decap}(sk, \psi_0)$; then K and K' differ by a factor of Es, and $d(K, K') = \text{wt}(Es)$, hence we just need to bound the weight of this product. Remember that E and s are distributed, respectively, according to $\chi_\rho^{\ell \times n}$ and χ_τ^n, where $\rho = O(n^{-1/2-\varepsilon})$ and $\tau = \gamma\rho$ for $\gamma > 0$. We now use a result from Döttling, Müller-Quade and Nascimento [8]. A matrix $X \in \mathbb{F}_2^{\ell \times n}$ is said to be (β, ϵ)-*good* if for a fixed constant β and $\epsilon = \epsilon(n)$ it holds that for all $s \in \mathbb{F}_2^n$ if $\text{wt}(s) \leq \epsilon n$ then $\text{wt}(Xs) \leq \beta\ell$. It is proved in [8] that when $\rho = O(n^{-1/2-\varepsilon})$ and n is sufficiently large, for any fixed $\beta, \gamma > 0$ a matrix sampled from $\chi_\rho^{\ell \times n}$ is $(\beta, \gamma\rho)$-good with overwhelming probability. Thus in our case we will have $\text{wt}(Es) \leq t$ for $t = \beta\ell$, and this concludes the proof.

Table 2. Code-based HPS

Setup	Public parameters are a matrix $A \xleftarrow{\$} \mathbb{F}_2^{k \times n}$ and integers k, n, ℓ with $k < n$, $\ell > k$. Let δ be the minimum distance of the code having A as generator matrix and set $\rho = \delta/n$ and $\tau = \gamma\rho$ for a certain $\gamma > 0$. The set of encapsulated keys is defined as $\mathsf{K} = \mathbb{F}_2^{\ell}$.
KeyGen	selects matrices $M \xleftarrow{\$} \mathbb{F}_2^{\ell \times k}$ and $E \leftarrow \chi_\rho^{\ell \times n}$ and outputs the private key $\mathsf{sk} = M$ and the public key $\mathsf{pk} = MA + E$.
Encap	chooses $s \leftarrow \chi_\tau^n$ and returns the ciphertext/key pair (ψ_0, K) where $\psi_0 = As$ and $K = \mathsf{pk} \cdot s$.
Encap*	chooses $r \xleftarrow{\$} \mathbb{F}_2^k$ and returns the invalid ciphertext $\psi_0 = r$.
Decap	takes as input the private key sk and a ciphertext ψ_0 and obtains K' as $\mathsf{sk} \cdot \psi_0$.

Universality. A defines a random linear code $\mathcal{C}$, hence its minimum distance δ is on the GV bound with high probability. Consider the expected number of codewords in $\mathcal{B}(x, r)$ for x chosen uniformly at random, $\mu_\mathcal{C}(r) = \mathbb{E}_{x \in \mathbb{F}_q^n}[|\mathcal{C} \cap \mathcal{B}(x, r)|]$. Following Dumer, Micciancio and Sudan [9], we know that $\mu_\mathcal{C}(r) = 2^{k-n} \cdot |\mathcal{B}(0, r)|$ (we are interested in the case $q = 2$), and that for $r = \delta$ this number is equal to a certain constant $\mu > 1$. Since each row of M is chosen independently, it holds $H_\infty(\mathsf{sk}) \geq \mu^\ell$. This completes the first part. For the second part, recall that $\mathsf{Decap}(\mathsf{sk}, \psi_0) = M\psi_0$. Consider two private keys $M \neq M'$: then $\mathsf{Decap}(\mathsf{sk}, \psi_0) = \mathsf{Decap}(\mathsf{sk}', \psi_0) \iff M\psi_0 = M'\psi_0 \iff (M - M')\psi_0 = 0$. Now, $\ell > k$ and both M and M' are generated uniformly at random, so the matrix $N = (M - M')$ is of full rank k with high probability [5], say p. It follows that $(M - M')\psi_0 = 0 \iff \psi_0 = 0$. We conclude that the code-based HPS is (η, ν)-universal, for $\eta = \mu^\ell$ and $\nu = 1 - p$.

Ciphertext Indistinguishability. We know that $\rho = O(n^{-1/2-\varepsilon})$, thus choosing s according to χ_ρ produces a vector with weight below the GV bound. As proved by Fischer and Stern in [11], the vector $\psi_0 = As$ is pseudorandom. Ciphertext indistinguishability follows directly since clearly the private key M doesn't carry information about the ciphertext.

Remark 2. We remark that the t-approximate correctness of the scheme relies heavily on a careful choice of the values ρ and τ, which are selected such that s and the rows of E have very low weight. It is easy to see that, if this condition is not respected, the weight of the corresponding product Es grows very quickly. One could in fact imagine an attack scenario aimed at obtaining an alternative decapsulation key K'', in which the attacker produces a vector $s' \neq s$ such that $As' = As$, and subsequently uses s' to get K'' as $\mathsf{pk} \cdot s'$. Because of the hardness of SDP, though, such an attacker would only be able to recover a vector s' having high weight; for the above argument, the difference factor $E(s + s')$ would also have high weight, hence this attack would not work in practice.

6   The Scheme

In this section, we show how to use the HPS that we presented above to achieve leakage-resilient public-key encryption. In addition to the "standard" protocol presented in [2], we have to include an error-correcting code to deal with the error coming from the approximate correctness. High error-correction capacity can be achieved, for example, by using list-decodable codes; Guruswami and Rudra in [15] show how it is possible to obtain codes that are list-decodable up to a radius $1 - R - \varepsilon$, for any $\varepsilon > 0$.

Table 3. Leakage-Resilient Public-Key Encryption Scheme

Setup	Set public parameters as in Table 2, and let m be the length of the plaintexts. Fix an integer t' and set $t'' = t + t'$, then select an $[\ell, m]$ linear code $\mathcal{C}$ which is decodable up to the radius t''.
KeyGen	Run $\mathsf{KeyGen}^{\mathsf{HPS}}$ and return the private key $\mathsf{sk} = M$ and the public key $\mathsf{pk} = MA + E$.
Enc	On input a plaintext $\phi \in \{0,1\}^m$, run $\mathsf{Encap}(\mathsf{pk})$ to obtain the pair (ψ_0, K), sample a random vector $z \xleftarrow{\$} \mathbb{F}_2^\ell$ having $\mathsf{wt}(z) \leq t'$, then set $\psi_1 = K + z + \mathsf{Encode}_{\mathcal{C}}(\phi)$. Finally, output the final ciphertext $\psi = (\psi_0, \psi_1)$.
Dec	On input a private key $\mathsf{sk} = M$ and a ciphertext $\psi = (\psi_0, \psi_1)$, calculate K' as $\mathsf{Decap}(\mathsf{sk}, \psi_0)$ and return the plaintext $\phi = \mathsf{Decode}_{\mathcal{C}}(K' + \psi_1)$.

As we mentioned above, the correctness of the scheme depends on the t-approximate correctness of the HPS, and the use of error-correcting codes. In fact $K' + \psi_1 = \mathsf{Encode}_{\mathcal{C}}(\phi) + Es + z$ and we expect Es to have weight less or equal to t and consequently $\mathsf{wt}(Es + z) \leq t + t' = t''$. Hence by applying the decoding algorithm is possible to recover the plaintext ϕ.

We now proceed to prove the security of the scheme. We start with a result from Alwen et al. [2, Theorem 3.1].

Theorem 1. *Let $\mathcal{H}$ be an (η, ν)-universal HPS with key space $K = \{0,1\}^\ell$. Then $\mathcal{H}$ is also λ-leakage smooth as long as $\lambda \leq \eta - \ell - \omega(\log \theta)$ and $\nu \leq 2^{-\ell}(1 + \mathsf{negl}(\theta))$.*

It is easy to see that the code-based HPS that we described in the previous section satisfies the conditions of Theorem 1. In addition, we will need the following computational assumption.

Assumption 1. *Let E, s and z be distributed as in Table 3. Then given E and $y = Es + z$ it is hard to recover s.*

One could think to use a generic decoding algorithm (e.g. Information Set Decoding [22]) or a dedicated decoding algorithm (e.g. bit flipping as for LDPC codes [12]); all these approaches, however, require at some point to check the syndrome equations. Because of the presence of z, these equations can't be trusted. The attacker would then need to guess the positions of z, either beforehand, or during the execution of the algorithm. In both cases, this implies a huge computational effort: there are in fact $N = \sum_{i=0}^{t'} \binom{n}{i}$ possibilities for z. Therefore, it is plausible to assume that there is no efficient way to recover s.

We are now ready to prove the following theorem.

Theorem 2. *Given that Assumption 1 holds, the scheme in Table 3 is semantically secure against λ-key-leakage attacks.*

Proof. For our security analysis we use a sequence of games. This is inspired by the proof of [2, Theorem 4.1], although a few *ad hoc* modifications are needed, due to the particular nature of our scheme.

Game 0: This is the semantic security game with leakage λ as presented in Definition 9.

Game 1: This game proceeds exactly as Game 0, except that we modify the encryption oracle as follows. We calculate $(\psi_0, K) = \mathsf{Encap}(\mathsf{pk})$ as usual, but instead of using K for encrypting the message, we use $K' = \mathsf{Decap}(\mathsf{sk}, \psi_0)$. Because of the approximate correctness, we have to artificially add some noise to preserve the structure of the ciphertext. We thus generate a random vector y of weight less or equal to t'', according to the same distribution of $Es + z$. The challenge ciphertext will then be (ψ_0^*, ψ_1^*), where $\psi_0^* = \psi_0$ and $\psi_1^* = K' + y + \mathsf{Encode}_\mathcal{C}(\phi_b)$. Now, suppose the adversary is in possession of the private key. In order to distinguish between the two games, it could easily recover E from pk and y from ψ_1^* and try to solve for s. However, because of Assumption 1, we claim that there is no efficient way to do this. Hence, the two games are computationally indistinguishable.

Game 2: This is the same as Game 1, but we modify again the encryption oracle, now replacing a valid ciphertext with an invalid one. More precisely, we calculate $\psi_0 = \mathsf{Encap}^*(\mathsf{pk})$ and $K' = \mathsf{Decap}(\mathsf{sk}, \psi_0)$, then return the challenge ciphertext (ψ_0^*, ψ_1^*) where $\psi_0^* = \psi_0$ and $\psi_1^* = K' + y + \mathsf{Encode}_\mathcal{C}(\phi_b)$. By the ciphertext indistinguishability property of the scheme, the two games are computationally indistinguishable. Note that, by definition, this indistinguishability holds even if the whole private key is revealed, hence in particular it holds for any bounded leakage $f(\mathsf{sk})$.

Game 3: In Game 3 we proceed as in Game 2, but now we generate ψ_1^* as a uniformly random string. That is, we calculate $\psi_0^* = \mathsf{Encap}^*(\mathsf{pk})$ and $\psi_1^* \xleftarrow{\$} \mathbb{F}_2^m$, then return the challenge ciphertext (ψ_0^*, ψ_1^*). Game 2 and Game 3 are statistically indistinguishable because of the leakage smoothness property.

Finally, in Game 3 the advantage of any adversary $\mathcal{A}$ is equal to 0, since this is independent from the chosen bit b. This completes the proof. $\square$

7 Conclusions

We have shown how to construct an HPS based on coding theory assumptions. The public-key encryption scheme that is based on it is inspired by a framework from Alwen et al. [2]; however we do not need to use randomness extractors to achieve semantic security against key-leakage attacks. This is because of the universality of our HPS construction. We remark that our scheme is but a first step towards achieving efficient leakage-resilient code-based encryption schemes. We thus hope to stimulate discussion about some open questions that stem from this work. For example, it would be important to improve the scheme in order to resist chosen-ciphertext attacks, without having to use impractical variants such as the one based on the Naor-Yung "double encryption" paradigm presented in [21].

References

1. Akavia, A., Goldwasser, S., Vaikuntanathan, V.: Simultaneous Hardcore Bits and Cryptography against Memory Attacks. In: Reingold, O. (ed.) TCC 2009. LNCS, vol. 5444, pp. 474–495. Springer, Heidelberg (2009)
2. Alwen, J., Dodis, Y., Naor, M., Segev, G., Walfish, S., Wichs, D.: Public-Key Encryption in the Bounded-Retrieval Model. In: Gilbert, H. (ed.) EUROCRYPT 2010. LNCS, vol. 6110, pp. 113–134. Springer, Heidelberg (2010)
3. Alwen, J., Dodis, Y., Wichs, D.: Leakage-Resilient Public-Key Cryptography in the Bounded-Retrieval Model. In: Halevi (ed.) [17], pp. 36–54
4. Berlekamp, E., McEliece, R., van Tilborg, H.: On the inherent intractability of certain coding problems. IEEE Transactions on Information Theory 24(3), 384–386 (1978)
5. Blake, I.F., Studholme, C.: Properties of random matrices and applications (2006), Unpublished report available at http://www.cs.toronto.edu/~cvs/coding
6. Cramer, R., Shoup, V.: Universal Hash Proofs and a Paradigm for Adaptive Chosen Ciphertext Secure Public-Key Encryption. In: Knudsen, L.R. (ed.) EUROCRYPT 2002. LNCS, vol. 2332, pp. 45–64. Springer, Heidelberg (2002)
7. Di Crescenzo, G., Lipton, R.J., Walfish, S.: Perfectly Secure Password Protocols in the Bounded Retrieval Model. In: Halevi, Rabin (eds.) [18], pp. 225–244
8. Döttling, N., Müller-Quade, J., Nascimento, A.C.A.: IND-CCA Secure Cryptography Based on a Variant of the LPN Problem. In: Wang, X., Sako, K. (eds.) ASIACRYPT 2012. LNCS, vol. 7658, pp. 485–503. Springer, Heidelberg (2012)
9. Dumer, I., Micciancio, D., Sudan, M.: Hardness of approximating the minimum distance of a linear code. IEEE Transactions on Information Theory 49(1), 22–37 (2003)
10. Dziembowski, S.: Intrusion-Resilience Via the Bounded-Storage Model. In: Halevi, Rabin (eds.) [18], pp. 207–224
11. Fischer, J.-B., Stern, J.: An Efficient Pseudo-Random Generator Provably as Secure as Syndrome Decoding. In: Maurer, U.M. (ed.) EUROCRYPT 1996. LNCS, vol. 1070, pp. 245–255. Springer, Heidelberg (1996)
12. Gallager, R.: Low-density parity-check codes. IRE Transactions on Information Theory 8(1), 21–28 (1962)

13. Gentry, C., Peikert, C., Vaikuntanathan, V.: Trapdoors for hard lattices and new cryptographic constructions. In: Dwork, C. (ed.) STOC, pp. 197–206. ACM (2008)
14. Goldwasser, S., Micali, S.: Probabilistic Encryption. J. Comput. Syst. Sci. 28(2), 270–299 (1984)
15. Guruswami, V., Rudra, A.: Explicit capacity-achieving list-decodable codes. In: Kleinberg, J.M. (ed.) STOC, pp. 1–10. ACM (2006)
16. Halderman, J.A., Schoen, S.D., Heninger, N., Clarkson, W., Paul, W., Calandrino, J.A., Feldman, A.J., Appelbaum, J., Felten, E.W.: Lest We Remember: Cold Boot Attacks on Encryption Keys. In: van Oorschot, P.C. (ed.) USENIX Security Symposium, pp. 45–60. USENIX Association (2008)
17. Halevi, S. (ed.): CRYPTO 2009. LNCS, vol. 5677. Springer, Heidelberg (2009)
18. Halevi, S., Rabin, T. (eds.): TCC 2006. LNCS, vol. 3876. Springer, Heidelberg (2006)
19. Katz, J., Vaikuntanathan, V.: Smooth Projective Hashing and Password-Based Authenticated Key Exchange from Lattices. In: Matsui, M. (ed.) ASIACRYPT 2009. LNCS, vol. 5912, pp. 636–652. Springer, Heidelberg (2009)
20. Kiltz, E., Pietrzak, K., Stam, M., Yung, M.: A New Randomness Extraction Paradigm for Hybrid Encryption. In: Joux, A. (ed.) EUROCRYPT 2009. LNCS, vol. 5479, pp. 590–609. Springer, Heidelberg (2009)
21. Naor, M., Segev, G.: Public-Key Cryptosystems Resilient to Key Leakage. In: Halevi [17], pp. 18–35.
22. C. Peters. Information-Set Decoding for Linear Codes over F_q. In N. Sendrier, editor, *PQCrypto*, volume 6061 of *Lecture Notes in Computer Science*, pages 81–94. Springer, 2010.
23. Regev, O.: On lattices, learning with errors, random linear codes, and cryptography. In: Gabow, H.N., Fagin, R. (eds.) STOC, pp. 84–93. ACM (2005)

Packed Homomorphic Encryption Based on Ideal Lattices and Its Application to Biometrics

Masaya Yasuda[1], Takeshi Shimoyama[1], Jun Kogure[1],
Kazuhiro Yokoyama[2], and Takeshi Koshiba[3]

[1] FUJITSU LABORATORIES LTD.,
1-1, Kamikodanaka 4-chome, Nakahara-ku, Kawasaki, 211-8588, Japan
{yasuda.masaya,shimo-shimo,kogure}@jp.fujitsu.com
[2] Department of Mathematics, Rikkyo University,
Nishi-Ikebukuro, Tokyo 171-8501, Japan
kazuhiro@rikkyo.ac.jp
[3] Division of Mathematics, Electronics and Informatics,
Graduate School of Science and Engineering, Saitama University,
255 Shimo-Okubo, Sakura, Saitama, 338-8570, Japan
koshiba@mail.saitama-u.ac.jp

Abstract. Among many approaches for privacy-preserving biometric authentication, we focus on the approach with homomorphic encryption, which is public key encryption supporting some operations on encrypted data. In biometric authentication, the Hamming distance is often used as a metric to compare two biometric feature vectors. In this paper, we propose an efficient method to compute the Hamming distance on encrypted data using the homomorphic encryption based on ideal lattices. In our implementation of secure Hamming distance of 2048-bit binary vectors with a lattice of 4096 dimension, encryption of a vector, secure Hamming distance, and decryption respectively take about 19.89, 18.10, and 9.08 milliseconds (ms) on an Intel Xeon X3480 at 3.07 GHz. We also propose a privacy-preserving biometric authentication protocol using our method, and compare it with related protocols. Our protocol has faster performance and shorter ciphertext size than the state-of-the-art prior work using homomorphic encryption.

Keywords: somewhat homomorphic encryption, ideal lattices, packed ciphertexts, secure Hamming distance, privacy-preserving biometrics.

1 Introduction

Biometric authentication (or biometrics) is an identification of clients by their physical characteristics such as fingerprint, iris, vein and DNA. Since biometric authentication has the advantage that clients do not need to remember their long and complex passwords compared to the commonly used ID/password authentication, the use of biometric authentication is now expanding (see US-VISIT [29] for a typical example). On the other hand, concerns about the security and the privacy are increasing. Especially, it is important to protect *templates*, which

A. Cuzzocrea et al. (Eds.): CD-ARES 2013 Workshops, LNCS 8128, pp. 55–74, 2013.
© IFIP International Federation for Information Processing 2013

are stored biometric feature data, since once leaked templates can be neither revoked nor replaced. At present, there are the following three main approaches for privacy-preserving biometric authentication (see [1] or [17] for the details):

- *Feature transformation approach*, in which biometric feature data are transformed to random data by using a client-specific key or password. Cancelable biometrics [26] and biohashing [1, Section 3.3] are typical examples in this approach. This approach is practical in performance, but it is no longer secure if the client-specific key is compromised.
- *Biometric cryptosystem approach*, which is based on error-correcting codes. This approach includes fuzzy vault [19] and fuzzy commitment [20]. Since this approach needs to have strong restriction of authentication accuracy, both practical and security issues are controversial.
- *Homomorphic encryption approach*, on which we focus in this paper. In this approach, biometric feature data are protected by homomorphic encryption, and similarity of two feature data is measured on encrypted data by metrics such as the Hamming and the Euclidean distances. This approach enables biometric authentication system to be considerably secure as long as the secret key is securely managed by the trusted party. The performance and the encrypted data size are main issues for the practical use of this approach.

1.1   Related Work on Homomorphic Encryption Approach

We summarize privacy-preserving biometric authentication protocols known so far based on homomorphic encryption approach. In 2006, Schoenmakers and Tuyls in [27] proposed secure computations suitable for privacy-preserving biometric authentication using the Paillier scheme [24], which is additively homomorphic. In 2010, Osadchy et al. in [23] designed a new face recognition algorithm and proposed an efficient secure face identification system, called *SCiFI*, with the Paillier scheme and the oblivious transfer protocol. Their secure two-party computation is based on the work in [18]. In SCiFI, a feature vector extracted from face image is always represented as a binary vector of 900-bit, and the Hamming distance is used as a metric to compare two feature vectors. Their implementation showed that it took 310 ms to compute their secure Hamming distance. At present, SCiFI is known as one of the state-of-the-art privacy-preserving biometric authentication systems suitable for real life. In 2011, Blanton and Gasti in [2] developed secure protocols for iris and fingerprints. Their secure computation is similar to SCiFI, but they use the DGK scheme [10], which is an additively homomorphic encryption with shorter ciphertexts than the Paillier scheme. In their protocol, an iris feature vector is always represented as a binary vector of 2048-bit and the Hamming distance is used as in SCiFI. Their implementation showed that it took 150 ms to compute their secure Hamming distance.

1.2   Our Contributions

After Gentry's breakthrough work [13] of constructing a fully homomorphic encryption (FHE) scheme, three main variants of FHE have been proposed so far; one based on ideal lattices [13, 14], another one based on integers [9, 11], and the last one based on the ring learning with errors (ring-LWE) assumption [5–7]. Those FHE schemes start from a somewhat homomorphic encryption (SHE) scheme, which can support only limited number of additions and multiplications on encrypted data but can be much more practical than FHE. To achieve faster secure Hamming distance, we rather use the SHE scheme based on ideal lattices (it is faster and easier to implement than the other SHE schemes). We propose an implementation of Gentry's scheme [13] for applying it to biometrics. Our variant is based mainly on Gentry-Halevi's [14], but is somewhat different from it because ours is tailored to faster secure computation. We also note that our variant is still provably secure in the sense of IND-CPA under the assumption that the ideal coset problem (ICP) [13, Section 3.2] is intractable. In this work, we will not refer to how to generate feature vectors as in [27], and assume that feature vectors are always represented as binary vectors of 2048-bit, whose length can be applied to various biometrics. Our main contributions are as follows:

- **Packing method for secure Hamming distance.** When we encrypt a feature vector bit by bit, we need to handle a large number of ciphertexts only for one feature vector and hence it would take much time to compute the Hamming distance on encrypted data. In contrast, we propose a new method to pack a feature vector into a single ciphertext, which also enables us to compute secure Hamming distance efficiently (our packing method can be applied in the SHE scheme based on the ring-LWE assumption, and results using the ring-LWE based scheme will be discussed in our next paper).
- **Privacy-preserving protocol using the SHE scheme.** We propose a new privacy-preserving biometric authentication protocol using our variant SHE scheme. We also give concrete parameters of our variant scheme with reasonable security, and demonstrate the efficiency of our packing method. Our implementation result shows that our protocol has both faster performance and shorter size of encrypted feature vectors than the state-of-the-art prior work. Furthermore, we believe that our protocol could give a new template protection technique due to our asymmetric packing methods to encrypt a feature vector in enrollment and authentication phases.

Comparison with Known Packing Methods. Smart and Vercauteren in [28] propose a packing method based on polynomial-CRT (Chinese Remainder Theorem) for packing many elements in a single ciphertext, which can be applied to perform SIMD (Single Instruction - Multiple Data) operations on encrypted data. The polynomial-CRT packing method is applied in the work [15] to evaluate the AES circuit homomorphically with a leveled FHE scheme of [5]. Furthermore, while the polynomial-CRT packing method can be applied only in ring-LWE based schemes, Brakerski, Gentry and Halevi extend the SIMD notions to the standard LWE based scheme of [7] using the packing method of [25]. Unlike the polynomial-CRT packing method, our method cannot be applied for SIMD operations, but it is very easier to handle and much more efficient for evaluating fundamental computations such as the Hamming distance (it would be more interesting to combine our packing method with the polynomial-CRT method). In their work [21], Lauter, Naehrig and Vaikuntanathan also present some message encoding techniques in the ring-LWE based scheme, and their technique is to encode integers in a single ciphertext so that it enables us to efficiently compute their sums and products over the integers. When we ignore the difference of homomorphic encryption schemes, our packing method can be considered as an extension of their techniques. Our extension is to give two types of packed ciphertexts, and combinations of two types of our packed ciphertexts give efficient computations such as the inner product and the Hamming distance.

2 Preliminaries

We fix our standard notation. The symbols $\mathbb{Z}$, $\mathbb{Q}$, $\mathbb{R}$, and $\mathbb{C}$ denote the ring of integers, the field of rational numbers, the field of real numbers, and the field of complex numbers, respectively. For a prime number p, the finite field with p elements is denoted by $\mathbb{F}_p$. For two integers z and d, let $[z]_d$ denote the reduction of z modulo d included in the interval $[-d/2, d/2)$ as in [14] (let $z \bmod d$ denote the usual reduction included in the interval $[0, d)$). For a rational number $q \in \mathbb{Q}$, we denote by $\lceil q \rfloor$ the rounding of q to the nearest integer, and by $[q]$ the fractional part of q. These notations are extended to vectors and matrices in the natural way. For a vector $a = (a_1, a_2, \ldots, a_n) \in \mathbb{R}^n$, let $\|a\|$ denote the Euclidean norm defined by $\sqrt{\sum_{i=1}^{n} a_i^2}$. Furthermore, we let $\|a\|_1$ and $\|a\|_\infty$ denote the 1-norm defined by $\sum_{i=1}^{n} |a_i|$ and ∞-norm defined by $\max_i |a_i|$, respectively.

2.1 Definitions and Notation in Lattices

Fix an integer number n. Let $B \in \mathbb{R}^{n \times n}$ be a matrix and let $\mathbf{b}_i \in \mathbb{R}^n$ denote the i-th row of B for $i = 1, \ldots, n$. Denote by

$$\mathcal{L}(B) = \left\{ \sum_{i=1}^{n} m_i \mathbf{b}_i : m_i \in \mathbb{Z} \right\}$$

the set of all integral linear combinations of the $\mathbf{b}_i$'s, which is a subgroup of $\mathbb{R}^n$. We say that the subgroup $\mathcal{L}(B)$ is a (full-rank) lattice of dimension n if $\mathbf{b}_1, \ldots, \mathbf{b}_n$ are linearly independent. In this case, we say that the matrix B is a basis of the lattice $\mathcal{L}(B)$. Every lattice has infinitely many lattice bases. If B_1 and B_2 are two bases of a lattice L, then there exists a unimodular matrix $U \in \mathrm{GL}_n(\mathbb{Z})$ satisfying $B_1 = U B_2$. Since we have $\det(U) = \pm 1$, the absolute value $|\det(B)|$ is invariant for any basis B of L and denoted by $\det(L)$. For a basis B, we let

$$\mathcal{P}(B) = \left\{ \sum_{i=1}^{n} x_i \mathbf{b}_i : x_i \in [-1/2, 1/2) \right\}$$

denote its associated half-open parallelepiped. Every lattice L has a unique Hermite normal form basis $\mathrm{HNF}(L) = (b_{ij})$, where $b_{ij} = 0$ for all $i < j$, $b_{jj} > 0$ for all j, and $b_{ij} \in [-b_{jj}/2, b_{jj}/2)$ for all $i > j$. Given any basis of L, we can compute the basis $\mathrm{HNF}(L)$ by Gaussian elimination. Note that the basis $\mathrm{HNF}(L)$ typically serves as the public key representation of the lattice.

By lattice reduction, we mean an operation that computes a basis $B = [\mathbf{b}_1, \ldots, \mathbf{b}_n]^t$ of L with short and nearly orthogonal vectors $\mathbf{b}_1, \ldots, \mathbf{b}_n$ from a given basis of L. Lattice reduction algorithms are often used for breaking lattice cryptosystems. The *root Hermite factor* of a lattice reduction algorithm is defined by $\|\mathbf{b}_1\| / \det(L)^{1/n}$ with the output basis $[\mathbf{b}_1, \ldots, \mathbf{b}_n]^t$. It is an index to measure the output quality of a lattice reduction algorithm (the output quality is better as the root Hermite factor is smaller). The most practical lattice reduction algorithms are the LLL and the BKZ algorithms.

2.2 Basic Construction of SHE Scheme

We present the basic construction of our variant of the SHE scheme based on ideal lattices (see §3 for some improvements). Our variant is based mainly on Gentry-Halevi's [14], but ours can use a more general ciphertext space for faster secure computation. For a 2-power integer $n = 2^m$, let $R := \mathbb{Z}[x]/(f_n(x))$ denote the polynomial ring modulo $f_n(x) := x^n + 1$, which is an irreducible polynomial. Since a map

$$\ni v(x) = v_0 + v_1 x + \cdots v_{n-1} x^{n-1} \mapsto \boldsymbol{v} = (v_0, v_1, \ldots, v_{n-1}) \in \mathbb{Z}^n \qquad (1)$$

gives an isomorphism $R \simeq \mathbb{Z}^n$ as $\mathbb{Z}$-modules, we can view each element of R as both a polynomial $v(x)$ and a vector $\boldsymbol{v}$.

Key Generation. To generate the public and the secret keys, we need key parameters (n, t, s), where $n = 2^m$ is the lattice dimension of 2-power, t is the bit length of coefficients in so called the generating polynomial $v(x)$, and s is the size of the plaintext space. The following construction is based on the sub-optimal key generation described in [14, Section 3] (see §3.3 for our improved key generation):

Step 1. We first choose an n-dimensional vector $\boldsymbol{v} = (v_0, v_1, \ldots, v_{n-1}) \in \mathbb{Z}^n$, where v_i is randomly chosen satisfying the condition $|v_i| \leq 2^t$ for any i. Set $v(x) = \sum_{i=0}^{n-1} v_i x^i \in R$ as a generating polynomial. Consider the rotation matrix

$$V := \mathrm{rot}(\boldsymbol{v}) = \begin{pmatrix} v_0 & v_1 & v_2 & \cdots & v_{n-1} \\ -v_{n-1} & v_0 & v_1 & \cdots & v_{n-2} \\ -v_{n-2} & -v_{n-1} & v_0 & \cdots & v_{n-3} \\ \vdots & \vdots & \vdots & \ddots & \vdots \\ -v_1 & -v_2 & -v_3 & \cdots & v_0 \end{pmatrix}. \qquad (2)$$

Since the i-th row of V corresponds to the polynomial $v(x) \times x^i \in R$ under the isomorphism (1), the subgroup $L := \mathcal{L}(V) \subset \mathbb{Z}^n$ is a lattice of dimension n and we have the relation $R \supset (v(x)) \simeq L \subset \mathbb{Z}^n$, where $(v(x))$ denotes the principal ideal of R generated by $v(x)$.

Step 2. By applying the extended Euclidean-GCD algorithm for polynomials, we compute the scaled inverse $w(x)$ of $v(x)$ modulo $f_n(x)$ satisfying

$$w(x) \times v(x) \equiv d \bmod f_n(x).$$

Note that d is the resultant of $v(x)$ and $f_n(x)$, which is also equal to the determinant $\det(L) = |\det(V)|$ of the lattice L. If $\gcd(d, s) \neq 1$, go back to Step 1 and generate another $\boldsymbol{v}$ (we can decrypt a ciphertext without the secret key when s divides d). Let $\boldsymbol{w} = (w_0, w_1, \ldots, w_{n-1})$ denote the vector corresponding to $w(x)$. Then the matrix $W := \mathrm{rot}(\boldsymbol{w})$ satisfies $W \times V = V \times W = d \cdot I$, where I is the $n \times n$ identity matrix.

Step 3. We give the following definition and lemma given in [14, Section 3]:

Definition 1 (goodness of $v(x)$). *We say that $v(x)$ is good if the Hermite normal form basis $B := \mathrm{HNF}(L)$ of the lattice $L = \mathcal{L}(V)$ has the form*

$$B = \begin{pmatrix} d & 0 & 0 & \cdots & 0 \\ -r & 1 & 0 & \cdots & 0 \\ * & 0 & 1 & \cdots & 0 \\ \vdots & \vdots & \vdots & \ddots & \vdots \\ * & 0 & 0 & \cdots & 1 \end{pmatrix}. \tag{3}$$

Lemma 1. *A generating polynomial $v(x)$ is good if and only if L contains a vector of the form $(-r', 1, 0, \ldots, 0)$. Furthermore, if $v(x)$ is good, we have that $r := w_1/w_0 = w_2/w_1 = \cdots = w_{n-1}/w_{n-2} = -w_0/w_{n-1} \bmod d$ and the element r satisfies the condition $r^n \equiv -1 \bmod d$.*

In this step, we check whether $v(x)$ is good or not. For checking it, we only test that $r := w_1/w_0 \bmod d$ satisfies $r^n \equiv -1 \bmod d$; If $r^n \equiv -1 \bmod d$, go to the next step. Otherwise, go back to Step 1 and generate another $\boldsymbol{v}$.

Step 4. We set V, W (resp. B) as the secret key (resp. the public key). We here call V, W (resp. B) the *secret key matrices* (resp. the *public key matrix*). Due to the special form (3) of B, we only need to set $\mathsf{sk} = w_i$ as the secret key and $\mathsf{pk} = (d, r, n, s)$ as the public key, where w_i is a single coefficient of $\boldsymbol{w}$ satisfying $\gcd(w_i, s) = 1$ (see Decryption below).

Encryption. To encrypt a plaintext $b \in \mathbb{Z}/s\mathbb{Z} = \{0, 1, \ldots, s-1\}$ with $\mathsf{pk} = (d, r, n, s)$, we first choose a random "noise vector" $\boldsymbol{u} = (u_0, u_1, \ldots, u_{n-1})$ with $u_i \in \{0, \pm 1\}$ chosen as 0 with some probability q and as ± 1 with probability $(1-q)/2$ each. Then the ciphertext of b is given by the integer

$$\mathsf{Enc}(b) = \left[b + s \sum_{i=0}^{n-1} u_i r^i \right]_d.$$

Set $\boldsymbol{a} := s\boldsymbol{u} + b\boldsymbol{e}_1 = (su_0 + b, su_1, \ldots, su_{n-1})$ with $\boldsymbol{e}_1 = (1, 0, \ldots, 0)$, and let $a(x) \in R$ denote the corresponding polynomial. Then we have $\mathsf{Enc}(b) = [a(r)]_d$ and the vector $(\mathsf{Enc}(b), 0, \ldots, 0)$ is equal to $\boldsymbol{a} \bmod B := \boldsymbol{a} - (\lceil \boldsymbol{a} \times B^{-1} \rfloor \times B) \in \mathcal{P}(B)$, which is the ciphertext vector generated by the public key matrix B (see [14, Section 5] for details).

Definition 2 (masked plaintext). *We call the vector $\boldsymbol{a}$ (or the polynomial $a(x)$) the masked plaintext corresponding to a ciphertext* ct.

We need to choose the probability q to make it hard to recover the original noise vector from a ciphertext c. Against exhaustive-search and birthday attacks, we set a security parameter λ, where we need to set q satisfying $2^{(1-q)n} \cdot \binom{n}{qn} > 2^{2\lambda}$ [14, Section 5.2]. Furthermore, Gentry and Halevi in [14] considered the hybrid attack, whose method is to choose a random subset of the powers of r including all the noise coefficients and search for a small vector in this low-dimension lattice (e.g., dimension 200). It is sufficient to set q satisfying $\left(\frac{n}{200}\right)^{qn} \geq 2^\lambda$ against the hybrid attack. For $\lambda = 80$ and $n \geq 1024$, the above two inequalities are satisfied if $q = \frac{1}{3}$. In this paper, we fix

$$q = \frac{1}{3}$$

for higher security. In contrast, Gentry and Halevi in [14] take an aggressive setting where the number of nonzero entries in the noise vectors is between 15 and 20 for FHE public challenges).

Decryption. To decrypt a ciphertext $\mathsf{Enc}(b)$ with the secret key matrices V, W, we first recover the corresponding masked plaintext by $\boldsymbol{a} = \boldsymbol{c} \bmod V = \boldsymbol{c} - \left(\lceil \boldsymbol{c} \times V^{-1} \rceil \times V\right) = [\boldsymbol{c} \times W/d] \times V$ with the ciphertext vector $\boldsymbol{c} = (\mathsf{Enc}(b), 0, \ldots, 0)$. It follows from [14, Section 6] that we can recover the masked plaintext $\boldsymbol{a}$ if every entry in $\boldsymbol{a} \times W$ is less than $d/2$ in absolute value. For $\boldsymbol{a} = (a_0, a_1, \ldots, a_{n-1})$, we then output $b = a_0 \bmod s \in \mathbb{Z}/s\mathbb{Z}$ as the decryption result.

In [14, Section 6.1], Gentry and Halevi proposed an optimized decryption procedure in the case $s = 2$. We can extend their method to our variant scheme; Let $\boldsymbol{a} = s\boldsymbol{u} + b\boldsymbol{e}_1$ be the masked plaintext of a ciphertext $\mathsf{Enc}(b)$. From a similar argument of [14, Section 6.1], we have

$$[\boldsymbol{c} \times W]_d = \boldsymbol{a} \times W = s\boldsymbol{u} \times W + b \cdot (w_0, w_1, \ldots, w_{n-1})$$

if every entry in $\boldsymbol{a} \times W$ is less than $d/2$ in absolute value. Since $[\boldsymbol{c} \times W]_d = ([\mathsf{Enc}(b) \cdot w_0]_d, [\mathsf{Enc}(b) \cdot w_1]_d, \ldots, [\mathsf{Enc}(b) \cdot w_{n-1}]_d)$, we have $[\mathsf{Enc}(b) \cdot w_i]_d \equiv b \cdot w_i \bmod s$ for any i. It is therefore sufficient to keep one coefficient w_i of $\boldsymbol{w}$ with $\gcd(w_i, s) = 1$ as the secret key sk, and then we can recover b by computing

$$[\mathsf{Enc}(b) \cdot \mathsf{sk}]_d \cdot \mathsf{sk}^{-1} \bmod s. \tag{4}$$

Note that there always exists w_i satisfying $\gcd(w_i, s) = 1$ if we take $s = 2^k$.

Homomorphic Operations. For two ciphertexts $\mathsf{Enc}(b_1)$ and $\mathsf{Enc}(b_2)$, the homomorphic addition "$\dotplus$" is defined by

$$\mathsf{Enc}(b_1) \dotplus \mathsf{Enc}(b_2) := [\mathsf{Enc}(b_1) + \mathsf{Enc}(b_2)]_d.$$

The homomorphic subtraction is also defined by $\mathsf{Enc}(b_1) \dotminus \mathsf{Enc}(b_2) := [\mathsf{Enc}(b_1) - \mathsf{Enc}(b_2)]_d$. Similarly, the homomorphic multiplication "$*$" is defined by

$$\mathsf{Enc}(b_1) * \mathsf{Enc}(b_2) := [\mathsf{Enc}(b_1) \cdot \mathsf{Enc}(b_2)]_d.$$

Let $a_1, a_2 \in R$ denote the masked plaintexts corresponding to $\mathsf{Enc}(b_1), \mathsf{Enc}(b_2)$, respectively. Then we see that the vectors $([\mathsf{Enc}(b_1) + \mathsf{Enc}(b_2)]_d, 0, \dots, 0)$ and $([\mathsf{Enc}(b_1) \cdot \mathsf{Enc}(b_2)]_d, 0, \dots, 0)$ are equal to $a_1 + a_2 \bmod B$ and $a_1 \times a_2 \bmod B$ respectively, where "$\times$" denotes the multiplication operation in the ring R. This shows that the homomorphic operations correspond to the ring structure of R, from which the homomorphic property of our variant scheme follows. However, homomorphic operations make the size of the noise vector in the corresponding masked plaintext larger. Therefore it is only possible to add and multiply ciphertexts before the size of the noise vector grows beyond the decryption range.

3 Some Improvements of SHE Scheme

In this section, we give some improvements of our variant SHE scheme described in §2.2, mainly for an efficient computation of secure Hamming distance.

3.1 Theoretical Evaluation of Decryption Range

In applying the SHE scheme to a concrete application scenario, the size of its decryption range is the most important in choosing key parameters suitable for the scenario. Under the condition $|v_i| \leq 2^t$, Gentry and Halevi in [14, Section 7] experimentally estimate that the decryption range is roughly equal to 2^t and it succeeds to decrypt a ciphertext ct if the corresponding masked plaintext a satisfies $||a|| \leq 2^t$. In contrast, we give a theoretical evaluation of the range under a certain condition in choosing a generating polynomial $v(x) = \sum_{i=0}^{n-1} v_i x^i \in R$ (cf. Key Generation in §2.2). In the following, we give our technical result without a proof due to lack of space (a complete proof will be given in our forthcoming paper):

Proposition 1. *Assume the condition*

$$(\clubsuit): \quad T = |v_{n-1}| = 2^t(1 + \varepsilon_{n-1}) \text{ and } v_i = T\varepsilon_i$$
$$\text{with } |\varepsilon_i| < \tfrac{1}{4n} \text{ for } 0 \leq i \leq n-2 \text{ and } \varepsilon_{n-1} > 0.$$

Then the decryption of a ciphertext ct *succeeds if the corresponding masked plaintext* a *satisfies either*

$$||a||_1 < \frac{11 \cdot 2^{t-1}}{13} \quad or \quad ||a||_\infty < \frac{11n \cdot 2^{t-1}}{19n - 6}. \tag{5}$$

Since we have $|v_{n-1}| = T \approx 2^t$ and $|v_i| < T/4n$ for $0 \leq i \leq n-1$ under the condition ($\clubsuit$) for sufficiently small $\varepsilon_{n-1} > 0$, we can consider our condition as a restricted version of Gentry-Halevi's condition $|v_i| \leq 2^t$. Our theoretical evaluation gives the same level as Gentry-Halevi's experimental one, and especially it enables us to use the ∞-norm evaluation, which is independent of the noise probability q in encryption (Gentry-Halevi's evaluation uses the Euclidean norm, and it is deeply related with q). Hence our evaluation makes it easier to choose key parameters in applying our variant SHE scheme to a concrete scenario (in particular, the ∞-norm evaluation makes it easy in the noise management of ciphertexts).

3.2 Packing Method for Secure Hamming Distance

As described in Encryption of §2.2, we can only encrypt an element of $\mathbb{Z}/s\mathbb{Z}$ in our variant scheme. In contrast, we propose a new method to pack a binary vector in a single ciphertext, which is also suitable for an efficient computation of both secure inner product and secure Hamming distance. Our packing method is to transform a binary vector into a certain polynomial of the ring R, and to encrypt the transformed polynomial. Furthermore, for efficient secure computation, we make use of polynomial operations in the ring R. As described in §1.2, our packing method can be considered as an extension of the method proposed in [21], and our main extension is to give two types of packed ciphertexts. However, our packing method causes a difficulty that it is not straightforward to apply the optimized decryption procedure (4) described in Decryption of §2.2. To overcome the problem, we need to take a generating polynomial $v(x)$ satisfying a certain condition (see Proposition 3 below). We begin with our packing method and efficient computation of the secure inner product. As remarked in §1.2, we only consider 2048-bit binary vectors for securing the Hamming distance often used in biometrics.

Definition 3 (packing method vEnc$_i$). *Assume $n \geq 2048$. We define two types of packing method as follows (cf. Encryption of §2.2):*

Type 1. *For a binary vector A, let $F_1 : A = (A_0, \ldots, A_{2047}) \mapsto \sum_{i=0}^{2047} A_i x^i \in R = \mathbb{Z}[x]/(f_n(x))$. Then its packed ciphertext is defined by the integer*

$$\mathsf{vEnc}_1(A) := [F_1(A)(r) + su_1(r)]_d = \left[\sum_{i=0}^{2047} A_i r^i + su_1(r) \right]_d \qquad (6)$$

using the public key $\mathsf{pk} = (d, r, n, s)$, where $u_1(x) \in R$ denotes a noise polynomial. We note that the masked plaintext of $\mathsf{vEnc}_1(A)$ corresponds to the polynomial $F_1(A) + su_1(x) \in R$.

Type 2. *For a binary vector B, let $F_2 : B = (B_0, \ldots, B_{2047}) \mapsto -\sum_{i=0}^{2047} B_i x^{n-i}$. Then its packed ciphertext is defined by the integer*

$$\mathsf{vEnc}_2(B) := [F_2(B)(r) + su_2(r)]_d = \left[-\sum_{i=0}^{2047} B_i r^{n-i} + su_2(r) \right]_d, \qquad (7)$$

where $u_2(x)$ denotes a noise polynomial. We also note that the masked plaintext of $\mathsf{vEnc}_2(B)$ corresponds to the polynomial $F_2(B) + su_2(x) \in R$.

Proposition 2 (secure inner product). *Assume $n \geq 2048$. Let ct be the ciphertext given by the homomorphic multiplication of $\mathsf{vEnc}_1(A)$ and $\mathsf{vEnc}_2(B)$. Let $\boldsymbol{a} = (a_0, \ldots, a_{n-1}) \in R = \mathbb{Z}^n$ denote the masked plaintext corresponding to ct. Then we have*

$$a_0 \equiv \sum_{i=0}^{2047} A_i B_i \bmod s.$$

Proof. The homomorphic multiplication corresponds to the multiplication in the ring R. This shows that $\boldsymbol{a} = (F_1(A) + su_1(x)) \times (F_2(B) + su_2(x)) \in R$ and we have $\boldsymbol{a} \equiv F_1(A) \times F_2(B) \bmod s$. We easily see that the constant term of

$$F_1(A) \times F_2(B) = \sum_{i=0}^{2047} A_i x^i \times \sum_{j=0}^{2047} B_j x^{n-j}$$

is equal to $\sum_{i=0}^{2047} A_i B_i$ since $x^n = -1$ in the ring R.   □

Let ct and $\boldsymbol{a} = (a_0, \ldots, a_{n-1})$ be as in Proposition 2. By Proposition 2, we only need to recover $a_0 \bmod s$ with the secret key sk to obtain the inner product. However, it is not straightforward to apply the optimized decryption procedure (4) described in Decryption of §2.2 since the masked plaintext $\boldsymbol{a} \in R$ is not of the form $s\boldsymbol{u} + b\boldsymbol{e}_1$, which we handle for the usual encryption Enc(b) described in Encryption of §2.2. To apply the optimized decryption (4) for the recovery of $a_0 \bmod s$ with sk, we need the following result:

Proposition 3 (suitable condition for decryption). *Let* ct *and* $\boldsymbol{a}$ *be as in Proposition 2. For a generating polynomial* $v(x) = \sum_{i=0}^{n-1} v_i x^i \in R$, *we assume* $v_i \in s\mathbb{Z}$ *for* $i = 1, \ldots, n-1$ *(but we take* $v_0 \notin s\mathbb{Z}$). *Let* $\boldsymbol{w} = (w_0, w_1, \ldots, w_{n-1})$ *be the vector generated in* Key Generation *of §2.2, and we take* w_0 *as the secret key* sk. *Then we can recover* $a_0 \bmod s$ *with* sk *by computing*

$$[\mathsf{ct} \cdot \mathsf{sk}]_d \cdot v_0 \cdot d^{-1} \bmod s.$$

In particular, we can recover $a_0 \bmod s$ *with* sk *by computing* $[\mathsf{ct} \cdot \mathsf{sk}]_d \bmod s$ *if we take* v_0 *satisfying* $v_0 \in 1 + s\mathbb{Z}$.

Proof. For $\boldsymbol{v} = (v_0, \ldots, v_{n-1})$, let $V = \mathrm{rot}(\boldsymbol{v})$ and $W = \mathrm{rot}(\boldsymbol{w})$ be the secret key matrices. For the ciphertext vector $\boldsymbol{c} = (\mathsf{ct}, 0, \ldots, 0)$, it follows from a similar argument of Decryption of §2.2 that

$$[\boldsymbol{c} \times W]_d = \boldsymbol{a} \times W \Longleftrightarrow$$
$$([\mathsf{ct} \cdot w_0]_d, \ldots, [\mathsf{ct} \cdot w_{n-1}]_d) \cdot V = \boldsymbol{a} \times W \times V = (da_0, \ldots, da_{n-1}) \qquad (8)$$

if every entry in $\boldsymbol{a} \times W$ is less than $d/2$ in absolute value (note that we have $W \times V = d \cdot I$). By comparing the first entry of the vectors in the right hand side of (8), we have $[\mathsf{ct} \cdot w_0]_d \cdot v_0 \equiv da_0 \bmod s$ by the assumption $v_i \in s\mathbb{Z}$ for $i = 1, \ldots, n-1$. Hence we can recover $a_0 \bmod s$ by computing $[\mathsf{ct} \cdot w_0]_d \cdot v_0 \cdot d^{-1} \bmod s$. In particular, if $v_0 \in 1 + s\mathbb{Z}$, we have $v_0 \cdot d^{-1} \equiv 1 \bmod s$ since $d \equiv v_0^n \equiv 1 \bmod s$ by $d = \det(V)$ and $v_i \in s\mathbb{Z}$ for $i = 1, \ldots, n-1$. This completes the proof.   □

Secure Hamming Distance. We apply our packing method to compute the Hamming distance on encrypted data. Assume $n, s \geq 2048$. For the guarantee of both the theoretical decryption range of Proposition 1 and the success of the decryption, we need to take a generating polynomial $v(x)$ under the condition

$(\spadesuit) : v_0 \in 1 + s\mathbb{Z}$, $v_i \in s\mathbb{Z}$ for $1 \leq i \leq n-1$, and the condition ($\clubsuit$).

Take w_0 as the secret key sk as in Proposition 3. For two binary vectors A and B, the Hamming distance $d_H(A, B)$ can be computed by $\sum_{i=0}^{2047}(A_i + B_i - 2A_iB_i) =$ $\mathrm{HW}(A) + \mathrm{HW}(B) - 2\sum_{i=0}^{2047} A_iB_i$, where $\mathrm{HW}(\cdot)$ denotes the Hamming weight of a binary vector. For computing the Hamming distance on encrypted data, we consider two integers

$$C_1 := \left[\sum_{i=0}^{n-1} r^i\right]_d \quad \text{and } C_2 := [-C_1 + 2]_d$$

with the public key $\mathsf{pk} = (d, r, n, s)$. Set $c_1(x) := \sum_{i=0}^{n-1} x^i$ and $c_2(x) := -c_1(x) + 2 = 1 - \sum_{j=1}^{n-1} x^j$ in the ring R. From a similar argument in the proof of Proposition 2, the homomorphic multiplication of $\mathsf{vEnc}_1(A)$ and C_2 (resp. $\mathsf{vEnc}_2(B)$ and C_1) corresponds to the masked plaintext $(F_1(A) + su_1(x)) \times c_2(x)$ (resp. $(F_2(B) + su_2(x)) \times c_1(x)$), whose constant term modulo s is equal to $\mathrm{HW}(A)$ (resp. $\mathrm{HW}(B)$). Therefore the encrypted Hamming distance is computed by

$$\mathsf{ct}_H = C_2 * \mathsf{vEnc}_1(A) + C_1 * \mathsf{vEnc}_2(B) + (-2\mathsf{vEnc}_1(A) * \mathsf{vEnc}_2(B))$$
$$= C_1 * (-\mathsf{vEnc}_1(A) + \mathsf{vEnc}_2(B)) + 2\mathsf{vEnc}_1(A) * (1 - \mathsf{vEnc}_2(B)) \quad (9)$$

which only requires two homomorphic multiplications, two homomorphic additions and one left-shift of a ciphertext if we precompute the integer C_1. For the masked plaintext $\boldsymbol{a}_H \in R = \mathbb{Z}^n$ corresponding to ct_H, we see that the first entry of $\boldsymbol{a}_H$ modulo s is equal to the Hamming distance $d_H(A, B)$ by Proposition 2. By Proposition 3, we can recover $d_H(A, B)$ with sk by computing

$$[\mathsf{ct}_H \cdot \mathsf{sk}]_d \bmod s \quad (10)$$

if $\boldsymbol{a}_H$ is included in the theoretical decryption range of Proposition 1. The following diagram represents the computation procedure of secure Hamming distance with our packing method:

Remark 1. As mentioned in §1.2, our variant is just an instantiation of Gentry's abstract scheme described in [13, Section 3.1] (of course, ours provides an "efficient" implementation). Since Gentry's scheme is provably secure in the sense of IND-CPA under the ICP assumption even in the abstract level (see [13, Section 3.2] for the detail). Thus ours inherits the provable security from Gentry's (we note that Gentry's scheme is not IND-CCA1 [22]).

3.3 Improving Key Generation

The problem of the construction of our variant scheme described in §2.2 is the slow key generation. Based on Gentry-Halevi's optimized key generation [14, Section 4], we give some improvements for faster key generation than their one, and also guarantee the theoretical decryption range of Proposition 1. The main idea of Gentry-Halevi's optimized key generation is as follows: For a lattice dimension $n = 2^m$, fix a primitive $2n$-th root ρ of $f_n(x) = x^n + 1$ and set $\rho_i = \rho^{2i+1}$ for $i = 0, 1, \ldots, n-1$, which are the roots of $f_n(x)$ in the field $\mathbb{C}$ of complex numbers. To generate the key pair (pk, sk), we consider two polynomials

$$g(z) := \prod_{i=0}^{n-1} (v(\rho_i) - z) \text{ and } h(z) := \prod_{i=0}^{n-1} (v(\rho_i) - z/\rho_i)$$

for a generating polynomial $v(x)$. Although $g(z)$ and $h(z)$ are defined by $\rho_i \in \mathbb{C}$, the coefficients of $g(z)$ and $h(z)$ are all integers. Let g_i (resp. h_i) denote the coefficient of z^i in $g(z)$ (resp. $h(z)$). By [14, Section 4], we have $d = g_0$, $w_0 = -g_1/n$ and $w_1 = -h_1/n$ if $v(x)$ is square-free. Since $w_1/w_0 = \cdots = w_{n-1}/w_{n-2} = -w_0/w_{n-1} \bmod d$ in the case where $v(x)$ is good by Lemma 1, we can recover the rest of w_i from the triple (d, w_0, w_1). After recovering the triple (d, w_0, w_1), we therefore compute the ratio $r = w_1/w_0 \bmod d$ and verify that $r^n \equiv -1 \bmod d$, which is the condition for testing that $r \cdot w_i = w_{i+1} \bmod d$. In the following, we give our improvements:

3.3.1 Simultaneous Computation of $g(z), h(z) \bmod z^2$

From the above argument, we need to consider $g(z), h(z) \bmod z^2$ to obtain the triple (d, w_0, w_1). In [14, Section 4.1], Gentry and Halevi showed a method to compute $g(z), h(z) \bmod z^2$ separately. In contrast, we give a method to compute $g(z), h(z) \bmod z^2$ at the same time: Set $U_0(x) = 1$, $V_0(x) = v(x)$ and $W_0(x) = -x^{n-1}$. For $0 \le j \le m$, let

$$\begin{cases} V_j(x) \cdot V_j(-x) \bmod f_{n_j}(x) = \sum_{i=0}^{n_j-1} a_i^{(j)} x^i, \\ U_j(x) \cdot V_j(-x) + U_j(-x) \cdot V_j(x) \bmod f_{n_j}(x) = \sum_{i=0}^{n_j-1} b_i^{(j)} x^i, \\ W_j(x) \cdot V_j(-x) + W_j(-x) \cdot V_j(x) \bmod f_{n_j}(x) = \sum_{i=0}^{n_j-1} c_i^{(j)} x^i, \end{cases}$$

and $U_{j+1}(x) = \sum_{k=0}^{n_j/2-1} b_{2k}^{(j)} x^k$, $V_{j+1}(x) = \sum_{k=0}^{n_j/2-1} a_{2k}^{(j)} x^k$, $W_{j+1}(x) = \sum_{k=0}^{n_j/2-1} c_{2k}^{(j)} x^k$, where $f_{n_j}(x) := x^{n_j} + 1$ with $n_j = n/2^j$. Then we have

$$g_j(z) := \prod_{i=0}^{n_j-1} \left(V_j(\rho_i^{2^j}) - z U_j(\rho_i^{2^j}) \right) \equiv g(z) \bmod z^2, \tag{11}$$

$$h_j(z) := \prod_{i=0}^{n_j-1} \left(V_j(\rho_i^{2^j}) - z W_j(\rho_i^{2^j}) \right) \equiv g(z) \bmod z^2 \tag{12}$$

by a similar argument of [14, Section 4.1]. Since the degree of $U_m(x)$, $V_m(x)$ and $W_m(x)$ is equal to 0, we can consider these polynomials as integers U_m, V_m and W_m respectively, and we have $g_0 = h_0 = V_m$, $g_1 = U_m$ and $h_1 = W_m$ by the equations (11) and (12). Therefore we only need to compute $U_j(x)$, $V_j(x)$ and $W_j(x)$ to obtain the triple (d, w_0, w_1).

3.3.2 Quick Test of Goodness

In the optimal key generation of [14], after computing (d, w_0, w_1), we test the condition $r^n \equiv -1 \bmod d$ to check that $v(x)$ is not good (see also **Key Genera-tion** of §2.2). In the case where $r^n \not\equiv -1 \bmod d$, we need to compute the triple (d, w_0, w_1) again for another generating polynomial $v(x)$. Since the cost of com-puting the triple (d, w_0, w_1) is dominant in the key generation, we consider a method to check that $v(x)$ is not good without computing the triple (d, w_0, w_1) exactly. We give the following lemma:

Lemma 2. *If $v(x)$ is good, we have $d \equiv 1 \bmod 2n$.*

Proof. Assume that $v(x)$ is good, namely, the public key matrix B has the form (3). Then we see that $f_n(x) \bmod d$ is split completely. This shows that $f_n(x) \bmod p$ is split completely for the primes $p \mid d$. By the theory of cyclotomic fields, we have that $p \equiv 1 \bmod 2n$ for the primes $p \mid d$, which shows that $d \equiv 1 \bmod 2n$. □

To check that $v(x)$ is not good, we test the condition $d \equiv 1 \bmod 2n$. In testing $d \equiv 1 \bmod 2n$, we only need to compute $d \bmod 2n$. By using $V_j(x) \bmod 2n \in (\mathbb{Z}/2n\mathbb{Z})[x]$ to compute $d \bmod 2n$, we can check it in lower cost (after obtaining the triple (d, w_0, w_1), we can check the goodness of $v(x)$ exactly by testing the condition that $v(x) \cdot w(x) \equiv d \bmod f_n(x)$, where $w(x) = \sum_{i=0}^{n-1} w_i x^i$ with $r = w_1/w_0 \bmod d$ and $w_i = r^i \cdot w_0$ for $i \geq 1$).

3.3.3 Guarantee of Theoretical Decryption Range

We give a method to choose a generating polynomial $v(x)$ in order to guar-antee the theoretical decryption range of Proposition 1. In the key generation, we choose a generating polynomial $v(x) = \sum_{i=0}^{n-1} v_i x^i \in R$, where $v_i \in \mathbb{Z}$ is randomly chosen with the condition (♠) for our secure Hamming distance (see Proposition 3). Then we can use the theoretical evaluation of the decryption range of Proposition 1.

Improved Key Generation Algorithm. In Algorithm 1, we give a concrete algo-rithm of our key generation. Using our key generation, we can generate a good generating polynomial $v(x)$ with higher probability than the key generation of [14]. Since $v(x)$ with $d \equiv 1 \bmod 2n$ satisfies the condition $r^n \equiv -1 \bmod d$ with very high probability, we hardly go back to Step 1 in Step 4 of Algorithm 1, which shows that Step 2 has the advantage of the processing performance. n particular, our experiment shows that our algorithm is 25% faster on average than the case without Step 2 for input $(n, t, s) = (4096, 37, 2048)$.

Algorithm 1. Improved key generation of our variant SHE scheme

---

Input: (n, t, s): key parameters (for simplicity, assume that s is a 2-power integer)
Output: The public key $\mathsf{pk} = (d, r, n, s)$ and the secret key $\mathsf{sk} = w$.

1: Generate a random vector $\boldsymbol{v} = (v_0, v_1, \ldots, v_{n-1}) \in \mathbb{Z}^n$, where $v_i \in \mathbb{Z}$ is chosen under the condition (♣) (or (♠) for secure Hamming distance), and set $v(x) = \sum_{i=0}^{n-1} v_i x^i$.
2: By computing the followings, we verify that $d = \mathrm{res}(f_n(x), v(x)) \equiv 1 \bmod 2n$:

    (2-a) $S_0(x) \leftarrow v(x) \bmod 2n \in (\mathbb{Z}/2n\mathbb{Z})[x]$.
    (2-b) For $j = 0$ to $m - 1$, do

          i. Set $f_{n_j}(x) = x^{n_j} + 1$ with $n_j = n/2^j$. Compute $T_j(x) = S_j(x) \cdot S_j(-x) \bmod (2n, f_{n_j}(x)) = \sum_{i=0}^{n_j-1} t_i x^i$ with $t_i \in \{0, 1, \ldots, 2n - 1\}$.
          ii. $S_{j+1}(x) \leftarrow \sum_{k=0}^{n_j/2-1} t_{2k} x^k$.

    (2-c) Then $d \equiv S_m \bmod 2n$. If $S_m \not\equiv 1 \bmod 2n$, go back to Step 1.

3: Compute the triple (d, w_0, w_1) as follows:

    (3-a) $U_0(x) \leftarrow 1$, $V_0(x) \leftarrow v(x)$, $W_0(x) \leftarrow -x^{n-1}$.
    (3-b) For $j = 0$ to $m - 1$, do

          i. As in (2-b), set $f_{n_j}(x) = x^{n_j} + 1$ with $n_j = n/2^j$. Compute $A_j(x) = V_j(x) \cdot V_j(-x) \bmod f_{n_j}(x) = \sum_{i=0}^{n_j-1} a_i x^i$, $B_j(x) = U_j(x) \cdot V_j(-x) + U_j(-x) \cdot V_j(x) \bmod f_{n_j}(x) = \sum_{i=0}^{n_j-1} b_i x^i$ and $C_j(x) = W_j(x) \cdot V_j(-x) + W_j(-x) \cdot V_j(x) \bmod f_{n_j}(x) = \sum_{i=0}^{n_j-1} c_i x^i$.
          ii. $U_{j+1}(x) \leftarrow \sum_{k=0}^{n_j/2-1} b_{2k} x^k$, $V_{j+1}(x) \leftarrow \sum_{k=0}^{n_j/2-1} a_{2k} x^k$, $W_{j+1}(x) \leftarrow \sum_{k=0}^{n_j/2-1} c_{2k} x^k$.

    (3-c) Then $d = V_m$, $g_1 = U_m$, $h_1 = W_m$, and hence $w_0 = -g_1/n$, $w_1 = -h_1/n$.

4: Set $r = w_1/w_0 \bmod d$ and verify that $r^n \equiv -1 \bmod d$. If $r^n \equiv -1 \bmod d$, set $\mathsf{pk} = (d, r, n, s)$. Otherwise, go back to Step 1.
5: For $i = 0$ to $n-1$, find $w_i = r^i \cdot w_0 \bmod d$ with $\gcd([w_i]_d, s) = 1$. If $\gcd([w_i]_d, s) = 1$, set w_i as the secret key sk (in using the condition (♠), we set w_0 as sk).

---

4 Application to Biometric Authentication

In this section, we propose a privacy-preserving biometric authentication protocol using our variant SHE scheme with our packing method. We also compare our protocol with the related protocols described in §1.1, and demonstrate the efficiency of our packing method.

4.1 Protocol Using SHE Scheme Based on Ideal Lattices

Unlike SCiFI and the protocol of [2], our protocol involves three parties, a client server $\mathcal{C}$, a computation server $\mathcal{S}$, and an authentication server $\mathcal{A}$. We assume that the authentication server $\mathcal{A}$ is a trusted party to manage the secret key of homomorphic encryption. Our protocol is based on the work in [16] using generic 2-DNF (disjunctive normal form) homomorphic encryption such as the BGN scheme [3], which can support additions and one depth multiplications on encrypted data. In contrast to their work, we use the SHE scheme based on ideal lattices. In the following, we give a construction of our protocol of biometric authentication with ID, namely, one-to-one authentication protocol:

Setup Phase. The authentication server $\mathcal{A}$ generates the public key pk and the secret key sk of our variant scheme. Then the server $\mathcal{A}$ distributes only the public key pk to both the client server $\mathcal{C}$ and the computation server $\mathcal{S}$.

Enrollment Phase

1. The client server $\mathcal{C}$ generates a feature vector A of 2048-bit from client's biometric data such as fingerprints, encrypts A using our packing method of type 1 (see Definition 3), and sends the encrypted feature vector $\mathsf{vEnc}_1(A)$ with client's ID to the computation server $\mathcal{S}$.
2. The computation server $\mathcal{S}$ stores the encrypted feature vector $\mathsf{vEnc}_1(A)$ in the database D as a template with client's ID.

Authentication Phase

1. As in the enrollment phase, the client server $\mathcal{C}$ generates a feature vector B of 2048-bit from client's biometric data, encrypts B using our packing method of type 2 (note that it is different from the encryption method in the enrollment phase), and sends the encrypted feature vector $\mathsf{vEnc}_2(B)$ with client's ID to the computation server $\mathcal{S}$.
2. The computation server $\mathcal{S}$ extracts the template $\mathsf{vEnc}_1(A)$ corresponding to client's ID from the database D. Then the server $\mathcal{S}$ computes the encrypted Hamming distance ct_H of $\mathsf{vEnc}_1(A)$ and $\mathsf{vEnc}_2(B)$ defined by the equation (9), and sends only the encrypted data ct_H to the authentication server $\mathcal{A}$.
3. The authentication server $\mathcal{A}$ decrypts the encrypted data ct_H with the secret key sk to obtain the Hamming distance $d_H(A, B)$. Finally, the server $\mathcal{A}$ returns the authentication result 'OK' (resp. 'NG') if $d_H(A, B) \leq \sigma$ (resp. otherwise), where let σ denote pre-defined threshold.

In our protocol, all feature vectors handled by the computation server $\mathcal{S}$ are protected by homomorphic encryption, and hence we hope that we could use the cloud as the server $\mathcal{S}$ for outsourcing storage of templates and computation resources of secure Hamming distance. Furthermore, since the method $\mathsf{vEnc}_1(A)$ to encrypt a feature vector A in the enrollment phase is asymmetric to the method $\mathsf{vEnc}_2(B)$ in the authentication phase, our protocol is expected to have the additional advantage that identity theft is harder than the conventional protocols even if templates are leaked to attackers (even if an attacker steals a template $\mathsf{vEnc}_1(A)$ from the database $\mathcal{D}$ and sends it to the computation server $\mathcal{S}$ instead of $\mathsf{vEnc}_2(B)$ in the authentication phase, the authentication would fail with very high probability since the decryption result in the authentication server $\mathcal{A}$ is not by the Hamming distance between A and A due to lack of $\mathsf{vEnc}_2(A)$). From the above discussions, we believe that our protocol would be secure as long as the authentication server $\mathcal{A}$ manages the secret key sk correctly.

4.2   Choosing Parameters and Security Analysis

In this section, we describe a method to choose key parameters for secure Hamming distance described in §3.2, and estimate their security level.

Key Parameters. We give key parameters (n, t, s) suitable for secure Hamming distance ct_H given in the equation (9). Our chosen key parameters are

$$(n, t, s) = (2048, 37, 2048) \text{ and } (4096, 37, 2048). \tag{13}$$

These key parameters are estimated to have more than 80-bit security against exhaustive-search and birthday attacks on $v(x)$ generated under the condition (♠) since $2^t = 2^{37}$ is enough large compared with $4n \cdot s = 2^{24}$ or 2^{25} (for example, exhaustive-search attack takes $(2^t/(4n \cdot s))^n = (2^{13})^{2048}$ or $(2^{12})^{4096}$).

The method to choose the key parameters (13) is as follows: Since $0 \leq d_H(A, B) \leq 2048$, we set $s = 2048$ to avoid expensive carry operations. To encrypt a 2048-bit binary vector in a single ciphertext, we should take $n \geq 2048$ and we only consider the two cases $n = 2048$ and 4096 for the practical use (see also Definition 3). Let a_H be the masked plaintext corresponding to the encrypted Hamming distance ct_H as in §3.2. We let a_1 and b_1 denote the masked plaintexts corresponding to $\mathsf{vEnc}_1(A)$ and $\mathsf{vEnc}_2(B)$, respectively. We also let a_2 and b_2 denote the masked plaintexts corresponding to the homomorphically operated ciphertexts $C_2 * \mathsf{vEnc}_1(A)$ and $C_1 * \mathsf{vEnc}_2(B)$, respectively. Then we have

$$a_H = a_2 + b_2 - 2a_1 \times b_1 \in R$$

by the equation (9). By evaluating the ∞-norm size of a_H, we determine suitable t for decryption success of the ciphertext ct_H. For any two elements $a, b \in R$, we have $||a + b||_\infty \leq ||a||_\infty + ||b||_\infty$, $||a \times b||_\infty \leq n \cdot ||a||_\infty \cdot ||b||_\infty$ (see [21, Lemma 3.2]). Since we only consider $n = 2048$ and 4096, we have

$$\begin{aligned} ||a_H||_\infty &\leq ||a_2||_\infty + ||b_2||_\infty + 2n \cdot ||a_1||_\infty \cdot ||b_1||_\infty \\ &\leq 2n \cdot (2^{11} + 1) + 2n \cdot (2^{11} + 1)^2 \leq 2^{26} + 2^{35}. \end{aligned}$$

Note that we have $||a_1||_\infty, ||b_1||_\infty \leq 2^{11} + 1$ and $||a_2||_\infty, ||b_2||_\infty \leq n \cdot (2^{11} + 1)$ due to $s = 2^{11}$. By the ∞-norm evaluation of Proposition 1, we estimate that the decryption of ct_H succeeds if we take $t \geq 37$, and then we fix $t = 37$ for better performance and shorter ciphertexts.

Security Analysis against Lattice Reduction Attack. By using lattice reduction algorithms with considerably small root Hermite factor (see §2.1 for the root Hermite factor), we can recover the plaintext from a ciphertext without the secret key, which we simply call a lattice reduction attack. We note that the hardness of the lattice reduction attack is closely related to the ICP assumption, on which the provable security of our variant scheme relies (see Remark 1). We estimate the security level of our key parameters (13) against the attack.

Its security is based on the hardness of the lattice problem γ-BDDP [14, Section 2.2] with the parameter

$$\gamma = \frac{d^{1/n}}{\min \|\boldsymbol{a}\|} \approx \frac{(2^{tn})^{1/n}}{s \cdot \sqrt{2n/3}} = \frac{2^t}{s \cdot \sqrt{2n/3}}, \tag{14}$$

where $\min \|\boldsymbol{a}\|$ denotes the minimal Euclidean norm of the masked plaintexts. Note that $\min \|\boldsymbol{a}\| = \|\boldsymbol{a}_1\|$ or $\|\boldsymbol{b}_1\| \approx s \cdot \sqrt{2n/3}$ due to the probability $q = \frac{1}{3}$, where $\boldsymbol{a}_1$ (resp. $\boldsymbol{b}_1$) denotes the masked plaintext corresponding to $\mathsf{vEnc}_1(A)$ (resp. $\mathsf{vEnc}_2(B)$). BDDP is intuitively the analogue of the lattice problem unique-SVP, and it can be solved by lattice reduction algorithms with the root Hermite factor smaller than γ [12].

The case $(n, t, s) = (2048, 37, 2048)$. We have $\gamma = 1.0071^n$ by the equation (14). Since the root Hermite factor of LLL (resp. BKZ with $\beta = 20$) is practically 1.02^n (resp. 1.0128^n) on average (see experimental results of the work in [12]), it cannot be solved by LLL and BKZ with $\beta = 20$. At present, BKZ 2.0 is the state-of-the-art implementation of BKZ with large $\beta \geq 50$. The approximate root Hermite factor achieved by BKZ 2.0 is shown in [8, Table 2]. According to [8, Table 2], the BKZ blocksize $\beta \approx 160$ is needed to solve this case (the root Hermite factor of BKZ 2.0 with $\beta = 168$ is predicted to be 1.007^n). The approximate running time of BKZ 2.0 is given by $z \times \dim \times e$, where z is the number of rounds, "dim" is the lattice dimension and e is the approximate running time of the enumeration subroutine of blocksize β (see [8] for details). Since a few rounds are sufficient to achieve an enough performance of BKZ 2.0, we assume $z = 1$ for simplicity. As for e, Chen and Nguyen in [8, Table 3] gave an estimated upper bound on the cost of the enumeration subroutine. From [8, Table 3], we have that the enumeration subroutine of BKZ 2.0 with $\beta = 160$ is estimated at $2^{84.7}$ nodes at maximum. Since they also reported that one node requires about 200 clock cycles, we estimate that $e \leq 200 \times 2^{84.7} \approx 2^{92.3}$ clock cycles for BKZ 2.0 with $\beta = 160$. Therefore we estimate that the running time of BKZ 2.0 with $\beta = 160$ is at most $2^{11} \times 2^{92.3} = 2^{103.3}$ cycles in dimension 2048, which shows that this case may reach 80-bit security against BKZ 2.0. We remark that this estimation is just an upper bound cost of BKZ 2.0.

The case $(n, t, s) = (4096, 37, 2048)$. We have $\gamma = 1.0034^n$ in this case. The BKZ blocksize $\beta \geq 280$ is needed to solve this case from [8, Table 2] (the root Hermite factor of BKZ 2.0 with $\beta = 286$ is predicted to be 1.005^n). In contrast to [8, Table 3], they in [8, Table 4] also gave an estimated lower bound of the cost of e. According to [8, Table 4], the cost of e for BKZ 2.0 with $\beta = 280$ is estimated at $2^{79.8}$ nodes at lowest. From a similar argument as above, we estimate $e \geq 200 \times 2^{79.8} \approx 2^{87.4}$ clock cycles. Therefore we estimate that the running time of BKZ 2.0 with $\beta = 280$ is at least $2^{12} \times 2^{87.4} \approx 2^{99.4}$ clock cycles in dimension 4096. Hence we conclude that this case is estimated at 80-bit security with an enough margin (we can estimate from [8, Table 3] that this case has more than 192-bit security against BKZ 2.0).

Table 1. Performance and ciphertext size of our variant scheme

Parameters (n, t, s)	Key gen. (Alg. 1)	Precomp. Table	Packed Enc.	Secure Hamming	Dec.	Cipher. size	BDDP instance
$(2048, 37, 2048)$	220 ms	5.20 sec	6.20 ms	4.98 ms	2.51 ms	9.5 KB	1.0071^n
$(4096, 37, 2048)$	870 ms	38.15 sec	19.89 ms	18.10 ms	9.08 ms	19 KB	1.0034^n

4.3   Implementation Results

We implemented our variant scheme for the key parameters (13). The performance and the ciphertext size are shown in Table 1. We remark that the packed encryption $vEnc_i$ is computed by the equation (6) or (7), the secure Hamming distance is computed by the equation (9) using the precomputed integer C_1, and the decryption of the encrypted Hamming distance ct_H is computed by (10) with the secret key sk. In particular, the homomorphic addition takes about 0.004 ms (resp. 0.007 ms), and the homomorphic multiplication takes about 2.46 ms (resp. 9.00 ms) for $(n, t, s) = (2048, 37, 2048)$ (resp. $(n, t, s) = (4096, 37, 2048)$). In our implementation, we used our software library written with assembly language x86_64 for all computations in the base ring $R/(v(x)) \simeq \mathbb{Z}/d\mathbb{Z}$ (cf. see also [21] for its implementation result of the SHE scheme based on the ring-LWE problem). Our experiments ran on an Intel Xeon X3480 at 3.07 GHz with 16 GByte memory. We also implemented Karatsuba Multiplication and Montgomery Reduction algorithm for efficient multiplication in the base ring $\mathbb{Z}/d\mathbb{Z}$. Furthermore, we used a precomputed table $T = \{1, [r]_d, [r^2]_d, \ldots, [r^{n-1}]_d\}$ to make the encryption and the homomorphic operations much faster.

4.4   Comparison to Related Work

In Table 2, we give a comparison of our protocol using a lattice of 4096 dimension with the related protocols described in §1.1, with respect to the performance and the ciphertext size, which are main issues for the practical use of homomorphic encryption as remarked in §1 (all encryption schemes in Table 2 are estimated to have 80-bit security). From Table 2, our protocol has faster performance and shorter size than SCiFI and the protocol of [2]. In particular, our protocol is about 8 times faster and about 14 times shorter than the protocol of [2] when we ignore the difference of the PC performance. This is mainly due to our packing method since a feature vector can only be encrypted bit by bit due to the property of additive encryption schemes in SCiFI and the protocol of [2].

Furthermore, let us compare our protocol with one using the BGN scheme [3] such as the work in [16]. The BGN scheme is based on bilinear pairings on elliptic curves, and it requires a pairing computation for its homomorphic multiplication. According to [21, Section 1.2], the homomorphic multiplication of the BGN scheme is very slower than that of lattice-based homomorphic encryption. Furthermore, we can not use our packing method in the BGN scheme, and hence it needs 2048 homomorphic multiplications for secure Hamming distance of two vectors of 2048-bit. Even if we use very fast implementation taking 1 ms for

Table 2. Comparison to protocols using homomorphic encryption

Protocols (feature vector size)	Performance of Secure Hamming	Size increase rate by encryption* (cipher. size)	Homomorphic encryption scheme
SCiFI [23] (900-bit)	310 ms$^{(a)}$	2048 times (230 KByte)	Paillier-1024 (additive scheme)
Protocol of [2] (2048-bit)	150 ms$^{(b)}$	1024 times (262 KByte)	DGK-1024 (additive scheme)
Ours (2048-bit)	**18.10 ms**$^{(c)}$	≈ **80 times** (**19 KByte**)	**ideal lattices-4096** (**SHE scheme**)

*denotes the ratio of (encrypted feature vector size)/(plain feature vector size)
$^{(a)}$on an 8 core machine of 2.6 GHz AMD Opteron processors with 1 GByte memory
$^{(b)}$on an Intel Core 2 Duo 2.13 GHz with 3 GByte memory
$^{(c)}$on an Intel Xeon X3480 at 3.07 GHz with 16 GByte memory

one pairing computation, it takes about 2048 ms ≈ 2 sec for secure Hamming distance. Therefore we estimate that our protocol is at least about 100 times faster than one using the BGN scheme (our protocol is also estimated to have shorter size than one using the BGN scheme due to our packing method).

References

1. Belguechi, R., Alimi, V., Cherrier, E., Lacharme, P., Rosenberger, C.: An overview on privacy preserving biometrics, http://cdn.intechopen.com/pdfs/17038/InTech-An_overview_on_privacy_preserving_biometrics.pdf
2. Blanton, M., Gasti, P.: Secure and efficient protocols for iris and fingerprint identification. In: Atluri, V., Diaz, C. (eds.) ESORICS 2011. LNCS, vol. 6879, pp. 190–209. Springer, Heidelberg (2011)
3. Boneh, D., Goh, E.-J., Nissim, K.: Evaluating 2-DNF formulas on ciphertexts. In: Kilian, J. (ed.) TCC 2005. LNCS, vol. 3378, pp. 325–341. Springer, Heidelberg (2005)
4. Brakerski, Z., Gentry, C., Halevi, S.: Packed ciphertexts in LWE-based homomorphic encryption. In: Kurosawa, K., Hanaoka, G. (eds.) PKC 2013. LNCS, vol. 7778, pp. 1–13. Springer, Heidelberg (2013)
5. Brakerski, Z., Gentry, C., Vaikuntanathan, V.: (Leveled) fully homomorphic encryption without bootstrapping. In: Innovations in Theoretical Computer Science–ITCS 2012, pp. 309–325 (2012)
6. Brakerski, Z., Vaikuntanathan, V.: Fully homomorphic encryption from ring-LWE and security for key dependent message. In: Rogaway, P. (ed.) CRYPTO 2011. LNCS, vol. 6841, pp. 505–524. Springer, Heidelberg (2011)
7. Brakerski, Z., Vaikuntanathan, V.: Efficient fully homomorphic encryption from (standard) LWE. In: Foundations of Computer Science–FOCS 2011, pp. 97–106 (2011)
8. Chen, Y., Nguyen, P.Q.: BKZ 2.0: Better lattice security estimates. In: Lee, D.H., Wang, X. (eds.) ASIACRYPT 2011. LNCS, vol. 7073, pp. 1–20. Springer, Heidelberg (2011)
9. Coron, J.-S., Mandal, A., Naccache, D., Tibouchi, M.: Fully homomorphic encryption over the integers with shorter public keys. In: Rogaway, P. (ed.) CRYPTO 2011. LNCS, vol. 6841, pp. 487–504. Springer, Heidelberg (2011)
10. Damgård, I., Geisler, M., Krøigård, M.: Homomorphic encryption and secure comparison. Journal of Applied Cryptography 1(1), 22–31(2008)

11. van Dijk, M., Gentry, C., Halevi, S., Vaikuntanathan, V.: Fully homomorphic encryption over the integers. In: Gilbert, H. (ed.) EUROCRYPT 2010. LNCS, vol. 6110, pp. 24–43. Springer, Heidelberg (2010)

12. Gama, N., Nguyen, P.Q.: Predicting lattice reduction. In: Smart, N.P. (ed.) EUROCRYPT 2008. LNCS, vol. 4965, pp. 31–51. Springer, Heidelberg (2008)

13. Gentry, C.: Fully homomorphic encryption using ideal lattices. In: Symposium on Theory of Computing–STOC 2009, pp. 169–178. ACM (2009)

14. Gentry, C., Halevi, S.: Implementing Gentry's fully-homomorphic encryption scheme. In: Paterson, K.G. (ed.) EUROCRYPT 2011. LNCS, vol. 6632, pp. 129–148. Springer, Heidelberg (2011)

15. Gentry, C., Halevi, S., Smart, N.P.: Homomorphic evaluation of the AES circuit. In: Safavi-Naini, R., Canetti, R. (eds.) CRYPTO 2012. LNCS, vol. 7417, pp. 850–867. Springer, Heidelberg (2012)

16. Hattori, M., Matsuda, N., Ito, T., Takashima, K., Yoneda, T.: Provably-secure cancelable biometrics using 2-DNF evaluation. Journal of Information Processing 20(2), 496–507 (2012)

17. Jain, A.K., Nandakumar, K., Nagar, A.: Biometric template security (review article). EURASIP Journal on Advances in Signal Processing, 1–17 (2008)

18. Jarrous, A., Pinkas, B.: Secure hamming distance based computation and its applications. In: Abdalla, M., Pointcheval, D., Fouque, P.-A., Vergnaud, D. (eds.) ACNS 2009. LNCS, vol. 5536, pp. 107–124. Springer, Heidelberg (2009)

19. Juels, A., Sudan, M.: A fuzzy vault scheme. Designs, Codes and Cryptography 38(2), 237–257 (2006)

20. Juels, A., Wattenberg, M.: A fuzzy commitment scheme. In: ACM CCS 1999, pp. 28–36 (1999)

21. Lauter, K., Naehrig, M., Vaikuntanathan, V.: Can homomorphic encryption be practical? In: Proceedings of the 3rd ACM Workshop on Cloud Computing Security Workshop, pp. 113–124 (2011)

22. Loftus, J., May, A., Smart, N.P., Vercauteren, F.: On CCA-secure somewhat homomorphic encryption. In: Miri, A., Vaudenay, S. (eds.) SAC 2011. LNCS, vol. 7118, pp. 55–72. Springer, Heidelberg (2012)

23. Osadchy, M., Pinkas, B., Jarrous, A., Moskovich, B.: SCiFI - A system for secure face identification. In: IEEE Symposium on Security and Privacy, pp. 239–254 (2010)

24. Paillier, P.: Public-key cryptosystems based on composite degree residuosity classes. In: Stern, J. (ed.) EUROCRYPT 1999. LNCS, vol. 1592, pp. 223–238. Springer, Heidelberg (1999)

25. Peikert, C., Vaikuntanathan, V., Waters, B.: A framework for efficient and composable oblivious transfer. In: Wagner, D. (ed.) CRYPTO 2008. LNCS, vol. 5157, pp. 554–571. Springer, Heidelberg (2008)

26. Ratha, N., Connelle, J., Bolle, R.: Enhansing security and privacy in biometrics-based authentication system. IBM Systems J. 37(11), 2245–2255 (2001)

27. Schoenmakers, B., Tuyls, P.: Efficient binary conversion for paillier encrypted values. In: Vaudenay, S. (ed.) EUROCRYPT 2006. LNCS, vol. 4004, pp. 522–537. Springer, Heidelberg (2006)

28. Smart, N.P., Vercauteren, F.: Fully homomorphic SIMD operations. Designs, Codes and Cryptography (to appear)

29. U.S. Department of Homeland Security, Privacy impact assessment for the biometric storage system, http://www.dhs.gov/xlibrary/assets/privacy/privacy_pia_cis_bss.pdf (March 28, 2007)

A Comparison between Two Off-the-Shelf Algebraic Tools for Extraction of Cryptographic Keys from Corrupted Memory Images

Abdel Alim Kamal[1], Roger Zahno[2], and Amr M. Youssef[2]

[1] Faculty of Computers and Information, Menofia University, Shebin El-kom,
Menofia, 32511 Egypt
a_kamala@ci.menofia.edu.eg
[2] Institute for Information Systems Engineering, Concordia University, Montreal,
Quebec, H3G 1M8 Canada
{r_zahno,youssef}@ciise.concordia.ca

Abstract. Cold boot attack is a class of side channel attacks which exploits the data remanence property of random access memory (RAM) to retrieve its contents which remain readable shortly after its power has been removed. Specialized algorithms have been previously proposed to recover cryptographic keys of several ciphers from decayed memory images. However, these techniques were cipher-dependent and certainly uneasy to develop and fine tune. On the other hand, for symmetric ciphers, the relations that have to be satisfied between the subround key bits in the key schedule always correspond to a set of nonlinear Boolean equations. In this paper, we investigate the use of an off-the-shelf SAT solver (CryptoMiniSat), and an open source Gröbner basis tool (PolyBoRi) to solve the resulting system of equations. We also provide the pros and cons of both approaches and present some simulation results for the extraction of AES and Serpent keys from decayed memory images using these tools.

1 Introduction

Cryptanalytic attacks can be classified into pure mathematical attacks and side channel attacks. Pure mathematical attacks, are traditional cryptanalytic techniques that rely only on known or chosen input-output pairs of the cryptographic function, and exploit the inner structure of the cipher to reveal secret key information. On the other hand, in side channel attacks, it is assumed that the attacker has some physical access to the cryptographic device through one or more side channel. Well-known side channels, which can leak critical information about the encryption state, include timing information [1] and power consumption [2].

In addition to these commonly exploited side channels, the remanence effect of random access memory (RAM) is a highly critical side channel that has been recently exploited by cold boot attacks [3][4] to retrieve secret keys from RAM. Although dynamic RAMs (DRAMs) become less reliable when its contents are

A. Cuzzocrea et al. (Eds.): CD-ARES 2013 Workshops, LNCS 8128, pp. 75–90, 2013.

not refreshed, they are not immediately erased. In fact, contrary to popular belief, DRAMs may retain their contents for seconds to minutes after power is lost and even if they are removed from the computer motherboard. A cold boot attack is launched by removing the memory module, after cooling it, from the target system and immediately plugging it in another system under the adversarys control. This system is then booted to access the memory. Another possible approach to execute the attack is to cold boot the target machine by cycling its power off and then on without letting it shut down properly. Upon reboot, a lightweight operating system is instantly booted where the contents of targeted memory are dumped to a file.

Experimental results in [5] show how data are retained for a relatively long time in computer memories after a system power off. However, the first work explicitly exploiting those observations to recover cryptographic keys from the memory was reported by Halderman *et al.* [3] where they presented proof of concept experiments which showed that it is practically feasible to perform cold boot attacks exploiting the remanence effect of RAMs to recover secret keys of DES, AES and RSA. After the publication of Halderman *et al.* [3], several other authors (e.g., [6], [7] [4]) further improved upon this proof of concept and presented algorithms that solved cases with higher decay factors. However, almost all these previously proposed techniques were cipher-dependent and certainly uneasy to develop and fine tune. On the other hand, for symmetric ciphers, the relations that have to be satisfied between the subround key bits in the key schedule always correspond to a set of nonlinear Boolean equations. In this paper, we investigate the use of an off-the-shelf SAT solver (CryptoMiniSat [8]), and an open source Gröbner basis tool (PolyBoRi [9]) to solve the resulting system of equations. We also discuss the pros and cons of both tools and present some experimental results for the extraction of AES and Serpent keys from decayed memory images.

The remainder of the paper is organized as follows. In section 2 we briefly review some related works. SAT solvers and Gröbner basis tools, and their applications in cryptography, are discussed in section 3. Relevant details of the the structure of the AES and Serpent key schedules are discussed in section 4. Our experimental results are presented and discussed in section 5. Finally, our conclusion is given in section 6.

2   Related Work

Cryptographic key recovery from memory or memory dumps, for malicious or forensic purposes, has attracted great attention of security professionals and cryptographic researchers. In [10], Shamir and van Someren considered the problem of locating cryptographic keys hidden in large amount of data, such as the complete file system of a computer system. In addition to efficient algebraic attacks locating secret RSA keys in long bit strings, they also presented more general statistical attacks which can be used to find arbitrary cryptographic keys embedded in large files. This statistical approach relies on the simple fact that good cryptographic keys pose high entropy. Areas with unusually high entropy can be located by searching for unique byte patterns in sliding windows and then selecting those windows with the highest numbers of unique bytes as a potential places for the key. Moe *et al.* [11] developed a proof of concept tool, *Interrogate*, which implements several search methods for a set of key schedules. To verify the effectiveness of the developed tool, they investigated key recovery for systems running in different states (live, screen-saver, dismounted, hibernation, terminated, logged out, reboot, and boot states). Another proof of concept tool, *Disk Decryptor*, which can extract Pretty Good Privacy (PGP) and Whole Disk Encryption (WDE) keys from dumps of volatile memories was presented in [12].

All the above techniques and tools took another dimension after the publication of the cold boot attack by Halderman *et al.* [3]. While the remanence effect of RAM has already been known since decades [5], it attracted greater attention in cryptography only after Halderman *et al.* work in 2008, which explicitly exploited those observations to recover cryptographic keys from the memory. They developed tools which capture everything present in RAM before power was cut off and developed proof of concept tools which can analyze these memory copies to extract secret DES, AES and RSA keys.

In particular, Heninger *et al.* showed that an RSA private key with small public exponent can be efficiently recovered given a 27% fraction of its bits at random. They have also developed a recovery algorithm for the 128-bit version of AES (AES-128) that recovers keys from 30% decayed AES-128 Key Schedule images in less than 20 minutes for half of the simulated cases. Tsow [6] further improved upon the proof of concept in Halderman *et al.* and presented a heuristic algorithm that solved all cases at 50% decay in under half a second. At 60% decay, Tsow recovered the worst case in 35.5 seconds while solving the average case in 0.174 seconds. At the extended decay rate of 70%, recovery time averages grew to over 6 minutes with the median time at about five seconds.

In [7], Albrecht *et al.* proposed methods for key recovery of ciphers (AES, Serpent and Twofish) used in Full Disk Encryption (FDE) products where they applied a method for solving a set of non-linear algebraic equations with noise based on mixed integer programming. To improve the running time of their algorithms, they only considered a reduced number of rounds. Applying their algorithms, they obtained satisfactory success rates for key recovery using the Serpent key schedule up to 30% decay and for the AES up to 40% decay.

3   Modern Algebraic Tools and Their Applications to Cryptography

The use of SAT solvers and Gröbner basis in cryptanalysis has recently attracted the attention of cryptanalysts. Courtois *et al.* [13] demonstrated a weakness in KeeLog by presenting an attack which requires about 2^{32} known plaintexts. For 30% of all keys, the full key can be recovered against a complexity of 2^{28} KeeLoq encryptions. In [14], 6 rounds of DES are attacked with only a single known plaintext/ciphertext pair using a SAT solver. Erickson *et al.* [15] used the

SAT solver and Gröbner basis [16] attacks against SMS4 on equation system over GF(2) and GF(2^8). In [17], a practical Gröbner basis [16] attack using Magma was applied against the ciphers Flurry and Curry, recovering the full cipher key by requiring only a minimal number of plaintext/ciphertext pairs.

SAT solvers and Gröbner basis have also been applied to the cryptanalysis of stream ciphers. Eibach *et al.* [18] presented experimental results on attacking a reduced version of Trivium (Bivium) using exhaustive search, a SAT solver, a binary decision diagram (BDD) based attack, a graph theoretic approach, and Gröbner basis. Their result implies that the usage of the SAT solver is faster than the other attacks. The full key of Hitag2 stream cipher is recovered in a few hours using MiniSat 2.0 [19]. In [20], the full 48-bit key of the MiFareCrypto 1 algorithm was recovered in 200 seconds on a PC, given 1 known initial vector (IV) from one single encryption. In [21], Velichkov *et al.* applied the Gröbner basis on a reduced 16 bit version of the stream cipher Lex.

Mironov and Zhang [22] described some initial results on using SAT solvers to automate certain components in cryptanalysis of hash functions of the MD and SHA families. De *et al.* [23] presented heuristics for solving inversion problems for functions that satisfy certain statistical properties similar to that of random functions. They demonstrate that this technique can be used to solve the hard case of inverting a popular secure hash function and were able to invert MD4 up to 2 rounds and 7 steps in less than 8 hours. In [24], Sugita *et al.* used the Gröbner basis to improve the attack on the 58-round SHA-1 hash function to 2^{31} computations instead of 2^{34} in Wang's method [25].

3.1   Gröbner Basis and PolyBoRi

A Gröbner basis is a set of multivariate polynomials that have desirable algorithmic properties. In what follows, we briefly review some basic definitions and algebraic preliminaries related to Gröbner basis as presented in [26].

Let K be any field (in here we are interested in the case where $K = \mathbb{F}_2$.) We write $K[x_1, ..., x_n]$ for the ring of polynomials in n for the variables x_i having its coefficients in the field K.

Definition 1. *A subset $I \subset K[x_1, ..., x_n]$ is an ideal if it satisfies:*

1. *$0 \in I$.*
2. *if $f, g \in I$, then $f + g \in I$.*
3. *if $f \in I$ and $h \in K[x_1, ..., x_n]$, then $hf \in I$.*

Definition 2. *Let $f_1, ..., f_m$ be polynomials in $K[x_1, ..., x_n]$. Define the ideal $\langle f_1, ..., f_m \rangle = \{\sum_{i=1}^{m} h_i f_i : h_1, ..., h_m \in K[x_1, ..., x_n] \}$. If there exists a finite set of polynomials in $K[x_1, ..., x_n]$ that generate the given ideal, we call this set a basis.*

Definition 3. *A monomial ordering on $K[x_1, ..., x_n]$ is any relation $>$ on $\mathbb{Z}_{\geq 0}^n$, or equivalently, any relation on the set of monomials x^α, $\alpha \in \mathbb{Z}_{\geq 0}^n$, satisfying:*

1. $>$ is a total ordering on $\mathbb{Z}^n_{\geq 0}$.
2. if $\alpha > \beta$ and $\alpha, \beta, \gamma \in \mathbb{Z}^n_{\geq 0}$, then $\alpha + \gamma > \beta + \gamma$.
3. $>$ is a well ordering on $\mathbb{Z}^n_{\geq 0}$. That is every nonempty subset of $\mathbb{Z}^n_{\geq 0}$ has a smallest element with respect to $>$.

An example of monomial ordering for our application is lexicographic order which is defined as follows:

Definition 4. (Lexicographic Order (lex)). Let $\alpha = (\alpha_1, ..., \alpha_n)$, and $\beta = (\beta_1, ..., \beta_n) \in \mathbb{Z}^n_{\geq 0}$. We say $\alpha >_{lex} \beta$ if, in the vector difference $\alpha - \beta \in \mathbb{Z}^n$, the left-most nonzero entry is positive. We will write $x^\alpha >_{lex} x^\beta$ if $\alpha >_{lex} \beta$.

Definition 5. Let $f = \Sigma_\alpha a_\alpha x^\alpha$ be a non-zero polynomial in P and let $>$ be a monomial order. The multidegree of f is $multideg(f) = max_>(\alpha \in \mathbb{Z}^n_{\geq 0} : a_\alpha \neq 0)$.

Definition 6. (leading term of a polynomial). Let $f(x) = \sum_{i=1}^m c_\alpha x^\alpha : c_\alpha \in K$ is non-zero and $>$ is the order relation defined for the monomials of the polynomial $f(x)$. The greatest monomial in $f(x)$, regarding to the order relation $>$, is called the leading monomial for the polynomial $f(x)$ and is represented by $LM(f) = x^{multideg(f)}$. Also the set $M(f)$ consists of all monomials of $f(x)$ and $T(f)$ denote the set of all terms of $f(x)$. The coefficient of the leading monomial is represented by $LC(f) = a_{multideg(f)} \in K$ and called the leading coefficient. The term containing both the leading coefficient and leading monomial is called the leading term, represented by $LT(f) = LC(f) \cdot LM(f)$.

The idea of Gröbner basis was first proposed by Buchberger [16] to study the membership of a polynomial in the ideal of the polynomial ring.

Definition 7. (Gröbner basis) Let an ideal I be generated by $G = g_1, ..., g_m$, where g_i, $1 \leq i \leq m$ is a polynomial. G is called the Gröbner basis for the ideal I, if:

$$\langle LT(I) \rangle = \langle LT(g_1), ..., LT(g_m) \rangle,$$

where $\langle LT(I) \rangle$ denotes the ideal generated by the leading terms of the members in I.

One can view Gröbner basis as a multivariate, non-linear generalization of the Euclidean algorithm for computation of univariate greatest common divisors, Gaussian elimination for linear systems, and integer programming problems. In this work, we use Gröbner basis as an algebraic tool that allows us to solve non-linear Boolean equations by using the PolyBoRi framework.

The following example explains the main involved steps and commands for the PolyBoRi framework in Sage [27] to solve a given system of nonlinear Boolean equations.

Example 8. Consider the following system of non-linear Boolean equations

$$\begin{aligned}
x_1 x_2 \oplus x_3 x_4 &= 1, \\
x_1 x_3 x_5 \oplus x_4 x_5 &= 0, \\
x_1 x_2 x_5 \oplus x_3 x_5 &= 0, \\
x_2 x_3 \oplus x_3 x_4 x_5 &= 1,
\end{aligned} \tag{1}$$

```
c   Lines starting with 'c' are comments
c   Step 1 defines the Polynomial Ring; where GF(2) defines the Galois field (GF)
c   of 2 elements as the base ring, 5 is the number of variables and order = 'lex'
c   sets the order to lexical order
c   Step 2 defines the Ideal taking a set of homogeneous equations
c   as calling parameter
c   Step 3 combines the ideal I with the field ideal;
c   limiting the solution range to F₂
c   Step 4 executes the Gröbner basis returning the result

sage: PR.<x1,x2,x3,x4,x5> = PolynomialRing(GF(2), 5, order='lex')
sage: I = ideal([x1*x2 + x3*x4 + 1, x1*x3*x5 + x4*x5,
        x1*x2*x5 + x3*x5, x2*x3 + x3*x4*x5 + 1])
sage: J = I + sage.rings.ideal.FieldIdeal(PR)
sage: J.groebner_basis()
```

Fig. 1. Working with PolyBoRi to solve the systems of equations in (1)

Figure 1 shows the steps to be executed in PolyBoRi to solve the Gröbner basis. As shown in the figure, the function *ideal()* in step 2 takes the corresponding homogeneous system of equations as a calling parameter.

The resulting Gröbner basis is given by $[x_1 + x_4 + 1, x_2 + 1, x_3 + 1, x_4^2 + x_4, x_5]$. In this notation, x_i appearing in a separate term by itself implies that the system of equations under consideration can be solved by setting $x_i = 0$. Similarly, $x_i + 1$ implies that $x_i = 1$. Also, the notation $x_i + x_i^2$ implies that x_i can be assigned a 0 or a 1. Thus the above basis corresponds to the following two independent solutions: $\{x_1 = 1, x_2 = 1, x_3 = 1, x_4 = 0, x_5 = 0\}$ and $\{x_1 = 0, x_2 = 1, x_3 = 1, x_4 = 1, x_5 = 0\}$.

3.2   The SAT Problem and CryptoMiniSat

The Boolean satisfiability (SAT) problem [28] is defined as follows: Given a Boolean formula, check whether an assignment of Boolean values to the propositional variables in the formula exists such that the formula evaluates to true. If such an assignment exists, the formula is said to be satisfiable; otherwise, it is unsatisfiable. For a formula with m variables, there are 2^m possible truth assignments. The conjunctive normal form (CNF) is frequently used for representing Boolean formulas. In CNF, the variables of the formula appear in literals (e.g., x) or their negation (e.g., $\overline{x}$). Literals are grouped into clauses, which represent a disjunction (logical *OR*) of the literals they contain. A single literal can appear in any number of clauses. The conjunction (logical *AND*) of all clauses represents a formula. For example, the CNF formula $(x_1) \wedge (\overline{x}_2 \vee \overline{x}_3) \wedge (x_1 \vee x_3)$ contains three clauses: x_1, $\overline{x}_2 \vee \overline{x}_3$ and $x_1 \vee x_3$. Two literals in these clauses are positive (x_1, x_3) and two are negative $(\overline{x}_2, \overline{x}_3)$. For a variable assignment to satisfy a CNF formula, it must satisfy each of its clauses. For example, if x_1 is true and x_2 is false, then all three clauses are satisfied, regardless of the value of x_3.

While the SAT problem has been shown to be NP-complete [28], efficient heuristics exist that can solve many real-life SAT formulations. Furthermore, the wide range of target applications of SAT have motivated advances in SAT solving techniques that have been incorporated into freely-available SAT solvers such as the CryptoMiniSat.

When preparing the input to the SAT solver, the terms of quadratic and higher degree are handled by noting that (for example) the logical expression

$$(x_1 \vee \overline{T})(x_2 \vee \overline{T})(x_3 \vee \overline{T})(x_4 \vee \overline{T})(T \vee \overline{x}_1 \vee \overline{x}_2 \vee \overline{x}_3 \vee \overline{x}_4) \qquad (2)$$

is tautologically equivalent to $T \Leftrightarrow (x_1 \wedge x_2 \wedge x_3 \wedge x_4)$, or the $GF(2)$ equation $T = x_1 x_2 x_3 x_4$. Similar expressions exist for higher order terms. Thus, the system of equations obtained in this step can be linearized by introducing new variables as illustrated by the following example.

Example 9. Suppose we would like to find the Boolean variable assignment that satisfies the following formula

$$x_0 \oplus x_1 x_2 \oplus x_0 x_1 x_2 = 0.$$

Then, using the approach illustrated in (2), we introduce two linearization variables, $T_0 = x_1 x_2$ and $T_1 = x_0 x_1 x_2$. Thus we have

$$\begin{aligned}
&x_0 \oplus T_0 \oplus T_1 = 0, \\
&(\overline{T}_0 \vee x_1) \wedge (\overline{T}_0 \vee x_2) \wedge (T_0 \vee \overline{x}_1 \vee \overline{x}_2) = 1, \\
&(\overline{T}_1 \vee x_0) \wedge (\overline{T}_1 \vee x_1) \wedge (\overline{T}_1 \vee x_2) \wedge \\
&(T_1 \vee \overline{x}_0 \vee \overline{x}_1 \vee \overline{x}_2) = 1.
\end{aligned} \qquad (3)$$

Since the CryptoMiniSAT expects only positive clauses and the CNF form does not have any constants, we need to overcome the problem that the first line in (3) corresponds to a negative, i.e., false, clause. Adding the clause consisting of a dummy variable, d, or equivalently $(d \wedge d \cdots \wedge d)$ would require the variable d to be true in any satisfying solution, since all clauses must be true in any satisfying solution. In other words, the variable d will serve the place of the constant 1.

Therefore, the above formula can be expressed as

$$\begin{aligned}
&d = 1, \\
&x_0 \oplus T_0 \oplus T_1 \oplus d = 1, \\
&(\overline{T}_0 \vee x_1) \wedge (\overline{T}_0 \vee x_2) \wedge (T_0 \vee \overline{x}_1 \vee \overline{x}_2) = 1, \\
&(\overline{T}_1 \vee x_0) \wedge (\overline{T}_1 \vee x_1) \wedge (\overline{T}_1 \vee x_2) \wedge \\
&(T_1 \vee \overline{x}_0 \vee \overline{x}_1 \vee \overline{x}_2) = 1.
\end{aligned}$$

Applying the same logic to the system of equations in (1), we obtain

$$d = 1,$$
$$T_1 \oplus T_2 = 1,$$
$$(\overline{T_1} \vee x_1) \wedge (\overline{T_1} \vee x_2) \wedge (T_1 \vee \overline{x_1} \vee \overline{x_2}) = 1,$$
$$(\overline{T_2} \vee x_3) \wedge (\overline{T_2} \vee x_4) \wedge (T_2 \vee \overline{x_3} \vee \overline{x_4}) = 1,$$
$$T_3 \oplus T_4 \oplus d = 1,$$
$$(\overline{T_3} \vee x_1) \wedge (\overline{T_3} \vee x_3) \wedge (\overline{T_3} \vee x_5) \wedge$$
$$(T_3 \vee \overline{x_1} \vee \overline{x_3} \vee \overline{x_5}) = 1,$$
$$(\overline{T_4} \vee x_4) \wedge (\overline{T_4} \vee x_5) \wedge (T_4 \vee \overline{x_4} \vee \overline{x_5}) = 1,$$
$$T_5 \oplus T_6 \oplus d = 1,$$
$$(\overline{T_5} \vee x_1) \wedge (\overline{T_5} \vee x_2) \wedge (\overline{T_5} \vee x_5) \wedge$$
$$(T_3 \vee \overline{x_1} \vee \overline{x_2} \vee \overline{x_5}) = 1,$$
$$(\overline{T_6} \vee x_3) \wedge (\overline{T_6} \vee x_5) \wedge (T_6 \vee \overline{x_3} \vee \overline{x_5}) = 1,$$
$$T_7 \oplus T_8 = 1,$$
$$(\overline{T_7} \vee x_2) \wedge (\overline{T_7} \vee x_3) \wedge (T_7 \vee \overline{x_2} \vee \overline{x_3}) = 1,$$
$$(\overline{T_8} \vee x_3) \wedge (\overline{T_8} \vee x_4) \wedge (\overline{T_8} \vee x_5) \wedge$$
$$(T_8 \vee \overline{x_3} \vee \overline{x_4} \vee \overline{x_5}) = 1,$$

Figure 2 shows the CryptoMiniSat input file corresponding to the above system of equations. As shown in the figure, a negative number implies that the variables assumes a value $= 0$ and a positive number implies a value $= 1$. Lines starting with 'x' denote an XOR equation and each lines is terminated with '0'.

From the above examples, its is clear that, compared to PolyBoRi, preparing the input for the CryptoMiniSat requires relatively longer pre-processing steps. Also, unlike the Gröbner basis approach which returns the general form of the solution, CryptoMiniSat returns one valid solution. To find the other solutions, the already found solutions have to be negated and added to the SAT solver input file. In the example above, the first solution returned by the CryptoMiniSat ({1, −2, 3, 4, 5, −6, −7, 8, −9, −10, −11, −12, 13, −14}) is negated ({−1, 2, −3, −4, −5, 6, 7, −8, 9, 10, 11, 12, −13, 14}) and added to the SAT solver input file as a new entry. When running the SAT solver again, this added entry forces the SAT solver to eliminate this as a possible solution and search for a new one that solves the SAT problem. When doing so, the SAT solver returns the second possible solution ({1, 2, 3, 4, −5, −6, 7, −8, −9, −10, −11, −12, 13, −14}).

4   Structure of the AES-128 and Serpent Key Schedules

In this section, we briefly review the relevant details of the AES-128 and Serpent key schedules.

4.1   Key Schedule of AES-128

In the following we describe the AES-128 key scheduler [29], [30]. AES-128 works with a user key (Master Key) of 128 bits (16 bytes) represented by a 4x4 array

```
c    Lines starting with 'c' are comments
c    The first line in the SAT file is in the form: 'p cnf # variables # clause'
c    Each line ends with '0' and lines starting with 'x' denote XOR equations
c    True variables are denoted by positive numbers and False variables
c    are denoted by negating the number; example: x₁ → 2; (x̄₂ → -3)
c    d → 1, x₁ → 2, x₂ → 3, ... , T₆ → 12, T₇ → 13, T₈ → 14

p cnf 14 32
1 0
x 7 8 0
-7 2 0
-7 3 0
7 -2 -3 0
-8 4 0
-8 5 0
8 -4 -5 0
x 9 10 1 0
-9 2 0
-9 4 0
-9 6 0
9 -2 -4 -6 0
-10 5 0
-10 6 0
10 -5 -6 0
x 11 12 1 0
-11 2 0
-11 3 0
-11 6 0
11 -2 -3 -6 0
-12 4 0
-12 6 0
12 -4 -6 0
x 13 14 0
-13 3 0
-13 4 0
13 -3 -4 0
-14 4 0
-14 5 0
-14 6 0
14 -4 -5 -6 0
```

Fig. 2. CryptoMiniSat input file corresponding to the system of equations in (1)

$K_{i,j}^0$, the AES state matrix; with $0 \leq i, j \leq 3$ where i and j denote the row and column indices, respectively. $K_{i,j}^{r+1}$ denotes the bijective mapping of the user key to the 10 sub-round keys, where $0 \leq r \leq 9$ denotes the number of the rounds. The rth key schedule round is defined by the following transformations:

$$
\begin{aligned}
K_{0,0}^{r+1} &\leftarrow S(K_{1,3}^r) \oplus K_{0,0}^r \oplus Rcon(r+1) \\
K_{i,0}^{r+1} &\leftarrow S(K_{(i+1)mod4,3}^r) \oplus K_{i,0}^r, 1 \leq i \leq 3 \\
K_{i,j}^{r+1} &\leftarrow K_{i,j-1}^{r+1} \oplus K_{i,j}^r, 0 \leq i \leq 3, 1 \leq j \leq 3
\end{aligned}
\tag{4}
$$

where $Rcon(\cdot)$ denotes a round-dependent constant and $S(\cdot)$ represents the S-box operations based on the 8×8 Rijndael S-box [29]. Figure 3 shows the transformations given by equation 4.

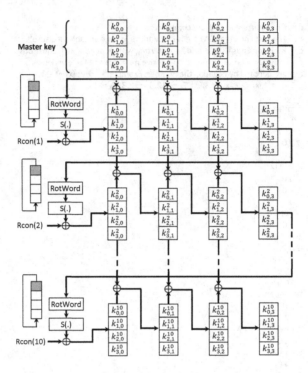

Fig. 3. AES Key Scheduler

4.2 Key Schedule of Serpent

Serpent [31] is a 32 round block cipher based on a substitution permutation network (SPN) structure with an Initial Permutation (IP) and a Final Permutation (FP). It has 32 rounds, each consists of a key mixing operation, a pass through S-boxes, and (in all but the last round) a linear transformation. In the last round, this linear transformation is replaced by an additional key mixing operation. The cipher accepts a variable user key length that is always padded up to 256 bits by appending one bit-value '1' to the end of the most significant bit followed by bit-values '0'. To obtain the 33 128-bit subkeys $K_0, ..., K_{32}$, the user key is divided into eight 32-bit words $w_{-8}, w_{-7}, ..., w_{-1}$, from which the 132 intermediate keys or pre-keys ($w_0...w_{131}$) are derived as follows:

$$w_i := (w_{i-8} \oplus w_{i-5} \oplus w_{i-3} \oplus w_{i-1} \oplus \phi \oplus i) <<< 11 \tag{5}$$

where ϕ is a constant formed by the fractional part of the golden ratio $(\sqrt{5}+1)/2$ or 0x9e3779b9 in hexadecimal.

The round keys k_i are evaluated from the pre-keys by first calling one of the eight 4×4 S-boxes in bit slice mode. In bit slice mode, each input of the S-box comes from a different 32-bit word and each output goes to a different 32-bit word. The 4x32 bits per round are all handled by the same S-box. A group of four input or

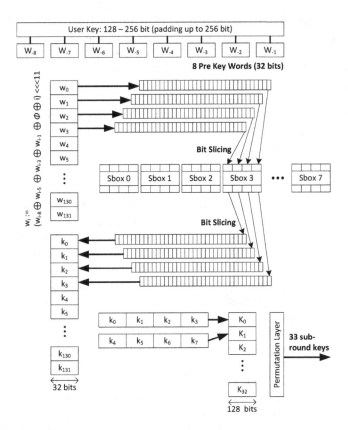

Fig. 4. Serpent Key Scheduler

four output words defines a unit that is handled together. The transformation from pre-keys w_i into words k_j of round keys is performed as follows:

$$
\begin{aligned}
\{k_0; k_1; k_2; k_3\} &= S_3(w_0; w_1; w_2; w_3) \\
\{k_4; k_5; k_6; k_7\} &= S_2(w_4; w_5; w_6; w_7) \\
\{k_8; k_9; k_{10}; k_{11}\} &= S_1(w_8; w_9; w_{10}; w_{11}) \\
\{k_{12}; k_{13}; k_{14}; k_{15}\} &= S_0(w_{12}; w_{13}; w_{14}; w_{15}) \\
\{k_{16}; k_{17}; k_{18}; k_{19}\} &= S_7(w_{16}; w_{17}; w_{18}; w_{19}) \\
&\ \ \vdots \\
\{k_{124}; k_{125}; k_{126}; k_{127}\} &= S_4(w_{124}; w_{125}; w_{126}; w_{127}) \\
\{k_{128}; k_{129}; k_{130}; k_{131}\} &= S_3(w_{128}; w_{129}; w_{130}; w_{131})
\end{aligned}
\tag{6}
$$

where S_i denotes the ith s-box of Serpent. The round keys K_i are then formed by regrouping the 32-bit values k_j as 128-bit sub-keys K_i (for i $\in$ 0,.., r) as follows:

$$
K_i := \{k_{4i}; k_{4i+1}; k_{4i+2}; k_{4i+3}\}
\tag{7}
$$

Finally, we apply IP to the round keys K_i in order to place the key bits in the correct column, i.e., $\hat{K}_i = \text{IP}(K_i)$. Figure 4 depicts the described key scheduler of Serpent.

By exploiting the asymmetric decay of the memory images and the redundancy of key material inherent in the key schedule of both algorithms above, rectifying the faults in the corrupted memory images of the the key schedule is formulated as a Boolean satisfiability problem which can be solved efficiently for relatively large decay factors.

5   Experimental Results

Because of the nature of the cold boot attack, it is realistic to assume that only a corrupted image of the contents of memory is available to the attacker, i.e., a fraction of the memory bits will be flipped. Halderman *et al.* [3] observed that, within a specific memory region, the decay is overwhelmingly asymmetric, i.e., either $0 \to 1$ or $1 \to 0$. When trying to retrieve cryptographic keys, the decay direction for a region can be determined by comparing the number of 0s and 1s since in an uncorrupted key, the expected number of 0s and 1s should approximately be equal.

Similar to the previous work in [3] [6] [32], throughout our experimental results, we assume an asymmetric decay model where bits overwhelmingly decay to their ground state rather than their charged state. Using this model, only the bits that remain in their charged state are useful to the cryptanalyst since one cannot be sure about the original values of the 0 bits, i.e., whether they were originally 0's or decayed 1's. Let β denote the fraction of decayed bits. If the percentage of 0's and 1's in the original key schedule bits is p_z and $1 - p_z$, respectively, then the fraction, f, of key bits that can be assumed to be known by examining the decayed memory of the key schedule is given by

$$f = 1 - (p_z + \beta \times (1 - p_z)) = (1 - p_z) \times (1 - \beta).$$

Since in an uncorrupted key schedule key, we expect the number of 0's and 1's to be approximately equal, i.e., $p_z \approx 1/2$, then we have $f \approx (1 - \beta)/2$.

In our experiments, the input files for the CryptoMiniSAT contained 5,144 and 18,500 clauses for AES and Serpent, respectively. For PolyBoRi, 1,280 equations with 1,728 variables were defined for AES and 8,448 equations with 8,704 variables were defined for Serpent.

Tables 1, 2, 3 [32] and 4 show statistics for the run time required to recover the key of AES and Serpent from the corresponding corrupted memory images for different decay factors. These runtime statistics were obtained using PolyBoRi and CryptoMiniSat running on a Dell Precision 370 workstation with a 3.0 GHz Intel Pentium 4 CPU and 1 GB of RAM. Examining the results in the tables reveal the following observations:

– While the resource requirements of both tools (time for CryptoMiniSat, and time and memory for PloyBoRi) seem to grow exponentially with the decay factor, for practical values of the decay factor, both tools require reasonably short time to recover the secret keys from corrupted memory images.

- The simple and high redundancy in the AES key schedule allows for faster recovery of the key from corrupted memory images. This makes AES more prone to these attacks as compared to other AES finalist such as Serpent. In fact, our initial experiments with Twofish [33] indicate that its relatively more complex key schedule limits the practical applications of these tools to very small values of the decay factor.

- CryptoMiniSat seems to be more suitable for applications in this type of attacks. In particular, every time we tried to push the decay factor higher than the values reported in Table 1, the PolyBoRi tool always crashed after few minutes due to the excessive memory consumption. This behavior also persisted on a 64 bit Linux operating systems with a freshly compiled PolyBoRi/sage system and 8 GB RAM. The question remains if solutions for a higher decay factor can be achieved in a reasonable time if this memory limitations is fixed in the tool.

Table 1. Run-time statistics using Gröbner basis for AES

Decay	10%	20%	30%	40%	50%	60%	70%
Min	0.4	0.6	0.8	1.3	2.2	3.5	7
Max	0.7	0.9	1.1	2.1	3.6	7.6	45
Avg.	0.6	0.7	0.9	1.7	2.9	5.6	21
St.Dev	0.1	0.1	0.1	0.3	0.5	1.2	13
Med.	0.5	0.7	0.9	1.7	2.9	5.3	15

Table 2. Run-time statistics using Gröbner basis for Serpent

Decay	10%	20%	30%	40%	50%	60%	70%
Min	8	9	17	56	114	417	-
Max	9	34	50	2075	2812	578	-
Avg.	8	15	36	328	399	507	-
St.Dev	0.3	7	11	656	764	47	-
Med.	8	12	40	107	131	504	-

Table 3. Run-time statistics using SAT-solver for AES

Decay	30%	40%	50%	60%	70%
Min	0.046	0.046	0.062	0.062	0.078
Max	0.593	0.140	0.187	0.593	207.171
Avg.	0.064	0.066	0.074	0.102	1.233
St.Dev	0.009	0.007	0.008	0.028	4.899
Med.	0.062	0.062	0.078	0.093	0.359

Table 4. Run-time statistics using SAT-solver for Serpent

Decay	10%	20%	30%	40%	50%	60%	70%
Min	0.4	0.4	0.5	0.5	0.7	0.9	4
Max	0.7	0.8	1.2	1.6	8.0	69	35282
Avg.	0.6	0.6	0.7	0.9	1.9	8	1278
St.Dev	0.05	0.07	0.10	0.22	1.30	11	4402
Med.	0.15	0.17	0.20	0.35	1.18	9	27706

6 Conclusion

In this work, we investigated the suitability of two off-the-shelf Algebraic tools for extraction of cryptographic keys from corrupted memory images. Based on our experimental results, it is clear that while the CryptoMiniSat requires a slightly longer preprocessing step to prepare its input file, this step is done only once and the tool runs much faster than the Gröbner basis PolyBoRi tool. Furthermore, CryptoMiniSat does not require a large amount of memory during run time. However, if several solutions were possible for the SAT problem in question, only one result is returned by the solver and the additional solutions have to be explicitly searched again by re-running the tool after appending some extra constraints to exclude already found solutions. On the other hand, Gröbner basis returns a general form representing all possible solutions. However, PolyBoRi requires large memory and usually crashes when the memory requirements is exceeded which limits its applications for solving large problems. It should also be noted that, given the high redundancy of the key schedules of the considered ciphers, the advantage of being able to return all possible solutions does not seem to be very significant since in all the instances we considered, only one possible solution exists.

References

1. Kocher, P.C.: Timing Attacks on Implementations of Diffie-Hellman, RSA, DSS, and Other Systems. In: Koblitz, N. (ed.) CRYPTO 1996. LNCS, vol. 1109, pp. 104–113. Springer, Heidelberg (1996)
2. Kocher, P.C., Jaffe, J., Jun, B.: Differential Power Analysis. In: Wiener, M.J. (ed.) CRYPTO 1999. LNCS, vol. 1666, pp. 388–397. Springer, Heidelberg (1999)
3. Halderman, J.A., Schoen, S.D., Heninger, N., Clarkson, W., Paul, W., Calandrino, J.A., Feldman, A.J., Appelbaum, J., Felten, E.W.: Lest We Remember: Cold Boot Attacks on Encryption Keys. In: van Oorschot, P.C. (ed.) USENIX Security Symposium, pp. 45–60. USENIX Association (2008)
4. Heninger, N., Shacham, H.: Reconstructing RSA Private Keys from Random Key Bits. In: Halevi, S. (ed.) CRYPTO 2009. LNCS, vol. 5677, pp. 1–17. Springer, Heidelberg (2009)
5. Skorobogatov, S.: Low temperature data remanence in static RAM. Technical Report UCAM-CL-TR-536, University of Cambridge, Computer Laboratory (2002)
6. Tsow, A.: An Improved Recovery Algorithm for Decayed AES Key Schedule Images. In: Jacobson Jr., M.J., Rijmen, V., Safavi-Naini, R. (eds.) SAC 2009. LNCS, vol. 5867, pp. 215–230. Springer, Heidelberg (2009)
7. Albrecht, M., Cid, C.: Cold Boot Key Recovery by Solving Polynomial Systems with Noise. In: Lopez, J., Tsudik, G. (eds.) ACNS 2011. LNCS, vol. 6715, pp. 57–72. Springer, Heidelberg (2011)
8. CryptoMiniSat, http://www.msoos.org/cryptominisat2/ (accessed November 2012)
9. Brickenstein, M., Dreyer, A.: PolyBoRi: A framework for Gröbner-basis computations with Boolean polynomials. Journal of Symbolic Computation, 1326–1345 (September 2009)
10. Shamir, A., van Someren, N.: Playing 'Hide and Seek' with Stored Keys. In: Franklin, M. (ed.) FC 1999. LNCS, vol. 1648, pp. 118–124. Springer, Heidelberg (1999)
11. Maartmann-Moe, C., Thorkildsen, S.E., Årnes, A.: The persistence of memory: Forensic identification and extraction of cryptographic keys. Digital Investigation, 132–140 (2009)

12. Kaplan, B.: RAM is Key, Extracting Disk Encryption Keys From Volatile Memory. Master's thesis, Carnegie Mellon University (May 2007)
13. Courtois, N.T., Bard, G.V., Wagner, D.: Algebraic and Slide Attacks on KeeLoq. In: Nyberg, K. (ed.) FSE 2008. LNCS, vol. 5086, pp. 97–115. Springer, Heidelberg (2008)
14. Courtois, N.T., Bard, G.V.: Algebraic Cryptanalysis of the Data Encryption Standard. In: Galbraith, S.D. (ed.) Cryptography and Coding 2007. LNCS, vol. 4887, pp. 152–169. Springer, Heidelberg (2007)
15. Erickson, J., Ding, J., Christensen, C.: Algebraic Cryptanalysis of SMS4: Gröbner Basis Attack and SAT Attack Compared. In: Lee, D., Hong, S. (eds.) ICISC 2009. LNCS, vol. 5984, pp. 73–86. Springer, Heidelberg (2010)
16. Buchberger, B.: Gröbner-Bases: An Algorithmic Method in Polynomial Ideal Theory, ch. 6, pp. 184–232. Reidel Publishing Company, Dodrecht (1985)
17. Buchmann, J., Pyshkin, A., Weinmann, R.-P.: Block Ciphers Sensitive to Gröbner Basis Attacks. In: Pointcheval, D. (ed.) CT-RSA 2006. LNCS, vol. 3860, pp. 313–331. Springer, Heidelberg (2006)
18. Eibach, T., Pilz, E., Völkel, G.: Attacking Bivium using SAT solvers. In: Kleine Büning, H., Zhao, X. (eds.) SAT 2008. LNCS, vol. 4996, pp. 63–76. Springer, Heidelberg (2008)
19. Courtois, N.T., O'Neil, S., Quisquater, J.-J.: Practical Algebraic Attacks on the Hitag2 Stream Cipher. In: Samarati, P., Yung, M., Martinelli, F., Ardagna, C.A. (eds.) ISC 2009. LNCS, vol. 5735, pp. 167–176. Springer, Heidelberg (2009)
20. Courtois, N.T., Nohl, K., O'Neil, S.: Algebraic Attacks on the Crypto-1 Stream Cipher in MiFare Classic and Oyster Cards. Cryptology ePrint Archive, Report 2008/166 (2008)
21. Velichkov, V., Rijmen, V., Preneel, B.: Algebraic cryptanalysis of a small-scale version of stream cipher Lex. IET Information Security, 49–61 (June 2010)
22. Mironov, I., Zhang, L.: Applications of SAT Solvers to Cryptanalysis of Hash Functions. In: Biere, A., Gomes, C.P. (eds.) SAT 2006. LNCS, vol. 4121, pp. 102–115. Springer, Heidelberg (2006)
23. De, D., Kumarasubramanian, A., Venkatesan, R.: Inversion Attacks on Secure Hash Functions Using SAT Solvers. In: Marques-Silva, J., Sakallah, K.A. (eds.) SAT 2007. LNCS, vol. 4501, pp. 377–382. Springer, Heidelberg (2007)
24. Sugita, M., Kawazoe, M., Perret, L., Imai, H.: Algebraic Cryptanalysis of 58-Round SHA-1. In: Biryukov, A. (ed.) FSE 2007. LNCS, vol. 4593, pp. 349–365. Springer, Heidelberg (2007)
25. Wang, X., Yin, Y.L., Yu, H.: Finding Collisions in the Full SHA-1. In: Shoup, V. (ed.) CRYPTO 2005. LNCS, vol. 3621, pp. 17–36. Springer, Heidelberg (2005)
26. Segers, A.: Algebraic Attacks from a Groebner Basis Perspective. Master's thesis, Technische Universiteit Eindhoven (October 2004)
27. Boolean Polynomials, Sage Reference Manual V4.7.2, http://www.sagemath.org/doc/reference/sage/rings/polynomial/pbori.html (accessed November 2012)
28. Cook, S.A.: The complexity of theorem-proving procedures. In: Proceedings of the Third Annual ACM Symposium on Theory of Computing, STOC 1971, pp. 151–158. ACM, New York (1971)
29. Daemen, J., Rijmen, V.: The Design of Rijndael: AES - The Advanced Encryption Standard. Springer (2002)
30. Federal Information Processing Standards Publication (FIPS 197). Advanced Encryption Standard, AES (2001)

31. Anderson, R., Biham, E., Knudsen, L.: Serpent: A Proposal for the Advanced Encryption Standard, http://www.cl.cam.ac.uk/~rja14/serpent.html (accessed October 2012)
32. Kamal, A., Youssef, A.: Applications of SAT Solvers to AES Key Recovery from Decayed Key Schedule Images. In: 2010 Fourth International Conference on Emerging Security Information Systems and Technologies (SECURWARE), pp. 216–220 (July 2010)
33. Twofish, http://www.schneier.com/twofish.html (accessed September 2012)

Cryptanalysis of 2-Layer Nonlinear Piece in Hand Method

Xuyun Nie[1,2,3,4], Albrecht Petzoldt[2], and Johannes Buchmann[2]

[1] School of Computer Science and Engineering,
University of Electronic Science and Technology of China, Chengdu 611731, China
[2] Technische Universität Darmstadt, Department of Computer Science,
Hochschulstraße 10, 64289 Darmstadt, Germany
[3] State Key Laboratory of Information Security, Institute of Information Engineering,
Chinese Academy of Sciences, Beijing 100093, China
[4] Network and Data Security Key Laboratory of Sichuan Province
xynie@uestc.edu.cn, {apetzoldt,buchmann}@cdc.informatik.tu-darmstadt.de

Abstract. Piece in Hand method is a security enhancement method for Multivariate Public Key Cryptosystems (MPKCs). Since 2004, many types of this method have been proposed. In this paper, we consider the 2-layer nonlinear Piece in Hand method as proposed by Tsuji et al. in 2009. The key point of this method is to introduce an invertible quadratic polynomial map on the plaintext variables to construct perturbation of the original MPKC. Through our analysis, we find that the security of the enhanced scheme is mainly relying on the quadratic polynomials of this auxiliary map. The two examples proposed by Tsuji et al. for this map can not resist the Linearization Equation attack. Given a valid ciphertext, we can easily get a public key which is equivalent to the original MPKC. If there is an algorithm that can recover the plaintext corresponding to a valid ciphertext of the original MPKC, we can construct an algorithm that can recover the plaintext corresponding to a valid ciphertext of the enhanced MPKC.

Keywords: Multivariate Cryptography, Quadratic Polynomial, Algebraic Cryptanalysis, Linearization Equation, Piece in Hand.

1 Introduction

Multivariate Public Key Cryptosystems (MPKCs) are promising candidates to resist the quantum computer attack [1]. The security of these schemes is based on the difficulty of solving systems of multivariate quadratic (MQ) equations over a finite field, which is an NP-hard problem in general.

Since 1988, many MPKCs have been proposed, such as MI [15], HFE [20], MFE [26], TTM [16], Rainbow [5], MQQ [13]etc. However, many of these schemes have shown to be insecure [19, 11, 6, 17, 2, 14]. In order to enhance the security of MPKCs, many enhancement methods were proposed. There are plus/minus [22, 21], internal perturbation [3, 4], Extended Multivariate public key Cryptosystems (EMC) [27] etc. All of these methods are subjected to different levels of attacks [12, 7, 9, 8, 18].

A. Cuzzocrea et al. (Eds.): CD-ARES 2013 Workshops, LNCS 8128, pp. 91–104, 2013.
© IFIP International Federation for Information Processing 2013

Piece in Hand (PH) method is another security enhancement method introduced and studied in a series of papers [23, 24, 10, 25]. In [25], Tsuji et al. proposed the 2-layer nonlinear Piece in Hand method. For this, they introduced two vectors of polynomials: an auxiliary polynomial vector and a perturbation polynomial vector. The perturbation polynomial vector is used to add perturbation to the underlying MPKC, whereas the auxiliary polynomial vector is constructed to be efficiently invertible which will be used during the decryption process.

Since the information of the auxiliary polynomial vector is part of the public key, the security of the whole scheme relies on the structure of this vector. In their paper [25], the authors gave two examples for this vector, called H_1 and H_2.

In this paper we show that both H_1 and H_2 satisfy Linearization Equations (LEs) of the form

$$\sum a_{ij} \cdot x_i \cdot y_j + \sum b_i \cdot x_i + \sum c_j \cdot y_j + d = 0, \qquad (1)$$

where x_i are the plaintext variables and y_j are the ciphertext variables.

After finding all the LEs and substituting a valid ciphertext into these equations, we can get a system of linear equations in the plaintext variables. By solving this system, we can represent some of the plaintext variables by linear combinations of the other plaintext variables. Hence, we can do elimination on the public key. And we can perform a similar analysis on the eliminated public key to check if there are Linearization Equations satisfied by the simplified public key.

In the case of H_1, given a valid ciphertext, we can, after two eliminations on the public key, find a public key equivalent to that of the original MPKC. In the case of H_2, given a valid ciphertext, we can achieve the same goal using three eliminations on the public key. This means that Piece in Hand method using these two auxiliary polynomial vectors can not enhance the security of the underlying MPKC. So, we must be very careful when designing the auxiliary polynomial vector of PH method.

The rest of this paper is organized as follows. In Section 2 we give a brief description of MPKCs and Linearization Equations. Section 3 introduces the 2-layer nonlinear Piece in Hand method. In Section 4, we present our cryptanalysis of the enhanced scheme and present the results of our computer experiments. Finally, in Section 5, we conclude the paper.

2   Preliminaries

2.1   Multivariate Public Key Cryptography

To build a multivariate public key cryptosystem (MPKC), one starts with an easily invertible map $\mathcal{F} : \mathbb{F}^n \to \mathbb{F}^m$ (central map). To hide the structure of $\mathcal{F}$ in the public key, one combines it with two invertible affine maps $\mathcal{T} : \mathbb{F}^m \to \mathbb{F}^m$ and $\mathcal{U} : \mathbb{F}^n \to \mathbb{F}^n$. Therefore the public key has the form

$$\mathcal{E} : \mathbb{F}^n \to \mathbb{F}^m, \; \mathbf{y} = (y_1, \ldots, y_m) = \mathcal{E}(x_1, \ldots, x_n) = \mathcal{T} \circ \mathcal{F} \circ \mathcal{U}(x_1, \ldots, x_n). \quad (2)$$

The private key consists out of the three maps $\mathcal{T}, \mathcal{F}$ and $\mathcal{U}$ and therefore allows to invert the public key.

2.2   Linearization Equations

For MPKCs, a Linearization Equation (LE) is an equation in the $n + m$ plaintext/ciphertext variables $x_1, x_2, \ldots, x_n, y_1, y_2, \ldots, y_m$ of the form

$$\sum_{i=1}^{n}\sum_{j=1}^{t} a_{ij} \cdot x_i \cdot g_j(y_1, y_2, \ldots, y_m) + \sum_{j=1}^{l} c_j \cdot f_j(y_1, y_2, \ldots, y_m) + d = 0. \qquad (3)$$

where f_j $(1 \le j \le l)$, g_j $(1 \le j \le l)$, are polynomial functions in the ciphertext variables. The highest degree of g_j, $1 \le j \le l$ is called the order of the LE.

For example, a First Order Linearization Equation (FOLE) looks like

$$\sum_{i=1}^{n}\sum_{j=1}^{m} a_{ij} \cdot x_i \cdot y_j + \sum_{i=1}^{n} b_i \cdot x_i + \sum_{j=1}^{m} c_j \cdot y_j + d = 0. \qquad (4)$$

Note that, given a valid ciphertext $\mathbf{y}' = (y_1', y_2', \ldots, y_m')$, we can substitute it into equation (3) to get a linear equation in the plaintext variables. By finding all these equations we get a linear system which can be solved by Gaussian Elimination. After having found a solution, we can do elimination on the public key.

3   2-Layer Piece in Hand Method

We use the same notation as in [25].

Let $\mathcal{E} : \mathbb{F}^n \to \mathbb{F}^m$ be the public map of a multivariate public key encryption scheme with $\{x_1, \ldots, x_n\}$ and $\{y_1, \ldots, y_m\}$ being the plaintext and ciphertext variables repectively and l be a positive integer.

To enhance the security of the MPKC, the inventors of the 2-layer nonlinear Piece in Hand method introduced an auxiliary polynomial vector $\boldsymbol{H}$ of l components and a perturbation polynomial vector $\boldsymbol{J}$. The elements of the auxiliary polynomial vector $\boldsymbol{H}$ are products of two random linear polynomials h_i and h_j, where the functions h_i are given by $h_i = \sum_{j=1}^{n} s_{ij} \cdot x_j$ $(i = 1, \ldots, l)$ with $s_{ij} \in_R \mathbb{F}$. The perturbation polynomial vector $\boldsymbol{J}$ is a vector with $l(l-1)/2$ components constructed from the polynomials $h_i \cdot h_j$ $(1 \le i < j \le l)$. Note that the polynomial components of the vector $\boldsymbol{H}$ are designed to be easily invertible for decryption. Therefore, one can use the vector $\boldsymbol{H}$ to compute the values of h_i $(i = 1, \ldots, l)$ and sequentially calculate the value of the vector $\boldsymbol{J}$. By the above construction, one gets an enhanced public key $\tilde{\mathcal{E}} : \mathbb{F}^n \to \mathbb{F}^{m+l}$ of the form

$$\tilde{\mathcal{E}}(x_1, \ldots, x_n) = B\begin{pmatrix} \mathcal{E}(x_1, \ldots, x_n) + D\boldsymbol{J} \\ C\boldsymbol{H} \end{pmatrix} \qquad (5)$$

where B is an $(m + l) \times (m + l)$ invertible matrix over $\mathbb{F}$, D is an $m \times \frac{l \cdot (l-1)}{2}$ matrix over $\mathbb{F}$, and C is an $l \times l$ invertible matrix over $\mathbb{F}$.

Secret Key: The secret key includes

- the secret key of the underlying MPKC
- the matrices B, C and D
- the auxiliary polynomial vector $\boldsymbol{H}$ and
- the perturbation polynomial vector $\boldsymbol{J}$.

Public Key: The $m + l$ components of the function $\tilde{\mathcal{E}}$.
Encryption: Given a plaintext $\boldsymbol{x}' = (x'_1, \ldots, x'_n)$, compute

$$\boldsymbol{y}' = (y'_1, \ldots, y'_{m+l}) = \tilde{\mathcal{E}}(x'_1, \ldots, x'_n).$$

Decryption: Given a valid ciphertext $\boldsymbol{y}' = (y'_1, \ldots, y'_{m+l})$, decryption includes the following steps:

1. Compute $\boldsymbol{v}' = (v'_1, \ldots, v'_{m+l}) = B^{-1}(y'_1, \ldots, y'_{m+l})^T$;
2. Compute $\boldsymbol{H} = C^{-1}(v'_{m+1}, \ldots, v'_{m+l})^T$ and get the values of h_i $(i = 1, \ldots, l)$;
3. Compute the value of $\boldsymbol{J}$ by substituting the values of h_i $(i = 1, \ldots, l)$ into its components;
4. Compute $\boldsymbol{x}' = (x'_1, \ldots, x'_n) = \mathcal{E}^{-1}(v'_1 - dj_1, \ldots, v'_m - dj_m)$, where $(dj_1, \ldots, dj_m)^T = DJ$.

Examples for the auxiliary vector H and the perturbation vector J

In [25], the authors gave two examples for the choice of the auxiliary vector $\boldsymbol{H}$, denoted by $\boldsymbol{H}_1$ and $\boldsymbol{H}_2$, respectively.
For arbitrary l, the vector $\boldsymbol{H}_1$ is given by

$$\boldsymbol{H}_1 = (u_1, \ldots, u_l)^T = \begin{pmatrix} h_1 h_2 + \alpha_1 \\ h_2 h_3 + \alpha_2 \\ h_3 h_1 + \alpha_3 \\ h_1 h_4 + \alpha_4 \\ h_1 h_5 + \alpha_5 \\ \vdots \\ h_1 h_{l-1} + \alpha_{l-1} \\ h_1 h_l + \alpha_l \end{pmatrix}. \tag{6}$$

with $\alpha_1, \ldots, \alpha_l \in_R \mathbb{F}$. For our experiments (see Subsection 4.3) we use the value $l = 8$.
Apparently, given the value of the vector $(u_1, \ldots, u_l)$, we can get from the first three equations of (6)

$$h_1 = \left(\frac{(u_1 - \alpha_1)(u_3 - \alpha_3)}{(u_2 - \alpha_2)} \right)^{\frac{1}{2}} \tag{7}$$

and then get the values of $h_2, h_3, \ldots, h_l$ in turn.

For the auxiliary map H_2, the value l is fixed to 15. We have

$$H_2 = (u_1, \ldots, u_{15})^T = \begin{pmatrix} h_1 h_2 + \alpha_1 \\ h_2 h_3 + \alpha_2 \\ h_3 h_4 + \alpha_3 \\ h_4 h_5 + \alpha_4 \\ h_5 h_1 + \alpha_5 \\ h_6^2 + h_1 h_3 + \alpha_6 \\ h_7^2 + h_3 h_5 + \alpha_7 \\ h_8^2 + h_5 h_2 + \alpha_8 \\ h_9^2 + h_2 h_4 + \alpha_9 \\ h_{10}^2 + h_4 h_1 + \alpha_{10} \\ h_1 h_{10} + h_6 h_{11} + \alpha_{11} \\ h_2 h_9 + h_7 h_{12} + \alpha_{12} \\ h_3 h_8 + h_8 h_{13} + \alpha_{13} \\ h_4 h_7 + h_9 h_{14} + \alpha_{14} \\ h_5 h_6 + h_{10} h_{15} + \alpha_{15} \end{pmatrix} \tag{8}$$

where $\alpha_i \in_R \mathbb{F}$ $(i = 1, \ldots, l)$. Similarly to H_1, H_2 can be easily inverted. The perturbation vector J used in [25] is given as follows:

$$J = (j_1, j_2, \ldots, j_{l(l-1)/2}) = \begin{pmatrix} h_1 h_2 + \beta_1 \\ h_1 h_3 + \beta_2 \\ \vdots \\ h_1 h_l + \beta_{l-1} \\ h_2 h_3 + \beta_l \\ \vdots \\ h_2 h_l + \beta_{2l-3} \\ h_3 h_4 + \beta_{2l-2} \\ \vdots \\ h_{l-1} h_l + \beta_{l(l-1)/2} \end{pmatrix} \tag{9}$$

where $\beta_i \in_R \mathbb{F}$ $(i = 1, \ldots, l(l-1)/2)$.

4   Cryptanalysis of the 2-Layer PH Method

Although the perturbation map J can hide the weak point of the underlying MPKC scheme, the security of the enhanced scheme depends mainly on the design of the auxiliary map H. Bad design of the vector H will bring some new security problems to the scheme. Both vectors H_1 and H_2 of [25] are not properly chosen to enhance the security of the underlying scheme, since they satisfy Linearization Equations.

In this section, we present our cryptanalysis of the 2-layer PH method with auxiliary polynomial vector H_1 and H_2, respectively. Given a valid ciphertext

$y' = (y'_1, \ldots, y'_{m+l})^T$, our goal is to find the corresponding plaintext. Namely, we have to solve the system

$$\begin{cases} y'_1 = \tilde{\mathcal{E}}_1(x_1, \ldots, x_n) \\ \quad\vdots \\ y'_{m+l} = \tilde{\mathcal{E}}_{m+l}(x_1, \ldots, x_n) \end{cases} . \tag{10}$$

4.1   Case of H_1

Through theoretical analysis, we find that the system $\tilde{\mathcal{E}}$ satisfies Linearization Equations, which are brought in by the vector H_1. Given a valid ciphertext we can, after finding all FOLEs, recover the corresponding plaintext easily.

Linearization Equations

In the expression of the polynomial vector H_1 (see (6)), we have

$$u_1 = h_1 h_2 + \alpha_1 \text{ and } u_2 = h_2 h_3 + \alpha_2.$$

Hence we get

$$h_3(u_1 - \alpha_1) = h_1(u_2 - \alpha_2). \tag{11}$$

Since the matrices B and C are invertible, the elements u_i $(i = 1, \ldots, l)$ can be expressed by linear equations in the ciphertext variables, namely $u_i = \sum_{j=1}^{m+l} t_{ij} \cdot y_j$ $(i = 1, \ldots, l)$. Analogously we get $h_i = \sum_{j=1}^{n} s_{ij} \cdot x_j$ $(i = 1, \ldots, l)$. Hence equation (11) implies that the plaintext variables $\{x_1, \ldots, x_n\}$ and ciphertext variables $\{y_1, \ldots, y_{m+l}\}$ satisfy an equation of the form:

$$\sum_{i=1}^{n}\sum_{j=1}^{m+l} a_{ij} \cdot x_i \cdot y_j + \sum_{i=1}^{n} b_i \cdot x_i + \sum_{j=1}^{m+l} c_j \cdot y_j + d = 0. \tag{12}$$

This equation is exactly a FOLE. Similarly, from each of the pairs $h_j(u_i - \alpha_i) = h_i(u_j - \alpha_j)$ $(1 \leq i < j \leq l, i \neq 2)$ and the pair $h_1(u_2 - \alpha_2) = h_2(u_3 - \alpha_3)$, we can get an additional FOLE. Hence there exist at least $(l-2)(l-1)/2 + 1$ linear independent Linearization Equations of type (12).

To find these FOLEs, we randomly generate $D_1 \geq n(m+l) + n + m + l + 1$ plaintext/ciphertext pairs and substitute them into equation (12). By doing so, we get a system of D_1 linear equations in the $n(m+l) + n + m + l + 1$ unknowns a_{ij}, b_i, c_j and d which can be solved by Gaussian Elimination. We denote the solution space by V and its dimension by D. Hence, we derive D linearly independent equations of type (12) in the plaintext and ciphertext variables.

The work above depends only on the public key and can be done once for a given public key.

By substituting the given ciphertext $\mathbf{y}' = (y'_1, \ldots, y'_{m+l})$ into the Linearization Equations found above we get D linear equations in the plaintext variables. Let's assume that t_1 of these equations are linearly independent.

First Elimination

By substituting the t_1 equations found above into the public key $\tilde{\mathcal{E}}$ of the 2-layer nonlinear PH scheme, we can eliminate t_1 equations from $\tilde{\mathcal{E}}$. By doing so, we get a simplified public key $\tilde{\mathcal{E}}'$ of the form

$$\begin{cases} y'_j = \tilde{\mathcal{E}}'_j(w_1, \ldots, w_{n-t_1}) \\ 1 \le j \le m + l \end{cases}. \tag{13}$$

Second Elimination

In the practical setting of [25], the characteristic of the underlying field $\mathbb{F}$ was chosen to be 2. Using this property, we can find another type of Linearization Equations satisfied by the simplified public key $\tilde{\mathcal{E}}'$.

We denote by u'_i ($i = 1, \ldots, l$) the value of u_i corresponding to the given ciphertext $\mathbf{y}' = (y'_1, \ldots, y'_{m+l})$. Such we get

$$\begin{cases} u'_1 = h_1 h_2 + \alpha_1 \\ u'_2 = h_2 h_3 + \alpha_2 \\ u'_3 = h_3 h_1 + \alpha_3 \\ u'_4 = h_1 h_4 + \alpha_4 \\ u'_5 = h_1 h_5 + \alpha_5 \\ \quad\vdots \\ u'_{l-1} = h_1 h_{l-1} + \alpha_{l-1} \\ u'_l = h_1 h_l + \alpha_l \end{cases} \tag{14}$$

According to FOLEs similar to equation (11), we find

$$\begin{cases} h_2 = \frac{u'_2 - \alpha_2}{u'_3 - \alpha_3} h_1 \\ h_3 = \frac{u'_2 - \alpha_2}{u'_1 - \alpha_1} h_1 \\ h_4 = \frac{u'_4 - \alpha_4}{u'_1 - \alpha_1} \cdot \frac{u'_2 - \alpha_2}{u'_3 - \alpha_3} h_1 \\ h_5 = \frac{u'_5 - \alpha_5}{u'_1 - \alpha_1} \cdot \frac{u'_2 - \alpha_2}{u'_3 - \alpha_3} h_1 \\ \quad\vdots \\ h_l = \frac{u'_l - \alpha_l}{u'_1 - \alpha_1} \cdot \frac{u'_2 - \alpha_2}{u'_3 - \alpha_3} h_1 \end{cases} \tag{15}$$

By substituting (15) into (6), we get

$$
\begin{cases}
u_1 = \frac{u_2' - \alpha_2}{u_3' - \alpha_3} h_1^2 + \alpha_1 \\[4pt]
u_2 = \frac{u_2' - \alpha_2}{u_1' - \alpha_1} \cdot \frac{u_2' - \alpha_2}{u_3' - \alpha_3} h_1^2 + \alpha_2 \\[4pt]
u_3 = \frac{u_2' - \alpha_2}{u_1' - \alpha_1} h_1^2 + \alpha_3 \\[4pt]
u_4 = \frac{u_4' - \alpha_4}{u_1' - \alpha_1} \cdot \frac{u_2' - \alpha_2}{u_3' - \alpha_3} h_1^2 + \alpha_4 \\[4pt]
u_5 = \frac{u_5' - \alpha_5}{u_1' - \alpha_1} \cdot \frac{u_2' - \alpha_2}{u_3' - \alpha_3} h_1^2 + \alpha_5 \\[4pt]
\vdots \\[4pt]
u_l = \frac{u_l' - \alpha_l}{u_1' - \alpha_1} \cdot \frac{u_2' - \alpha_2}{u_3' - \alpha_3} h_1^2 + \alpha_l
\end{cases}
\tag{16}
$$

Due to $u_i = \sum_{j=1}^{m+l} t_{ij} \cdot y_j$ $(i = 1, \ldots, l)$ and $h_i = \sum_{j=1}^{n} s_{ij} \cdot x_j$ $(i = 1, \ldots, l)$ and using the fact that squaring is a linear operation on a field of characteristic 2, we have at least one equation satisfied by ciphertext variables and the remaining plaintext variables of the form

$$
\begin{cases}
\sum_{j=1}^{m+l} \tilde{a}_j \cdot y_j' + \sum_{i=1}^{n-t_1} \tilde{b}_i \cdot w_i^2 + \tilde{c} = 0 \\
\forall w_1, \ldots, w_{n-t_1} \in \mathbb{F}
\end{cases}
\tag{17}
$$

It is easy to solve the above linear system for the $\tilde{a}_i$, $\tilde{b}_j$ and $\tilde{c}$. Let $\{\tilde{a}_1^{(\rho)}, \cdots, \tilde{a}_{m+l}^{(\rho)}, \tilde{b}_1^{(\rho)}, \cdots, \tilde{b}_{n-t_1}^{(\rho)}, \tilde{c}^{(\rho)}, \ 1 \le \rho \le r\}$ be a basis of the solution space of the system (17). Set

$$
\begin{cases}
\sum_{j=1}^{n-t_1} (\tilde{b}_j^{(\rho)})^{1/2} \cdot w_j + \left(\sum_{i=1}^{m+l} \tilde{a}_i^{(\rho)} \cdot y_i' + \tilde{c}^{(\rho)} \right)^{1/2} = 0 \\
1 \le \rho \le r
\end{cases}
\tag{18}
$$

For any vector $\mathbf{w} = (w_1, \ldots w_{n-t_1})$, $\mathbf{w}$ and the corresponding ciphertext $(y_1, \ldots, y_{m+l}) = \tilde{\mathcal{E}}'(\mathbf{w})$ satisfy equation (18). Therefore we can represent at least one variable of the set $\{w_1, \ldots, w_{n-t_1}\}$ as a linear equation in the remaining variables. Denote the remaining variables by $v_1, \ldots, v_{n-t_1-1}$.

Substituting this linear expression into the system (13), we can get a new public key with $(n - t_1 - 1)$ unknowns, denoted as

$$
\begin{cases}
y_j' = \tilde{\mathcal{E}}_j''(v_1, \ldots, v_{n-t_1-1}) \\
1 \le j \le m + l
\end{cases}
\tag{19}
$$

Eliminating Perturbation

Furthermore, after two eliminations, the vector $\boldsymbol{J}$ becomes a constant vector, namely, the perturbation of Piece in Hand method is eliminated. The reason for this is shown as follows. From (16), we get

$$
h_1 = \left(\frac{(u_1' - \alpha_1)(u_3' - \alpha_3)}{u_2' - \alpha_2} \right)^{1/2}.
\tag{20}
$$

Substituting (20) and (15) into (9), the vector $\boldsymbol{J}$ becomes a constant vector on $\mathbb{F}$. For example,

$$j_1 = h_1 h_2 + \beta_1 = u_1' - \alpha_1 + \beta_1,$$

$$j_{l+1} = h_2 h_4 + \beta_{l+1} = \left(\frac{(u_2' - \alpha_2)(u_4' - \alpha_4)}{u_3' - \alpha_3} \right) + \beta_{l+1}.$$

Hence, the public key $\tilde{\mathcal{E}}''$ of equation (19) is equivalent to the public key of the underlying MPKC scheme.

If there exists an algorithm which recovers the plaintext corresponding to a valid ciphertext for the underlying MPKC scheme, we can therefore find the values of the variables $v_1, \ldots, v_{n-t_1-1}$ corresponding to the valid ciphertext $\mathbf{y}'$. Using the linear equations found during the two eliminations above, we can recover the values of the remaining plaintexts variables.

4.2   Case of H_2

Let $y' = (y_1', \ldots, y_{m+15}')$ be a valid ciphertext of the Piece in Hand MPKC with auxiliary map $\boldsymbol{H}_2$. Again we want to find the corresponding plaintext $x' = (x_1', \ldots, x_n')$ by solving the system (10).

Similarly to the case of $\boldsymbol{H}_1$, from the first five equations in (8), we can get five FOLEs between u_i and h_i $(1 \leq i \leq 5)$ by

$$\begin{cases} h_3(u_1 - \alpha_1) = h_1(u_2 - \alpha_2) \\ h_4(u_2 - \alpha_2) = h_2(u_3 - \alpha_3) \\ h_5(u_3 - \alpha_3) = h_3(u_4 - \alpha_4) \\ h_1(u_4 - \alpha_4) = h_4(u_5 - \alpha_5) \\ h_2(u_5 - \alpha_5) = h_5(u_1 - \alpha_1) \end{cases}.$$

Apparently, these five equations are linearly independent. Hence, we can get at least five Linearization Equations satisfied by plain- and ciphertext variables of the form (12).

Using the same method as in Subsection 4.1, we do the first elimination on the system (10). Suppose we eliminated $t_1 \geq 4$ variables in the system. Denote the remaining plaintext variables by $w_1, \ldots, w_{n-t_1}$ and let

$$\begin{cases} y_j' = \tilde{\mathcal{E}}_j'(w_1, \ldots, w_{n-t_1}) \\ 1 \leq j \leq m + 15 \end{cases} \tag{21}$$

be the simplified public key.

Using a similar method as in Subsection 4.1, we can perform two additional eliminations on the system (21). Due to the limitation of paper size, we omit the details of this part here. We will present them in the full version of this paper. But we should point out the following facts.

For the public key $\tilde{\mathcal{E}}_j'(w_1, \ldots, w_{n-t_1})$, plain- and ciphertext variables satisfy equations of the form

$$\sum_{j=1}^{m+l} \tilde{a}_j \cdot y_j + \sum_{i=1}^{n-t_1} \tilde{b}_i \cdot w_i^2 + \tilde{c} = 0. \tag{22}$$

By substituting the ciphertext $\mathbf{y}'$ into these equations and using the fact that squaring is a linear function over fields of characteristic 2, we can find $t_2 \geq 6$ linear equations in the plaintext variables. We can therefore eliminate t_2 variables from the public key. After this elimination, the simplified public key has the form

$$\begin{cases} y'_j = \tilde{\mathcal{E}}''_j(v_1, \ldots, v_{n-t_1-t_2}) \\ 1 \leq j \leq m+15 \end{cases}. \tag{23}$$

The public key $\tilde{\mathcal{E}}''$ satisfies equations of the form

$$\sum_{j=1}^{m+15} \tilde{\tilde{a}}_j \cdot y_j + \sum_{i=1}^{n-t_1-t_2} \tilde{\tilde{b}}_i \cdot v_i + \tilde{\tilde{c}} = 0. \tag{24}$$

By substituting the ciphertext $\mathbf{y}'$ into these equations, we can find $t_3 \geq 5$ linear equations in the variables $v_1, \ldots, v_{n-t_1-t_2}$. Therefore, we can eliminate t_3 variables from the system (23) and get a new public key $\tilde{\mathcal{E}}'''$ of the form

$$\begin{cases} y'_j = \tilde{\mathcal{E}}'''_j(u_1, \ldots, u_{n-t_1-t_2-t_3}) \\ 1 \leq j \leq m+15 \end{cases}. \tag{25}$$

For the public key $\tilde{\mathcal{E}}'''$, the perturbation vector $\mathbf{J}$ becomes a constant vector. Hence, $\tilde{\mathcal{E}}'''$ is equivalent to the public key of the underlying MPKC.

Analogously to Subsection 4.1 we can therefore, under the assumption that there exists an algorithm which, for the underlying MPKC, finds for a given ciphertext the corresponding plaintext, construct an algorithm which, for any given ciphertext $\mathbf{y}' = (y'_1, \ldots, y'_{m+15})$, recovers the corresponding plaintext $\mathbf{x}' = (x'_1, \ldots, x'_n)$.

4.3   Complexity and Experimental Verification

In our concrete attack scenario we set $\mathbb{F} = GF(256)$ and $m = n = 25$. As the underlying MPKC we used the $C^\star$ scheme of Matsumoto and Imai. We implemented the Piece in Hand cryptosystem in two different ways using $\mathbf{H}_1$ (with $l = 8$) and $\mathbf{H}_2$ as auxiliary matrix respectively. For our attack we chose randomly a valid ciphertext $\mathbf{y}' = (y'_1, \ldots, y'_{m+l}) \in \mathbb{F}^{m+l}$. Our goal was to find the corresponding plaintext $\mathbf{x}' = (x'_1, \ldots, x'_n) \in \mathbb{F}^n$.

Case of $\mathbf{H}_1$. In the first step we computed 900 ($> n(m+l)+n+m+l+1 = 884$) plaintext/ciphertext pairs and substituted them into the Linearization Equation of type (12). We did Gaussian Elimination on this linear system and found a basis of all FOLEs. The complexity of the Gaussian Elimination is equal to $(n(m+l)+n+m+l+1)^3$ operations on the finite field $\mathbb{F}$. In our experiments,

$$(n(m+l)+n+m+l+1)^3 = 884^3 \leq 2^{30}.$$

We found that the dimension of the space spanned by all FOLEs is $D = (l-2)(l-1)/2 = 22$.

Computing the plaintext/ciphertext pairs and solving this large linear system proved to be the most time-consuming step of our attack. In our experiments, it took about 70 seconds, where it took about 68 seconds on generating the plaintext/ciphertext pairs and about 2 seconds on the Gaussian Elimination. This step is independent of the given ciphertext $\mathbf{y}'$ and has to be done for a given public key only once.

After substituting the ciphertext $\mathbf{y}'$ into these equations we obtained 7 linear equations in the plaintext variables.

In the second step we computed 100 plaintext/ciphertext pairs and substituted them into the Linearization Equation of type (17). By doing so, we got 15 linearly independent equations of the form (17). By evaluating equation (18), we got 1 linear equation in the plaintext variables.

We substituted the 8 linear equations found in the previous steps into the public key and obtained a new public key $\tilde{\mathcal{E}}''$ of 33 equations in 17 variables, which proved to be of the form of a $C^\star$ public key (i.e. the perturbation was eliminated).

In the last step of the attack, we attacked the new public key $\tilde{\mathcal{E}}''$ with the Linearization Equation attack of Patarin [19]. We computed 500 plaintext/ciphertext pairs and substituted them into the Linearization Equation of type (12). By doing so, we got 25 linear independent equations of type (12). After substituting the ciphertext y' we obtained 17 linear equations in the plaintext variables which enabled us to reconstruct the plaintext $\mathbf{x}'$.

The running time of the whole attack was about 90 seconds.

Case of H_2. In the first step we computed 1100 $(> (n(m+15)+n+m+15+1) = 1066)$ plaintext/ciphertext pairs and substituted them into the Linearization Equation of type (12). We solved the resulting linear system for the variables a_{ij}, b_i, c_j and d to find a basis of all FOLEs. By doing so, we found 5 linear independent Linearization Equations. After substituting the ciphertext $\mathbf{y}'$ into these equations we obtained 4 linear equations in the plaintext variables. The complexity of this step is equal to $1066^3 \leq 2^{31}$. It took about 104 seconds in our experiments, where it took about 102 seconds on generating the plaintext/ciphertext pairs and about 2 second on the Gaussian Elimination. This step has to be performed for each public key only once.

In the second step we computed 100 plaintext/ciphertext pairs and substituted them into the Linearization Equation of type (22). By doing so, we got 14 linear independent equations of form (22). After substituting the ciphertext $\mathbf{y}'$, we got 6 linear equations in the plaintext variables.

In the third step we computed again 100 plaintext/ciphertext pairs and substituted them into the Linearization Equation of type (24). We obtained 25 linear independent equations. By substituting the ciphertext $\mathbf{y}'$ into these equations, we got 5 linear equations in the plaintext variables.

We substituted the 15 linear equations found in the previous steps into the public key and obtained a new public key $\tilde{\mathcal{E}}'''$ of 40 equations in 10 variables, which proved to be of the form of a $C^\star$ public key (i.e. the perturbation was eliminated).

In the last step of the attack, we attacked the new key $\tilde{\mathcal{E}}'''$ with the Linearization Equation attack of Patarin [19]. We computed 500 plaintext/ciphertext pairs and substituted them into the Linearization Equation of type (12). By doing so, we obtained 25 linear independent equations. After substituting the ciphertext $\mathbf{y}'$ we got 10 linear equations in the plaintext variables which enabled us to reconstruct the plaintext $\mathbf{x}'$.

The running time of the whole attack was about 127 seconds.

All experiments were performed on a server with 24 AMD Opteron processors and 128 GB RAM. However, for our experiments we used only a single core. The attack was programmed in Magma code and required about 120 MB of memory.

5   Conclusion

In this paper, we presented the cryptanalysis of two examples of the 2-layer nonlinear Piece in Hand method. As we showed, both examples do not enhance the security of the underlying MPKC because they can not resist Linearization Equation attacks. From this paper, we find that the security of the 2-layer nonlinear Piece in Hand method depends mainly on the construction of the auxiliary polynomial vector $\boldsymbol{H}$. We should therefore design the auxiliary polynomial vector $\boldsymbol{H}$ in such a way that it resists existing attacks.

Acknowledgements. We want to thank the anonymous reviewers for their comments which helped to improve the paper. The first author is supported by the National Key Basic Research Program of China (2013CB834203), the National Natural Science Foundation of China (No. 61103205), the Fundamental Research Funds for the Central Universities under Grant ZYGX2010J069. The second author thanks the Horst Görtz Foundation for financial support.

References

[1]   Bernstein, D., Buchmann, J., Dahmen, E. (eds.): Post-Quantum Cryptography. Springer (2009)

[2]   Billet, O., Gilbert, H.: Cryptanalysis of Rainbow. In: De Prisco, R., Yung, M. (eds.) SCN 2006. LNCS, vol. 4116, pp. 336–347. Springer, Heidelberg (2006)

[3]   Ding, J.: A new variant of the Matsumoto-Imai cryptosystem through perturbation. In: Bao, F., Deng, R., Zhou, J. (eds.) PKC 2004. LNCS, vol. 2947, pp. 305–318. Springer, Heidelberg (2004)

[4]   Ding, J., Schmidt, D.: Cryptanalysis of HFEv and internal perturbation of HFE. In: Vaudenay, S. (ed.) PKC 2005. LNCS, vol. 3386, pp. 288–301. Springer, Heidelberg (2005)

[5]   Ding, J., Schmidt, D.: Rainbow, a new multivariate public key signature scheme. In: Ioannidis, J., Keromytis, A.D., Yung, M. (eds.) ACNS 2005. LNCS, vol. 3531, pp. 164–175. Springer, Heidelberg (2005)

[6]   Ding, J., Hu, L., Nie, X., Li, J., Wagner, J.: High Order Linearization Equation (HOLE) Attack on Multivariate Public Key Cryptosystems. In: Okamoto, T., Wang, X. (eds.) PKC 2007. LNCS, vol. 4450, pp. 233–248. Springer, Heidelberg (2007)

[7] Dubois, V., Fouque, P., Shamir, A., Stern, J.: Practical Cryptanalysis of SFLASH. In: Menezes, A. (ed.) CRYPTO 2007. LNCS, vol. 4622, pp. 1–12. Springer, Heidelberg (2007)

[8] Dubois, V., Granboulan, L., Stern, J.: Cryptanalysis of HFE with Internal Perturbation. In: Okamoto, T., Wang, X. (eds.) PKC 2007. LNCS, vol. 4450, pp. 249–265. Springer, Heidelberg (2007)

[9] Fouque, P.-A., Granboulan, L., Stern, J.: Differential Cryptanalysis for Multivariate Schemes. In: Cramer, R. (ed.) EUROCRYPT 2005. LNCS, vol. 3494, pp. 341–353. Springer, Heidelberg (2005)

[10] Fujita, R., Tadaki, K., Tsujii, S.: Nonlinear piece in hand perturbation vector method for enhancing security of multivariate public key cryptosystems. In: Buchmann, J., Ding, J. (eds.) PQCrypto 2008. LNCS, vol. 5299, pp. 148–164. Springer, Heidelberg (2008)

[11] Faugère, J.-C., Joux, A.: Algebraic Cryptanalysis of Hidden Field Equation (HFE) Cryptosystems Using Gröbner bases. In: Boneh, D. (ed.) CRYPTO 2003. LNCS, vol. 2729, pp. 44–60. Springer, Heidelberg (2003)

[12] Faugère, J.-C., Joux, A., Perret, L., Treger, J.: Cryptanalysis of the Hidden Matrix Cryptosystem. In: Abdalla, M., Barreto, P.S.L.M. (eds.) LATINCRYPT 2010. LNCS, vol. 6212, pp. 241–254. Springer, Heidelberg (2010)

[13] Gligoroski, D., Markovski, S., Knapskog, S.: Multivariate Quadratic Trapdoor Functions Based on Multivariate Quadratic Quasigroups. In: Proceedings of the American Conference on Applied Mathematics (MATH 2008), Cambridge, Massachusetts, USA (March 2008)

[14] Mohamed, M.S.E., Ding, J., Buchmann, J., Werner, F.: Algebraic Attack on the MQQ Public Key Cryptosystem. In: Garay, J.A., Miyaji, A., Otsuka, A. (eds.) CANS 2009. LNCS, vol. 5888, pp. 392–401. Springer, Heidelberg (2009)

[15] Matsumoto, T., Imai, H.: Public quadratic polynomial-tuples for efficient signature-verification and message-encryption. In: Günther, C.G. (ed.) EUROCRYPT 1988. LNCS, vol. 330, pp. 419–453. Springer, Heidelberg (1988)

[16] Moh, T.: A fast public key system with signature and master key functions. Lecture Notes at EE department of Stanford University (May 1999), http://www.usdsi.com/ttm.html

[17] Nie, X., Hu, L., Li, J., Updegrove, C., Ding, J.: Breaking a New Instance of TTM Cryptosystems. In: Zhou, J., Yung, M., Bao, F. (eds.) ACNS 2006. LNCS, vol. 3989, pp. 210–225. Springer, Heidelberg (2006)

[18] Nie, X., Xu, Z., Buchmann, J.: Cryptanalysis of Hash-based Tamed Transformation and Minus Signature Scheme. In: Gaborit, P. (ed.) PQCrypto 2013. LNCS, vol. 7932, pp. 155–164. Springer, Heidelberg (2013)

[19] Patarin, J.: Cryptanalysis of the Matsumoto and Imai public key scheme of Eurocrypt '88. In: Coppersmith, D. (ed.) CRYPTO 1995. LNCS, vol. 963, pp. 248–261. Springer, Heidelberg (1995)

[20] Patarin, J.: Hidden fields equations (HFE) and isomorphisms of polynomials (IP): Two new families of asymmetric algorithms. In: Maurer, U. (ed.) EUROCRYPT 1996. LNCS, vol. 1070, pp. 33–48. Springer, Heidelberg (1996)

[21] Patarin, J., Courtois, N., Goubin, L.: Flash, a fast multivariate signature algorithm. In: Naccache, D. (ed.) CT-RSA 2001. LNCS, vol. 2020, pp. 298–307. Springer, Heidelberg (2001)

[22] Patarin, J., Goubin, L., Courtois, N.: C^*_{-+} and HM: Variations around two schemes of T. Matsumoto and H. Imai. In: Ohta, K., Pei, D. (eds.) ASIACRYPT 1998. LNCS, vol. 1514, pp. 35–50. Springer, Heidelberg (1998)

[23] Tsujii, S., Tadaki, K., Fujioka, R.: Piece in Hand concept for enhanceing the security of multivariate type public key cryptosystem: public key without containing all the information of secret key. IACR eprint 2004/366, http://eprint.iacr.org

[24] Tsujii, S., Tadaki, K., Fujioka, R.: Proposal for piece in hand matrix ver.2: General concept for enhancing security of multivariate pulic key cryptosystem. IACR eprint 2006/051, http://eprint.iacr.org

[25] Tsujii, S., Tadaki, K., Fujita, R., Gotaishi, M., Kaneko, T.: Security Enhancement of Various MPKCs by 2-layer Nonlinear Piece in Hand Method. IEICE Trans. Fundamentals E92-A(10), 2438–2447 (2009)

[26] Wang, L.-C., Yang, B.-Y., Hu, Y.-H., Lai, F.: A "Medium-Field" Multivariate Public-Key Encryption Scheme. In: Pointcheval, D. (ed.) CT-RSA 2006. LNCS, vol. 3860, pp. 132–149. Springer, Heidelberg (2006)

[27] Wang, H., Zhang, H., Wang, Z., Tang, M.: Extended multivariate public key cryptosystems with secure encryption function. Science China Information Sciences 54(6), 1161–1171 (2011)

On the Security of LBlock against the Cube Attack and Side Channel Cube Attack

Saad Islam, Mehreen Afzal, and Adnan Rashdi

National University of Sciences and Technology, Islamabad, Pakistan
{saadislam,mehreenafzal,adnanrashdi}@mcs.edu.pk

Abstract. In this research, a recently proposed lightweight block cipher LBlock, not tested against the cube attack has been analyzed. 7, 8 and 9 round LBlock have been successfully attacked with complexities of $O(2^{10.76})$, $O(2^{11.11})$ and $O(2^{47.00})$ respectively. For the case of side channel cube attack, full version of LBlock has been attacked using a single bit leakage model with the complexity of $O(2^{55.00})$ cipher evaluations. For this purpose, a generic practical platform has been developed to test various stream and block ciphers against the latest cube attack.

Keywords: Cube attack, Side channel cube attack, Lightweight block ciphers, LBlock.

1 Introduction

Cube attack has been recently introduced by Dinur and Shamir in 2009 [1,2]. Preliminarily cube attack has been applied successfully on stream ciphers. Several results can be found on the stream cipher Trivium [3,4], one of the finalists of the estream project [5]. Reduced versions of Trivium having 672, 735 and 767 initialization rounds have been attacked. In a similar research, Vielhaber worked on the concept named AIDA (Algebraic IV Differential Attack) and attacked One.Fivium(a variant of Trivium) [6]. His other contributions include [7,8,9,10]. Zhe et al. further improved results of Vielhaber on One.Fivium [11]. Other predecessors of cube attack include the work of Englund et al. who showed statistical weaknesses of Trivium up to 736 initialization rounds [12] and the attack on 672 round Trivium by Fischer et al. [13]. In 2011, Mroczkowski and Szmidt evaluated Trivium by applying the cube attack and used the concept of quadraticity tests [14]. Another LFSR-based lightweight stream cipher Hitag2 has been analyzed by Sun et al. against the cube attack in 2011 [15]. MICKEY [16], also a finalist of the estream project has been found secure by Stefan in [17].

After successful results of cube attack on Trivium, Shamir et al. proposed the concept of Cube testers in 2009 [18]. Cube testers are based on efficient property-testing algorithm. They detect nonrandom behavior rather than performing key extraction. They can also attack cryptographic schemes described by nonrandom polynomials of relatively high degree. The targets of the authors in the mentioned paper are Trivium and MD6 [19]. In 2010, Li et al. worked on cube testers on Bivium [20]. Shamir et al. worked on Grain-128 [21] and gave results for

A. Cuzzocrea et al. (Eds.): CD-ARES 2013 Workshops, LNCS 8128, pp. 105–121, 2013.

cube testers and dynamic cube attack in [22] and [23]. Conditional differential cryptanalysis by Knellwolf et al. is a predecessor to dynamic cube attack [24]. Standard cube attack finds the key by solving a system of linear equations in terms of key bits whereas the dynamic cube attack recovers the secret key by exploiting distinguishers obtained from cube testers. Recently in 2012, Shamir et al. has proposed the concept of robust cube attacks for stream ciphers in realistic scenarios and also suggested the use of generalized linearity tests instead of BLR tests [25].

For block ciphers, Dinur and Shamir proposed the idea of side channel cube attack model in which only one bit of information is available to the attacker after each round [26]. The time complexities for AES [27] and SERPENT [28] are found to be $O(2^{38})$ and $O(2^{18})$ for full key recovery. Due to the exponential increase in degree after every round, the standard cube attack becomes limited to reduced versions only while the side channel attack model is applicable to the full versions and thus more practical.

Lightweight block ciphers, which provide a good trade off between security and efficiency, have attained significant attention of researchers. These ciphers are mostly used in resource-constraint environments like RFID and sensor networks. RFID technology has been used in many aspects of life, such as access control, parking management, identification, goods tracking etc. The lightweight block ciphers evaluated against the cube attack include the KATAN family [29], NOEKEON [30], PRESENT [31] and Hummingbird-2 [32] in [33,34,35,36,37,38]. Mroczkowski and Szmidt have attacked the Courtois Toy Cipher CTC, designed by Courtois [39] against the cube attack [40,41]. Lightweight block ciphers which are not evaluated against the cube attack so far include LED [42], EPCBC [43], PRINCE [44], Piccolo [45], mCrypton [46], TWIS [47], MIBS [48], CGEN [49], PRINTcipher [50], KLEIN [51], FOX [52], HIGHT [53], ICEBERG [54], LCASE [55], MISTY [56], PUFFIN [57], SEA [58], TEA [59] and CLEFIA [60].

LBlock, a lightweight block cipher recently proposed in 2011 by Wu et al. has not yet been tested against the cube attack [61]. In the security evaluation of LBlock by the authors, five cryptanalysis techniques have been used. For differential cryptanalysis, there is no useful 15-round differential characteristic for LBlock. For linear cryptanalysis, it is difficult to find useful 15-round linear-hulls which can be used to distinguish LBlock from a random permutation. For impossible differential cryptanalysis, attacks on 20-round LBlock has been mounted using 14-round impossible differential distinguishers. Integral attack goes up to 20 rounds and the related key attack goes up to 14 rounds of LBlock. Impossible differential attack has been improved up to 21 and 22-round LBlock in [62] and [63]. Minier et al. improved the related key attack to 22 rounds of LBlock [64]. Liu et al. also worked on a similar concept on 22-round LBlock [65]. Biclique cryptanalysis has been performed by the authors of LBlock and new key scheduling algorithm has been proposed in [66].

The cube attack implementations include Paul Crowley's implementation [67,68] and a practical platform developed by Bo Zhu [69]. Zhu et al. has also created an online application which only works for Trivium and checks the cubes for linearity and generate the linear expressions [70]. However, the tool is not suitable to be extended for the complete cube attack on any generic structure. Cryptool 2.0 [71] includes the cube attack block having the option for Trivium and DES only.

Our Contribution. LBlock has been evaluated against the developed tool. We are able to successfully attack 7, 8 and 9 round LBlock with complexities of just $O(2^{10.76})$, $O(2^{11.11})$ and $O(2^{47.00})$ cipher evaluations. Full version of LBlock has been attacked using the single bit leakage side channel cube attack model with the complexity of $O(2^{55.00})$. Cube attack may also be extended to further rounds by using more efficient hardware resources like super computer, the use of GPUs and the concept of distributed computing.

We have developed a graphical user interface toolkit which can load any stream or block cipher into it(as a function) and can check its resistance against the cube attack. The tool shows how may rounds of the cipher can be attacked, and it outputs the cube expressions found in a text file. The options such as cube size, number of linearity tests, output bit index, public bit size and secret bit size can be set from the GUI. The tool is user friendly and can be used easily without the help of the developers. The developed tool is capable of detecting the total number of processors in the machine and can utilize all of them for efficient execution. The tool works on both x86 and x64 systems having any windows version as it is just an executable file. The algorithm of cube attack used in our implementation can be found in [17].

Organization of the Paper. The cube attack has been explained in Section 2. An introduction of the cipher LBlock is given in Section 3 and the results of cube attack against LBlock are given in Section 4. Section 5 contains the results of side channel cube attack against LBlock. Detail of our software toolkit is given in Section 6. Section 7 concludes the article and proposes some future work.

2 The Cube Attack

The Cube Attack is a chosen public key attack which means chosen IV attack for stream ciphers and chosen plaintext attack for block ciphers. Ciphers can be represented as black box polynomials in terms of secret and private variables. These black boxes can be attacked by hitting them with chosen input values and obtaining the output.

Definition 1. Assume some polynomial $p(x_1, ..., x_n)$ and a set $I \subseteq \{1, ...n\}$ of indices to the variables of p Let t_I be a subterm of p which is the product of the variables indexed by I. Then factorizing p by t_I yields Equation 1.

$$p(x_1, ..., x_n) = t_I.p_{S(I)} + q(x_1, ..., x_n) \tag{1}$$

where $p_{S(I)}$ is the superpoly of I in p and q is the linear combination of all terms which do not contain t_I.

For detailed description of the attack, refer to [2]. The attack consists of two phases, the preprocessing phase and the online phase.

2.1   Preprocessing Phase

In the Preprocessing stage of the attack, the target is to find the maximum number of linearly independent expressions in terms of key bits. These expressions are called maxterm equations. This phase is time consuming and may take several weeks. The precomputation phase consists of two parts, finding maxterms and the superpoly reconstruction.

Finding Maxterms. A maxterm or a cube is a set of positions of plaintext block bits for which $2^{cubesize}$ crafted plaintexts are generated. These plaintexts P_i are generated by inserting all the possible values at cube positions keeping all other positions zero or constant. Summing a fixed output bit C_j for all P_i's while setting a same random key K in $GF(2)$ is called a cube sum for key K with output bit index j. Cube sum or summing over a cube is an important terminology. Linear cubes are searched whose cube sums satisfy the linearity tests(Blum Luby Rubinfeld tests) [72]. BLR test checks for the condition $f(0) \oplus f(K_1) \oplus f(K_2) = f(K_1 \oplus K_2)$ where K_1 and K_2 are random keys and f is the cube sum with a certain key over a cube to be tested. The probability that f is linear for $3N$ tests is $1 - 2^{-N}$. If a cube satisfies all the linearity tests, it is placed in the results table with the corresponding output bit index and the reconstructed maxterm equation which is explained in the next part. For the selection of cubes, the authors have proposed a random walk process in [2].

Reconstructing Maxterm Equations. Reconstructing maxterm equations or the superpoly reconstruction in terms of key bits (e.g $1 \oplus k_3 \oplus k_4$) is the second part of the preprocessing phase. According to Theorem 2 in [2], the constant term can be easily computed by setting $K = 0$ and calculating the cube sum. If the sum is 1, the maxterm contains the free term 1, otherwise not. The coefficients of the key bit variables k_i can be found by setting each k_i to one and remaining zeros and calculating the cube sums. If the sum is different from that for $K = 0$, that k_i will be the part of the maxterm equation. This is because if the value of a variable in a linear expression is flipped, the value of the expression is also flipped.

2.2   Online Phase

In the online phase there is an unknown set key which has to be recovered and the adversary can only tweak the plaintext bits. The target of this phase is to determine the right hand sides of the found expressions and their solution. This stage consists of two phases, forming and solving a system of linear equations.

Forming System of Linear Equations. In this part, cube sums are calculated for the same cubes found in the preprocessing stage and their relevant output bit index. These sums make the right hand side of the expressions making a system of linear equations (e.g $1 \oplus k_3 \oplus k_4 = 0$).

Solving System of Linear Equations. The system of linear equations may be solved using Gaussian elimination. The number of key bits recovered is equal to the number of linearly independent relations found in the preprocessing phase. For finding further relations the time consumed by the first phase increases exponentially.

Attack Complexity. The attack complexity includes two things. One is the number of iterations of the cipher carried out in the formation of system of linear equations and the other is the complexity to solve the linear relations in the online phase. Hence, the total complexity becomes $O(2^{d-1}n + n^2)$ where d is the degree of the cryptosystem and n is the number of secret bits. Brute force complexity of the remaining unknown key bits is also added to the total.

3 LBlock: A Lightweight Block Cipher

LBlock, LuBan LOCK or Lightweight BLOCK cipher has been proposed by Wu and Zhang in 2011 [61]. The cipher is a good trade off between efficiency and security. The hardware implementation of LBlock requires about $1320GE$ on $0.18\mu m$ technology with a throughput of $200Kbps$ at $100KHz$ and its software implementation on 8-bit microcontroller requires about 3955 clock cycles to encrypt a plaintext block.

3.1 Specification of LBlock

LBlock has a Fiestel structure having block length of 64-bit, key length of 80-bit and 32 rounds see Figure 1, where concatenation of X_1 and X_0 represents the plaintext block, $K_1 - K_{32}$ are the 32 subkeys generated through a key scheduling procedure, $<<< 8$ sign indicates 8-bit left cyclic shift operation, $\oplus$ is the XOR operation, X_{32} and X_{33} represents the concatenated ciphertext block. The round function F contains the confusion layer having eight 4×4 S-Boxes and a diffusion layer having permutation of eight 4-bit words.

4 The Cube Attack on LBlock

We have applied the cube attack on LBlock having 7, 8 and 9 rounds. The machine used throughout our analysis is Dell XPS 17 Laptop, 2nd generation Intel Core i7 2.20 GHz, 8GB DDR3, NVIDIA GeForce GT 550M 1GB graphics. Extension of the attack to further rounds has been constrained by the available computational capability. However, the concept of supercomputing and GPUs can greatly reduce the simulation time.

4.1 Results of the Preprocessing Phase

70 linearly independent relations in terms of key bits can be found in the preprocessing part for 8-round LBlock as shown in Table 1. 100 linearity tests have

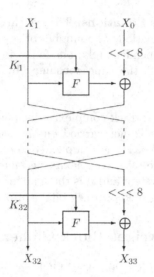

Fig. 1. Encryption Procedure for LBlock

been passed by each cube. The results have been confirmed by testing the attack for various random keys. Results for the preprocessing phase for 7 and 9 round LBlock are shown in Table 4 and Table 5 in Appendix-A.

4.2   Results of the Online Phase

In the online phase of the attack, the set of expressions obtained in the preprocessing phase are converted into the system of linear equations by determining the right hand sides. The values have been found by setting a random test key and summing over the same cubes found in the first phase. The example equations are shown below:

$$x1 = 0, x2 = 0, 1 + x3 + x4 = 1, x4 = 0, x5 = 0, x6 = 0, x7 = 0, x8 = 1,$$
$$1 + x9 = 1, x10 = 0, 1 + x11 = 0, x12 = 0, 1 + x13 = 1, x14 = 0,$$
$$1 + x15 + x16 = 1, x16 = 1, x17 = 0, x18 = 1, 1 + x19 = 1, 1 + x20 = 1,$$
$$x21 = 0, x22 = 1, x23 + x24 = 1, 1 + x24 = 0, 1 + x25 = 1, x26 = 1,$$
$$1 + x27 + x28 = 0, x28 = 0, x29 = 0, x30 = 1, 1 + x31 + x32 = 1, 1 + x32 = 0,$$
$$x38 = 0, x2 + x39 = 0, x40 + x41 = 0, x41 = 1, x42 = 0, x43 = 1,$$
$$1 + x10 + x44 + x45 = 0, x45 = 1, 1 + x46 = 1, x47 = 1, x47 + x48 + x49 = 1,$$
$$1 + x22 + x49 = 1, x50 = 1, x30 + x51 = 1, 1 + x52 + x53 = 0, x53 = 1,$$
$$x18 + x54 = 0, x55 = 0, 1 + x17 + x56 + x57 = 1, x57 = 1, x58 = 1,$$
$$x26 + x59 = 0, 1 + x60 + x61 = 0, 1 + x61 = 0, x67 = 1, 1 + x68 = 0,$$
$$x69 + x70 = 0, x70 = 1, x71 = 1, x72 = 0, x71 + x73 + x74 = 1, x74 = 1,$$
$$1 + x75 = 1, x76 = 1, x76 + x77 + x78 = 1, x76 + x78 = 0, x79 = 0,$$
$$x79 + x80 = 0 \tag{2}$$

Table 1. Maxterms for 8-Round LBlock

Maxterm Equations	Cube Indexes	Output Index	Maxterm Equations	Cube Indexes	Output Index
x1	2,4,23,51	25	x41	2,3,4,23	25
x2	1,3,51,52	11	x42	9,10,11,15	15
1+x3+x4	1,2,51,52	11	x43	9,11,14,56	13
x4	1,2,51,52	12	1+x10+x44+x45	11,12,14,54	15
x5	6,7,19,43	1	x45	11,12,15,54	15
x6	5,7,19,43	1	1+x46	2,22,23,24	18
x7	5,6,19,43	1	x47	3,21,22,23	18
x8	5,6,18,42	4	x47+x48+x49	3,21,22,24	18
1+x9	10,11,15,54	13	1+x22+x49	2,23,24,57	18
x10	11,41,55,56	1	x50	26,29,31,32	6
1+x11	9,10,15,54	13	x30+x51	27,31,32,63	5
x12	9,10,14,55	13	1+x52+x53	27,30,31,32	5
1+x13	14,15,45,48	5	x53	27,29,31,62	6
x14	6,13,33,47	10	x18+x54	5,19,20,36	12
1+x15+x16	10,14,46,47	21	x55	6,17,18,19	9
x16	13,14,47,48	23	1+x17+x56+x57	7,18,19,33	9
x17	7,18,19,35	10	x57	7,18,19,33	10
x18	6,17,19,34	9	x58	25,27,28,31	29
1+x19	6,17,18,34	9	x26+x59	27,28,31,40	29
1+x20	17,18,33,36	9	1+x60+x61	26,27,28,31	29
x21	2,22,23,59	18	1+x61	26,27,28,31	30
x22	21,23,58,59	1	x67	41,43,44,62	60
x23+x24	3,21,22,58	18	1+x68	41,43,55,56	13
1+x24	21,22,59,60	1	x69+x70	42,43,44,62	60
1+x25	26,27,39,40	14	x70	42,43,44,63	57
x26	27,37,38,57	3	x71	49,50,51,55	47
1+x27+x28	25,26,39,40	14	x72	50,51,52,54	47
x28	25,26,30,38	29	x71+x73+x74	22,49,50,52,54	47
x29	31,32,50,51	27	x74	22,51,52,55,56	31
x30	26,28,29,62	5	1+x75	42,62,63,64	50
1+x31+x32	29,30,63,64	6	x76	43,61,62,63	50
1+x32	27,29,30,63	6	x76+x77+x78	43,61,62,64	50
x38	1,3,4,22	28	x76+x78	25,42,61,62,64	50
x2+x39	3,4,23,52	25	x79	34,37,39,40	38
x40+x41	2,3,4,22	28	x79+x80	31,35,37,38,40	37

Solving Equations 2, 70 key bits are recovered as shown below:
$x1 = 0, x2 = 0, x3 = 0, x4 = 0, x5 = 0, x6 = 0, x7 = 0, x8 = 1, x9 = 0, x10 = 0, x11 = 1, x12 = 0, x13 = 0, x14 = 0, x15 = 1, x16 = 1, x17 = 0, x18 = 1, x19 = 0, x20 = 0, x21 = 0, x22 = 1, x23 = 0, x24 = 1, x25 = 0, x26 = 1, x27 = 1, x28 = 0, x29 = 0, x30 = 1, x31 = 1, x32 = 1, x38 = 0, x39 = 0, x40 = 1, x41 = 1, x42 = 0, x43 = 1, x44 = 0, x45 = 1, x46 = 0, x47 = 1, x48 = 1, x49 = 1, x50 = 1, x51 = 0, x52 = 0, x53 = 1, x54 = 1, x55 = 0, x56 = 1, x57 = 1, x58 = 1, x59 = 1, x60 =$

$0, x61 = 1, x67 = 1, x68 = 1, x69 = 1, x70 = 1, x71 = 1, x72 = 0, x73 = 1, x74 = 1, x75 = 0, x76 = 1, x77 = 1, x78 = 1, x79 = 0, x80 = 0$

Remaining bits $x33, ..., x37, x62, ...x66$ may be recovered using quadraticity tests [14] or brute force search. The recovered bits can be further compared with the test key. The test key may be set to any random value. The online phase is not computationally expensive and just takes fraction of a second.

4.3   Attack Complexity

The total complexity includes the complexity of the online phase and of the brute force search. Precomputation is the one time effort and thus not included in the calculations. 66 out of 70 cubes are of size 4 having complexity equal to $66 \times 2^4 = 1056$. 4 out of 70 cubes are of size 5 having complexity equal to $4 \times 2^5 = 128$. Total becomes $1056 + 128 = 1184$ iterations of LBlock. Brute force complexity for remaining 10 bits is 2^{10}. So final complexity becomes $1184 + 2^{10} = 2208$ approximately equal to $O(2^{11.11})$ which is quite less. Similarly for 7-round LBlock the complexity becomes $17 \times 2^2 + 32 \times 2^3 + 18 \times 2^4 + 3 \times 2^5 + 2^{10} \approx O\left(2^{10.76}\right)$. For 9-round LBlock the complexity is $12 \times 2^4 + 11 \times 2^5 + 10 \times 2^6 + 2^{47} \approx O\left(2^{47.00}\right)$.

5   The Side Channel Cube Attack on LBlock

The side channel cube attack is a variant of the standard cube attack which is more practical in realistic scenarios. The standard cube attack is restricted on the reduced versions of the ciphers whereas the side channel cube attack is a threat in practical situations for the full versions. In this type of attack the adversary is able to get one bit of leakage information of the state after each round of an iterated block cipher. The process may be made possible via physical probing, power measurement, or any other type of side channel. However, this information is quite noisy and this problem is addressed by using error correction techniques like erasure codes [73].

5.1   Results of the Preprocessing Phase

LBlock achieves complete diffusion after 8 rounds, as mentioned by the authors of LBlock [61]. So, a single bit leakage after 8th round may give maximum number of linear relations as compared to inner rounds. We have taken the MSB of the right half X_R of the state after 8th round as the leakage bit and used for our analysis. Thousands of linear relations have been found but 25 linearly independent have been extracted using Gaussian elimination technique. The results of the preprocessing phase for full version of LBlock are shown in Table 3. Time consumed for searching all possible combinations for various cube sizes is shown in Table 2 where the number of linearity tests has been set to 100. The results are for the single core execution with the multi-processing feature disabled.

Table 2. Elapsed Times against the Cube Sizes for Preprocessing

Cube Size	Time in Seconds
3	2
4	53
5	1667
6	28739
7	704582

5.2   Attack Complexity

10 out of 25 cubes are of size 4 having complexity $= 10 \times 2^4 = 160$. Remaining 15 cubes are of sizes 5, 6, 7 and 8 having complexities, $5 \times 2^5 = 160, 4 \times 2^6 = 256, 3 \times 2^7 = 384$ and $3 \times 2^8 = 768$ respectively. Total becomes $160 + 160 + 256 + 384 + 768 = 1728$ iterations of LBlock. Brute force complexity for remaining 55 bits $= 2^{55}$. So final complexity becomes $1728 + 2^{55}$ approximately equal to $O(2^{55.00})$.

Table 3. Maxterms for Full LBlock using Leakage Bit after 8th Round

Maxterm Equations	Cube Indexes	Maxterm Equations	Cube Indexes
x1	3,4,21,41,54,55	x22	21,23,58,59
x2	3,19,23,49,50,55	1+x23+x24	21,22,58,59
1+x3+x4	1,2,19,51,52,55	1+x24	21,22,59,60
x1+x4	3,18,23,50,51,55	x25+x26+x28	27,31,62,63,64
x5	6,7,19,43	x38	1,3,4,18,22,41,55
x6	5,7,19,43	1+x38+x39	1,2,4,23,41,52,55,56
x7	5,6,19,43	1+x40+x41	1,2,3,21,41,54,55
1+x5+x8	7,18,42,43	x41	1,2,3,9,23,24,41,49
1+x9	10,11,41,54,56	1+x71+x72	19,49,50,51,55
x10	11,41,55,56	1+x72	19,50,51,52,54
1+x11+x12	10,41,55,56	x71+x73+x74	1,2,3,17,18,22,50,54
x12	9,10,18,41,55	x74	1,2,3,19,22,50,55
1+x21	22,24,59,60		

6   Cube Attack Software Toolkit

We have developed a GUI based software tool using the MFC application in Microsoft Visual Studio 2010 Professional. There is a function named *cipher* which is to be replaced by any stream or block cipher to be tested. The function is capable of taking the plaintext, key and number of rounds as input and should return the ciphertext as the output. All inputs/outputs have to be in hexadecimal notation. After replacing the function, one has to start debugging and an executable file is made as the output. This executable will be able to run on any Windows version on both x86 and x64 platforms. In the GUI, we have five inputs public bit size, secret bit size, cube size, number of linearity tests and the number of rounds which can be set to any desired position. The results are compiled in a text file at the end of the simulation which include the cubes found, the output bit indexes, total simulation time in seconds and the reconstructed maxterms, see Figure 2.

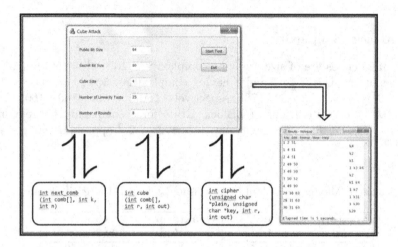

Fig. 2. Cube Attack Implementation Architecture

- After debugging the project with the embedded cipher function, the GUI is created and launched.
- The GUI takes the parameters from the user and interacts with the three functions next_comb, cube and cipher.
- next_comb function is responsible for randomly generating different cubes of the required size.
- cube function is responsible for testing the cubes for the linearity tests.
- cipher function is invoked millions of times to get the required output bits for the crafted plaintexts.
- Results are written in the results.txt file at the end of the simulation.

The number of rounds in the GUI represents the initialization or setup rounds in case of stream ciphers and the main rounds in case of block ciphers. Hence, the tool is generalized for both of them. The option to set number of rounds is for the variants or reduced versions of ciphers. This helps in better understanding about the resistivity of the ciphers.

The tool is intelligent to use all the available CPU cores in a system, thus decreasing the simulation time to a great extent. OpenMP (Open Multiprocessing) has been used to implement this task [74]. Another option has been added in the tool to work on multiple output bits on each iteration. The standard cube attack works on a single output bit model and the remaining block is not utilized. The concept has been explained in Figure 3. The same concept holds true for the stream ciphers and thus complete reinitialization of the cipher is not required to get each output bit. This feature increased the speed of the simulation 27 times in our experiments. The option is turned off when working on single bit leakage models.

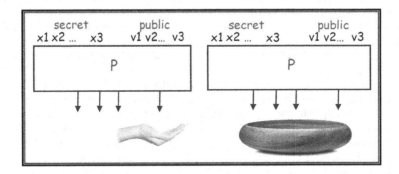

Fig. 3. Attacking Multiple Output Bits

7 Conclusion and Future Work

Cube Attack is a relatively new technique of cryptanalysis and its application on different new ciphers is important. 7, 8 and 9 rounds of LBlock have been attacked. The complexities of the attack for the three versions are $O(2^{10.76})$, $O(2^{11.11})$ and $O(2^{47.00})$ respectively. Full version of LBlock has been attacked using single bit side information after 8 rounds with a complexity of $O(2^{55})$. A software tool has been developed for the application of cube attack to any black box cipher. The tool can be easily used for testing and evaluation purposes.

Higher order tests like quadraticity tests may be implemented to recover more number of key bits where linearity tests have failed to produce the linear relations. BLR tests may be replaced by generalized linearity tests. The efficiency of the tool may be increased by the use of GPUs as their highly parallel structure makes them more effective than CPUs. The task can also be divided to a number of computers connected in a network, a concept known as distributed computing. Another solution is to use a super computer having a number of processors having multiple cores along with the powerful GPUs. Cube testers and dynamic cube attacks are the next steps after the cube attack.

Acknowledgments. We are thankful to the authors of LBlock especially Lei Zhang. They confirmed us that the security analysis of LBlock against the cube attack has not been done yet and we may try. We are also thankful to Michael Vielhaber, Deian Stefan and Bo Zhu who coordinated with us on email that helped us in understanding the cube attack.

References

1. Dinur, I., Shamir, A.: Cube attacks on tweakable black box polynomials. Cryptology ePrint Archive, Report 2008/385 (2008), http://eprint.iacr.org/
2. Dinur, I., Shamir, A.: Cube attacks on tweakable black box polynomials. In: Joux, A. (ed.) EUROCRYPT 2009. LNCS, vol. 5479, pp. 278–299. Springer, Heidelberg (2009)
3. De Cannière, C., Preneel, B.: Trivium specifications. ECRYPT Stream Cipher Project Report 2005/030 (2005)
4. De Cannière, C.: TRIVIUM: A stream cipher construction inspired by block cipher design principles. In: Katsikas, S.K., López, J., Backes, M., Gritzalis, S., Preneel, B. (eds.) ISC 2006. LNCS, vol. 4176, pp. 171–186. Springer, Heidelberg (2006)
5. eSTREAM: The ecrypt stream cipher project
6. Vielhaber, M.: Breaking one.fivium by aida an algebraic iv differential attack. Cryptology ePrint Archive, Report 2007/413 (2007), http://eprint.iacr.org/
7. Vielhaber, M.: Speeding up aida the algebraic iv differential attack by the fast reedmuller transform. In: Intelligent Decision Making Systems. World Scientific Proceedings Series on Computer Engineering and Information Science, vol. 2. World Scientific Publishing Co. (2010)
8. Vielhaber, M.: Aida vs. trivium 793: 1152 final score 980: 1152. Eurocrypt 2009 rump session (April 2009), http://eurocrypt2009rump.cr.yp.to/
9. Vielhaber, M.: Aida breaks bivium (a&b) in 1 minute dual core cpu time. Cryptology ePrint Archive, Report 2009/402 (2009), http://eprint.iacr.org/
10. Vielhaber, M.: Shamir's "cube attack": A remake of aida, the algebraic iv differential attack (2009)
11. Zhe, S., Shi-Wu, Z., Lei, W.: Chosen iv algebraic attack on one.fivium. In: 3rd International Conference on Intelligent System and Knowledge Engineering, ISKE 2008, pp. 1427–1431 (November 2008)
12. Englund, H., Johansson, T., Sönmez Turan, M.: A framework for chosen IV statistical analysis of stream ciphers. In: Srinathan, K., Pandu Rangan, C., Yung, M. (eds.) INDOCRYPT 2007. LNCS, vol. 4859, pp. 268–281. Springer, Heidelberg (2007)
13. Fischer, S., Khazaei, S., Meier, W.: Chosen IV statistical analysis for key recovery attacks on stream ciphers. In: Vaudenay, S. (ed.) AFRICACRYPT 2008. LNCS, vol. 5023, pp. 236–245. Springer, Heidelberg (2008)
14. Mroczkowski, P., Szmidt, J.: Corrigendum to: The cube attack on stream cipher trivium and quadraticity tests. Cryptology ePrint Archive, Report 2011/032 (2011), http://eprint.iacr.org/
15. Sun, S., Hu, L., Xie, Y., Zeng, X.: Cube cryptanalysis of hitag2 stream cipher. In: Lin, D., Tsudik, G., Wang, X. (eds.) CANS 2011. LNCS, vol. 7092, pp. 15–25. Springer, Heidelberg (2011)
16. Babbage, S., Dodd, M.: The MICKEY stream ciphers. In: Robshaw, M., Billet, O. (eds.) New Stream Cipher Designs. LNCS, vol. 4986, pp. 191–209. Springer, Heidelberg (2008)
17. Stefan, D.: Analysis and Implementation of ESTREAM and SHA-3 Cryptographic Algorithms. Cooper Union for the Advancement of Science and Art, Albert Nerken School of Engineering, Graduate Division (2011)
18. Aumasson, J.P., Dinur, I., Meier, W., Shamir, A.: Cube testers and key recovery attacks on reduced-round md6 and trivium. In: Dunkelman, O. (ed.) FSE 2009. LNCS, vol. 5665, pp. 1–22. Springer, Heidelberg (2009)

19. Rivest, R.L., Agre, B., Bailey, D.V., Crutchfield, C., Dodis, Y., Elliott, K., Khan, F.A., Krishnamurthy, J., Lin, Y., Reyzin, L., Shen, E., Sukha, J., Sutherland, D., Tromer, E., Yin, Y.L.: The md6 hash function a proposal to nist for sha-3 (2008)

20. Li, S., Wang, Y., Peng, J.: Cube testers on bivium. In: 2010 International Conference on Communications and Intelligence Information Security (ICCIIS), pp. 121–124 (October 2010)

21. Hell, M., Johansson, T., Maximov, E., Meier, W.: A stream cipher proposal: Grain-128. In: ISIT

22. Aumasson, J.P., Dinur, I., Henzen, L., Meier, W., Shamir, A.: Efficient fpga implementations of high-dimensional cube testers on the stream cipher grain-128. Cryptology ePrint Archive, Report 2009/218 (2009), http://eprint.iacr.org/

23. Dinur, I., Shamir, A.: Breaking grain-128 with dynamic cube attacks. In: Joux, A. (ed.) FSE 2011. LNCS, vol. 6733, pp. 167–187. Springer, Heidelberg (2011)

24. Knellwolf, S., Meier, W., Naya-Plasencia, M.: Conditional differential cryptanalysis of NLFSR-based cryptosystems. In: Abe, M. (ed.) ASIACRYPT 2010. LNCS, vol. 6477, pp. 130–145. Springer, Heidelberg (2010)

25. Dinur, I., Shamir, A.: Applying cube attacks to stream ciphers in realistic scenarios. Cryptography and Communications 4, 217–232 (2012)

26. Dinur, I., Shamir, A.: Side channel cube attacks on block ciphers. Cryptology ePrint Archive, Report 2009/127 (2009), http://eprint.iacr.org/

27. Daemen, J., Rijmen, V.: Aes proposal: Rijndael (1998)

28. Biham, E., Anderson, R.J., Knudsen, L.R.: Serpent: A new block cipher proposal. In: Vaudenay, S. (ed.) FSE 1998. LNCS, vol. 1372, pp. 222–238. Springer, Heidelberg (1998)

29. De Cannière, C., Dunkelman, O., Knežević, M.: KATAN and KTANTAN — A family of small and efficient hardware-oriented block ciphers. In: Clavier, C., Gaj, K. (eds.) CHES 2009. LNCS, vol. 5747, pp. 272–288. Springer, Heidelberg (2009)

30. Daemen, J., Peeters, M., Vanassche, G.: Nessie proposal: Noekeon. Submitted as an NESSIE Candidate Algorithm, http://www.cryptonessie.org

31. Bogdanov, A., Knudsen, L.R., Leander, G., Paar, C., Poschmann, A., Robshaw, M.J.B., Seurin, Y., Vikkelsoe, C.: PRESENT: An ultra-lightweight block cipher. In: Paillier, P., Verbauwhede, I. (eds.) CHES 2007. LNCS, vol. 4727, pp. 450–466. Springer, Heidelberg (2007)

32. Engels, D., Saarinen, M.-J.O., Schweitzer, P., Smith, E.M.: The hummingbird-2 lightweight authenticated encryption algorithm. In: Juels, A., Paar, C. (eds.) RFIDSec 2011. LNCS, vol. 7055, pp. 19–31. Springer, Heidelberg (2012)

33. Bard, G.V., Courtois, N.T., Nakahara Jr., J., Sepehrdad, P., Zhang, B.: Algebraic, AIDA/Cube and side channel analysis of KATAN family of block ciphers. In: Gong, G., Gupta, K.C. (eds.) INDOCRYPT 2010. LNCS, vol. 6498, pp. 176–196. Springer, Heidelberg (2010)

34. Mroczkowski, P., Szmidt, J.: The algebraic cryptanalysis of the block cipher katan32 using modofied cube attack. In: Concepts and Implementations for Innovative Military Communications (2011)

35. Abdul-Latip, S., Reyhanitabar, M., Susilo, W., Seberry, J.: On the security of noekeon against side channel cube attacks. In: Kwak, J., Deng, R.H., Won, Y., Wang, G. (eds.) ISPEC 2010. LNCS, vol. 6047, pp. 45–55. Springer, Heidelberg (2010)

36. Yang, L., Wang, M., Qiao, S.: Side channel cube attack on present. In: Garay, J.A., Miyaji, A., Otsuka, A. (eds.) CANS 2009. LNCS, vol. 5888, pp. 379–391. Springer, Heidelberg (2009)

37. Zhao, X., Wang, T., Guo, S.: Improved side channel cube attacks on present. Cryptology ePrint Archive, Report 2011/165 (2011), http://eprint.iacr.org/
38. Fan, X., Gong, G.: On the security of hummingbird-2 against side channel cube attacks. In: Armknecht, F., Lucks, S. (eds.) WEWoRC 2011. LNCS, vol. 7242, pp. 18–29. Springer, Heidelberg (2012)
39. Courtois, N.T.: How fast can be algebraic attacks on block ciphers? In: Online Proceedings of Dagstuhl Seminar 07021, Symmetric Cryptography, pp. 7–12 (2006)
40. Mroczkowski, P., Szmidt, J.: Cube attack on courtois toy cipher. Cryptology ePrint Archive, Report 2009/497 (2009), http://eprint.iacr.org/
41. Mroczkowski, P., Szmidt, J.: The cube attack in the algebraic cryptanalysis of ctc2. Concepts and Implementations for Innovative Military Communications (2011)
42. Guo, J., Peyrin, T., Poschmann, A., Robshaw, M.: The LED block cipher. In: Preneel, B., Takagi, T. (eds.) CHES 2011. LNCS, vol. 6917, pp. 326–341. Springer, Heidelberg (2011)
43. Yap, H., Khoo, K., Poschmann, A., Henricksen, M.: EPCBC - A block cipher suitable for electronic product code encryption. In: Lin, D., Tsudik, G., Wang, X. (eds.) CANS 2011. LNCS, vol. 7092, pp. 76–97. Springer, Heidelberg (2011)
44. Borghoff, J., et al.: PRINCE – A low-latency block cipher for pervasive computing applications. In: Wang, X., Sako, K. (eds.) ASIACRYPT 2012. LNCS, vol. 7658, pp. 208–225. Springer, Heidelberg (2012)
45. Shibutani, K., Isobe, T., Hiwatari, H., Mitsuda, A., Akishita, T., Shirai, T.: Piccolo: An ultra-lightweight blockcipher. In: Preneel, B., Takagi, T. (eds.) CHES 2011. LNCS, vol. 6917, pp. 342–357. Springer, Heidelberg (2011)
46. Lim, C.H., Korkishko, T.: mCrypton – A lightweight block cipher for security of low-cost RFID tags and sensors. In: Song, J.-S., Kwon, T., Yung, M. (eds.) WISA 2005. LNCS, vol. 3786, pp. 243–258. Springer, Heidelberg (2006)
47. Ojha, S.K., Kumar, N., Jain, K., Sangeeta: TWIS – A lightweight block cipher. In: Prakash, A., Sen Gupta, I. (eds.) ICISS 2009. LNCS, vol. 5905, pp. 280–291. Springer, Heidelberg (2009)
48. Izadi, M., Sadeghiyan, B., Sadeghian, S., Khanooki, H.: MIBS: A new lightweight block cipher. In: Garay, J.A., Miyaji, A., Otsuka, A. (eds.) CANS 2009. LNCS, vol. 5888, pp. 334–348. Springer, Heidelberg (2009)
49. Robshaw, M.J.B.: Searching for compact algorithms: CGEN. In: Nguyên, P.Q. (ed.) VIETCRYPT 2006. LNCS, vol. 4341, pp. 37–49. Springer, Heidelberg (2006)
50. Knudsen, L., Leander, G., Poschmann, A., Robshaw, M.J.B.: PRINTCIPHER: A block cipher for IC-printing. In: Mangard, S., Standaert, F.-X. (eds.) CHES 2010. LNCS, vol. 6225, pp. 16–32. Springer, Heidelberg (2010)
51. Gong, Z., Nikova, S., Law, Y.: Klein: A new family of lightweight block ciphers. In: Juels, A., Paar, C. (eds.) RFIDSec 2011. LNCS, vol. 7055, pp. 1–18. Springer, Heidelberg (2012)
52. Junod, P., Vaudenay, S.: FOX: A new family of block ciphers. In: Handschuh, H., Hasan, M.A. (eds.) SAC 2004. LNCS, vol. 3357, pp. 114–129. Springer, Heidelberg (2004)
53. Hong, D., et al.: Hight: A new block cipher suitable for low-resource device. In: Goubin, L., Matsui, M. (eds.) CHES 2006. LNCS, vol. 4249, pp. 46–59. Springer, Heidelberg (2006)
54. Standaert, F.-X., Piret, G., Rouvroy, G., Quisquater, J.-J., Legat, J.-D.: ICEBERG: An involutional cipher efficient for block encryption in reconfigurable hardware. In: Roy, B., Meier, W. (eds.) FSE 2004. LNCS, vol. 3017, pp. 279–299. Springer, Heidelberg (2004)

55. Tripathy, S., Nandi, S.: Lcase: Lightweight cellular automata-based symmetric-key encryption (2008)
56. Matsui, M.: New block encryption algorithm MISTY. In: Biham, E. (ed.) FSE 1997. LNCS, vol. 1267, pp. 54–68. Springer, Heidelberg (1997)
57. Cheng, H., Heys, H.M., Wang, C.: Puffin: A novel compact block cipher targeted to embedded digital systems. In: Proceedings of the 2008 11th EUROMICRO Conference on Digital System Design Architectures, Methods and Tools, DSD 2008, pp. 383–390. IEEE Computer Society, Washington, DC (2008)
58. Standaert, F.X., Piret, G., Gershenfeld, N., Quisquater, J.J.: Sea: A scalable encryption algorithm for small embedded applications. In: Domingo-Ferrer, J., Posegga, J., Schreckling, D. (eds.) CARDIS 2006. LNCS, vol. 3928, pp. 222–236. Springer, Heidelberg (2006)
59. Wheeler, D., Needham, R.: Tea, a tiny encryption algorithm. In: Preneel, B. (ed.) FSE 1994. LNCS, vol. 1008, pp. 363–366. Springer, Heidelberg (1995)
60. Shirai, T., Shibutani, K., Akishita, T., Moriai, S., Iwata, T.: The 128-bit blockcipher CLEFIA (extended abstract). In: Biryukov, A. (ed.) FSE 2007. LNCS, vol. 4593, pp. 181–195. Springer, Heidelberg (2007)
61. Wu, W., Zhang, L.: Lblock: A lightweight block cipher. In: Lopez, J., Tsudik, G. (eds.) ACNS 2011. LNCS, vol. 6715, pp. 327–344. Springer, Heidelberg (2011)
62. Liu, Y., Gu, D., Liu, Z., Li, W.: Impossible differential attacks on reduced-round Lblock. In: Ryan, M.D., Smyth, B., Wang, G. (eds.) ISPEC 2012. LNCS, vol. 7232, pp. 97–108. Springer, Heidelberg (2012)
63. Karakoç, F., Demirci, H., Harmancı, A.E.: Impossible differential cryptanalysis of reduced-round LBlock. In: Askoxylakis, I., Pöhls, H.C., Posegga, J. (eds.) WISTP 2012. LNCS, vol. 7322, pp. 179–188. Springer, Heidelberg (2012)
64. Minier, M., Naya-Plasencia, M.: A related key impossible differential attack against 22 rounds of the lightweight block cipher Lblock. Inf. Process. Lett. 112(16), 624–629 (2012)
65. Liu, S., Gong, Z., Wang, L.: Improved related-key differential attacks on reducedround Lblock. In: Chim, T.W., Yuen, T.H. (eds.) ICICS 2012. LNCS, vol. 7618, pp. 58–69. Springer, Heidelberg (2012)
66. Wang, Y., Wu, W., Yu, X., Zhang, L.: Security on LBlock against biclique cryptanalysis. In: Lee, D.H., Yung, M. (eds.) WISA 2012. LNCS, vol. 7690, pp. 1–14. Springer, Heidelberg (2012)
67. Crowley, P.: Trivium, sse2, corepy, and the "cube attack" (December 2008), http://www.lshift.net/blog/2008/12/09/trivium-sse2-corepy-and-the-cube-attack
68. Corepy: Assembly programming in python, http://www.corepy.org/
69. Zhu, B., Yu, W., Wang, T.: A practical platform for cube-attack-like cryptanalyses. Cryptology ePrint Archive, Report 2010/644 (2010), http://eprint.iacr.org/
70. Zhu, B., Yu, W., Wang, T.: A practical platform for cube-attack-like cryptanalyses, http://cube-attack.appspot.com
71. Cryptool 2 cryptography for everybody, http://www.cryptool.org/en/cryptool2
72. Blum, M., Luby, M., Rubinfeld, R.: Self-testing/correcting with applications to numerical problems. In: Proceedings of the Twenty-Second Annual ACM Symposium on Theory of Computing, STOC 1990, pp. 73–83. ACM, New York (1990)
73. Luby, M., Mitzenmacher, M., Shokrollahi, M., Spielman, D.: Efficient erasure correcting codes. IEEE Transactions on Information Theory 47(2), 569–584 (2001)
74. The openmp api specification for parallel programming, http://openmp.org/wp/

Appendix-A

Table 4. Maxterms for 7-Round LBlock

Maxterm Equations	Cube Indexes	Output Index	Maxterm Equations	Cube Indexes	Output Index
x1	3,4	4	x41	3,4,23,50	57
x2	1,50	4	x42	9,10,11,54	23
1+x3+x4	2,49,50	1	x43	10,11,12	23
1+x4	3,50	3	x10+x44+x45	11,12,54	23
x5	7,8	24	1+x45	50,51,63,64	39
x6	7,42	24	1+x46	23,24,60	11
1+x7+x8	6,41,42	21	x21+x47	22,23,60	11
x8	5,6,42	28	x22+x48+x49	1,23,24,46	15
1+x9	10,12,55	25	1+x22+x49	23,24,57	11
x10	11,53	27	x50	29,30,31,63	4
1+x11+x12	10,53	27	x30+x51	31,32,64	4
x12	9,10,55	25	1+x52+x53	31,32,62	4
1+x13	14,15,45	13	x53	27,29,31,62	38
x14	13,47	13	1+x18+x54	19,20,36	41
1+x15+x16	14,46	16	1+x55	19,20,33	14
x16	13,14,47	15	1+x17+x56+x57	18,19,33	14
1+x17	18,20,34	20	x57	7,18,19,33	41
x18	20,35	16	x58	25,26,27,40	5
1+x17+x19	6,20,34	41	1+x26+x59	27,28,40	5
x17+x20	19,34	18	1+x60+x61	26,27,28,31	61
x21	22,23,59	5	x61	26,27,28	5
x22	23,58	8	x67	41,43,44,62	4
1+x23+x24	22,58	8	1+x68	41,43,55,56	45
1+x24	21,22,59	6	x69+x70	18,43,44,62	3
x25	27,28	9	x70	18,43,44,63	1
x26	25,38	9	x71	49,50,51,55	23
x27	25,26,39	5	1+x72	49,52,55	21
1+x28	25,26,39	10	x71+x73+x74	50,52,55	21
x29	31,32	29	x74	22,51,52,55	23
x30	29,62	29	1+x75	27,43,63,64	21
1+x31	29,30,63	1	x76	41,42,62,63	21
x32	29,30,62	32	x76+x77+x78	14,41,61,65,64	47
x38	1,3,4,22	60	x76+x78	25,42,61,62,64	24
x2+x39	3,4,51	31	x79	34,37,39,40	14
x40+x41	3,4,50	31	x79+x80	31,35,37,38,40	13

Table 5. Maxterms for 9-Round LBlock

Maxterm Equations	Cube Indexes	Output Index	Maxterm Equations	Cube Indexes	Output Index
x1	2,3,41,43,44	28	x30	29,32,41,43,44,64	25
x2	29,35,37,38,39	6	x32	29,30,41,43,44,64	25
1+x3+x4	1,2,41,43,44	28	x67	41,43,44,62	28
x4	46,57,58,59	9	x67+x68	41,42,44,61,62	25
x5	6,7,41,61,63,64	17	x69+x70	42,43,44,62	28
x6	2,47,57,58,59	10	x70	42,43,44,63	25
x7	33,35,36,39	29	x71	49,50,51,55	15
x7+x8	7,33,34,36,39	29	x72	50,51,52,54	15
1+x9+x10	34,35,36,39	29	x71+x73+x74	22,49,50,52,54	15
x10	34,35,36,38	32	x74	22,49,50,52,55	15
1+x17	18,19,31,37,39,40	5	x75	26,42,61,62,63	18
x18	17,19,31,37,39,40	5	x76	43,61,62,63	18
x25	8,26,27,34,35,36	32	x76+x77+x78	43,61,62,64	18
x26	5,28,33,35,36,37	30	x76+x78	25,42,61,62,64	18
x9+x10+x27+x28	25,26,34,35,36,37	30	x79	34,37,39,40	6
1+x25+x28	27,39,40,57,59,60	11	x79+x80	31,35,37,38,40	5
x29	30,32,41,43,44,64	25			

Code-Based Identification and Signature Schemes in Software

Sidi Mohamed El Yousfi Alaoui[1], Pierre-Louis Cayrel[2],
Rachid El Bansarkhani[3], and Gerhard Hoffmann[3]

[1] CASED-Center for Advanced Security Research Darmstadt,
Mornewegstraße, 32 64293 Darmstadt, Germany
elyousfi@cased.de
[2] Laboratoire Hubert Curien, UMR CNRS 5516,
Bâtiment F 18 rue du professeur Benoît Lauras, 42000 Saint-Etienne
pierre.louis.cayrel@univ-st-etienne.fr
[3] Technische Universität Darmstadt, Fachbereich Informatik Kryptographie und
Computeralgebra,
Hochschulstraße 10 64289 Darmstadt, Germany

Abstract. In this paper we present efficient implementations of several code-based identification schemes, namely the Stern scheme, the Véron scheme and the Cayrel-Véron-El Yousfi scheme. We also explain how to derive and implement signature schemes from the previous identification schemes using the Fiat-Shamir transformation. For a security of 80 bits and a document to be signed of size 1 kByte, we reach a signature in about 4 ms on a standard CPU.

Keywords: Cryptography, zero-knowledge identification, signatures, coding theory, efficient implementation.

1 Introduction

Identification schemes are very useful and fundamental tools in many applications such as electronic fund transfer and online systems for preventing data access by invalid users. Such schemes are typical applications of zero-knowledge interactive proofs [15], which are two-party protocols allowing a party called a prover to convince another party called a verifier, that it knows some secret piece of information, without the verifier being able to learn anything about the secret value except for what is revealed by the prover itself. Zero-knowledge identification schemes are of particular interest because it is possible to convert them into secure signature schemes through the very famous Fiat-Shamir paradigm [13].

Quantum computation arises much interest in cryptography, since Peter Shor found a polynomial-time algorithm to solve the factoring and discrete logarithm problems using quantum computers [21]. Therefore, it is of extreme importance to come up with cryptosystems that remain secure even when the adversary has access to a quantum computer; such systems are called post-quantum cryptosystems. One promising candidate is based on codes, since no quantum attack

A. Cuzzocrea et al. (Eds.): CD-ARES 2013 Workshops, LNCS 8128, pp. 122–136, 2013.
© IFIP International Federation for Information Processing 2013

exists so far to solve the syndrome decoding problem on which the code-based cryptosystems are based.

Besides the fact that designing code-based identification schemes offer security against quantum attacks, these schemes have other good features. First, they are usually very fast and easy to implement compared to schemes based on number-theoretic problems as they use only matrix-vector multiplications. Second, their security is directly related to the syndrome decoding problem. Finally, the complexity of attacks against code-based identification schemes can be given in the expected number of binary operations and not only through asymptotic estimations, as in the case of lattice-based cryptosystems for example.

In 1993, Stern proposed in [23] the first efficient zero-knowledge identification scheme based on the hardness of the binary syndrome decoding problem. A few years later, Véron in [25] has designed a scheme with a lower communication cost. Recently, Cayrel-Véron-El Yousfi in [11] have designed a scheme which reduces this communication cost even more.

Code-based cryptosystems suffer from a major drawback: they require a very large public key which makes them very difficult to use in many practical situations. Using quasi-cyclic and quasi-dyadic constructions, several new constructions like [4,17] permits to reduce the size of the public matrices. Recently, there have been several structural attacks against such constructions, the first attack presented by Gauthier et al. in [24] and the second attack is due to Faugère et al. [12]; these attacks extract the private key of some parameters of these variants. We should mention that schemes using binary codes are so far unaffected by such attacks.

Our Contribution. In this paper we provide efficient implementations of the Stern, the Véron and the Cayrel-Véron-El Yousfi schemes. We also explain how to derive signature schemes from the previous identification schemes using the Fiat-Shamir paradigm. In a previous work [9], we have used Keccak [14] for the generation orandom vectors and hash values. Now we use RFSB [8] for the same purpose and juxtapose the results. In [10], the authors presented a smart implementation of the Stern scheme, but it was more a proof of concept than an efficient implementation.

Organization of the Paper. First, we give in Section 2 a general overview of code-based cryptography. Section 3 describes the Stern, Véron and Cayrel-Véron-El Yousfi (CVE) schemes. The results of our implementations will be described in Section 4. Finally, we conclude the paper in Section 5.

2   Background of Coding Theory

In this section, we recall basic facts about code-based cryptography. We refer to [6] for a general introduction to these issues.

2.1   Definitions

Linear codes are k-dimensional subspaces of an n-dimensional vector space over a finite field $\mathbb{F}_q$, where k and n are positive integers with $k < n$, and q a prime power. The theoretical error-correcting capability of such a code is the maximum number ω of errors that the code is able to decode. In short, linear codes with these parameters are denoted (n, k)-codes or $(n, n - r)$-codes, where r is the codimension of a code with $r = n - k$.

Definition 1 (Hamming weight). *The (Hamming) weight of an arbitrary vector $x \in \mathbb{F}_q^n$ is the number of its non-zero entries. We use $\mathsf{wt}(x)$ to denote the Hamming weight of x.*

The distance of vectors $x, y \in \mathbb{F}_q^n$ is defined as $\mathsf{wt}(x - y)$. The weight of $x \in \mathbb{F}_q^n$ is therefore just its distance from the null-vector $0 \in \mathbb{F}_q^n$. The minimal distance of a linear code $\mathcal{C}$ is defined as $d := \min_{x \in \mathcal{C}, x \neq 0} \mathsf{wt}(x)$. The error-correcting capability of a linear code $\mathcal{C}$ can be expressed as $\omega = \lfloor \frac{d-1}{2} \rfloor$.

Definition 2 (Generator and Parity Check Matrix). *Let $\mathcal{C}$ be a linear (n, k)-code over $\mathbb{F}_q$. A matrix $G \in \mathbb{F}_q^{k \times n}$ is called a generator matrix of $\mathcal{C}$ if its rows form a basis of $\mathcal{C}$:*

$$\mathcal{C} = \{xG : x \in \mathbb{F}_q^k\}.$$

Vectors $x \in \mathcal{C}$ are called codewords. A matrix $H \in \mathbb{F}_q^{r \times n}$ is called a parity-check matrix of $\mathcal{C}$ if

$$\mathcal{C} = \{x \in \mathbb{F}_q^n : Hx^T = 0\}.$$

In other words, H is a parity-check matrix, if $GH^T = 0$ holds. A parity-check matrix H generates the dual space $\mathcal{C}^\perp$ of $\mathcal{C}$, the space perpendicular to $\mathcal{C}$.

As we have already mentioned, there have been some proposals to use quasi-cyclic or quasi-dyadic codes in order to reduce the public key size of code-based cryptosystems. The idea is to replace codes having a random parity-check matrix H by particular type of codes with a very compact representation, namely quasi-cyclic or quasi-dyadic codes. In both variants, the matrix has the form $H = (I_r | R)$, where I_r denotes the $r \times r$ identity matrix and $R \in \mathbb{F}_q^{r \times k}$ is a quasi-circulant respectively quasi-dyadic matrix. A quasi-cyclic matrix (resp. quasi-dyadic matrix) is a block matrix whose component blocks are circulant (resp. dyadic) submatrices.

A circulant matrix is defined by a vector $(a_1, a_2, \ldots, a_r) \in \mathbb{F}_q^r$ and has the following form:

$$R = \begin{pmatrix} a_1 & a_2 & a_3 & \ldots & a_r \\ a_r & a_1 & a_2 & \ldots & a_{r-1} \\ \vdots & \vdots & \vdots & \vdots & \vdots \\ a_2 & a_3 & a_4 & \ldots & a_1 \end{pmatrix}.$$

A dyadic matrix is recursively defined: any 1×1 matrix is dyadic and for $p > 1$, a $2^p \times 2^p$ dyadic matrix has the form:

$$R = \begin{pmatrix} B & C \\ C & B \end{pmatrix},$$

where B and C are $2^{p-1} \times 2^{p-1}$ dyadic matrices. To give an example, an 4×4 dyadic matrix has the following form:

$$R = \begin{pmatrix} a & b & c & d \\ b & a & d & c \\ c & d & a & b \\ d & c & b & a \end{pmatrix},$$

where $a, b, c, d \in \mathbb{F}_q$.

The advantage of a circulant resp. dyadic matrix is the fact that the whole matrix can be reconstructed from the knowledge of its first row alone. This is the trick to reduce a public key element.

We describe in the following the main hard problems on which the security of code-based schemes presented in this paper relies. We denote by $x \xleftarrow{\$} A$ the uniform random choice of x among the elements of a set A, and "$\oplus$" the exclusive disjunction (XOR) operation.

Definition 3 (Binary Syndrome Decoding Problem (SD)).
Input : $H \xleftarrow{\$} \mathbb{F}_2^{r \times n}$, $y \xleftarrow{\$} \mathbb{F}_2^r$, and an integer $\omega > 0$.
Find :   a word $s \in \mathbb{F}_2^n$ such that $wt(s) \leq \omega$ and $Hs^T = y$.

This problem was proven to be NP-hard in 1978 [5]. A dual version of the previous problem, using the generator matrix G instead of the parity-check matrix H of the code $\mathcal{C}$, can be defined as follows.

Definition 4 (General Decoding Problem (GD)).
Input : $G \xleftarrow{\$} \mathbb{F}_2^{k \times n}$, $y \xleftarrow{\$} \mathbb{F}_2^n$, and an integer $\omega > 0$.
Find :   A pair $(m, e) \in \mathbb{F}_2^k \times \mathbb{F}_2^n$, where $wt(e) \leq \omega$ s.t $mG \oplus e = y$.

Note that $x := mG \in \mathbb{F}_2^n$ for $m \in \mathbb{F}_2^k$ is by definition a codeword. In other words, GD states that given a vector $y \in \mathbb{F}_2^n$, find the (unique) codeword $x \in \mathcal{C}$, such that $wt(x - y)$ is minimal. GD is also proven to be NP-hard. Moreover, it is assumed that it is hard not only for some worst-case instances, but hard on average.

An extension of the binary syndrome decoding (SD) problem over an arbitrary finite field can be formulated as well. It was proven to be NP-hard by A. Barg in 1994 [2, in russian].

Definition 5 (q-ary Syndrome Decoding (qSD) problem).

Input : $H \xleftarrow{\$} \mathbb{F}_q^{r \times n}$, $y \xleftarrow{\$} \mathbb{F}_q^r$, and an integer $\omega > 0$.
Find : a word $s \in \mathbb{F}_q^n$ such that $wt(s) \leq \omega$ and $Hs^T = y$.

Best known attack. The most efficient known algorithm to attack code-based schemes is the Information Set Decoding (ISD) algorithm. Some improvement of this algorithm have been developed by Peters [19], Niebuhr et al. [18], and Bernstein et al. [7], and recently in [16] and [3]. The main idea of the ISD algorithm consists in recovering the $n - r$ information symbols as follows: the first step is to pick r of the n coordinates randomly in the hope that most of them are error-free, then try to recover the message by solving an $r \times r$ linear system (binary or over $\mathbb{F}_q$). The recent results of this attack are taken into account when choosing our parameters in order to determine the security level needed. We denote the workfactor of the Information Set Decoding algorithm by WF_{ISD}.

3   Code-Based Zero-Knowledge Identification Schemes

In code-based cryptography, there have been many attempts to design identification schemes. In such constructions, there are two main goals: on the one hand, a prover $\mathcal{P}$ wants to convince a verifier $\mathcal{V}$ of its identity. On the other hand, $\mathcal{P}$ does not want to reveal any additional information that might be used by an impersonator.

For a fixed positive integer n; let S_n denote the symmetric group of $n!$ permutations on n symbols, and let h be a public hash function. In the following, we will give an overview of three proposals in this area. The symbol "$||$" denotes the concatenating operator.

3.1   Stern Scheme

The first code-based zero-knowledge identification scheme was presented by Stern [23] at Crypto'93, its security is based on the syndrome decoding (SD) problem.

Description. The Stern scheme has two parts: a key generation algorithm, shown in Fig. 1, and an identification protocol as given in Fig. 2. It uses a public parity-check matrix H of the code over the binary field $\mathbb{F}_2$.

The scheme is a multiple-rounds identification protocol, where each round is a three-pass interaction between the prover and the verifier. A cheater has a probability of 2/3 per round to succeed in the protocol without the knowledge of the secret key (sk). The number of rounds depends on the impersonation resistance required. For instance to achieve the weak and strong authentication probabilities of 2^{-16} and 2^{-32} according the norm ISO/IEC-9798-5, one needs respectively 28 and 56 rounds. Stern proposed another identification protocol with five-pass [23] (like CVE in section 3.3), but it is inefficient.

KeyGen:

Let κ be the security parameter

Choose n, r, ω, such that $\mathrm{WF_{ISD}}(n, r, \omega, 2) \geq 2^{\kappa}$

$H \xleftarrow{\$} \mathbb{F}_2^{r \times n}$

$s \xleftarrow{\$} \mathbb{F}_2^n$, s.t. $\mathsf{wt}(s) = \omega$.

$y \leftarrow Hs^T$

Output $(\mathrm{sk}, \mathrm{pk}) = (s, (y, H, \omega))$

Fig. 1. Stern key generation algorithm

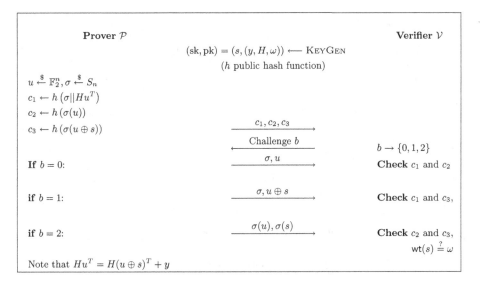

Fig. 2. Stern identification protocol

3.2   Véron Scheme

In 1996, Véron proposed in [25] a dual version of Stern's scheme, its security is based on general decoding problem (GD).

Description. The scheme uses a generator matrix instead of a parity-check matrix of the code, which has the advantage to reduce slightly the communication costs. The Véron scheme, as the Stern's one, is a multiple rounds zero-knowledge protocol, where each round is a three-pass interaction between the prover and the verifier, for which the success probability for a cheater is $2/3$ in one round. The key generation algorithm part Fig. 3 and the identification protocol part Fig. 4 of the Véron's scheme are given as follows.

KEYGEN:

Let κ be the security parameter

Choose $n, k,$ and ω such that $\mathrm{WF}_{\mathrm{ISD}}(n, k, \omega, 2) \geq 2^\kappa$

$G \leftarrow \mathbb{F}_2^{k \times n}$

$(m, e) \leftarrow \mathbb{F}_2^k \times \mathbb{F}_2^n,$ s.t. $\mathsf{wt}(e) = \omega$ $((m, e)$ secret key$)$

$y \leftarrow mG \oplus e$ $(y$ public key$)$

Output $(\mathrm{sk}, \mathrm{pk}) = ((m, e), (y, G, \omega))$

Fig. 3. Véron key generation algorithm

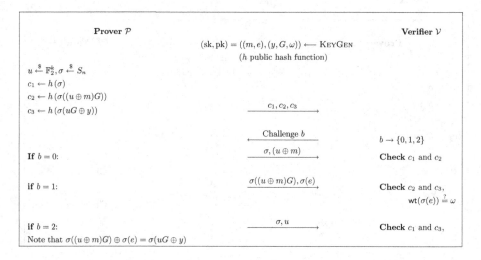

Fig. 4. Véron identification protocol

3.3 CVE Identification Scheme

In 2010, Cayrel, Véron, and El Yousfi presented in [11] a five-pass identification protocol using q-ary codes instead of binary codes.

In addition to the new way of computing the commitments, the idea of this protocol uses another improvement which is inspired by [20,22]. The main achievement of this proposal is to decrease the cheating probability of each round from 2/3 for the Stern and Véron schemes to 1/2. This allows to decrease the communication complexity by obtaining the same impersonation probability in fewer rounds compared to Stern and Véron constructions.

Furthermore, this scheme offers a small public key size, about 4 kBytes, whereas that of Stern and Véron scheme is almost 15 kBytes for the same level of security. It is proven in [11] that this scheme verifies the zero-knowledge proof and its security is based on the hardness of the q-ary Syndrome Decoding (qSD) problem.

Before presenting the CVE identification scheme, we first introduce a special transformation that will be used in the protocol.

Definition 6. *Let $\Sigma \in S_n$ and $\gamma = (\gamma_1, \ldots, \gamma_n) \in (\mathbb{F}_q^*)^n$ such that $\gamma_i \neq 0$ for all i. The transformation $\Pi_{\gamma, \Sigma}$ is defined as follows:*

$$\Pi_{\gamma, \Sigma} : \mathbb{F}_q^n \longrightarrow \mathbb{F}_q^n$$
$$v \mapsto \left(\gamma_{\Sigma(1)} v_{\Sigma(1)}, \ldots, \gamma_{\Sigma(n)} v_{\Sigma(n)}\right)$$

Notice that $\forall \alpha \in \mathbb{F}_q$, $\forall v \in \mathbb{F}_q^n$, $\Pi_{\gamma, \Sigma}(\alpha v) = \alpha \Pi_{\gamma, \Sigma}(v)$, and $\mathsf{wt}(\Pi_{\gamma, \Sigma}(v)) = \mathsf{wt}(v)$.

Description. The key generation algorithm is as follows: in a first step choose randomly a parity-check matrix $H \in \mathbb{F}_q^{r \times n}$ and a vector $s \in \mathbb{F}_q^n$ with weight $\mathsf{wt}(s) = \omega$. s identifies the secret key. Finally, perform Hs^T to get the vector $y \in \mathbb{F}_q^r$. The public key consists of y, H and ω (see Figure 5).

KEYGEN:

Choose n, r, ω, and q such that $\mathrm{WF}_{\mathrm{ISD}}(n, r, \omega, q) \geq 2^\kappa$

$H \xleftarrow{\$} \mathbb{F}_q^{r \times n}$

$s \xleftarrow{\$} \mathbb{F}_q^n$, s.t. $\mathsf{wt}(s) = \omega$.

$y \leftarrow Hs^T$

Output $(\mathrm{sk}, \mathrm{pk}) = (s, (y, H, \omega))$

Fig. 5. CVE key generation algorithm

Prover $\mathcal{P}$		**Verifier** $\mathcal{V}$
	$(\mathrm{sk}, \mathrm{pk}) = (s, (y, H, \omega)) \longleftarrow$ KEYGEN	
	(h public hash function)	
$u \xleftarrow{\$} \mathbb{F}_q^n, \Sigma \xleftarrow{\$} S_n$		
$\gamma \xleftarrow{\$} (\mathbb{F}_q^*)^n$		
$c_1 \leftarrow h\left(\Sigma, \gamma, Hu^T\right)$		
$c_2 \leftarrow h\left(\Pi_{\gamma, \Sigma}(u), \Pi_{\gamma, \Sigma}(s)\right)$	$\xrightarrow{\quad c_1, c_2 \quad}$	
	$\xleftarrow{\quad \alpha \quad}$	$\alpha \xleftarrow{\$} \mathbb{F}_q^*$
$\beta \longleftarrow \Pi_{\gamma, \Sigma}(u + \alpha s)$	$\xrightarrow{\quad \beta \quad}$	
	$\xleftarrow{\text{Challenge } b}$	$b \xleftarrow{\$} \{0, 1\}$
If $b = 0$:	$\xrightarrow{\quad \Sigma, \gamma \quad}$	**Check** $c_1 \overset{?}{=} h(\Sigma, \gamma, H\Pi_{\gamma, \Sigma}^{-1}(\beta)^T - \alpha y)$
Else:	$\xrightarrow{\quad \Pi_{\gamma, \Sigma}(s) \quad}$	**Check** $c_2 \overset{?}{=} h(\beta - \alpha \Pi_{\gamma, \Sigma}(s), \Pi_{\gamma, \Sigma}(s))$,
		$\mathsf{wt}(\Pi_{\gamma, \Sigma}(s)) \overset{?}{=} \omega$

Fig. 6. CVE identification protocol

3.4 Signature Schemes via the Fiat-Shamir Transform

Using the Fiat-Shamir transform [13], respectively its extended version [1], it is possible to transform the Stern and Véron schemes, respectively the CVE scheme, given above into signature schemes. The idea of this transformation is to split the identification scheme in two parts.

In the first part, the signer runs the identification scheme as before, but without any verifier involved. Instead, the signer has to generate the challenges on his own, for instance using a stream cipher with a predefined start value, which includes the message to sign. On the one hand, the signer can not predict the next challenge bits, and on the other hand, the procedure must be repeatable by the verifier. In other words, concerning the challenges, the signer is simulating the role of the verifier, and recording the responses without any checks.

In the second part, the verifier uses the same stream cipher and starting value and replays the protocol with the saved responses and performs the necessary checks. This also explains the relatively big signature sizes of schemes based on the Fiat-Shamir transform as the signer is recording a history of the actions involved. This history is used by the verifier in the verification process. It also shows the varying sizes of the signatures, as the given responses change from run to run with high probability.

4 Implementation

In total, six different schemes have been implemented in **C**: the Stern, Véron and CVE identification schemes and the corresponding signature schemes based on the Fiat-Shamir transform [13,1].

The implementation assumes that the dimensions of the matrices are a multiple of 64. The public keys G and H are given in systematic form, i.e. $G = [I_k | R]$ and $H = [I_{n-k} | R]$ respectively, where only the redundant part R is used. In the quasi-cyclic and quasi-dyadic cases, the matrices G and H consist of cyclic and dyadic submatrices of size 64×64, because 64 is the natural number to use on a 64-bit machine.

For the generation of random vectors and hash values, we deployed the code-based RFSB-509 hash function presented by Bernstein et al. [8]. This choice is driven by the intension to base the security of the schemes on only one hardness assumption, namely the hardness of solving the syndrome decoding problem. But note that it can be replaced by any other suitable scheme providing the necessary functionality: for comparison, we also implemented the signature schemes using Keccak [14].

The experiments were performed on an Intel Xeon E5-1602 running at 2.80 GHz, having 8 GB of RAM and running a 64bit version of Debian 6.0.6.

4.1 Identification Schemes

Stern Scheme. This scheme uses a binary parity check matrix $H = [I_{n-k} | R]$ of size $r \times n$, where $r = n - k$ and $k = n/2$. For the implementation we used

$n = 768$ and $k = 384$. Due to the row-major order of $\mathbf{C}$, the product sH^T is more efficient as Hs^T ($s \in \mathbb{F}_2^n$). Hence, the implementation uses the transposed matrix H^T instead of H.

Table 1. Stern timing results for 28 rounds when the impersonation probability is bounded by 2^{-16}

Matrix Type	Dimension $[n \times r]$	Weight	Time $[ms]$	Sec. Level$_{[bits]}$
Random	768×384	76	2.79	80
Quasi-cyclic	768×384	76	2.57	80
Quasi-dyadic	768×384	76	3.78	80

Véron Scheme: This scheme uses a binary generator matrix $G = [I_k | R]$ of dimensions $k \times n$, where $k = n/2$. Again, in the quasi-cyclic and quasi-dyadic case, the cyclic and dyadic submatrices have a size of 64×64 bits, $n = 768$ and $k = 384$. As in Stern, if G is quasi-cyclic or quasi-dyadic, then the submatrix R would consist of 36 cyclic or dyadic submatrices of size 64×64 bits.

Table 2. Véron timing results for 28 rounds when the impersonation probability is bounded by 2^{-16}

Matrix Type	Dimension $[k \times n]$	Weight	Time $[ms]$	Sec. Level$_{[bits]}$
Random	768×384	76	2.65	80
Quasi-cyclic	768×384	76	2.47	80
Quasi-dyadic	768×384	76	3.57	80

Memory Requirements. The memory requirements for the Stern and Véron scheme are as follows: using a random matrix $384 \times 384 = 147.456$ bits are necessary to store the redundancy part R of H resp. G. Using quasi-cyclic (quasi-dyadic) matrices, the memory footprint for the matrices drops by a factor of 64. Only $6 \times 6 \times 64 = 2.304 = 147.456/64$ bits are needed. Hence, although the timings using quasi-cyclic (quasi-dyadic) matrices are worse than for random matrices, in some environments the smaller memory footprint might compensate for the loss in performance.

CVE Scheme. It uses a parity check matrix H of size $r \times n$ over $\mathbb{F}_q$, where $q = 2^m$, $1 \leq m \leq 16$, $r = n - k$ and $k = n/2$. As in the Stern scheme, the implementation uses the transposed matrix H^T instead of H. If H is quasi-cyclic or quasi-dyadic, then the submatrix R would consist of 81 cyclic or dyadic submatrices of 8×8 field elements.

The matrix size is always measured in numbers of field elements. Each field element occupies invariably 2 bytes of memory. Strictly speaking, this would be necessary only in the case $m = 16$. However, using only the necessary bits would complicate the code and slow down the computation. In environments in which memory is a very valuable resource, this fact had to be taken into account.

For the measurements we used $m = 8$.

Table 3. CVE timing results for 16 rounds when the impersonation probability is bounded by 2^{-16}

Matrix Type	Dimension $[n \times r]$	Degree $q = 2^m$	Weight	Time $[ms]$	Sec. Level$_{[bits]}$
Random	144×72	256	55	1.40	80
Quasi-cyclic	144×72	256	55	1.38	80
Quasi-dyadic	144×72	256	55	1.67	80

Memory Requirements for the CVE Scheme. Using a random matrix, $72 \times 72 \times 2 = 10.368$ bytes are necessary to store the redundancy part R of H resp. G. Using quasi-cyclic (quasi-dyadic) matrices, the memory footprint for the matrices drops by a factor of 8, because in this case only $9 \times 9 \times 8 \times 2 = 1.296 = 10.368/8$ bytes are needed. Again, as with the Stern and Véron scheme, memory savings using the structured matrix types might be more important than the loss in runtime.

4.2   Signature Schemes Based on Fiat-Shamir Transform

Using the Fiat-Shamir transform [13], one can transform identification schemes to signature schemes. We describe the process in detail for the Stern scheme (respectively Véron scheme). It is straightforward to adapt it to the non canonical (more than three-pass) CVE case, see [1] for more details.

Note that the signer and verifier parts are always located in the same executable, thus the two parts can communicate in almost no time. In reality, they would reside on different machines, such that additional costs over some communication link had to be taken into account.

4.3   The Signing Procedure

Let δ the number of rounds needed to achieve the required cheating probability. In a first step, a commitment CMT is computed as

$$\text{CMT} = (c_{01}, c_{02}, c_{03}) \, || \, (c_{11}, c_{12}, c_{13}) \, || \, \cdots \, || \, (c_{\delta-1,1}, c_{\delta-1,2}, c_{\delta-1,3}).$$

More precisely, in each round we run one of the above identification schemes to generate a corresponding commitment (c_{i1}, c_{i2}, c_{i3}), where $0 \le i \le \delta - 1$. Note that the c_{i1}, c_{i2} and c_{i3} are hashed values (using RFSB-509) and that each such triple has $3 \times 160 = 480$ bits. The number of rounds δ is a predefined value (e.g. 141 for Stern and Véron schemes or 80 for the CVE scheme to achieve a impersonation resistance of $1/2^{80}$). All round-triples together form the compound commitment CMT.

In a second step, we compute the challenge CH $= h($CMT $\| M)$, where h denotes the RFSB-509 hash function and M is the message, typically the content of some file. CH has a length such that it consists of twice as many bits as there are rounds, because for each round the signer needs a new challenge. Each two bits of CH give a partial challenge, where the bit pattern 11 is mapped to $b \in \{0, 1, 2\}$ in a cyclic fashion.

Finally, compute for each partial challenge b the response according to the deployed identification scheme. Note that the response size for each b varies depending on its actual value of 0, 1 or 2. Denote all responses by RSP $= (r_0 \| r_1 \| \ldots \| r_{\delta-1})$. The final signature is (CMT $\|$ RSP).

4.4 The Verification Procedure

Upon receiving the signature, the verifier extracts CMT and computes CH $= h($CMT $\| M)$. As in the signing step, the verifier uses the individual bytes of CH modulo 3 to obtain δ many challenges $b \in \{0, 1, 2\}$. Using b, the verifier extracts the corresponding response contained in RSP and calculates the commitment c_{ij}, where $j = b$ and i denotes the current round. Finally, the verifier computes $h(c_{ij})$ of CMT and compares this value with the c_{ij} contained in the triple (c_{i1}, c_{i2}, c_{i3}). We identify here the value $h(c_{ij})$ and c_{ij}. In case the values of c_{ij} match for all rounds, the signature is considered valid.

In the following, tables are given for runtime measurement of the three signature schemes derived from the corresponding identification schemes using the Fiat-Shamir transform.

4.5 Signature Scheme Timings

Table 4. Stern timing results: separate signing and verification time (s/v) for 141 rounds

Matrix Type	Dimension$_{[n \times r]}$	Weight	Time$_{[ms]}$				Msg.$_{[kBytes]}$	Sec.$_{[bits]}$
			Keccak		RFSB			
Random	768×384	76	7.18	3.57	7.67	4.88	1	80
	768×384	76	7.32	3.92	7.88	3.70	10	80
	768×384	76	7.49	4.02	8.11	3.93	25	80
Quasi-cyclic	768×384	76	6.59	3.25	7.01	4.59	1	80
	768×384	76	6.70	3.35	7.18	4.16	10	80
	768×384	76	6.84	3.49	7.44	4.03	25	80
Quasi-dyadic	768×384	76	10.13	5.61	10.46	6.07	1	80
	768×384	76	10.25	5.64	10.87	4.71	10	80
	768×384	76	10.49	5.65	10.97	7.77	25	80

4.6   Remarks

The signature size in the Stern and Véron schemes is about 25 kBytes and respectively 19 kBytes in the CVE scheme for 80-bit security. The numbers mean an average value of several runs over 141 resp. 80 rounds. Note that the signature size is independent from the message to be signed.

Table 5. Véron timing results: separate signing and verification time (s/v) for 141 rounds

Matrix Type	Dimension$_{[n \times r]}$	Weight	Time$_{[ms]}$				Msg.$_{[kBytes]}$	Sec.$_{[bits]}$
			Keccak		RFSB			
Random	768 × 384	76	10.26	4.86	7.98	3.76	1	80
	768 × 384	76	10.37	5.53	7.99	4.22	10	80
	768 × 384	76	10.55	5.26	8.33	4.14	25	80
Quasi-cyclic	768 × 384	76	9.37	4.80	6.87	3.89	1	80
	768 × 384	76	9.47	4.92	7.25	3.33	10	80
	768 × 384	76	9.64	5.07	7.35	3.89	25	80
Quasi-dyadic	768 × 384	76	13.79	6.23	11.66	4.17	1	80
	768 × 384	76	14.23	7.01	11.99	3.88	10	80
	768 × 384	76	14.02	6.13	12.40	3.65	25	80

Table 6. CVE timing results: separate signing and verification time (s/v) for 80 rounds

Matrix Type	Dimension$_{[n \times r]}$	Weight	Time$_{[ms]}$				Msg.$_{[kBytes]}$	Sec.$_{[bits]}$
			Keccak		RFSB			
Random	144 × 72	55	4.25	1.90	4.21	3.73	1	80
	144 × 72	55	4.38	2.03	4.36	2.40	10	80
	144 × 72	55	4.59	2.97	4.59	2.30	25	80
Quasi-cyclic	144 × 72	55	5.21	2.42	5.20	2.62	1	80
	144 × 72	55	5.32	2.51	5.31	3.02	10	80
	144 × 72	55	5.56	3.70	5.55	2.80	25	80
Quasi-dyadic	144 × 72	55	4.44	2.07	4.41	2.18	1	80
	144 × 72	55	4.58	2.13	4.56	2.53	10	80
	144 × 72	55	4.79	3.13	4.77	2.42	25	80

The runtime is dominated by RFSB creating random vectors $u[0], \ldots, u[\delta - 1]$ before entering the loop of 141 resp. 80 rounds, which could also be confirmed profiling the implementation directly with gprof, the profiler contained in gcc.

5   Conclusion

In this paper, we have described three existing code-based identification and their corresponding signature schemes and provided running times of their implementation. As a result, we obtain three very fast signature schemes. Depending on the message size it is possible to sign and verify in the order of milliseconds, but at the cost of very long signature sizes: typically 19 kBytes for CVE and 25 kBytes bytes for Stern resp. Véron.

The source code of the **C** implementation is available under the following link: http://cayrel.net/research/code-based-cryptography/code-based-cryptosystems/article/implementation-of-code-based-zero.

References

1. El Yousfi Alaoui, S.M., Dagdelen, Ö., Véron, P., Galindo, D., Cayrel, P.-L.: Extended security arguments for signature schemes. In: Mitrokotsa, A., Vaudenay, S. (eds.) AFRICACRYPT 2012. LNCS, vol. 7374, pp. 19–34. Springer, Heidelberg (2012)
2. Barg, S.: Some new NP-complete coding problems. Probl. Peredachi Inf. 30, 23–28 (1994)
3. Becker, A., Joux, A., May, A., Meurer, A.: Decoding random binary linear codes in $2^{(n/20)}$: How 1+1=0 improves information set decoding. In: Pointcheval, D., Johansson, T. (eds.) EUROCRYPT 2012. LNCS, vol. 7237, pp. 520–536. Springer, Heidelberg (2012)
4. Berger, T.P., Cayrel, P.-L., Gaborit, P., Otmani, A.: Reducing Key Length of the McEliece Cryptosystem. In: Preneel, B. (ed.) AFRICACRYPT 2009. LNCS, vol. 5580, pp. 77–97. Springer, Heidelberg (2009)
5. Berlekamp, E., McEliece, R., van Tilborg, H.: On the Inherent Intractability of Certain Coding Problems. IEEE Transactions on Information Theory 24(3), 384–386 (1978)
6. Bernstein, D.J., Buchmann, J., Dahmen, E.: Post-Quantum Cryptography. Springer (2008)
7. Bernstein, D.J., Lange, T., Peters, C.: Smaller decoding exponents: ball-collision decoding. In: Rogaway, P. (ed.) CRYPTO 2011. LNCS, vol. 6841, pp. 743–760. Springer, Heidelberg (2011)
8. Bernstein, D.J., Lange, T., Peters, C., Schwabe, P.: Really fast syndrome-based hashing. In: Nitaj, A., Pointcheval, D. (eds.) AFRICACRYPT 2011. LNCS, vol. 6737, pp. 134–152. Springer, Heidelberg (2011)
9. Cayrel, P.-L., El Yousfi Alaoui, S.M., Günther, F., Hoffmann, G., Rother, H.: Efficient implementation of code-based identification schemes (2011), http://cayrel.net/PublicationsCayrel/2011-Efficient%implementation%of%code-based%identification%schemes.pdf
10. Cayrel, P.-L., Gaborit, P., Prouff, E.: Secure Implementation of the Stern Authentication and Signature Schemes for Low-Resource Devices. In: Grimaud, G., Standaert, F.-X. (eds.) CARDIS 2008. LNCS, vol. 5189, pp. 191–205. Springer, Heidelberg (2008)
11. Cayrel, P.-L., Véron, P., El Yousfi Alaoui, S.M.: A Zero-Knowledge Identification Scheme Based on the q-ary Syndrome Decoding Problem. In: Biryukov, A., Gong, G., Stinson, D.R. (eds.) SAC 2010. LNCS, vol. 6544, pp. 171–186. Springer, Heidelberg (2011)

12. Faugère, J.-C., Otmani, A., Perret, L., Tillich, J.-P.: Algebraic cryptanalysis of mceliece variants with compact keys. In: Gilbert, H. (ed.) EUROCRYPT 2010. LNCS, vol. 6110, pp. 279–298. Springer, Heidelberg (2010)
13. Fiat, A., Shamir, A.: How To Prove Yourself: Practical Solutions to Identification and Signature Problems. In: Odlyzko, A.M. (ed.) CRYPTO 1986. LNCS, vol. 263, pp. 186–194. Springer, Heidelberg (1987)
14. Bertoni, G., Daemen, J., Peeters, M., Assche, G.V.: The Keccak sponge function family, http://keccak.noekeon.org/
15. Goldwasser, S., Micali, S., Rackoff, C.: The knowledge complexity of interactive proof-systems. In: STOC 1985. acmid, vol. 22178, pp. 291–304. ACM (1985)
16. May, A., Meurer, A., Thomae, E.: Decoding random linear codes in $\tilde{O}(2^{0.054n})$. In: Lee, D.H., Wang, X. (eds.) ASIACRYPT 2011. LNCS, vol. 7073, pp. 107–124. Springer, Heidelberg (2011)
17. Misoczki, R., Barreto, P.S.L.M.: Compact McEliece keys from Goppa Codes. In: Jacobson Jr., M.J., Rijmen, V., Safavi-Naini, R. (eds.) SAC 2009. LNCS, vol. 5867, pp. 376–392. Springer, Heidelberg (2009)
18. Niebuhr, R., Cayrel, P.-L., Bulygin, S., Buchmann, J.: On Lower Bounds for Information Set Decoding over $\mathbb{F}_q$. In: SCC 2010, Rhul, London, UK (2010)
19. Peters, C.: Information-Set Decoding for Linear Codes over $\mathbb{F}_q$. In: Sendrier, N. (ed.) PQCrypto 2010. LNCS, vol. 6061, pp. 81–94. Springer, Heidelberg (2010)
20. Shamir, A.: An efficient identification scheme based on permuted kernels (extended abstract). In: Brassard, G. (ed.) CRYPTO 1989. LNCS, vol. 435, pp. 606–609. Springer, Heidelberg (1990)
21. Shor, P.W.: Polynomial-Time Algorithms for Prime Factorization and Discrete Logarithms on a Quantum Computer. SIAM Journal on Computing 26, 1484–1509 (1995)
22. Stern, J.: Designing Identification Schemes with Keys of Short Size. In: Desmedt, Y.G. (ed.) CRYPTO 1994. LNCS, vol. 839, pp. 164–173. Springer, Heidelberg (1994)
23. Stern, J.: A New Identification Scheme Based on Syndrome Decoding. In: Stinson, D.R. (ed.) CRYPTO 1993. LNCS, vol. 773, pp. 13–21. Springer, Heidelberg (1994)
24. Gauthier Umana, V., Leander, G.: Practical key recovery attacks on two McEliece variants. IACR Cryptology ePrint Archive, Report 2009/509 (2009)
25. Véron, P.: Improved Identification Schemes Based on Error-Correcting Codes. Appl. Algebra Eng. Commun. Comput. 8(1), 57–69 (1996)

Fast Software Polynomial Multiplication on ARM Processors Using the NEON Engine

Danilo Câmara, Conrado P. L. Gouvêa*, Julio López**, and Ricardo Dahab

University of Campinas (Unicamp)
{dfcamara,conradoplg,jlopez,rdahab}@ic.unicamp.br

Abstract. Efficient algorithms for binary field operations are required in several cryptographic operations such as digital signatures over binary elliptic curves and encryption. The main performance-critical operation in these fields is the multiplication, since most processors do not support instructions to carry out a polynomial multiplication. In this paper we describe a novel software multiplier for performing a polynomial multiplication of two 64-bit binary polynomials based on the VMULL instruction included in the NEON engine supported in many ARM processors. This multiplier is then used as a building block to obtain a fast software multiplication in the binary field $\mathbb{F}_{2^m}$, which is up to 45% faster compared to the best known algorithm. We also illustrate the performance improvement in point multiplication on binary elliptic curves using the new multiplier, improving the performance of standard NIST curves at the 128- and 256-bit levels of security. The impact on the GCM authenticated encryption scheme is also studied, with new speed records. We present timing results of our software implementation on the ARM Cortex-A8, A9 and A15 processors.

Keywords: binary field arithmetic, ARM NEON, elliptic curve cryptography, authenticated encryption, software implementation.

1 Introduction

Mobile devices such as smartphones and tablets are becoming ubiquitous. While these devices are relatively powerful, they still are constrained in some aspects such as power consumption. Due to the wireless nature of their communication, it is very important to secure all messages in order to prevent eavesdropping and disclosure of personal information. For this reason, the research of efficient software implementation of cryptography in those devices becomes relevant. Both public key and symmetric cryptography are cornerstones of most cryptographic solutions; in particular, the public-key elliptic curve schemes and the symmetric authenticated encryption schemes are often used due to their high efficiency. Elliptic curve schemes include the well known Elliptic Curve Digital Signature

* Supported by FAPESP grant 2010/15340-3.
** Partially supported by a research productivity scholarship from CNPq-Brazil.

A. Cuzzocrea et al. (Eds.): CD-ARES 2013 Workshops, LNCS 8128, pp. 137–154, 2013.

Algorithm (ECDSA) and the Elliptic Curve Diffie Hellman (ECDH) key agreement scheme; while the Galois/Counter Mode (GCM) is an important example of authenticated encryption scheme which is included in many standards such as IPSec and TLS.

A significant portion of mobile devices uses processors based on the 32-bit RISC ARM architecture, suitable for low-power applications due to its relatively simple design, making it an appropriate choice of target platform for efficient implementation. Many ARM processors are equipped with a NEON engine, which is a set of instructions and large registers that supports operations in multiple data using a single instruction. Thus, our objective is to provide an efficient software implementation of cryptography for the ARM architecture, taking advantage of the NEON engine. We have aimed for standard protection against basic side-channel attacks (timing and cache-leakage). Our main contributions are: (i) to describe a new technique to carry out polynomial multiplication by taking advantage of the VMULL NEON instruction, achieving a binary field multiplication that is up to 45% faster than a state-of-the-art LD [15] multiplication also using NEON; (ii) using the new multiplier, to achieve speed records of elliptic curve schemes on standard NIST curves and of authenticated encryption with GCM; (iii) to offer, for the first time in the literarure, comprehensive timings for four binary NIST elliptic curves and one non-standard curve, on three different ARM Cortex processors. With this contributions, we advance the state of the art of elliptic curve cryptography using binary fields, offering an improved comparison with the (already highly optimized) implementations using prime fields present in the literature. Our code will be available[1] to allow reproduction of results.

Related Work. Morozov et al. [20] have implemented ECC for the OMAP 3530 platform, which features a 500 MHz ARM Cortex-A8 core and a DSP core. Taking advantage of the XORMPY instruction of the DSP core, they achieve 2,106 μs in the B-163 elliptic curve and 7,965 μs in the B-283 curve to compute a shared key, which should scale to 1,053 and 3,982 Kcycles respectively.

Bernstein and Schwabe [6] have described an efficient implementation of non-standard cryptographic primitives using the NEON engine on a Cortex-A8 at the 128-bit security level, using Montgomery and Edwards elliptic curves over the prime field $\mathbb{F}_{(2^{255}-19)}$. The primitives offer basic resistance against side-channel attacks. They obtain 527 Kcycles to compute a shared secret key, 368 Kcycles to sign a message and 650 Kcycles to verify a signature.

Hamburg [9] has also efficiently implemented non-standard cryptographic primitives on a Cortex-A9 *without* NEON support at the 128-bit security level, using Montgomery and Edwards Curves over the prime field $\mathbb{F}_{(2^{252}-2^{232}-1)}$, with basic resistance against side-channel attacks. He obtains 616 Kcycles to compute a shared key, 262 Kcycles to sign a message and 605 Kcycles to verify a signature.

Faz-Hernández et al. [7] have targeted the 128-bit security level with a GLV-GLS curve over the prime field $\mathbb{F}_{(2^{127}-5997)^2}$, which supports a four dimensional

---

[1] http://conradoplg.cryptoland.net/ecc-and-ae-for-arm-neon/

decomposition of the scalar for speeding up point multiplication. The implementation also provides basic resistance against side-channel attacks. They have obtained 417 and 244 Kcycles for random point multiplication on the Cortex-A9 and A15 respectively; 172 and 100 Kcycles for fixed point multiplication and 463 and 266 Kcycles for simultaneous point multiplication.

Krovetz and Rogaway [13] studied the software performance of three authenticated encryption modes (CCM, GCM and OCB3) in many platforms. In particular, they report 50.8 cycles per byte (cpb) for GCM over AES with large messages using the Cortex-A8; an overhead of 25.4 cpb over unauthenticated AES encryption.

Polyakov [22] has contributed a NEON implementation of GHASH, the authentication code used by GCM, to the OpenSSL project. He reports a 15 cpb performance on the Cortex-A8.

Paper Structure. This paper is organized as follows. In Section 2 we describe the ARM architecture. In Section 3, the binary field arithmetic is explained, along with our new multiplier based on the the VMULL instruction. Section 4 describes the high-level algorithms used and Section 5 presents our results. Finally, concluding remarks are given in Section 6.

2   ARM Architecture

The ARM is a RISC architecture known for enabling the production of low-power processors and is widely spread in mobile devices. It features a fairly usual instruction set with some interesting characteristics such as integrated shifts, conditional execution of most instructions, and optional update of condition codes by arithmetic instructions. There are sixteen 32-bit registers (R0–R15), thirteen of which are general-purpose. The version 7 of the ARM architecture has added an advanced Single Instruction, Multiple Data (SIMD) extension referred as "NEON engine", which is composed of a collection of SIMD instructions using 64- or 128-bit operands and a bank of sixteen 128-bit registers. These are named Q0–Q15 when viewed as 128-bit, and D0–D31 when viewed as 64-bit. There are many CPU designs based on the ARM architecture such as the ARM7, ARM9, ARM11 and the ARM Cortex series. In this work, we used three ARM Cortex devices, which we now describe.

Cortex-A8. The ARM Cortex-A8 processor is a full implementation of the ARMv7 architecture including the NEON engine. Compared to previous ARM cores the Cortex-A8 is dual-issue superscalar, achieving up to twice the instructions executed per clock cycle. Some pairs of NEON instructions can also be dual-issued, mainly a load/store or permutation instruction together with a data-processing instruction. Its pipeline has 13 stages followed by 10 NEON stages; its L2 cache is internal. The Cortex-A8 is used by devices such as the iPad, iPhone 4, Galaxy Tab, and Nexus S.

Cortex-A9. The ARM Cortex-A9 shares the same instruction set with the Cortex-A8, but it features up to four cores. It no longer supports NEON dual-issue and its L2 cache is external. However, it supports out-of-order execution of regular ARM instructions and register renaming, and has a 9–12 stage pipeline (more for NEON, we were unable to find how many). Devices that feature the Cortex-A9 include the iPad 2, iPhone 4S, Galaxy S II, and Kindle Fire.

Cortex-A15. Implements the ARMv7 architecture, provides dual-issue and out-of-order execution for most NEON instructions and can feature up to four cores. Its pipeline is wider, with 15 to 25 stages. The Cortex-A15 is present in devices such as the Chromebook, Nexus 10, and Galaxy S4.

Instructions. We highlight the NEON instructions which are important in this work, also illustrated in Figure 1. The VMULL instruction is able to carry out several multiplications in parallel; the VMULL.P8 version takes as input two 64-bit input vectors A and B of eight 8-bit binary polynomials and returns a 128-bit output vector C of eight 16-bit binary polynomials, where the i-th element of C is the multiplication of the i-th elements from each input.

The VEXT instruction, for two 64-bit registers and an immediate integer i, outputs a 64-bit value which is the concatenation of lower $8i$ bits of the first register and the higher $64 - 8i$ bits of the second register. Note that if the inputs are the same register then the VEXT instruction computes right bit rotation by multiples of 8 bits. The instruction also supports 128-bit registers, with similar functionality.

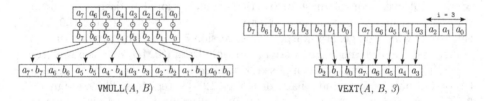

VMULL(A, B)   VEXT(A, B, 3)

Fig. 1. Main NEON instructions in this work: VMULL.P8 (shortened as VMULL) and VEXT. Each square is 8 bits; rectangles are 16 bits.

3   Binary Field Arithmetic

Binary field arithmetic is traditionally implemented in software using polynomial basis representation, where elements of $\mathbb{F}_{2^m}$ are represented by polynomials of degree at most $m - 1$ over $\mathbb{F}_2$. Assuming a platform with a W-bit architecture ($W = 32$ for ARM), a binary field element $a(z) = a_{m-1}z^{m-1} + \cdots + a_2 z^2 + a_1 z + a_0$ may be represented by a binary vector $a = (a_{m-1}, \ldots, a_2, a_1, a_0)$ of length m using $t = \lceil m/W \rceil$ words. Remaining $s = Wt - m$ bits are left unused.

Multiplication in $\mathbb{F}_{2^m}$ (*field multiplication*) is performed modulo $f(z) = z^m + r(z)$, an irreducible binary polynomial of degree m. This multiplication can be carried out in two steps: first, the polynomial multiplication of the operands; second, the polynomial reduction modulo $f(z)$. The basic method for computing the polynomial multiplication of $c(z) = a(z)b(z)$ is to read each i-th bit of $b(z)$ and, if it is 1, xor $a(z) \ll i$ into an accumulator. However, since the left-shifting operations are in general expensive, faster variations of this method have been developed. One of the fastest known methods for software implementation is the López-Dahab (LD) algorithm [15], which processes multiple bits in each iteration. We have implemented it using the NEON engine, taking advantage of the VEXT instruction and larger number of registers.

While the LD algorithm is often the fastest in many platforms, the presence of the VMULL.P8 NEON instruction has the potential to change this landscape. However, it is not obvious how to build a n-bit polynomial multiplier for cryptographic applications ($n \geq 128$) using the eight parallel 8-bit multiplications provided by VMULL.P8. Our solution is a combination of the Karatsuba algorithm and a multiplier based on VMULL.P8 which we have named the Karatsuba/NEON/VMULL multiplier (KNV), described below.

3.1   New Karatsuba/NEON/VMULL (KNV) Multiplier

Our new approach was to built a 64-bit polynomial multiplier, which computes the 128-bit product of two 64-bit polynomials. This multiplier was then combined with the Karatsuba algorithm [11] in order to provide the full multiplication.

The 64-bit multiplier was built using the VMULL.P8 instruction (VMULL for short) as follows. Consider two 64-bit polynomials $a(z)$ and $b(z)$ over $\mathbb{F}_2$ represented as vectors of eight 8-bit polynomials:

$$A = (a_7, a_6, a_5, a_4, a_3, a_2, a_1, a_0); \quad B = (b_7, b_6, b_5, b_4, b_3, b_2, b_1, b_0).$$

To compute the polynomial multiplication $c(z) = a(z) \cdot b(z)$ (represented as a vector C), the schoolbook method would require sixty-four 8-bit multiplications with every (a_i, b_j) combination, where each product is xored into an accumulator in the appropriate position. In our proposal, these multiplications can be done with eight executions of VMULL by rearranging the inputs. Let $\ggg$ denote a circular right shift; compute $A_1 = A \ggg 8$, $A_2 = A \ggg 16$, $A_3 = A \ggg 24$, $B_1 = B \ggg 8$, $B_2 = B \ggg 16$, $B_3 = B \ggg 24$ and $B_4 = B \ggg 32$ using VEXT. This results in:

$$A_1 = (a_0, a_7, a_6, a_5, a_4, a_3, a_2, a_1); \quad B_1 = (b_0, b_7, b_6, b_5, b_4, b_3, b_2, b_1);$$
$$A_2 = (a_1, a_0, a_7, a_6, a_5, a_4, a_3, a_2); \quad B_2 = (b_1, b_0, b_7, b_6, b_5, b_4, b_3, b_2);$$
$$A_3 = (a_2, a_1, a_0, a_7, a_6, a_5, a_4, a_3); \quad B_3 = (b_2, b_1, b_0, b_7, b_6, b_5, b_4, b_3);$$
$$B_4 = (b_3, b_2, b_1, b_0, b_7, b_6, b_5, b_4).$$

Now compute these VMULL products:

$$D = \text{VMULL}(A, B) \quad = (a_7b_7, a_6b_6, a_5b_5, a_4b_4, a_3b_3, a_2b_2, a_1b_1, a_0b_0);$$
$$E = \text{VMULL}(A, B_1) \quad = (a_7b_0, a_6b_7, a_5b_6, a_4b_5, a_3b_4, a_2b_3, a_1b_2, a_0b_1);$$
$$F = \text{VMULL}(A_1, B) \quad = (a_0b_7, a_7b_6, a_6b_5, a_5b_4, a_4b_3, a_3b_2, a_2b_1, a_1b_0);$$
$$G = \text{VMULL}(A, B_2) \quad = (a_7b_1, a_6b_0, a_5b_7, a_4b_6, a_3b_5, a_2b_4, a_1b_3, a_0b_2);$$
$$H = \text{VMULL}(A_2, B) \quad = (a_1b_7, a_0b_6, a_7b_5, a_6b_4, a_5b_3, a_4b_2, a_3b_1, a_2b_0);$$
$$I = \text{VMULL}(A, B_3) \quad = (a_7b_2, a_6b_1, a_5b_0, a_4b_7, a_3b_6, a_2b_5, a_1b_4, a_0b_3);$$
$$J = \text{VMULL}(A_3, B) \quad = (a_2b_7, a_1b_6, a_0b_5, a_7b_4, a_6b_3, a_5b_2, a_4b_1, a_3b_0);$$
$$K = \text{VMULL}(A, B_4) \quad = (a_7b_3, a_6b_2, a_5b_1, a_4b_0, a_3b_7, a_2b_6, a_1b_5, a_0b_4).$$

These vectors of eight 16-bit polynomials contain the product of every (a_i, b_j) combination, as required. We now need to xor everything into place. Let $L = E + F$, $M = G + H$ and $N = I + J$. Let k_i be the i-th element of vector K and analogously to L, M and N. Now, compute:

$$P_0 = (0, \ 0, \ 0, \ 0, \ \ell_7, \ 0, \ 0, \ 0); \quad P_4 = (0, \ 0, \ 0, \ 0, \ n_7, \ n_6, \ n_5, \ 0);$$
$$P_1 = (0, \ \ell_6, \ \ell_5, \ \ell_4, \ \ell_3, \ \ell_2, \ \ell_1, \ \ell_0); \quad P_5 = (0, \ 0, \ 0, n_4, \ n_3, \ n_2, \ n_1, n_0);$$
$$P_2 = (0, \ 0, \ 0, \ 0, m_7, m_6, \ 0, \ 0); \quad P_6 = (0, \ 0, \ 0, \ 0, \ k_7, \ k_6, \ k_5, \ k_4);$$
$$P_3 = (0, \ 0, m_5, m_4, m_3, m_2, m_1, m_0); \quad P_7 = (0, \ 0, \ 0, \ 0, \ k_3, \ k_2, \ k_1, k_0).$$

The final result is obtained with:

$$C = A \cdot B = D + (P_0 + P_1) \ll 8 + (P_2 + P_3) \ll 16 + (P_4 + P_5) \ll 24 + (P_6 + P_7) \ll 32.$$

The expansion of the above equation produces the same results of the schoolbook method for multiplication, verifying its correctness. The whole process is illustrated in Figure 2, and Algorithm 6 in the Appendix lists the assembly code for reference. The partial results $(P_0 + P_1) \ll 8$, $(P_2 + P_3) \ll 16$ or $(P_4 + P_5) \ll 24$ can each be computed from L, M or N with four instructions (two xors, one mask operation and one shift). The partial result $(P_6 + P_7) \ll 32$ can be computed from K with three instructions (one xor, one mask operation and one shift). To clarify our approach, we list the assembly code used in the computation of L and $(P_0 + P_1) \ll 8$ from A and B in Algorithm 1 and describe it below.

In Algorithm 1, the 128-bit NEON register tq can be viewed as two 64-bit registers such that tq = th||tl where tl is the lower part and th is the higher part; the same applies to other registers. In line 1, the VEXT instruction concatenates the lower 8 bits of A with the higher $(64 - 8) = 56$ bits of A, resulting in the value A_1 being stored in tl. Line 2 computes $F = \text{VMULL}(A_1, B)$ in the tq register. Lines 3 and 4 compute B_1 and then $E = \text{VMULL}(A, B_1)$ in the uq register, while line 5 computes $L = E + F$ in the tq register. Observe that the result we want, $(P_0 + P_1)$, can be viewed as $(0, \ell_6, \ell_5, \ell_4, \ell_3 + \ell_7, \ell_2, \ell_1, \ell_0)$. The straightforward way to compute $(P_0 + P_1)$ from L would be to use a mask operation to isolate ℓ_7, xor it to tq in the appropriate position and do another mask operation to clear the highest 16 bits. However, we use another approach

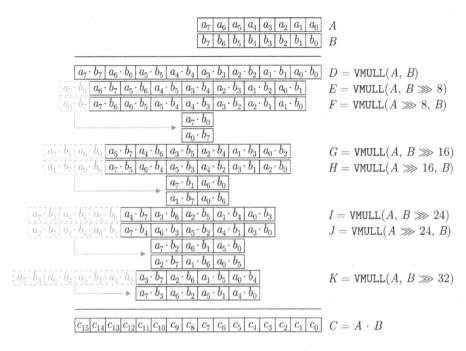

Fig. 2. The 64×64-bit polynomial multiplier using VMULL

which does not need a temporary register, described as follows. In line 6, we xor the higher part of tq into the lower part, obtaining $(\ell_7, \ell_6, \ell_5, \ell_4, \ell_3 + \ell_7, \ell_2 + \ell_6, \ell_1 + \ell_5, \ell_0 + \ell_4)$. Line 7 uses a mask operation to clear the higher 16 bits of tq, which now holds $(0, \ell_6, \ell_5, \ell_4, \ell_3 + \ell_7, \ell_2 + \ell_6, \ell_1 + \ell_5, \ell_0 + \ell_4)$. In line 8, the higher part of tq is again xored into the lower part, resulting in the expected $(0, \ell_6, \ell_5, \ell_4, \ell_3 + \ell_7, \ell_2, \ell_1, \ell_0)$ which is finally shifted 8 bits to the left with the VEXT instruction in line 9.

3.2 Additional Binary Field Operations

Squaring a binary polynomial corresponds to inserting a 0 bit between every consecutive bits of the input, which often requires precomputed tables. The VMULL instruction can improve squaring since, when using the same 64-bit value as the two operands, it computes the 128-bit polynomial square of that value.

Multiplication and squaring of binary polynomials produce values of degree at most $2m - 2$, which must be reduced modulo $f(z) = z^m + r(z)$. Since $z^m \equiv r(z)$ (mod $f(z)$), the usual approach is to multiply the upper part by $r(z)$ using shift and xors. For small polynomials $r(z)$ it is possible to use the VMULL instruction to carry out multiplication by $r(z)$ with a special 8×64-bit multiplier; this was done for $\mathbb{F}_{2^{128}}$ ($r(z) = z^7 + z^2 + z + 1$) and $\mathbb{F}_{2^{251}}$ ($r(z) = z^7 + z^4 + z^2 + 1$). Reduction in $\mathbb{F}_{2^{283}}$ takes advantage of the factorization of $r(z) = z^{12} + z^7 + z^5 + 1 = (z^7 + 1)(z^5 + 1)$ as described in [2]. For $\mathbb{F}_{2^{571}}$, $r(z) = z^{10} + z^5 + z^2 + 1$, and its reduction is computed with the usual shifts and xors.

Algorithm 1. Computation of L and $(P_0 + P_1) \ll 8$ from A and B

Input: 64-bit registers ad (holding A), bd (holding B) and k48 (holding the constant 0x0000FFFFFFFFFFFF)

Output: 128-bit register tq (th|tl) (holding $(P_0 + P_1) \ll 8$)

```
1: vext.8    tl, ad, ad, $1
2: vmull.p8  tq, tl, bd
3: vext.8    ul, bd, bd, $1
4: vmull.p8  uq, ad, ul
5: veor      tq, tq, uq
6: veor      tl, tl, th
7: vand      th, th, k48
8: veor      tl, tl, th
9: vext.8    tq, tq, tq, $15
```

Field inversion is commonly carried out with the well-known extended Euclidean algorithm, but it does not take constant time and may be vulnerable to side channel attacks. For this reason, we have used the Itoh-Tsujii algorithm [10], which is an optimization of inversion through Fermat's little theorem $(a(x)^{-1} = a(x)^{2^m - 2})$. The algorithm uses a repeated field squaring operation $a(x)^{2^k}$ for some values of k; we have implemented a special function where field squaring is completely done using NEON instruction and registers using the same techniques described for squaring and reduction, but avoiding reads and writes to memory.

4 Algorithms

The KNV multiplier was used as the building block for a implementation of Elliptic Curve Cryptography (ECC) and of authenticated encryption (AE), which we now describe together with our implementation of side-channel resistance.

4.1 Side-channel Resistance

Side-channel attacks [12] are a serious threat for cryptographic implementations; different attacks require different levels of protection. Here we consider the basic level of resistance which avoids: branching on secret data, algorithms with timings dependent on secret data, and accessing table indexes with secret indices.

The building block of a side-channel resistant (SCR) implementation can be considered the "select" operation $t \leftarrow \text{SELECT}(a, b, v)$, which copies a into t if the bit v is 0 or copies b if v is 1. This operation can be implemented without branching as described in [14] and listed for reference in Algorithm 3 in the Appendix. In ARM assembly, SELECT can be implemented easily since most instructions can be made conditional to a previous register comparison. However, a faster approach is to use the NEON instruction VBIT Qd, Qn, Qm (bitwise insert if false) — it inserts each bit in Qn into Qd if the corresponding bit in Qm is 1, otherwise it leaves the corresponding bit in Qd unchanged. If the m value from Algorithm 3 is stored in Qm, then VBIT is precisely the SELECT operation restricted to the case where t and a refer to the same location (which is often the case).

Some of the algorithms we will describe use precomputed tables to improve performance. However, looking up a table entry may leak its index through side-channels, since it affects the contents of the processor cache. For this reason, we employ a side-channel resistant table lookup. We follow the strategy found in the source code of [6], listed for reference in Algorithm 4 in the Appendix, where s can be computed without branches by copying the sign bit of r (e.g. in the C language, convert r to unsigned and right shift the result in order to get the highest bit). We have implemented the SCR table lookup for elliptic curve points entirely in assembly with the VBIT instruction. It is possible to hold the entire t value (a point) in NEON registers, without any memory writes except for the final result.

4.2 Elliptic Curve Cryptography

Elliptic Curve Cryptography is composed of public key cryptographic schemes using the arithmetic of points on elliptic curves over finite fields, and it uses shorter keys at the same security level in comparison to alternative public-key systems such as RSA and DSA. Two types of fields are mainly used: prime fields (with p elements, where p is prime) and binary fields (with 2^m elements for some m). While prime fields are used more often (and most literature on ECC for ARM uses them), we decided to study the efficiency of ECC using binary fields with our KNV multiplier.

Four standardized curves for Elliptic Curve Cryptography (ECC) [21] were implemented: the random curves B-283 and B-571 which provide 128 and 256 bits of security respectively; and the Koblitz curves K-283 and K-571 which provide the same bits of security respectively. A non-standard curve over $\mathbb{F}_{2^{251}}$ [5] ("B-251", roughly 128 bits of security) was also implemented, due to its high efficiency.

The main algorithm in ECC is the point multiplication, which often appears in three different cases: the random point multiplication kP (k terms of the elliptic point P are summed), where the point P is not known in advance; the fixed point multiplication kG, where G is fixed; and the simultaneous point multiplication $kP + \ell G$ where P is random and G is fixed. In the random point case, we chose the Montgomery-LD multiplication [16] which offers high efficiency and basic side-channel resistance (SCR) without precomputed tables. In the fixed point case, the signed multi-table Comb method is employed [9], with side-channel resistant table lookups. It uses t tables with 2^{w-1} points. For simultaneous point multiplication, we have used the interleaving method [8,18] of w-(T)NAF. It employs two window sizes: d for the fixed point (requiring a precomputed table with 2^{d-2} elements) and w for the random point (requiring a on-the-fly table with 2^{w-2} elements). SCR is not required in this case since the algorithm is only used for signature verification, whose inputs are public.

The main advantage of Koblitz curves is the existence of specialized algorithms for point multiplication which take advantage of the efficient endomorphism τ present in those curves [24]. However, we have not used these algorithms since we are not aware of any SCR methods for recoding the scalar k into the representation required by them. Therefore, the only performance gain in those curves were obtained using a special doubling formula with two field multiplications; see Algorithm 2. Montgomery-LD also requires one less multiplication per iteration in Koblitz curves.

Algorithm 2. Our proposed point doubling on the Koblitz curve $E_a\colon y^2 + xy = x^3 + ax^2 + 1$, $a \in \{0,1\}$ over $\mathbb{F}_{2^m}$ using LD projective coordinates

Input: Point $P = (X_1, Y_1, Z_1) \in E_a(\mathbb{F}_{2^m})$
Output: Point $Q = (X_3, Y_3, Z_3) = 2P$
1: $S \leftarrow X_1 Z_1$
2: $T \leftarrow (X_1 + Z_1)^2$
3: $X_3 \leftarrow T^2$
4: $Z_3 \leftarrow S^2$
5: **if** $a = 0$ **then**
6:     $Y_3 \leftarrow ((Y_1 + T)(Y_1 + S) + Z_3)^2$
7: **else**
8:     $Y_3 \leftarrow (Y_1(Y_1 + S + T))^2$
9: **return** (X_3, Y_3, Z_3)

We have selected the three following well known ECC protocols. The Elliptic Curve Digital Signature Algorithm (ECDSA) requires a fixed point multiplication for signing and a simultaneous point multiplication for verification. The Elliptic Curve Diffie-Hellman (ECDH) [4] is a key agreement scheme which requires a random point multiplication, and the Elliptic Curve Schnorr Signature (ECSS) [23] is similar to ECDSA but does not require an inversion modulo the elliptic curve order.

4.3   Inversion Modulo the Elliptic Curve Order

When signing, the ECDSA generates a random secret value k which is multiplied by the generator point; this requires side-channel resistance since if k leaks then it is possible to compute the signer's private key. However, an often overlooked point is that ECDSA also requires the inversion of k modulo the elliptic curve order n. This is usually carried out with the extended Euclidean algorithm, whose number of steps are input-dependent and therefore theoretically susceptible to side-channel attacks. While we are not aware of any concrete attacks exploiting this issue, we are also not aware of any arguments for the impossibility of such an attack. Therefore, we believe it is safer to use a SCR inversion.

The obvious approach for SCR inversion would be to use Fermat's little theorem ($a^{-1} \equiv a^{n-2} \pmod{n}$), which would require a very fast multiplier modulo

n to be efficient. However, we have found a simple variant of the binary extended Euclidean algorithm by Niels Möller [19] which takes a fixed number of steps. For reference, it is described in Algorithm 5 in the Appendix, where branches are used for clarity and can be avoided with SELECT. The algorithm is built entirely upon four operations over integers with the same size as n: addition, subtraction, negation and right shift by one bit. These can be implemented in assembly for speed; alternatively the whole algorithm can be implemented in assembly in order to avoid reads and writes by keeping operands (a, b, u and v) in NEON registers. We have followed the latter approach for fields at the 128-bit level of security, and the former approach for the 256-bit level, since the operands are then too big to fit in registers.

Interestingly, implementing this algorithm raised a few issues with NEON. The right shift and SELECT can be implemented efficiently using NEON; however, we had to resort to regular ARM instructions for addition and subtraction, since it is difficult to handle carries with NEON. This requires moving data back and forth from NEON to ARM registers; which can be costly. In the Cortex A8, since the NEON pipeline starts after the ARM pipeline, a move from NEON to ARM causes a 15+ cycles stall. The obvious approach to mitigate this would be to move from NEON to ARM beforehand, but this is difficult due to the limited number of ARM registers. Our approach was then to partially revert to storing operands in memory since it becomes faster to read from cached memory than to move data between NEON and ARM. In the Cortex A9 we followed the same approach, but with smaller gains, since the ARM and NEON pipelines are partly parallel and moving from NEON to ARM is not that costly (around 4 cycles of latency). However, the Cortex A15 is much more optimized in this sense and our original approach of keeping operands in registers was faster.

4.4 Authenticated Encryption

An authenticated encryption (AE) symmetric scheme provides both encryption and authentication using a single key, and is often more efficient and easy to employ than using two separate encryption and authentication schemes (e.g. AES-CTR with HMAC). The Galois/Counter Mode (GCM) [17] is an AE scheme which is built upon a block cipher, usually AES. It was standardized by NIST and is used in IPSec, SSH and TLS. For each message block, GCM encrypts it using the underlying block cipher in CTR mode and xors the ciphertext into an accumulator, which is then multiplied in $\mathbb{F}_{2^{128}}$ by a key-dependent constant. After processing the last block, this accumulator is used to generate the authentication tag.

We have implemented the $\mathbb{F}_{2^{128}}$ multiplication using the same techniques described above; modular reduction took advantage of the VMULL instruction since $r(z)$ in this field is small. We remark that our implementation does not uses precomputed tables (as it is often required for GCM) and is side-channel resistant (if the underlying block cipher also is). For benchmarking, we have used an assembly implementation of AES from OpenSSL without SCR; however this is not an issue since we are more interested in the overhead added by GCM to the plain AES encryption.

5   Results

To evaluate our software implementation, we have used a DevKit8000 board with an 600 MHz ARM Cortex-A8 processor, a PandaBoard board with a 1 GHz ARM Cortex-A9 processor and an Arndale board with a 1.7 GHz ARM Cortex-A15 processor. We have used the GCC 4.5.1 compiler. Our optimized code is written in the C and assembly languages using the RELIC library [1]. Each function is benchmarked with two nested loops with n iterations each; inside the outer loop, an input is randomly generated; and the given operation is executed n times in the inner loop using this input. The total time taken by this procedure, given by the clock_gettime function in nanoseconds, is divided by n^2 in order to give the final result for the given operation. We chose $n = 1024$ for measuring fast operations such as finite field arithmetic, and $n = 64$ for the slower operations such as point multiplication.

Table 1 presents the timings of field operations used in ECC. Our new Karatsuba/NEON/VMULL (KNV) multiplication gives a up to 45% improvement compared to the LD/NEON implementation. For field squaring, we have obtained a significant improvement of up to 70% compared to the conventional table lookup approach. The very fast squaring made the Itoh-Tsujii inversion feasible.

Timings for ECC protocols are listed in Table 2, while Figure 3 plots the 128-bit level timings to aid visualization. Compared to the LD/NEON multiplier

Table 1. Our timings in cycles for binary field arithmetic

Algorithm/Processor		$\mathbb{F}_{2^{251}}$	$\mathbb{F}_{2^{283}}$	$\mathbb{F}_{2^{571}}$
Multiplication (LD)	A8	671	1,032	3,071
	A9	774	1,208	3,140
	A15	412	595	1,424
Multiplication (KNV)	A8	385	558	1,506
	A9	491	701	1,889
	A15	317	446	1,103
Squaring (Table)	A8	155	179	349
	A9	168	197	394
	A15	128	151	282
Squaring (VMULL)	A8	57	53	126
	A9	63	59	146
	A15	43	42	99
Inversion (Itoh-Tsujii)	A8	18,190	20,777	90,936
	A9	19,565	22,356	97,913
	A15	13,709	16,803	71,220

Table 2. Our timings in 10^3 cycles for elliptic curve protocols

Algorithm/Processor		B-251	B-283	K-283	B-571	K-571
ECDH Agreement	A8	657	1,097	934	5,731	4,870
	A9	789	1,350	1,148	7,094	6,018
	A15	511	866	736	4,242	3,603
ECDSA Sign	A8	458	624	606	2,770	2,673
	A9	442	612	602	2,880	2,816
	A15	233	337	330	1,740	1,688
ECSS Sign	A8	270	389	371	1,944	1,846
	A9	285	414	404	2,137	2,073
	A15	186	270	263	1,264	1,212
ECDSA Verify	A8	943	1,397	791	6,673	3,069
	A9	1,100	1,644	887	8,171	3,581
	A15	715	1,064	583	4,882	2,237
ECSS Verify	A8	933	1,337	735	6,338	3,064
	A9	1,086	1,572	827	7,776	3,602
	A15	715	1,022	546	4,623	2,228

with table-based squaring, the KNV multiplication with VMULL-based squaring improved the point multiplication by up to 50%. ECDSA is 25–70% slower than ECSS due to the SCR modular inversion required.

When limited to standard NIST elliptic curves, our ECDH over K-283 is 70% faster than the results of Morozov et al. [20]. Considering non-standard curves, we now compare our binary B-251 to the prime curves in the state of the art; this is also shown in Table 3. On the A8, compared to Bernstein and Schwabe's [6], our key agreement is 25% slower; our signing is 26% faster; and our verification is 43% slower. On the A9, compared to Faz-Hernández et al. [7], our random point multiplication is 88% slower, our fixed point multiplication is 53% slower; and our simultaneous point multiplication is 132% slower. On the A15, also compared to Faz-Hernández et al. [7], our random point multiplication is 108% slower, our fixed point multiplication is 72% slower; and our simultaneous point multiplication is 162% slower. We remark that this is a comparison of our implementation of binary elliptic curves with the state-of-the-art prime elliptic curve implementations, which are very different. In particular, note that the arithmetic of prime curves can take advantage of native 32×32-bit and 64×64-bit multiply instructions.

For the GCM authenticated encryption scheme, we have obtained 38.6, 41.9 and 31.1 cycles per byte for large messages, for the A8, A9 and A15 respectively; a 13.7, 13.6 and 9.2 cpb overhead to AES-CTR. Our A8 overhead is 46% faster than the timing reported by Krovetz and Rogaway's [13] and 8.6% faster than [22].

It is interesting to compare the timings across Cortex processors. The A9 results are often slower than the A8 results: while the A9 improved performance

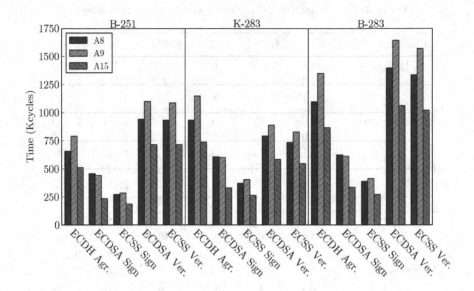

Fig. 3. Our timings for ECC algorithms at the 128-bit level of security

Table 3. Our best ECC timings (on the non-standard elliptic curve B-251 over binary field) compared to state-of-the-art timings using non-standard elliptic curves over prime fields, at the 128-bit level of security, in 10^3 cycles

Algorithm/Processor		Ours	[6]	[9]	[7]
Key Agreement	A8	657	527		
	A9	789		616	417
	A15	511			244
Sign	A8	270	368		
	A9	285		262	172
	A15	186			100
Verify	A8	933	650		
	A9	1,086		605	463
	A15	715			266

of regular ARM code, the lack of partial dual issue in NEON caused a visible drop in performance in NEON-based code, which is our case. (The exception is ECDSA signing where the A8 currently does not have much advantage in the modular inversion, which dilutes any savings in the point multiplication.) On the other hand, the return and expansion of NEON dual issue in A15 caused great performance gains (up to 40%).

6 Conclusions and Future Work

In this paper we have introduced a new multiplier for 64-bit binary polynomial multiplication using the VMULL instruction, part of the NEON engine present in many ARM processors in the Cortex-A series. We then explain how to use the new multiplier to improve the performance of finite field multiplication in $\mathbb{F}_{2^m}$. We have also shown the performance gains by the new multiplier in elliptic curve cryptography and authenticated encryption with GCM. We were unable to break speed records for non-standard elliptic curves, but we believe this work offers a useful insight in how binary curves compare to prime curves in ARM processors. For standard curves we were able to improve the state of the art, as well for the GCM authenticated encryption scheme.

An interesting venue for future research is on the implementation of standard prime curves for ARM, which seems to be lacking in the literature. In addition, the arrival of ARMv8 processors in the future (including the Cortex A53 and A57) may provide great speed up to binary ECC, since the architecture will provide two instructions for the full 64-bit binary multiplier (PMULL and PMULL2) and will double the number of NEON registers [3].

References

1. Aranha, D.F., Gouvêa, C.P.L.: RELIC is an Efficient LIbrary for Cryptography, http://code.google.com/p/relic-toolkit/
2. Aranha, D.F., Faz-Hernández, A., López, J., Rodríguez-Henríquez, F.: Faster implementation of scalar multiplication on Koblitz curves. In: Hevia, A., Neven, G. (eds.) LatinCrypt 2012. LNCS, vol. 7533, pp. 177–193. Springer, Heidelberg (2012)
3. ARM Limited: ARMv8 instruction set overview (2012)
4. Barker, E., Johnson, D., Smid, M.: NIST SP 800-56A: Recommendation for pairwise key establishment schemes using discrete logarithm cryptography (March 2007)
5. Bernstein, D.J.: Batch binary Edwards. In: Halevi, S. (ed.) CRYPTO 2009. LNCS, vol. 5677, pp. 317–336. Springer, Heidelberg (2009)
6. Bernstein, D.J., Schwabe, P.: NEON crypto. In: Prouff, E., Schaumont, P. (eds.) CHES 2012. LNCS, vol. 7428, pp. 320–339. Springer, Heidelberg (2012)
7. Faz-Hernández, A., Longa, P., Sánchez, A.H.: Efficient and secure algorithms for GLV-based scalar multiplication and their implementation on GLV-GLS curves. Cryptology ePrint Archive, Report 2013/158 (2013), http://eprint.iacr.org/
8. Gallant, R.P., Lambert, R.J., Vanstone, S.A.: Faster point multiplication on elliptic curves with efficient endomorphisms. In: Kilian, J. (ed.) CRYPTO 2001. LNCS, vol. 2139, pp. 190–200. Springer, Heidelberg (2001)
9. Hamburg, M.: Fast and compact elliptic-curve cryptography. Cryptology ePrint Archive, Report 2012/309 (2012), http://eprint.iacr.org/
10. Itoh, T., Tsujii, S.: A fast algorithm for computing multiplicative inverses in $GF(2^m)$ using normal bases. Information and Computation 78(3), 171–177 (1988)
11. Karatsuba, A., Ofman, Y.: Multiplication of multidigit numbers on automata. Soviet Physics Doklady 7, 595 (1963)

12. Kocher, P.C.: Timing attacks on implementations of Diffie-hellman, RSA, DSS, and other systems. In: Koblitz, N. (ed.) CRYPTO 1996. LNCS, vol. 1109, pp. 104–113. Springer, Heidelberg (1996), http://dx.doi.org/10.1007/3-540-68697-5_9

13. Krovetz, T., Rogaway, P.: The software performance of authenticated-encryption modes. In: Joux, A. (ed.) FSE 2011. LNCS, vol. 6733, pp. 306–327. Springer, Heidelberg (2011)

14. Käsper, E.: Fast elliptic curve cryptography in OpenSSL. In: Danezis, G., Dietrich, S., Sako, K. (eds.) FC 2011 Workshops. LNCS, vol. 7126, pp. 27–39. Springer, Heidelberg (2012)

15. López, J., Dahab, R.: High-speed software multiplication in $\mathbb{F}_{2^m}$. In: Roy, B., Okamoto, E. (eds.) INDOCRYPT 2000. LNCS, vol. 1977, pp. 203–212. Springer, Heidelberg (2000)

16. López, J., Dahab, R.: Fast multiplication on elliptic curves over $GF(2^m)$ without precomputation. In: Koç, Ç.K., Paar, C. (eds.) CHES 1999. LNCS, vol. 1717, pp. 316–327. Springer, Heidelberg (1999)

17. McGrew, D.A., Viega, J.: The Security and Performance of the Galois/Counter Mode (GCM) of Operation. In: Canteaut, A., Viswanathan, K. (eds.) INDOCRYPT 2004. LNCS, vol. 3348, pp. 343–355. Springer, Heidelberg (2004)

18. Möller, B.: Algorithms for multi-exponentiation. In: Vaudenay, S., Youssef, A.M. (eds.) SAC 2001. LNCS, vol. 2259, pp. 165–180. Springer, Heidelberg (2001)

19. Möller, N.: Nettle, low-level cryptographics library. Nettle Git repository (2013), http://git.lysator.liu.se/nettle/nettle/blobs/ 9422a55130ba65f73a053f063efa6226f945b4f1/sec-modinv.c#line67

20. Morozov, S., Tergino, C., Schaumont, P.: System integration of elliptic curve cryptography on an OMAP platform. In: 2011 IEEE 9th Symposium on Application Specific Processors (SASP), pp. 52–57. IEEE (2011)

21. National Institute of Standards and Technology: FIPS 186-3: Digital signature standard (DSS) (June 2009), http://www.itl.nist.gov

22. Polyakov, A.: The OpenSSL project. OpenSSL Git repository (2013), http://git.openssl.org/gitweb/?p=openssl.git;a=blob;f=crypto/modes/ asm/ghash-armv4.pl;h=d91586ee2925bb695899b17bb8a7242aa3bf9150; hb=9575d1a91ad9dd6eb5c964365dfbb72dbd3d1333#135

23. Schnorr, C.P.: Efficient signature generation by smart cards. Journal of Cryptology 4(3), 161–174 (1991)

24. Solinas, J.A.: Efficient arithmetic on Koblitz curves. Designs, Codes and Cryptography 19(2), 195–249 (2000)

A   Reference Algorithms

Listed below are algorithms for reference and the full code of our multiplier.

Algorithm 3. Branchless select, described by Emilia Käsper in [14]

Input: W-bit words a, b, v, with $v \in \{0, 1\}$
Output: b if v, else a
1: **function** SELECT(a, b, v)
2:     $m \leftarrow$ TWOSCOMPLEMENT($-v, W$)   ▷ convert $-v$ to W-bit two's complement
3:     $t \leftarrow (m \mathrel{\&} (a \oplus b)) \oplus a$
4:     **return** t

Algorithm 4. SCR table lookup, contained in the source code of Bernstein and Schwabe's [6]

Input: array a with n elements of any fixed type, desired index k, $0 \leq k < n$
Output: $a[k]$
1: **function** CHOOSE(a, n, k)
2:     $t \leftarrow a[0]$
3:     **for** $i \leftarrow 1$ **to** $n - 1$ **do**
4:         $r \leftarrow (i \oplus k) - 1$
5:         $s \leftarrow (r < 0)$ ▷ s holds whether i is equal to k
6:         $t \leftarrow$ SELECT($t, a[i], s$)
7:     **return** t

Algorithm 5. SCR modular inversion algorithm by Niels Möller in the Nettle library [19]

Input: integer x, odd integer n, $x < n$
Output: $x^{-1} \pmod{n}$
1: **function** MODINV(x, n)
2:     $(a, b, u, v) \leftarrow (x, n, 1, 1)$
3:     $\ell \leftarrow \lfloor \log_2 n \rfloor + 1$ ▷ number of bits in n
4:     **for** $i \leftarrow 0$ **to** $2\ell - 1$ **do**
5:         odd $\leftarrow a \mathrel{\&} 1$
6:         **if** odd **and** $a \geq b$ **then**
7:             $a \leftarrow a - b$
8:         **else if** odd **and** $a < b$ **then**
9:             $(a, b, u, v) \leftarrow (b - a, a, v, u)$
10:         $a \leftarrow a \gg 1$
11:         **if** odd **then** $u \leftarrow u - v$
12:         **if** $u < 0$ **then** $u \leftarrow u + n$
13:         **if** $u \mathrel{\&} 1$ **then** $u \leftarrow u + n$
14:         $u \leftarrow u \gg 1$
15:     **return** v

Algorithm 6. Our proposed ARM NEON 64-bit binary multiplication $C = A \cdot B$ with 128-bit result

---

Input: 64-bit registers ad (holding A), bd (holding B), k16 (holding the constant 0xFFFF), k32 (holding 0xFFFFFFFF), k48 (holding the constant 0xFFFFFFFFFFFF).

Output: 128-bit register rq (rh|rl) (holding A).

Uses temporary 128-bit registers t0q (t0h|t0l), t1q (t1h|t1l), t2q (t2h|t2l), t3q (t3h|t3l).

```
 1: vext.8    t0l, ad, ad, $1                              ▷ A1
 2: vmull.p8  t0q, t0l, bd                          ▷ F = A1*B
 3: vext.8    rl, bd, bd, $1                               ▷ B1
 4: vmull.p8  rq, ad, rl                            ▷ E = A*B1
 5: vext.8    t1l, ad, ad, $2                              ▷ A2
 6: vmull.p8  t1q, t1l, bd                          ▷ H = A2*B
 7: vext.8    t3l, bd, bd, $2                              ▷ B2
 8: vmull.p8  t3q, ad, t3l                          ▷ G = A*B2
 9: vext.8    t2l, ad, ad, $3                              ▷ A3
10: vmull.p8  t2q, t2l, bd                          ▷ J = A3*B
11: veor      t0q, t0q, rq                          ▷ L = E + F
12: vext.8    rl, bd, bd, $3                               ▷ B3
13: vmull.p8  rq, ad, rl                            ▷ I = A*B3
14: veor      t1q, t1q, t3q                         ▷ M = G + H
15: vext.8    t3l, bd, bd, $4                              ▷ B4
16: vmull.p8  t3q, ad, t3l                          ▷ K = A*B4
17: veor      t0l, t0l, t0h          ▷ t0 = (L) (P0 + P1) << 8
18: vand      t0h, t0h, k48
19: veor      t1l, t1l, t1h         ▷ t1 = (M) (P2 + P3) << 16
20: vand      t1h, t1h, k32
21: veor      t2q, t2q, rq                  ▷ N = I + J
22: veor      t0l, t0l, t0h
23: veor      t1l, t1l, t1h
24: veor      t2l, t2l, t2h         ▷ t2 = (N) (P4 + P5) << 24
25: vand      t2h, t2h, k16
26: veor      t3l, t3l, t3h         ▷ t3 = (K) (P6 + P7) << 32
27: vmov.i64  t3h, $0
28: vext.8    t0q, t0q, t0q, $15
29: veor      t2l, t2l, t2h
30: vext.8    t1q, t1q, t1q, $14
31: vmull.p8  rq, ad, bd                            ▷ D = A*B
32: vext.8    t2q, t2q, t2q, $13
33: vext.8    t3q, t3q, t3q, $12
34: veor      t0q, t0q, t1q
35: veor      t2q, t2q, t3q
36: veor      rq, rq, t0q
37: veor      rq, rq, t2q
```

Improving the Efficiency of Elliptic Curve Scalar Multiplication Using Binary Huff Curves

Gerwin Gsenger and Christian Hanser

Institute for Applied Information Processing and Communications (IAIK),
Graz University of Technology (TUG), Inffeldgasse 16a, 8010 Graz, Austria
gerwin.gsenger@student.tugraz.at, christian.hanser@iaik.tugraz.at

Abstract. In 2010, Joye et. al brought the so-called Huff curve model, which was originally proposed in 1948 for the studies of diophantine equations, into the context of elliptic curve cryptography. Their initial work describes Huff curves over fields of large prime characteristic and details unified addition laws. Devigne and Joye subsequently extended the model to elliptic curves over binary fields and proposed fast differential addition formulas that are well-suited for use with the Montgomery ladder, which is a side-channel attack resistant scalar multiplication algorithm. Moreover, they showed that, in contrast to Huff curves over prime fields, it is possible to convert (almost) all binary Weierstrass curves into Huff form.

We have implemented generalized binary Huff curves in software using a differential Montgomery ladder and detail the implementation as well as the optimizations to it. We provide timings, which show speed-ups of up to 7.4% for binary NIST curves in Huff form compared to the reference implementation on Weierstrass curves. Furthermore, we present fast formulas for mapping between binary Weierstrass and generalized binary Huff curves and vice versa, where in the back conversion step an implicit y-coordinate recovery is performed. With these formulas, the implementation of the differential Montgomery ladder on Huff curves does not require more effort than its counterpart on Weierstrass curves. Thus, given the performance gains discussed in this paper, such an implementation is an interesting alternative to conventional implementations. Finally, we give a list of Huff curve parameters corresponding to the binary NIST curves specified in FIPS 186-3.

1 Introduction

In 1985, Neal Koblitz [10] and Victor S. Miller [14] both discovered independently that elliptic curves over finite fields can be used for public key cryptography. By now, elliptic curves have become an important concept within public key cryptography. This is mainly due to small key sizes compared to other public key cryptosystems, such as RSA, which lower the requirements for CPUs as well as the memory footprint. Elliptic curves have a group structure and their cryptographic security relies on the difficulty of solving the elliptic curve discrete logarithm problem (ECDLP). Traditionally, Weierstrass equations have been

A. Cuzzocrea et al. (Eds.): CD-ARES 2013 Workshops, LNCS 8128, pp. 155–167, 2013.

used to describe elliptic curves. Nevertheless, over time, especially in the last couple of decades, new models to describe elliptic curves have been found, such as the Montgomery form, the Edwards form [2] and the like.

In 1948, Huff was studying a diophantine problem, for which he introduced a new elliptic curve model [8]. In 2010, Joye et. al [9], studied Huff's model over fields of odd characteristic and introduced formulas for fast point arithmetics. Each Huff curve defined over $\mathbb{F}_p$ contains a subgroup isomorphic to $\mathbb{Z}_4 \times \mathbb{Z}_2$ which, unfortunately, implies that there are no standardized prime curves that can be expressed in Huff form, as all these curves have cofactors equal to one. The Huff model has subsequently been extended by Devigne and Joye [5] to cover elliptic curves defined over binary fields $\mathbb{F}_{2^m}$. Furthermore, in [5], they present a unified addition law and give very fast differential addition formulas for binary Huff curves, which are well-suited for use with the Montgomery ladder, which is a side-channel attack resistant scalar multiplication algorithm.

For $m \geq 4$, every Weierstrass curve over $\mathbb{F}_{2^m}$ is birationally equivalent to a generalized Huff curve. Therefore, we are free to convert all standardized binary curves into corresponding (generalized) binary Huff curves. The authors of [5], give formulas for mapping points between binary Weierstrass curves and binary Huff curves, using an intermediate Weierstrass curve isomorphic to the original curve in short Weierstrass form.

1.1   Contribution

We have implemented generalized binary Huff curves in software, where for scalar multiplication we use a differential Montgomery ladder, which is a good choice for software implementations running in server environments, as it is resistant to remote timing attacks [4,3,18]. The differential Montgomery ladder is based on the differential addition formulas given by Devigne and Joye in [5]. The timings show that for the binary NIST curves, this implementation is up to 7.4% faster than the reference implementation of the differential Montgomery ladder on the original Weierstrass curves, to which we have applied the same optimizations.

The conversion between binary Weierstrass and generalized binary Huff curves requires two steps. As generalized binary Huff curves are birationally equivalent to a class of Weierstrass curves, which are themselves isomorphic to curves in short Weierstrass form, it is necessary to apply a birational equivalence as well as an isomorphism for the conversion. Additionally, after applying the differential Montgomery ladder on binary Huff curves and mapping the result back to the corresponding Weierstrass curve, a y-coordinate recovery is necessary. We address this issue by providing fast all-in-one, back-and-forth conversion formulas. These back-and-forth conversions turn out to be almost as efficient as the y-coordinate recovery on Weierstrass curves, which is required anyway after using the differential Montgomery ladder on Weierstrass curves, which preserves most of the savings obtained through the faster differential addition formulas. When using the formulas presented in this paper, the implementation of the differential Montgomery ladder on Huff curves does not require more effort than its counterpart on Weierstrass curves. Thus, given the performance gains discussed in this paper such an implementation is an interesting alternative to conventional implementations.

Finally, we present curve parameters for Huff curves, which are birationally equivalent to the NIST-recommended binary Weierstrass curves specified in FIPS 186-3 [6].

1.2 Outline

In Section 2 and 3 we are going to talk about elliptic curves in general and the Huff curve model in particular. Section 4 gives the Huff curve parameters we have derived for the NIST-recommended curves. It details the implementation, the improvements we have achieved, shows the benchmark results and draws a comparison to the reference implementation. At last, Section 5 concludes the paper.

2 Preliminaries

An elliptic curve over the field $\mathbb{K}$ is a plane, smooth curve described by the Weierstrass equation:

$$E : Y^2 + a'_1 XY + a'_3 Y = X^3 + a'_2 X^2 + a'_4 X + a'_6, \tag{1}$$

where $a'_1, a'_2, a'_3, a'_4, a'_6 \in \mathbb{K}$. The set $E(\mathbb{K})$ of points $(x, y) \in \mathbb{K}^2$ satisfying Equation (1) plus the point at infinity $\mathcal{O} = (0 : 1 : 0)$, which is the neutral element, forms an additive Abelian group. The addition of points on an elliptic curve is achieved using the *chord-and-tangent* method [16].

For cryptographic purposes, we are interested in elliptic curves over finite fields $\mathbb{F}_q$, especially in curves over fields $\mathbb{F}_{2^m}$ and $\mathbb{F}_p$ with p being a large prime number. The security of elliptic curve cryptography is based on the assumption that in general there is no subexponential-time algorithm to solve the discrete logarithm problem in elliptic curve groups (ECDLP). Given $Q, P \in E(\mathbb{F}_q)$ the ECDLP constitutes the problem of finding a scalar $k \in \mathbb{Z}$ such that $Q = k \cdot P$.

In cryptography, usually non-supersingular curves are being used, as supersingular curves turned out to be susceptible to the MOV attack [13], which reduces the ECDLP to the DLP on finite fields, for which an efficient subexponential-time algorithm is known. Non-supersingular curves defined over $\mathbb{F}_{2^m}$, are described using the following short form of Equation (1):

$$Y^2 + XY = X^3 + a_2 X^2 + a_6, \tag{2}$$

where $a_2, a_6 \in \mathbb{F}_{2^m}$ and $a_6 \neq 0$.

For binary field multiplications we are using the windowed left-to-right comb multiplier as detailed in [7]. This algorithm uses lookup-tables, which can be cached and reused to speed up multiplications with frequently used values, such as curve parameters. In the following, let **M** and **S** denote the costs of one field multiplication and one field squaring, respectively. Moreover, let $\mathbf{m_w}$ stand for the cost of the multiplication with some value, for which the lookup table of window size w has already been calculated.

2.1   Differential Addition and the Montgomery Ladder

Scalar multiplication is the most crucial and at the same time the most costly operation on elliptic curves and there are many ways to perform elliptic curve scalar multiplications. One way to do so is the so-called Montgomery ladder, which is both side-channel resistant and reasonably fast. Its side-channel resistance is due to the fact that at each ladder step, regardless of the currently processed bit of the scalar k, one point doubling operation as well as one point addition operation are performed and only the order of execution is changed. Thus, in order to mitigate side-channel attacks, the Montgomery ladder is widely used, especially in hardware implementations. In the context of software implementations, side-channel resistance is less important. Still, there are scenarios, such as cryptographic implementations running on servers, where remote timing attacks can be performed (cf. [4,3,18]) and, therefore, timing-attack proof implementations are required. This issue can again be addressed with the use of the Montgomery ladder, as its execution time is constant for fixed scalar lengths.

For the fast application of the Montgomery ladder, differential addition and doubling formulas are necessary. Luckily, these two operations can be performed very efficiently on Huff curves. By *differential point addition*, we mean the computation of $w(P + Q)$ from $w(P)$, $w(Q)$, and $w(P - Q)$, where $w(\cdot)$ is a coordinate function for which typically $w(P) = w(-P)$ is demanded. Note that the difference $w(P - Q)$ required for the differential addition steps within the Montgomery ladder is fixed, i.e., the difference of the resulting points stays invariant throughout the whole process. For differential addition on Weierstrass curves, the knowledge of y-coordinates is irrelevant, as the computation of x-coordinates does not involve them, which is reflected in the definition of $w(\cdot)$. Clearly, this saves computational effort, as the y-coordinate of intermediate results is not computed. Analogously, we mean by differential doubling the computation of $w(2P)$ from $w(P)$.

On Weierstrass curves, the fastest differential addition formulas are due to Bernstein and Lange (see [1]). From the results of Stam [17], they derive a representation, called XZ-coordinates, featuring fast differential addition and doubling formulas. Per bit of scalar k, these formulas require $\mathbf{5M + 1m_8 + 4S}$ for P known a priori and $\mathbf{6M + 2m_8 + 5S}$ otherwise.

The Montgomery ladder for projective differential addition formulas is shown in Algorithm 1. Here, the addition and the doubling steps are carried out using differential addition and differential doubling formulas, where in the former case the input is $W(2P)$, $W(P)$ and the invariant, consequently, is $W(P)$. Note that $W(\cdot)$ stands for the projective version of the coordinate function $w(\cdot)$.

After application of the Montgomery ladder, the y-coordinate of the product $k \cdot P = (x_1, y_1)$ can be restored efficiently and, hence, there is no need to compute it in the intermediate steps. Restoring the y-coordinate for affine coordinates, also means simultaneously scaling the x-coordinate, in order to avoid multiple inversions. It works in the following way, as detailed in [11] and in [17]:

Algorithm 1. Differential Montgomery Ladder

Require: A point P on E and a scalar $k = (k_{l-1}, \ldots, k_0)_2 \in \mathbb{Z}$
Ensure: $W(k \cdot P) = (X_1 : Z_1)$
  $(X_1 : Z_1) = W(P)$ and $(X_2 : Z_2) = W(2P)$
  for $i = l - 2$ **downto** 0 **do**
    if $k_i = 0$ **then**
      $(X_1 : Z_1) = 2(X_1 : Z_1)$, and
      $(X_2 : Z_2) = (X_1 : Z_1) + (X_2 : Z_2)$
    else
      $(X_1 : Z_1) = (X_1 : Z_1) + (X_2 : Z_2)$, and
      $(X_2 : Z_2) = 2(X_2 : Z_2)$
    end if
  end for

$$x_1 = \frac{\bar{Z}\bar{X}Z_2 X_1}{\bar{Z}\bar{X}Z_2 Z_1} \quad \text{and} \quad y_1 = \bar{Y} + \frac{\gamma((X_1\bar{Z} + \bar{X}Z_1)\gamma + Z_1 Z_2 \bar{X}^2 + Z_1 Z_2 \bar{Z}\bar{Y})}{\bar{Z}\bar{X}Z_2 Z_1},$$

where $\gamma = X_2\bar{Z} + \bar{X}Z_2$ and $P = (\bar{X} : \bar{Y} : \bar{Z}) \neq \mathcal{O}$. There are two special cases to check, see [11] for more details on that. Using these formulas requires $\mathbf{1I + 10M}$, when assuming $\bar{Z} = 1$, i.e., P to be scaled.

3   The Binary Huff Curve Model

This section is mainly a recapitulation of the research done by Joye et. al in [5] and [9], since we need these facts in Section 4 in order to derive compact formulas for mapping between binary Weierstrass and binary Huff curves.

As defined in [5], binary Huff curves are a new class of elliptic curves. For every Weierstrass curve defined over $\mathbb{F}_{2^m}$ with $m \geq 4$, there is a birationally equivalent generalized binary Huff curve. A *generalized binary Huff curve* is given by the set of projective points $(X : Y : Z)$ over $\mathbb{F}_{2^m}$ satisfying the subsequent equation:

$$E_H : aX(Y^2 + fYZ + Z^2) = bY(X^2 + fXZ + Z^2) \tag{3}$$

with $a, b, f \in \mathbb{F}_{2^m}^*$ and $a \neq b$. Three points at infinity, i.e., $(1 : 0 : 0), (0 : 1 : 0)$, and $(a : b : 0)$, satisfy Equation (3). The affine version of Equation (3) is birationally equivalent to the subsequent binary Weierstrass curve:

$$E_{W'} : v(v + (a + b)fu) = u(u + a^2)(u + b^2), \tag{4}$$

which itself is isomorphic to the short Weierstrass form through the following isomorphism:

$$\Theta : E_W(\mathbb{F}_{2^m}) \longrightarrow E_{W'}(\mathbb{F}_{2^m})$$
$$(u, v) \longmapsto \left(\mu^2 u, \mu^3 \left(v + su + \sqrt{a_6}\right)\right),$$

and its inverse:

$$\Omega : E_{W'}(\mathbb{F}_{2^m}) \longrightarrow E_W(\mathbb{F}_{2^m})$$
$$(u', v') \longmapsto (\nu^2 u', \nu^3 v' + s\nu^2 u' + \sqrt{a_6})$$

with $\mu = (a + b) f$, $\nu = \mu^{-1}$, and $s \in \mathbb{F}_{2^m}$ satisfying $s^2 + s = a_2 + f^{-2}$. The birational equivalence

$$\Phi : E_{W'}(\mathbb{F}_{2^m}) \longrightarrow E_H(\mathbb{F}_{2^m}),$$
$$(u, v) \longmapsto \left(\frac{b(u + a^2)}{v}, \frac{a(u + b^2)}{v + (a + b) fu} \right),$$

maps from the Weierstrass curve $E_{W'}$ onto the Huff curve E_H. Its inverse looks as follows:

$$\Psi : E_H(\mathbb{F}_{2^m}) \longrightarrow E_{W'}(\mathbb{F}_{2^m}),$$
$$(x, y) \longmapsto \left(\frac{ab}{xy}, \frac{ab(axy + b)}{x^2 y} \right).$$

The neutral element is $(0, 0)$ and the group law is based on the chord-and-tangent rule. Note, however, that the birational equivalences are not line-preserving. The inverse of some affine point $P = (x_1, y_1) \in E_H$ is

$$-P = \left(y_1 \frac{(\alpha x_1 + 1)}{(\beta y_1 + 1)}, x_1 \frac{(\beta x_1 + 1)}{(\alpha x_1 + 1)} \right), \tag{5}$$

with $\alpha = \frac{a+b}{b \cdot f}$ and $\beta = \frac{a+b}{a \cdot f}$. The projective homogenization of Equation (5) can be evaluated using $\mathbf{4M + 4m_8}$. Furthermore, there are four exceptional cases, which have to be dealt with separately. We refer the reader to [5] for more details on that. Compared to binary Weierstrass curves, where point inversion costs at most one field addition and, hence, is negligible, this operation is very expensive on binary Huff curves.

Projective point doubling, and point addition take $\mathbf{6M + 2m_8 + 6S}$ and $\mathbf{15M + 3S}$, respectively. The affine doubling formula looks as follows:

$$2P = \begin{cases} (1 : 0 : 0) & \text{if } x_1 = 1, \\ (0 : 1 : 0) & \text{if } y_1 = 1, \\ (a : b : 0) & \text{if } x_1 y_1 = 1, \text{ and} \\ \left(\frac{f(a+b)x_1^2(1+y_1)^2}{b(1+x_1)^2(1+x_1 y_1)^2}, \frac{f(a+b)y_1^2(1+x_1)^2}{a(1+y_1)^2(1+x_1 y_1)^2} \right) & \text{otherwise.} \end{cases} \tag{6}$$

where $P = (x_1, y_1) \in E_H$. Also note that for subgroups not including the points at infinity a complete addition law exists, i.e., it can also be used for point doublings.

3.1 Differential Addition

For Huff curves, the authors of [5] give differential addition formulas for use with the Montgomery ladder. To do so, they introduce the coordinate function $w(x, y) = xy$, which fulfills the condition $w(P) = w(-P)$. From Formula (6), they derive the following differential doubling formula:

$$w(2P) = \begin{cases} \gamma \cdot \frac{w_1^2}{(1+w_1)^4} & \text{if } w_1 \neq 1, \text{ and} \\ (1 : 0) & \text{otherwise.} \end{cases} \tag{7}$$

where $\gamma = \frac{(a+b)^2}{ab}$ and $w_1 = w(P)$. Using the birational equivalence Φ and the multiplicative differential addition formula from [17], the authors of [5] obtain the subsequent addition formula:

$$w(P + Q) = \begin{cases} \frac{(w_1+w_2)^2}{\bar{w}(1+w_1w_2)^2} & \text{if } w_1w_2 \neq 1, \text{ and} \\ (1 : 0) & \text{otherwise.} \end{cases} \tag{8}$$

where $P \neq Q$, $w_1 = w(P)$, $w_2 = w(Q)$, and $\bar{w} = w(P - Q)$.

Working with affine coordinates is less satisfying due to the costly inversion required in each step. Hence, Devigne and Joye introduce projective WZ-coordinates. A point $P = (\frac{X_1}{Z_1}, \frac{Y_1}{Z_1}) \in E_H$ in WZ-coordinates, is represented by the tuple

$$(W : Z) = \begin{cases} (\theta w(P) : \theta) = (\theta X_1 Y_1 : \theta Z_1^2) & \text{if } P \neq (a : b : 0), \text{ and} \\ (\theta : 0) & \text{otherwise.} \end{cases}$$

for some $\theta \in \mathbb{F}_{2^m}^*$. Now, when given $P = (W_1 : Z_1)$ and $Q = (W_2 : Z_2)$, the projective differential addition formulas look as follows:

$$\begin{cases} W(2P) = \gamma \cdot (W_1 Z_1)^2 \\ Z(2P) = (W_1 + Z_1)^4 \end{cases} \text{and} \begin{cases} W(P + Q) = \bar{Z}(W_1 Z_2 + W_2 Z_1)^2 \\ Z(P + Q) = \bar{W}(W_1 W_2 + Z_1 Z_2)^2, \end{cases}$$

where $W(P - Q) = (\bar{W}, \bar{Z})$ are the WZ-coordinates of $P - Q$. Obviously, the first requires $\mathbf{1M + 1m_8 + 3S}$, whereas the latter requires $\mathbf{6M + 2S}$, which can be improved to $\mathbf{4M + 2S}$ by computing $W_1 Z_2 + W_2 Z_1$ as $(W_1 + Z_1)(W_2 + Z_2) + (W_1 W_2 + Z_1 Z_2)$ and scaling the coordinate $(\bar{W} : \bar{Z})$, since it remains constant throughout the whole Montgomery ladder process.

4 Contribution

In this section we are going to describe a Huff curve implementation and the optimizations we have applied to it. Furthermore, we contrast its performance with a reference implementation that is based on Weierstrass curves, to which we have applied the same set of optimizations. Then, we present timings of both implementations, which show that for the binary NIST curves, the Huff curve implementation is up to 7.4% faster than the reference implementation.

We also present the curve parameters for the binary Huff curves corresponding to the binary NIST curves and give formulas for back-and-forth conversion between binary Huff curves and binary curves in short Weierstrass form.

4.1   Deriving Curve Parameters

Deriving curve parameters $a, b, f \in \mathbb{F}_{2^m}$ from a given binary Weierstrass curve with parameters $a_2, a_6 \in \mathbb{F}_{2^m}$, works as follows [5, Proof of Proposition 2]:

1. Select an arbitrary $f \in \mathbb{F}_{2^m}$ so that $Tr(f^{-1}) = Tr(a_2)$ and $Tr(f^8 a_6) = 0$,
2. find a solution $t \in \mathbb{F}_{2^m}$ to the equation $t^2 + \left(f^4 \sqrt{a_6}\right)^{-1} t + 1 = 0$, and
3. determine $a, b \in \mathbb{F}_{2^m}$ such that $\sqrt{t} = ab^{-1}$,

where $Tr(\cdot)$ is the trace function $Tr : \mathbb{F}_{2^m} \to \mathbb{F}_2, x \mapsto \sum_{i=0}^{m-1} x^{2^i}$. The parameters we have obtained for the NIST-recommended curves [6] plus the value s needed for Ω and Θ are listed in Table 1 and in Table 2, respectively.

4.2   Mapping between Huff and Weierstrass Curves

Let $P_W = (u, v)$ be a point on $E_W(\mathbb{F}_{2^m})$, $P_{W'} = (u', v') = \Theta(P_W) \in E_{W'}(\mathbb{F}_{2^m})$ and $P = \Omega(P_{W'})$ be the corresponding point on $E_H(\mathbb{F}_{2^m})$.

Weierstrass to Huff Curve: From the birational equivalence $\Phi \circ \Theta$, we derive the following formula for directly mapping P_W to WZ-coordinates:

$$(W:Z) = \left(ab\left(\mu^2 u + a^2\right)\left(\mu^2 u + b^2\right) : \mu^6\left(v + su + \sqrt{a_6}\right)\left(\left(v + su + \sqrt{a_6}\right) + u\right)\right)$$

Through decomposition we get:

- $A = \mu^2 u$,
- $B = (A + a^2)$, $C = (A + b^2)$,
- $D = v_1 + su + \sqrt{a_6}$, $E = D + u$,
- $W = ab \cdot B \cdot C$, and
- $Z = \mu^6 \cdot D \cdot E$.

The values a^2, b^2, and $\sqrt{a_6}$ as well as the multiplication lookup tables for the values μ^2, μ^6, s, and ab can be determined a priori. For this setting, we get a total of $\mathbf{2M + 4m_8}$ for obtaining the WZ-coordinates of P_W. Of course, if P_W is fixed, one can precompute its scaled WZ-coordinates.

Huff to Weierstrass Curves: In order to convert the result $W(k \cdot P) = (W_1 : Z_1)$, obtained from applying the differential Montgomery ladder on E_H, back to E_W, we need to evaluate the birational equivalence $\Omega \circ \Psi$. The naive approach would be to, firstly, compute the x-coordinate of the corresponding point on $E_{W'}$ as $u_1 = \frac{ab}{w(k \cdot P)}$ then, secondly, to map the result from $E_{W'}$ to E_W, and, finally, to recover its y-coordinate v_1 using the formula from [11]:

$$v_1 = \frac{(u_1 + u)\left((u_1 + u)(u_2 + u) + u^2 + v\right)}{u} + v, \tag{9}$$

which requires the additional value $u_2 = \frac{ab}{w((k+1) \cdot P)}$, which can be computed using the point $W((k+1)P) = (W_2 : Z_2)$ from the last step of the Montgomery ladder. All in all, this would require several inversions, which can be saved by

Table 1. Generalized Huff curve parameters for NIST-recommended binary curves (cf. [6])

Curve	a	b	f
B-163	0x1	0x253f3c45a6d779b47e63758c35336f0679b42f4c0	0x6
K-163	0x1	0x20000000000000000000000000000000000000033	0x6
B-233	0x1	0x115b7c737bec7a5cc19212911c2bd03cadb9a29ddf9b1dc64b\ 8b3550fb3	0x3
K-233	0x1	0x1e5ff5c884156aaebbd38370425882dff04f04ba05a7f40740\ 82385c149	0x2
B-283	0x1	0x6a263cdd28c309d3d3068046747abe51375b0d763dccc64868\ 251918d59c21842dd4fe1	0x3
K-283	0x1	0x7a0fa1ffdaf44208a4efb593c405714e0fbc4423dd0db57384\ 89cb583073c2cae153d0d	0x2
B-409	0x1	0x3f2918c0e689aca093d4cf5a389aeda96eb5cdcb930617991d\ 09111a3f91dc7283123ef8ab912744e193c34c9bd3cd532e17b7	0x9
K-409	0x1	0x846538361ed11b7c42b9e302169a3ea16009df82f80a155d56\ 39d78d4ba8dd02284110d6b3fbc05dda9c0ed1c0d6316c72d676	0x2
B-571	0x1	0x3c0904534c17c94a947b971ee5e6a3f3fb917dd3b57d7ad1f6\ ea35ec2593bae024934b8efe08d2a5bb97c4286665408d50f80c\ afc8dfbee0011c03e785fe39c94c977d5e3a7f065	0xf
K-571	0x1	0x6a28a2cf6fb77a9485f438a79f8832d86c465b689fd80b3d9c\ 4b1ef40380b5d92f85044e450336618a69b209eb37ecdd23da7b\ f7ee9e0fc1e98248edb0dc92f3510027be50cd2bb	0x2

Table 2. Auxiliary parameter s for mapping between NIST-recommended binary Weierstrass curves (cf. [6]) and the corresponding binary Huff curves

Curve	s
B-163	0x4058c6f9ae170f30f3ec9def6b2ddf2a28f0c0872
K-163	0x4058c6f9ae170f30f3ec9def6b2ddf2a28f0c0872
B-233	0xe7b4bcdb4af3163783507af91971d49927298e32e548d55b3a0b602a42
K-233	0xb1ce7164613a37fed984a32b18d265ada947ed207757d373d4e139835a
B-283	0x21b24c4336e195a894fc9021fabac4e6988ff780c29522af3261508be\ fb321108eda3fa
K-283	0x387fd1da986a7fa48458bf27d26d9162d60c2f7f6e3da61f30d215c6b\ 193e73f223326e
B-409	0x106176448c66d8e7d0ddc074d76277a7ac8093ee53499d108099266d9\ 82c68dae5cb61d5054b30ecfce3c3beebc8cbecb904fd0
K-409	0x15dedff38eafec7e43a277eea795fbb1d52e6075a8bfe6a275be0dcba\ f6b781f8c9d37e4f414e8de3634d946434d9b6a6d62e20
B-571	0x12007d9377488ff6122ccce941d1cef856279188c8e82a6696a918b2f\ ccd78353385beb5e972f83d491d22db627117ab1580dabd23c6e8adeb99\ d3bdbc95d6fb645833ba6b4f182
K-571	0x2780c6d786569591600518d211a5d6fbd900d9b44a1e4e65016d2331d\ d243a6b31db129832a46326c7e3fd9b43f900ee58ed165e550a3cc3a41f\ b88b001fa79f398351bb7c35dea

combining the formulas. To do so, one can replace $u_1 = \frac{ab}{w(k \cdot P)}$ with $u_1 = \frac{\delta \cdot Z_1}{W_1}$, where $w(k \cdot P) = \frac{W_1}{Z_1}$ as $W(k \cdot P) = (W_1 : Z_1)$, $\delta = \frac{ab}{\mu^2}$ and $\mu = (a+b)f$, and so implicitly apply Ω. By inserting it into Equation (9), one derives the following formula:

$$v_1 = \frac{(\delta Z_1 + uW_1)\left((\delta Z_1 + uW_1)(\delta Z_2 + uW_2) + (u^2 + v)W_1 W_2\right)}{uW_1^2 W_2} + v,$$

Now, one can compute

$$U_1 = \delta Z_1 uW_1 W_2 \quad \text{and} \quad V_1 = \beta\left(\beta(\delta Z_2 + uW_2) + (u^2 + v)W_1 W_2\right) + uvW_1^2 W_2$$

with $\beta = \delta Z_1 + uW_1$ and obtain $(u_1, v_1) = \left(\frac{U_1}{uW_1^2 W_2}, \frac{V_1}{uW_1^2 W_2}\right)$. Common sub-expression elimination yields the following relations:

- $A = \delta Z_1$, $B = \delta Z_2$,
- $C = uW_1$, $D = uW_2$,
- $E = A + C$, $F = B + D$,
- $G = W_1 W_2$, $H = (u^2 + v)$,
- $I = (C \cdot G)^{-1}$, $J = A \cdot G$,
- $K = J \cdot I$, $L = E \cdot I$,
- $u_1 = uK$, and
- $v_1 = L \cdot (E \cdot F + H \cdot G) + v$.

During the computation one can save the lookup tables of the intermediate values I and G, replacing **4M** by **2M + 2m$_4$**. Moreover, δ is constant and multiplications with it require **1m$_8$**. Finally, we recycle the lookup table of u_1, exchanging **3M** for **1M + 2m$_4$**. In case the point $P_W = (u, v)$ is fixed, one can precompute the lookup tables of u and H using $w = 8$. Thus, one can trade **1M + 3m$_4$ + 1S** for **4m$_8$**. To sum this up, the back-conversion including the y-coordinate recovery costs **1I + 6M + 5m$_4$ + 2m$_8$ + 1S** in general, and **1I + 5M + 2m$_4$ + 6m$_8$** for P_W fixed.

Implications: If the point P_W is not fixed, in which case one needs both back and forth conversions including a y-coordinate recovery, one obtains total costs of at most **1I + 8M + 5m$_4$ + 6m$_8$ + 1S**. Using XZ-coordinates on short Weierstrass curves, the formulas for restoring the y-coordinate turn out to be faster by only **2m$_8$** and, hence, this difference is negligible. Taking the conversion to WZ-coordinates into account, one gets a small difference of **2M + 6m$_8$**, which only becomes significant if P_W is not known a priori. This minimal overhead for the conversion pays off, as for the scalar multiplication using WZ-coordinates one has **4M + 2m$_8$ + 5S** contrary to **5M + 1m$_8$ + 4S** per bit of the scalar k when using XZ-coordinates.

4.3   Implementation Details and Optimizations

The implementation is written in Java and is based on the NIST recommended elliptic curves B–163, B–233, B–283, B–409 and B–571 [6]. We are using fast reductions for the underlying binary fields and `long`-arrays for values thereof, which are in polynomial representation. Furthermore, we perform squarings in linear time using table lookups [15] and multiplications using the windowed left-to-right comb multiplier. The latter works with precomputed multiplication lookup tables and is due to Lim and Lee (cf. [12,7]). For ordinary binary field multiplications we use windows of size $w = 4$ and for multiplications with values known beforehand, such as curve parameters and combinations thereof, we use windows of size $w = 8$. Additionally, we cache these lookup tables for curve parameters and recurring intermediate values in the addition/doubling formulas resulting in a quite reasonable speedup. We point out that both implementations only restore the y-coordinates without scaling the result and, thus, return projective coordinates. The coordinate $W(2P - P) = W(P) = (\bar{W} : \bar{Z})$ gets scaled and, thus, one can ignore $\bar{Z}$. Furthermore, $\bar{W}$ is either fixed because of P being the base point, or fixed throughout the whole ladder steps as the point difference stays the same. In both cases one can store the multiplication lookup tables for $w = 8$. Hence, the costs of the differential addition drop from $4\mathbf{M} + 2\mathbf{S}$ to $3\mathbf{M} + 1\mathbf{m_8} + 2\mathbf{S}$. With differential doubling requiring $1\mathbf{M} + 1\mathbf{m_8} + 3\mathbf{S}$, one gets an overall of $4\mathbf{M} + 2\mathbf{m_8} + 5\mathbf{S}$ per bit of scalar k. In case P is not fixed, one has additional one-time costs for scaling $(\bar{W} : \bar{Z})$, that is $1\mathbf{I} + 1\mathbf{M}$, and one-time costs for assembling its lookup tables with window size $w = 8$.

Finally, we emphasize that the implementation of the differential Montgomery ladder on Huff curves is straight-forward and does not require more effort than its counterpart on Weierstrass curves, especially when the all-in-one formulas presented in this paper are being used.

Timings: All benchmarks were carried out on an Intel Core i5-2540M running Ubuntu Linux 12.10/amd64 and OpenJDK 7u15/amd64 in server mode. Table 3 shows the timings of one application of the Montgomery ladder on the test platform using both WZ and XZ-coordinates on the binary NIST curves, where in the former case we present the timings for both cases, i.e., for fixed P fixed and random P. The performance gains achieved through precomputations, which are possible in case of fixed P, are reflected in the timings. Furthermore, all timings include the recovery of the y-coordinate as well as in case of WZ-coordinates the back-and-forth conversion between Weierstrass and Huff curves.

Table 3. Timings of the Montgomery ladder for WZ and XZ coordinates using binary NIST curves

Coordinates	B-163 [ms]	B-233 [ms]	B-283 [ms]	B-409 [ms]	B-571 [ms]
XZ	0.709	1.315	1.896	4.203	8.403
WZ	0.692	1.251	1.826	4.040	8.143
Speedup	**2.46%**	**5.12%**	**3.83%**	**4.03%**	**3.19%**
WZ (P fixed)	0.662	1.224	1.778	3.928	8.039
Speedup	**7.10%**	**7.43%**	**6.64%**	**7.00%**	**4.53%**

In Table 4, one can see the relative costs of one squaring and one multiplication with a curve parameter compared to an ordinary field multiplication. This analysis shows that trading $1M$ for $1m_8 + 1S$ per ladder iteration, as done by using WZ instead of XZ-coordinates, saves up to $0.54M$ per ladder step on the test platform.

Table 4. Costs of squarings and multiplications with curve parameters in relation to ordinary multiplications

	$\mathbb{F}_{2^{163}}$	$\mathbb{F}_{2^{233}}$	$\mathbb{F}_{2^{283}}$	$\mathbb{F}_{2^{409}}$	$\mathbb{F}_{2^{571}}$
$1S =$	0.094M	0.080M	0.077M	0.061M	0.055M
$1m_8 =$	0.369M	0.411M	0.387M	0.418M	0.430M

5   Conclusions

We have implemented binary Huff curves in software. For scalar multiplication, we were using a differential Montgomery ladder, based on the differential addition formulas given by Devigne and Joye in [5]. The timings show that for the binary NIST curves, this implementation is up to 7.4% faster than the reference implementation of the differential Montgomery ladder on the corresponding Weierstrass curves, to which we have applied the same set of optimizations.

We have presented fast all-in-one back-and-forth conversion formulas, which implicitly include the recovery of the y-coordinate. These conversions turn out to be almost as efficient as the y-coordinate recovery on Weierstrass curves, which is required anyway after using the Montgomery ladder on Weierstrass curves. This preserves most of the savings obtained through the faster differential addition formulas. Furthermore, we have presented curve parameters for Huff curves, which are birationally equivalent to the NIST-recommended binary Weierstrass curves.

Finally, we emphasize that when using the formulas presented in this paper, the implementation of the differential Montgomery ladder on Huff curves does not require more effort than its counterpart on Weierstrass curves. Thus, given the performance gains discussed in this paper such an implementation is an interesting alternative to conventional implementations.

References

1. Bernstein, D.J., Lange, T.: Explicit-formulas database,
   http://www.hyperelliptic.org/EFD/index.html
2. Bernstein, D.J., Lange, T.: Faster addition and doubling on elliptic curves. In: Kurosawa, K. (ed.) ASIACRYPT 2007. LNCS, vol. 4833, pp. 29–50. Springer, Heidelberg (2007)
3. Brumley, B.B., Tuveri, N.: Remote timing attacks are still practical. In: Atluri, V., Diaz, C. (eds.) ESORICS 2011. LNCS, vol. 6879, pp. 355–371. Springer, Heidelberg (2011)

4. Brumley, D., Boneh, D.: Remote timing attacks are practical. Computer Networks 48(5), 701–716 (2005)
5. Devigne, J., Joye, M.: Binary Huff curves. In: Kiayias, A. (ed.) CT-RSA 2011. LNCS, vol. 6558, pp. 340–355. Springer, Heidelberg (2011)
6. Gallagher, P., Furlani, C.: Fips pub 186-3 federal information processing standards publication digital signature standard, dss (2009)
7. Hankerson, D., Menezes, A.J., Vanstone, S.: Guide to Elliptic Curve Cryptography. Springer-Verlag New York, Inc., Secaucus (2003)
8. Huff, G.B.: Diophantine problems in geometry and elliptic ternary forms. Duke Math. J. 15, 443–453 (1948)
9. Joye, M., Tibouchi, M., Vergnaud, D.: Huff's model for elliptic curves. In: Hanrot, G., Morain, F., Thomé, E. (eds.) ANTS-IX 2010. LNCS, vol. 6197, pp. 234–250. Springer, Heidelberg (2010)
10. Koblitz, N.: Elliptic curve cryptosystems. Mathematics of Computation 48(177), 203–209 (1987)
11. López, J., Dahab, R.: Fast multiplication on elliptic curves over $GF(2^m)$ without precomputation. In: Koç, Ç.K., Paar, C. (eds.) CHES 1999. LNCS, vol. 1717, pp. 316–327. Springer, Heidelberg (1999)
12. López, J., Dahab, R.: High-speed software multiplication in F_{2^m}. In: Roy, B., Okamoto, E. (eds.) INDOCRYPT 2000. LNCS, vol. 1977, pp. 203–212. Springer, Heidelberg (2000)
13. Menezes, A., Okamoto, T., Vanstone, S.: Reducing elliptic curve logarithms to logarithms in a finite field. In: Proceedings of the Twenty-Third Annual ACM Symposium on Theory of Computing, STOC 1991, pp. 80–89. ACM, New York (1991)
14. Miller, V.S.: Use of elliptic curves in cryptography. In: Williams, H.C. (ed.) CRYPTO 1985. LNCS, vol. 218, pp. 417–426. Springer, Heidelberg (1986)
15. Schroeppel, R., Orman, H., O'Malley, S., Spatscheck, O.: Fast key exchange with elliptic curve systems. In: Coppersmith, D. (ed.) CRYPTO 1995. LNCS, vol. 963, pp. 43–56. Springer, Heidelberg (1995)
16. Silverman, J.: The Arithmetic of Elliptic Curves, Graduate Texts in Mathematics, vol. 106. Springer (1986)
17. Stam, M.: On montgomery-like representationsfor elliptic curves over $GF(2^k)$. In: Desmedt, Y.G. (ed.) PKC 2003. LNCS, vol. 2567, pp. 240–253. Springer, Heidelberg (2003)
18. Zhang, Y., Juels, A., Reiter, M.K., Ristenpart, T.: Cross-vm side channels and their use to extract private keys. In: ACM Conference on Computer and Communications Security, pp. 305–316 (2012)

Speeding Up the Fixed-Base Comb Method for Faster Scalar Multiplication on Koblitz Curves

Christian Hanser and Christian Wagner

Institute for Applied Information Processing and Communications (IAIK),
Graz University of Technology (TUG), Inffeldgasse 16a, 8010 Graz, Austria
{christian.hanser,christian.wagner}@iaik.tugraz.at

Abstract. Scalar multiplication is the most expensive arithmetical operation on elliptic curves. There are various methods available, which are optimized for different settings, such as high speed, side-channel resistance and small memory footprint. One of the fastest methods for fixed-base scalar multiplications is the so-called fixed-base comb scalar multiplication method, which is due to Lim and Lee. In this paper, we present a modification to this method, which exploits the possibility of exchanging doublings for much cheaper applications of the Frobenius endomorphism on binary Koblitz curves. We have implemented the findings in software and compare the performance of the implementation to the performance of the reference WTNAF implementation and the performance of the conventional comb multiplication methods. For single scalar multiplications, we are able to achieve performance improvements over the WTNAF method of up to 25% and of up to 42% over the conventional comb methods. Finally, we emphasize that the implementation of the τ-comb method is straight-forward and requires only little effort. All in all, this makes it a good alternative to other fixed-base multiplication methods.

Keywords: ECC, scalar multiplication, Lim-Lee method, comb method, Koblitz curves, Frobenius endomorphism, τ-adic representation.

1 Introduction

In 1985, Neal Koblitz [8] and Victor S. Miller [14] both discovered independently that elliptic curves over finite fields can be used for public key cryptography. By now, elliptic curves have become an important concept within public key cryptography. This is mainly due to small key sizes compared to other public key cryptosystems, such as RSA, which lower the requirements for CPUs as well as the memory footprint. Elliptic curves have a group structure and their cryptographic security relies on the difficulty of solving the elliptic curve discrete logarithm problem (ECDLP).

The most expensive, yet, at the same time most important operation, on elliptic curves is the scalar multiplication. There are plenty of different techniques achieving optimizations for different settings, such as high speed through the

A. Cuzzocrea et al. (Eds.): CD-ARES 2013 Workshops, LNCS 8128, pp. 168–179, 2013.
© IFIP International Federation for Information Processing 2013

reduction of group operations, side-channel resistance and small memory footprint. In this paper we are focusing solely on the performance aspects of scalar multiplication. Koblitz curves allow trading the doubling operation for another operation, that is, the application of the so-called Frobenius endomorphism, which is inexpensive compared to point doubling. In the context of Koblitz curves, many multiplication methods relying on a non-adjacent form (NAF), such as windowed non-adjacent form (WNAF), interleaved simultaneous point multiplication, etc., have been adapted, so that doublings can be replaced by far more efficient applications of the Frobenius endomorphism. Yet, to the best of our knowledge, no such modification to the fixed-base comb method, which is also referred to as Lim-Lee method [10], has been proposed until now. This algorithm achieves very high speed at the cost of precomputations and increased memory usage due to lookup tables.

1.1 Contribution

In this paper, we are going to introduce an improvement of the fixed-base comb method on Koblitz curves. In this context, we show how point doublings can be traded for applications of the Frobenius endomorphism. To do so, we use scalar recoding to obtain an unsigned τ-adic representation of scalars, which allows us to exchange the doubling steps within the comb methods for the application of the Frobenius endomorphism. We detail the scalar recoding algorithm and describe the modified fixed-base comb method. Furthermore, we have implemented this method as well as the WTNAF method in software. We give a detailed performance comparison and illustrate the performance gains we have achieved with respect to the WTNAF and the conventional fixed-base comb methods. In the former case, we achieve performance improvements of up to 25% and in the latter case improvements of up to 42%.

1.2 Outline

In Section 2, we are going to talk about elliptic curves in general, binary Koblitz curves and the fixed-base comb multiplication methods. Section 3 discusses the improvements we have achieved and Section 4 details the implementation, presents the benchmark results and compares the findings to the conventional comb multiplier variants. At last, Section 5 concludes the paper.

2   Preliminaries

An elliptic curve over a field $\mathbb{K}$ is a plane, smooth curve described by the Weierstrass equation:

$$E : Y^2 + a'_1 XY + a'_3 Y = X^3 + a'_2 X^2 + a'_4 X + a'_6, \tag{1}$$

where $a'_1, a'_2, a'_3, a'_4, a'_6 \in \mathbb{K}$. The set $E(\mathbb{K})$ of points $(x, y) \in \mathbb{K}^2$ satisfying Equation (1) plus the point at infinity $\mathcal{O} = (0 : 1 : 0)$, which is the neutral element, forms an additive Abelian group. The addition of points on an elliptic curve is achieved using the *chord-and-tangent* method [17].

For cryptographic purposes, one is interested in elliptic curves over finite fields $\mathbb{F}_q$, especially in curves over fields $\mathbb{F}_{2^m}$ with m being prime and $\mathbb{F}_p$ with p being a large prime number. The security of elliptic curve cryptography is based on the assumption that in general there is no subexponential-time algorithm to solve the discrete logarithm problem in elliptic curve groups (ECDLP). Given $P, Q \in E(\mathbb{F}_q)$ with P being a generator of a subgroup of $E(\mathbb{F}_q)$ of large prime order n, the ECDLP constitutes the problem of finding a scalar $k \in \mathbb{Z}_n$ such that $Q = k \cdot P$. In the following, we use $E(\mathbb{F}_q)[n]$ to denote this n-order subgroup of $E(\mathbb{F}_q)$.

In cryptography, we usually use non-supersingular curves, as supersingular curves turned out to be susceptible to the MOV attack [13], which reduces the ECDLP to the DLP on finite fields for which an efficient subexponential-time algorithm is known. Non-supersingular curves defined over $\mathbb{F}_{2^m}$, are described using the following short form of Equation (1):

$$Y^2 + XY = X^3 + a_2 X^2 + a_6, \tag{2}$$

where $a_2, a_6 \in \mathbb{F}_{2^m}$ and $a_6 \neq 0$.

The most important and at the same time most expensive operation on elliptic curves is the scalar multiplication, that is, computing $k \cdot P$ from some point $P \in E(\mathbb{F}_q)$ and some scalar $k \in \mathbb{Z}_n$. For this purpose, many different algorithms for different goals, such as small or even constant memory footprint, high speed or side-channel resistance, have been invented.

Basic algorithms for scalar multiplication are the double-and-add and the NAF method. In the former case, one is given an unsigned binary representation of the scalar and per bit of the scalar a doubling is performed, where for bits set to 1 an additional point addition is carried out. In the latter, the unsigned scalar representation is replaced by a signed representation, i.e., bits can now take values in $\{0, \pm 1\}$, where for negative bit values point subtractions instead of additions have to be performed. This way, the Hamming weight of the scalar can be reduced to $1/3$, which gives a major speedup by reducing the number of additions. Further speed-ups can be achieved by reducing the number of additions, which is done by the windowed-NAF (WNAF) method at the expense of some precomputations (cf. [6,4]).

Subsequently, we are dealing with so-called fixed-base comb multipliers, which are very fast methods for multiplications with some fixed-point P (mostly a fixed generator of $E(\mathbb{F}_q)[n]$), and with scalar multiplications on Koblitz curves, for which enormous speed improvements exist already.

2.1   Fixed-Base Comb Multiplication

The fixed-base comb multiplier is due to Lim and Lee [10] and is one of the fastest scalar multiplication methods available. As it requires intense precomputations, it is only used for multiplications with a fixed point, which is in most cases a generator of an elliptic curve (sub-)group.

In the fixed-base comb method, the bit representation of a scalar k of maximum bitsize t (where t is the curve's group order in bits) is prepended with 0s, such that the length of k is a multiple of the window size w and then split into w blocks K_i with $0 \le i < w$ of size $d = \lceil t/w \rceil$, so that

$$k = K_{w-1} \| \cdots \| K_1 \| K_0.$$

Each bitstring K_i represents one row of a binary matrix with w rows and d columns:

$$
\begin{bmatrix} K_0 \\ \vdots \\ K_i \\ \vdots \\ K_{w-1} \end{bmatrix}
=
\begin{bmatrix} K_{0,d-1} & \cdots & K_{0,0} \\ \vdots & & \vdots \\ K_{i,d-1} & \cdots & K_{i,0} \\ \vdots & & \vdots \\ K_{w-1,d-1} & \cdots & K_{w-1,0} \end{bmatrix}
=
\begin{bmatrix} k_{d-1} & \cdots & k_0 \\ \vdots & & \vdots \\ k_{(i+1)d-1} & \cdots & k_{id} \\ \vdots & & \vdots \\ k_{wd-1} & \cdots & k_{(w-1)d} \end{bmatrix}
\tag{3}
$$

Here, $K_{j,i}$ denotes the i-th bit of the bitstring K_j and k_i denotes the i-th bit of the unsigned binary representation of the scalar k. The columns of this matrix are then processed one at a time. By precomputing the points

$$[a_{w-1}, \ldots, a_2, a_1, a_0]_2 P = a_{w-1} 2^{(w-1)d} P + \cdots + a_2 2^{2d} P + a_1 2^d P + a_0 P,$$

for all possible bitstrings $(a_{w-1}, \ldots, a_1, a_0)$ the actual computation can be accelerated. This method is summarized in Algorithm 1. The *Multiply* step of Algorithm 1 has an expected running time of

---

Algorithm 1. Fixed-base comb method ([10,6])

Precompute:

Input: Window width w, $d = \lceil t/w \rceil$, $P \in E(\mathbb{F}_q)$.
Output: Table T holding $[a_{w-1}, \ldots, a_0]_2 P$ for all length w bitstrings $(a_{w-1}, \ldots, a_0)$.

Multiply:

Input: Window width w, $d = \lceil t/w \rceil$, $k = (k_{t-1}, \ldots, k_1, k_0)_2$, lookup table T generated via *Precompute* with respect to $P \in E(\mathbb{F}_q)$.
Output: kP.
1: If necessary, pad k on the left with 0s, interpret k as $K_{w-1} \| \cdots \| K_1 \| K_0$, where each K_j is a length d bitstring, where $K_{j,i}$ denotes the i-th bit of K_j.
2: $Q = \mathcal{O}$.
3: **for** $i = d - 1$ **downto** 0 **do**
4:     $Q = 2Q$
5:     $Q = Q + [K_{w-1,i}, \ldots, K_{1,i}, K_{0,i}]_2 P = Q + T_{\sum_{j=0}^{w-1} K_{j,i} 2^j}$
6: **end for**
7: **return** Q

$$\left(\frac{2^w - 1}{2^w}d - 1\right) A + (d - 1)D, \tag{4}$$

where A and D stand for the costs of a (mixed) point addition and a point doubling, respectively. Inside the main loop, the fixed-base comb method has the same number of point additions and point doublings. To reduce the number of point doublings by half, the so-called fixed-base comb method with two tables has been introduced, which makes use of an additional table of the same size as the first table. This method gives a benefit over the conventional comb method whenever w is chosen such that

$$\frac{2^{w-1}(w - 2)}{2^w - w - 1} \geq \frac{A}{D}, \tag{5}$$

For instance, in case of López-Dahab coordinates, $w \geq 6$ must hold for the two-table comb method to be faster than the comb method, since $A/D \approx 2$ [6].

2.2   Koblitz Curves

Binary Koblitz curves are defined by Equation (2), where the curve equation is defined over $\mathbb{F}_2$, that is $a_2 \in \{0,1\}$ and $a_6 = 1$. The group of these curves is defined over $\mathbb{F}_{2^m}$ with m prime. For cryptographic purposes, $E(\mathbb{F}_{2^m})$ is required to have almost prime group order, meaning that $E(\mathbb{F}_{2^m}) = hn$, where n is a large prime and the cofactor $h \leq 4$.

On Koblitz curves, the map $\tau : E(\mathbb{F}_{2^m}) \to E(\mathbb{F}_{2^m})$ with:

$$P \mapsto \begin{cases} (x^2, y^2) & \text{if } P = (x, y), \text{ and} \\ \mathcal{O} & \text{if } P = \mathcal{O}, \end{cases}$$

is an endomorphism, which is called *Frobenius endomorphism*. It can be used to achieve tremendous speedups for scalar multiplications on this curve type. Note that all of the remaining techniques in this section are being discussed in detail by Solinas [18].

The characteristic polynomial of τ is $\tau^2 - \mu\tau + 2$ with $\mu = (-1)^{1-a_2}$. Thus, the relation $2P = \mu\tau(P) - \tau^2(P)$ holds for all $P \in E(\mathbb{F}_{2^m})$. Since squaring is inexpensive in binary fields, the costs of applying τ are insignificant compared to other operations, such as point doubling, which suggests trading point doublings for applications of τ within multiplications by some scalar k. This way, one can trade $3M + 5S$ required for a doubling on Koblitz curves in López-Dahab coordinates ([9,4,7]) for $3S$ required for one evaluation of τ, where M stands for the costs of one multiplication and S for the costs of one squaring. However, to be able to do so, k needs to be converted to a value $k' = \sum_{i=0}^{l-1} u_i \tau^i \in \mathbb{Z}[\tau]$, which is said to be in τ-adic representation.

The τ-adic Representation: Now, in order to convert scalars from base 2 to base τ, we need to introduce the norm function on $\mathbb{Z}[\tau]$. The norm of an element $\alpha = a_0 + a_1\tau \in \mathbb{Z}[\tau]$ (note that every element of $\mathbb{Z}[\tau]$ can be written this way) is the integer product of α and its complex conjugate $\bar{\alpha} = a_0 + a_1\bar{\tau} \in \mathbb{Z}[\tau]$, i.e., $N : \mathbb{Z}[\tau] \to \mathbb{Z}$ with $N(a_0 + a_1\tau) = a_0^2 + \mu a_0 a_1 + 2a_1^2$. The ring $\mathbb{Z}[\tau]$ is Euclidean with respect to $N(\cdot)$, i.e., it is possible to perform division with remainder in $\mathbb{Z}[\tau]$ so that the norm of the remainder is smaller than the norm of the divisor. In particular, an element $\alpha = a_0 + a_1\tau \in \mathbb{Z}[\tau]$ is divisible by τ if and only if a_0 is even. If so, then $\alpha/\tau = (a_1 + \mu a_0/2) - (a_0/2)\tau$. Note that this also enables us to repeatedly divide $k \in \mathbb{Z}$ by τ, which is necessary to derive the τ-adic representation $k' = \sum_{i=0}^{l-1} u_i\tau^i$ of a scalar k. As $N(\tau) = 2$, the remainder in the i-th division u_i is either an element of $\{0, \pm 1\}$ in case of signed representations or an element of $\{0, 1\}$ in case of unsigned representations.

So far, there is, however, one problem with this representation, namely, the length of the resulting τ-adic representation is twice the length of the corresponding base 2 representation. In case of the NAF, this means that replacing NAF(k) by the τ-adic NAF (also known as TNAF) will eliminate one doubling for two applications of τ, but will double the number of additions in the scalar multiplication method. To overcome this problem, Solinas introduced the reduced τ-adic NAF in [18], leading to a τ-adic NAF representation half the length of the original representation and, therefore, of roughly the size of an ordinary NAF representation. Here, an element $\rho \in \mathbb{Z}[\tau]$ of smallest possible norm so that $\rho \equiv k$ mod δ with $\delta = \frac{\tau^m - 1}{\tau - 1}$ is computed. Then, for all points $P \in E(\mathbb{F}_{2^m})[n]$ it holds that $kP = \rho P$. From the resulting value ρ, the TNAF representation TNAF(ρ) is derived, where the length of TNAF(ρ) is bounded by $m + a_2$.

In practice, often a partial reduction (cf. [18]) is being performed in order to avoid multiprecision integer divisions. Here, one computes an element $\rho' \in \mathbb{Z}[\tau]$ that is congruent to k modulo δ, but does not necessarily have the smallest possible norm. After the partial reduction, the length of TNAF(ρ') is bounded by $m + a_2 + 3$ and is, in general, the same as the length of TNAF(ρ).

The Windowed τ-adic NAF Method: The windowed τ-adic NAF or WT-NAF method is the τ-adic analogue of the ordinary width-w NAF (WNAF). The goal of this method, is to replace doublings by evaluations of the map τ and at the same time to reduce the number of additions through windowing. We do not discuss this method in detail here, but refer the reader to [6,18].

As with the WNAF, a representation of the scalar, having at most one nonzero coefficient among w consecutive coefficients, is derived. Like before, a scalar $k \in \mathbb{Z}$ is (partially) reduced modulo $\delta = \frac{\tau^m - 1}{\tau - 1}$, and thereby an element $\rho \in \mathbb{Z}[\tau]$ is obtained. For $w > 1$, ρ can be expressed in the form $\rho = \sum_{i=0}^{l-1} u_i\tau^i$ where $u_{l-1} \neq 0$ and $u_i \in \{0\} \cup \{\pm\alpha_u : \alpha_u \in \pi\}$ with $\pi = \{\alpha_u \equiv u \mod \tau^w : u = 1, 3, \ldots, 2^{w-1} - 1\}$. Thus, the number of additions in the multiplication step is reduced in favor of the precomputation of the points $\alpha_u P$ for $\alpha_u \in \pi$. As in case of the fixed-base comb methods, these points can be computed beforehand for points known a priori, such as generators. In this case, the WTNAF method has the following expected costs:

$$\frac{l}{w+1}A + lT, \qquad (6)$$

where T denotes the cost of one evaluation of τ.

3 Fixed-Base Comb Method on Koblitz Curves

We now show how the fixed-base comb multiplier can be modified to take advantage of the Frobenius endomorphism on Koblitz curves, i.e., how in this context doublings can be traded for evaluations of the map τ. Subsequently, we refer to this method as fixed-base τ-comb method. Both the precomputation and multiplication step benefit tremendously from this measure. See Section 4 for more details on the achieved performance improvements.

In order to combine the advantages of Koblitz curves with the fast fixed-based comb method, the scalar representation has to be modified. Obviously, it is necessary to obtain an unsigned τ-adic representation of scalar k, that is $k = \sum_{i=0}^{l-1} u_i \tau^i$, with $u_i \in \{0,1\}$. This representation can be obtained with a small modification to the TNAF algorithm specified by Solinas in [18], which is summarized in Algorithm 2, where we only allow u_i to be 1 in Step 4. As with TNAF, the size of this representation is approximately twice the size of the ordinary binary representation. This is why we need to perform a reduction by $\delta = \frac{\tau^m - 1}{\tau - 1}$ beforehand, in order to reduce the size of the resulting representation. As we have obtained an unsigned τ-adic scalar representation, the doublings in the precomputation need to be replaced by evaluations of τ, i.e.,

$$[a_{w-1}, \ldots, a_2, a_1, a_0]_\tau P = a_{w-1}\tau^{(w-1)d}(P) + \cdots + a_2\tau^{2d}(P) + a_1\tau^d(P) + a_0 P.$$

Algorithm 2. Computing the unsigned τ-adic representation

Input: $\kappa = r_0 + r_1\tau \in \mathbb{Z}[\tau]$
Output: κ represented as bitstring $u = (u_{t-1}, \ldots, u_1, u_0)_\tau$.
1: $i = 0$
2: **while** $(r_0 \neq 0 \lor r_1 \neq 0)$ **do**
3:     **if** $r_0 \equiv 1 \mod 2$ **then**
4:         $u_i = 1, r_0 = r_0 - 1$
5:     **else**
6:         $u_i = 0$
7:     **end if**
8:     $tmp = r_0, r_0 = \mu r_0, r_0 = r_1 + r_0/2, r_1 = -tmp/2$
9:     $i = i + 1$
10: **end while**
11: **return** $(u_{i-1}, u_{i-2}, \ldots, u_1, u_0)$

Algorithm 3 shows the fixed-base τ-comb multiplier, where doublings are replaced by evaluations of the Frobenius endomorphism τ.

We note that due to the small costs for τ, the right hand-side of Equation (5) gets large, and, thus, the two-table τ-comb method does not give an advantage over Algorithm 3 for window sizes used in practice.

Algorithm 3. Fixed-base comb method on Koblitz curves

Precompute:

Input: Window width w, $d = \lceil t/w \rceil$, $P \in E(\mathbb{F}_q)$.
Output: Table T holding $[a_{w-1}, \ldots, a_0]_\tau P$ for all length w bitstrings $(a_{w-1}, \ldots, a_0)$.

Multiply:

Input: Window width w, $d = \lceil t/w \rceil$, $k = (k_{t-1}, \ldots, k_1, k_0)_\tau$, lookup table T generated
    via *Precompute* with respect to $P \in E(\mathbb{F}_q)$.
Output: kP.
1: If necessary, pad k on the left with 0s, interpret k as $K_{w-1} \| \cdots \| K_1 \| K_0$, where
    each K_j is a length d bitstring, where $K_{j,i}$ denotes the i-th bit of K_j.
2: $Q = \mathcal{O}$.
3: **for** $i = d - 1$ **downto** 0 **do**
4:     $Q = \tau Q$
5:     $Q = Q + [K_{w-1,i}, \ldots, K_{1,i}, K_{0,i}]_\tau P = Q + T_{\sum_{j=0}^{w-1} K_{j,i} 2^j}$
6: **end for**
7: **return** Q

---

4   Implementation Results

In this section, we are detailing the implementation of the τ-comb multiplication algorithm and contrast its performance to the reference implementations of the WTNAF method and the conventional comb method.

4.1   Implementation Details

We have implemented the NIST-recommended elliptic curves K-163, K-233, K-283, K-409 and K-571 [5] in Java. We are using fast reductions for the underlying binary fields and `long`-arrays for values thereof, which are in polynomial representation. We perform squarings in linear time complexity using table lookups [16] and multiplications using the windowed left-to-right comb multiplier, which works with precomputed multiplication lookup tables and is also due to Lim and Lee (cf. [12,6]). For field multiplications, we use windows of size $w = 4$ and cache these lookup tables for recurring intermediate values in the addition/doubling formulas. Furthermore, we use partial reductions to derive the unsigned τ-adic representations (see Section 2.2).

We use López-Dahab coordinates [11] with the fast formulas given by Lange and Doche in [9,4] as well as Higuchi and Takagi in [7] and perform mixed additions in all implementations. Using this coordinate type, mixed additions take $8M + 5S$, where the multiplication lookup tables for two intermediate values can be used twice, lowering the costs to $6M + 2m + 5S$. The evaluation of τ takes $3S$ and point doublings take $3M + 5S$, which are necessary for the conventional comb methods.

Finally, we emphasize that the implementation of the τ-comb method is straight-forward and requires only little effort, which makes it a good alternative to other fixed-base multiplication methods.

4.2   Estimated Costs and Timings

Here, we present rough estimates for the scalar multiplication costs of the discussed scalar multiplication algorithms and the corresponding timings of our software implementations. As test platform served an Intel Core i5-2540M running Ubuntu Linux 12.10/amd64 and OpenJDK 7u15/amd64 in server mode.

Table 1 lists the costs of squarings and multiplications with already precomputed lookup tables in relation to the costs of multiplications on the test platform. Thus, on the test platform, we get at most $A = 8.2M$, $D = 3.5M$ and $T = 0.3M$ per mixed addition, per doubling and per evaluation of τ, respectively.

Table 1. Costs of squarings in relation to multiplications, where S denotes the cost of one squaring, M the cost of a multiplication and m the cost of a multiplication using cached precomputation tables of window size $w = 4$

	$\mathbb{F}_{2^{163}}$	$\mathbb{F}_{2^{233}}$	$\mathbb{F}_{2^{283}}$	$\mathbb{F}_{2^{409}}$	$\mathbb{F}_{2^{571}}$
$1S =$	0.094M	0.080M	0.077M	0.061M	0.055M
$1m =$	0.643M	0.717M	0.761M	0.829M	0.939M

In the following, we give some rough estimates of point multiplication costs of the WTNAF and the τ-comb method based on the relative costs given in Table 1. So, for instance, on curve K-233 with $w = 7$ the WTNAF method has expected costs of 284.09M, whereas the τ-comb method has expected costs of 264.36M giving an advantage of 7.46%. For $w = 8$, the expected runtime of the WTNAF method on K-283 is 314.00M, whereas the τ-comb method requires only 283.72M resulting in a performance gain of 10.67%. For $w = 9$ and curve K-233, we have 238.45M compared to 201.45M resulting in a speed-up of 18.37% and on curve K-409 with $w = 9$ we get 400.53M compared to 365.85M giving a speed-up of 9.48%.

Table 2 compares the timings of one fixed-base scalar multiplication of the τ-comb method with the WTNAF method and the conventional comb method. As Table 2 shows, in the former case, we achieve performance improvements of up to 25% and in the latter case improvements of up to 42%.

Table 2. Comparison of the multiplication timings of the comb, the τ-comb and the WTNAF methods

Curve	Window size	Comb [μs]	τ-Comb [μs]	WTNAF [μs]	Speedup w.r.t Comb	Speedup w.r.t WTNAF
K-163	w=6	276.50	209.06	241.77	1.32x	1.16x
	w=7	237.03	196.51	208.73	1.21x	1.06x
	w=8	211.65	168.13	194.55	1.26x	1.16x
	w=9	192.83	152.97	187.38	1.26x	1.22x
K-233	w=6	511.96	398.87	405.49	1.28x	1.02x
	w=7	455.76	341.16	386.22	1.34x	1.13x
	w=8	383.59	299.29	356.87	1.28x	1.19x
	w=9	343.87	266.21	332.61	1.29x	1.25x
K-283	w=6	738.62	544.43	583.54	1.36x	1.07x
	w=7	653.78	489.27	527.23	1.34x	1.08x
	w=8	582.79	430.37	509.92	1.35x	1.18x
	w=9	508.49	393.47	448.91	1.29x	1.14x
K-409	w=6	1581.53	1113.97	1284.27	1.42x	1.15x
	w=7	1383.75	1024.39	1110.81	1.35x	1.08x
	w=8	1203.60	889.96	1077.14	1.35x	1.21x
	w=9	1060.99	807.13	938.07	1.31x	1.16x
K-571	w=6	3026.80	2135.81	2280.14	1.42x	1.07x
	w=7	2627.00	1903.24	2061.80	1.38x	1.08x
	w=8	2336.93	1675.88	1865.80	1.39x	1.11x
	w=9	2048.58	1581.32	1816.99	1.30x	1.15x

5 Conclusions

In this paper we have presented a modification to the fixed-base comb method, which allows us to benefit from speedups available on Koblitz curves, i.e., the possibility of replacing point doublings with applications of the far more efficient Frobenius endomorphism τ. In order to do so, one has to perform scalar recoding from base 2 to an unsigned base τ representation, for which we presented the respective algorithm. We have implemented the findings in Java, which allowed us to draw a detailed performance comparison. The implementation timings showed a speedup of up to 42% for single scalar multiplications over the conventional comb method and of up to 25% over the WTNAF method. Finally, we emphasize that the implementation of the τ-comb method is straight-forward and requires only little effort. All in all, this makes it a good alternative to other fixed-base multiplication methods.

5.1 Related and Future Work

The authors of [2] showed how τ-adic representations can be optimized using telescopic sums in combination with a single point halving operation giving a speedup of $\approx 12.5\%$ over the conventional TNAF method. Later on, this approach was refined in [3] resulting in about 25% less group operations. In [1], the authors study how the Frobenius endomorphism τ can be efficiently combined with the GLV-method by using powers of τ. This way, they are able to decompose scalars and apply interleaved point multiplication on the decomposed smaller scalars, setting new speed records using a low-level implementation. Implementing the aforementioned approaches and drawing comparisons to the method proposed in this paper are issues for future work.

The authors of [15] proposed a new, fast fixed-base comb method, which combines the Lim-Lee and the Tsaur-Chou method [19]. Future work includes adapting this new fixed-base comb multiplier to work with the Frobenius endomorphism.

References

1. Aranha, D.F., Faz-Hernández, A., López, J., Rodríguez-Henríquez, F.: Faster implementation of scalar multiplication on Koblitz curves. In: Hevia, A., Neven, G. (eds.) LatinCrypt 2012. LNCS, vol. 7533, pp. 177–193. Springer, Heidelberg (2012)
2. Avanzi, R.M., Ciet, M., Sica, F.: Faster scalar multiplication on Koblitz curves combining point halving with the Frobenius endomorphism. In: Bao, F., Deng, R., Zhou, J. (eds.) PKC 2004. LNCS, vol. 2947, pp. 28–40. Springer, Heidelberg (2004), http://www.iacr.org/cryptodb/archive/2004/PKC/3329/3329.pdf
3. Avanzi, R.M., Heuberger, C., Prodinger, H.: Minimality of the hamming weight of the τ-NAF for koblitz curves and improved combination with point halving. In: Preneel, B., Tavares, S. (eds.) SAC 2005. LNCS, vol. 3897, pp. 332–344. Springer, Heidelberg (2006)
4. Cohen, H., Frey, G., Avanzi, R., Doche, C., Lange, T., Nguyen, K., Vercauteren, F.: Handbook of Elliptic and Hyperelliptic Curve Cryptography. CRC Press (2005)
5. Gallagher, P., Furlani, C.: FIPS PUB 186-3 federal information processing standards publication digital signature standard, dss (2009)
6. Hankerson, D., Menezes, A.J., Vanstone, S.: Guide to Elliptic Curve Cryptography. Springer-Verlag New York, Inc., Secaucus (2003)
7. Higuchi, A., Takagi, N.: A fast addition algorithm for elliptic curve arithmetic in $GF(2^n)$ using projective coordinates. Inf. Process. Lett. 76(3), 101–103 (2000)
8. Koblitz, N.: Elliptic curve cryptosystems. Mathematics of Computation 48(177), 203–209 (1987)
9. Lange, T.: A note on López-Dahab coordinates. IACR Cryptology ePrint Archive 2004, 323 (2004)
10. Lim, C.H., Lee, P.J.: More flexible exponentiation with precomputation. In: Desmedt, Y.G. (ed.) CRYPTO 1994. LNCS, vol. 839, pp. 95–107. Springer, Heidelberg (1994)
11. López, J., Dahab, R.: Improved algorithms for elliptic curve arithmetic in $GF(2^n)$. In: Tavares, S., Meijer, H. (eds.) SAC 1998. LNCS, vol. 1556, pp. 201–212. Springer, Heidelberg (1999)
12. López, J., Dahab, R.: High-speed software multiplication in F_{2^m}. In: Roy, B., Okamoto, E. (eds.) INDOCRYPT 2000. LNCS, vol. 1977, pp. 203–212. Springer, Heidelberg (2000)
13. Menezes, A., Okamoto, T., Vanstone, S.: Reducing elliptic curve logarithms to logarithms in a finite field. In: Proceedings of the Twenty-third Annual ACM Symposium on Theory of Computing, STOC 1991, pp. 80–89. ACM, New York (1991)
14. Miller, V.S.: Use of elliptic curves in cryptography. In: Williams, H.C. (ed.) CRYPTO 1985. LNCS, vol. 218, pp. 417–426. Springer, Heidelberg (1986)
15. Mohamed, N.A.F., Hashim, M.H.A., Hutter, M.: Improved fixed-base comb method for fast scalar multiplication. In: Mitrokotsa, A., Vaudenay, S. (eds.) AFRICACRYPT 2012. LNCS, vol. 7374, pp. 342–359. Springer, Heidelberg (2012)

16. Schroeppel, R., Orman, H., O'Malley, S., Spatscheck, O.: Fast key exchange with elliptic curve systems. In: Coppersmith, D. (ed.) CRYPTO 1995. LNCS, vol. 963, pp. 43–56. Springer, Heidelberg (1995)
17. Silverman, J.: The Arithmetic of Elliptic Curves. Graduate Texts in Mathematics, vol. 106. Springer (1986)
18. Solinas, J.A.: Efficient arithmetic on Koblitz curves. Des. Codes Cryptography 19(2/3), 195–249 (2000)
19. Tsaur, W.J., Chou, C.H.: Efficient algorithms for speeding up the computations of elliptic curve cryptosystems. Applied Mathematics and Computation 168(2), 1045–1064 (2005), http://www.sciencedirect.com/science/article/pii/S0096300304006629

Cumulus4j: A Provably Secure Database Abstraction Layer

Matthias Huber, Matthias Gabel, Marco Schulze, and Alexander Bieber

Karlsruhe Institute of Technology (KIT), NightLabs Consulting GmbH
name.surname@kit.edu, surname@nightlabs.de

Abstract. Cloud Computing has huge impact on IT systems. It offers advantages like flexibility and reduced costs. Privacy and security issues, however, remain a major drawback. While data can be secured against external threats using standard techniques, service providers themselves have to be trusted to ensure privacy.

In this paper, we present a novel technique for secure database outsourcing. We provide the security notion Ind-ICP that focuses on hiding relations between values. We prove the security of our approach and present benchmarks showing the practicability of this solution. Furthermore, we developed a plug-in for a persistence layer. Our plug-in de- and encrypts sensitive data transparently to the client application. By using encrypted indices, queries can still be executed efficiently.

1 Introduction

Cloud Computing enables a more efficient use of storage and computing resources by sharing them between multiple applications and clients. Outsourcing and pay-per-use payment models cause reduced cost for IT infrastructures. Also, the risk of fatal data loss is minimized due to specialization of the individual providers.

Huge impediments for the adoption of Cloud Computing, however, are security concerns. A client using a cloud service, loses control over his data. He cannot control whether its data is copied or misused. A malicious system administrator may copy sensitive data and sell it to e.g. competitors. Providers may even be required by law to disclose the data of their clients to government agencies.

Current security measures of Cloud Computing providers focus on *external adversaries*. Authentication and authorization mechanisms prohibit access for unauthorized clients. Measures against *internal adversaries* mostly try to restrict physical access to servers to authorized staff. Examples like Wikileaks, however, show that legal insiders also have to be taken into account.

In this paper, we present a novel approach to secure database outsourcing. Intuitively, our scheme hides associations like *Alice* ↔ *Bob* rather than hiding the values *Alice* and *Bob* themselves. In order to achieve security as well as efficiency, we use a combination of encryption and index generation. We provide the security notion Ind-ICP that informally hides relations between data values. Furthermore, we prove that our approach fulfills this new security notion.

A. Cuzzocrea et al. (Eds.): CD-ARES 2013 Workshops, LNCS 8128, pp. 180–193, 2013.

In order to demonstrate the practicability of our approach, we provide Cumulus4j [1], an implementation of our approach for data objects. We implemented Cumulus4j as a plug-in for DataNucleus [2]. DataNucleus is an open-source database abstraction layer that implements the latest versions of JPA [4] and JDO [3]. Our plug-in transparently encrypts data before it is stored in the database back-end, while providing provable security. The overhead introduced by Cumulus4j depends on the query type and the data structure. We define the overhead as the fraction time with Cumulus4j over time without Cumulus4j. Our benchmarks show that Cumulus4j has no impact on select and update queries but takes 5 times longer for inserts. Cumulus4j is open source under the GNU Affero General Public License, and can be downloaded from [1].

This paper is structured as follows: In Section 2, we will discuss related work. We present the data model used by Cumulus4j in Section 3 and the architecture in Section 4. In Section 5, we prove the security of Cumulus4j. We present and discuss benchmark results in Section 6. Section 7 concludes.

2   Related Work

The problem of secure database outsourcing emerged early in 2002 [13]. Consequently, there is a rich body of research on this problem. Most of the approaches rely either on indices or on fragmentation.

There are also well-known cryptographic schemes, that could be used to implement secure database outsourcing, namely secure multi party computations and fully homomorphic encryption [11,10]. While providing provable security, the huge overhead of these schemes would cancel out the benefits of outsourcing.

More practical approaches try to find a trade-off between security, performance, and efficient support for as many query types as possible. An efficient and practical database outsourcing scheme should provide support for sub-linear query execution time in the size of the database [16].

To our knowledge, the first practical approach to the problem of secure database outsourcing was presented by Hacigümüs et. al. in [13]. Based on this approach, additional solutions have been suggested [12,8,14].

The idea of these solutions is to create indices in order to support efficient query processing. These indices are coarse-grained. They contain keywords, ranges, or other identifiers and row ids of the rows in the database where the keywords occur. An adapter handles query transformation and sorts out false positives. Depending on the indices and the queries this can lead to a large overhead. Furthermore, it is unclear what level of security these approaches provide for realistic scenarios.

Another idea found in literature is to achieve privacy by data partitioning. The approaches in [7,9,20] introduce privacy constraints that can be fulfilled by fragmenting or encrypting the data [7,9] or fragmentation and addition of dummy data [20]. In [18], Nergiz et. al. use the Anatomy approach [21] to achieve privacy in a database outsourcing scenario. The level of privacy achieved by these partition-based approaches depends on the actual data and user defined privacy constraints. They do not provide any security notion beyond that.

Different to the approaches described above is CryptDB [19]. It does not rely on explicit indices or fragmentation. It uses the interesting concept of onions of encryptions. CryptDB proposes to encrypt the database attribute wise. Furthermore, it uses different encryption schemes that for example allow for exact match or for range queries of encrypted values. These encryptions are nested with the clear text in the middle. If a query cannot be executed because of the current encryption level of an attribute, the database removes the outermost layer of all entries of this attribute. Therefore, the security of this approach depends on how the database is used (i.e. what type of queries are issued to the database). The CryptDB approach does not provide any security notion.

3 Data Model

In order to store data objects securely in a database, we need to transform them. In this section, we describe the data model of Cumulus4j, the transformation and encryption of data objects, as well as retrieval of stored data.

A difference between relational data and objects is that objects can hold references to other objects. In order to serialize objects we serialize these references. We also need to serialize references for the indices we create. We will explain this process in the next subsection.

3.1 Serializing References

In contrast to plain fields such as int, char or boolean, references to other objects cannot be encrypted directly. They need to be serialized first. Therefore, we replace the reference with a field containing the id of the referenced object. Consider Figure 1(a). There are two objects, each with an unique *id*. These ids are provided by DataNucleus as specified in JDO and JPA. The object A has a reference to object B. Cumulus4j replaces this reference with an additional field in object A' containing the object id of object B.

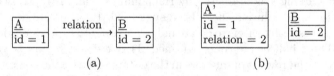

(a)   (b)

Fig. 1. Two objects A and B (a). Each object has a unique id. Object A has a reference *relation* to object B. In Figure (b), the reference has been replaced. A' contains an additional field with the id of object B.

Encrypting this field prevents an adversary from learning the relation of object A to object B. With the encryption key Cumulus4j can, however, reconstruct the original object A from the object A'.

Note that this procedure can also be recursively applied to more complex data structures.

3.2   The Cumulus4j Transformation

Cumulus4j transforms data objects into the data structure depicted in Figure 2. This transformation is done in three steps:

1. **Data object transformation and encryption**
   Cumulus4j serializes data objects, encrypts the serialization, and stores it in wrapper objects of the type *DataEntry*. References to other objects are serialized by replacing them with their wrapper objects' IDs.
2. **Meta data class creation**
   For each data object class a *ClassMeta* object and for each field of each class a *FieldMeta* object is created. These objects contain metadata such as the name of the class/field. Additionally *ClassMeta* objects contain references to their *FieldMeta* objects.
3. **Index generation**
   For each field in a data object, an *IndexEntry* object is created. This object contains the value of the field together with serialized (cf. Section 3.1) and encrypted references to those *DataEntry* wrapper objects containing the indexed field value. There are different types of *IndexEntry* classes. For example an *IndexEntryDouble* objects contains a double value, while an *IndexEntryString* object contains a string value. Each *IndexEntry* object contains a reference to its *FieldMeta* object.

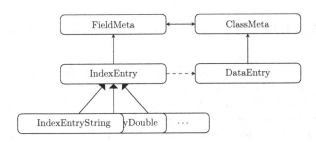

Fig. 2. The Cumulus4j data model stored in the back-end. The dashed arrow represents a serialized and encrypted reference. The *DataEntry* classes contain encrypted serializations of data objects.

After this transformation, due to the encrypted references in the *IndexEntry* objects and the encrypted data objects, an adversary only learns the field values of the original objects, but not which values occurred in the same object. Cumulus4j, however, can reconstruct the original objects. Note, that this transformation can also be applied to relational data interpreted as data objects (cf. Section 5.1). We use this in our security proof in Section 5.3.

For increased security, the index generation step can be suppressed with annotations in data object classes. In this case no index will be generated. Cumulus4j allows for suppression of index generation on field level. This has implications for security as well as performance. Not generating an index results in faster writes and increased security. This is an option for fields that are confidential by itself, and will not be part of conditions in queries (e.g. credit card numbers).

3.3 Data Retrieval

In the last section, we described the transformation that is used in order to store data objects. In this section, we describe the retrieval of data objects. This is done by the Cumulus4j plug-in that intercepts issued queries and rewrites them. The transformation of data retrieval queries is depicted as pseudocode in Figure 3.

Data: retrieval query q with conditions C and boolean operators OP
Result: result set S
exp = {} ;   /* empty expression of algebra of sets */
foreach $c_i \in C$ **do**
 | $ind \leftarrow$ retrieve and decrypt *IndexEntry* objects with matching condition c_i;
 | **if** i = 1 **then** $exp = ind$;
 | **else** $exp = exp\ op_{i-1}\ ind$;
end
ids = evaluate exp ;   /* set of ids */
$data \leftarrow$ retrieve and decrypt *DataEntry* objects with ids in ids;
$S \leftarrow q(data)$;   /* remaining evaluation of q with $data$ */
return S;

Fig. 3. Pseudocode for data retrieval queries in Cumulus4j

Consider the following example selection query for objects of a class C: $\sigma_{A=x\ op\ B<y}(C)$, where A and B are attributes, x and y are attribute values from the domain of A and B, respectively, and op is a boolean operator. In order to execute this query, Cumulus4j issues queries to the IndexEntries for indices of Class C and field A with value x and for field B with value $< y$. This procedure can be parallelized. Then Cumulus4j decrypts the indices and applies the boolean operator op to the decrypted sets of indices. The result is the set of indices of DataEntries that satisfies the query. After retrieval and decryption of these DataEntries, Cumulus4j returns them. If the issued query contains an aggregation (e.g. count), we use in memory evaluation before returning the result.

4   Architecture

We implemented Cumulus4j as a plug-in for the database abstraction layer DataNucleus. Cumulus4j integrates into DataNucleus as an OSGi plug-in. Consider the architecture depicted in Figure 4. The application component accesses DataNucleus and DataNucleus accesses the underlying database. Cumulus4j enhances DataNucleus.

The integration of our plug-in, and therefore the encryption of the underlying database, is fully transparent to the application (except for a minimum of Cumulus4j API calls controlling the key management). Thus, existing applications using DataNucleus can be easily enhanced with Cumulus4j.

In one database, thousands or more different keys are used to encrypt different records. During a database operation, only those encryption keys are in the memory of the server Cumulus4j is deployed to which are needed for the current operation. Therefore, an attacker taking a memory dump can only compromise a subset of the keys and thus decrypt only a part of the database.

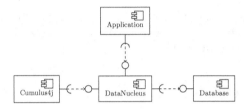

Fig. 4. Coarse architecture of DataNucleus with Cumulus4j. The integration of Cumulus4j as a plug-in for DataNucleus is transparent for the application.

Cumulus4j requires a key server that manages encryption keys. Cumulus4j supports deployment of the key server on the client as well as deployment of the key server on a separate server.

Key Server Deployed on the Client. In order to communicate with the server, the client establishes a communication channel with the server. Without a dedicated key server, the client will initiate a second communication channel. This channel is dedicated for key requests issued by the server and responses from the client (cf. Figure 5(a)). Key requests are issued by the server whenever it has to encrypt or decrypt data and therefore needs access to certain keys.

Dedicated Key Server. Alternatively to holding the keys on every client, it is possible to run a dedicated key-server (cf. Figure 5(b)). Then, clients need to establish crypto sessions with the key server. Since the keys are password protected, the key server only sends issued keys to the server if there is a corresponding crypto session with a client.

To increase security, the presence of a crypto-session (i.e. an authenticated user) is not sufficient for the key server to respond to key requests. Only, if the client is currently expecting the application server to perform database operations on his behalf, access to the key server is granted. This is done by temporarily unlocking the current crypto-session. It is locked again immediately after the application server finished its database operation. Therefore, a user does not need to log out in order to deny access to the keys on his behalf. His crypto-session is always locked whenever the user is not actively using the application.

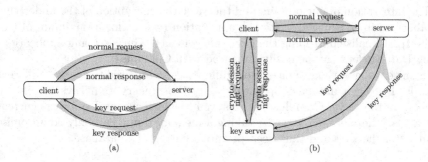

Fig. 5. Key management for different deployment Scenarios: Without a dedicated key server (a) clients handle key management. With a dedicated key-server (b) clients establish a crypto session with the key server.

5   Security of Cumulus4j

In this section, we introduce a novel security notion for outsourced databases, called Ind-ICP (Indistinguishability under Independent Column Permutation). Informally, this notion hides relations between attribute values. Furthermore, we argue that the Cumulus4j transformation we presented in Section 3.2 adheres this security notion. In order to do so, we interpret objects as rows in a table with a scheme defined by the class of the object.

5.1   Interpretation of Objects as Relational Data

Data objects contain either primitive values (e.g. int, boolean, char) or references to other objects. In order to prove the security of Cumulus4j, we interpret objects as rows in tables of a relational database. The representation we choose is as follows: Tables represent classes, attributes represent fields of classes, and attribute values represent field values of objects. Therefore, an object is represented by a row in the table of its class. Consider for example Figures 6(a) and 6(b).

Alice:Person		Bob:Person
name = Alice	← friends with →	name = Bob
surname = Smith		surname = Smith

id	name	surname	friends with
1	Alice	Smith	2
2	Bob	Smith	1

(a)   (b)

Fig. 6. An example of two objects of type *Person* (a) and a tabular representation (b) of these objects

Figure 6(a) depicts two objects of the class Person. These objects have the field *name, surname* and a *friends with* reference to each other.

These objects can be represented by rows in the table depicted in figure 6(b). Each row has a unique *id*. The references are replaced with the *id*s of the objects or rather rows.

Note, that the mapping of data objects to relational data is bijective. Therefore, a proof of security properties of objects represented this way, also applies to the objects itself.

5.2   A Security Notion for Outsourced Databases: Ind-ICP

In this section, we will present Ind-ICP, a security notion applicable to secure database outsourcing. We already introduced Ind-ICP in [15]. In this paper, we will do this more formally. We do not distinguish between a table and a database, since a (finite) set of tables always can be normalized to a universal relation. For the definition of our security notion, we define a database as a multiset of tuples:

Definition 1. *A database* $d = \{t_1, t_2, \ldots, t_n\}$ *is a multiset of tuples with attributes* $A_1, A_2, \ldots, A_m$. *We denote the value of attribute* A_i *in tuple* t_j *as* $d_{i,j}$. *We call the set of all i-th elements of each tuple in d the i-th column of d. We call the set of all databases DB.*

Throughout this paper, we use the terms tuple and row interchangeably. When interpreting objects as rows of a database, the Cumulus4j transformation presented in Section 3.2 takes databases as input and outputs also databases. We define this process as a database transformation:

Definition 2. *A database transformation is a transformation* $f : DB \to DB$. *We call* $\mathcal{F}$ *the set of all database transformations. If f is a function, we call f a database function.*

Note that not all database transformations are functions. Consider for example transformations that involve probabilistic processes. In order to define a security notion for database outsourcing, we define a relation for databases that should be indistinguishable after the Cumulus4j transformation. This relation is implied by the following database function:

Definition 3. *Let* $\Pi \subset \mathcal{F}$ *be the set of database functions* $\mathfrak{p} : DB \to DB$ *such that each* $\mathfrak{p} \in \Pi$ *independently permutes the entries within each column of a database. We call* $\mathfrak{p}$ *an independent column permutation (ICP).*

$$
\begin{array}{ccc}
\begin{array}{|c|c|c|}
\hline
\alpha & a & \mathfrak{a} \\
\beta & b & \mathfrak{b} \\
\gamma & c & \mathfrak{c} \\
\hline
\end{array}
&
\begin{array}{|c|c|c|}
\hline
\gamma & c & \mathfrak{a} \\
\beta & a & \mathfrak{b} \\
\alpha & b & \mathfrak{c} \\
\hline
\end{array}
\\
\text{(a)} & \text{(b)}
\end{array}
$$

Fig. 7. An example for a database before (a) and after (b) an independent column permutation

Consider for example the databases depicted in Figure 7. The right database (b) is the result of applying the independent column permutation $\mathfrak{p} = (\mathfrak{p}_1, \mathfrak{p}_2, \mathfrak{p}_3)$ with $\mathfrak{p}_1 = (13)$, $\mathfrak{p}_2 = (123)$, and $\mathfrak{p}_3 = id$ to the one (a).

Based on Definition 3, we define the following experiment:

Definition 4. *Let $d \in DB$ be a database, $f \in \mathcal{F}$ a database transformation, $\mathfrak{p} \in \Pi$ a independent column permutation, $\mathcal{A}$ an adversary and $i \in \{0, 1\}$. We define the experiment Ind-ICP$_{\mathcal{A}}^i$ as follows:*

$\quad Ind\text{-}ICP_{\mathcal{A}}^i(d):$
$\qquad d_0 \leftarrow f(d)$
$\qquad d_1 \leftarrow f(\mathfrak{p}(d))$
$\qquad b \leftarrow \mathcal{A}(d_i)$
$\qquad return\ b$

In this experiment, an adversary $\mathcal{A}$ guesses whether an ICP $\mathfrak{p}$ has been applied to a database d before applying f. Now, we can define our security notion:

Definition 5. *For a database transformation f, Indistinguishability under Independent Column Permutation (Ind-ICP) holds iff for each polynomially restricted adversary $\mathcal{A}$, for each database $d \in DB$, and each ICP $\mathfrak{p} \in \Pi$ the following holds:*

$$\mathrm{Adv}_{\mathcal{A}}^{Ind\text{-}ICP}(d) :=$$

$$\left| Pr[Ind\text{-}ICP_{\mathcal{A}}^1(d) = 1] - Pr[Ind\text{-}ICP_{\mathcal{A}}^0(d) = 1] \right|$$

is negligible.

Informally, a database transformation fulfills Ind-ICP if, given the transformed database, an adversary cannot infer the relations of the attribute values of the original database, since the relations are destroyed by independent column permutations. This security notion is weaker than classical cryptographic security notion (e.g. Ind-CCA). It, however, allows for schemes that support efficient execution of queries on the *encrypted* data.

Please note, that Ind-ICP does not compose with background knowledge. According to the No-Free-Lunch Theorem [17], this is not possible for an scheme that maintains some utility. Because of this, in our implementation we introduced annotations that allow for suppression of index generation.

5.3   Cumulus4j Fulfills Ind-ICP

In Section 5.1, we argued that data objects also can be interpreted as relational data. In this section, we apply the Cumulus4j transformation to arbitrary relational data and prove that it adheres Ind-ICP. For this proof, we assume that all tables are sorted lexicographically and that the adversary has no background knowledge about the database.

Consider Figure 8: Figure 8(a) depicts an arbitrary table with attributes a_i and attribute values $v_{i,j}$. Figure 8(b) depicts the table from Figure 8(a) after applying an arbitrary independent column permutation (cf. Section 5.2). We now apply the Cumulus4j transformation to these two tables and show, that the results are indistinguishable for any polynomial time adversary. Thus, proving that the Cumulus4j transformation fulfills Ind-ICP.

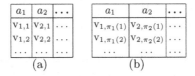

Fig. 8. A table with attributes a_i and values $v_{i,j}$ (a) and the same table after applying an independent column permutation (b). Not depicted: The meta data associated with the tables and its attributes.

Interpreting the tables in Figure 8 as objects, applying the Cumulus4j transformation (cf. Section 3.2) and reinterpreting the result as relational data yields tables depicted in Figures 9 and 10. For the sake of simplicity and w.l.o.g., we assume each attribute value to be unique.

Fig. 9. A relational representation of the result of the application of the Cumulus4j transformation (cf. Section 3.2) to the table in Figure 8(a) assuming the attribute values $v_{i,j}$ are different

Fig. 10. The result of the application of the Cumulus4j transformation to the table in Figure 8(b) assuming the attribute values $v_{i,j}$ are different

Cumulus4j encrypts each row of the original table (*DataEntry*), generates indices (*IndexEntry*) with encrypted keys for every attribute value, and generates the meta data tables. The meta data tables contain keys, meta data about the original table, as well as meta data about attributes.

The tables in Figures 9 and 10 are identical except for the encrypted entries. Therefore, breaking the Ind-ICP property of Cumulus4j implies breaking the underlying encryption scheme.

6 Performance

In order to predict the performance of an application after migrating to Cumulus4j, we measure the performance with a generic benchmark suite. For this, we use the open-source database benchmark suite PolePosition [5], which can be easily used with DataNucleus. We compare two engines: DataNucleus without Cumulus4j and DataNucleus with Cumulus4j. The benchmark is run multiple times for each engine and averaged. This way, effects of the OS and the Java garbage collection are minimized. Different scenarios (called *circuits*) are considered in order to better understand the impact on a complex application later. The full source code – including the benchmarks – can be downloaded at [1]. We measure the time for four different circuits (for details cf. [6]):

- **Complex** uses a deep object graph of different classes with an inheritance hierarchy of five levels.
- **Flatobject** uses simple flat objects with indexed fields.
- **Inheritancehierarchy** operates on objects of a class hierarchy with a depth of five levels.
- **Nestetdlists** uses a deep graph of lists for traversing.

We describe the operations performed in the different circuits:

- **write** stores all objects into an initially empty database.
- **read** loads all attached objects into memory and traverses them, by calculating a checksum over all objects.
- **query** queries for instances over an indexed field.
- **update** traverses all objects, updates a field in each object.
- **delete** traverses all objects and deletes each object individually.
- **queryIndexedString** simulates querying for a number of flat objects by an indexed string member.
- **queryIndexedInt** simulates querying for a number of flat objects by an indexed int member.

DataNucleus translates all above queries into rapidly processable exact match queries (`attr = param`).

The setup is as follows: The benchmark is run on an application and benchmark server (Intel Core i7-2700K, 3.5 GHz, 16 GB RAM). A database server (AMD Phenom II X6, 0.8 GHz, 8 GB RAM) hosts the MySQL 5.5 database. They are connected via Gigabit Ethernet. The setup divides the servers into two zones: The trusted zone running the DataNucleus+Cumulus4j middleware and the untrusted storage back-end.

The results are shown in Figure 11 in appendix A. In oder to cope with outliers, the mean time for all operations is shown on a logarithmic scale in order to cope with outliers. The introduction of the Cumulus4j plug-in makes the creation of the initial datasets more complex, thus consuming more time. Data encryption and the creation of indices result in an overhead of factor 5. MySQL does not use any indices per default. But due to the implicit use of indices in Cumulus4j, query operations run faster on the Cumulus4j engine for all circuits. Updates take almost the same amount of time while deletes are marginally slower with Cumulus4j. It is currently unknown why the read operations in the *Inheritance-hierarchy* are much slower than without Cumulus4j.

We can confer that the use of the Cumulus4j plug-in in DataNucleus does not introduce high overhead in any scenario. It is best suited for applications with many read and few write queries, but it can be used in every scenario.

When using Cumulus4j in web application, the user would probably not notice any slowdown at all, because the overall response time is only marginally affected by Cumulus4j.

7   Conclusion and Future Work

In this paper, we introduced a new approach for securing outsourced databases. While taking insider-attacks into account, we focused on privacy – a major concern when dealing with Cloud Computing.

We presented Cumulus4j, a plug-in for the database abstraction layer DataNucleus. It serializes and encrypts data objects and generates meta data that enables fast query processing. Cumulus4j handles encryption, decryption and query translation transparently and requires only minimal changes to the original application. We defined a novel security notion, Ind-ICP, which informally is fulfilled if relations between attribute values are hidden. We proved that Cumulus4j achieves this kind of security. Finally, we showed that the solution is practical by comparing it with an unsecured database in several benchmark scenarios.

Planned future improvements are optimizations of the index structure as well as additional annotations in order to allow for even faster queries execution.

Acknowledgements. We wish to thank Andy Jefferson and Jan Mortensen of NightLabs Consulting GmbH their support with the implementation of Cumulus4j and with the benchmarks. This work has been partially funded by the Federal Ministry of Education and Research, Germany (BMBF, Contract No. 01IS10037) and KASTEL (BMBF, Contract No. 16BY1172). The responsibility for the content of this article lies solely with the authors.

References

1. Cumulus4j, http://www.cumulus4j.org/
2. Data Nucleus Access Plattform, http://www.datanucleus.org/
3. Java Data Objects (JDO), http://db.apache.org/jdo/
4. Java Persistence API (JPA), http://www.oracle.com/technetwork/java/javaee/tech/persistence-jsp-140049.html
5. PolePosition, http://polepos.sourceforge.net
6. PolePosition Circuits, http://polepos.sourceforge.net/circuits.html
7. Aggarwal, G., Bawa, M., Ganesan, P., Garcia-Molina, H., Kenthapadi, K., Motwani, R., Srivastava, U., Thomas, D., Xu, Y.: Two can keep a secret: A distributed architecture for secure database services. In: CIDR 2005 (2005)

8. Damiani, E., De Capitani di Vimercati, S., Jajodia, S., Paraboschi, S., Samarati, P.: Balancing confidentiality and efficiency in untrusted relational DBMSs (2003)
9. De Capitani di Vimercati, S., Foresti, S., Jajodia, S., Paraboschi, S., Samarati, P.: Fragments and loose associations: respecting privacy in data publishing. Proc. VLDB Endow. 3(1-2), 1370–1381 (2010)
10. Gentry, C.: Fully homomorphic encryption using ideal lattices. In: Proceedings of the 41st Annual ACM Symposium on Theory of Computing, STOC 2009, pp. 169–178. ACM, New York (2009)
11. Goldreich, O., Micali, S., Wigderson, A.: How to play any mental game or a completeness theorem for protocols with honest majority. In: Proceedings of the Nineteenth Annual ACM Symposium on Theory of Computing, pp. 218–229. ACM, New York (1987)
12. Hacigümüs, H., Iyer, B., Li, C., Mehrotra, S.: Executing SQL over encrypted data in the database-service-provider model. In: Proceedings of the 2002 ACM SIGMOD International Conference on Management of Data, pp. 216–227. ACM (2002)
13. Hacigümüs, H., Iyer, B., Mehrotra, S.: Providing database as a service. In: ICDE 2002: Proceedings of the 18th International Conference on Data Engineering, p. 29. IEEE Computer Society, Washington, DC (2002)
14. Hore, B., Mehrotra, S., Tsudik, G.: A privacy-preserving index for range queries. In: VLDB 2004: Proceedings of the Thirtieth International Conference on Very Large Data Bases, pp. 720–731. VLDB Endowment (2004)
15. Huber, M., Henrich, C., Müller-Quade, J., Kempka, C.: Towards secure cloud computing through a separation of duties. In: Informatik 2011 (2011)
16. Kantarcioglu, M., Clifton, C.: Security issues in querying encrypted data. Technical report (2004)
17. Kifer, D., Machanavajjhala, A.: No free lunch in data privacy. In: Proceedings of the 2011 ACM SIGMOD International Conference on Management of Data, SIGMOD 2011, pp. 193–204. ACM, New York (2011)
18. Nergiz, A.E., Clifton, C.: Query processing in private data outsourcing using anonymization. In: Li, Y. (ed.) Data and Applications Security and Privacy XXV. LNCS, vol. 6818, pp. 138–153. Springer, Heidelberg (2011)
19. Popa, R.A., Redfield, C.M.S., Zeldovich, N., Balakrishnan, H.: Cryptdb: protecting confidentiality with encrypted query processing. In: Proceedings of the Twenty-Third ACM Symposium on Operating Systems Principles, SOSP 2011, pp. 85–100. ACM, New York (2011)
20. Soodejani, A.T., Hadavi, M.A., Jalili, R.: k-anonymity-based horizontal fragmentation to preserve privacy in data outsourcing. In: Cuppens-Boulahia, N., Cuppens, F., Garcia-Alfaro, J. (eds.) DBSec 2012. LNCS, vol. 7371, pp. 263–273. Springer, Heidelberg (2012)
21. Xiao, X., Tao, Y.: Anatomy: simple and effective privacy preservation. In: Proceedings of the 32nd International Conference on Very Large Data Bases, VLDB 2006, pp. 139–150. VLDB Endowment (2006)

A Benchmark Results

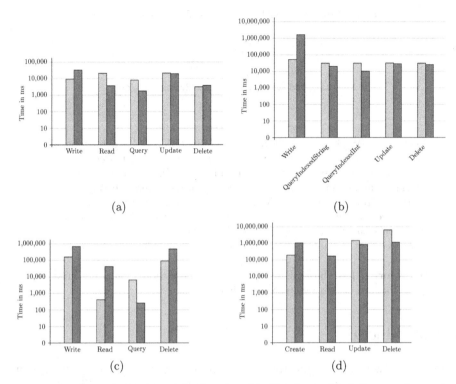

Fig. 11. Benchmark of circuit (a) *Complex*, (b) *Flatobject*, (c) *Inheritancehierarchy*, and (d) *Nestedlists* of JDO/DataNucleus without (light gray) and with the Cumulus4j plug-in (dark gray)

Optimal Parameters for XMSS^{MT}

Andreas Hülsing[*], Lea Rausch, and Johannes Buchmann

Cryptography and Computeralgebra
Department of Computer Science
TU Darmstadt, Germany
huelsing@cdc.informatik.tu-darmstadt.de

Abstract. We introduce Multi Tree XMSS (XMSS^{MT}), a hash-based
signature scheme that can be used to sign a virtually unlimited number
of messages. It is provably forward and hence EU-CMA secure in the
standard model and improves key and signature generation times compared to previous schemes. XMSS^{MT} has — like all practical hash-based
signature schemes — a lot of parameters that control different trade-offs
between security, runtimes and sizes. Using linear optimization, we show
how to select provably optimal parameter sets for different use cases.

Keywords: hash-based signatures, parameter selection, linear optimization, forward secure signatures, implementation.

1 Introduction

Digital signatures are among the most important cryptographic primitives in
practice. They are used to secure communication protocols like SSL/TLS and
SSH, software updates, or to replace handwritten signatures. Hash-based signature schemes are an interesting alternative to the signature schemes used today.
Not only because they are assumed to resist quantum computer aided attacks,
but also because of their fast signature generation and verification times as well
as their strong security guarantees. The latest hash-based signature schemes [3,9]
come with a standard model security proof and outperform RSA in many settings regarding runtimes.

Practical hash-based signature schemes have a lot of parameters that control
several trade-offs between runtimes and sizes. Hence, an important open problem
on the way of making hash-based signatures practical is parameter selection. In
previous works [3,4,6,7,9] it was shown how to select secure parameters using
the exact security reductions, but this still leaves too many possible parameter
choices to apply a brute-force search. Even applying reasonable restrictions on
the parameters, the search space can easily grow to the order of 2^{80} and more.
In this work we introduce Multi Tree XMSS (XMSS^{MT}), a new hash-based
signature scheme that contains the latest hash-based signature schemes XMSS

---

[*] Supported by grant no. BU 630/19-1 of the German Research Foundation
(www.dfg.de).

A. Cuzzocrea et al. (Eds.): CD-ARES 2013 Workshops, LNCS 8128, pp. 194–208, 2013.

and XMSS$^+$ as special cases and propose a systematic way to select the optimal parameter set for a given scenario for XMSS^{MT}.

XMSS^{MT} improves XMSS in a way, that it allows for a virtually unlimited number of signatures, while it preserves its desirable properties. XMSS^{MT} has minimal security requirements, i.e. it can be proven EU-CMA secure in the standard model, when instantiated with a pseudorandom function family and a second preimage resistant hash function. Moreover, XMSS^{MT} is forward secure [1] and introduces a new trade-off between signature and key generation time on the one hand and signature size on the other hand. XMSS^{MT} can be viewed as applying the tree chaining idea introduced in [6] to XMSS and combine it with the improved distributed signature generation proposed in [9].

For XMSS^{MT}, we show how to model the parameter selection problem as a linear optimization problem. A straight forward approach would lead many nonlinear constraints. To overcome this problem, we use the generalized lambda method [13] for linearization. The resulting model can then be solved using the Simplex algorithm [8]. As the general lambda method is exact, the Simplex algorithm outputs a provably optimal solution under the given constraints. We made the model flexible, such that it can be used for different use cases with different requirements using different inputs. We present results for demonstrative use cases and compare them to possible parameter choices from previous work. However, the code is available on the corresponding authors home page and can be used to select optimal parameters for other use cases. Linear optimization was used before in [4] to find optimal parameters. Unfortunately, the results given there do not carry over to the new hash-based signature schemes, as less parameters were taken into account and the authors of [4] do not provide details about how to model the problem.

Organization. We start with an introduction to XMSS^{MT} in Section 2, where we also discuss theoretical runtimes and parameter sizes as well as security and correctness of the scheme. In Section 3 we show how to model the parameter selection problem for XMSS^{MT} as a linear optimization problem and present optimal parameters for exemplary use cases in Section 4. We discuss our results and draw a conclusion in Section 5.

2   Multi Tree XMSS - XMSS^{MT}

In this section we introduce XMSS^{MT}. For a better understanding, we first give a brief description of the scheme. A hash-based signature scheme starts with a one-time signature scheme (OTS). To obtain a many time signature scheme, many instances of the OTS are used and their public key are authenticated using a binary hash tree, called Merkle-Tree. The root of the tree is the public key of the scheme and the secret key is the seed of a pseudorandom generator that is used to generate the OTS secret keys. A signature contains an index, the OTS signature, and the so called authentication path which contains the siblings of the nodes on the way from the used OTS key pair to the root. For XMSS^{MT} we extend this using many layers of trees. The trees on the lowest layer are used to sign the messages and the trees on higher layers are used to sign the roots of the trees on the layer below. The public key contains only the root of the tree on the top layer. A signature consists of all the signatures on the way to the highest tree. A graphical representation of the scheme can be found in Appendix E. In the following we describe the construction in detail, starting with the description of some building blocks. Afterwards we describe the algorithms of the scheme and present an theoretical analysis of its performance, security and correctness.

Parameters. For security parameter $n \in \mathbb{N}$, the basic building blocks of XMSS^{MT} are a pseudorandom function family $\mathcal{F}_n = \{F_K : \{0,1\}^n \to \{0,1\}^n | K \in \{0,1\}^n\}$, and a second preimage resistant hash function $H : \{0,1\}^{2n} \to \{0,1\}^n$. Further parameters are the number of layers $d \in \mathbb{N}$, the binary message length m and one parameter set per layer. For a layer $0 \leq i \leq d-1$ a parameter set contains the tree height $h_i \in \mathbb{N}$, the so called BDS parameter $k_i \in \mathbb{N}$ with the restrictions $k_i < h_i$ and $h_i - k_i$ is even and the Winternitz parameter $w_i \in \mathbb{N}, w_i \geq 2$. To enable improved distributed signature generation we require $(h_{i+1} - k_{i+1} + 6)/2 \leq 2^{h_i - k_i + 1}$ for $0 \leq i < d - 1$, as well as $(h_0 - k_0)/2 \geq d - 1$. A XMSS^{MT} key pair can be used to sign $h = \sum_{i=0}^{d-1} h_i$ messages of m bits. The remaining parameters define the various trade-offs explained below. These parameters are publicly known.

Winternitz OTS. XMSS^{MT} uses the Winternitz-OTS (W-OTS) from [2]. W-OTS uses the function family $\mathcal{F}_n$ and a value $X \in \{0,1\}^n$ that is chosen during XMSS key generation. Besides message length m and Winternitz parameter w it has another parameter $\ell = \ell(m, w)$ that is a function of m and w. The W-OTS secret key, public key and signatures consist of ℓ bit strings of length n. An important property of W-OTS is that the public key can be computed from a valid signature. The sizes of signature, public, and secret key are ℓn bits. The runtimes for key generation, signature generation and signature verification are all bounded by $\ell(w - 1)$ evaluations of elements from $\mathcal{F}_n$. The Winternitz parameter w controls a time - space trade-off, as ℓ shrinks logarithmically in w. For more detailed information see Appendix A.

XMSS Tree. XMSS^{MT} uses the XMSS tree construction, originally proposed in [7]. An XMSS tree of height h is a binary tree with $h + 1$ levels. The leaves are on level 0, the root on level h. The nodes on level j, are denoted by $N_{i,j}$, for $0 \leq i < 2^{h-j}, 0 \leq j \leq h$. To construct the tree, h bit masks $B_j \in \{0,1\}^{2n}$, $0 < j \leq h$ and the hash function H, are used. $N_{i,j}$, for $0 < j \leq h$, is computed as $N_{i,j} = H((N_{2i,j-1}||N_{2i+1,j-1}) \oplus B_j)$.

Leaf Construction. The leaves of a XMSS tree are the hash values of W-OTS public keys. To avoid the need of a collision resistant hash function, another XMSS tree is used, called L-tree. The ℓ leaves of an L-tree are the ℓ bit strings $(\mathsf{pk}_0, \ldots, \mathsf{pk}_\ell)$ from the corresponding public key. If ℓ is not a power of 2, a left node that has no right sibling is lifted to a higher level of the L-tree until it becomes the right sibling of another node. For the L-tree, the same hash function as above but $\lceil \log \ell \rceil$ new bitmasks are used. These bitmasks are the same for all L-trees.

Pseudorandom Generator. The W-OTS key pairs belonging to one XMSS tree are generated using two pseudorandom generators (PRG) build using $\mathcal{F}$. The stateful forward secure PRG FsGEN : $\{0,1\}^n \to \{0,1\}^n \times \{0,1\}^n$ is used to generate one seed value per W-OTS keypair. Then the seed is expanded to the ℓ W-OTS secret key bit strings using $\mathcal{F}_n$. FsGEN starts from a uniformly random state $S_0 \xleftarrow{\$} \{0,1\}^n$. On input of a state S_i, FsGEN generates a new state S_{i+1} and a pseudorandom output R_i: FsGEN$(S_i) = (S_{i+1}||R_i) = (\mathrm{F}_{S_i}(0)||\mathrm{F}_{S_i}(1))$. The output R_i is used to generate the ith W-OTS secret key $(\mathsf{sk}_1, \ldots, \mathsf{sk}_\ell)$ as $\mathsf{sk}_j = \mathrm{F}_{R_i}(j-1), 1 \leq j \leq \ell$.

Tree Traversal - The BDS Algorithm. To compute the authentication paths for the W-OTS key pairs of one XMSS tree, XMSS^{MT} uses the BDS algorithm [5]. The choice of this algorithm is already a time - memory trade-off. Instead of computing every node of the authentication path when needed, BDS uses some storage to decrease the worst case runtime. The BDS algorithm uses the TREEHASH algorithm (see Algorithm 1) as a subroutine. The BDS algorithm reduces the worst case signing time from $2^h - 1$ to $(h - k)/2$ leaf computations and evaluations of TREEHASH. More specifically, the BDS algorithm does three things. First, it uses the fact that a node that is a left child can be computed from values that occurred in an authentication path before, spending only one evaluation of H. Second, it stores the right nodes from the top k levels of the tree during key generation. Third, it distributes the computations for right child nodes among previous authentication path computations. It schedules one instance of TREEHASH per tree level. The computation of the next right node on a level starts, when the last computed right node becomes part of the authentication path. BDS uses a state State$_{\mathrm{BDS}}$ of $2(h - k)$ states of FsGEN and at most $\left(3h + \lfloor \frac{h}{2} \rfloor - 3k - 2 + 2^k\right)$ tree nodes that is initialized during key generation. To compute the authentication paths, the BDS algorithm spends $(h-k)/2$ leaf computations and evaluations of TREEHASH as well as $(h - k)$ calls to F to update its state per signature. For more details see [5].

Algorithm 1. TREEHASH

Input: Stack Stack, node N_1
Output: Updated stack Stack

1. **While** top node on Stack has same height as N_1 **do**
   (a) $t \longleftarrow N_1.height() + 1$
   (b) $N_1 \longleftarrow \mathrm{H}\left((\mathsf{Stack}.pop()||N_1) \oplus B_t\right)$
2. Stack.$push(N_1)$
3. **Return** Stack

Key Generation. The XMSS^{MT} key generation algorithm takes as input all of the above parameters. First, the $\max_{0 \le i \le d-1}\{h_i + \lceil \log \ell_i \rceil\}$ bitmasks and X are chosen uniformly at random. The same bitmasks and X are used for all layers. Then, the root of the first XMSS tree on each layer is computed. This is done in an ordered way, starting from layer 0. For the tree TREE$_i$ on layer i the initial state of FSGEN, $S_{0,i}$ is chosen uniformly at random and a copy of it is stored as part of the secret key SK. The tree is constructed using the TREEHASH algorithm above. Starting with an empty stack Stack$_i$ and $S_{0,i}$, all 2^{h_i} leaves are successively generated and used as input to the TREEHASH algorithm to update Stack$_i$. This is done updating S_i and generating the W-OTS key pairs using its output. The W-OTS public key is then used to compute the corresponding leaf using an L-tree which in turn is used to update the current Stack$_i$ using TREEHASH. Then the W-OTS key pair is deleted. After all 2^{h_i} leaves were processed by TREEHASH, the only value on Stack$_i$ is the root ROOT$_i$ of TREE$_i$. When ROOT$_i$ $0 \le i < d-1$, is computed, it is signed using the first W-OTS key pair of TREE$_{i+1}$, which is computed next. This signature σ_{i+1} can be extracted while TREE$_i$ is generated and hence does not need any additional computation. Then σ_{i+1} is stored as part of SK. If the highest layer $d-1$ is reached, ROOT$_{d-1}$ is stored in the public key PK. During the computation of ROOT$_i$, the state of the BDS algorithm State$_{\text{BDS},i}$ is initialized. For details see [5].

Finally, the data structures for the next trees are initialized: For the next tree NEXT$_i$ on each layer $0 \le i < d-1$ a FSGEN state $S_{n,i}$ is chosen uniformly at random and a new TREEHASH stack Stack$_{next,i}$ is initialized. Summing up, SK consists of the states $(S_{0,i}, \text{State}_{\text{BDS},i}), 0 \le i \le d-1$ and the $d-1$ signatures σ_i, $0 < i \le d-1$. Additionally, it contains $d-1$ FSGEN states $S_{n,i}, d-1$ TREEHASH stacks Stack$_{next,i}$ and $d-1$ BDS states State$_{\text{BDS},n,i}$ for the next trees NEXT$_i$ on layer $0 \le i < d-1$. The public key PK consists of the $\max_{0 \le i \le d-1}\{h_i + \lceil \log \ell_i \rceil\}$ bitmasks, the value X and ROOT$_{d-1}$.

Signature generation. The signature generation algorithm takes as input a m bit message M, the secret key SK, and the index i, indicating that this is the ith message signed with this keypair. The signature generation algorithm consists of two phases. First, M is signed. A XMSS^{MT} signature $\Sigma = (i, \sigma_0, \text{Auth}_0, \sigma_1, \text{Auth}_1, \ldots, \sigma_d, \text{Auth}_d)$ contains the index i, the W-OTS signature σ_0 on the message M, the corresponding authentication path for TREE$_0$ and the W-OTS signatures on the roots of the currently used trees together with the corresponding authentication paths. The only thing that has to be computed is σ_0 — the W-OTS signature on message M using the ith W-OTS key pair on the lowest layer. All authentications paths and the W-OTS signatures on higher layers are already part of the current secret key.

The second phase is used to update the secret key. Therefor BDS is initialized with State$_{\text{BDS},0}$ and receives $(h_0 - k_0)/2$ updates. If not all of these updates are needed to update State$_{\text{BDS},0}$, i.e. all scheduled TREEHASH instances are finished and there are still updates left, the remaining updates are used for the upper trees. On the upper layers, not only the BDS state has to be updated, but while one leaf is used, one leaf in the next tree must be computed and $h_i - k_i$

FsGen states must be updated. This means that remaining updates from layer zero are first used to update $\mathsf{State}_{BDS,1}$. If all scheduled TreeHash instances in $\mathsf{State}_{BDS,1}$ are finished, one update is used to compute a new leaf for Next_1 and to update $\mathsf{Stack}_{next,1}$ afterwards. The next update is used to for the FsGen states. If layer 1 does not need anymore updates, the remaining updates are forwarded to layer 2 and so on, until either all updates are used or all tasks are done. Finally, one leaf of the next tree is computed and used as input for TreeHash to update $\mathsf{Stack}_{next,0}$.

A special case occurs if $i \bmod 2^{h_0} = 2^{h_0} - 1$. In this case, the last W-OTS key pair of the current Tree_0 was used. This means that for the next signature a new tree is needed on every layer j with $i \bmod 2^{h_j} = 2^{h_j} - 1$. For all these layers, $\mathsf{Stack}_{next,j}$ already contains the root of Next_j. So, Tree_{j+1} is used to sign Root_j. Each signature is counted as one update. In case not all updates are needed, remaining updates are forwarded to the first layer that did not get a new tree. In SK, $\mathsf{State}_{BDS,j}$, S_j, and Σ_j are replaced by the newly computed data. Afterwards, new data structures for the next tree on layer j are initialized and used to replace the ones in SK. Finally, the signature SIG, the updated secret key SK and $i + 1$ are returned.

Signature verification. The signature verification algorithm takes as input a signature $\Sigma = (i, \sigma_0, \mathsf{Auth}_0, \sigma_1, \mathsf{Auth}_1, \ldots, \sigma_d, \mathsf{Auth}_d)$, the message M and the public key PK. To verify the signature, σ_0 and M are used to compute the corresponding W-OTS public key. The corresponding leaf $N_{0,j}$ of Tree_0 is constructed and used together with Auth_0 to compute the path $(P_0, \ldots, P_{h_0})$ to the root of Tree_0, where $P_0 = N_{0,j}$, $j = i \bmod 2^{h_0}$ and

$$P_c = \begin{cases} \mathrm{H}((P_{c-1} \| \mathsf{Auth}_{c-1,0}) \oplus B_c), & \text{if } \lfloor j/2^c \rfloor \equiv 0 \mod 2 \\ \mathrm{H}((\mathsf{Auth}_{c-1,0} \| P_{c-1}) \oplus B_c), & \text{if } \lfloor j/2^c \rfloor \equiv 1 \mod 2 \end{cases}$$

for $0 \leq c \leq h_0$. This process is then iterated for $1 \leq a \leq d-1$, using the output of the last iteration $P_{h_{a-1}} = \mathrm{Root}_{a-1}$ as message, σ_a, Auth_a and $j = \left\lfloor i/2^{\sum_{b=0}^{a-1} h_b} \right\rfloor$ mod 2^{h_a}. If the output of the last iteration $P_{h_{d-1}}$ equals the root value contained in PK, Root_{d-1}, the signature is assumed to be valid and the algorithm returns 1. In any other case it returns 0.

2.1   Analysis

In the following we provide an analysis of XMSS^{MT}. A discussion of correctness and security can be found in appendices B, C and D. In the following we discuss key and signature sizes and the runtimes of the algorithms.

First we look at the sizes. A signature contains the index and d pairs of W-OTS signature and authentication path. Hence a signature takes $24 + n \cdot \sum_{i=0}^{d-1}(\ell_i + h_i)$ bits, assuming we reserve three bytes for the index. The public key contains the bitmasks, X and Root_{d-1}. Thus, the public key size is $n \cdot (\max_{0 \leq i \leq d-1}\{h_i + \lceil \log \ell_i \rceil\} + 2)$ bits. The secret key contains one FsGen state and one BDS state consisting of $2(h_i - k_i)$ FsGen states and no more than $(3h_i + \lfloor \frac{h_i}{2} \rfloor - 3k_i - 2 + 2^{k_i})$

tree nodes [5] per currently used tree TREE_i. In addition it contains the $d - 1$ W-OTS signatures $\sigma_1, \ldots, \sigma_{d-1}$ which have a total size of $n \cdot \sum_{i=1}^{d-1} \ell_i$ bits and the structures for upcoming trees. As observed by the authors of [9], these structures do not require a full BDS state, as some of the structures are not filled during initialization and the space to store the k top levels of nodes can be shared with the current tree. Thus, these structures require only $(h_i - k_i + 1)$ FSGEN states (one for building the tree and the remaining as storage for the BDS state) and no more than $3h_i - k_i + 1$ tree nodes per TREE_i, $0 \le i < d - 1$. The secret key size is

$$n \cdot \left(\sum_{i=0}^{d-1} \left[\left(5h_i + \left\lfloor \frac{h_i}{2} \right\rfloor - 5k_i - 2 + 2^{k_i} \right) + 1 \right] + \sum_{i=0}^{d-2} (\ell_{i+1} + 4h_i - 2k_i + 2) \right)$$

bits. For the runtimes we only look at the worst case times and get the following. During key generation, the first tree on each layer has to be computed. This means, that each of the 2^h W-OTS key pairs has to be generated, including the execution of the PRGs. Further, the leaves of the trees have to be computed and all internal nodes of the tree, to obtain the root. If key generation generates the trees in order, starting from the first one, the W-OTS signatures on the roots of lower trees need no additional computation, as the signature can be extracted while the corresponding W-OTS key pair is generated. The key generation time is

$$t_{\text{Kg}} \le t_{\text{H}} \left(\sum_{i=0}^{d-1} \left(2^{h_i} (\ell_i + 1) \right) \right) + t_{\text{F}} \left(\sum_{i=1}^{d-1} \left(2^{h_i} (2 + \ell_i (w_i + 1)) \right) \right),$$

where t_{H} and t_{F} denote the runtimes of one evaluation of H and F, respectively. During one call to Sign, a W-OTS signature on the message must be generated, including generation of the key $(t_{\text{F}}(2 + \ell_0(w_0 + 1)))$, the BDS algorithm receives $(h_0 - k_0)/2$ updates, one leaf of the next tree on layer 0 must be computed and the BDS algorithm updates $h_0 - k_0$ upcoming seeds $(t_{\text{F}}(h_0 - k_0))$. The worst case signing time is bounded by

$$t_{\text{Sign}} \le \max_{i \in [0, d-1]} \left\{ \begin{array}{l} t_{\text{H}} \left(\frac{h_0 - k_0 + 2}{2} \cdot (h_i - k_i + \ell_i) + h_0 \right) \\ + t_{\text{F}} \left(\frac{h_0 - k_0 + 4}{2} \cdot (\ell_i (w_i + 1)) + h_0 - k_0 \right) \end{array} \right\}$$

Signature verification consists of computing d W-OTS public keys and the corresponding leafs plus hashing to the root. Summing up verification takes $t_{\text{vf}} \le \sum_{i=0}^{d-1} (t_{\text{H}} (\ell_i + h_i) + t_{\text{F}} (\ell_i w_i))$ in the worst case.

3   Optimization

Given the theoretical formulas for runtimes and sizes from the last section, we now show how to use them to model the parameter selection problem as linear optimization problem. There are parameters which control different trade-offs. The BDS parameters $k_i \in \mathbb{N}$ control a trade-off between signature time and secret key size, the Winternitz parameters $w_i \in \mathbb{N}$ control a trade-off between runtimes and signature size and the number of layers d determines a trade-off between key generation and signature time on the one hand and signature size on the other hand. Moreover there are the different tree heights h_i that do not define any obvious trade-off, but influence the security as well as the performance of the scheme. The goal of the optimization is to choose these parameters. The function families $\mathcal{F}_n$ and H can be instantiated, either using a cryptographic hash function or a block cipher. Hence the security parameter n is restricted to the output size of such functions. We choose 128 and 256 bit corresponding to AES and SHA-2 for our optimization, respectively.

Optimization Model. To find good parameter choices, we use linear optimization. In the following we discuss how we model the problem of optimal parameter choices as a linear optimization problem. As objective function of our problem we chose a weighted sum of all runtimes and sizes that should be minimized. Using the weights it is possible to control the importance of minimizing a certain parameter and thereby using the model for different scenarios. We further allow to apply absolute bounds on the runtimes and sizes. The formulas for runtimes and sizes are modeled as constraints as well as the parameter restrictions and the formula for bit security (see Appendix D). The input to the model are the runtimes of $\mathcal{F}$ and $\mathcal{H}$ for $n = 128$ and $n = 256$, the overall height h, the message length m and a value b as lower bound on the bit security.

As many of our initial constraints are not linear, we have to linearize all functions and restrictions. This is done using the generalized lambda method [13]. In addition, we split the problem into sub problems each having some decision variables fixed. The optimization problem contains the parameters of the scheme (d, n, the h_i, k_i, w_i for all layer) as decisions variables which are determined by solving the optimization. Further the message length m_i on each layer has to be modelled as a decision variable. Since solving the optimization problem takes much time and memory, we split the problem into sub problems by fixing the decision variables n and d. Therefore, we receive one sub problem for each combination of possible values of n and d. The resulting sub problems are solved independently and the best of their solutions is chosen as global solution of the original optimization problem.

The next step is to linearize the remaining sub problems by using the generalized lambda method. Therefore, we introduce a grid point for each possible combination of the remaining variables h, k, w and m on each layer i. For each grid point we have a binary variable $\lambda_{h,k,w,m,i}$ which takes value 1 if the combination of h, k, w, m is chosen on layer i. Otherwise, it takes value 0. Since we need one choice of h, k, w, m for each $i \in [0, d-1]$, d λ's must be chosen.

We use those lambdas to calculate the functions describing the problem. Thus, before optimizing we determine the values of the functions for each possible values of their variables. To make this feasible, we have to introduce bounds on the decision variables. We bound the tree height per layer layer by 24. As $k \leq h$ this bound also applies to k. For w we chose 255. These bounds are reasonable for the scenarios of the next section. For different scenarios they might have to be changed. Then, to model the needed space of signatures $\sum_{i=0}^{d-1} (\ell_i + h_i) \cdot n$, we formulate the constraint

$$SpaceSig == \sum_{i=0}^{d-1} \sum_{h=1}^{24} \sum_{k=1}^{24} \sum_{w=2}^{512} \sum_{m \in \{128,256\}} \lambda_{h,k,w,m,i} \cdot \underbrace{f_{SpaceSig}(w,h,m)}_{pre-calculated}$$

in the optimizing model, where $f_{SpaceSig}(w,h,m) = (\ell + h)n$. Thus, $SpaceSig$ gives the exact value of the needed space of signatures for the choice of lambda's and can be used in constraints and objective function.

To linearize a condition containing the maximum of some terms, such as the public key size $n \cdot (\max_{0 \leq i \leq d-1}\{h_i + \lceil \log \ell_i \rceil\} + 2)$, we write the following constraint:

$$\forall i \in \{1, ..., T\}$$

$$SpacePK \geq \sum_{h=1}^{24} \sum_{k=1}^{24} \sum_{w=2}^{512} \sum_{m \in \{128,256\}} \lambda_{h,k,w,m,i} \cdot (\underbrace{f_{\lceil \log \ell \rceil}(w,m)}_{pre-calculated} + h + 2)n$$

Hence, $SpacePK$ gives the public key size for the choice of lambda's. This constraint pushes the value of $SpacePK$ up high and due to the objective function the value will be pushed down as low as possible, so that in the end it takes the exact value.

4   Optimization Results

In this section we present optimal parameters for two exemplary use cases. More results will be included in the full version of this paper. To solve the optimization problem, we used the IBM Cplex solver [10], that implements the Simplex algorithm [8] with some improvements. The linearization described in the last section is exact. Thus, there is no loss of information or error. Therefore, it can be proven that the solution found by linear optimization based on the Simplex algorithm is the best possible solution. In the following we present the results and compare them with the results for parameter sets proposed in [3] and [9]. We choose a message length of 256 bits for all use cases assuming that the message is the output of a collision resistant hash function. Moreover we use 80 bits as lower bound for the provable bit security. This seems reasonable, as the used bit security represents a provable lower bound on the security of the scheme and is not related to any known attacks. We used the instantiations for $\mathcal{F}$ and $\mathcal{H}$ proposed in [3] with AES and SHA2 for $n = 128$ and $n = 256$, respectively and measured the resulting runtimes on a Laptop with Intel(R) Core(TM) i5-2520M CPU @2.5 GHz and 8 GB RAM. We got $t_F = 0.000225ms$ and $t_H = 0.00045ms$ for $n = 128$ as well as $t_F = 0.00169ms$ and $t_H = 0.000845ms$ for $n = 256$.

The first use case we look at meets the requirements of a document or code signature. We assume that the most important parameters are signature size and verification time and try to minimize them, while keeping reasonable bounds on the remaining parameters. We used the bounds $t_{Sign} < 1000ms, t_{Vf} < 1000ms, t_{Kg} < 60s, sk < 25kB, pk < 1.25kB, \sigma < 100kB$ and the weights $t_{Sign} = 0.00000001, t_{Vf} = 0.00090000, t_{Kg} = 0.00000001, sk = 0.00000001, \sigma = 0.99909996, pk = 0.00000001$ for $h = 20$. We chose different weights for t_{Vf} and σ, because the optimization internally counts in bits and milliseconds. We set the weights such that $1ms$ costs the same as 1000 bit. The remaining weights are not set to zero but to $1.0e-8$, the smallest possible value that we allow. This is necessary to ensure that our implementation of inequalities in the model works. This also ensures that within the optimal solutions regarding t_{Vf} and σ, the best one regarding the remaining parameters is chosen. It turns out, that the optimization can be solved for $d \geq 2$. For $d = 1$ the bound on the key generation time cannot be achieved for the required height. If we relax this bound to be $t_{Kg} < 600s$, i.e. 10 minutes, the problem can be solved for $n = 128$ using AES. For $d \geq 2$ this relaxation does not change the results. The optimal parameters for this setting are $n = 128, d = 2, h_0 = 17, k_0 = 5, w_0 = 5$ and $h_1 = 3, k_1 = 3, w_1 = 22$. For comparison we use a parameter set from [9] that matches the bound on the bit security ($n = 128, d = 2, h_0 = h_1 = 10, k_0 = k_1 = 4, w_0 = w_1 = 4$). The resulting runtimes and sizes are shown in Table 1. The results show that it is possible to reduce the signature size by almost one kilo byte, changing the other parameters within their bounds and increasing the second important parameter, the verification time, by 0.08 milliseconds.

As a second use case we take a total tree height of 80 and aim for a balanced performance over all parameters. This use cases corresponds to the use in a communication protocol. Again, we choose the weights such that $1ms$ costs the same as 1000 bit, but this time we use the same weights for all runtimes and for all sizes. For comparison we use parameters from [4] ($d = 4, h_0 = h_1 = h_2 = h_3 = 20, w_0 = 5, w_1 = w_2 = w_3 = 8, k_0 = k_1 = k_2 = k_3 = 4$). As they do not use a BDS parameter, we choose $k = 4$ on all layers. To make a fair comparison, we limited our optimization also to four layers. The optimal parameters returned by the optimization are $h_0 = h_1 = h_2 = h_3 = 20, w_0 = 14, w_1 = w_2 = w_3 = 24$ and $k_0 = k_1 = k_2 = 4, k_3 = 2$. The results are shown in Table 1. It turns out, that again, by trading some runtime, the signature size can be significantly reduced.

Table 1. Runtimes and sizes for optimized parameters and parameters proposed in previous works

Use case	Runtimes (ms)			Sizes (bit)		
	t_{Kg}	t_{Sign}	t_{Vf}	σ	PK	SK
$UC1$ optimal	27251	1.65	0.36	21376	6144	25472
$UC1$ from [9]	326	1.00	0.28	28288	4608	25856
$UC2$ optimal	166min	25.55	9.13	83968	13824	209152
$UC2$ from [4]	98min	14.53	5.01	119040	13824	233472

5 Conclusion

With XMSS^{MT} we presented a new hash-based signature scheme, that allows to use a key pair for 2^{80} signatures, which is a virtually unlimited number of signatures in practice. The new scheme is highly flexible and can be parameterized to meet the requirements of any use case for digital signatures. In order to get the maximum benefit from this parameterization, we showed how to use linear optimization to obtain provably optimal parameter sets. We have shown the strength and functionality of our approach by presenting the parameter sets for two different use cases. Comparing our results to parameter sets from other works, it turns out that there is a lot of space for optimization.

References

1. Bellare, M., Miner, S.: A forward-secure digital signature scheme. In: Wiener, M. (ed.) CRYPTO 1999. LNCS, vol. 1666, pp. 431–448. Springer, Heidelberg (1999)
2. Buchmann, J., Dahmen, E., Ereth, S., Hülsing, A., Rückert, M.: On the security of the Winternitz one-time signature scheme. In: Nitaj, A., Pointcheval, D. (eds.) AFRICACRYPT 2011. LNCS, vol. 6737, pp. 363–378. Springer, Heidelberg (2011)
3. Buchmann, J., Dahmen, E., Hülsing, A.: XMSS - A practical forward secure signature scheme based on minimal security assumptions. In: Yang, B.-Y. (ed.) PQCrypto 2011. LNCS, vol. 7071, pp. 117–129. Springer, Heidelberg (2011)
4. Buchmann, J., Dahmen, E., Klintsevich, E., Okeya, K., Vuillaume, C.: Merkle signatures with virtually unlimited signature capacity. In: Katz, J., Yung, M. (eds.) ACNS 2007. LNCS, vol. 4521, pp. 31–45. Springer, Heidelberg (2007)
5. Buchmann, J., Dahmen, E., Schneider, M.: Merkle tree traversal revisited. In: Buchmann, J., Ding, J. (eds.) PQCrypto 2008. LNCS, vol. 5299, pp. 63–78. Springer, Heidelberg (2008)
6. Buchmann, J., Coronado García, L.C., Dahmen, E., Döring, M., Klintsevich, E.: CMSS – an improved merkle signature scheme. In: Barua, R., Lange, T. (eds.) INDOCRYPT 2006. LNCS, vol. 4329, pp. 349–363. Springer, Heidelberg (2006)
7. Dahmen, E., Okeya, K., Takagi, T., Vuillaume, C.: Digital signatures out of second-preimage resistant hash functions. In: Buchmann, J., Ding, J. (eds.) PQCrypto 2008. LNCS, vol. 5299, pp. 109–123. Springer, Heidelberg (2008)
8. Dantzig, G.B.: Linear Programming And Extensions. Princeton University Press (1963)
9. Hülsing, A., Busold, C., Buchmann, J.: Forward secure signatures on smart cards. In: Knudsen, L.R., Wu, H. (eds.) SAC 2012. LNCS, vol. 7707, pp. 66–80. Springer, Heidelberg (2013)
10. IBM. IBM ILOG CPLEX Optimizer, http://www-01.ibm.com/software/integration/optimization/cplex-optimizer/ (accessed Januray 2013)
11. Lenstra, A.K.: Key lengths. Contribution to The Handbook of Information Security (2004)
12. Malkin, T., Micciancio, D., Miner, S.: Efficient generic forward-secure signatures with an unbounded number of time periods. In: Knudsen, L.R. (ed.) EUROCRYPT 2002. LNCS, vol. 2332, pp. 400–417. Springer, Heidelberg (2002)
13. Moritz, S.: A Mixed Integer Approach for the Transient Case of Gas Network Optimization. PhD thesis, TU Darmstadt (February 2007)

A   Winternitz OTS

XMSS^{MT} uses the Winternitz-OTS (W-OTS) from [2]. W-OTS uses the function family $\mathcal{F}_n$ and a value $X \in \{0,1\}^n$ that is chosen during XMSS key generation. For $K, X \in \{0,1\}^n$, $e \in \mathbb{N}$, and $F_K \in \mathcal{F}_n$ we define $F_K^e(X)$ as follows. We set $F_K^0(X) = K$ and for $e > 0$ we define $K' = F_K^{e-1}(X)$ and $F_K^e(X) = F_{K'}(X)$. Also, define

$$\ell_1 = \left\lceil \frac{m}{\log(w)} \right\rceil, \quad \ell_2 = \left\lfloor \frac{\log(\ell_1(w-1))}{\log(w)} \right\rfloor + 1, \quad \ell = \ell_1 + \ell_2.$$

The secret signature key of W-OTS consists of ℓ n-bit strings sk_i, $1 \leq i \leq \ell$. The generation of the sk_i will be explained later. The public verification key is computed as

$$\mathsf{pk} = (\mathsf{pk}_1, \ldots, \mathsf{pk}_\ell) = (F_{\mathsf{sk}_1}^{w-1}(X), \ldots, F_{\mathsf{sk}_\ell}^{w-1}(X)),$$

with F^{w-1} as defined above. W-OTS signs messages of binary length m. They are processed in base w representation. They are of the form $M = (M_1 \ldots M_{\ell_1})$, $M_i \in \{0, \ldots, w-1\}$. The checksum $C = \sum_{i=1}^{\ell_1}(w - 1 - M_i)$ in base w representation is appended to M. It is of length ℓ_2. The result is a sequence of ℓ base w numbers, denoted by $(T_1, \ldots, T_\ell)$. The signature of M is

$$\sigma = (\sigma_1, \ldots, \sigma_\ell) = (F_{\mathsf{sk}_1}^{T_1}(X), \ldots, F_{\mathsf{sk}_\ell}^{T_\ell}(X)).$$

It is verified by constructing $(T_1 \ldots, T_\ell)$ and checking

$$(F_{\sigma_1}^{w-1-T_1}(X), \ldots, F_{\sigma_\ell}^{w-1-T_\ell}(X)) \stackrel{?}{=} (\mathsf{pk}_1, \ldots, \mathsf{pk}_\ell).$$

The sizes of signature, public, and secret key are ℓn bits. The runtimes for key generation, signature generation and signature verification are all bounded by $\ell(w-1)$ evaluations of elements from $\mathcal{F}_n$. The Winternitz parameter w controls a time - space trade-off, as ℓ shrinks logarithmically in w. For more detailed information see [2].

B   Correctness

In the following we argue that the BDS state on every layer receives its $(h-k)/2$ updates between two signatures. The authors of [9] showed that there is a gap between the updates a XMSS key pair receives over its lifetime and the updates it really uses. Namely, for $2 \leq k \leq h$ there are 2^{h-k+1} unused updates. For every tree on a layer other than 0, $h - k + 3$ updates are needed. The first $h - k$ updates are needed to update the TREEHASH instances in the BDS state. Further one update is needed to compute a node in the next tree, to update the FsGen states in the BDS state and to sign the root of the next tree on the lower layer, respectively. Between two signatures of a tree on layer $i + 1$, a whole tree on layer i is used, so if we ensure that $(h_{i+1} - k_{i+1} + 6)/2 \leq 2^{h_i - k_i + 1}$, as we do, the $(h_i - k_i)/2$ updates TREE_i receives over its lifetime leave enough unused updates such that TREE_{i+1} receives the required updates. There would still occur a problem, if the number of updates per signature would be smaller than $d - 1$. The reason is, that this would mean that the roots of the new trees on different layers could not always be signed using the updates of the last signature before the change. In this case the private storage would grow, as we would need some intermediate storage for the new signatures. This is the reason why the second condition $((h_0 - k_0)/2 \geq d - 1)$ is needed.

C   Security

For the security, the argument is similar to that of [9]. In [3], an exact proof is given which shows that XMSS is forward secure, if $\mathcal{F}$ is a pseudorandom function family and $\mathcal{H}$ a second preimage resistant hash function family. The tree chaining technique corresponds to the product composition from [12]. In [12] the authors give an exact proof for the forward security of the product composition if the underlying signature schemes are forward secure. It is straight forward to combine both security proofs to obtain an exact proof for the forward security of XMSS^{MT}. In contrast to the case of XMSS^+, for XMSS^{MT} the product composition is applied not only once, but $d - 1$ times. As forward security implies EU-CMA security, this also shows that XMSS^{MT} is EU-CMA secure.

D   Security Level

We compute the security level in the sense of [11]. This allows a comparison of the security of XMSS^{MT} with the security of a symmetric primitive like a block cipher for given security parameters. Following [11], we say that XMSS^{MT} has security level b if a successful attack on the scheme can be expected to require approximately 2^{b-1} evaluations of functions from $\mathcal{F}_n$ and $\mathcal{H}_n$. Following the reasoning in [11], we only take into account generic attacks on $\mathcal{H}_n$ and $\mathcal{F}_n$. A lower bound for the security level of XMSS was computed in [3]. For XMSS^{MT}, we combined the exact security proofs from [3] and [12]. Following the computation in [3], we can lower bound the security level b by

$$b \geq \min_{0 \leq i \leq d-1} \left\{ n - 4 - w_i - 2log(\ell_i w_i) - \sum_{j=i}^{d-1} h_j \right\}$$

for the used parameter sets.

E   XMSS^{MT} in Graphics

Here we included some graphics for a better understanding of XMSS^{MT}. Figure 1 shows the construction of the XMSS tree. An authentication path is shown in Figure 2. And finally Figure 3 shows a schematic representation of a XMSS^{MT} instance with four layers.

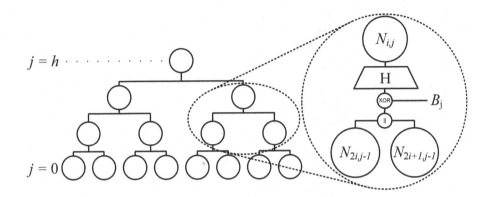

Fig. 1. The XMSS tree construction

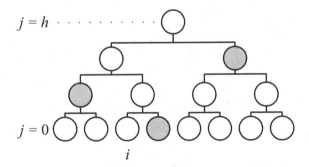

Fig. 2. The authentication path for a leaf i

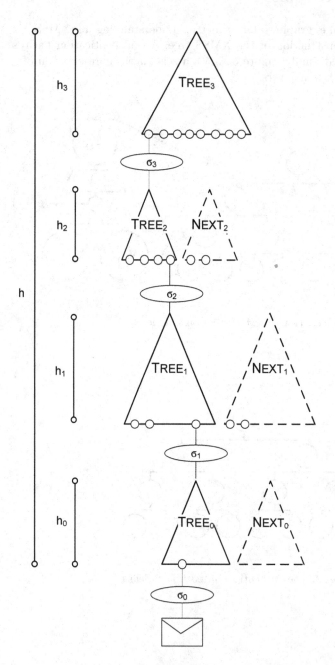

Fig. 3. A schematic representation of a XMSS^{MT} instance with four layers

Solving the Discrete Logarithm Problem for Packing Candidate Preferences

James Heather[1], Chris Culnane[1], Steve Schneider[1], Sriramkrishnan Srinivasan, and Zhe Xia[2,*]

[1] Department of Computing, University of Surrey, Guildford GU2 7XH, U.K.
{j.heather,c.culnane,s.schneider}@surrey.ac.uk
[2] Department of Computing, Wuhan University of Technology, 430063, China
xiazhe@whut.edu.cn

Abstract. Ranked elections are used in many places across the world, and a number of end-to-end verifiable voting systems have been proposed to handle these elections recently. One example is the vVote system designed for the Victorian State Election, Australia. In this system, many voters will give a full ranking of up to 38 candidates. The easiest way to do this is to ask each voter to reorder ciphertexts representing the different candidates, so that the ciphertext ordering represents the candidate ranking. But this requires sending 38 ciphertexts per voter through the mixnets, which will take a long time. In this paper, we explore how to "pack" multiple candidate preferences into a single ciphertext, so that these preferences can be represented in the least number of ciphertexts possible, while maintaining efficient decryption. Both the packing and the unpacking procedure are performed publicly: we still provide 38 ciphertexts, but they are combined appropriately before they enter the mixnets, and after decryption, a meet-in-the-middle algorithm can be used to recover the full candidate preferences despite the discrete logarithm problem.

1 Introduction

Ranked elections are currently used in various elections across the world. For example, they can be found in some local government elections in the US, Scotland, Northern Ireland, New Zealand and Malta. Also, they are used to elect the lower house of parliament in some territories in Australia. Recently, several end-to-end verifiable (e2e) voting systems have been proposed to handle ranked elections. One example is the vVote system [7], [6], which is designed for the Victorian State Election, Australia. In this election, there are around 10 parties and up to 38 candidates. The ballot form consists of two parts: the Above-The-Line (ATL) part lists the parties and the Below-The-Line (BTL) part lists the candidates. The voter can cast her vote using either the ATL part or the BTL part. If a voter chooses to use the ATL part, she simply selects a single party and her vote

---

* Corresponding author.

A. Cuzzocrea et al. (Eds.): CD-ARES 2013 Workshops, LNCS 8128, pp. 209–221, 2013.

will be interpreted according to this party's pre-published candidate ranking. If this voter does not agree on any pre-published candidate ranking, she can cast her vote by expressing a full ranking of the candidates in the BTL part. After all votes are received, the election result will be tallied using the Single Transferable Vote (STV) method. According to the historical data, among the 430,000 voters in that election, about 95% of them will cast ATL votes and the others will cast BTL votes. To design an e2e voting solution for the vVote system, both situations need to be considered. In theory, the ATL votes can be tallied simply using the homomorphic property [9], [10]. However, since the BTL vote contains a full ranking of a very large number of candidates, how to tally these votes in an efficient manner is not so straightforward, and this has been overlooked in many existing schemes.

1.1 Design Decisions in the vVote System

The vVote system [7], [6] is not designed as some theoretical concept, but it aims to be used in the real elections in the State of Victoria, Australia. Hence not only security issues but also efficiency and usability issues have been considered. Here, we review some of the design decisions in the vVote system and briefly explain why they have been made.

- **Prêt à Voter style ballot form:** the voters will cast their votes using the Prêt à Voter [8], [21], [20] style ballot form. The main reason for this design decision is that in Prêt à Voter, the vote casting and the ballot auditing are nicely separated, and the ballots can be audited without the vote choices being given. Compared with some other e2e schemes, e.g. the Benaloh scheme [4], Helios [1] and Wombat [24], in which voters need to fill in their choices before deciding whether to audit the ballots or to cast them, the Prêt à Voter approach is more appropriate in this case because the voter will only need to give a full ranking of 38 candidates once.
- **Italian attack:** if the election consists of a large number of candidates, a very large number of possible candidate rankings exist. Adversaries can force voters to cast their votes using specific orderings, and check whether ballots with these unique orderings appear among the cast ballots. This has been referred to as the Italian attack in the literature. Recently, existing techniques [23], [5] have been introduced to solve the Italian attack. However, these techniques are computationally expensive and are not practical to be used in large scale elections. Hence, some compromise needs to be made between security and efficiency: the vVote system has decided not to address the Italian attack.
- **Mixnets vs. homomorphic encryption** in e2e voting schemes, the vote tally phase is normally designed either using mixnets [22], [17], [13] or homomorphic encryption [3], [10], [2]. However, when the election is tallied using the STV method, votes may need to be transferred during the vote tally phase. Thus, each vote has to be kept separated from the other ones. To hide the voter-vote relationships, mixnets are used to shuffle the received votes.

- **ElGamal encryption vs. Paillier encryption** ElGamal [12] has been selected in the system design. The main reason for this design decision is that compared with Paillier [18], ElGamal is not only more computationally efficient but also easier to implement. For example, in order to achieve the 128-bit security level[1], 4096-bit p and 256-bit q are normally used in ElGamal, while in Paillier, the size of n is normally chosen to be 4096 bits. Therefore, in ElGamal and Paillier, the size of exponentiation is 256 bits and 4096 bits respectively, and the size of modulus is 4096 bits and 8192 bits respectively. Therefore, when using ElGamal, the re-encryption computation in the shuffle will be several dozen times quicker than using Paillier. Moreover, the implementation of distributed key generation and threshold decryption in ElGamal is much more straightforward than those in Paillier.

1.2 Our Contribution

Based on the above design decisions, the BTL vote will be handled using the Prêt à Voter style ballot form. The "onions" in the ballot form are encrypted using ElGamal encryption. The received votes are shuffled using mixnets in the vote tally phase. However, if the Prêt à Voter scheme is used in ranked elections, the candidate ordering on the ballot form needs to be randomly permuted rather than just be cyclicly shifted. Otherwise, if the adversaries know who is the voter's most/least preferred candidate, they can find out the rest of this voter's ranking just by accessing her receipt. A simple method to design the randomly permuted candidate ordering is to assign a ciphertext next to each candidate. The voter's ranking will be used to reorder these ciphertexts (this is demonstrated in Figure 1). But this means that for each ballot, a 38-ciphertext tuple will be inserted into the mixnets, and after the shuffle, each of the ciphertext needs to be decrypted. Obviously, this will take a long time.

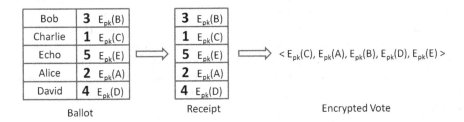

Fig. 1. The ciphertext ranking represents the candidate ordering

---

[1] Considering that the encrypted votes will be published on the web bulletin board. Some people argue that 128-bit security level is not enough since the votes may need to be protected far into the future. Here, the 128-bit security level is only used as an example.

If multiple candidate references can be packed into one ciphertext before the shuffle, fewer ciphertexts will be sent to the mixnets, and fewer ciphertexts need to be decrypted after the shuffle. To make this idea work, we need to use the additive homomorphic property when packing the ciphertexts. This requires us to use the exponential ElGamal encryption. However, because of the discrete logarithm problem, there does not exist an efficient algorithm to retrieve the voter's rankings after the ciphertext is decrypted.

In this paper, we investigate how to pack the sequence of 38 ciphertexts into the least number of ciphertexts possible, so that they can be mixed and decrypted more efficiently. We also introduce a meet-in-the-middle algorithm that enables the full candidate preferences to be recovered despite the discrete logarithm problem. Note that although our technique is developed using the vVote system as an example, it is applicable to many other ranked elections with a large number of candidates.

1.3   Structure of the Paper

In Section 2, we briefly review the meet-in-the-middle techniques, especially the Baby-Step-Giant-Step algorithm. This is followed by describing the system parameters in Section 3. Our method to recover the candidate preferences despite the discrete logarithm problem will be introduced in Section 4. We then provide some discussions in Section 5 before concluding in Section 6.

2   Meet-in-the-middle Review

In the literature, many meet-in-the-middle methods have been introduced. A common property of these methods is that trade-off can be made between time and memory. The benefit is that the search time can be dramatically reduced at the cost of extra storage. For example, because of the meet-in-the-middle attack, double DES is not more secure than the standard DES although its keysize is doubled [11]. Triple DES with two keys is also unable to improve security over the standard DES when considering the chosen plaintext attack [16].

Another famous example of the meet-in-the-middle method is Shank's Baby-Step-Giant-Step (BSGS) algorithm, which is used to solve the discrete logarithm problem. Since it shares some similarities with our proposed technique, we briefly review this algorithm here. In BSGS, the discrete logarithm $x = log_g y$ is represented as follows:

$$x = x_\alpha \cdot \gamma + x_\beta \qquad \text{where } 0 \leq x_\alpha, x_\beta < \gamma$$

The value γ is chosen to be the size of the square root of the group order $\lceil \sqrt{|\mathbb{G}|} \rceil$. This ensures that the value x will span across the entire group. Now, if we denote $T = g^x = g^{x_\alpha \cdot \gamma + x_\beta}$, the above equation can be re-written as follows:

$$T \cdot (g^{-\gamma})^{x_\alpha} = g^{x_\beta}$$

Thus, in order to find $x \in \mathbb{G}$, we need to find a pair (x_α, x_β) that satisfies the above equation. To achieve this, we first build a lookup table that stores all possible mappings from g^{x_β} to x_β, where $0 \leq x_\beta < \gamma$. Note that the size of this table is $\sqrt{|\mathbb{G}|}$. Then, we can try all possible x_α values in the range $0 \leq x_\alpha < \gamma$, until we find a hit in the lookup table that satisfies $T \cdot (g^{-\gamma})^{x_\alpha} = g^{x_\beta}$. If we find such a pair, x can be calculated as $x = x_\alpha \cdot \gamma + x_\beta$.

When using the brute force search to solve the discrete logarithm problem, the computational cost is $|\mathbb{G}|$. By using the Baby-Step-Giant-Step algorithm, the cost can be reduced to $\sqrt{|\mathbb{G}|}$, and the extra cost is to build a lookup table of size $\sqrt{|\mathbb{G}|}$.

3   System Parameters

All these parameters are selected publicly before the election.

Crypto parameters: Let p, q be two large primes such that $q|p-1$. We denote $\mathbb{G}_q$ as the subgroup of $\mathbb{Z}_p^*$ of order q. Let g be a generator of $\mathbb{G}_q$. The public key pk is (p, q, g, y), where $y = g^x \pmod{p}$ and the secret key x is threshold shared among a number of parties [19], [14]. In order to achieve the 128-bit security level, p and q are suggested to be chosen as 4096 and 256 bits respectively[2].

Candidate parameters: Following the idea in [9], [2], we choose a value M which is larger than the number of candidates. Hence in our case, if there are $n = 38$ candidates, M can be chosen as $n + 1 = 39$. After the candidates are sorted into the canonical order, the first candidate will be assigned value $M^0 \pmod{q}$, the second candidate $M^1 \pmod{q}$, and so on. If we generalise this, the i-th candidate will be assigned the value $M^{i-1} \pmod{q}$.

Encryption The exponential ElGamal cipher [12] will be used for encryption thanks to its additive homomorphic property, i.e. for two messages $m_1, m_2 \in \mathbb{Z}_q$, their ciphertexts can be denoted as $\mathsf{E}_{pk}(m_1) = (g^{m_1}y^{r_1}, g^{r_1}), \mathsf{E}_{pk}(m_2) = (g^{m_2}y^{r_2}, g^{r_2})$ respectively[3], and we have the property that $\mathsf{E}_{pk}(m_1) \cdot \mathsf{E}_{pk}(m_2) = \mathsf{E}_{pk}(m_1 + m_2 \pmod{q})$. For the candidates in the canonical order, the ciphertext assigned to the first candidate is $C_1 = \mathsf{E}_{pk}(M^0)$, the ciphertext assigned to the second candidate is $C_2 = \mathsf{E}_{pk}(M^1)$, and so on. If we generalise this, the ciphertext assigned for the i-th candidate is $C_i = \mathsf{E}_{pk}(M^{i-1})$.

4   Ciphertext Packing

To make the explanation clear, we describe the "ciphertext packing" technique step by step, where each step improves its previous step.

---

[2] For more information about the recommended key length by NIST and ECRYPT II, please refer to http://www.keylength.com/

[3] In this document, we assume all arithmetic to be modulo p where applicable, unless otherwise stated.

4.1 Packing All 38 Ciphertexts into 1 Ciphertext

Theoretically, it is possible to pack all the 38 ciphertexts as well as the voter's rankings into a single ciphertext. For example, we first sort the ciphertexts of a received vote based on its rankings, and the result can be represented as $\{C_{\pi(1)}, C_{\pi(2)}, \ldots, C_{\pi(38)}\}$, where $\pi(i)$ denotes the i-th candidate in the voter's rankings. Then the set of ciphertexts can be packed as

$$\widehat{C} = \prod_{i=1}^{n} C_{\pi(i)}{}^{i}$$

When the above ciphertext is decrypted, we will get the plaintext as $g^{\sum_{i=1}^{n} i \cdot M^{\pi(i)-1}}$. However, because of the discrete logarithm problem, there is no efficient method to retrieve $\sum_{i=1}^{n} i \cdot M^{\pi(i)-1} \pmod{q}$ from the decrypted plaintext. One method is to build a lookup table to store all the possible mappings from g^{ρ} to ρ. In our case, the 38 candidates can be ranked in any order. Thus, there will be $n! = 38! \approx 2^{148}$ possible ρ values. Obviously, it is not feasible to build such a lookup table in practice.

Example 1. *Suppose there are 5 candidates, and the voter's ranking is $\langle 4, 5, 2, 1, 3 \rangle$ (so that $\pi(1) = 4$, $\pi(2) = 5$ and so on). Then the packing becomes*

$$E_{pk}(M^3)^1 \cdot E_{pk}(M^4)^2 \cdot E_{pk}(M^1)^3 \cdot E_{pk}(M^0)^4 \cdot E_{pk}(M^2)^5$$
$$= \quad E_{pk}(1 \cdot M^3 + 2 \cdot M^4 + 3 \cdot M^1 + 4 \cdot M^0 + 5 \cdot M^2)$$

4.2 Packing Every α Ciphertexts into 1 Ciphertext

Alternatively, once we have the ciphertext list $\{C_{\pi(1)}, C_{\pi(2)}, \ldots, C_{\pi(38)}\}$ sorted according to the voter's ranking, starting from the first ciphertext, we can make every α ciphertexts as a group

$$\{(C_{\pi(1)}, C_{\pi(2)}, \ldots, C_{\pi(\alpha)}), (C_{\pi(\alpha+1)}, C_{\pi(\alpha+2)}, \ldots, C_{\pi(2\alpha)}), \ldots\}$$

For each group of α ciphertexts, we treat their rankings as values from 1 to α, and we pack these α ciphertexts into one as

$$\widehat{C_j} = \prod_{i=1}^{\alpha} C_{\pi(j\alpha+i)}{}^{i}$$

where $j = 0, 1, \ldots, \lceil \frac{n}{\alpha} \rceil - 1$. When the ciphertext $\widehat{C_j}$ is decrypted, the plaintext is $g^{\sum_{i=1}^{\alpha} i \cdot M^{\pi(j\alpha+i)-1}}$. Similarly, we need to build a lookup table to retrieve $\sum_{i=1}^{\alpha} i \cdot M^{\pi(j\alpha+i)-1} \pmod{q}$ from the decrypted plaintext. In this case, the size of the lookup table is $n!/(n-\alpha)!$ which is smaller than $n!$. Hence by selecting different value α, we can adjust not only the packing ratio (how many ciphertexts to be packed into one) but also the size of the lookup table: to increase the value α, both the packing ratio and the size of the lookup table increase, and the reverse is true as well. For example, if there are 38 candidates and $\alpha = 6$, all 38 ciphertexts in a ballot can be packed into $\lceil \frac{38}{6} \rceil = 7$ ciphertexts, and the size of the lookup table will be $38!/(38-6)! \approx 2^{31}$. Since the lookup table can be generated in advance (e.g. before the election) and it only needs to be generated once, the construction of such a lookup table is within the computational capacity of modern computers.

Example 2. *Suppose there are 6 candidates and $\alpha = 3$. The voter's ranking is $\langle 4, 5, 2, 1, 3, 6 \rangle$. The packing becomes*

$$\langle (\mathsf{E}_{pk}(\mathsf{M}^3)^1 \cdot \mathsf{E}_{pk}(\mathsf{M}^4)^2 \cdot \mathsf{E}_{pk}(\mathsf{M}^1)^3), \quad (\mathsf{E}_{pk}(\mathsf{M}^0)^1 \cdot \mathsf{E}_{pk}(\mathsf{M}^2)^2 \cdot \mathsf{E}_{pk}(\mathsf{M}^5)^3) \rangle$$
$$= \quad \langle \mathsf{E}_{pk}(1 \cdot \mathsf{M}^3 + 2 \cdot \mathsf{M}^4 + 3 \cdot \mathsf{M}^1), \quad \mathsf{E}_{pk}(1 \cdot \mathsf{M}^0 + 2 \cdot \mathsf{M}^2 + 3 \cdot \mathsf{M}^5) \rangle$$

4.3   Packing Every $\alpha + \beta$ Ciphertexts into 1 Ciphertext

Now, we improve the above packing method a step further: we show how the packing ratio can be increased without increasing the size of the lookup table. Similar to the existing meet-in-the-middle methods, our search method is also a trade-off between time and memory. Suppose the ciphertext list $\{C_{\pi(1)}, C_{\pi(2)}, \ldots, C_{\pi(38)}\}$ has been sorted according to the voter's ranking. Starting from the first ciphertext, we make every $\alpha + \beta$ ciphertexts as a group

$$\{(C_{\pi(1)}, \ldots, C_{\pi(\alpha)}, C_{\pi(\alpha+1)}, \ldots, C_{\pi(\alpha+\beta)}), (C_{\pi(\alpha+\beta+1)}, \ldots, C_{\pi(2\alpha+\beta)}, C_{\pi(2\alpha+\beta+1)}, \ldots, C_{\pi(2\alpha+2\beta)}) \ldots\}$$

For each group of $\alpha + \beta$ ciphertexts, we treat their rankings as values from 1 to $\alpha + \beta$, and we can pack these $\alpha + \beta$ ciphertexts into one ciphertext as

$$\widehat{C_j} = \prod_{i=1}^{\alpha+\beta} C_{\pi(j(\alpha+\beta)+i)}{}^i = \prod_{s=1}^{\alpha} C_{\pi(j(\alpha+\beta)+s)}{}^s \cdot \prod_{t=\alpha+1}^{\alpha+\beta} C_{\pi(j(\alpha+\beta)+t)}{}^t$$

where $j = 0, 1, \ldots, \lceil \frac{n}{\alpha+\beta} \rceil - 1$. When the ciphertext $\widehat{C_j}$ is decrypted, the plaintext is

$$g^{\sum_{i=1}^{\alpha+\beta} i \cdot \mathsf{M}^{\pi(j(\alpha+\beta)+i)-1}} = g^{\sum_{s=1}^{\alpha} s \cdot \mathsf{M}^{\pi(j(\alpha+\beta)+s)-1}} \cdot g^{\sum_{t=\alpha+1}^{\alpha+\beta} t \cdot \mathsf{M}^{\pi(j(\alpha+\beta)+t)-1}}$$

where we have

$$\sum_{s=1}^{\alpha} s \cdot \mathsf{M}^{\pi(j(\alpha+\beta)+s)-1} = \sum_{i=1}^{\alpha+\beta} i \cdot \mathsf{M}^{\pi(j(\alpha+\beta)+i)-1} - \sum_{t=\alpha+1}^{\alpha+\beta} t \cdot \mathsf{M}^{\pi(j(\alpha+\beta)+t)-1} \pmod{q}$$

Now we build up two lookup tables: the α-table stores all the possible mappings from g^ρ to ρ, where ρ is in the form:

$$\rho = \sum_{i=1}^{\alpha} i \cdot \mathsf{M}^{\pi(i)-1} \pmod{q}$$

and the β-table stores all the possible mappings from g^δ to δ, where δ is in the form:

$$\delta = - \sum_{j=\alpha+1}^{\alpha+\beta} j \cdot \mathsf{M}^{\pi(j)-1} \pmod q$$

Hence to retrieve the exponent value from the decrypted plaintext

$$m = g^{\sum_{i=1}^{\alpha+\beta} i \cdot \mathsf{M}^{\pi(j(\alpha+\beta)+i)-1}}$$

we can try $m \cdot g^\delta$ for all the possible δ values in the β-table until the result is in the α-table. In this case, suppose the particular values in the α-table and β-table are ρ' and δ' respectively, we will have $m = g^{\rho'-\delta'}$. Hence, $\rho' - \delta' \pmod q$ is the desired exponent value of the decrypted plaintext m.

For an election with $n = 38$ candidates, if we use $\alpha = 6$ and $\beta = 4$, we can pack every 10 ciphertexts into one ciphertext. The size of the α-table is $n!/(n-\alpha)! = 38!/(38-6)! \approx 2^{31}$ and the size of the β-table is $n!/(n-\beta)! = 38!/(38-4)! \approx 2^{21}$. And both tables can be generated in advance before the election. After the shuffle, when decrypting a ciphertext and extracting its exponent, we need to try $m \cdot g^\delta$ roughly for half of the possible values in the β-table until the result is in the α-table. Hence we need to repeat the test roughly 2^{20} times.

5   Discussion

5.1   Shrink the α-table

When p and q are chosen as 4096 bit and 256 bit respectively, for both the α-table and β-table, each row consists of a 256-bit value and a 4096-bit value. Hence the data size for a row is 544 bytes, which is roughly 0.5 KB. If $\alpha = 6$ and $\beta = 4$, the α-table contains 2^{31} rows and its total size is roughly 1 TB. The β-table contains 2^{21} rows where its total size is roughly 1 GB.

Note that in the β-table, we will use the g^δ value in the calculation $m \cdot g^\delta$. Thus we have to keep this value intact. However, we can shrink the g^ρ value in the α-table by keeping its last κ bits. The only requirement is that the remaining κ bits of each value is still unique. To check whether $m \cdot g^\delta$ is in the α-table, we only need to check whether its last κ bits are in the α-table. In practice, we can shrink the g^ρ value in the α-table by keeping removing its leading bit when its remaining bits are still unique across the table. Since the size of the α-table is 2^{31}, according to the birthday paradox, if $\kappa = 62$, there is a 50% chance that every remaining value is unique. In this case, the data size for a row is 40 bytes, and the data size for the entire α-table can shrunk to 80 GB.

5.2   Shrink the β-table

Although we mentioned earlier that each value in the β-table has to be kept intact, we can shrink the β-table by reducing the number of rows rather than reducing the size of each row. This can be achieved by applying the Steinhaus-Johnson-Trotter (SJT) algorithm [15] as follows: denote $\Delta_{i,j,l} = g^{i*M^l + j*M^{l+1}}$ for $i, j = -\beta, \ldots, 0, \ldots, \beta$ and $l = 0, 1, \ldots, n - 1$. The mappings between (i, j, l) and $\Delta_{i,j,l}$ are stored in the β-table. By multiplying with a single element $\Delta_{i,j,l}$ of this table, we can execute an adjacent transposition in the exponent. Thus, starting from any g^δ, we can generate the next possible sequence using a single multiplication. Hence the running time of this approach remains the same, but the number of rows in the β-table has been reduced from $n!/(n-\beta!)$ to $(2\beta)^2 * n$. In case where there are 38 candidates and $\beta = 4$, the number of rows have been reduced from 2^{21} to 2432 which is negligible.

5.3   What if $(\alpha + \beta) \nmid n$?

Previously, we deliberately ignored the case that $(\alpha + \beta) \nmid n$. However, this is an issue we should consider in practice. There are two methods to address this issue: one with padding and one without padding.

Method with Padding. We can simply append the ciphertext list by repeating the list from the left side until it exactly divides $\alpha + \beta$. For example, suppose the sorted ciphertext list is $\{C_{\pi(1)}, C_{\pi(2)}, \ldots, C_{\pi(38)}\}$, where $\alpha = 6$ and $\beta = 4$. In this case, we treat every 10 ciphertexts as a group and pack them into one ciphertext. If we copy the first two ciphertexts and append them to the end of the list, all the groups will have exactly 10 ciphertexts. After decryption, the repeated candidate preferences can be removed. This method is very simple, and it always works if the number of candidates is larger than $\alpha + \beta$. Next, we introduce another method without using padding.

Method without Padding. Denote the number of candidates $n = k(\alpha+\beta)+r$ for some integer k. We now discuss the following various situations:

- When $r = \alpha$: after every $(\alpha + \beta)$ ciphertexts have been packed, there will be exactly α ciphertexts remaining, and they will be packed into a single ciphertext. After this packed ciphertext is decrypted, we can use the α-table to retrieve the exponent part of its plaintext.
- When $0 < r < \alpha$: after every $(\alpha+\beta)$ ciphertexts have been packed, there will be less than α ciphertexts remaining, and they will be packed into a single ciphertext. After this packed ciphertext is decrypted, neither the α-table nor the β-table can be used to retrieve the exponent part of the plaintext. To solve this problem, we need to build another lookup table, called α'-table, which stores all the possible mappings from $g^{\rho'}$ to ρ'. And there will be $\sum_{i=1}^{\alpha-1} n!/(n-i)!$ number of possible ρ' values. In case there are 38 candidates and $\alpha = 6$, the α'-table will contain roughly 2^{26} rows, and the size of the α'-table is roughly 2.5 GB. Note that the technique introduced in the previous section can be used to shrink the α'-table.
- When $\alpha < r < \alpha + \beta$: after every $(\alpha + \beta)$ ciphertexts have been packed, there will be more than α ciphertexts remaining, and they will be packed

into a single ciphertext. After this packed ciphertext is decrypted, we need to build another lookup table, called β'-table, and use this table along with the α-table to retrieve the exponent part of the plaintext. The β'-table stores all the possible mappings from $g^{\delta'}$ to δ', and there will be $\sum_{i=1}^{\beta-1} n!/(n-i)!$ number of possible δ' values. To retrieve the exponent part of the plaintext m, we test $m \cdot g^{\delta'}$ for all the possible δ' values in the β'-table until the result is in the α-table. In case there are 38 candidates and $\beta = 4$, the β'-table contains roughly 2^{16} rows, and the size of the β'-table is roughly 32 MB. Note that the SJT algorithm introduced above also can be applied here to further reduce the β'-table.

5.4   Constructing the Tables

It is possible to construct the tables without requiring a large number of exponentiations. Here, we only informally describe how to build the α-table. The other tables can be built similarly.

Firstly, we build a temporary table of values of the form $g^{j \cdot M^i}$ where $0 \leq i < n$ and $1 \leq j \leq \alpha$. Then, building the α-table requires $\alpha - 1$ group multiplications from these values. This removes the need for many unnecessary exponentiations. By using a recursive algorithm to build the table, the computational cost can be reduced even further:

1. Set $r = 1$ (the group identity element) and $s = \alpha$ (the packing ratio), the candidate set $\mathsf{C} = \{1, 2, \ldots, n\}$, and the preference set $\mathsf{P} = \{1, 2, \ldots, \alpha\}$.
2. For each candidate $i \in \mathsf{C}$:
   (a) Remove i from C and compute $s = s - 1$.
   (b) For each preference $j \in \mathsf{P}$:
       i. Remove j from P.
       ii. Set $r \leftarrow r \cdot g^{j \cdot M^{i-1}}$.
       iii. If $s > 0$, recursively run from step 2; otherwise:
           A. Output r.
           B. Restore r and s to values at previous recursive step.
           C. Add j back to P.
           D. Add i back to C.

We have written a program to build the α-table in Java using a standard laptop (Intel i7 processor with 4 cores at 2.7GHz, 8 GB memory, and 64-bit Windows 7). Our assumption is that there are 38 candidates and $\alpha = 6$. Our test shows that the time spent to build the table is just under 10 hours, and it costs slightly more than 3 hours to sort the table (this is a necessary step for binary search). The total size of the table is 100.8GB, and an average search in the table takes 49ms.

5.5   Related Work

As described in Section 2, the BSGS algorithm is an important technique to solve the discrete logarithm problem. Our introduced method shares some similarities with BSGS. However, there are also some differences between them. Firstly, BSGS searches the entire group, while our method makes use of the structure of the plaintext and only searches a much smaller subgroup. Thus our method will be quicker when used in unpacking candidate preferences. Secondly, compared with BSGS, our method is more flexible since the sizes of the two lookup tables can be easily adjusted according to different cases.

Packing different votes in the homomorphic fashion was first introduced in [9], and our method follows this approach. Later, it was briefly mentioned in [10] that the meet-in-the-middle trick can be used to solve the discrete logarithm problem if votes are packed homomorphicly using the exponential ElGamal encryption. However, no technical detail was given about how this can be done. Moreover, in both these works, the ciphertext packing technique was only designed for the First-Past-The-Post (FPTP) elections, while ranked elections were not considered. Our work in this paper can be considered as some extension to these two existing works.

6   Conclusion

In this paper, we have explored the details to "pack" multiple candidate preferences into the least number of ciphertext. The benefit is that fewer ciphertexts need to be shuffled and decrypted. After decryption, the full candidate preferences can be retrieved using a meet-in-the-middle algorithm despite the discrete logarithm problem. The vVote system was used as an example, and the parameters were carefully chosen accordingly. But the method present here is generic in nature and it has the potential to be applied in many other ranked elections with a large number of candidates.

Acknowledgement. Dr. Sriramkrishnan Srinivasan was at the University of Surrey when this work was carried out. This work was funded by the UK Engineering and Physical Sciences Research Council (EPSRC) under grant EP/G025797/1, and we are grateful to the anonymous reviewers for their valuable comments on the paper.

References

1. Adida, B.: Helios: web-based open-audit voting. In: Proceedings of the 17th conference on Security Symposium (SS 2008), Berkeley, CA, pp. 335–348 (2008)
2. Baudron, O., Fouque, P.-A., Pointcheval, D., Stern, J., Poupard, G.: Practical multi-candidate election system. In: Proceedings of the 20th ACM Symposium on Principles of Distributed Computing (PODC 2001), New York, NY, USA, pp. 274–283 (2001)
3. Benaloh, J.C.: Secret sharing homomorphisms: Keeping shares of a secret secret (Extended Abstract). In: Odlyzko, A.M. (ed.) CRYPTO 1986. LNCS, vol. 263, pp. 251–260. Springer, Heidelberg (1987)

4. Benaloh, J.: Towards simple verifiable elections. In: Proceedings of IAVoSS Workshop on Trustworthy Election (WOTE 2006), Cambridge, UK, pp. 61–68 (2006)
5. Benaloh, J., Moran, T., Naish, L., Ramchen, K., Teague, V.: Shuffle-sum: coercion-resistant verifiable tallying for STV voting. IEEE Transactions on Information Forensics and Security 4(4), 685–698 (2009)
6. Burton, C., Culnane, C., Heather, J., Peacock, T., Ryan, P.Y.A., Schneider, S., Srinivasan, S., Teague, V., Wen, R., Xia, Z.: A supervised verifiable voting protocol for the Victorian Electoral Commission. In: The 5th International Conference on Electronic Voting, EVOTE 2012 (2012)
7. Burton, C., Culnane, C., Heather, J., Peacock, T., Ryan, P.Y.A., Schneider, S., Srinivasan, S., Teague, V., Wen, R., Xia, Z.: Using Prêt à Voter in the Victorian State elections. In: The 2012 USENIX/ACCURATE Electronic Voting Technology Workshop, EVT 2012 (2012)
8. Chaum, D., Ryan, P.Y.A., Schneider, S.: A practical voter-verifiable election scheme. In: De Capitani di Vimercati, S., Syverson, P.F., Gollmann, D. (eds.) ESORICS 2005. LNCS, vol. 3679, pp. 118–139. Springer, Heidelberg (2005)
9. Cramer, R., Franklin, M., Schoenmakers, B., Yung, M.: Multi-authority secret-ballot elections with linear work. In: Maurer, U.M. (ed.) EUROCRYPT 1996. LNCS, vol. 1070, pp. 72–83. Springer, Heidelberg (1996)
10. Cramer, R., Gennaro, R., Schoenmakers, B.: A secure and optimally efficient multi-authority election scheme. In: Fumy, W. (ed.) EUROCRYPT 1997. LNCS, vol. 1233, pp. 103–118. Springer, Heidelberg (1997)
11. Diffie, W., Hellman, M.: Exhaustive cryptanalysis of the nbs data encryption standard. Journal of Computer 10(6), 74–84 (1977)
12. ElGamal, T.: A public key cryptosystem and a signature scheme based on discrete logarithms. IEEE Transactions on IT 31(4), 467–472 (1985)
13. Furukawa, J., Sako, K.: An efficient scheme for proving a shuffle. In: Kilian, J. (ed.) CRYPTO 2001. LNCS, vol. 2139, pp. 368–387. Springer, Heidelberg (2001)
14. Gennaro, R., Jarecki, S., Krawczyk, H., Rabin, T.: Secure distributed key generation for discrete-log based cryptosystems. In: Stern, J. (ed.) EUROCRYPT 1999. LNCS, vol. 1592, pp. 295–310. Springer, Heidelberg (1999)
15. Knuth, D.E.: The Art of Computer Programming, 2nd edn. Seminumerical Algorithms, vol. II. Addison-Wesley (1981)
16. Merkle, R., Hellman, M.: On the security of multiple encryption. Communications of the ACM 24(7) (1981)
17. Andrew Nef, C.: A verifiable secret shuffle and its application to e-voting. In: Proceedings of the 8th ACM Conference on Computer and Communications Security (CSS 2001), pp. 116–125 (2001)
18. Paillier, P.: Public-key cryptosystems based on composite degree residuosity classes. In: Stern, J. (ed.) EUROCRYPT 1999. LNCS, vol. 1592, pp. 223–238. Springer, Heidelberg (1999)
19. Pedersen, T.P.: A threshold cryptosystem without a trusted party. In: Davies, D.W. (ed.) EUROCRYPT 1991. LNCS, vol. 547, pp. 522–526. Springer, Heidelberg (1991)
20. Ryan, P.Y.A., Bismark, D., Heather, J., Schneider, S., Xia, Z.: Prêt à Voter: a Voter-Verifiable Voting System. IEEE Transactions on Information Forensics and Security (Special Issue on Electronic Voting) 4(4), 662–673 (2009)
21. Ryan, P.Y.A., Schneider, S.A.: Prêt à voter with re-encryption mixes. In: Gollmann, D., Meier, J., Sabelfeld, A. (eds.) ESORICS 2006. LNCS, vol. 4189, pp. 313–326. Springer, Heidelberg (2006)

22. Sako, K., Kilian, J.: Receipt-free mix-type voting scheme. In: Guillou, L.C., Quisquater, J.-J. (eds.) EUROCRYPT 1995. LNCS, vol. 921, pp. 393–403. Springer, Heidelberg (1995)
23. Teague, V., Ramchen, K., Naish, L.: Corcion-resistant tallying for STV voting. In: 2008 USENIX/ACCURATE Electronic Voting Workshop (EVT 2008), San Jose, CA, US (2008)
24. Wombat, http://www.wombat-voting.com

SPA on MIST Exponentiation Algorithm with Multiple Computational Sequences*

Chien-Ning Chen[1], Jheng-Hong Tu[2], and Sung-Ming Yen[2]

[1] Physical Analysis & Cryptographic Engineering (PACE)
Nanyang Technological University, Singapore
chienning@ntu.edu.sg
[2] Laboratory of Cryptography and Information Security (LCIS)
Dept of Computer Science and Information Engineering
National Central University, Chung-Li, Taiwan
{jhtu,yensm}@csie.ncu.edu.tw

Abstract. The MIST algorithm is a randomized version of the division chain exponentiation algorithm and is a side-channel countermeasure. When analyzing the MIST algorithm by ordinary simple power analysis (with only one square-multiply sequence obtained), an attacker cannot retrieve the secret exponent due to the ambiguous relationship between the square-multiply sequence and the computation. We point out the MIST algorithm is still vulnerable to simple power analysis observing multiple power consumption traces and propose a practical method with detailed steps to deduce the secret exponent from multiple square-multiply sequences. Further countermeasures such as exponent blinding are required to prevent the analysis proposed in this paper.

Keywords: division chain, exponentiation, MIST algorithm, side-channel analysis, simple power analysis.

1 Introduction

Exponentiation evaluation is a fundamental computation in most public-key cryptography. Conventional exponentiation algorithms are vulnerable to simple power analysis (SPA) [3], differential power analysis (DPA) [3] and other side-channel attacks, which break a cryptosystem by analyzing side-channel leakages from their implementation. SPA assumes that an attacker can distinguish power consumption patterns generated by different operations. When analyzing exponentiation computation, if a fast squaring algorithm is adopted, the attacker can distinguish the power consumption pattern of a squaring from that of a multiplication and then obtain a computational sequence composed of squarings and multiplications (abbreviated to "SM sequence"). Since a multiplication indicates

---

* Some part of this research was done while Chien-Ning Chen was a postdoctoral research fellow at the National Central University. The research of Jheng-Hong Tu and Sung-Ming Yen on this work were supported by the National Science Council of the Republic of China under contract NSC 101-2221-E-008-111-MY2.

A. Cuzzocrea et al. (Eds.): CD-ARES 2013 Workshops, LNCS 8128, pp. 222–235, 2013.

a nonzero bit in the exponent, an attacker can deduce the secret exponent or partial information about the secret exponent from the SM sequence.

Many research results of countermeasures against side-channel attacks can be found in the literature. The square-and-multiply-always algorithm [2] is a well-known method against SPA. It performs a dummy multiplication when the corresponding bit of the exponent is zero, i.e., there are always a squaring and a multiplication in each iteration. An attacker cannot retrieve any information about the secret exponent from a regular SM sequence.

The MIST algorithm [4] proposed by Walter is an efficient exponentiation algorithm and also a countermeasure against side-channel attacks. Conventional exponentiation algorithms have exponents in binary and scan one or more bits per iteration. In contrast, the MIST algorithm represents exponents in mixed-radix. Mixed-radix representation means that the radix varies from position to position. An application of mixed-radix is the representation of dates and times, for example, 18429 seconds can be represented as $(0100011111111101)_2$ in binary or as $(5_{24}7_{60}9_{60})$, 5 hours 7 minutes 9 seconds in the mixed-radix clock system. The radixes in the MIST algorithm are randomly selected from small integers, and the radixes $\{2, 3, 5\}$ are used in [4]. Side-channel attacks which average a number of power consumption traces (e.g., DPA) are infeasible because the computation varies among each exponentiation evaluation.

The MIST algorithm is also immune to ordinary SPA due to the ambiguous relationship between an observed SM sequence and the computation. For example, the pattern SM (a squaring followed by a multiplication) in a sequence corresponds to either 1_2 (digit 1 with radix 2) or 0_3 (digit 0 with radix 3). While analyzing an SM sequence of the MIST algorithm with the exponent smaller than 2^n, the average number of exponents which may possibly generate this sequence is about $2^{3n/5}$ [6], i.e., there are $2^{3n/5}$ candidates of the exponent. A unique candidate might be deduced from multiple SM sequences, but it is infeasible to find the intersection of sets of $2^{3n/5}$ candidates. Walter claimed analyzing multiple sequences is an open problem, and Okeya [5] also observed that a small portion of the exponent reveals when analyzing multiple sequences. Besides the analysis by Walter, Oswald pointed out the security margin provided in [6] is wrong (might be lower) [8]. Sim et al. [9] also analyzed the MIST algorithm with an additional assumption which is similar to the doubling attack [7].

This paper presents a multi-sequence SPA on the MIST algorithm. We assume that an attacker can collect multiple power consumption traces generated by the MIST algorithm with the same exponent and then obtain SM sequences by the same technique used in ordinary SPA. In contrast with finding the intersection of sets of candidates after analyzing all sequences individually, the proposed method simultaneously analyzes multiple sequences and finds candidates satisfying all sequences. The proposed analysis employs the residue class operations and is a practical method to deduce the exponent directly from multiple SM sequences. Our implementation results show that around 25 sequences are sufficient to deduce a 1024-bit exponent in less than two hours by using a modern desktop PC in 2012.

The remaining parts of this paper are organized as follows. We review the MIST algorithm as well as some operations of residue class in Sect. 2. Section 3 describes our analysis, a theoretical attack with one SM sequence, followed by the extended attack exploiting multiple sequences. Section 4 provides the implementation results and also some tricks to reduce the memory requirement. Finally, Sect. 5 concludes this paper.

2   Preliminary and Background

2.1   MIST Exponentiation Algorithm

In 1998, Walter proposed an algorithm – exponentiation using division chain [1] which is a predecessor of the MIST exponentiation algorithm. In both algorithms, an exponentiation x^e is decomposed into $x^{(e \bmod d)} \times \left(x^d\right)^{\lfloor \frac{e}{d} \rfloor}$ where d is a small positive integer. The two small exponentiations $x^{(e \bmod d)}$ and x^d are computed by using a computational sequence $\{x, x^2, \cdots, x^d\}$ in which the exponents $\{1, 2, \cdots, d\}$ form an addition sequence containing $(e \bmod d)$ and d, i.e., $x^{(e \bmod d)}$ can be obtained during the evaluation of x^d without any cost. By repeating the above procedure, we have

$$x^e = A_i \times x_i{}^{q_i} = \left(A_i \times x_i{}^{r_i}\right) \times \left(x_i{}^{d_i}\right)^{\lfloor \frac{q_i}{d_i} \rfloor} \qquad (1)$$
$$= A_{i+1} \times x_{i+1}{}^{q_{i+1}} = \cdots$$

with the base number $x_{i+1} = x_i{}^{d_i}$ initialized by $x_1 = x$; the accumulator $A_{i+1} = A_i \times x_i{}^{r_i}$ initialized by $A_1 = 1$; the quotient $q_{i+1} = \lfloor \frac{q_i}{d_i} \rfloor$ initialized by $q_1 = e$; and the remainder $r_i = q_i \bmod d_i$. The quotient q_i is the *remaining exponent* in the i-th iteration of the computation, and we have $q_i = \left((r_{\text{MSB}})_{d_{\text{MSB}}} \cdots (r_i)_{d_i}\right)$ in mixed-radix representation. The divisors d_i are small integers. The MIST algorithm in [4] selects d_i from $\{2, 3, 5\}$ randomly and is a randomized version of its predecessor (exponentiation using division chain).

INPUT: x and e
OUTPUT: x^e

---

01 A $= 1$, X $= x$, Q $= e$
02 while (Q > 0)
03   Randomly choose d from $\{2, 3, 5\}$
04    $r =$ Q mod d
05   Compute A $=$ A $\times$ X^r and X $=$ X^d together†
06   Q $= \lfloor$Q$/d\rfloor$
07 return A

---

†Referring to Fig.2 for the detailed computational sequence

Fig. 1. The MIST exponentiation algorithm

Figure 1 is the sketch of the MIST algorithm, and Fig. 2 provides the detailed computation of the MIST algorithm for various divisor-remainder pairs (abbreviated to "DR pair"). In the column of register sequence, X and A are the two variables used in the algorithm in Fig. 1, and T is the temporary variable. The computation XX→T denotes that the result of the multiplication (squaring) X × X is stored in T. The addition sequence and the square-multiply pattern (abbreviated to "SM pattern") generated by the computation are also provided.

DR pair (d_i, r_i)	Addition sequence	Register sequence	SM pattern
$(2,0)$	12	XX→X	S
$(2,1)$	12	XX→T, XA→A, (T→X)	SM
$(3,0)$	123	XX→T, XT→X	
$(3,1)$	123	XX→T, XA→A, XT→X	
$(3,2)$	123	XX→T, TA→A, XT→X	SMM
$(5,0)$	1235	XX→T, XT→X, XT→X	
$(5,1)$	1235	XX→T, XA→A, XT→X, XT→X	
$(5,2)$	1235	XX→T, TA→A, XT→X, XT→X	SMMM
$(5,3)$	1235	XX→T, XT→X, XA→A, XT→X	
$(5,4)$	1245	XX→T, TT→T, TA→A, XT→X	SSMM

Fig. 2. Computation in the MIST algorithm

Since the MIST algorithm selects the divisors d_i randomly, it is naturally immune to power analysis which averages over a number of power consumption traces, e.g., differential power analysis. Simple power analysis is the other category of power analysis which assumes the power consumption trace of multiplications is distinguishable from that of squarings. However, an attacker cannot uniquely determine the secret exponent by analyzing one SM sequence of the MIST algorithm due to the ambiguous relationship between an observed SM pattern and the exact computation. As shown in Fig. 2, each of the patterns SM, SMM, SMMM corresponds to two or three DR pairs, and the pattern SSMM corresponds to either the DR pair $(5,4)$ or a squaring (S) followed by the pattern SMM. In [6], Walter pointed out that on average $2^{3n/5}$ candidates will remain for an n-bit exponent after analyzing one SM sequence.

2.2   Operations of Residue Class

The proposed analysis represents the candidates of the exponent as a collection of residue classes, which is much more efficient than enumerating and storing all candidates. In this paper, a residue class $\langle M, N \rangle$ denotes a set consisting of nonnegative integers congruent to the nonnegative integer N modulo the positive integer M $(0 \leq N < M)$, i.e., $\langle M, N \rangle = \{kM + N | k \in \mathbf{Z}, k \geq 0\}$. The following operations are used in the proposed analysis.

The first operation is *split* which splits a residue class $\langle M, N \rangle$ into ε subsets by expanding the modulus M to εM. Since $kM + N = \lfloor \frac{k}{\varepsilon} \rfloor \varepsilon M + (k \bmod \varepsilon) M + N$, $\langle M, N \rangle$ can be split into the collection of distinct subsets

$$\langle M, N \rangle = \bigcup_{\delta=0}^{\varepsilon-1} \langle \varepsilon M, \delta M + N \rangle,$$

and $split(\langle M, N \rangle, \varepsilon, \delta) = \langle \varepsilon M, \delta M + N \rangle$ is defined as the δ-th subset of $\langle M, N \rangle$.

The second operation is *integer division*, i.e., dividing all numbers in a residue class $\langle M, N \rangle$ by a given divisor d and obtaining the integer quotients. Suppose $\varepsilon M = \mathrm{lcm}(M, d)$, the least common multiple of M and d. Since $\lfloor \frac{kM+N}{d} \rfloor = \lfloor \frac{(k'\varepsilon+\delta)M+N}{d} \rfloor = k'(\frac{\varepsilon M}{d}) + \lfloor \frac{\delta M+N}{d} \rfloor$ where $k' = \lfloor \frac{k}{\varepsilon} \rfloor$ and $\delta = k \bmod \varepsilon$, we have

$$\langle M, N \rangle \div d = \left\{ \lfloor \frac{kM+N}{d} \rfloor \middle| k = 1, 2, \cdots \right\} = \bigcup_{i=0}^{\varepsilon-1} \left\langle \frac{\varepsilon M}{d}, \lfloor \frac{iM+N}{d} \rfloor \right\rangle.$$

For example, $\langle 10, 7 \rangle$ represents integers $\{7, 17, 27, \cdots\}$. When dividing by 6, $\langle 10, 7 \rangle$ will be split to a collection $\langle 30, 7 \rangle \cup \langle 30, 17 \rangle \cup \langle 30, 27 \rangle$, and then we have $\langle 10, 7 \rangle \div 6 = \langle 5, 1 \rangle \cup \langle 5, 2 \rangle \cup \langle 5, 4 \rangle$ which represents integers $\{1, 2, 4, 6, 7, 9, \cdots\}$.

The last two operations are to find *union* and *intersection*[1] of two residue classes. Before finding union or intersection, the moduli of the two sets should be expanded to their least common multiple by using the first operation. For example, $\langle 2, 1 \rangle = \langle 6, 1 \rangle \cup \langle 6, 3 \rangle \cup \langle 6, 5 \rangle$ and $\langle 3, 2 \rangle = \langle 6, 2 \rangle \cup \langle 6, 5 \rangle$, and we have $\langle 2, 1 \rangle \cup \langle 3, 2 \rangle = \langle 6, 1 \rangle \cup \langle 6, 2 \rangle \cup \langle 6, 3 \rangle \cup \langle 6, 5 \rangle$ as well as $\langle 2, 1 \rangle \cap \langle 3, 2 \rangle = \langle 6, 5 \rangle$.

3   Analysis to MIST by Using Residue Class

The MIST algorithm with a given exponent can generate various SM sequences due to its randomness. These SM sequences are the potential SM sequences associated with the given exponent, and one of them will be generated during each computation. On the other hand, an SM sequence generated by the MIST algorithm is associated with more than one exponents due to the ambiguous relationship between the SM pattern and the computation. The MIST algorithm with these exponents may possibly generate this SM sequence. When an SM sequence is observed by SPA, all these exponents associated with this observed SM sequence are candidates of the secret exponent, and we say these candidates satisfy this SM sequence. The proposed analysis will find the candidates simultaneously satisfying multiple SM sequences.

The observed SM sequences should be decomposed into small blocks before the analysis. Each block contains one SM pattern listed in Fig. 2 and corresponds to one iteration of the MIST algorithm. However, the pattern SSMM can

---

[1] The *intersection* operation is similar to solving the simultaneous congruences in the Chinese remainder theorem. However, in the proposed analysis, the moduli may not be relatively prime.

be interpreted as either an atomic pattern or two patterns S-SMM. It should be identified as a special block prior to other SM patterns. The proposed analysis deals with one block per iteration from the first to the last block of each SM sequence. Since there will be some special blocks SSMM, the block number in the proposed analysis is different from the iteration number in the MIST algorithm.

In the first step, the proposed analysis will find candidates of the exponent simultaneously satisfying the first block of every observed SM sequence.[2] These candidates can be divided into one or more residue classes, and each residue class is a candidate set. After analyzing the first i blocks of the observed SM sequences and obtaining the candidate sets satisfying the first i blocks, we inspect the subsets of each candidate set and then obtain the candidate sets satisfying the first $(i + 1)$ blocks. After analyzing from the first to the last block of the observed SM sequences, we obtain the candidates of the exponent satisfying whole blocks of the observed SM sequences.

The candidates of the exponent in the proposed analysis are organized into one or more candidate sets (represented by using residue class) instead of enumerating all of them. A candidate set will contain more than one candidates when its modulus M is smaller than the upper limit of the exponent of the cryptosystem. The number of candidate sets does not indicate how much exhaustive search required, for example, we can use only one residue class $\langle 1, 0 \rangle$ to represent all exponents smaller than the upper limit.

The details of the analysis is provided in the following subsections. The theoretical analysis with one SM sequence is introduced in Sect. 3.1, and the practical analysis of exploiting multiple SM sequences is presented in Sect. 3.2.

3.1   Single-sequence Analysis to MIST

Referring to the equation (1), the computation of the MIST algorithm is controlled by the DR pairs (d_i, r_i). The potential DR pairs associated with the block of SM patterns S, SM, SMM, SMMM are listed in Fig. 2, and the DR pairs associated with the special block SSMM are $(5, 4)$, $(6, 2)$, $(6, 4)$, and $(10, 0)$.[3] The variable for the potential DR pair as well as some other variables is defined below.

Definition 1. *Let* $\mathrm{DR}_i{}^{(\gamma)} = (d_i{}^{(\gamma)}, r_i{}^{(\gamma)})$ *be the γ-th potential DR pair associated with the i-th block of the SM sequence.*

Definition 2. *Let* $e_i{}^{(\alpha)} = \left\langle M_i{}^{(\alpha)}, N_i{}^{(\alpha)} \right\rangle$ *be the α-th candidate set of the exponent satisfying the first $(i - 1)$ blocks of the SM sequence.*

---

[2] A candidate of the exponent satisfying the first i blocks of an observed SM sequence means there is at least one potential SM sequence associated with this candidate, of which the first i blocks are identical to the first i blocks of the observed SM sequence.

[3] The DR pair $(5, 4)$ is associated with the atomic pattern SSMM. In contrast, when a block SSMM is composed of two patterns S-SMM, the remaining exponent will satisfy $q_i \bmod 2 = 0$ as well as one of the three equations $\frac{q_i}{2} \bmod 3 = 1$, $\frac{q_i}{2} \bmod 3 = 2$, and $\frac{q_i}{2} \bmod 5 = 0$. The DR pairs associated with S-SMM are $(6, 2)$, $(6, 4)$, and $(10, 0)$.

If the exponent belongs to a candidate set $e_i^{(\alpha)}$, the remaining exponent q_i in the i-th iteration will belong to $e_i^{(\alpha)} \div (d_1^{(\gamma_1)} \cdots d_{i-1}^{(\gamma_{i-1})})$ for all enumerations of products $(d_1^{(\gamma_1)} \cdots d_{i-1}^{(\gamma_{i-1})})$. These potential values $e_i^{(\alpha)} \div (d_1^{(\gamma_1)} \cdots d_{i-1}^{(\gamma_{i-1})})$ can be divided into several residue classes, and each one is a candidate set of the remaining exponent.

Definition 3. *Let* $q_i^{(\alpha\text{-}\beta)} = \langle m_i^{(\alpha\text{-}\beta)}, n_i^{(\alpha\text{-}\beta)} \rangle$ *be the β-th candidate set of the remaining exponent in the i-th iteration, associated with* $e_i^{(\alpha)}$.

The superscript, (γ), (α), $(\alpha\text{-}\beta)$, in variables indicates a specified DR pair or candidate set. We also use $(*)$ to indicate an arbitrary one among these DR pairs or candidate sets. For example, $q_i^{(*\text{-}*)}$ is an arbitrary candidate set of q_i, and $q_i^{(\alpha\text{-}*)}$ is an arbitrary one associated with $e_i^{(\alpha)}$.

The following is an example of the proposed analysis. Suppose the first few operations of an SM sequence are SSMSMMS. The initial candidate set of the exponent and that of the remaining exponent associated are

$$e_1^{(1)} = \langle 1, 0 \rangle \text{ and } q_1^{(1\text{-}1)} = \langle 1, 0 \rangle.$$

The DR pair associated with the first block S is $(d_1^{(1)}, r_1^{(1)}) = (2, 0)$, and we have the expansion factor $\varepsilon_{1,1} = 2$ when finding $q_1^{(1\text{-}1)} \div d_1^{(1)}$. Since only $split(q_1^{(1\text{-}1)}, 2, 0) \cap \langle d_1^{(1)}, r_1^{(1)} \rangle = \langle 2, 0 \rangle$ is nonempty, the candidate sets of the exponent and the associated remaining exponent satisfying the first block are

$$e_2^{(1)} = split(e_1^{(1)}, 2, 0) = \langle 2, 0 \rangle, q_2^{(1\text{-}1)} = split(q_1^{(1\text{-}1)}, 2, 0) \div d_1^{(1)} = \langle 1, 0 \rangle.$$

When analyzing the second block SM, the potential DR pairs are $(d_2^{(1)}, r_2^{(1)}) = (2, 1)$ and $(d_2^{(2)}, r_2^{(2)}) = (3, 0)$. We have $\varepsilon_{2,1} = 6$, and $e_2^{(1)}$ will be split into six subsets. Four of these subsets will satisfy the first two blocks, and they are

$$e_3^{(1)} = split(e_2^{(1)}, 6, 0) = \langle 12, 0 \rangle, q_3^{(1\text{-}1)} = split(q_2^{(1\text{-}1)}, 6, 0) \div 3 = \langle 2, 0 \rangle;$$

$$e_3^{(2)} = split(e_2^{(1)}, 6, 1) = \langle 12, 2 \rangle, q_3^{(2\text{-}1)} = split(q_2^{(1\text{-}1)}, 6, 1) \div 2 = \langle 3, 0 \rangle;$$

$$e_3^{(3)} = split(e_2^{(1)}, 6, 3) = \langle 12, 6 \rangle, \begin{cases} q_3^{(3\text{-}1)} = split(q_2^{(1\text{-}1)}, 6, 3) \div 2 = \langle 3, 1 \rangle \\ q_3^{(3\text{-}2)} = split(q_2^{(1\text{-}1)}, 6, 3) \div 3 = \langle 2, 1 \rangle \end{cases};$$

$$e_3^{(4)} = split(e_2^{(1)}, 6, 5) = \langle 12, 10 \rangle, q_3^{(4\text{-}1)} = split(q_2^{(1\text{-}1)}, 6, 5) \div 2 = \langle 3, 2 \rangle.$$

When analyzing the third block SMM, the potential DR pairs are $(3, 1)$, $(3, 2)$, and $(5, 0)$. The sets $e_3^{(1)}$, $e_3^{(2)}$, $e_3^{(3)}$, $e_3^{(4)}$ will be split into $\varepsilon_{3,1} = 15$, $\varepsilon_{3,2} = 5$, $\varepsilon_{3,3} = 15$, $\varepsilon_{3,4} = 5$ subsets, and 11, 1, 15, 5 subsets will satisfy the first three blocks, respectively. We only demonstrate how to inspect the subset $split(e_3^{(2)}, 5, 0)$ of $e_3^{(2)}$ and the fourth subset $split(e_3^{(3)}, 15, 3)$ of $e_3^{(3)}$. Since $split(q_3^{(2\text{-}1)}, 5, 0) = \langle 15, 0 \rangle \subset \langle 5, 0 \rangle$, we have

$$e_4^{(12)} = split(e_3^{(2)}, 5, 0) = \langle 60, 2 \rangle, q_4^{(12\text{-}1)} = split(q_3^{(2\text{-}1)}, 5, 0) \div 5 = \langle 3, 0 \rangle.$$

Since $split(q_3^{(3-1)}, 15, 3) = \langle 45, 10 \rangle \subset \langle 3, 1 \rangle$, $\langle 45, 10 \rangle \subset \langle 5, 0 \rangle$, and $split(q_3^{(3-2)}, 15, 3) = \langle 30, 7 \rangle \subset \langle 3, 1 \rangle$, we have

$$e_4^{(16)} = split(e_3^{(3)}, 15, 3) = \langle 180, 42 \rangle, \begin{cases} q_4^{(16-1)} = \langle 45, 10 \rangle \div 3 = \langle 15, 3 \rangle \\ q_4^{(16-2)} = \langle 45, 10 \rangle \div 5 = \langle 9, 2 \rangle \\ q_4^{(16-3)} = \langle 30, 7 \rangle \div 3 = \langle 10, 2 \rangle \end{cases}.$$

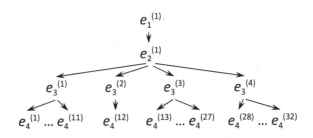

Fig. 3. Candidate sets satisfying the SM sequence SSMSMMS

Figure 3 sketches the relationship between the candidate sets in the above example, which forms a tree. Each child node is a subset of its parent node and will satisfy one more block of the SM sequence than its parent node. The proposed analysis is a breadth-first search, starting from the root $e_1^{(1)}$. Suppose we have obtained all $e_i^{(*)}$ as well as all $q_i^{(\alpha-*)}$ associated with each $e_i^{(\alpha)}$. We can find all $e_{i+1}^{(*)}$ as well as all $q_{i+1}^{(*-*)}$ by the following steps.

Step 1. Select one $e_i^{(*)}$

Step 2. Suppose $e_i^{(\alpha)}$ is selected. Find the smallest positive integer $\varepsilon_{i,\alpha}$ satisfying $d_i^{(\gamma)} \mid \varepsilon_{i,\alpha} m_i^{(\alpha-\beta)}$ for all γ and β (i.e., for all DR$_i^{(*)}$ and $q_i^{(\alpha-*)}$. Split $e_i^{(\alpha)}$ and all $q_i^{(\alpha-*)}$ by the factor $\varepsilon_{i,\alpha}$.

Step 3. Select one subset of $e_i^{(\alpha)}$, i.e., select an integer $\delta \in [0, \varepsilon_{i,\alpha} - 1]$ and then compute $split(e_i^{(\alpha)}, \varepsilon_{i,\alpha}, \delta) = \left\langle \varepsilon_{i,\alpha} M_i^{(\alpha)}, \delta M_i^{(\alpha)} + N_i^{(\alpha)} \right\rangle$.

Step 4. Inspect whether the selected $split(e_i^{(\alpha)}, \varepsilon_{i,\alpha}, \delta)$ satisfies the first i blocks of the SM sequence (i.e., whether it is a valid $e_{i+1}^{(*)}$).
If $\bigcup_{\beta,\gamma} \left(split(q_i^{(\alpha-\beta)}, \varepsilon_{i,\alpha}, \delta) \cap \left\langle d_i^{(\gamma)}, r_i^{(\gamma)} \right\rangle \right) \neq \emptyset$, then $split(e_i^{(\alpha)}, \varepsilon_{i,\alpha}, \delta)$ is one $e_{i+1}^{(*)}$, and $\bigcup_{\beta,\gamma} \left(\left(split(q_i^{(\alpha-\beta)}, \varepsilon_{i,\alpha}, \delta) \cap \left\langle d_i^{(\gamma)}, r_i^{(\gamma)} \right\rangle \right) \div d_i^{(\gamma)} \right)$ represents all $q_{i+1}^{(*-*)}$ associated with $split(e_i^{(\alpha)}, \varepsilon_{i,\alpha}, \delta)$. Otherwise, discard $split(e_i^{(\alpha)}, \varepsilon_{i,\alpha}, \delta)$.

Step 5. Select another subset of $e_i^{(\alpha)}$ and go back to step 4 until all subsets are processed.

Step 6. Select another $e_i^{(*)}$ and go back to step 2 until all $e_i^{(*)}$ are processed.

Each $e_i^{(*)}$ is split into several subsets in step 2, and whether each subset is a valid $e_{i+1}^{(*)}$ is inspected in step 4. Since the remaining exponent should satisfy

$q_i \bmod d_i = r_i$, a subset $split(e_i^{(\alpha)}, \varepsilon_{i,\alpha}, \delta)$ is one $e_{i+1}^{(*)}$ if and only if we can find at least one $q_i^{(\alpha-\beta)}$ (i.e., $\exists \beta$) satisfying $split(q_i^{(\alpha-\beta)}, \varepsilon_{i,\alpha}, \delta) \subset \bigcup_\gamma \left\langle d_i^{(\gamma)}, r_i^{(\gamma)} \right\rangle$. When s subset $split(q_i^{(\alpha-\beta)}, \varepsilon_{i,\alpha}, \delta) \subset \left\langle d_i^{(\gamma)}, r_i^{(\gamma)} \right\rangle$, $split(q_i^{(\alpha-\beta)}, \varepsilon_{i,\alpha}, \delta) \div d_i^{(\gamma)}$ is one $q_{i+1}^{(*-*)}$ associated with $split(e_i^{(\alpha)}, \varepsilon_{i,\alpha}, \delta)$.

The candidate sets $e_{\mathsf{end}+1}^{(*)}$ satisfying the whole SM sequence can be obtained by repeating the above steps. In the last few iterations of the analysis, the modulus $M_i^{(*)}$ of each $e_i^{(*)}$ will be greater than the upper limit of the exponent, and each $e_i^{(*)}$ can be simplified by $e_i^{(\alpha)} = N_i^{(\alpha)}$ because $(\delta M_i^{(\alpha)} + N_i^{(\alpha)})$ with $\delta \geq 1$ is not a valid exponent. The associated $q_i^{(*-*)}$ can be also simplified by $q_i^{(\alpha-\beta)} = n_i^{(\alpha-\beta)}$. In the last iteration, the DR pair $(d_{\mathsf{end}}^{(*)}, r_{\mathsf{end}}^{(*)})$ should further satisfy $r_{\mathsf{end}}^{(*)} \neq 0$ because of $q_{\mathsf{end}} = d_{\mathsf{end}} q_{\mathsf{end}+1} + r_{\mathsf{end}} \neq 0$ and $q_{\mathsf{end}+1} = 0$. After analyzing the whole SM sequence, we have the candidates $\bigcup_\alpha N_{\mathsf{end}+1}^{(\alpha)}$ of the exponent.

The proposed analysis assumes the attacker can distinguish squaring and multiplication in a power consumption trace. However, some operations might not be identified exactly. Ambiguous SM patterns will be isolated and processed by the method similar to that analyzing the special pattern SSMM. For example, when an SM sequence is SSMS?MS, the fourth to sixth operations S?M will be isolated, and they are either SMM or SSM. The potential DR pairs are $(3, 1)$, $(3, 2)$, $(5, 0)$ for the first case and $(4, 2)$, $(6, 0)$ for the second case.

Some exponentiation algorithms employ uniform computation for both squarings and multiplications to prevent SPA, e.g., the side-channel atomicity [10]. However, the divisions $q_i = \lfloor \frac{q_{i-1}}{d_{i-1}} \rfloor$ in the MIST algorithm still reveal information. If the divisions are evaluated during the computation and the power consumption trace of divisions can be recognized, the SM patterns S, SM, and SMM can be determined by the number of squarings/multiplications between two divisions. In addition, some special chosen messages will cause revelation of computational sequence [11], e.g., $-1 \equiv n - 1 \pmod{n}$ and faulty elliptic curve points of small orders [12]. If the exponent is an odd integer and the input message (base number) is -1, referring to Fig. 2, there are only two types of computation, $1 \times 1 = 1$ and $1 \times (-1) = (-1)$. The computations XA→A and TA→A can be identified because A is always equal to -1. The analysis based on the observation of divisions or the special chosen message is similar to the proposed analysis.

The proposed analysis is an implementation of the exhaustive search in [6, Section 8]. In the next subsection, we will introduce how to exploit multiple SM sequences simultaneously.

3.2   Multi-sequence Analysis to MIST

The straightforward method to exploit multiple SM sequences is to find the candidates satisfying each SM sequence individually and then find the intersection of these candidates. In contrast, the proposed method directly finds the candidates satisfying all observed SM sequences. Since multiple SM sequences are handled simultaneously, the additional subscript j is employed to indicate variables associated with the j-th SM sequence. Some variables are redefined below, and the steps 2 and 4 of the analysis in Sec. 3.1 are also modified.

Definition 4. *When analyzing the i-th block of the j-th SM sequence, let $DR_{j,i}^{(\gamma)} = (d_{j,i}^{(\gamma)}, r_{j,i}^{(\gamma)})$ be the γ-th potential DR pair; $q_{j,i}$ be the remaining exponent; $q_{j,i}^{(\alpha-\beta)} = \langle m_{j,i}^{(\alpha-\beta)}, n_{j,i}^{(\alpha-\beta)}\rangle$ be the β-th candidate set of $q_{j,i}$ associated with $e_i^{(\alpha)}$.*

Step 2. Suppose $e_i^{(\alpha)}$ is selected. Find the smallest positive integer $\varepsilon_{i,\alpha}$ satisfying $d_{j,i}^{(\gamma)}|\varepsilon_{i,\alpha}m_{j,i}^{(\alpha-\beta)}$ for all $DR_{*,i}^{(*)}$ and $q_{*,i}^{(\alpha-*)}$ and for all SM sequences (i.e. $\forall j, \gamma, \beta$). Split $e_i^{(\alpha)}$ and all $q_{*,i}^{(\alpha-*)}$ by the factor $\varepsilon_{i,\alpha}$.

Step 4. Inspect whether the selected $split(e_i^{(\alpha)}, \varepsilon_{i,\alpha}, \delta)$ satisfies the first i blocks of all SM sequences (i.e., whether it is one $e_{i+1}^{(*)}$).

If $\bigcup_{\beta,\gamma}\left(split(q_{j,i}^{(\alpha-\beta)}, \varepsilon_{i,\alpha}, \delta) \cap \langle d_{j,i}^{(\gamma)}, r_{j,i}^{(\gamma)}\rangle\right) \neq \emptyset$ for all j (i.e., for all SM sequences), then $split(e_i^{(\alpha)}, \varepsilon_{i,\alpha}, \delta)$ is one $e_{i+1}^{(*)}$, and

$\bigcup_{\beta,\gamma}\left(\left(split(q_{j,i}^{(\alpha-\beta)}, \varepsilon_{i,\alpha}, \delta) \cap \langle d_{j,i}^{(\gamma)}, r_{j,i}^{(\gamma)}\rangle\right) \div d_{j,i}^{(\gamma)}\right)$ represents all $q_{j,i+1}^{(*-*)}$

associated with $split(e_i^{(\alpha)}, \varepsilon_{i,\alpha}, \delta)$ for the j-th SM sequence.
Otherwise, discard $split(e_i^{(\alpha)}, \varepsilon_{i,\alpha}, \delta)$.

Since each $e_i^{(*)}$ should satisfy all SM sequences, in the modified step 2, all candidate sets are split with the same factor $\varepsilon_{i,\alpha}$ instead of various factors for each SM sequence. In the modified step 4, $split(e_i^{(\alpha)}, \varepsilon_{i,\alpha}, \delta)$ is one $e_{i+1}^{(*)}$ if the candidate set of remaining exponent $q_{j,i+1}^{(\alpha-*)}$ exists for every SM sequence.

According to [6, Theorem 9], the expected number of exponents satisfying a given SM sequence is about $2^{3n/5}$ for an n-bit exponent, i.e., an arbitrary exponent will satisfy a given SM sequence with the probability $2^{-0.4n}$. Three to five SM sequences might be sufficient to obtain a unique candidate of the exponent. In the next section, we will provide some implementation results and discuss the feasibility.

4   Results and Discussions

The proposed analysis is implemented in C++ and executes on PC with 3.1GHz CPU and 8GB RAM. It uses the *list container* of Standard Template Library to store candidate sets. Each candidate set of exponent $e_i^{(\alpha)}$ is associated with one or more candidate sets of remaining exponent $q_{j,i}^{(\alpha-*)}$ for every SM sequence j. For a candidate set, the modulus M in the residue class $\langle M, N\rangle$ is represented as the form $2^a 3^b 5^c$, and the remainder N is represented by 240-base number system. Figure 4 sketches the data structure in our implementation.

Figure 5 provides three results of finding 256-bit exponent by analyzing five SM sequences. Each time, we randomly generate a 256-bit exponent, and then the MIST algorithm executes five times to collect five SM sequences associated with this exponent. The figure illustrates the number of the candidate sets $e_i^{(*)}$

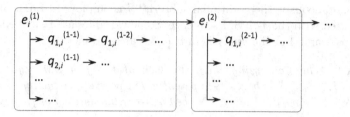

Fig. 4. Data structure for storing candidate sets

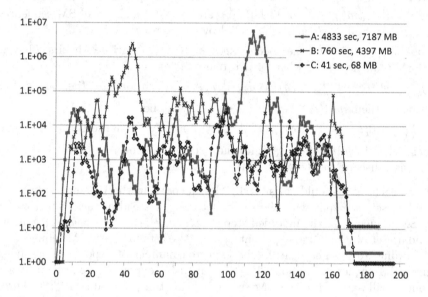

Fig. 5. Results of finding 256-bit exponent with 5 SM sequences

in each iteration, where the x-axis indicates the iteration i, and the logarithmic-scale y-axis indicates the number of $e_i^{(*)}$. The execution time (single thread execution) and peak memory usage are also provided. Figure 6 provides results with various numbers of SM sequences. We collect ten SM sequences associated with a 256-bit exponent and then perform analysis with 6/8/10 SM sequences.

The number of candidate sets during the analysis is determined by two factors, the ratio $\mathcal{E}_i$ of expansion in step 2 and the ratio $\mathcal{F}_i$ of filtering in step 4. The product $\mathcal{E}_i \times \mathcal{F}_i$ is the ratio between the number of $e_i^{(*)}$ and $e_{i+1}^{(*)}$. However, the implementation results show that the number of candidate sets in each iteration is irregular and depends on combination of observed SM sequences. There is no obvious trend of the number, except after nearly the 160th iteration, it decreases continually because expansion is not required when the modulus $M_i^{(*)}$ in each $e_i^{(*)}$ is greater than the upper limit of the exponent. Exploiting more SM sequences will remove more subsets in step 4, i.e., $\mathcal{F}_i$ gets smaller, but also generate more subsets in step 2, i.e., $\mathcal{E}_i$ gets larger. For example, between the

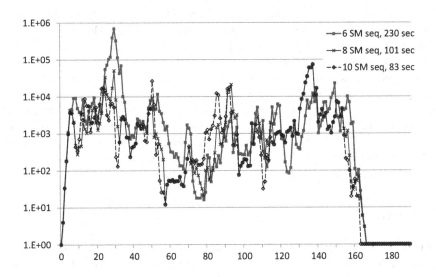

Fig. 6. Results of finding 256-bit exponent with 6/8/10 SM sequences

130th and 140th iteration of Fig. 6, there are more candidate sets in the analysis
with 10 SM sequences than with 6 or 8 SM sequences.

The execution time depends on the total number of candidate sets during
the analysis, and the peak memory usage depends on the maximum number
of candidate sets in an iteration. When the exponent is 1024-bit or longer, the
analysis program might spend too much memory and also extreme long time.
In order to reduce the number of candidate sets, we can employ supplement SM
sequences to inspect candidate sets. Unlike ordinary SM sequences, supplement
SM sequences do not allow to split candidate sets of the exponent, i.e., they only
reduce the filter factor $\mathcal{F}_i$ but not increase the expansion factor $\mathcal{E}_i$. Suppose the
i-th iteration of the analysis with the ordinary SM sequences has finished. For
each $e_i^{(\alpha)}$, we initialize $q_{\mathsf{sup},1}^{(\alpha-1)} = e_i^{(\alpha)}$ and find all $q_{\mathsf{sup},2}^{(\alpha-*)}$, ..., $q_{\mathsf{sup},i'}^{(\alpha-*)}$
relating to a supplement SM sequence until splitting is required (i.e., $\varepsilon_{i'+1,\alpha} \neq 1$
in step 2) to find $q_{\mathsf{sup},i'+1}^{(\alpha-*)}$. A candidate set $e_i^{(\alpha)}$ is valid if there is at least
one $q_{\mathsf{sup},i'}^{(\alpha-*)}$, i.e., $e_i^{(\alpha)}$ satisfies the first $(i-1)$ blocks of the supplement SM
sequence. After inspecting all candidate sets $e_i^{(*)}$ by a supplement SM sequence,
we can filter them again by another supplement SM sequence. Since $q_{\mathsf{sup},i'}^{(*-*)}$
arc not stored after analyzing a supplement SM sequence, exploiting supplement
SM sequences only slightly increases the memory requirement.

According to our implementation results, five ordinary SM sequences and
twenty supplement SM sequences are enough to deduce a 1024-bit exponent.
We start to exploit supplement SM sequences when the number of candidate
sets is more than 10,000 and until it is less than 5,000. These supplement SM
sequences are circularly reused during the analysis. In the ten implementation
results, the average execution time is 3,353 seconds (between 1,386 seconds and
5,719 seconds), and the average peak memory usage is 415 MB (between 214

MB and 872 MB). Exploiting more supplement SM sequences definitely reduces the number of candidate sets, but it might increase the execution time.

The proposed analysis is a breadth-first search (referring to Fig. 3). The breadth-first search requires a queue to store all nodes of a level, and the peak memory usage is determined by the maximum number of nodes of a level. The memory usage can be reduced by converting the proposed analysis to a depth-first search. When traversing to a child node, we only need to store its parent node and the index of the child node, i.e., storing $e_i^{(\alpha)}$ and δ when traversing to $split(e_i^{(\alpha)}, \varepsilon_{i,\alpha}, \delta)$. The maximum number of nodes stored is equal to the maximum number of blocks of SM sequences, and the execution time is roughly the same as the original method.

5   Conclusions

When designing an exponentiation algorithm with immunity to SPA, removing the explicit relationship between the computational sequence and the secret exponent is a widely used method. However, an attacker can still obtain partial information about the secret exponent from a computational sequence. He might be able to integrate information collected from several computations if the algorithm is nondeterministic, i.e., randomized.

This paper proposes the first practical multi-sequence SPA against the MIST algorithm. Further countermeasures such as exponent blinding are required to prevent the attacker from collecting multiple SM sequences corresponding to the same exponent. The proposed method is an example that a randomized algorithm with immunity to single-sequence SPA might be vulnerable to multi-sequence SPA due to its randomness. Randomized exponentiation algorithms is not an elixir of preventing side-channel attacks.

References

1. Walter, C.D.: Exponentiation using Division Chains. IEEE Transactions on Computers 47(7) (July 1998)
2. Coron, J.-S.: Resistance against Differential Power Analysis for Elliptic Curve Cryptosystems. In: Koç, Ç.K., Paar, C. (eds.) CHES 1999. LNCS, vol. 1717, pp. 292–302. Springer, Heidelberg (1999)
3. Kocher, P.C., Jaffe, J., Jun, B.: Differential power analysis. In: Wiener, M. (ed.) CRYPTO 1999. LNCS, vol. 1666, pp. 388–397. Springer, Heidelberg (1999)
4. Walter, C.D.: MIST: An Efficient, Randomized Exponentiation Algorithm for Resisting Power Analysis. In: Preneel, B. (ed.) CT-RSA 2002. LNCS, vol. 2271, pp. 53–66. Springer, Heidelberg (2002)
5. Okeya, K.: A Multiple Power Analysis Attack against Side Channel Attack Countermeasure MIST. Technical Report of IEICE, ISEC2002-104, 53–58 (2002) (in Japanese)
6. Walter, C.D.: Some security aspects of the MIST randomized exponentiation algorithm. In: Kaliski Jr., B.S., Koç, Ç.K., Paar, C. (eds.) CHES 2002. LNCS, vol. 2523, pp. 276–290. Springer, Heidelberg (2003)

7. Fouque, P.-A., Valette, F.: The Doubling Attack – Why Upwards Is Better than Downwards. In: Walter, C.D., Koç, Ç.K., Paar, C. (eds.) CHES 2003. LNCS, vol. 2779, pp. 269–280. Springer, Heidelberg (2003)

8. Oswald, E., Preneel, B.: A Survey on Passive Side-Channel Attacks and their Countermeasures for the NESSIE Public-Key Cryptosystems. Public Reports of the NESSIE Project (2003), `https://www.cosic.esat.kuleuven.be/nessie/reports/`

9. Sim, S.G., Park, D.J., Lee, P.J.: New Power Analysis on the Ha-Moon Algorithm and the MIST Algorithm. In: López, J., Qing, S., Okamoto, E. (eds.) ICICS 2004. LNCS, vol. 3269, pp. 291–304. Springer, Heidelberg (2004)

10. Chevallier-Mames, B., Ciet, M., Joye, M.: Low-Cost Solutions for Preventing Simple Side-Channel Analysis: Side-Channel Atomicity. IEEE Transaction on Computers 53(6), 760–768 (2004)

11. Courrège, J.-C., Feix, B., Roussellet, M.: Simple Power Analysis on Exponentiation Revisited. In: Gollmann, D., Lanet, J.-L., Iguchi-Cartigny, J. (eds.) CARDIS 2010. LNCS, vol. 6035, pp. 65–79. Springer, Heidelberg (2010)

12. Yen, S.-M., Lien, W.-C., Chen, C.-N.: Modified Doubling Attack by Exploiting Chosen Ciphertext of Small Order. IEICE Transactions 94-A(10), 1981–1990 (2011)

Cyber Threats Monitoring: Experimental Analysis of Malware Behavior in Cyberspace

Clara Maria Colombini[1], Antonio Colella[2,*],
Marco Mattiucci[3], and Aniello Castiglione[4]

[1] University of Milan, External Researcher, I-20122 Milano, Italy
cmcolombini@email.it
[2] Italian Army, Via XX Settembre, 123, I-00187, Rome, Italy
antonio.colella@esercito.difesa.it
[3] High Tech Crime Department (RTI), Arma dei Carabinieri
Caserma Palidoro, Viale di Tor di Quinto, 119, I-00191, Rome, Italy
marco.mattiucci@carabinieri.it
[4] Dipartimento di Informatica, Università di Salerno
Via Ponte don Melillo, I-84084, Fisciano (SA), Italy
castiglione@ieee.org

Abstract. Cyberspace is a borderless new universe in which all actors, including States, share information and communications technologies, now indispensable to the modern lifestyle. Starting from the beginning of the 21st century, the ability to leverage the cyberspace has become the most important source of power. Due to the proliferation of ICT systems into all aspects of life, the importance of information for political matters has increased awfully. State and non-State actors can use this power to achieve objectives into cyberspace and physical world. Low cost and high potential impact make cyber-power attractive to all actors. In fact, cyber threats have grown exponentially with the proliferation of the cyberspace infrastructures. Consequently, cyberspace has become a war-fighting domain with the potential to destroy or make useless logical, physical, technical, and virtual infrastructure, damaging in fact critical National capabilities.

This scenario forces all national institutions to a review of their defense strategies, because of the difficulties to identify the actors of a cyber-attack. It then becomes necessary to gain a broader view of the problem to acquire more detailed information, useful to identify such sources of cyber-attacks. This new point of view can be achieved by using the analytical method developed by the authors and applied to data streams flowing across the cyberspace. In this way we can collect, detect, isolate and analyze the behavior of those malware that are acting as cyber weapons, through the implementation of an honeypot-based system such as the one presented in this paper.

Keywords: Cyberspace, Digital Profiling, Malware, Cyber Threat, Honeypot, Cyber Weapon, Digital Behavior.

* Corresponding author.

A. Cuzzocrea et al. (Eds.): CD-ARES 2013 Workshops, LNCS 8128, pp. 236–252, 2013.

1   Introduction

Cyberspace is a unique domain that does not occupy a physical space. It does, however, depend on physical nodes, servers, and terminals that are located in Nations that exert control and sometimes ownership, as described by the definition of the U.S. Department of Defense: "Cyber-space is a global domain within the broader universe of information, and consists of a network of interdependent infrastructures, including telecommunications networks, computer systems, processors, and embedded controllers" [1]. This definition let to discern between the place *cyberspace* and the activities that occur within it. This means that cyberspace, unlike the well-known physical space, has no national boundaries. In fact, while it is possible to isolate or disable one or more parts of a compromised network, its functions and data continue to exist. This unique feature of the cyberspace influences any defensive strategy we want to implement [2]. In such a scenario, cyber threats have grown exponentially. Consequently, cyberspace has become a war-fighting domain with the potential to destroy or make useless logical, physical, and virtual infrastructure, and to damage critical national capabilities [3].

Threats within cyberspace are disparate, diffuse, and some may also be disproportionate in the harm they could cause: this means that the correct description of cyber weapons becomes primarily important to assess, on the one hand the level of threat from cyber-attacks, and on the other hand the most appropriate countermeasures to adopt, for both preventive and defensive purposes. Weapons in general are instruments through which, within a specific context, a person can bring harm to another person or object, or defend themselves from attacks. Attacks made by means of cyber weapons, in the same way as conflicts of conventional type, are designed to cause damage only to a specific opponent, often in a situation of tension or crisis already underway or about to be born, in order to obtain some kind of advantage [4].

In this paper we develop a method based on the extrapolation of the digital behavior from data streams flowing over the Internet [5]. The entire tests are carried out by implementing a set of virtual honeypots, specifically configured with different known vulnerabilities. The purpose is to collect log files, detect malware, and finally isolate those one that are acting as cyber weapons through the application of the obtained information. The purpose of the tests is to obtain valuable information about the actors of a cyber conflict, giving in real-time the vision of possible attack situations and the ability to implement an effective system of cyber defense that is pre-configurable on specific threats that are to be contrasted.

Clearly, the problem of containing large-scale malware and worms over the Internet has been addressed by several works, some of one by using a cooperative distribution of traffic filtering policies [6], others by using automatic security assessment [7]. Moreover, a part of the literature considers as a best practice to adopt audit-based access control [8] or use network anomaly detection methods [9], [10].

Section 2 shows the scenario in which we operate, the cyberspace, its unique characteristics, with respect to the proposed analytical method, while Section 3 briefly describes the method of analysis with its components: the study of the characteristics of cyber weapons, the analysis of their lifetime in cyberspace, the problems of a cyber defense, and the implementation of the filters. Section 4 introduces the experimental tests and Section 5 explains how to construct the profile of an attacker. Finally, in Section 6 are drawn the conclusions.

2   Profiling the Cyberspace

One of the biggest problems of cyber defense is represented by its anonymity with the resulting non-imputability that cyberspace can offer to the responsible of a cyber threat. In that case, it is difficult, if not impossible, to identify the enemy, because many of the challenges of traditional warfare are highlighted and amplified into cyberspace. One of the most important aspect is the challenge of situational awareness, which is defined as "the continuous extraction of environmental information, the integration of this information with previous knowledge to form a coherent mental picture, and the use of that picture in directing further perception and anticipating future event." [11]. It is therefore essential to gain the view that allows to acquire those information. This can be achieved by using the method of analysis proposed in several studies about the Digital Profiling paradigm [12], [13], [14], that gives a more detailed description of a threat in the cyberspace. This approach is based on the assessments made by the behavioral analysis of the cyber threat's main actors. We extrapolate their characteristics, in relation to their lifetime in the cyberspace. This action is made starting from two points of view: the ICT one, which analyzes software properties, and the strategic one, which reveals the strategic/military use of them as real weapons of offense. The union of the two aspects allows us to reveal new additional properties. The analysis of these new properties, together with the old ones, allow us to extrapolate the behavior of a cyber weapon. Therefore, the results of the cyber-profile are composed by a series of information that can be used as "filters" for the monitoring and the analysis of data streams [5], [15], in order to have a more efficient identification of the actors of a cyber conflict. In fact, this type of profile allows a real-time awareness of possible situations of attack and facilitate the implementation of an effective dynamic system of cyber defense.

3   The Method of Analysis

The method to extrapolate the behavior of a cyber weapon consists of the following four steps. The first one is to analyze the properties of a cyber weapon, which provides detailed features. This is followed by the analysis of the timeline of a cyber-attack. It uses the features resulted from the previous step to extrapolate comprehensive information that help to delineate the behavioral pattern of an attack. The third step is to analyze the cyber defense, considering the information gathered in the second step. Finally, the fourth step is the implementation of filters for monitoring and analysis of cyber threats, through the profile obtained from all the previous steps.

3.1   Analysis of Properties of a Cyber Weapon

The study of the characteristics of cyber weapons is based on the properties coming from an evaluation performed by using two different points of view. The *ICT* point of view, which describes the malware as any set of computer instructions designed to unlawfully damage a computer system. The cyber weapons are in fact an evolution of malware with all their properties. The *strategic/military* point of view that reveals the impact of cyber-attacks and the expected damages brought at the enemy target. This perspective adds further information about targets, such as critical infrastructures, data or programs contained therein or pertaining thereto, by using the common methods of military strategy.

A cyber weapon is a set of instructions compiled into a programming language, and thus can be disassembled, analyzed and modified. Unlike the common malware that affects either any computer system, without any type of control or advantage, it is specially customized for the characteristics of the systems to hit, with the aim to reach a specific advantage. The program code of the cyber weapons differs for each attack and is able to deal with different form of attacks simultaneously.

The impact of the caused damage is publicly revealed with a lag: similarly to all crimes, the victim is not willing to reveal his vulnerability. Furthermore, source and path are difficult to find, because their authors can take advantage of the anonymity offered by the Internet architecture. A cyber weapon can destroy itself after the attack, leaving no traces in the infected system. Any trace eventually left after the attack can easily be created ad hoc for deceiving any attempt to identify it.

Cyber weapons are often used as part of a larger conventional attack in support of it within a conflict, to gain more advantage over the enemy. They may act at a certain time, remaining "silent" until the right moment for the actions of attack comes, adapting themselves to the state of the systems in which it is introduced, and changing in response to the variables that meets. These properties make them intelligent agents, similar to "fire and forget" weapons [16]. Usually, they have a very short life, just the duration of the attack. Its discovery decrees an immediate reaction to correct any exploited vulnerability. For such a reason, cyber weapons should not be reused at a later time without substantial changes. The implementation of a cyber weapon is a very complex task. Differently from a common malware that can be created and launched by a single individual, it requires a C4ISTAR command & control (C&C) structure [1] such those one present in some advanced botnet architectures [17].

3.2   Analysis of Lifetime of a Cyber Weapon

The above features make possible to describe in detail when a cyber weapon was introduced in the wild. Analyzing the following six steps, we can exploit the actions that characterize the cyber weapon's lifetime.

Target Choice. Often the design of a cyber-attack takes place in a strategic way, from the originating motivations to the management of the entire attack. Initially, the choice of the targets is related to the enemy structure and its criticality as well as it is closely linked to the reasons of attack. It can be possible to describe the targets choice with the answer to the following four questions. *Where* is physical location of the target? *What* is the target functions? *Who* are the owner and the users of the target? *Why* such attack is performed? In this respect, it can be determined the type of damage to cause, which can be *digital* with the unauthorized access to confidential data, delay or interruption of service, modification, damage or destruction of a computer code or *physical* with the destruction of the devices and the equipment. In addition, the damage is measured in terms of *severity* of the effects caused by attack [18] and of the *persistence* of the effects that can be permanent, temporary or transient [19].

Acquisition of Information. The phase related to the acquisition of information about the chosen target is essential for the construction of the weapon itself, since its ability to effectively hit a specific target is proportional to the nature and quality of the collected information. Such information can be derived mainly from the *intelligence* point of view (e.g., information on choosing the target, its location, any access road, systems of physical protection, best time for attack, etc.) or from the *technical* point of view (e.g., technical characteristics of the selected target, its vulnerability and protection systems hardware and software).

Source Code Analysis. The majority of cyber weapons are specifically built for their purpose: more and more often we find specific cyber weapons for specific targets to hit. This makes a cyber weapon more effective. In fact, when a cyber weapon is discovered, specific defensive countermeasures are taken. This makes it no longer able to act also if the quality of the cyber weapon was high. The code that composes it is implemented by considering the type of intrusion, which can be:

- *direct*: connection to the target system with a device that transmits it (USB mass storage, CDROM, etc.);
- *semi-direct*: sent over the network from a non-critical location;
- *indirect*: sent through cyberspace.

In addition, this "armed code" must implement those properties that distinguish it from a common malware and make it an effective weapon, anonymous and difficult to detect. Namely, an effective implementation of a good cyber weapon having the above characteristics should consider when it have to be launched (immediately, delayed or repeated) and should adapt itself to the conditions of the targeted system, including a mechanism of self-destruction and the possibility to connect to a C&C server. In addition, no unwanted and uncontrollable collateral damages as well as no traces are left on the attacked system and in the cyberspace.

Simulation and Testing. A cyber-attack must succeed at the first attempt, otherwise it can be easily neutralized. Its realization must include, as with any other software, a test phase, before the real attack. Initially it takes place in a virtual environment, in order to test the functionalities of the implemented code, but it then needs to be tested into the cyberspace, to correct any eventual error, and especially to adapt it to the changes that may have occurred in the configuration of the security measures taken by the target system. The aim is to gain information on the effectiveness of the penetration methods and on the intended damages, in order to ensure the success of the attack against the real target. At this stage the type of attack is similar to a real one. In fact, the target system is composed of a set of systems similar to the chosen one.

Attacks. The most important phase in the timeline analysis is the attack, in which all the prepared actions, tested in the previous stages, are implemented. The aim is to effectively hit the chosen target and get a response as close as possible to the expected result in the prescribed manner and time, avoiding any unwanted side-effect.

Results Evaluation. The last phase consist on evaluating, both in the actual state and in the near future, the success of the attack by comparing the expected results against the real obtained ones. The first step verifies the successful reaching of the intended target, followed by the assessment of the time of the attack, the type, the duration, and costs of caused damage on the target system. Later on, have been also considered the effects of damage on the infected system, the building that houses it, and any impact in the short, medium and long term, such as side effects inside and outside the target system, impact of the attack (military/political/social), and the eventual countermeasures (active/passive). The assessments in the above paragraphs lead to an overall evaluation of the attack in terms of analysis of cost/benefit as well as in term of real gained advantages.

3.3   Cyber Defense Analysis

In order to have a more comprehensive analysis of cyber-attacks, the evaluation of its characteristics from the point of view of the structure responsible for the defense is of fundamental importance. The study of known cyber weapons (from the DDoS attacks in Estonia up to the Stuxnet worm) [20], [21], [22], [23], confirmed that the weapon *computer* is mostly often used as part of a larger conventional attack in support of it. This observation leads to the creation of a monitoring system that can be useful to extrapolate those indicators that show the possibility of a cyber-attack on critical infrastructures, through the analysis of available information from different type of sources. Such sources can be *open*, if publicly available (such as national reports coming from companies producing antivirus, national and international newspapers, websites dealing with political, economical and social analysis), *semi-open* when consist on websites of hackers' groups, antagonists, extremists, fundamentalists, and *closed* when it is part of a strategic/military documentation.

The obtained information should be able to answer to the following seven questions:

- *who*: the identification of possible attackers;
- *why*: the reasons of the attack;
- *where*: the identification of critical infrastructures that are possible targets;
- *how*: the intrusion mode;
- *what*: the damage type;
- *when*: the attack time;
- *results*: the damage extent and possible disadvantage;
- *reaction*: response actions.

3.4   Implementation of Filters to Monitor Data Flow

The information obtained from the above-mentioned analysis constitutes a first set of filters applicable in the analysis of data streams to detect those signals that indicate the possibility of a cyber-attack in the near future. The main step consists on detecting the presence of a cyber weapon through the analysis of characteristics of its behavior, which distinguish it from a common malware. The possible identification of targets may be exploited detecting properties in common among different malware. In particular, the possible targets are: limited in number and restricted to a particular type, geographically distributed, with similar processes or critical data, with the same OS, with similar policy and security systems and, finally, with the same vulnerabilities.

In Table 1 are listed the behavioral characteristics of the malware detected by the analysis that reveals the activity of cyber weapons. Furthermore, the real target (according to the properties of the cyber weapons) undergoes the highest number of attacks, is repeatedly attacked in different times, can be identified in a later time upon an intrusion or an attack, reveals stepwise refinements in the malware code and is related to the reasons of tensions/crisis/conflicts/antagonisms, either national or international.

The information obtained upon analyzing the content of its source code, can provide the profile of the detected cyber weapon. The indicators that can be extracted from it, can be used as filters for the recognition of a cyber-attack that is in progress or about to be launched. Such filters can be applied to the log files related to the attempts of intrusion into the domain of interest.

Table 1. The meaning of each detected feature in the malware behavior

Feature	Meaning
Incomplete code	- developing code
Simultaneous diffusion of the same code in a limited number of objectives	- malware test on a controllable number of objective similar to target - refine tuning of malware code - deception - reduction of target reaction response time
Repeated attacks over time for the same purposes	- code corrections - deception
More attacks on the chosen target	- customize code on actual configuration of real target
No major damage caused as a results of the intrusion or attack	- decrease the possibility of detection by antivirus softwares - reduction of target reaction response time

4   The Experiments

The main goal of the experiments is to illustrate the application of the method introduced in the previous sections. This will be used to implement a system to monitor and analyze data streams flowing through Internet. The experiments were conducted on a small-scale only from a technical point of view, applying those filters derived from the information extracted from the analysis of the characteristics of the detected cyber-attacks. To develop the experiments, we implemented a network of *honeypot* (called *honeynet*) through which collect, detect, extract and analyze malicious codes launched against it. A honeypot is a machine connected to a network that emulates system vulnerabilities in order to attract, capture and analyze cyber-attacks. If a connection occurs, it can be, at best an accidental connection or, more likely, an attempt to attack the machine. Briefly, we can classify honeypots firstly into two groups, based on their deployment. The *production honeypots* are used in a company's internal network to improve the security of the whole network. In addition, the *research honeypots* are more complex of the production ones, and provide a detailed information about the attacks and are used by research, military and government organizations.

The second criterion classifies honeypots based on their design criteria. The *pure honeypots* are full production systems, so no other software needs to be installed. The *high-interaction honeypots* use non-emulated OSes with multiple services which can be exploited by the attacker. Also, the *low-interaction honeypots* emulate the part of the system and services most frequently used [24].

4.1   Honeypots Implementation

We used the tools contained into the "Mercury Live DVD" [25]. It comprises valuable tools for digital forensics, data recovery, network monitoring, spoofing, reverse engineering, and four different type of honeypots: Honeyd, Nephentes, Dionaea, and Kippo. In particular, Honeyd is a low-interaction honeypot that comprises several components (see Figure 1(a)): configuration database, a central packet dispatcher, protocol handlers and a personality engine. Incoming packets first go through the central packet dispatcher. It is able of dealing with three protocols, TCP, UDP and ICMP. The dispatcher queries the configuration corresponding to the destination address. Then it passes the packet to the protocol-specific handler. On receiving a TCP or UDP packet, the handler manages the connections to different services. The framework checks if a specific packet is part of an already started service application. If so, all packets are redirected to the service, otherwise a new service is started. The handler also helps in connections' redirection. Then the packet is sent to the personality engine which manipulates its content to make it appear similar to the one originated from the network stack. Through Honeyd we implemented a network with three routers and four simulated hosts, as in Figure 1(b). The Honeyd implementation also includes two hosts configured with two different versions of Microsoft Windows, one as a server and the other as a client. What follows is an example of configuration.

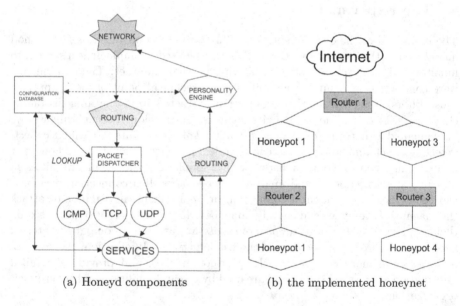

(a) Honeyd components   (b) the implemented honeynet

Fig. 1. Architectural sketch of the Honeyd components (a) and the scheme of the implemented honeynet (b)

```
# Windows 2000 Server SP3 WebServer
create windows2000
set windows2000 personality "Microsoft Windows 2000 Server SP3"
add windows2000 tcp port 80 "perl scripts/iis-0.95/iisemul8.pl"
add windows2000 tcp port 139 open
add windows2000 tcp port 137 open
add windows2000 udp port 137 open
add windows2000 udp port 135 open
set windows2000 default tcp action reset
set windows2000 default udp action reset
```

To improve the reality of the implemented honeynet, Honeyd allows to simulate all the standard devices connected to a network, such as "Cisco" routers as shown in the following example:

```
# Cisco Router
create routerCisco
set routerCisco personality "Cisco IOS 11.3 - 12.0(11)"
set routerCisco default tcp action reset
set routerCisco default udp action reset
add routerCisco tcp port 23 "/usr/bin/perl scripts/router-telnet.pl"
set routerCisco uid 32767 gid 32767
set routerCisco uptime 1327650
```

All configurations are contained in a simple text file (name.conf) that must be read by the program, and according to which all details of the simulated network are created. This is in fact a sort of *false digital profile* offered to the attackers, to increase the realism of the honeypots. This concept is similar to the one of the *false digital alibi* in which it is shown how simple is to setup false digital evidence on different systems (such as Mac OS X [26], Android devices [27], and different flavor of the Microsoft Windows OSes [28], [29], [30]) in order to claim a false alibi to be used in several scenarios. In the case of the honeynet, since the attackers often try to remotely fingerprint OSes by using tools like nmap or X probe, Honeyd takes the same fingerprint database used by nmap to spoof the response of any OS it is emulating by providing false evidence about the running OS.

In order to present simple but effective experimental results, we focuses our attention on the study of the behavior of malicious attacks performed against the SSH service. Also, the experiments let to inspect the activities performed by the attackers once they gain access to the system and try to progress in their intrusion [31], configuring the machine to record the password along with the account name that was used in the login attempt [32], [33]. In order to better analyze the behavior of the attacks, we implemented two identical honeypots, into two different subnets, with two different SSH user account configurations, in order to obtain two different profiles of the same attack to compare. In the first one (see Figure 2(a)) there exist 8 user accounts and their relatives passwords composed by very common words, in order to offer a high level of vulnerability. On the contrary, the second one ((see Figure 2(b))) also contains the same 8 user accounts, but with 8 complex passwords, composed by letters, digits, and special symbols, to resemble to a more protected system.

Here we present the results of the analysis of captured data in the two honeypots during 30 days, focusing in particular on the log files containing the authentication requests to the SSH server: date, time, the IP address from which the login attempt originated, the result of the request (failure or success), the account name and the password used for the authentication request as follows:

```
Jan 16 03:36:45 basta sshd[2308]: PW-ATTEMPT: 1234
Jan 16 03:36:45 basta sshd[2308]: Failed password for root from 10.0.160.14 port 39529 ssh2
Jan 16 03:17:11 basta sshd[2310]: Illegal user password from 10.0.160.14
Jan 16 03:17:11 basta sshd[2308]: PW-ATTEMPT: password
Jan 16 03:17:11 basta sshd[2308]: Failed password for illegal user password from 10.0.160.14 port 40444 ssh2
```

honeypot1	
Account Name	*Password*
root	root
admin	1234
user	0000
guest	password
password	123456
test	qwerty
administrator	654321
webmaster	abc123

(a) weak account names and passwords

honeypot2	
Account Name	*Password*
root	JotCR4E->
admin	mC3bum@:
user	ZR?s25{_
guest	k6r@bPr6
password	[Ea~K^#_
test	{Q};Dced
administrator	:3h!t>VD
webmaster	c)isWAr?

(b) weak account names with strong passwords

Fig. 2. Configurations of the SSH service on honeypot1 (a) and on honeypot2 (b)

4.2   Experimental Results: Statistical Aspects and Analysis

In this section are presented the results of our experiments, that start with a statistical overview of the activities observed on the two honeypots continuing with the analysis of the activities performed after the intrusions.

In the examined period of 30 days, the two honeypots were contacted by 237 different IP addresses. They recorded 74201 login attempts on SSH, capturing in total 2548 different account names and 4231 passwords. We processed the raw data in order to use it as filters to extract relevant information. Such data range from usernames and passwords, the attack types and also the activities performed after the intrusion. As stated above, honeypot1 contained weak accounts names and passwords, while honeypot2 contained weak accounts names but complex passwords. Referring to the SSH login account of the honeypot1, the first success occurred with the same username and password: "root", after only 23 attempts by only one attack. Thus the remaining 7 accounts were all detected and used to access the machine after about 50-100 attempts. In relation to honeypot2, only one account was successfully detected after 4452 attempts, the one with username "root" and password JotCR4E->.

Regarding the date and time of the connections, considering the database of the 74201 login attempts on SSH, filtering them by date, we analyzed the distribution of the attacks in the 30 days (see Fig. 3), in which we observed that honeypot1 was hit with 57457 login attempts with a rate of 1915 attempt per day (with an increasing trend), while for honeypot2 there were 16744 login attempts with a rate of 558 attempt per day (showing an initial increase, followed by a decrease, probably due to the complexity of passwords).

Analyzing duration and frequency of the attempts, we can split them into two separate groups. The first one comprises attacks performed without interruptions for a period of time (days), with an high frequency and the same interval of time among them. In addition, the second one is composed by attacks realized from time to time, with a low frequency and different intervals of time among them.

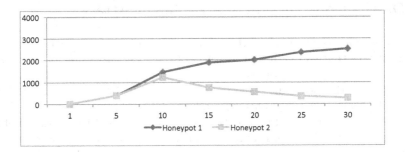

Fig. 3. Trend of access attempts on the two honeypots along the 30 days timeline

Regarding the location (i.e., the IP address) of the attacker, during the examined period of 30 days, the two honeypots were contacted by 437 different IP addresses. All of them attacked the `honeypot1`, but only 76 attempted to access the `honeypot2`. Using the tool GeoIP, we could geographically locate the machines performing the attacks, not necessary the real origin of them. We realized that the intrusion tentatives come from several countries, that is 21% from USA, 19% from China, 15% from Netherlands 11% from Romania, 9% from the United Kingdom, 7% from Germany, and so on.

Analyzing the total number of login attempts, we recognized from one side a 9% of real-time intrusions, recognized by their behavior, processing username and password in a slow way with different breaks, containing also some typing errors, while on the other site, the 91% were performed by dictionary attacks. Applying "`IP addresses`" and "`honeypot1`" as filters to the list of dictionary attacks, we found that 106 of their attempts had these characteristics, which let us to recognize them as performed by automatic scripts. In fact, such connections were only targeted against port 22, thousands of usernames and passwords were processed in a very short time, no pauses were found between attempts and weak usernames and passwords were found in a very short time. The login attempts against the `honeypot2` were performed from 76 IP addresses, which used 233 dictionary attacks, 17 real-time intrusions, and 52 scanning activities. Referring to `honeypot1`, only 8 real-time attacks, performed by two different IP addresses, were able to compromise the system, while all the 106 dictionary attacks violated the machine.

4.3 Analysis of the Activities Performed after the Intrusions

After a successful intrusion, a series of activities were performed by the attackers on the violated host. The attackers first of all change the password of the hacked account and try to acquire the *root* privileges. After that, start exploring the filesystem and start downloading files by means of the commands `wget` and `sftp`. Also, create and hide new directories where to store malicious software that usually is used to scan the networks and to create backdoors. Often, such software includes an IRC client to join a botnets and some tools useful to execute lot of scanning activities.

5   On the Construction of a Profile of Attack

Upon performing the analysis of the attacks, it is possible to extract lot of interesting features that can be useful to start constructing the profile of the attack. First of all, the IP address of the attacker machine and the associated "owner" of such IP together with the geographical location of the attacker machine are extracted. Clearly, the type of attack can be a real-time attack or one based on a dictionary. All the temporal information, such as attack lifetime, duration of the attack with the complete hour and day time are easily calculated since the honeypots have been synchronized with a trusted external source of time. From such temporal data it is possible to have the frequency of the attempts of intrusion giving an idea of its regularity and occurrence. Analyzing whether the attack was successful or not, it can be seen the activities performed after the intrusion that may range from (internal/external) network scan, download of files, system exploration, directory creation, malicious software upload and installation. At last but not least, it can be analyzed the type of installed malicious software, the activities performed by the malicious software and, more importantly, the traces and evidence left on the attacked host.

The information extracted from above-mentioned features allow us to build the profile of the attack. First of all, we recognized two main groups: *real-time* or *automatic* attacks. We want here to focus attention on the second group, to which we applied, as filters, the following features: high frequency attacks, fast guessing of usernames and passwords, network scanning, creation of new directories/files, successful passwords guessing, upload of files, no errors encountered, success of the intrusion and no traces left.

5.1   Profile Analysis to Detect the Presence of a Cyber Threat

The obtained results brought to our attention one intruder, the only one able to compromise the `honeypot2`. Its IP origin seems to be in Shaoxing, located in the province of Zhejiang, China. Here we show a detailed timeline of its activity:

- Jan 6 2013, 02:00 A.M.: the attacker machine launched a dictionary attack against `honeypot1`, breaking one login account in 21 minutes (username: `test` password: `0000`).
- Jan 6 2013, 02:22 A.M.: it changed the password in `N!ka@mikk@2112`, then it closed the connection.
- Jan 7 2013, 02:00 A.M.: the same machine entered the system with its new account and began to scan the network finding `honeypot2` and its open port 22.
- Jan 7 2013, 02:07 A.M.: It began a dictionary attack to SSH login account on the `honeypot2`, finding the username `root` in about 10 minutes.
- Jan 7 2013, 02:18 A.M. it continued its attack against the password, processing thousands of words in a very fast way with high frequency attempts, and stopped at 5:00.
- Jan 8 2013, 01:00 A.M.: it resumed its attack stopping it at 5:00.

He attacked the system in a continuous way for 11 days, from 0:00 to 6:00 A.M. until the right password `JotCR4E->` was guessed. After the intrusion, it did not changed the password, but created into the home directory a new directory named "MY_OLD_DOCS", in which a file named "11022012doc_old.pdf" was uploaded before stopping the connection. We did not detected other any other connection until the end of the experimentation on the two honeypots. Submitting that file (named "11022012doc_old.pdf") to a forensic analysis, we extracted the MD5 (0xD1E7C8A8D857E097EEF8922F41074E80), the SHA-1 (0xA1339C48B7D8A9F8C7358DA6C3C620F63BE25A51) and filesize (253.952 bytes). This allow us to discover that it was a known cyber threat, named IXESHE [34], that is a backdoor/trojan born in China. This malware communicates with remote servers and receives instructions, acting as in a botnet. It may download and run other malware. The Trend Micro reported [35] that such a trojan is often attached to email messages as a simple PDF file, coming from a compromised or spoofed account. Once opened, the PDF either displays a blank or dummy page, but the code inside it starts the malware. Once installed, IXESHE starts communicating with compromised machines hosted on previously infiltrated networks. Such a dangerous backdoor is the trojan horse named IXESHE, hidden into a PDF file with a very common name capable to connect to a remote C&C server [36] to transmit and receive information to be used during future attacks. It is worth to highlight that very often PDF files are used to convey different kind of malware. The reader can find an interesting study on some security issues that can be exploited by means of PDF files in [37].

Although this type of malware is almost sent by email messages as attachment, here we saw that it was uploaded, but not executed, into a directory with a very ordinary name, probably for several reasons. In fact, spreading such a malware in the ordinary way may not be effective because it could be easily detected by antivirus checking emails and attachments. Also, the attacker did not started the malware immediately for several reasons: to observe how long it will remain undetected, to wait for some user to open such file resulting in the malware installation, or to test a new infection method on some compromised machines to improve it and use at a later time on different targeted systems. Moreover, due to the massive spread of mobile devices and its ubiquitous nature, particular attention should be also paid in protecting such mobile equipment from malware attacks [38], [39].

6   Conclusions

In this paper, we have presented the application of an analytical method to monitor the data streams flowing in cyberspace. The experimental tests were performed by implementing an honeynet system. The results have been obtained from tests conducted for 30 days by using two honeypots, configured to trap SSH intrusion attempts in two different ways. This let us to analyze the behavior of the attacks, step by step, from login attempts to the activities after the intrusion. Clearly, this represents a simple scenario that can be expanded in further researches. However, these tests, although small, allowed us to detect, extract, and analyze the behavior of one cyber-attack used to compromise systems that are well protected, in a very little time by means of a dictionary-based attack against the SSH service, acting only during the night in a increasing way to stay inconspicuous.

It is important to highlight that, in order to study attacks against a predetermined system, it could be also useful to use tools and methods that record all the packet traffic going to the system under attack [40]. Any way, such approach could not be useful when there is the need of a broader point of view. The information deriving from the use of our method can be used to implement a series of effective countermeasures for the protection and the prevention of cyber-attacks, by improving the physical protection of critical infrastructures, as well as the resolution of digital vulnerabilities of critical systems and the implementation of new security policies for protecting critical data. From a defensive point of view, the possibility to be aware, in real-time, of the presence of forthcoming attacks allows the implementation of an effective system of cyber defense in a dynamic way.

References

1. U.S. Department of Defense: Joint Publication 1-02, Dictionary of Military and Associated Terms, http://www.dtic.mil/doctrine/new_pubs/jp1_02.pdf (November 2010)
2. Fahrenkrug, D.T.: Countering the Offensive Advantage in Cyber-space: An Integrated Defensive Strategy. In: 4th International Conference on Cyber Conflict, NATO CCD COE Publications, Tallinn, pp. 197–207 (2012)
3. Klimburg, A.: National Cyber Security Framework Manual. NATO CCD COE Publications (December 2012), http://www.ccdcoe.org/369.html
4. Saalbach, K.: Cyber-war. Methods and Practice, version 6.0 (January 2013), http://www.dirk-koentopp.com/downloads/saalbach-cyberwar-methods-and-practice.pdf
5. Colombini, C., Colella, A., Mattiucci, M.: Cyber-war Profiling, a new Method for the Analysis of a Cyber-Conflict. To appear on NATO CCD COE, Tallinn (January 2013)
6. Palmieri, F., Fiore, U.: Containing large-scale worm spreading in the Internet by cooperative distribution of traffic filtering policies. Computers & Security 27(1-2), 48–62 (2008)
7. Palmieri, F., Fiore, U., Castiglione, A.: Automatic security assessment for next generation wireless mobile networks. Mobile Information Systems 7(3), 217–239 (2011)
8. Palmieri, F., Fiore, U.: Audit-Based Access Control in Nomadic Wireless Environments. In: Gavrilova, M., Gervasi, O., Kumar, V., Tan, C.J.K., Taniar, D., Laganá, A., Mun, Y., Choo, H. (eds.) ICCSA 2006. LNCS, vol. 3982, pp. 537–545. Springer, Heidelberg (2006)
9. Palmieri, F., Fiore, U.: Network anomaly detection through nonlinear analysis. Computers & Security 29(7), 737–755 (2010)
10. Fiore, U., Palmieri, F., Castiglione, A., De Santis, A.: Network anomaly detection with the restricted Boltzmann machine. Neurocomputing (2013), http://dx.doi.org/10.1016/j.neucom.2012.11.050, doi:10.1016/j.neucom.2012.11.050

11. Vidulich, M., Dominguez, C., Vogel, E., McMillian, G.: Situation Awareness: Papers and Annotated Bibliography, U.S. Department of Defense, Defense Technical Information Center (DTIC) (June 1994), http://www.dtic.mil/dtic/tr/fulltext/u2/a284752.pdf

12. Colombini, C.M., Colella, A.: Digital Profiling: A Computer Forensics Approach. In: Tjoa, A.M., Quirchmayr, G., You, I., Xu, L. (eds.) ARES 2011. LNCS, vol. 6908, pp. 330–343. Springer, Heidelberg (2011)

13. Colombini, C., Colella, A., Castiglione, A., Scognamiglio, V.: The Digital Profiling Techniques Applied to the Analysis of a GPS Navigation Device. In: 2012 Sixth International Conference on Innovative Mobile and Internet Services in Ubiquitous Computing (IMIS), pp. 591–596 (2012)

14. Castiglione, A., De Santis, A., Fiore, U., Palmieri, F.: Device Tracking in Private Networks via NAPT Log Analysis. In: 2012 Sixth International Conference on Innovative Mobile and Internet Services in Ubiquitous Computing (IMIS), pp. 603–608 (2012)

15. Colombini, C.M., Colella, A., Mattiucci, M., Castiglione, A.: Network Profiling: Content Analysis of Users Behavior in Digital Communication Channel. In: Quirchmayr, G., Basl, J., You, I., Xu, L., Weippl, E. (eds.) CD-ARES 2012. LNCS, vol. 7465, pp. 416–429. Springer, Heidelberg (2012)

16. Matrosov, A., Rodionov, E., Harley, D., Malcho, J.: Stuxnet Under the Microscope, rev. 1.31, ESET LLC (2012), http://ece.wpi.edu/ dchasaki/papers/ Stuxnet_Under_the_Microscope.pdf

17. Castiglione, A., De Prisco, R., De Santis, A., Fiore, U., Palmieri, F.: A botnet-based command and control approach relying on swarm intelligence. Journal of Network and Computer Applications (2013), http://dx.doi.org/10.1016/j.jnca.2013.05.002, doi:10.1016/j.jnca.2013.05.002

18. Ziolkowski, K.: *Ius ad bellum* in Cyberspace - Some Thoughts on the "Schmitt-Criteria" for Use of Force. In: 4th International Conference on Cyber Conflict, NATO CCD COE Publications, Tallinn, pp. 295–309 (2012)

19. Fanelli, R., Conti, G.: A methodology for cyber operations targeting and control of collateral damage in the context of lawful armed conflict. In: 2012 4th International Conference on Cyber Conflict (CYCON), pp. 1–13 (2012)

20. CrySyS Lab: sKyWIper (a.k.a. Flame a.k.a. Flamer): A complex malware for targeted attacks (May 2012), http://www.crysys.hu/skywiper/skywiper.pdf

21. Bencsáth, B., Pék, G., Buttyán, L., Félegyházi, M.: Duqu: A Stuxnet-like malware found in the wild (October 2011), http://www.crysys.hu/publications/files/bencsathPBF11duqu.pdf

22. Kaspersky Lab, Global Research and Analysis Team: Gauss: Abnormal Distribution (August 2012), http://www.securelist.com/en/analysis/204792238/

23. Kaspersky Lab, Global Research and Analysis Team: The Mahdi Campaign (July 2012), http://www.securelist.com/en/blog/208193691/ The_Madi_Campaign_Part_II

24. Infosec Institute: Honeypots Resources (October 2012), http://resources.infosecinstitute.com/honeypots/

25. Moore, J.: Mercury Live DVD (2013), http://mercurylivedvd.sourceforge.net/

26. Castiglione, A., Cattaneo, G., De Prisco, R., De Santis, A., Yim, K.: How to Forge a Digital Alibi on Mac OS X. In: Quirchmayr, G., Basl, J., You, I., Xu, L., Weippl, E. (eds.) CD-ARES 2012. LNCS, vol. 7465, pp. 430–444. Springer, Heidelberg (2012)

27. Albano, P., Castiglione, A., Cattaneo, G., De Maio, G., De Santis, A.: On the Construction of a False Digital Alibi on the Android OS. In: Xhafa, F., Barolli, L., Köppen, M. (eds.) INCoS, pp. 685–690. IEEE (2011)

28. Castiglione, A., Cattaneo, G., De Maio, G., De Santis, A.: Automated Production of Predetermined Digital Evidence. IEEE Access 1, 216–231 (2013)

29. De Santis, A., Castiglione, A., Cattaneo, G., De Maio, G., Ianulardo, M.: Automated Construction of a False Digital Alibi. In: Tjoa, A.M., Quirchmayr, G., You, I., Xu, L. (eds.) ARES 2011. LNCS, vol. 6908, pp. 359–373. Springer, Heidelberg (2011)

30. Castiglione, A., Cattaneo, G., De Maio, G., De Santis, A., Costabile, G., Epifani, M.: The Forensic Analysis of a False Digital Alibi. In: 2012 Sixth International Conference on Innovative Mobile and Internet Services in Ubiquitous Computing (IMIS), pp. 114–121 (2012)

31. Nicomette, V., Kaâniche, M., Alata, E., Herrb, M.: Set-up and deployment of a high-interaction honeypot: experiment and lessons learned. Journal in Computer Virology 7(2), 143–157 (2011)

32. Li, C., Parsioan, T.: Profiling Honeynet Attackers. In: Proceedings of the Class of 2006 Senior Conference, pp. 19–26 (2005)

33. Seifert, C.: Analyzing Malicious SSH Login Attempts (November 2010), http://www.symantec.com/connect/articles/analyzing-malicious-ssh-login-attempts

34. Threat Expert Ltd.: Backdoor:Win32/Ixeshe.E (2013), http://www.threatexpert.com/report.aspx?md5=d1e7c8a8d857e097eef8922f41074e80

35. Sancho, D., dela Torre, J., Bakuei, M., Villeneuve, N., McArdle, R.: IXESHE An APT Campaign (2012), http://www.trendmicro.com/cloud-content/us/pdfs/security-intelligence/white-papers/wp_ixeshe.pdf

36. Tyugu, E.: Command and control of cyber weapons. In: 2012 4th International Conference on Cyber Conflict (CYCON), pp. 1–11 (2012)

37. Castiglione, A., De Santis, A., Soriente, C.: Security and privacy issues in the Portable Document Format. Journal of Systems and Software 83(10), 1813–1822 (2010)

38. Armando, A., Merlo, A., Migliardi, M., Verderame, L.: Would You Mind Forking This Process? A Denial of Service Attack on Android (and Some Countermeasures). In: Gritzalis, D., Furnell, S., Theoharidou, M. (eds.) SEC 2012. IFIP AICT, vol. 376, pp. 13–24. Springer, Heidelberg (2012)

39. Armando, A., Merlo, A., Migliardi, M., Verderame, L.: Breaking and fixing the Android Launching Flow. Computers & Security (2013)

40. Castiglione, A., Cattaneo, G., De Maio, G., De Santis, A.: Forensically-Sound Methods to Collect Live Network Evidence. In: 2013 IEEE 27th International Conference on Advanced Information Networking and Applications (AINA), pp. 405–412 (2013)

Analyzing the Internet Stability
in Presence of Disasters

Francesco Palmieri[1], Ugo Fiore[2,*], Aniello Castiglione[3], Fang-Yie Leu[4],
and Alfredo De Santis[3]

[1] Dipartimento di Ingegneria Industriale e dell'Informazione
Seconda Università di Napoli
Via Roma 29, Aversa (CE), I-81031, Italy
fpalmier@unina.it
[2] Information Services Center, Università Federico II
Via Cinthia 5, I-80126, Napoli, Italy
ufiore@unina.it
[3] Dipartimento di Informatica, Università di Salerno
Via Ponte don Melillo, I-84084, Fisciano (SA), Italy
castiglione@ieee.org, ads@dia.unisa.it
[4] Department of Computer Science, Tunghai University
No.1727, Sec.4, Taiwan Boulevard, Xitun District, Taichung 40704, Taiwan, R.O.C.
leufy@thu.edu.tw

Abstract. The Internet is now a critical infrastructure for the modern, information-based, e-Society. Stability and survivability of the Internet are thus important, especially in presence of catastrophic events which carry heavy societal and financial impacts. In this work, we analyze the stability of the inter-domain routing system during several large-scale catastrophic events that affected the connectivity of massive parts of the address space, with the objective of acquiring information about degradation of service and recovery capabilities.

Results show that the Internet has maintained good responsiveness: service disruption has been contained and recovery times have been fast, even after catastrophic events. However, combining the view provided by the routing table and the view originated by the analysis of the BGP updates is not a trivial task, as such phenomena need to be analyzed at multiple time scales.

Keywords: Internet Resilience, BGP, Disasters, Critical Infrastructures, Catastrophic Events.

1 Introduction

Much of the social life is now reliant on interactions carried out remotely, and a significant fraction of these interactions happen over the Internet that assumes the role of a critical infrastructure for the modern information-based e-Society.

---

* Corresponding author.

A. Cuzzocrea et al. (Eds.): CD-ARES 2013 Workshops, LNCS 8128, pp. 253–268, 2013.

This is also true for money-involving applications such as financial transactions, which make heavy use of the Internet infrastructures. Disruption of service on the Internet would carry catastrophic consequences over these activities: therefore, resilience and survivability of the Internet are now extremely important aspects, both at the business level and the government one.

The impact of an Internet outage on essential economic sectors may in fact be devastating for an entire country. Furthermore, to respond to emergencies in an effective and timely manner, availability of accurate information and ability to disseminate it are critical factors that both depend on the correct functioning of a communication infrastructure. The term *survivability* is generally referred to the ability, in the aftermath of a disruptive event, to recover and quickly return to service levels offered before. While the Internet has become a critical infrastructure, there is no comprehensive knowledge about its expected behavior during crises, particularly in terms of its survivability in presence of large-scale disruptions or failures over its fundamental transport infrastructure. Due to the distributed architecture of the Internet, there are many exchange points around the globe, owned by consortia of service providers who share costs and capacity, where a number of transmission links converge in order to connect networks operated by different organizations. In addition, there are critical connections such as undersea links, forming an essential part of the global Internet. These points and links assume the role of critical assets for the overall Internet coverage and operations, since their failure, due to fiber damage or power outages, may wreak havoc on connectivity of significant portions of the Internet. Fiber damages and power outages may be either due to natural phenomena, such as earthquakes, typhoons, and floods, or man-made disasters consequent to war or terrorist actions. Other service disruptions may originate from malware (e.g., worms) devouring all communication resources during their spread throughout the Internet.

In order to achieve a better understanding of the fundamental dynamics governing the Internet behavior, one must study historical data, recorded over the last decade, that describe the state and evolution of network reachability information, and correlate such data with knowledge about the events occurred at the time data were registered. With this in mind, we analyze the stability and behavior of the routing infrastructure, whose fundamental glue is the interdomain routing system, empowered by the Border Gateway Protocol (BGP), during several large-scale catastrophic events that affected the connectivity of large regions within the Internet, in order to acquire some information about its fundamental service degradation properties and fault recovery capabilities.

In this work we limit our study to catastrophic events originated by physical causes, disregarding any kind of malicious network/traffic activity that can adversely affect the Internet operations on a large scale. We are interested in analyzing the entity of damage to Internet connectivity, its distribution across the globe, and the time needed to recover together with the effects perceived on global reachability from several observation points scattered throughout the world.

2   Related Work

Several experiences available in literature focus their attention on the analysis of the Internet behavior in presence of large scale infrastructure failures due to both natural or human-driven causes, such as catastrophic events or worm/malware outbreaks. The study presented in [1] carefully analyzed the BGP system dynamics, during a power outage that affected the connectivity of 3,175 networks in a large number of cities in the eastern United States and Canada. The 2006 earthquake in Taiwan has been extensively analyzed from the BGP point of view in [2], largely focusing on an AS-based perspective. Similarly, in [3] a characterization is presented of BGP recovery times under large-scale failure scenarios associated to disasters or man-made events, resulting in substantial recovery times in presence of massive failures. In addition, the work in [4] evaluates the potentiality of BGP-compliant recovery schemes exploiting route diversity in order to recover from large-scale Internet failures. A survey on the security issues related to disasters, with emphasis on maintaining network access, is presented in [5]. From a more theoretical point of view, the contribution presented in [6] studied the stability of the Internet, as a scale free network with respect to crashes, such as random removal of sites, according to a percolation theory-driven approach. The effects of other kind of events, such as large worm outbreaks on Internet stability has been analyzed in [7].

3   Routing, BGP, and Stability

The number of services running on the Internet continually increases, and so does the network size. This continued growth challenges the capability of the routing layer to produce a stable, coherent, and reasonably efficient view of the topological structure of all portions of the network. This is an essential condition for continued delivery of packets to their destination addresses.

3.1   BGP

Adjacent Autonomous Systems (ASes) [8] exchange reachability information about destination Internet address blocks, so that routers can reach a consistent topological view of the network. In turn, this allows consistent routing decisions to be taken, without generating undesirable situations such as conflicts or loops. The de-facto standard protocol for inter-domain routing is the Border Gateway Protocol (BGP). A BGP announcement (BGP UPDATE message) concerns a route, and carries a set of attributes. A mandatory attribute is the AS-PATH, indicating the sequence of ASes to be traversed to reach the listed destinations. A BGP-speaking router within an AS, passing an announcement originated at another BGP peer, prepends its own AS number to the AS-PATH. Each AS makes its own routing decisions based on several factors, including financial considerations or various agreements with other ASes: the chosen route is not necessarily the shortest one, but it is the more *convenient*. BGP also provides network administrators with means to influence the routing selection process at other places. A comprehensive source of information about BGP and the network prefixes advertised and withdrawn can be found in the CIDR Report [9].

3.2   Routing Instability

Routing instability can be informally defined as the continuous, and sometimes rapid, change of topological information, so that network reachability fluctuates and cannot be controlled by network administrators: routes become unpredictable. While a small percentage of changes can be expected over all the network — due to normal building and maintenance operations as well as failures — instability may be localized or distributed. When a single router repeatedly withdraws some routes and re-announces them soon after, instability is localized and is then called *route flapping*. Here, we are considering distributed instability, measured at global or at least regional scale. To measure Internet instability, BGP routing statistics provide important data to work with. BGP statistics describe two aspects: the (global) routing table, i.e., the list of all reachable prefixes, and the number, and rates of change, of the routing information updates, i.e., prefix announcements and withdrawals in BGP UPDATE messages. Each of these aspects, if studied alone offers useful information to quantify instability. Analyzing both aspects in combination can provide additional insights.

- The *size of the global routing table* gives an overall measure of the reachability in terms of network prefixes that are announced. Keeping in mind that aggregated prefixes will still be announced even if more specific ones are no longer reachable, reachability of specific prefixes is a more reliable indicator of instability than it is reachability of aggregated prefixes.
- The *number of BGP updates* sent out and received per time unit is a fundamental metric in observing the dynamics of BGP, also providing an indication of whether BGP peers need to exchange fresh information or not, perhaps as a result of changes in reachability of their connected networks or of communication problems between the routers themselves. Sudden increases in the number of BGP updates per time unit indicate an increased signaling activity and this, in turn, suggests that something is happening which is worth investigating. BGP update message may bring two different kinds of routing information: *prefix announcements* and *withdrawals*. An announcement is a network reachability message, specifying the presence of a new network (identified by its own prefix) that becomes reachable through a specific route. Each time an available route/path for a particular network changes, eventually also due to traffic engineering/management activities, a new announcement is issued from the node ensuring the reachability for that network and propagated through BGP so far. On the other hand, withdrawals happen when a given path for reaching a particular prefix is no longer preferred or available. When a route fails, in absence of other paths, the BGP peer notifies other peers that the path is no longer valid. Although

backup systems or redundant routes/paths are commonly used within the Internet, we expect that a severe outage will have caused some networks to become unreachable due to the sustained nature of the outage, extending beyond backup capabilities or redundancies. BGP sessions that involve networks affected by the outage can thus be broken. When BGP routers peering with BGP routers from affected networks send out explicit withdrawals to notify other BGP routers, it will result in many withdrawal updates. The number of networks affected during the blackout directly affects the number of withdrawal updates.

- The *average AS-PATH length* over the whole Internet is another interesting metric that can be useful to depict the degree of interconnection at the global level. Due to the basic BGP route selection criterion based on preferring the "shortest AS path", when BGP determines the path connecting two different ASes it will select the one going through the least number of hops. Hence as the degree of interconnection between ASes grows, the average AS path tends to become shorter.

While the first two metrics (routing table size and updates count) are related, they do not necessarily agree. Misalignment may result from the superposition of the effects of different events happening simultaneously or from the different frequency of data collection.

4   Analyzing the Internet Stability Dynamics

The simplest way of understanding the fundamental dynamics characterizing the Internet routing system during critical situations, comes from the careful observation of BGP activities, by spotting its resilience and capacity of reacting to adverse conditions. In this study, BGP data collected by the Routing Information Service (RIS) project[1] from RIPE NCC have been used. The aim of RIS is providing Internet operators information about the global routing system current state and its evolution. Routing information is gathered by means of monitoring points. The RIPE RIS project maintains seventeen monitoring points (Remote Route Collectors) in major exchange points across the world. Ten monitoring points are in Europe, four in the US, one in Brazil, one in Japan, and one in Russia. Each monitoring point is basically a BGP-speaking router that makes no announcement of its own but listens to (and records) announcements from its peers. Both BGP updates and routing table dumps are collected and stored. Recall that routing decisions stem from the combination of several factors, which are dependent of the geographical location, the ASes involved, their relationships with other ASes and Tier-1 providers, and financial agreements. Thus, having more than one monitoring point means being able to observe a multifaceted phenomenon (the routing system) from different perspectives and situations. Analysis of routing information collected at each BGP monitoring point can

---

[1] https://labs.ripe.net/datarepository/data-sets/routing-information-
service-ris-raw-data-set

provide a great deal of information about the view that organizations at the collection point have of the Internet. By studying how this information evolves over time, insights can be obtained on the dynamics of path change, spotting trends, cyclic behavior, and periods of instability. In particular, we are interested in detecting, in correspondence of well-documented catastrophic events, compatibly long periods of growth and decay in the routing table dimensions and prefix announcement/withdrawal rates across multiple observation points, indicating a significant and widespread degradation in the overall connectivity and functional behavior of large sections of the Internet.

The advantage of having the monitoring point at a peering point is that the views of all the participants to peering may be observed and combined together. In particular, routing instabilities, even of considerable extent, that are localized to a single AS can be isolated from global failures that affect large portions of the Internet. The updates are collected with an interval of 5 minutes. The routing tables are instantaneous snapshots of the routing tables saved every 8 hours. The amount of data collected in a single monitoring point ranges from about 30 MByte/day for the updates to about 30-60 MByte/day for the routing tables.

It is useful to have a unified view of both the routing tables and the updates with the same sampling interval. Updates have thus been aggregated over the same interval of the routing tables, i.e., 8 hours. A side effect of this aggregation is that the effects of transient phenomena tend to be diluted, since these phenomena are unlikely to span over 8 hours or a significant fraction of that time. Occasional router malfunctions, data losses, link saturation, or router reloads affecting either the BGP speakers or the monitoring point, may in fact produce sudden apparent increases or decreases in the number of updates, thus raising false signals of instability that are unrelated to the disruptive effects of the events under observation. The smoothing effect of aggregation will reduce the influence of short-lived glitches, privileging large-scale changes. In addition, observing on a larger time scale will also reduce the effects of time synchronization issues. Unfortunately, in global-scale BGP analysis the observations are aggregated over all networks, and when the amount of BGP updates associated to the event of interest is only a very limited part of the whole baseline update activity propagating throughout the Internet, the statistical variations in the overall update rate introduced by the event of interest may be difficult to appreciate. In this case, in order to pinpoint the specific update activities related to the prefixes really affected from the event, refocusing out attention by restricting the analysis only on the prefixes of interest, to observe the BGP behavior at the individual prefix level, becomes of fundamental importance. This can be accomplished by geographically referencing the update data and observing them on a contextualized scale. That is, the updates have been mapped, depending on their prefixes, on a worldwide map to allow an observation of the involved phenomena based on geographical localization criteria. In order to refine our observations, we analyzed the BGP activity data collected before, during, and after the events of interest, so that the observations before the event can be used as a baseline of the assumed normal behavior. That is, routing tables and updates were collected for analysis over a time window starting three days before the day the critical event occurred and ending three days after. This allows an enough long time to observe the smoothing recovery. Since data have been collected also before critical events, by averaging over three days, it is possible to obtain a more smoothed baseline depicting the state of the network immediately before the event, to be compared with the one visible after the event. So the extent to which the situation returned to normality and the speed of this process can be evaluated. For each event, thus, 21 snapshots of the routing table (i.e., 7 days) and 2016 files containing updates have been analyzed.

4.1   The Events of Interest

The catastrophic events analyzed are different in nature, amplitude of the affected region, duration, and presence/absence of alternate routes. For example, a long-lasting blackout determines the outage of large areas and their address blocks, while a cable failure only involves the connected endpoints and the mutual reachability of networks that were using that connection, provided that no other path existed between them. The events analyzed are reported in Table 1. The significance of discussing two events of the same type (earthquakes) is that in one case the effects were more limited, because there were alternative routes available for many networks. Availability of Internet connection had indeed been, in that circumstance, an important factor for speeding up and coordinating rescue efforts to aid people who were affected in the disaster.

Table 1. The considered events

Type	Location	Date
Earthquake	Taiwan	27 Dec 2006
Earthquake	Japan	11 Mar 2011
Blackout	USA	08 Sep 2011

5   Results and Discussion

5.1   Earthquake in Taiwan

An earthquake off the southern coast of Taiwan, approximately 22.8 km southwest of Hengchun, struck on December 26, 2006 at 12:25 UTC (20:25 local time). The earthquake, of magnitude 7.1 on the Richter scale, damaged undersea cables, catastrophically disrupting communications across east Asia, affecting, in addition to Taiwan, also Malaysia, Singapore, Thailand and Hong Kong. Telephone and Internet problems were reported in Taiwan, South Korea, China and Japan. Eight submarine cables (see Fig. 1) were severed after the earthquake and its aftershocks, all of which were above magnitude 5 of the Richter scale. Some of the submarine networks affected had backup paths that helped limit the

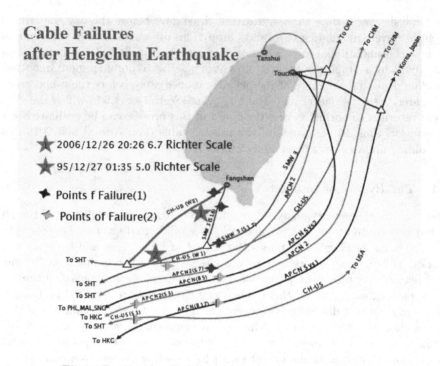

Fig. 1. Earthquake in Taiwan: Affected undersea cables [10]

extent of damage. The diversion of all traffic over the backup links caused congestion on these links, with a perceptible slowdown of communications. Links to Europe, in particular the FLAG Europe Asia link, had no such backup available. Communications over that links were thus interrupted and a significant part of Asia near Taiwan and China went back into the pre-Internet era. The effects of these phenomena have been immediately observed on the whole Internet in terms of both BGP update activity and reduction of the available number of prefixes in the routing table (see Figures 2 and 3). After all the strong aftershocks, the number of routes plummeted by about 800 in NY (Fig. 2(a)) and 1500 in Moscow (Fig. 2(b)).

Fig. 4 displays the number of IP addresses that became unreachable and their geographical location. A yellow tint on a country indicates the loss of a small number of IP addresses originating from that country; orange means a moderate loss, and red a significant loss. The number of IP addresses shown in Fig. 4 are measured from a monitoring point in Europe.

Looking in detail at Fig. 4, one may observe how a noticeable number of IP addresses from India became unreachable from Europe, as well as some from other countries along the FLAG Europe Asia cable. A large number of IP addresses lost came from the US. This can be explained because the coloring reflects the absolute, not the relative entity of loss. This, combined with the higher number of addresses originating from the US as compared with other countries, suggests that the US can be expected to exhibit a intense shade in the graphs.

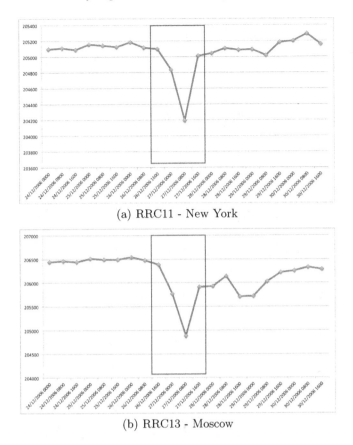

(a) RRC11 - New York

(b) RRC13 - Moscow

Fig. 2. Earthquake in Taiwan: Routing Table Sizes from NY (a) and Moscow (b) collectors

Finally, we remark that, interestingly, the average AS-PATH length has stayed steadily at the value 5 across all the analyzed time span. Looking at data more closely, the average AS-PATH length had been equal to 4 (instead of 5) for two 8-hour intervals (24/12/2006-2355 and 25/12/2006-0755), but these intervals preceded the earthquake. In conclusion, the global degree of network interconnection, as seen at the monitoring point, has undergone no significant variation.

5.2 Earthquake in Japan

On March 11, 2011, a tsunami, unleashed by one of the strongest earthquakes ever measured (magnitude 9.0), devastated the eastern coast of Honshu island, in Japan. Waves as high as 11 meters slammed the coastline and surged inland for several kilometers before retreating back to the sea carrying huge amounts of debris. The wave raced forward at speeds up to 800 km/h and was felt on the other side of the Pacific Ocean.

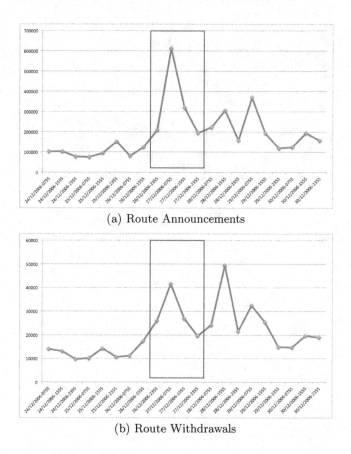

(a) Route Announcements

(b) Route Withdrawals

Fig. 3. Earthquake in Taiwan: updates from NY collector: Announcements (a) and Withdrawals (b)

Casualties and property damage were, unfortunately, dramatic. However, from BGP data one may see that most of the local and transit connections to the Internet stayed stable. In particular, observing the routing table size from most of the collectors no significant falls in the number of routes can be observed in correspondence with the earthquake (see the Amsterdam collector data in Fig. 5(b) as an example). In this case, Internet availability might well have been a factor that facilitated rescue operations. The seas around Japan are a major hub for undersea telecom cables, and a lot of redundant paths are available for the connections attaining to such area. While some undersea cables were damaged, other links stayed active. Though overloaded, those links provided Internet connectivity between the strained Japan and the rest of the world. However, 1969 distinct routes were withdrawn soon after the event, but within the next 8 hours they became available again, and this effect had only been appreciable on the NY collector (Fig. 5(a)).

Fig. 4. Earthquake in Taiwan: IP addresses unreachable from the monitoring point

While our analysis shows that in some places of the world route reachability metrics were not affected in a perceivable way during the event, a significant BGP update activity, in particular in terms of BGP announcements, mainly due to network engineering/rerouting operations has been observed (see Fig. 6). The number of announcements (Fig. 6(a)) grows much more than the number of withdrawals (Fig. 6(b)). There are two reasons for that. The first reason is that the only cancellations that give raise to withdrawals are those where no alternate path is available, whereas in the other case the backup path is simply advertised for the original prefix, thus substituting the previous route. The other reason is that network engineering activities aimed at restoring connectivity, started soon after the disaster had been detected and spanning the following hours, may have created new paths by temporarily relaxing policy-based constraints. This behavior is similar to the other monitoring points. Graphs displaying withdrawals have been omitted to save space.

By analyzing Figure 7(a), one can see that the number of IP addresses that became unreachable was massive. Japan was heavily struck, with 13,4 million IP addresses through 72 routes unreachable from the monitoring point. Note, however, that the monitoring point for Fig. 7(a) is located in the US, while the one for Fig. 4 is in Europe. Therefore the absolute values are not directly comparable. As confirmation of the hypothesis that the climb in the number of routes immediately following the disaster was due to traffic engineering activities, Fig. 7(b) depicts the number of IP addresses reachable through freshly announced routes in the 8 hours following the tsunami. The green shade indicates a large number of IP addresses recovered for a single country. As one can see, Fig. 7(a) and Fig. 7(b) are fairly complementary. The noticeable difference is in a fraction of Japanese addresses that stayed unreachable during the 8 hours immediately

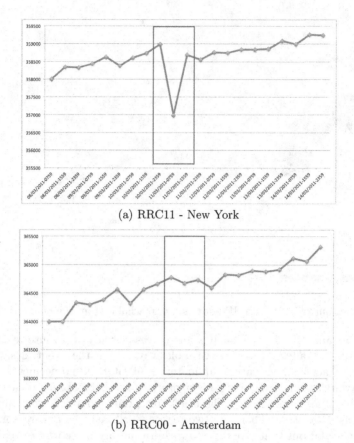

(a) RRC11 - New York

(b) RRC00 - Amsterdam

Fig. 5. Earthquake in Japan: Routing Table Sizes from NY (a) and Amsterdam (b) collectors

after the catastrophe, probably due to the structural damages provoked by the tsunami.

5.3 Blackout in the US

The last event that has been selected for the analysis is the blackout that hit Southern California, USA, on September 8, 2011. The reason why the blackout was chosen is that it represents an event of different nature. It is thus interesting to study its effects and the similarities and differences with respect to the earthquakes discussed above. The massive power outage left more than 8 million citizens without power, also disabling the telephone system, and most wireless phone service, putting people at a severe informational disadvantage [11]. San Diego Gas & Electric claimed that the replacement of faulty equipment at a power substation in Arizona triggered a chain of events that eventually shut down Southwest Powerlink, one of the two major transmission links that connect the San Diego area to the electrical grid for the western United States.

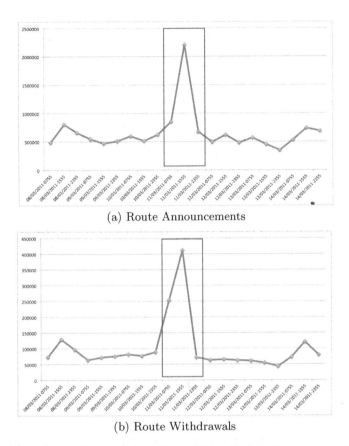

(a) Route Announcements

(b) Route Withdrawals

Fig. 6. Earthquake in Japan: updates from NY collector: Announcements (a) and Withdrawals (b)

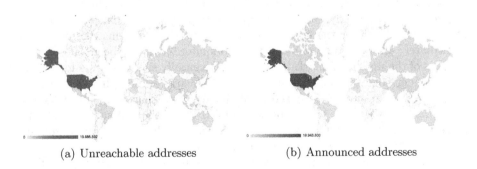

(a) Unreachable addresses   (b) Announced addresses

Fig. 7. Earthquake in Japan: IP addresses unreachable (a) and announced (b) at/from the monitoring point

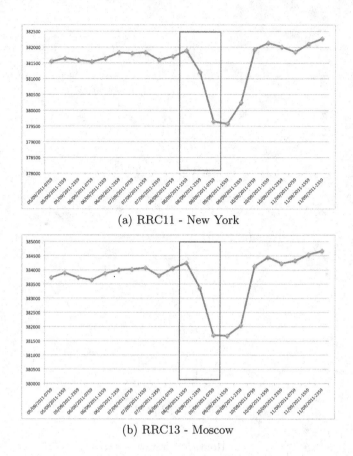

(a) RRC11 - New York

(b) RRC13 - Moscow

Fig. 8. Blackout in the US: Routing Table Sizes from NY (a) and Moscow (b) collectors

Looking at Fig. 8, a plunge of about 2000 routes is evident. In addition, the loss is gradual, especially as compared with the sudden declines visible in Figures 2 and 5. Possibly, this behavior is due to portions of the network turning unreachable only after the exhaustion of backup power systems, therefore not immediately after the outage but some hours later. As it has been said earlier, analysis of the updates remarkably shows substantially similar results for all the events under consideration. From Fig. 9, it is clearly evident that at the time of the event, the number of withdrawals undergoes a sharp increase, which is unsurprising. However, another peak preceded the event and some oscillatory behavior is visible after it. This suggests that other failures, possibly originated elsewhere in the world, were present at the same time.

Also in this case, the average AS-PATH length has not been affected at all by the event, indicating the absence of global degradation in the Internet connectivity within the interested area.

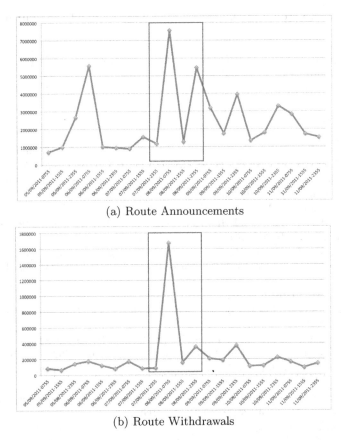

(a) Route Announcements

(b) Route Withdrawals

Fig. 9. Blackout in the US - updates from Moscow collector: Announcements (a) and Withdrawals (b)

6   Conclusions and Future Work

An analysis of Internet routing statistics when disasters occur, and immediately after, has been performed in this work. Catastrophic events have been selected for study because they are well documented, and usually there is a wealth of information related to their effects. After gathering BGP statistics and preprocessing data, the number of routes and geo-localization of IP addresses that became unreachable have been studied. Data show how catastrophic events impact on the reachability of network prefixes, the extent of damages to the Internet global connectivity, the geographical location of the most heavily struck addresses, and the time needed to recover.

Directions for future research include investigation on the degree of correlation, for the same event, between measurements taken at different monitoring points. Moreover, an evaluation of the behavior of BGP updates observed at several time scales would provide interesting insights about the dynamics of the update process.

Acknowledgements. The authors gratefully acknowledge Mr. G. Lanciato for his precious support in data collection.

References

1. Li, J., Wu, Z., Purpus, E.: Toward understanding the behavior of BGP during large-scale power outages. In: Proceedings of IEEE GLOBECOM (2006)
2. Popescu, A., Underwood, T., Zmijewski, E.: Quaking tables: The Taiwan earthquakes and the Internet routing table. In: APRICOT, Bali (2007)
3. Sahoo, A., Kant, K., Mohapatra, P.: Characterization of BGP recovery time under large-scale failures. In: IEEE International Conference on Communications, ICC 2006, vol. 2, pp. 949–954. IEEE (2006)
4. Hu, C., Chen, K., Chen, Y., Liu, B.: Evaluating potential routing diversity for internet failure recovery. In: 2010 Proceedings IEEE INFOCOM, pp. 1–5. IEEE (2010)
5. Kiyomoto, S., Fukushima, K., Miyake, Y.: Security issues on IT systems during disasters: a survey. Journal of Ambient Intelligence and Humanized Computing, 1–13 (2013)
6. Cohen, R., Erez, K., Ben-Avraham, D., Havlin, S.: Resilience of the internet to random breakdowns. Physical Review Letters 85(21), 4626–4628 (2000)
7. Palmieri, F.: Inter-domain Routing Stability Dynamics During Infrastructure Stress Events: The Internet Worm Menace. I. J. Network Security 6(1), 6–14 (2008)
8. Hawkinson, J., Bates, T.: RFC1930: Guidelines for creation, selection, and registration of an autonomous system (AS) (March 1996),
   http://tools.ietf.org/html/rfc1930
9. Bates, T., Smith, P., Huston, G.: CIDR report,
   http://www.cidr-report.org/as2.0/
10. Winston: Submarine Cables Cut after Taiwan Earthquake in December 2006,
   http://submarinenetworks.com/news/
   cables-cut-after-taiwan-earthquake-2006
11. Cerf, V.: Natural Disasters and Electric Infrastructure. IEEE Internet Computing 15(6), 103 (2011)

Dependency Analysis for Critical Infrastructure Security Modelling: A Case Study within the Grid'5000 Project

Thomas Schaberreiter[1,2,3], Sébastien Varrette[1], Pascal Bouvry[1], Juha Röning[2], and Djamel Khadraoui[3]

[1] University of Luxembourg, Computer Science and Communications Research Unit,
6 rue Richard Coudenhove-Kalergi, L-1359 Luxembourg
{firstname.lastname}@uni.lu
[2] University of Oulu, Department of Electrical and Information Engineering,
P.O.Box 4500, FIN-90014 University of Oulu, Finland
ouspg@ee.oulu.fi
[3] CRP Henri Tudor, Service Science & Innovation (SSI), 29,
avenue John F. Kennedy, L-1855 Luxembourg, Luxembourg
{firstname.lastname}@tudor.lu

Abstract. Critical infrastructure (CI) services (like electricity, telecommunication or transport) are constantly consumed by the society and are not expected to fail. A common definition states that CIs are so vital to our society that a disruption would have a severe impact on both the society and the economy. CI security modelling was introduced in previous work to enable on-line risk monitoring in CIs that depend on each other by exchanging on-line risk alerts expressed in terms of a breach of Confidentiality, a breach of Integrity and degrading Availability (CIA). One important aspect for the accuracy of the model is the decomposition of CIs into CI security modelling elements (CI services, base measurements and dependencies). To assist in CI decomposition and provide more accurate results a methodology based on dependency analysis was presented in previous work.

In this work a proof-of-concept validation of the CI decomposition methodology is presented. We conduct a case study in the context of the Grid'5000 project, an academic computing grid with clusters distributed at several locations in France and Luxembourg. We show how a CI security model can be established by following the proposed CI decomposition methodology and we provide a discussion of the resulting model as well as experiences during the case study.

Keywords: Critical infrastructures, dependency analysis, risk monitoring, security modelling.

1 Introduction

Critical infrastructures (CIs) are complex interacting systems on a nationwide or even international level that provide services to society and economy. More importantly, those infrastructures are so vital to society and economy that a failure

A. Cuzzocrea et al. (Eds.): CD-ARES 2013 Workshops, LNCS 8128, pp. 269–287, 2013.

in service delivery or a degradation of quality-of-service would have severe consequences.

CIs face a multitude of risks due to for example technical faults, human error or deliberate attacks. Furthermore, dependencies to services provided by other CIs can cascade risks from one CI to another which makes risk monitoring in CI services even more complex. In recent years, research on CI security modelling tried to evaluate on-line risks (breach of Confidentiality, breach of Integrity and degrading Availability - CIA) in complex systems like CIs on the CI service level. The basic idea of CI security modelling is to estimate the current risk of a CI service by observing the system state of the components that are used to provide the service as well as by observing the risk experienced by dependencies. The main components of the model are *CI services* (services provided to customers or internal services utilized to provide services to customers), *base measurements* (system measurements defining the state of a service) and *dependencies* among CI services. For each CI service, risk is derived from the observations using a Bayesian network based approach.

A crucial part for accuracy of risk estimates is a well performed analysis of a CI and its dependencies to be able to represent it as a CI security model. In complex systems like CIs, possibly operated on a national or even international level, this can be problematic. To assist with the decomposition necessary for the CI security model, a methodology based on dependency analysis was proposed in [1]. The main idea of this approach is to use a *socio-technological* approach of analysing a complex system, meaning that all possible information sources, reaching from written technical documentation or contracts to interviews with employees on all organizational levels of a CI are utilized to get a holistic view of the complex systems and its complex dependencies. Another important aspect of this methodology is a graphical representation of the findings to get a visual feedback of the analysis.

In this work we present a proof-of-concept validation of the dependency analysis methodology based on a case study conducted within the framework of the Grid'5000 platform. We show that we can decompose parts of the Grid'5000 platform into CI services, base measurements and dependencies and thus build a CI security model. To simplify our work, we only take availability risk into account. The Grid'5000 project maintains an academic computing grid with clusters distributed at several locations in France and Luxembourg to perform large-scale scientific experiments that require substantial processing power and/or storage. The sites of Grid'5000 are geographically distributed and connected via a dedicated high-speed network connection operated by an independent provider, which makes this case study especially interesting for validation of the CI security model since being able to model dependencies to external providers is a major goal of the CI security model. While Grid'5000 is not a CI in the narrow sense, because it lacks its importance to society and economy, it is similar to CIs of the computing or telecommunication sector in technical as well as organizational realization. Therefore the Grid'5000 project is an ideal candidate for validating research related to CIs having in mind that it is hard to get access to data coming from actual CIs. Furthermore, as a second contribution of this work, we provide an analysis of our case study experiences and we detail positive as well as negative aspects.

The remainder of the paper is organized as follows: Section 2 discusses related work. Section 3 introduces the previously proposed dependency analysis methodology as well as the CI security model. Section 4 presents the dependency analysis case study and Section 5 discusses case study results. Finally, Section 6 concludes the paper and gives an outlook on future work.

2   Related Work

Dependency analysis in CIs is a complex task. In [2] Rinaldi et al. provide an excellent introduction to the problem of CI (inter)dependency and its associated problems. Some authors propose CI models that focus on the interdependencies between CIs (e.g. [3], [4]), the main goal of those methods is to integrate CI sector-specific behaviour models with each other, whereas in CI security modelling we try to establish a CI model that uses model parameters (CI services and CIA risk) that are valid for each CI sector and thus allows to establish a cross-sector model. The first step of establishing such a model is to analyse the CIs and their dependencies to achieve an abstract representation of CIs as a modelling basis. In this work we use PROTOS-MATINE method for dependency analysis developed by OUSPG (Oulu University Secure Programming Group). The method was originally developed for identifying protocol dependencies [5] and is based on analysis of all available information sources to get a holistic picture of dependencies. The method has proven to be especially useful in combination with the semantic tool Graphingwiki [6] which allows to graphically represent the dependency model and refine the model whenever new information arrives. The PROTOS-MATINE method has furthermore been used to analyse critical dependencies in the context of antivirus software [7] and the socio-technical dependencies of a VoIP infrastructure [8]. In [1] the PROTOS-MATINE method was adapted to be used in the context of the CI security model [9], [10], [11].

The goal of CI security modelling is to propose a risk-based cross-sector CI model to be used for on-line risk monitoring. The model parameters are *CI services*, *dependencies* between CI services and *base measurements* (observable measures that define a CI service state). The model output is *CI service risk*, where risk is seen as a breach of Confidentiality, a breach of Integrity or degrading Availability (CIA). In [12] a Bayesian network based risk estimation methodology was introduced to the CI security model which provides a more sophisticated way of estimating risk as well as some advanced features like risk prediction. Some advantages of the CI security model compared to other CI models (e.g. [13], [14]) or CI risk models [15], [16] is the flexibility of the approach that allows to model CI systems to the desired level of detail, the comparability of different CI sectors due to abstraction to common, risk related indicators, and the ability to include dependent service risk in CI risk estimation.

3   CI Dependency Analysis

The dependency analysis method presented in [1] is used to find the modelling entities of the CI security model, the CI services, base measurements and dependencies. The core idea of the approach is to find a suitable model by combining information gathered from all available information sources at different organizational levels in a CI (preparedness and business continuity level, process level and technical level). The combination of internal (e.g. contracts, policies, expert interviews, manuals) and external (e.g. news, vulnerability feeds, laws/regulations) information sources provides a holistic view on the analysed system.

After gathering the information sources, the dependency analysis is carried out in an iterative manner. The first step is to generate a high level model of the system, finding the high level services and dependencies that define the system. In the next steps, the model is refined and detailed low level services/dependencies and base measurements are identified. During the process of better understanding the system by adding more detail, it is expected that the high level system model will be refined as well. It is expected that the high level system model will be mainly composed of services and dependencies, since the base measurements (e.g. sensor outputs), are expected to be rather available on the process level/ technical level than on the preparedness and business continuity level.

One important aspect of the proposed CI dependency analysis method is the graphical representation of the CI model. In order to facilitate discussion and expert input, the model has to be presented in a clear and intuitive way so that errors and wrong assumptions in the model are easier to identify. In this work the model is represented as a graph, where the CI services and base measurements represent nodes (CI services are visualized as elliptic shapes and base measurements as rectangle shapes) and the dependencies among services as well as among services and base measurements are represented as edges.

3.1   Bayesian Network Based CI Security Model

Since the publication of the CI dependency analysis method in [1], the CI security model was refined by adding a Bayesian network based component for risk estimation in [12]. The core concept of CI dependency analysis (identification of services, dependencies and base measurements) does not change compared to the original proposal, but the concept of how service risk is derived from dependent service risk and base measurement observations did change, therefore the integration of the Bayesian network based CI security model with the CI dependency analysis methodology is presented in this Section.

In the original proposal of the CI security model in [9], [10], [11], the service risk is calculated using a weighted sum method for which each dependency of a service (another CI service or a base measurement) is weighted by an expert based on the assumed importance to the service. In the Bayesian network based CI security model, service risk is estimated based on the state of dependencies, which is represented by the conditional probability table (CPT) of a node.

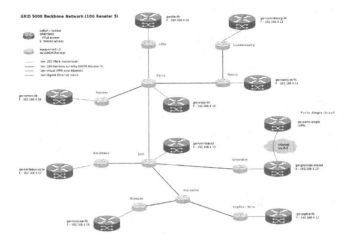

Fig. 1. Network backbone interconnection between the sites of the Grid'5000 platform

For each state combination of the dependencies of a service, the most probable service risk is estimated. Those probabilities can be learned from data records as well as estimated by experts where learning is not possible.

During the CI dependency analysis process, the Bayesian network based security model requires identification of following parameters:

- Normalization values for base measurements based on classification of normal operation/ allowed deviation from normal operation. To avoid state explosion, the CI security model requires that all base measurements are normalized to 5 discrete values, where 1 characterizes a base measurement value during normal operation and 5 the maximum allowed deviation. The classification of the boundaries is assumed to be done using technical specifications and expert estimation.
- For each service, the service risk has to be estimated for incidents that happened during the time period that is used to learn the risk probabilities from data. This is necessary since service risk is an abstract concept that can not be directly measured. Estimating service risk for past incidents will allow to learn the most probable service risk for each dependency state combination.
- In situations where service risk probabilities can not be learned from data due to missing data records or insufficient data, expert estimation is required to estimate the service risk probabilities for each missing dependency state combination.

In this case study we will, besides identifying the CI services, base measurements and dependencies, also describe the normalization process for each identified base measurement.

4   Grid'5000 Case Study

In this Section, the CI dependency analysis methodology is validated using the Grid'5000 platform[1] which provides the users with a fully customizable testbed to perform advanced experiments in all areas of computer science related to parallel, large-scale or distributed computing and networking. Grid'5000 is a distributed computing platform featuring clusters located in nine geographical sites – eight in France (Bordeaux, Grenoble, Lille, Lyon, Nancy, Reims, Rennes, Sophia, Toulouse) and one in Luxembourg. The interconnect backbone between all sites is illustrated in Figure 1. In addition, international connections to Brazil, Japan and the Netherlands operated via the site of Grenoble are available.

4.1   High-level Grid'5000 Security Model

The resulting CI security model of the highest decomposition level of Grid'5000 can be seen in Figure 2. The infrastructure is divided into two providers, the *Grid'5000* provider and the *Network provider*, since those infrastructures are operated by separate companies and therefore the organizational structure and day-to-day operation of the infrastructures differ greatly from each other.

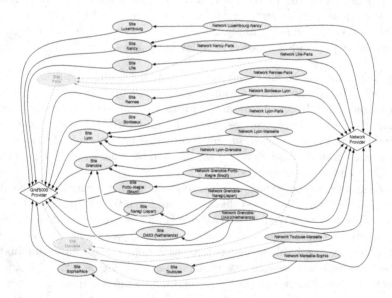

Fig. 2. Grid'5000 high level CI security model for availability risk indicator

Each site of Grid'5000 is represented as as service[2] that will aggregate service risk from the lower-level model described in the following Sections. The *Grid'5000*

---

[1] http://www.grid5000.fr

[2] The Sites represented by dotted lines in Figure 2 are part of the Grid'5000 project, but currently offline.

provider depends on all sites which allows to produce a global risk estimate for Grid'5000, taking the risk of the individual sites into account.

The network provider is modelled by defining each network link between two sites as a service. The risk estimate of each link aggregated from lower-level model of the network provider can be used at this decomposition level to estimate a risk for each network segment as well as a global risk estimate for the *Network provider*. Therefore, each service characterizing a network segment is modelled as a dependency of the *Network provider*. This representation was used since it follows the geographical structure of the network and it provides a good basis to model the lower decomposition levels as shown in the following Sections.

The dependencies between the network provider and the Grid'5000 provider were modelled in a way that each site physically connected to a network segment, depends on this network segment. In this way a changed risk in a network segment can be easily included in the risk estimation of the site that depends on this segment.

The main information sources to gather the information used at this decomposition level are the internal Grid'5000 documentation containing information about the high-level structure of Grid'5000, like the network backbone shown in Figure 1 and expert knowledge about Grid'5000 to account for the most recent changes in the the structure of Grid'5000.

4.2   The Network Backbone

Every network segment of the backbone presented in the Figure 1 is characterized by connection points within the dark fibre infrastructure provided by Renater[3] which allocates dedicated 10Gbit/s "lambdas" on a DWDM (Dense Wavelength Division Multiplexing) infrastructure for the Grid'5000 platform. Grid'5000 sites see each other inside the same VLAN at 10Gbps. A few bottleneck still exists, like the Lyon to Paris link, where the 10Gbps are shared between all the sites above Lyon and all the sites under Lyon.

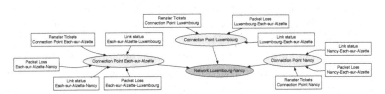

Fig. 3. CI security model for availability risk indicator of network segment Luxembourg-Nancy

Each network segment can be observed by incident monitoring as well as network performance measures, both of them performed by the backbone provider (Renater in France and Restena in Luxembourg). The incident monitoring takes the form of tickets which can be accessed by Grid'5000 administrators in real-time and are one of the following:

---

[3] http://www.renater.fr/

- *incident* : a sudden IP service disruption occurs on the network.
- *maintenance* : an operation will be performed on a network equipment that will (or not) interrupt the IP service.

Regarding backbone performance, Grid'5000 offers 3 different types of monitoring information: The *link status* (up or down), the *packet count* (reported by the SNMP counters of Renater/Restena switches) and the *packet loss* (PL) occurring on the link. Packet Loss can be caused by the saturation of a link. When router or switch buffers are unable to store packets, the packets are dropped. It may also be caused by a faulty equipment or a flapping link (link up/down/up/-down...).

4.3   The Network Backbone CI Security Model

The resulting CI security model for the network link Luxembourg-Nancy is presented in Figure 3. To account for space constraints in a publication, only the detailed decomposition of one network segment is presented in this work, but it should be noted here that the decomposition of all network segments follows a similar structure.

The network connection between the sites Luxembourg and Nancy is characterized by the three main connection points in Luxembourg, Esch-sur-Alzette and Nancy. In Figure 3 those are represented as services that are characterized by the measurements collected at the level of the routers at those locations (performance measures) and Restena tickets.

Normalization of base measurements according to the CI security model for Restena tickets is done following the information presented in Table 1. No ticket means normal operation or normalization level 1. A *maintenance* ticket is characterized as normalization level 3, since it will not interrupt the service, but a degradation in service can occur. An *incident* ticket is characterized as normalization level 5, since it implies an interruption of service.

From the performance measures presented in the previous Section, only *link status* and *packet loss* are taken into account, since they fully characterize the service availability status. *Link status*, as specified in Table 2a can be see as a binary base measurement where link up represents the normalized level 1 and link down represents level 5. The *Packet loss* measurement is normalized according to the boundaries presented in Table 2b, with rather restrictive bounds to reach level 1 or level 5.

Table 1. Base measurement normalization for Renater/Restina tickets

Level	Description
1	Normal
3	*maintenance* ticket for the link is pending
5	*incident* ticket for the link is pending

Table 2. (a): Base measurement normalization for link status. (b): Base measurement normalization for packet loss.

Level	Description
1	Normal: $PL = 0\%$
2	Degraded: $0 < PL \leq 33\%$
3	Really Degraded: $33\% < PL \leq 66\%$
4	Hightly Degraded: $66\% < PL \leq 99\%$
5	$PL > 99\%$

Level	Description
1	Link up
5	Link down

(a)

(b)

The main information sources at this level of decomposition were Grid'5000 as well as Restena network documentation (as far as available to the Grid'5000 project), manuals and documentation of the used monitoring tools (Passilo) and expert knowledge, especially to define the base measurement normalization bounds.

4.4   Grid'5000 Site Infrastructure

Each site of Grid'5000 holds one or several computing clusters. The hardware configuration of each site is depicted in Figure 4a and is typically organized in the following way:

- An *access* server which serves as an isolated user frontend to access the resources of the site;
- one or several *adminfront* server(s) holding a set of virtual machines dedicated to platform services.
- the *computing nodes*, split among one or more clusters (depending on the site capacity).
- an *NFS* server (together with its associated disk enclosure) that act as a centralized and shared storage area for the site.
- the *site router* which interconnects all site components and enables communication to other sites of Grid'5000.
- a *local interconnect switch*, which provides an isolated network for the site internal components.

Apart from the general structure, Grid'5000 consists of several elements crucial for operation, especially in the context of availability: The *Puppet infrastructure*[4] (responsible for the configuration and the deployment of all grid services within Grid'5000), the *Platform Monitoring infrastructure* (a set of monitoring tools such as Nagios[5] or Ganglia [17]), *OAR* [18] (the resource manager of Grid'5000) and *Kadeploy*[6] (piloting the deployment of the computing nodes) as well as the *technical committee* (engineers responsible for the maintenance and the development of the platform) and the *users* of Grid'5000.

---

[4] http://puppetlabs.com/
[5] http://www.nagios.org/
[6] http://kadeploy.gforge.inria.fr/

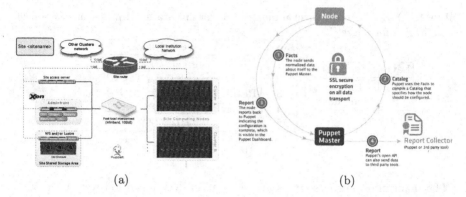

(a)   (b)

Fig. 4. (a): General overview of the hardware organization of each site. (b): General Puppet Workflow.

The Puppet Infrastructure. Puppet is an IT automation software based on a master/slave approach that helps system administrators to manage their infrastructure throughout its life cycle, from provisioning and configuration to patch management and compliance. Using Puppet, it is easy to automate repetitive tasks, quickly deploy critical applications, and pro-actively manage change in a scalable way. Puppet uses a declarative, model-based approach to IT automation. In particular, the desired state of the infrastructure's configuration is defined using Puppet's declarative configuration language. After a Puppet configuration is deployed, a Puppet agent is run on each node to automatically enforce the desired node state, correcting any configuration drift. As illustrated in Figure 4b, the Puppet agent of a node sends *Facts*, or data about its state, to the Puppet Master which compiles a *Catalog*, or detailed data about how the node should be configured, and sends this back to the Puppet agent. After making any changes to return to the desired state, the Puppet agent sends a complete Report back to the Puppet Master. In this work we propose to use the Puppet agent exit codes to classify the status of a given service. The exit codes are reported every time the Puppet agent is executed, which is every 30 minutes by default.

The Platform Monitoring Infrastructure. Many monitoring tools are used to reflect the status of the platform. The main one is Nagios which evaluates at the moment of writing 160 hosts and more than 629 service status. The different services currently monitored by Nagios plugins are summarized in Table 3.

Each service is checked by the Nagios daemon, either at regular intervals or On-demand as needed for predictive service dependency checks (such checks help to ensure that the dependency logic is as accurate as possible.) Services that are checked can be in one of four different states (OK, WARNING, UNKNOWN or CRITICAL).

Table 3. Nagios services monitored on Grid'5000

ID	Service	ID	Service	ID	Service	ID	Service
N1	APT	N6	/home usage	N11	LDAP	N16	NTP
N2	Conman consoles server	N7	Ganglia	N12	Load usage	N17	OAR
N3	Dhcp-proxy	N8	HTTP	N13	Mail server	N18	PING
N4	DNS	N9	Kadeploy	N14	MySQL	N19	Squid
N5	Filesystem usage	N10	KaVLAN server	N15	Nagios	N20	SSH

The OAR and Kadeploy Infrastructure. OAR is a versatile resource and task manager (also called a batch scheduler) for clusters and other computing infrastructures which is used in particular on Grid'5000 and provides a simple and flexible exploitation of a cluster. Its design is based on high level tools, more precisely a relational database engine (MySQL or PostgreSQL), a scripting language (Perl), a confinement system mechanism based on a feature proposed by recent (2.6) Linux kernels called cpuset and a scalable administrative tool (component of the Taktuk framework). It is composed of modules which interact only with the database and are executed as independent programs. Whereas the OAR service is managed by Puppet on Grid'5000, it integrates a set of internal checks of the computing nodes it pilots such that from the node status reported by OAR, it is possible to get information on the current status of the node.

For node deployment OAR is coupled with the Kadeploy middleware. Kadeploy belongs to the category of disk imaging and cloning tools and is used to install and customize servers. Users are able to deploy a new environment and customize computing nodes during their reservations. In parallel, other tools have been designed internally to qualify the good status of the computing nodes and detect altered environments. Among them, phoenix analyses the production environment deployed after user reservation and restarts the full deployment process up to 3 times if errors are detected (bad disk formatting, unhealthy system etc.), which can be used as measurement to determine the status of computing nodes.

4.5 Grid'5000 Site Infrastructure CI Security Model

For each site of Grid'5000 we identified 4 main factors that contribute to the availability risk of the site:

- **Cluster**: The hardware and software components that form a computing cluster.
- **Network connection**: The network interconnection between computing sites, as detailed in Section 4.2.
- **Environmental factors**: The supporting infrastructure needed to operate the computing cluster.

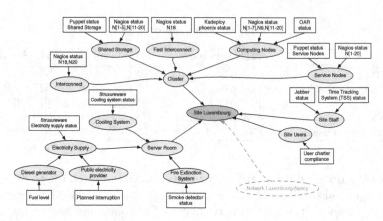

Fig. 5. Site Luxembourg CI security model for availability risk indicator

- **Human factor**: This describes how humans can influence the availability of the infrastructure. In Grid'5000, two types of human interaction was identified, by the *staff* operating and maintaining the grid and the *users* that can influence availability since they are granted substantial user rights to operate the grid.

The main information sources at this decomposition level were structural as well as organizational documentation of Grid'5000 as well as interviews with Grid'5000 administrators.

Each site of Grid'5000 follows the same basic structure, but further decomposition reveals differences in implementation details, for example different hardware components that allow different levels of monitoring as well as differences in the number of employed staff. In this work we illustrate the decomposition of the site Luxembourg and while the basic structure of the CI security model remains the same for each site, the outcome of the model depends on the actual implementation of the site.

The resulting CI security model for site Luxembourg can be seen in Figure 5. In the first level of decomposition, the node *Server Room* represents the environmental factors of the site, the *Site staff* and the *Site Users* represent the human factor, the *Network Luxembourg-Nancy* represents the network connection and the *Cluster* represents the actual computing cluster.

The main part of the site Luxembourg is the *Cluster* which can be further de-composed into the 5 major components (as illustrated in Figure 4a), the *Interconnect* (local interconnect to other institutions within site) and the *Fast Interconnect* (interconnect for site internal components), the *Computing Nodes*, the *Shared Storage* and the *Service Nodes* (a summation of supporting services like OAR, Puppet, Kadeploy, supervision or site access server, as listed in Figure 4a). The service state of the Interconnect and Fast Interconnect can be described by the the state of services they are composed of, monitored by nagios plugins N18 and N20 (Interconnect) and N18 (Fast Interconnect). The Shared Storage state can be characterized by the output of the puppet configuration status for shared storage and the state of the services monitored by nagios plugins N1-N5 and N11-N20. The state of the computing nodes can be described by the output of Kadeploy phoenix status, the node status as monitored by OAR[7] and the state of the services monitored by nagios plugins N1-N7, N9 and N11-N20. The Service Nodes state can be characterized by the puppet configuration status for each service node[8] as well as the status of the services monitored by the nagios plugins N1-N20.

The base measurement normalization for the output of the nagios plugins (N1-N20) is listed in Table 4a. The nagios plugins report 4 different states for the services they monitor which can be translated to normalization levels. Since only 4 states are available, normalization level 4 was omitted.

Puppet configuration, reports exit codes which are translated into normalization levels as illustrated in Table 4b.

Table 4. (a): Base measurement normalization for Nagios service checks. (b): Base measurement normalization for Puppet-managed services.

Level	Description
1	OK
2	WARNING
3	UNKNOWN
4	n/a
5	CRITICAL

(a)

Level	Description
1	Normal: exit code 0
2	Configuration changes: exit code 2
3	Puppet master is unreachable
4	Failures during the transaction: exit code 4
5	Configuration changes and failures during the transaction: exit code 6

(b)

The node status reported by OAR is translated into normalization levels according to Table 5a and Kadeploy phoenix node status is normalized according to Table 6a.

The main information sources to obtain the structure of the Cluster were structural documentation of Grid'5000 clusters, the technical documentations as well as log output of the platform monitoring tools to determine base measurements and base measurement normalization and expert interviews to verify the information.

---

[7] Each available computing node has a seperate Kadeploy phoenox as well as OAR status base measurement. To maintain readability of Figure 5, those base measurements are summarized by *"Kadeploy phoenix status"* and "OAR status".

[8] A puppet status base measurement for each monitored service is available. To maintain readability of Figure 5, only a single base measurement, *"Puppet status Service Nodes"* was introduced.

The second important aspect of each site are the environmental factors. The basic idea of this decomposition is to capture data from the environment the site is located in to be able to monitor not only the Cluster itself, but also be able to react to a changing environment that can influence the operation of the cluster (like for example fires or power shortage). At the site Luxembourg the main place to capture environmental factors is the *Server Room* the cluster is located in. We identified three main elements which would be *Cooling* of computing equipment, the *Fire Extinction System* and the *Electricity Supply*. The *Electricity Supply* of the Site Luxembourg is composed of the main public electricity supply as well as backup energy supply by a *Diesel generator*. The state of the electricity supply can on the one hand be determined by the output of Struxureware software[9], a tool that monitors several sensors and aggregates a risk level which is presented to the operator. On the other hand, additional information about the availability status of the public electricity provider as well as a backup diesel generator can be given by monitoring notifications about planned interruptions of public electricity supply as well as the diesel generator fuel level. The base measurement normalization of the Stuxureware risk levels can be found in Table 5b. The provided risk levels of low, medium and high are mapped to the normalization values 1, 3 and 5 respectively. The base measurement normalization for the planned public electricity supply can is presented in Table 6b. The normalization bounds result from the analysis of the electricity supply: For up to 5 minutes, batteries guarantee operation of the cluster and the backup diesel generator should provide backup electricity supply for up to 30 minutes. The base measurement normalization for the diesel generator fuel level can be seen in Table 7a. Unfortunately, the generator does not report fine grained fuel level status, but only *full* or *not full*. The cooling system status can be determined by Stuxureware alerts. The base measurement normalization is identical to the electricity supply status and can be seen in Table 5b. The fire extinction system status can be determined by the smoke detector status, each smoke detector can have three different states: *no alert, defect* or *alert*. The base measurement normalization for the smoke detector status can be found in Table 7b.

Table 5. (a): Base measurement normalization for OAR based node status checks. (b): Base measurement normalization for Struxureware monitored services.

Level	Description
1	Free: the node is unused and powered
2	Reserved: at least one job is running
3	Standby: the node is ready to wake up
4	Suspected
5	Down

(a)

Level	Description
1	Low Risk Assessment
3	Medium Risk Assessment
5	High Risk Assessment

(b)

---

[9] http://www.apc.com/.

Table 6. (a): Base measurement normalization for Kadeploy phoenix status. (b): Base measurement normalization for planned electricity supply interruption.

Level	Description
1	Node deployed without error
2	Node is re-deployed after error
3	Node is re-deployed a second time after error
4	Node is re-deployed a third time after error
5	Node is down

Level	Description
1	No interruption
2	0-5 Minutes
3	6-15 Minutes
4	16-30 Minutes
5	30 Minutes and more

(a)   (b)

The main information sources regarding identification of environmental factors were interviews with personal working in the server room as well as technical documentation of the server rack and the fire extinction system.

The human factor in a complex system is generally hard to quantify. In this case study, there are two separate groups that can influence the availability of the site Luxembourg: The *Site Staff* and the *Site Users*. We have identified that the main factor concerning availability in the Site Luxembourg caused by *Site Staff* is absence due to vacation or sick leave. Collecting and monitoring the availability of each staff member within Grid'5000 is performed via a time tracking system (TTS). Another interesting tool that help to monitor the staff presence is the Grid'5000 Jabber service (a messaging service similar to MSN or Skype). Monitoring the Jabber online status can add additional information about availability of site staff since in the computing sector personal can be available and resolve possible problems without physical presence.

The base measurement normalization of the Jabber and TTS status can be found in Tables 7c and 8a. Each member of the site staff will have a base measurement for *"Jabber status"* and *"Time Tracking System (TTS) status"*, even though in Figure 5 only one of each base measurements is introduced for the sake of readability.

Table 7. (a): Base measurement normalization for diesel generator fuel level. (b): Base measurement normalization for smoke detector status. (c): Base measurement normalization for Jabber status.

Level	Description
1	Full
5	Not full

Level	Description
1	No alert
3	Defect
5	Alert

Level	Description
1	Online
5	Offline

(a)   (b)   (c)

The influence of *Site Users* to the availability of site Luxembourg is hard to determine. On the one hand, due to the infrastructure-as-a-service approach of Grid'5000, site users have quite substantial rights to interact with Grid'5000 infrastructure. On the other hand, due to the academic nature of Grid'5000 there are not many tools in place to monitor user actions. One factor we could identify is *User charter compliance* measured by a script designed to check on a regular basis the compliance of the user behaviour with the user charter. The user charter compliance measurement normalization can be found in Table 8b. User charter compliance is measured for each user, but for readability reasons only one base measurement *"User Charter Compliance"* was introduced in Figure 5.

Table 8. (a): Base measurement normalization for Time Tracking System status. (b): Base measurement normalization for user charter compliance.

Level	Description
1	Available
5	Not Available

(a)

Level	Description
1	No violations of user charter compliance
2	1 violation of user charter compliance
3	2-3 violations of user charter compliance
4	4-5 violations of user charter compliance
5	5 or more violations of user charter compliance

(b)

5   Results and Discussion

In this Section we would like to discuss the observations made during the case study in more detail. We want to highlight which parts of the case study provided the expected results according to the proposed dependency analysis methodology, but we also want to highlight some problems and unexpected obstacles we experienced during the case study. At the end we want to summarize our findings and draw a conclusion regarding the feasibility of the proposed methodology.

On the positive side, by conducting this case study we have shown that it is possible to represent a complex system like Grid'5000 using the abstract elements of the CI security model (CI services, base measurements and dependencies) by following the steps of the presented dependency analysis methodology. We have successfully established a model that includes the socio-technical structure of Grid'5000 and takes technical as well as human and environmental components into account allowing us to provide a holistic view on the availability risk of CI services at different organizational levels. We have also shown that hierarchical decomposition in this context is possible by decomposing higher level services into sub-components and treating them as services they provide to higher level services. We have shown that we can identify base measurements within the CI systems to be able to observe the system state. And finally, we could show that we could identify enough information sources within Grid'5000 (e.g. documentation or expert interviews) or from external sources (e.g. manuals) to establish the

CI security model. It was experienced that expert interviews are a very valuable source of information, especially on the higher levels of decomposition. The lower, more technical levels are usually well described by documentation/manuals. In any case it was experienced that, as expected, the graphical representation of the CI security model is a very useful tool to discuss the model structure and find flaws in the representation.

Aside from the positive aspects, some observations were made during the course of the case study that could have a negative implication on the outcome of future case studies. One major observation was that not all information can be made available due to confidentiality or privacy reasons. This was even experienced in this case study (e.g. employee records due to privacy concerns) in an academic environment which is usually more open than a commercial operator. If the CI security model should be applied in a more competitive commercial environment, restricted access to information due to confidentiality reasons could pose a problem. Even though risk alerts are abstract metrics and should help to maintain source confidentiality, providers might be reluctant to provide the necessary structural information (CI services and dependencies) to business partners and possibly competitors.

Another observation made during the case study was that information gathering was generally more difficult and time consuming than expected. One problem contributing to this observation were for example the organizational structure of some of the sites. For example, the server room in one site was the responsibility of the universities maintenance department and the administration of the cluster is done by research personnel. Information requests regarding server room equipment and actual hardware caused substantial delays because those requests were treated with different urgency by the maintenance department for mainly two reasons: a) The employees were already overworked with other, more important tasks and b) since the maintenance department and research personnel of the university are organized in different branches of the organizational hierarchy, there is no direct authority which would give requests for information more urgency. Although this scenario was specific to this case study, similar challenges are expected to be experienced in other big companies or complex infrastructures.

The last observation that was made during the case study was that base measurements, although available and observable, are not always recorded. Before the case study it was assumed that sensor data is recorded for a certain time period. In the CI security model, recorded sensor data can be used to learn risk probabilities from events that happened in the past, but without data records learning is not possible. In this case, risk probabilities need to be estimated by experts which makes the estimates more inaccurate and error prone.

To conclude this Section, we want to state that this case study has shown that it is possible to represent complex infrastructures as CI security model, but it requires some effort and dedication by the operators to achieve the goal. We also recognize that every complex infrastructure is different and that one case study can not proof or disproof the validity of our approach, but we could make some general positive as well as negative observations that can serve as a basis for future discussions and case studies.

6   Conclusion and Future Work

In this work we presented a case study to provide a proof-of-concept validation of a CI dependency analysis methodology in the context of CI security modelling. CI security modelling provides a framework for on-line risk monitoring of CI services, taking into account the service state as well as the risk state of dependencies. A crucial part for the success of the model is a well performed CI analysis to identify the elements forming the CI security model, which are CI services (services provided to customers or internal services utilized to provide the service to the customer), base measurements (measurements to determine the state of a CI services) and dependencies between those elements. The presented case study was performed in the context of Grid'5000, a distributed academic computing grid operated by several universities in France and other countries like Luxembourg. The sites of the grid are connected by a dedicated high-speed fibre optic network connection. As a result of the case study, we have shown that, following the proposed dependency analysis methodology, it is possible to analyse a complex infrastructure and represent it as a CI security model. We have also seen that it is not trivial to gather the necessary information due to for example organizational reasons. Though it is not possible to provide a final verdict on the general feasibility of the methodology since every CI is different, the results suggest that the methodology will also work in other CI environments.

In future work, Bayesian network based risk estimation within the Grid'5000 CI security model as well as risk simulation based on attack or failure scenarios will be conducted. For this purpose a tool is currently implemented that allows risk estimation as well as risk simulation/emulation in the context of the CI security model. Given the opportunity, we also plan to conduct further case studies to validate the dependency analysis methodology as well as the CI security model in a broader context.

Acknowledgements. One of the authors would like to thank the Luxembourgish National Research Fund (FNR) for funding his PhD work under AFR grant number PHD-09-103.

References

1. Schaberreiter, T., Kittilä, K., Halunen, K., Röning, J., Khadraoui, D.: Risk assessment in critical infrastructure security modelling based on dependency analysis (short paper). In: 6th International Conference on Critical Information Infrastructure Security, CRITIS 2011 (2011)
2. Rinaldi, S.M., Peerenboom, J.P., Kelly, T.K.: Identifying, understanding, and analyzing critical infrastructure interdependencies. IEEE Control Systems Magazine (2001)

3. Panzieri, S., Setola, R., Ulivi, G.: An approach to model complex interdependent infrastructures. In: 16th IFAC World Congress (2005)
4. Tolone, W.J., Wilson, D., Raja, A., Xiang, W.-N., Hao, H., Phelps, S., Johnson, E.W.: Critical infrastructure integration modeling and simulation. In: Chen, H., Moore, R., Zeng, D.D., Leavitt, J. (eds.) ISI 2004. LNCS, vol. 3073, pp. 214–225. Springer, Heidelberg (2004)
5. Eronen, J., Laakso, M.: A case for protocol dependency. In: IEEE International Workshop on Critical Infrastructure Protection (2005)
6. Eronen, J., Röning, J.: Graphingwiki - a semantic wiki extension for visualising and inferring protocol dependency. In: Proceedings of the First Workshop on Semantic Wikis – From Wiki To Semantics. Workshop on Semantic Wikis (2006)
7. Eronen, J., Karjalainen, K., Puuperä, R., Kuusela, E., Halunen, K., Laakso, M., Röning, J.: Software vulnerability vs. critical infrastructure - a case study of antivirus software. International Journal on Advances in Security 2 (2009)
8. Pietikäinen, P., Karjalainen, K., Eronen, J., Röning, J.: Socio-technical security assessment of a voip system. In: The Fourth International Conference on Emerging Security Information, Systems and Technologies, SECURWARE 2010 (2010)
9. Aubert, J., Schaberreiter, T., Incoul, C., Khadraoui, D., Gateau, B.: Risk-based methodology for real-time security monitoring of interdependent services in critical infrastructures. In: International Conference on Availability, Reliability, and Security, ARES 2010 (2010)
10. Aubert, J., Schaberreiter, T., Incoul, C., Khadraoui, D.: Real-time security monitoring of interdependent services in critical infrastructures. Case study of a risk-based approach. In: 21th European Safety and Reliability Conference, ESREL 2010 (2010)
11. Schaberreiter, T., Aubert, J., Khadraoui, D.: Critical infrastructure security modelling and resci-monitor: A risk based critical infrastructure model. In: IST-Africa Conference Proceedings (2011)
12. Schaberreiter, T., Bouvry, P., Röning, J., Khadraoui, D.: A bayesian network based critical infrastructure model. In: Schütze, O., Coello Coello, C.A., Tantar, A.-A., Tantar, E., Bouvry, P., Del Moral, P., Legrand, P. (eds.) EVOLVE - A Bridge Between Probability. AISC, vol. 175, pp. 207–218. Springer, Heidelberg (2012)
13. Rinaldi, S.: Modeling and simulating critical infrastructures and their interdependencies. In: Proceedings of the 37th Annual Hawaii International Conference on System Sciences (2004)
14. Sokolowski, J., Turnitsa, C., Diallo, S.: A conceptual modeling method for critical infrastructure modeling. In: 41st Annual Simulation Symposium, ANSS 2008 (2008)
15. Tan, X., Zhang, Y., Cui, X., Xi, H.: Using hidden markov models to evaluate the real-time risks of network. In: IEEE International Symposium on Knowledge Acquisition and Modeling Workshop, KAM Workshop 2008 (2008)
16. Haslum, K., Årnes, A.: Multisensor real-time risk assessment using continuous-time hidden markov models. In: Wang, Y., Cheung, Y.-M., Liu, H. (eds.) CIS 2006. LNCS (LNAI), vol. 4456, pp. 694–703. Springer, Heidelberg (2007)
17. Massie, M.L., Chun, B.N., Culler, D.E.: The Ganglia Distributed Monitoring System: Design, Implementation, and Experience. Parallel Computing 30 (2004)
18. Capit, N., Da Costa, G., Georgiou, Y., Huard, G., Martin, C., Mounié, G., Neyron, P., Richard, O.: A batch scheduler with high level components. In: Cluster Computing and Grid 2005, CCGrid 2005 (2005)

How to Estimate a Technical VaR Using Conditional Probability, Attack Trees and a Crime Function

Wolfgang Boehmer

Technische Universität Darmstadt, Morneweg Str. 30,
CASED building, D-64293 Darmstadt, Germany
wboehmer@cdc.informatik.tu-darmstadt.de

Abstract. According to the Basel II Accord for banks and Solvency II for the insurance industry, not only should the market and financial risks for the institutions be determined, also the operational risks (opRisk). In recent decades, Value at Risk (VaR) has prevailed for market and financial risks as a basis for assessing the present risks. Occasionally, there are suggestions as to how the VaR is to be determined in the field of operational risk. However, existing proposals can only be applied to an IT infrastructure to a certain extent, or to parts of them e.g. such as VoIP telephony. In this article, a proposal is discussed to calculate a technical Value at Risk (t-VaR). This proposal is based on risk scenario technology and uses the conditional probability of the Bayes theorem. The vulnerabilities have been determined empirically for an insurance company in 2012. To determine the threats, attack trees and threat actors are used. The attack trees are weighted by a function that is called the criminal energy. To verify this approach the t-VaR was calculated for VoIP telephony for an insurance company. It turns out that this method achieves good and sufficient results for the IT infrastructure as an effective method to meet the Solvency II's requirements.

Keywords: Conditional probability, Bayes theorem, attack trees, threat actor, crime function, risk scenario technology.

1 Introduction

In the early days of protecting IT, i.e. in the early 90s, the focus was purely on technical security, because it was recognized that the IT is vulnerable. These often expensive safeguarding measures were not always bound by economic considerations and only a rudimentary relationship to the business processes was established. Therefore the Basel II Accord in 2004 represents a cornerstone, because it placed the operational risk (opRisk) equal to the market and financial risks. In the implementation of Basel II / Solvency II requirements for operational risks, it was recognized immediately that they should be treated differently than the market and financial risks. For while the market and financial risks can reference historical data, this is not possible for operational risk due to lack of data. Thus many projects have failed that tried to create a loss database in order to provide a database for operational risk. Additionally, for the operational risks, attempts have been made in several theoretical models to determine appropriate parameters for the VaR, which have never prevailed in practice. Consequently, the qualitative

A. Cuzzocrea et al. (Eds.): CD-ARES 2013 Workshops, LNCS 8128, pp. 288–304, 2013.
© IFIP International Federation for Information Processing 2013

and the quantitative risk procedures developed that still stand side by side today. The German Baseline Protection Manual, with his hazard analysis, can be considered a representative of the qualitative method and, to name a few examples for the quantitative method, there is the standard ISO 27005 or the standard ISO 31000. What the methods above have in common is that these do not calculate a VaR or similar parameter that is compatible with the parameters of the market and financial risks.

An important feature in the calculation of risk between the market and financial risks on the one hand and the operational risks on the other hand is the fact that the area of operational risk, the IT infrastructures are dominated by threats and existing vulnerabilities. Thus in the market and financial risks, the widespread approach of a Monte Carlo simulation to determine the probability distribution leads to unsatisfactory results when used for operational risks.

In general, the risk analysis is the consideration of two distributions. The first distribution describes the occurrence probability of risk events, and the second distribution represents the impact or outcome (consequence) of the risk event, if the risk is faced. Then the two distributions are convolved. This convolved distribution is a new distribution, the distribution of risk. If, for example, a 5% quantile (α - quantile as a confidence level) of this risk distribution is defined as the expected loss, the VaR is determined. But the question remains, how realistic input distributions are found. Furthermore, the type of the input distribution determines a specific part of the operational risk. The Basel II framework includes the operational risk (opRisk) and defines *opRisk as the risk of losses resulting from inadequate or failed internal processes, people and systems, or external events.* In this definition, legal risk is included. Strategic and reputational risks are excluded. Without entering into details, the main difference with market and credit risk is that, for opRisk, we only have losses, as P. Embrecht et al. argued in his paper [1].

The contribution of this paper is the development of a VaR for the system, or in detail, for the technical infrastructure, the t-VaR, that considers the characteristics of an IT infrastructure and is part of the opRisk, but is placed on a par with the VaR for the market and financial risks.

The rest of the article is organized as follows. In the next section, the underlying model is discussed. In section 3, the data collection for the identification of vulnerabilities, threats, and the application of the model to calculate the t-VaR is discussed using the VoIP telephony of an insurance company. The result is discussed in section 4, the relevant literature is discussed in section 5. The article concludes in section 6 with a brief summary, continuing considerations and proposals for further studies.

2 The Model

2.1 Basic Equations

Starting from the general linear relationship between the risk ($\mathcal{R}$), the probability (Pr) and the monetary outcome (impact) (I), as expressed in the equation 2.1,

$$\mathcal{R} = Pr \times I \ [\mathbb{R}], \qquad (2.1)$$

which is not directly used in this paper. We use instead 2.1 the loss distribution approach and the Lower Partial Moment, *cf.* Fig. 2, as expressed for a system Ψ in equation 2.2.

Because only the negative result for a system is considered, the Loss [$\mathbb{R}^-$], as is typical in the area of operational risk (see [1]).

$$\mathcal{R} = \left(Pr_E \times L\right)[\mathbb{R}^-] \mapsto \Psi \tag{2.2}$$

In 2.2 for the probability (Pr) of an event (E) instead the most frequent probability is, the conditional probability (Pr_E) in accordance with Bayes' Theorem is used.

According to the Bayesian statistics, a hypothesis is created that says here, that a vulnerability only can be exploited on the condition (|) if a threat exist with a matching threat agent. Or vice versa, that a threat with a threat agent can develop only if a corresponding vulnerability exists. The threat is indicated by (Thr) and the vulnerability by (Vul). Thus the equation 2.2 can be transformed into the equation 2.3.

$$\mathcal{R} = \left(Pr_E\left(Vul \mid Thr\right) \times L\right)[\mathbb{R}^-] \mapsto \Psi \tag{2.3}$$

Thus, the conditional probability that an existing vulnerability is exploited by a threat with a matching threat agent is described in equation 2.4

$$Pr_E(Vul \mid Thr) = \frac{Pr_E\left(Thr \cap Vul\right)}{Pr_E\left(Thr\right)}. \tag{2.4}$$

Hence the numerator describes in the equation 2.4 the intersection between the set of threats and set of vulnerabilities in the plane of the probability Pr_E (cf. Fig. 1). In this context, the vulnerability, the following definition is used.

Definition 2.1.01 (Vulnerabilities) are real (existing) and represent a weakness of an asset or represent a point at which the asset (component, system, process, employee) is technically or organizationally vulnerable. Vulnerability is a property of an asset and the security services of assets can be changed, circumvented or deceived (cf. ISO 27000:2012, p. 11).

Definition 2.1.02 (Threats) are not real (hypothetically) and aim at an asset (system or component) to exploit one or more weaknesses or vulnerabilities to a loss of data integrity, liability, confidentiality or availability. Threats can interact with an asset actively or passively (cf. ISO 27000:2012, p. 10).

The Figure 1 shows the conditional probability on a two dimensional level and the set of threats and vulnerabilities as well as their intersection. If now the equation (2.4) is used in the Def 2.2, the following equation (2.5) results for the system Ψ. Equation (2.5) states that the risk ($\mathcal{R}$) to face a loss (L [$\mathbb{R}^-$]) depends of the event (E), and a conditional probability (Pr) for the occurrence of the intersection of vulnerability (Vul) and threat (Thr) for the system Ψ.

$$\mathcal{R} = \left(\frac{Pr_E\left(Thr \cap Vul\right)}{Pr_E\left(Thr\right)}\right) \times L\,[\mathbb{R}^-] \mapsto \Psi. \tag{2.5}$$

From equation (2.5) individual risk scenarios $\mathcal{R} = \{R_{sz1}, ..., R_{szn}\}$ the Loss ($L = \{l_1, ..., l_n\}$) can be developed for different systems $\Psi = \{\psi_1, ..., \psi_n\}$, such as shown by the following equations (2.6) to (2.9).

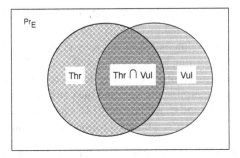

Fig. 1. Section and intersection of the set of threats and the set of vulnerabilities

$$R_{sz1} = PrE_{p1}(Vul_1 \mid Thr_1) \cdot l_1 \mapsto \psi_1 \tag{2.6}$$

$$R_{sz2} = PrE_{p2}(Vul_2 \mid Thr_1) \cdot l_2 \mapsto \psi_2 \tag{2.7}$$

$$R_{sz3} = PrE_{p3}(Vul_2 \mid Thr_2) \cdot l_3 \mapsto \psi_2 \tag{2.8}$$

$$\vdots$$

$$R_{szn} = PrE_{pn}(Vul_j \mid Thr_k) \cdot l_n \mapsto \psi_n \tag{2.9}$$

Summing up risk scenarios $R_{sz1}, ..., R_{szn}$ for an infinitely long period of time gives the maximum possible loss, such as the equation (2.10) expresses. For shorter periods e.g. for a fiscal year (T) a summation does not make sense; the risks must be aggregated as discussed in section 5.

$$\sum_{i=1}^{n} R_{sz_i} = PrE_{pi}\left(\sum_{Vul_{k=1}}^{n} \mid \sum_{Thr_{j=1}}^{n}\right) \cdot l_i \tag{2.10}$$

While vulnerabilities are real, threats are hypothetical. To obtain a quantitative assessment of the risk situation of a company, it is necessary to analyze the threats more accurately, because not every threat has an immediate and direct effect. It also assumes that behind every active threat, an actor must be present. Historically, the concept of the threat tree was first discussed in 1991 by J.D. Weis [2]. This concept is based on the theory of fault trees (Fault Tree Analysis, Event Tree Analysis FTA and ETA).

With risk (2.3) as a measure, it is associated as a universal measure of a probability space and is strongly related to the Loss Distribution Approach (LDA). The Loss Distribution Approach has been widely used in the financial and insurance industry for several decades and is as used for share portfolios. Thus it is natural to use this loss approach in the area of operational risk, but not for an equity portfolio, but for the value chain (production). In the literature, the topic is widely studied; significant work in this area has been performed by P. Embrecht et al. [1], M. Leipold and P. Vanini [3] and K. Böcker and C. Klüppelberg [4].

2.2 LDA Approach

The Loss Distribution Approach (LDA) refers to the bottom (marked in gray) part of Figure 2, which is the lower partial moment (LPM). For risk analysis, this means that two distributions are determined for a time period (T). First is the distribution of losses (Loss (T), *cf.* 2.2) and second is the probability distribution of events (Pr_E(T), *cf.* 2.2) which were mathematically composited in the grey dashed line in Figure 2 and is a joint distribution of risk according to the equations (2.6) to (2.9). The joint distribution is interpreted, which lead more often to minor losses and rarely major losses. This distribution is required to determine the VaR and the confidence level.

In the article by K. Böcker and C. Klüppelberg [4], a general summary of the standard LDA approach is given on page 6/7, which we follow here roughly.

1. The severities process $(l_k)_{k \in N}$ are positive independent and identically distributed (iid) random variables describing the magnitude of each loss event.
2. The number $N(x)$ of loss events (l_i) in the time interval $[t_1, t_2]$ for $t_2 \geq t_1$ is random (see Fig. 2). The resulting counting process $(N(x)_{t_2 \geq t_1})$, is generated by a sequence of points $(x_n)_{tn \geq 1}$ of non-negativ random variables, and
3. The severity process and the frequency process are assumed to be independent.
4. The aggregate loss process
   The aggregate loss $L(x)$ up to time T constitutes a process

$$L(T) = \sum_{i=1}^{N(x)} l_i, \quad x \geq 0. \tag{2.11}$$

2.3 Value at Risk

Illustrated in the equation 2.2, the risk represents the Lower Partial Moment (LPM), which as a downside risk measure only refers to a part of the total probability density (see Fig. 2). This covers only the negative deviations from a target size (e.g. a plan value of the reachability of the insurance company for their customers in a time interval) and evaluates all of the information of the probability distribution (up to the theoretically possible maximum outage). The random variable in the example in Figure 2 presents the reachability of the insurance company for their costumers in the unit of time. The reachability varies only in a small range $1 - \alpha$ for the planned insurance service and is shown as a random variable (X) for the period t_1, t_2. Figure 2 shows the normal distribution of the exogenous density function that results from the random variable (X). For this discrete random variable (X), the values $x_i, i =, 1, 2, 3$ and $x_i \neq x_j$ for $i \neq j$. The expected value (E_w^T) is defined for the discrete random variable (X) as the sum of their possible values, weighted by the respective probability. In the example of Figure 2, for the time period $t_1 \leq T \leq t_2$, this is represented by probability $1 \rightarrow \infty$ with

$$E_w^T = \sum_{i=1}^{\infty} x_i \cdot Pr(X - x_i). \tag{2.12}$$

For the random variable (X) as a placeholder, we can use the three protection goals of information security. These are defined e.g. in the standard ISO/IEC 27001:2005 as confidentiality (C), integrity (I), availability (A) [5]. Often referred to as the CIA Triad.

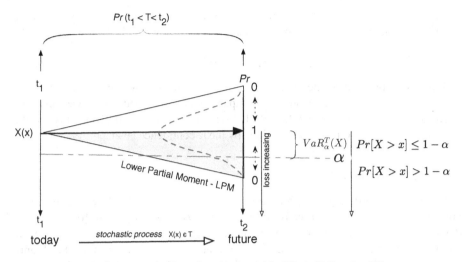

Fig. 2. Expected value of random variable (X), opVaR and opES

The statistical spread (σ) is the expectation of (E_w) expressed in the discrete case with the variance (Var), as shown in equation 2.13

$$Var(X) = \sigma_X^2 = \sum_{i=1}^{\infty}(x_i - E_w(X))^2 \cdot Pr\,(X = x_i).$$

(2.13)

The variance (Var) represents the average of the squared deviations from the mean of the random variable (X). The standard deviation is defined as the square root of the variance. The Discrete result values in the time interval T have been approximated by a normal distribution, so that in the Figure 2, the continuous course of the random variable is shown with density $f(x)$, so the expected value is obtained in this case E_w^T, as shown in equation 2.14

$$E_w^T = \int_{-\infty}^{+\infty} x \cdot f(x)\,dx.$$

(2.14)

In Fig. 2, the $opVaR_\alpha^T(X)$ and the $opES_\alpha^T(X)$ have been illustrated. This is where a VaR is a α-quantile. The α-quantile q_α of a distribution function $F(x)$ is the value of $\alpha\%$ below the mass of the probability mass that separates the upper $1 - \alpha\%$ from the probability mass. The random variable (X) with probability α then takes on a value less than or equal to q_α.

The formal definition of the α-quantile is shown as in infimum function in equation 2.15 with

$$q_\alpha = F^{-1}(\alpha).$$

(2.15)

F^{-1} it is the inverse function of the distribution function.

The *Value at Risk, VaR* is thus the α-quantile of a loss distribution. If a random variable (X) is given, the *OpVaR* for a time interval T is shown in the following equation 2.16

$$opVaR_\alpha^T(X) = inf\{x \in \mathbb{R} \mid P[X > x] \le 1 - \alpha\}. \tag{2.16}$$

$opVaR_\alpha^T(X)$ expresses that the smallest loss (for the example it would be the availability of the VoIP telephony of the insurance company) that corresponds to a lower limit and exceeds the loss with a probability of $(1 - \alpha)$. Hence the crucial probability for the calculation of $(opVaR_\alpha^T(X))$ is determined by the α confidence level.

2.4 Expected Shortfall

The Expected Shortfall (ES), often referred to as the *Conditional VaR, (CVaR)*, as a coherent risk measure, was already addressed in 1997 by Artzner et al. [6]. The ES is defined as the expected loss in the event that the VaR is actually exceeded. Thus, this is the probability-weighted average of all losses that are higher than the VaR. For Figure 2, the OpES for the random variable (X) with probability α for a time interval T is given in the equation 2.17.

$$opES_\alpha^T(X) = E_w^T[X \mid X \ge opVaR_\alpha^T(X)] \tag{2.17}$$

The expected value E_w^T for the time period T shown in Equation 2.17 corresponds to a conditional expectation of the random variable (X), for the case that $X \ge opVaR_\alpha^T(X)$ occurs. A risk scenario is understood under the conditional expectation of the random variable (X). For the very rare deviations of the extreme values of E_w^T a control circuit based Business Continuity Management System (BCMS) is used.

A major difference between the analysis of financial and market risks and operational risks, is that there are, firstly, no security protection concepts concerning the protection goals exist in the field of finance and mark risks, and secondly, there are no management systems that can respond to exogenous disturbances. Only the approach of H. Markowitz [7] in 1959 suggesting a risk diversification of a portfolio could, therefore, be considered as a measure to protect the invested capital (availability of capital), but for operational risks it would only be helpful in rare situations.

In the previous sections, the VaR and the OpVaR have been discussed along with application scenarios. The argument here, however, is that these considerations of VaR and the OpVaR could be transferred to information technology and information processing, but not easily, if at all.

One of the main differences is that the information technology of a company is exposed to, among other technical damage, passive and active threats, vulnerabilities and attacks. The literature in the field of OpVaR has barely considered these facts at all. Against this background, a technical VaR is proposed (t-VaR), which addresses the concerns of information technology and information processing as well as the demonstrated passive and active threats, vulnerabilities and attacks. This is based on the definition of risk, according to equation (2.2).

2.5   Attack Trees and Threat Agent

Equation (2.5) illustrated the Baysian view of a risk situation for a system Ψ. Exogenous knowledge is required for the intersection of vulnerability (Vul) and threat (Thr) for the Bayesian statistics. This required exogenous knowledge is filled with the attack trees, attack actors and a crime function. With this exogenous knowledge makes it possible to estimate the conditional probability of the intersection, as we will show in this section.

The idea of the attack trees goes back to the article by Weis in 1991 [2]. In this article he describes *threat logical trees*. Generally, attacks are modelled with graphical, mathematical, decision trees. A few years later, the idea of the threat trees was taken up by B. Schneier, among others, and developed [8]. This work by B. Schneier led to extensive additions and improvements to this technology, such as that published by A.P. Moore et al. [9]. Several tools have been developed and published; representative here of the work is [10, 11]; the authors provide an overview of the techniques and tools. The contribution of S. Mauw and M. Oostdijk [12] in 2005 formalize the concepts informally introduced by Schneier [8]. This formalization clarifies which manipulations of attack trees are allowed under which conditions. The commonality of attack trees and game theory has been elaborated on in 2010 by Kordy et al. [13]. Thus, a similar approach for the threat scenarios and threat agent are performed using the game theory.

In this work, we expand the idea of T. R. Ingoldsby [11] with conditional probability and the t-VaR. Threat trees generally have a root or target. Different branches (nodes) can lead to this target that are to be regarded as parts of goals and each start of a leaf. Each leaf is initiated by an attacker with different motives. The leaves and branches are weighted and equipped with an actor [12]. The weighting corresponds to the criminal energy (Criminal power, Cp), and contain three functions. The assessment of these three functions reflect the exogenous knowledge which is required in the Bayesian statistics (see equation (2.4)).

Already in 1985, A. Mosleh et al. pointed out the two main distributions for a risk analysis on the Bayesian statistic [14]. On the one hand, it is the probability distribution of the event occurring. Since these are rare events, the Poisson distribution is proposed here, which is later used by many other authors. The one-parameter Poisson distribution does a good job of providing the assessment, that small deviations occur more frequently than larger deviations, such as is expressed in Figure 2 with the lower partial moment (LPM). The challenge now is to get a good estimation of the parameters of the distribution. This assessment is made in this paper on the threats and attack trees in combination with the function of the criminal energy.

On the other hand, in the article by A. Mosleh et al. [14], the loss distribution is approximated by the log normal distribution. This distribution also corresponded to the idea that small losses occur more frequently than large losses for a long time. This idea has been revised by the Black Swan Theory [15] (extreme value theory) and is now often replaced by a Generalized Pareto Distribution (GPD).

Often, the loss distribution is easier to determine than the frequency distribution, if the loss is related to the value chain.

The function of the criminal energy (Cp), which in turn is composed of three additive functions, represents the expert knowledge for the Bayesian risk analysis (see equation (2.6 - 2.9)). The criminal energy is represented by the cost function (cost of attack *cf.*

Fig. 3), the technical feasibility function (technical function, Fig. 4) and the noticeability function, *cf.* Fig. 5. The three functions are mentioned by T. R. Ingoldsby [11] and have to be adjusted to the relevant inspection. The following Figures 3 - 5 describe the exogenous knowledge that focuses on the objective of VoIP telephony. This exogenous knowledge is important for the Bayesian approach.

Fig. 3 states that a threat agent (actor) for an attack on the VoIP telephony of the insurance company is willing to spend money on tools. This willingness varies between 0 - 1 (axis of ordinates) and decreases with increasing costs (axis of abscissae). This can be explained simply because on the internet there are a number of free tools that are all well-suited to threaten a VoIP telephony.

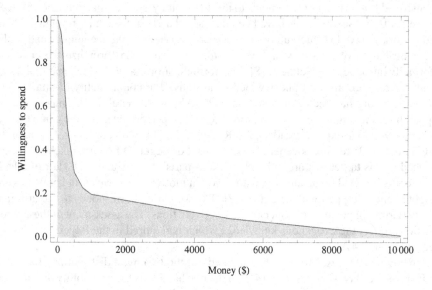

Fig. 3. Cost function

Figure 4 indicates how the tools are used and the technical possibilities that exist. It is a statement about the complexity of the tools and the willingness to make use of this complexity. The curve indicates that the greater the technical possibilities and the complexity of the tools, the more the willingness drops. I.e. it simple tools are preferred with simple operation.

Figure 5 shows the noticeability function expressing how an actor wants to disguise his attack, so that he could not be discovered. From of these three functions, the threat of an attack is determined more precisely. This is called the criminal energy. These functions must be adapted to each situation and reflect the exogenous knowledge again, which is necessary for the conditional probability.

As an example, we can estimate the technical ability rating of 5 (out of 10), and expose the miscreant at a 0.3 noticeability.

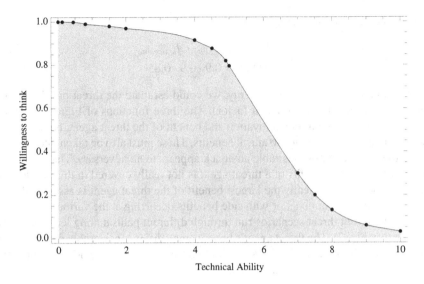

Fig. 4. Technical function

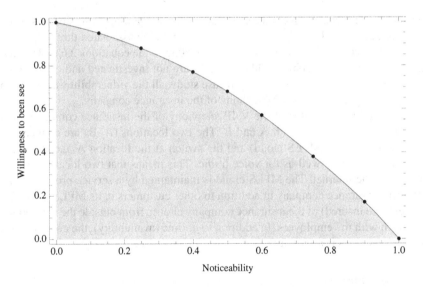

Fig. 5. Noticeability function

Using the utility functions shown, we discover that

$$f_{cost}(25) = 0.9 \tag{2.18}$$

$$f_{tech\,ability}(05) = 0.9 \tag{2.19}$$

$$f_{noticeabiity}(0.3) = 0.85 \tag{2.20}$$

and therefore the criminal energy with

$$Cp = f_{cost} \cdot f_{tech\,ability} \cdot f_{noticeabiity} \tag{2.21}$$
$$Cp = 0.6885 = 0.9 \cdot 0.9 \cdot 0.85 \tag{2.22}$$

With this function of the criminal energy, we could estimate the threat profile in conjunction with a specific threat agent (actor). The three functions of Figures 3 - 5 do not explain anything about the motivation and benefit of the threat agent, but the threat agent's motivation is correlated to attack benefits. These must also be taken into account in order to understand how desirable an attack appears to an adversary. The discussion of the motivation and benefits of a threat agent is not really covered in this article, due to lack of space. But, typically the largest benefit of the threat agent is associated with achieving the tree's root node, or with side benefits occurring at the various intermediate nodes. Different threat scenarios run through different paths among leaf nodes and root node (cfg Fig. 7). The threat agent's benefits may differ considerably depending on the threat scenario used. We will discuss different threat scenarios and different paths between leaf nodes and root in the next section.

3   Data Acquisition

According to the model (cf section 2), data acquisition regarding vulnerabilities is handled in this section and matched to the attack-tree with the associated threat agent (actor) and analyzed to develop risk scenarios according to the equations 2.6 to 2.9. Here, ψ represents the VoIP telephony. Other systems are not investigated and consequently $\Psi = \psi$. This means that in this real-world case study, all the vulnerabilities, threats and risk scenarios relate to ψ = VoIP telephony of the insurance company.

Figure 6 is a rough sketch of the VoIP telephony of the insurance company. There are two locations indicated with A and B. The two locations (A, B) are connected to a non-public network (MPLS cloud) and the switch at the location A and B are both used for data traffic as well as for voice traffic. This means that two locations are not connected to the internet. The MPLS cloud is maintained by a service provider which supplies the insurance company in addition to other customers in its MPLS cloud. The customers (the insured) of the insurance company choose from outside the softphone to get in touch with the employees. In addition to uptime (availability), the confidentiality of the conversations is a security objective for the insurance company.

3.1   Vulnerability Analysis

The empirical study in 2012 for the insurance company had to analyze the current target vulnerabilities within the scope of VoIP telephony. These weaknesses are discussed as an example in this section to show the procedure of the model. This analysis was carried out in two steps. In the first step, the VoIP module (B 4.7) of the baseline protection manual from the BSI was used [16, 17]. The technical department was interviewed. In the second step, a white box penetration testing was conducted to verify the statements and to find other vulnerabilities. It is worth mentioning that there is no connection between the VoIP telephony and the Internet.

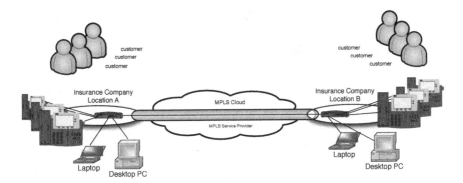

Fig. 6. VoIP Architecture

In our investigation in 2012 it was recognized, inter alia, that the voice data (RTP stream) transmitted without encryption and the ports at the Softphones and patch socket in the premises were not secured against unauthorized use (IEEE 802.1x, Port Based Network Control PBNC). Furthermore, we identified that there was no firewall between the MPLS network and the LAN of the insurance company and also the voice data was transmitted unecrypted in the MPLS network.

Based on these findings, the following threat analysis was performed.

3.2   Threat Analysis

The threat analysis is based on the identified vulnerabilities and contains three elements: the threat scenarios, the matching threat agent and the function of the criminal energy.

In our threat analysis, we show as an example, how the protection target – in this case, the confidentiality of VoIP Telephony – is given in the current threat situation for the insurance company. Confidentiality for VoIP telephony means that the phone calls between the employees of the insurance company and its insured cannot be intercepted. Similarly, the phone calls between sites A and B will be kept confidential, because the interception could have negative implications for the insurance company.

Figure 7 shows the potential threat paths for the insurance company from the leaf to the root. Between the paths are either "or" or "and" connections. The "and" connection means that the two paths connected with the "and" must be met in order to reach the next sub-goal. Between the sub-goals the function of the criminal energy will change. The individual leaves represents the threat agent and the root represents the target of the attack (interception of voice traffic). The numbers represent the function of the criminal energy and therefore the exogenous knowledge. The index (I) = Impossible and (P) = Possible differentiates possible paths that are possible or not possible due to policies or structural circumstances. The equations 2.18 - 2.20 were determined for each threat attack and different threat agent with a specific crime function (*cf.* 2.21). Inserting a set of risk scenarios for the VoIP-Telephony in the given situation into the set of equations 2.6 - 2.9 created equations 3.1 - 3.4.

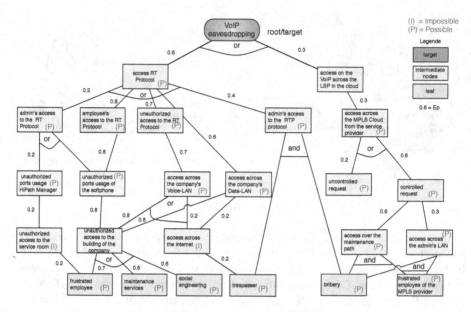

Fig. 7. Attack tree with the criminal energy

The actual risks of wiretapping the voice traffic in the real-world case study was estimated with risk scenarios (cf equations 3.1 - 3.4) according to the Bayesian statistics, with the attack trees, the threat agent and the criminal function (Cp). As a threat agent, an intruder from the inside the insurance company was postulated, because the unencrypted voice traffic is only in the LAN of the insurance company and is also transmitted unencrypted in the cloud provider's MPLS. However, no Internet connection exists for voice traffic to the insurance company and the MPLS cloud is also not connected to the Internet. Thus, as insiders only someone from the insurance company is eligible out of the environment (priviledged person) of the MPLS cloud providers.

The threat was assumed to be the interception (Thr_1) of sensitive voice data of the insurance company that could be performed by an internal perpetrator (threat agent). Likewise, the threat agent could also be represented by service personnel (Thr_2) or a trespasser (Thr_3). For each threat tree and threat agent a separate criminal function from Fig. 3, Fig. 4 and Fig. 5 is estimated with the equation 2.21. The leaves in Figure 7 represent the different threat agents. The behavior of insiders has already been addressed in a number of published articles, representative here is the article by I. J. Martinez-Moyano et al. [18]. ψ_1 denotes the VoIP infrastructure and refers to the vulnerability of the non-encrypted voice data with Vul_1.

The possible damage resulting for insurance company caused by insiders is the associated reputational damage if the intercepted voice data is given to the public. Given to the reputational damage for the voice data scenario, we made an assumption that 25 customers terminate their contract in the current year. The loss by termination is indicated with l_{25c}. The loss of 25 insurance contracts in a one-year period is also well above the normal turnover rate between 8 - 11 ($l_{8c} - l_{11c}$) contracts per year (T) and hence higher than the expected value of E_w^T (cf Eq. II.12).

We can use the equations 2.6 - 2.9 to express the risk scenarios $R_{sz1} - R_{szn}$ (3.1 - 3.4) with the potential loss of 25 contracts (l_{25c}) under consideration of Eq. 2.21 for the threat agents and the attack trees for our real-world case study of ψ = VoIP telephony of the insurance company:

$$R_{sz1} = PrE_{p1}(Vul_1 \mid Thr_1) \cdot l_{25c} \mapsto \text{VoIP-Telephony} \tag{3.1}$$

$$R_{sz2} = PrE_{p2}(Vul_1 \mid Thr_2) \cdot l_{25c} \mapsto \text{VoIP-Telephony} \tag{3.2}$$

$$R_{sz3} = PrE_{p3}(Vul_1 \mid Thr_3) \cdot l_{25c} \mapsto \text{VoIP-Telephony} \tag{3.3}$$

$$\vdots$$

$$R_{szn} = PrE_{pn}(Vul_n \mid Thr_n) \cdot l_{25c} \mapsto \text{VoIP-Telephony} \tag{3.4}$$

The probability $PrE_{p1} - PrE_{pn}$ is estimated as described above with the conditional probability of 2.4.

In addition to safeguarding the confidentiality and the risk scenarios as described with $R_{sz1} - R_{szn}$ (3.1 - 3.4), we also worked out the risk scenarios for the other two protection goals: the availability and integrity. Thus, for the protection of target availability and integrity, analogous threat trees were developed with appropriate threat agents and criminal functions in order to then determine the conditional probability and therefore the risk scenarios. Due to space limitations in this article, these analogous considerations will not be pursued further.

4   Results

In this section, we will discuss the results from the VoIP-Telephony investigation for our real-world case study.

The business success of a insurance company can be determined, inter alia, by the amount of insurance policies ($|C|$). The number of insurance policies ($c_i \in C$) fluctuates with 8 to 11 policy terminations. The target is expected to lose no more than 8 insurance policies per year, however, if the loss of 11 insurance policies occurs, this is also acceptable and the α value is achieved. Thus, the expected value of $E_w^T(C)$ for one year is 8 insurance policies and corresponds to the target value "1" in Figure 8. The period is one year (T).

The equation 4.1 describes the negative variation around the target value of 1 ((l_{c8} = 8 lost contracts). The possible new customers per year are not considered in our real-world case study. For this reason, only the lower distribution (LPM) is considered. The scattering width is 3 contracts and partly achieves the loss of 11 contracts per year. The equation 4.1 now describes the influence of the technical infrastructure with the control objectives (Confidentiality, Integrity, Availability) to the cardinality of the set of contracts $|C|$.

$$\text{t-Var(C)} = \sigma_C^2 = \sum_{i=1}^{|C|}(c_i - E_w^T(C))^2 \cdot Pr\,(C = c_i). \tag{4.1}$$

This experience of the turnover is derived from observations from the last 10 years.

For the insurance company, availability for your customers is very important. If customers cannot express their concerns over the phone, they are angry and are ready to switch to another insurance company in the current year.

The loss of confidentiality creates reputational damage for the insurance company and a number of customers cancel. There is an internal investigation of the insurance company, which proves this fact. This is one of reasons why the risk analysis was performed. It has been shown that, due to the risk scenarios in our real-world case study, there is the possibility losing a lot more contracts than expected. Figure 9 shows the distribution of the LPM in a different presentation. This presentation is done very often for loss considerations instead of Figure 8. These are the discrete values of the risk scenarios that have been analyzed in our real-world case study. It be shown that the expected loss of 8 to 11 insurance polices has been clearly exceeded. It is therefore an unexpected loss.

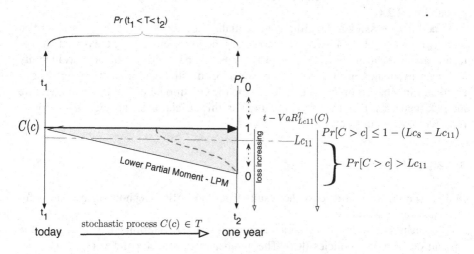

Fig. 8. Technical Value at Risk for the insured contracts

In conclusion, it can be said for our real-world case study that the insurance company has decided to take appropriate countermeasures in the field of encryption in the LAN and in the connection in the MPLS cloud. It was ensured that the cost of action does not exceed the potential unexpected losses.

5   Related Work

The concept of risk and its various considerations is a discussion of the past few decades in the literature as shown in the article 1980 of S. Kaplan and J. Garrick [19]. Also, the authors distinguish between risk and hazard. While the risk (R) contains the three items, the set of scenarios (S), probability (p) and loss (x), in a linear combination $R = \{\langle S_i, p_i, x_i \rangle\}$, the concept of hazard (H) contains only two items, the set of scenarios (S) and the loss (x) in a linear combination $H = \{\langle S_i, x_i \rangle\}$. Furthermore, the authors [19]

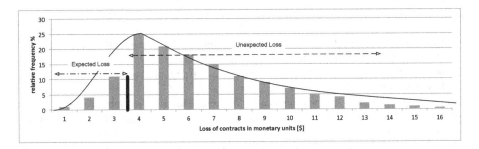

Fig. 9. Loss distribution for the contracts c_i due to breaches of confidentiality of the VoIP-Telephony

pointed out the difference between the probability according to the frequentist view of Laplace and the conditional probability of the Bayesian theory. For both of these views, there are a number of publications. Widespread is also the approach of Bayes. For this view, there are different ideas, to name a few: [14, 20–22].

Representative of many contributions to the provision of operational risk is the work of P. Embrecht et al. [1] or by K. Boecker and C. Klüppelberg [4]. The discussion about the coherent version of VaR was initiated by P. Atzner et al. [6]. In the area of operational risk, additional work should be mentioned that is related to this paper. Thus, the present paper follows broadly the doctoral thesis from 2010 of N. Poolsappasit [22] but expands on his idea, however, to the actor model and a weight function, which represents the criminal energy. Finally, it can be summarized that one unique way does not yet exist to satisfy answers to determine the operational risk.

6 Conclusion and Further Investigation

Over the past two decades the VaR and the coherent variant C-VaR have established themselves as a value for determining the risks associated with market and financial risks. According to BASEL II and/or Solvency II the operational risks should be determined in an appropriate manner. Once the standard approach to a loss database proved infeasible and unsuccessful, many institutes and industrial companies tried to follow BASEL II. However, the process of determining the VaR in the market and financial risks cannot be directly transferred to the technical infrastructure. In our view, the operational risk of the individual VaR must be assembled for systems, processes, people and external events. Therefore, in this article we present a method based on the Bayesian statistics, vulnerabilities, attack trees, an actor model and the function of criminal energy, that determines a technical VaR that is an appropriate response to the specific protection targets (confidentiality, integrity, availability) of an IT infrastructure. The real-world case study of VoIP telephony in an insurance company verified t-VaR for the protection target of confidentiality. As a result, it can be shown that the t-VaR is an appropriate method to determine the VaR for the IT infrastructure under operational risks. Other considerations now aim to determine a t-VaR for other areas of the IT infrastructure, and then conduct a risk aggregation to determine the overall risk in the technical area.

References

[1] Embrechts, P., Furrer, H., Kaufmann, R.: Quantifying regulatory capital for operational risk. Derivatives Use, Trading and Regulation 9, 217–233 (2003)
[2] Weis, J.D.: A system security engineering process. In: Proceedings of the 14th National Computer Security Conference (1991)
[3] Leippold, M., Vanini, P.: The quantification of operational risk (November 2003)
[4] Böcker, K., Klüppelberg, C.: Operational var: A closed-form approximation (December 2005)
[5] SC27, ISO/IEC 27001:2005, information technology - security techniques - information security management systems - requirements. Beuth-Verlag, Berlin (October 2005)
[6] Artzner, P., Delbaen, F., Eber, J.-M., Heath, D.: Coherent measures of risk. Math. Finance 9(3), 203–228 (2001)
[7] Markowitz, H.M.: Portfolio Selection: Efficient Diversification of Investment. Blackwell Publishers Ltd., Oxford (1991); Originally published in 1959 by John Wiley & Sons, Inc., New York
[8] Schneier, B.: Attack trees. Dr. Dobb' s Journal 24(12), 21–29 (1999)
[9] Moore, A.P., Ellison, R.J., Linger, R.C.: Attack modeling for information security and survivability, Technical Note CMU/SEI-2001- TN-001, Carnegie Mellon University (2001)
[10] Sheyner, O., Wing, J.: Tools for Generating and Analyzing Attack Graphs. In: de Boer, F.S., Bonsangue, M.M., Graf, S., de Roever, W.-P. (eds.) FMCO 2003. LNCS, vol. 3188, pp. 344–371. Springer, Heidelberg (2004)
[11] Ingoldsby, T.R.: Fundamentals of Capabilities-based Attack Tree Analysis. Amenaza Technologies Limited, 406–917 85th St SW, m/s 125
[12] Mauw, S., Oostdijk, M.: Foundations of Attack Trees. In: Won, D.H., Kim, S. (eds.) ICISC 2005. LNCS, vol. 3935, pp. 186–198. Springer, Heidelberg (2006)
[13] Kordy, B., Mauw, S., Melissen, M., Schweitzer, P.: Attack–defense trees and two-player binary zero-sum extensive form games are equivalent. In: Alpcan, T., Buttyán, L., Baras, J.S. (eds.) GameSec 2010. LNCS, vol. 6442, pp. 245–256. Springer, Heidelberg (2010)
[14] Mosleh, A., Hilton, E.R., Browne, P.S.: Bayesian probabilistic risk analysis. ACM SIGMETRICS – Performance Evaluation Review 13 (June 1985)
[15] Taleb, N.N.: The Black Swan. The Impact of the Highly Improbable. Random House Inc. (2008)
[16] Federal Office for Security in Information Technology, Baseline Protection Guide Germany. Bundesanzeiger (2006)
[17] Federal Office for Security in Information Technology, IT Baseline Protection Handbook, Bundesanzeiger, Cologne (2003-2005)
[18] Martinez-Moyano, I.J., Rich, E., Conrad, S., Andersen, D.F., Stewart, T.R.: A behavioral theory of insider-threat risks: A system dynamics approach. ACM Transactions on Modeling and Computer Simulation 18 (April 2008)
[19] Kaplan, S., Garrick, B.J.: On the quantitative definition of risk. Risk Analysis 1 (July 1980)
[20] Dalla Valle, L., Giudici, P.: A bayesian approach to estimate the marginal loss distributions in operational risk management. Comput. Stat. Data Anal. 52(6), 3107–3127 (2008)
[21] Alexander, C.: Bayesian methods for measuring operational risk, Discussion Papers in Finance (2000)
[22] Poolsappasit, N.: Towards an Efficient Vulnerability Analysis Methodology for better Security Risk Management. PhD thesis, Colorado State University (July 2010)

Using Probabilistic Analysis for the Certification of Machine Control Systems

Atif Mashkoor[1], Osman Hasan[2], and Wolfgang Beer[1]

[1] Software Competence Center Hagenberg,
Hagenberg, Austria
{firstname.lastname}@scch.at

[2] School of Electrical Engineering and Computer Science,
National University of Sciences and Technology,
Islamabad, Pakistan
{firstname.lastname}@seecs.nust.edu.pk

Abstract. Traditional testing techniques often reach their limits when employed for the assessment of critical Machine Control Systems as they contain a large amount of random and unpredictable components. The probabilistic analysis approach can assist in their evaluation by providing a subjective evidence of their safety and reliability. The synergy of probabilistic analysis and expressiveness of higher-order logic theorem proving results into convincing modelling and reasoning of several stringent safety cases that contribute towards the certification of high-assurance systems.

1 Introduction

Software-controlled systems have become ubiquitous in day to day affairs. The proliferation of software has spanned from transportation to industrial informatics and from power generation to homeland defence. While our domestic as well as defence activities increasingly depend on software-intensive systems, the safety-critical, distributed, heterogeneous, dynamic and often unpredictable nature of such systems produces several complex challenges.

The grand challenge of such systems is that their incorrect use or unsafe development may lead to a compromise on homeland defence and security. We often read such news related to cyber threats, unmanned aerial system crashes, and vulnerability of power generation and chemical plants against terrorist attacks.

One of the integral systems responsible for homeland defence and security is a Machine Control System (MCS). MCS is a device that manages, commands, directs or regulates the behaviour of various processing units. As shown by Figure 1, a typical MCS is composed of some realtime Programmable Logic Controllers (PLCs) and a non-realtime User Interface (UI) that helps interacting with PLCs. PLCs, in turn, are of two types. First type contains some domain-specific commands pertaining to the processing unit that control motors based on signals from sensors and actuators. The other type is comprised of stringent safety regulations that need to be certified before being functional.

A. Cuzzocrea et al. (Eds.): CD-ARES 2013 Workshops, LNCS 8128, pp. 305–320, 2013.

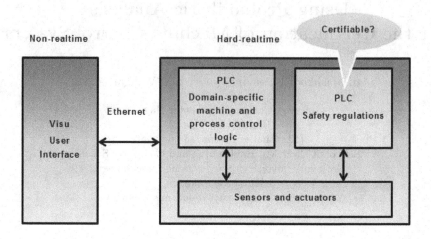

Fig. 1. A typical MCS

Besides threatening the homeland defence and security, a faulty MCS can also result into a minor injury, irreversible severe injury, amputation or even death. Although, we do not have detailed publicly available investigation reports of accidents caused by disturbances in MCS performing safety functions, yet some information is presented in [1]. The report is based on an analysis of 700 industrial incidents occurred between 1996-2002 in Poland alone. According to the report, 41% of severe accidents were caused by improper functioning of the system. Software faults were among the notable reasons.

Industrial incidents are not new phenomena. Standard techniques to avoid accidents [2] are in place since last several decades. However, with the proliferation of software, industry saw a paradigm shift when mechanical controls were replaced by their software counterparts and along new technology came new challenges. As software started becoming pervasive, it also became unprecedentedly complex.

Due to the critical nature of software components of MCS, there are numerous properties in which they must exceed other software systems, such as resilience, safety, security, and reliability. Such systems must also be certified. Certification, as defined by the charter of Software Certification Consortium (SCC)[1], demonstrates the assurance that the system has met its relevant technical standards and specifications, and it can be trusted to provide its services safely, securely and effectively.

There are several approaches towards software certification, e.g., argument-based, process-based and product-based. However, in the past few years, argument-based safety case approach [3] is gaining popularity among regularity regimes for the certification of software-intensive systems. It is also the explicit part of U.K. MoD Defence Standard 00-56. A safety case, in fact, is an evidence based on a convincing and valid argument that the designed system is adequately safe for a given application in the given environment.

---

[1] http://cps-vo.org/group/scc

Formal methods are usually the part of most of the software certification techniques. Their use is often recommended for the development of safety-critical systems involving higher Safety Integrity Level (SIL), IEC 61508, and DO-178C standards. Formal methods help specifying system requirements and properties using mathematical and logical notations which are then amenable to correctness. Correctness amounts to both verification, the practice where it is determined that product is being built correctly and meets its specification, and validation, the practice where it is ensured that the product meets customers requirements.

Standard verification and validation techniques are comprised of activities like standard theorem proving, model checking, animation and simulation. Each of these techniques has some inherent limitations and do not cope very well with the posed challenges in the development of highly complex and safety-critical MCS.

A standard method to guarantee the safety properties in a formal specification is to show that the invariant, a logical representation of safety, is preserved. We prove a theorem to satisfy the property. While adequate in most of the cases, less so to justify the absence of component failures and emergence of potential hazardous situations. In contrast to safety and deadlock-freedom, fairness and liveness proofs are not so straightforward. The techniques like animation, simulation, model checking can provide help in such cases but only up to some extent.

The problem with the animation is that currently available animators have strong limitations on the types of specifications they can animate. We have seen how the class of executable specifications can be extended with the help of few safe transformations [4]. Yet, there are some formal texts on which animators fail [5]. For those texts, we propose to use simulation rather than animation; the specification is translated into a program. But the problem with the translation is that currently available translators are in infancy stages and have their own weaknesses, such as expressiveness of the targeted languages. Approximation using closest counterparts does not fulfil the true purpose.

Model checking involves the construction of a precise state-based mathematical model of the given system. The state-space model is then subjected to exhaustive analysis to automatically verify that it satisfies a set of formally represented properties. The problem of this approach is that it can only be used to analyse systems that can be expressed as finite state machines. Another major limitation is the state-space explosion. The state-space of a real-world MCS can be very large, or sometimes even infinite and thus impossible to be explored completely within the limited resources of time and memory.

Higher-order theorem proving, on the other hand, is very flexible in terms of tackling a variety of systems, thanks to its expressiveness. However, this flexibility comes at the cost of enormous user efforts in terms of manual development of system models and interactive verification due to the undecidable nature of the underlying logic. Thus, developing realistic models of MCS, which usually involve significant amount of continuous and non-deterministic elements, and verifying them for all possible scenarios could be very tedious, if not impossible.

Probabilistic analysis overcomes the above mentioned limitations. Rather than ensuring absolute correctness, the main idea here is to ensure that the system behaves in the desired manner with an acceptable probability. This not only simplifies system modelling but also eases the verification task considerably. Probabilistic analysis is often used as an evidence to justify the claim of safety and reliability [3].

The main aim of this paper is to demonstrate how probabilistic analysis approach can provide a subjective evidence that can support the claim of system safety and reliability. Rest of the paper is organized as following: An overview of the existing formal analysis approaches is given in Section 2. Section 3 introduces the main concepts used in this paper, i.e., safety cases and higher-order logic theorem proving. Section 4 describes how probabilistic algorithms can be formalized. Section 5 presents the proposed formal probabilistic analysis approach. Section 6 applies the proposed approach to a simple case-study of multi-robot systems. The paper is finally concluded in Section 7.

2   Related Work

In recent years, the use of argument-based safety case approach has emerged as a popular technique for the certification of software-controlled critical systems. In [6], authors developed a conceptual model, based on the IEC 61508 standard, to characterize the chain of safety evidence that underlies safety arguments about software. In [7] and [8], authors present approaches that extend the border of safety case analysis towards general software properties. These approaches, though rigorous, are not fully formal.

In [9], an approach is presented to show how a safety case analysis based on SMT sovlers and infinite bounded model checkers can be used as a certification argument for the adaptive systems. The work is then extended in [10] with the proposition of a framework based on probabilistic analysis. The mathematics presented in [10] is then formalized by probabilistic kernels-based mathematical approach in [11]. The approach is illustrated using an example of a conflict detection system for an aircraft. Our proposed approach, as compared to these aforementioned works, is much more powerful in terms of handling a larger set of problems, for instance MCS. Moreover, unlike our approach, the mathematical framework of [11] has yet to be formalized in a theorem prover.

Probabilistic model checking [12,13] is the most widely used formal method for probabilistic analysis of systems that can be modelled as Markov chains. Like traditional model checking, it involves the construction of a precise state-based mathematical model of the given probabilistic system, which is then subjected to exhaustive analysis to verify if it satisfies a set of formally represented probabilistic properties. Some notable probabilistic model checkers include PRISM [14], Ymer [29] and VESTA [30].

Besides the accuracy of the results, the most promising feature of probabilistic model checking is the ability to perform the analysis automatically. But it is only limited to systems that can be expressed as Markov chains. Another major limitation of the probabilistic model checking approach is the state-space explosion. The state-space of a probabilistic system can be very large, or sometimes even infinite. Thus, at the outset, it is impossible to explore the entire state-space with limited resources of time and memory. Thus, the probabilistic model checking approach, even though capable of providing exact solutions, is quite limited in terms of handling a variety of probabilistic analysis problems.

Similarly, some algorithms implemented in model checking tools are based on numerical methods. For example, a well-known iterative method, the power method, is often applied to compute the steady-state probabilities (or limiting probabilities) of the Markov chain in PRISM . For this reason, most of the stationary properties analysed in model checkers are time bounded. Moreover, probabilistic model checking tools often utilize unverified algorithms and optimization techniques. Finally, probabilistic model checking cannot be used to verify generic mathematical expressions corresponding to probabilistic and statistical properties. Thus, the verified properties involve values that are expressed in a computer based notation, such as fixed or floating point numbers, which also introduces some degree of approximation in the results.

The B [15] and Event-B [16] methods have also been extended to support probabilistic analysis. The main idea here is either to use a probabilistic choice operator to reason about termination conditions [17] or to use the semantics of a Markov process to reason about the reliability or performance characteristics of the given system [18]. But these extensions of the B-method cannot be used to reason about generic mathematical expressions for probabilistic or statistical properties. Similarly, such formalisms are not mature enough yet to model and reason about all different kinds of continuous probability distributions. Due to the continuous nature of the MCS, both the probabilistic model checking and Event-B based techniques cannot be used to capture their true behaviour and thus, to the best of our knowledge, the use of probabilistic and quantitative assessment for the formal verification of MCS is almost non-existent.

The aforementioned limitations can be overcome by using higher-order logic theorem proving for conducting the formal probabilistic analysis. We can capture the true continuous and randomized behaviour of the given system in higher-order logic by leveraging upon its expressiveness. Moreover, generic mathematical expressions corresponding to the probabilistic and statistical properties of interest can be formally verified within the sound core of a theorem prover. Due to the formal nature of the models and properties and the inherent soundness of the theorem proving approach, probabilistic analysis carried out in this way will be free from any approximation and precision issues. The foremost criteria for conducting the formal probabilistic analysis of MCS in a theorem prover is the availability of a formalized probability theory, which will in turn allow us to express probabilistic notions in higher-order logic, and formal reasoning support for the probability distribution and statistical properties of random variables in a theorem prover.

Various higher-order-logic formalizations of probability theory can be found in the literature, e.g., [19,20,21]. The formalizations by Mhamdi [20] and Hölzl [21] are based on extended real numbers (including $\pm\infty$) and also include the formalization of Lebesgue integral for reasoning about statistical properties. This way, they are more mature than Hurd's [19] formalization of measure and probability theories, which is based on simple real numbers and offers a limited support for reasoning about statistical properties [22].

However, the former formalizations do not support a particular probability space like the one presented in Hurd's work. Due to this distinguishing feature, Hurd's formalization [19] has been utilized to verify sampling algorithms of a number of commonly used discrete and continuous random variables based on their probabilistic and statistical properties [22]. Since formalized random variables and their formally verified properties play a vital role in the probabilistic analysis of MCS systems, as illustrated later in this paper, we propose to utilize Hurd's formalization of measure and probability theories. Hurd's theories are already available in the HOL4 theorem prover therefore the current work make an extensive use of them.

3   Background

A brief introduction to safety cases and high-order logic theorem proving using the HOL4 theorem prover is provided in this section to facilitate the understanding of the paper.

3.1   Safety Case

A safety case, as described by [3], is an evidence that provides a convincing and valid argument about the safety of a system in a given domain. The main elements of a safety case are the claim about a property, its evidence, and its argument.

A claim is usually about a system meeting certain properties, such as reliability, availability, safety and accuracy. An evidence provides the basis of a safety argument. This can be either facts, assumptions, or even sub-claims. Arguments link an evidence to claims. An argument can either be deterministic, probabilistic, or qualitative. The choice of the argument will depend upon the available evidence and the type of claim. System reliability claims are often justified in terms of probability of failure of its components. Arguments can be based on the design of a system, its development process, or simulated and prior field experiences.

3.2   HOL4 Theorem Prover

HOL4 is an interactive theorem prover that allows conducting proofs in higher-order logic, which is implemented by using the simple type theory of Church [23] along with Hindley-Milner polymorphism [24]. The logic in HOL4 is represented by Meta Language (ML), which is a strongly-typed functional programming language. The core of HOL4 consists of only 5 axioms and 8 inference rules.

Building upon these foundations, HOL4 has been successfully used to formalize many classical mathematical theories and verify a wide variety of software and hardware systems.

HOL4 allows four kinds of terms, i.e., constants, variables, function applications, and lambda-expressions. It also supports polymorphism, i.e., types containing type variables, which is a distinguishing feature of higher-order logic. Semantically, types are denoted by sets and terms are denoted by memberships of these sets. Formulas, sequents, axioms, and theorems are represented by terms of Boolean types.

The formal definitions and theorems can be stored as a HOL4 theory file in computers. These theories can then be reused by loading them in a HOL4 session. This kind of reusability feature is very helpful in reducing the human interaction as we do not have to go through the tedious process of regenerating already available proofs using the basic axioms and primitive inference rules. Various classical mathematical results have been formalized and saved as HOL4 theories. The HOL4 theories that are of particular interest to the current work include the theory of Booleans, lists, positive integers and *real* analysis, measure and probability theory. One of the primary motivations of selecting the HOL4 theorem prover for our work was to benefit from these existing mathematical theories.

The formal proofs in HOL4 can be conducted in both forward and backward manner. In the forward proof method, the previously proven theorems are used along with the inference rules to verify the desired theorem. The forward proof method usually requires the exact details of a proof in advance and is thus not very straightforward. In the backward proof method, ML functions called *tactics* are used to break the main proof goals into simple sub-goals. Some of these intermediate sub-goals can be discharged by matching axioms or assumptions or by applying built-in automatic decision procedures. This process is repeated until all the sub goals are discharged, which concludes the proof for the given theorem.

4   Formalization of Probabilistic Algorithms

Building upon the recently developed measure-theoretic formalization of probability theory [19], we can conduct formal probabilistic analysis [25] in the sound core of a higher-order logic theorem prover. The system can be modelled as a probabilistic algorithm where its randomized components can be specified using appropriate random variables and its probabilistic and statistical properties can be verified using the proven probability axioms. The ability of higher-order logic to formalize continuous and randomized systems, and to verify all sorts of probabilistic and statistical properties makes it the meritorious approach for the formal probabilistic analysis of MCS.

The unpredictable components of a system can be modelled as higher-order logic functions that make random choices by using the required number of bits from an infinite sequence of random bits $\mathbb{B}^{\infty}$. These functions return the result along with the remaining portion of the infinite Boolean sequence to be used by other programs. Thus, the data type of a probabilistic algorithm that takes a parameter of type α and returns a value of type β is:

$$\mathcal{F} : \alpha \to \mathbb{B}^\infty \to \beta \times \mathbb{B}^\infty$$

For illustration, consider the example of a Bernoulli($\frac{1}{2}$) random variable that returns 1 or 0 with equal probability $\frac{1}{2}$. It can be formally modelled as follows:

⊢ bit s = (if shd s then 1 else 0, stl s)

where variable s represents the infinite Boolean sequence and functions shd and stl return the *head* and *tail* of their sequence argument, respectively. Probabilistic algorithms can be expressed in a more compact way without explicitly mentioning the Boolean sequence that is passed around by using more general state-transforming monads where the states are the infinite Boolean sequences.

⊢ ∀ a s. unit a s = (a,s)
⊢ ∀ f g s. bind f g s = g (fst (f s))
          (snd (f s))

The unit operator is used to lift values to the monad, and the bind is the monadic analogue of function application. The function *bit* can be defined using the monadic notation as:

⊢ bit_monad = bind sdest
          (λb.if b then unit 1 else unit 0)

where sdest provides the head and tail of a sequence as a pair (*shd* s, *stl* s).

Hurd [19] constructed a probability space on infinite Boolean sequence and formalized a measure theoretic formalization of probability theory in the higher-order-logic theorem prover HOL. Building upon these foundations, we can verify all the basic laws of probability as well as probabilistic properties of any algorithm that is specified using the infinite Boolean sequence. For example, we can verify the Probability Mass Function (PMF) of the function bit as:

⊢ $\mathbb{P}$ {s | fst (bit s) = 1} = $\frac{1}{2}$

where the HOL function fst selects the first component of a pair and $\mathbb{P}$ is the probability function that maps sets of infinite Boolean sequences to real numbers between 0 and 1 .

Just like the bit function, we can formalize and verify any random variable using the above mentioned approach. For example, the Bernoulli and Uniform random variables have been verified using the following PMF relations [19]:

Lemma 1: *PMF of Bernoulli(p) Random Variable*
⊢ ∀p. 0 ≤ p ∧ p ≤ 1 ⇒
     $\mathbb{P}$ {s | fst (bern_rv p s)=1} = p

Lemma 2: *PMF of Uniform(m) Random Variable*

⊢ ∀m x. x < m ⇒
    ℙ {s | fst (unif_rv m s) = x} = $\frac{1}{m}$

The function ber_rv models an experiment with two outcomes; 1 and 0, whereas p represents the probability of obtaining a 1. Similarly, the function unif_rv assigns equal probability to each element in the set $\{0, 1, \cdots, (m-1)\}$ and thus ranges over a finite number of positive integers. Such pre-formalized random variables and their proven properties greatly facilitate the analysis of MCS as, in most cases, the unpredictable nature of its components can be expressed in terms of well-known random variables.

Expectation theory also plays a vital role in probabilistic analysis as it is lot easier to judge performance issues based on the average of a characteristic, which is a single number, rather than its distribution function. The expectation of a discrete random variable can be defined as a higher-order logic function as follows [26]:

Definition 1: *Expectation of Discrete Random Variables*

⊢ ∀R. expec R =
    suminf (λn.n * ℙ {s | fst (R s) = n})

where suminf represents the HOL formalization of the infinite summation of a real sequence f, i.e., $\lim_{k \to \infty} \sum_{n=0}^{k} f(n)$. The function expec can be used to verify the expectation of any discrete random variable that attains values in positive integers. For example, the higher-order logic theorem corresponding to the expectation of the Bernoulli random variable has been formally verified in [26] as follows:

Lemma 3: *Expectation of Bernoulli(p) Random Variable*

⊢ ∀p. 0 ≤ p ∧ p ≤ 1 ⇒
    expec (λs.bern_rv p s) = p

where $(\lambda x.t)$ represents a lambda abstraction function in HOL that maps its argument x to $t(x)$.

The continuous random variables can also be formalized by building upon the above mentioned measure-theoretic formalization of probability theory. The main idea behind their formalization is to transform a Standard Uniform random variable to other continuous random variables based on the principles of the non-uniform random number generation [22]. The Standard Uniform random variable can be modeled by using the formalization approach for discrete random variables and the formalization of the mathematical concept of limit of a *real* sequence [27]:

$$\lim_{n \to \infty} (\lambda n. \sum_{k=0}^{n-1} (\frac{1}{2})^{k+1} X_k) \tag{1}$$

where X_k denotes the outcome of the kth random bit; *True* or *False* represented as 1 or 0, respectively. This formalization [22] is used along with the formalization of the CDF function to formally verify the correctness of the Inverse

Transform Method (ITM), i.e., a well known non-uniform random generation technique for generating non-uniform random variables for continuous probability distributions for which the inverse of the CDF can be represented in a closed mathematical form. Formally, it can be verified for a random variable X with CDF F using the Standard Uniform random variable U as follows [22].

$$Pr(F^{-1}(U) \leq x) = F(x) \tag{2}$$

The formalized Standard Uniform random variable can now be used to formally specify any continuous random variable for which the inverse of the CDF can be expressed in a closed mathematical form as $X = F^{-1}(U)$. Whereas, its CDF can be verified based on simple arithmetic reasoning, using the formally verified ITM, given in Equation (2). This approach has been successfully utilized to formalize and verify Exponential, Uniform, Rayleigh and Triangular random variables [22].

The expectation for a continuous random variable X is defined on a probability space (Ω, Σ, P) [22], is as follows:

$$E[X] = \int_\Omega X dP \tag{3}$$

where the integral represents the Lebesgue integral. In order to facilitate the formal reasoning about statistical properties of continuous random variables, the following two alternate expressions for the expectation have been verified [22]. The first expression is for the case when the given continuous random variable X is bounded in the positive interval $[a, b]$

$$E[X] = \lim_{n \to \infty} \sum_{i=0}^{2^n - 1} (a + \frac{i}{2^n}(b - a)) \\ \mathbb{P}\left\{ a + \frac{i}{2^n}(b - a) \leq X < a + \frac{i+1}{2^n}(b - a) \right\} \tag{4}$$

and the second one is for an unbounded positive random variable.

$$E[X] = \lim_{n \to \infty} \sum_{i=0}^{n2^n - 1} \frac{i}{2^n} \mathbb{P}\left\{ \frac{i}{2^n} \leq X < \frac{i+1}{2^n} \right\} + n\mathbb{P}(X \geq n) \tag{5}$$

Both of the above expressions do not involve any concepts from Lebesgue integration theory and are based on the well-known arithmetic operations like summation, limit of a real sequence, etc. Thus, users can simply utilize them, instead of Equation (3), to reason about the expectation properties of their random variables and gain the benefits of the original Lebesgue based definition. The formal verification details for these expressions are given in [22]. These expressions are further utilized to verify the expected values of Uniform, Triangular and Exponential random variables [22].

The above mentioned formalization plays a pivotal role for the formal probabilistic analysis of MCS. In the next section, we illustrate the usefulness and practical effectiveness of the foundational formalization, presented in this section, by providing a step-wise approach for analyzing a MCS using HOL4.

5   The Triptych Analysis Approach

Figure 2 depicts the proposed triptych formal probabilistic analysis approach. It primarily builds upon the existing formalization of probability theory (including the infinite Boolean sequence space), and commonly used random variables and their proved properties. The approach is as follows:

1. The first step is to formalize the true behaviour of the given MCS including its unpredictable and continuous components in higher-order logic. The randomized behaviours would be captured using appropriate discrete [19] and continuous random variables [22] and the continuous aspects can be modeled using the formalized real numbers [27].
2. The second step is to utilize the formally specified model, i.e., the higher-order-logic function that represents the behavior of the given MCS, to formally express desired system properties as higher-order logic proof goals. Due to the random nature of the model, the properties are also either probabilistic or statistical. For this purpose, the existing higher-order-logic functions of probability [19], expectation and variance [22] can be utilized.
3. The third and final step is to formally verify the developed higher-order logic proof goals using a theorem prover. The existing theorems corresponding to probability distribution functions, expectation and variance of commonly used random variables [19,22] greatly facilitate in minimizing the required user interaction to prove these goals.

We now illustrate the utilization and practical effectiveness of this approach by providing a simple case study.

6   Collision Detection in Multi-robot Systems: A Case Study

Our case study is based on multi-robot systems described in [28]. The use of such systems is on rise in the development of MCS. They offer numerous advantages over single-robot systems, e.g., more spacial coverage, redundancy, reconfigurability and throughput. However, the design of these robots involves many challenges due to their potentially unknown and dynamic environments. Moreover, due to their autonomous nature, avoiding collisions with other robots of the system is also a major challenge. The number of robots and the arena size is chosen at the design time such that potential collisions are minimized. However, estimating these parameters is not a straightforward task due to the unpredictable nature of the potential collisions. Probabilistic techniques can help in this realm.

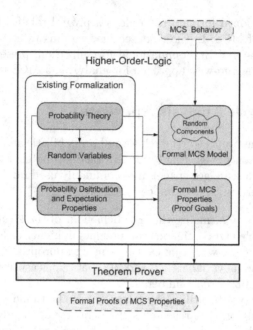

Fig. 2. The triptych probabilistic analysis of MCS

We are interested in finding the average number of collisions for the given system with k mobile robots moving in an arena of n distinct locations. A collision happens when two or more robots are on the same location at the same time. The randomized behavior of the collision can be modelled as a Bernoulli random variable X with two outcomes, 1 or 0, as follows:

$$X_{ij} = \begin{cases} 1 \text{ if robot } i \text{ and } j \text{ are using the same location;} \\ 0 \text{ otherwise.} \end{cases} \qquad (6)$$

corresponding to each pair (i, j) of the k robots in the group such that $0 \leq i \leq j < k$. We can reasonably assume that the location of any robot at any particular time instant is uniformly and independently distributed among the n available slots. Under these conditions, the total number of collisions can be computed as follows:

$$\sum_{i=0}^{k-1} \sum_{j=i+1}^{k-1} X_{ij} \qquad (7)$$

The formal probabilistic analysis of the above mentioned collision detection problem can now be done by following the triptych approach outlined in Figure 2. The first step is to formalize the system in higher-order logic. The behaviour of the given system can be expressed in terms of the Bernoulli and Uniform random variables using the following recursive functions.

Definition 2: *Collision Detection in Multi-Robot System*
```
⊢ (∀ n. col_detect_helper 0 n = unit 0) ∧
  (∀ k n. col_detect_helper(k+1) n =
   bind (col_detect_helper k n)
   (λa. bind (bern_rv
   (ℙ{s | fst(unif_rv n s) =
     fst(unif_rv n (snd (unif_rv n s)))}))
     (λb. unit (b + a))))
⊢ (∀ n. col_detect 0 n = unit 0) ∧
  (∀ k n. col_detect (k + 1) n =
   bind (col_detect k n)
     (λa. bind
     (col_detect_helper k n)
     (λb. unit (b + a))))
```

The functions `col_detect_helper` and `col_detect` model the inner and outer summations of Equation (7), respectively. The variable `bern_rv` models the randomness given in Equation (6), with the probability of success equal to the probability of the event when two independent Uniform(n) random variables generate the same values. The two Uniform random variables in the above definition correspond to the locations of two robots in the system based on the above mentioned assumptions. The independence between the two Uniform(n) random variables is ensured because of the fact that the second uniform random variable on the right-hand-side of the equality utilizes the remaining portion of the infinite Boolean sequence from the first Uniform(n) random variable that is on the left-hand-side of the equality. Thus, the function `col_detect` accepts two parameters k and n, which represents the number of robots in the system and the number of available locations in the areana, respectively, and it returns the total number of pairs of robots having the same location at a given time, which is the number of collisions.

The second step is to formalize the property of interest in higher-order logic. We are interested in the average number of collisions and that can be expressed using the expectation function, given in Definition 1, as follows:

Theorem 1: *Average Number of Collisions*
$$⊢ ∀k\ n.\ 0 < n ∧ 2 ≤ k ⇒$$
$$\text{expec (col\_detect } k\ n) = \frac{k(k-1)}{2n}$$

The assumptions in the above theorem ensure that the number of locations are more than 0 and the population is at least 2 in order to have 1 pair at minimum.

The third step is to verify the proof goal in a theorem prover. We verify it using the HOL4 theorem prover. The interactive reasoning process was primarily based on performing induction on the variable k, Lemmas 1, 2 and 3, and some formally verified probability theory laws like the linearity of expectation. The manually developed proof script for this verification relied heavily on already existing formalizations of probability theory [19] and random variables [22]. Theorem 1 provides very useful insights into the collision detection in a multi-robot system. It can be clearly observed that the expected number of collisions would be less than 1 if $k(k-1) \leq 2n$. This means that if we have $\sqrt{2n} + 1$ or more robots in the system, then on average we can expect at least one collision.

The above example clearly demonstrates the effectiveness of the proposed approach in analysing MCS. Due to the formal nature of the model and the inherent soundness of higher-order logic theorem proving, we have been able to verify the desired property with full precision. Same results could not be obtained using simulation or animation techniques, neither the problem could be described as a Markov chain and thus could not be analysed using a probabilistic model checker. Another distinguishing feature of Theorem 1 is its generic nature and the universal quantification on all the variables. Thus, the theorem can be instantiated with any possible values to obtain the average number of collisions for any specific system. Finally, the theorem explicitly provides all the assumptions under which it has been verified. This is usually not the case when we are verifying theorems by hand using the traditional paper-and-pencil proof methods as mathematicians may forget to pen down all the required assumptions that are required for the validity of their analysis. These missing assumptions may lead to erroneous designs as well and thus the proposed approach overcomes this problem.

These additional benefits have been gained at the cost of time and effort spent while formalizing the system and formally reasoning about its properties, by the user. But, the fact that we were building on top of already verified results in the theorem prover helped significantly in this regard as the analysis, described in this section, only consumed approximately 500 lines of HOL code and 30 man-hours by an expert HOL user.

7   Conclusion

We have presented a framework that enables us to unify the formal verification technique with quantitative reasoning for the engineering of safe and reliable MCS. The point is that in addition to analyse the absolute correctness, which at times is not possible, a probabilistic analysis can provide a better insight about the model. In this fashion, it is easier for stakeholders to obtain a probability of occurrence of a hazard in terms of the likelihood of components failures. We can now provide an evidence, as a certification argument, that the probability of violation of a safety requirement is sufficiently and acceptably small. Moreover, given the soundness of higher-order logic theorem proving, the analysis results are completely reliable. Similarly, the high expressiveness of higher-order logic enables us to analyse a wide range of MCS. Thus, the proposed approach can be beneficial for the analysis of industrial MCS where safety and reliability are coveted system traits.

Acknowledgement. This paper has been partially written with the support of the project Vertical Model Integration (VMI) that is financed within the program "Regionale Wettbewerbsfähigkeit OÖ 2007-2013" by the European Fund for Regional Development as well as the State of Upper Austria.

References

1. Dźwiarek, M.: An analysis of accidents caused by improper functioning of machine control systems. International Journal of Occupational Safety and Ergonomics 10(2), 129–136 (2004)
2. Heinrich, H.: Industrial Accident Prevention: A Scientific Approach. McGraw Hill Inc. (1941)
3. Bishop, P., Bloomfield, R.: A methodology for safety case development. In: Safety-Critical System Symposium, Birmingham, UK. Springer (1998)
4. Mashkoor, A., Jacquot, J.-P.: Stepwise validation of formal specifications. In: 18th Asia-Pacific Software Engineering Conference (APSEC 2011), Ho Chi Minh City, Vietnam. IEEE (2011)
5. Yang, F., Jacquot, J.-P.: Scaling up with Event-B: A case study. In: Bobaru, M., Havelund, K., Holzmann, G.J., Joshi, R. (eds.) NFM 2011. LNCS, vol. 6617, pp. 438–452. Springer, Heidelberg (2011)
6. Panesar-Walawege, R., Sabetzadeh, M., Briand, L., Coq, T.: Characterizing the chain of evidence for software safety cases: A conceptual model based on the IEC 61508 standard. In: 3rd International Conference on Software Testing, Verification and Validation (ICST 2010), pp. 335–344 (2010)
7. Fong, E., Kass, M., Rhodes, T., Boland, F.: Structured assurance case methodology for assessing software trustworthiness. In: 4th International Conference on Secure Software Integration and Reliability Improvement Companion (SSIRI-C 2010), pp. 32–33 (2010)
8. Graydon, P.J., Knight, J.C., Strunk, E.A.: Assurance-based development of critical systems. In: 37th International Conference on Dependable Systems and Networks (DSN 2007), pp. 347–357. IEEE, Washington, DC (2007)
9. Rushby, J.: A safety-case approach for certifying adaptive systems. In: AIAA Infotech@Aerospace Conference, American Institute of Aeronautics and Astronautics (2009)
10. Rushby, J.: Formalism in safety cases. In: Dale, C., Anderson, T. (eds.) 18th Safety-Critical Systems Symposium, Bristol, UK, pp. 3–17. Springer (2010)
11. Herencia-Zapana, H., Hagen, G., Narkawicz, A.: Formalizing probabilistic safety claims. In: Bobaru, M., Havelund, K., Holzmann, G.J., Joshi, R. (eds.) NFM 2011. LNCS, vol. 6617, pp. 162–176. Springer, Heidelberg (2011)
12. Baier, C., Haverkort, B., Hermanns, H., Katoen, J.P.: Model Checking Algorithms for Continuous time Markov Chains. IEEE Transactions on Software Engineering 29(4), 524–541 (2003)
13. Rutten, J., Kwaiatkowska, M., Normal, G., Parker, D.: Mathematical Techniques for Analyzing Concurrent and Probabilistic Systems. CRM Monograph Series, vol. 23. American Mathematical Society (2004)
14. Kwiatkowska, M., Norman, G., Parker, D.: Prism: Probabilistic symbolic model checker. In: Field, T., Harrison, P.G., Bradley, J., Harder, U. (eds.) TOOLS 2002. LNCS, vol. 2324, pp. 200–204. Springer, Heidelberg (2002)
15. Abrial, J.-R.: The B Book. Cambridge University Press (1996)
16. Abrial, J.-R.: Modelling in Event-B: System and Software Engineering. Cambridge University Press (2010)
17. Hallerstede, S., Hoang, T.S.: Qualitative probabilistic modelling in Event-B. In: Davies, J., Gibbons, J. (eds.) IFM 2007. LNCS, vol. 4591, pp. 293–312. Springer, Heidelberg (2007)

18. Tarasyuk, A., Troubitsyna, E., Laibinis, L.: Towards probabilistic modelling in Event-B. In: Méry, D., Merz, S. (eds.) IFM 2010. LNCS, vol. 6396, pp. 275–289. Springer, Heidelberg (2010)
19. Hurd, J.: Formal verification of probabilistic algorithms. PhD Thesis, University of Cambridge, Cambridge, UK (2002)
20. Mhamdi, T., Hasan, O., Tahar, S.: Formalization of Entropy Measures in HOL. In: van Eekelen, M., Geuvers, H., Schmaltz, J., Wiedijk, F. (eds.) ITP 2011. LNCS, vol. 6898, pp. 233–248. Springer, Heidelberg (2011)
21. Hölzl, J., Heller, A.: Three Chapters of Measure Theory in Isabelle/HOL. In: van Eekelen, M., Geuvers, H., Schmaltz, J., Wiedijk, F. (eds.) ITP 2011. LNCS, vol. 6898, pp. 135–151. Springer, Heidelberg (2011)
22. Hasan, O., Tahar, S.: Formal Probabilistic Analysis: A Higher-order Logic based approach. In: Frappier, M., Glässer, U., Khurshid, S., Laleau, R., Reeves, S. (eds.) ABZ 2010. LNCS, vol. 5977, pp. 2–19. Springer, Heidelberg (2010)
23. Church, A.: A Formulation of the Simple Theory of Types. Journal of Symbolic Logic 5, 56–68 (1940)
24. Milner, R.: A Theory of Type Polymorphism in Programming. Journal of Computer and System Sciences 17, 348–375 (1977)
25. Mashkoor, A., Hasan, O.: Formal probabilistic analysis of cyber-physical transportation systems. In: Murgante, B., Gervasi, O., Misra, S., Nedjah, N., Rocha, A.M.A.C., Taniar, D., Apduhan, B.O. (eds.) ICCSA 2012, Part III. LNCS, vol. 7335, pp. 419–434. Springer, Heidelberg (2012)
26. Hasan, O., Tahar, S.: Using theorem proving to verify expectation and variance for discrete random variables. J. Autom. Reasoning 41(3-4), 295–323 (2008)
27. Harrison, J.: Theorem Proving with the Real Numbers. Springer (1998)
28. Parker, L.E.: Multiple mobile robot teams, path planning and motion coordination. In: Encyclopedia of Complexity and Systems Science, pp. 5783–5800. Springer (2009)
29. Younes, H.L.S.: Ymer: A statistical model checker. In: Etessami, K., Rajamani, S.K. (eds.) CAV 2005. LNCS, vol. 3576, pp. 429–433. Springer, Heidelberg (2005)
30. Sen, K., Viswanathan, M., Agha, G.: Vesta: A statistical model-checker and analyzer for probabilistic systems. In: Second International Conference on the Quantitative Evaluation of Systems, pp. 251–252 (September 2005)

Experimental Investigation in the Impact on Security of the Release Order of Defensive Algorithms

Suliman A. Alsuhibany, Ahmad Alonaizi, Charles Morisset,
Chris Smith, and Aad van Moorsel

Centre for Cybercrime and Computer Security
Newcastle University, UK, School of Computing Science
Claremont Tower, NE1 7RU, United Kingdom
{suliman.alsuhibany,a.alonaizi,charles.morisset,
aad.vanmoorsel}@ncl.ac.uk

Abstract. In the practical use of security mechanisms such as CAPTCHAs and spam filters, attackers and defenders exchange 'victories,' each celebrating (temporary) success in breaking and defending. While most of security mechanisms rely on a single algorithm as a defense mechanism, we propose an approach based on a set of algorithms as a defense mechanism. When studying sets of algorithms various issues arise about how to construct the algorithms and in which order or in which combination to release them. In this paper, we consider the question of whether the order in which a set of defensive algorithms is released has a significant impact on the time taken by attackers to break the combined set of algorithms. The rationale behind our approach is that attackers learn from their attempts, and that the release schedule of defensive mechanisms can be adjusted so as to impair that learning process. This paper introduces this problem. We show that our hypothesis holds for an experiment using several simplified but representative spam filter algorithms—that is, the order in which spam filters are released has a statistically significant impact on the time attackers take to break all algorithms.

Keywords: Release Order of Defensive Algorithms, learning, Experimentation, Security and Protection.

1   Introduction

Many security solutions are based on algorithms that aim to protect system resources from misuse. These algorithms encode a set of rules that aim to characterize and recognize attempts of misuse, and prevent any adverse effect on system resources. Examples of such algorithms include spam-filters, CAPTCHAs and Anti-Phishing solutions. As attackers interact with the system, they receive feedback that augments their knowledge of the rules used by the system to characterize misuse. Accordingly, they are able to adapt their future interactions in accordance with this augmented knowledge, increasing their ability to break the defensive algorithms, until eventually reaching the point where the security mechanism is broken: the spam-filter rules are overridden, the CAPTCHAs are automatically deciphered, etc.

A. Cuzzocrea et al. (Eds.): CD-ARES 2013 Workshops, LNCS 8128, pp. 321–336, 2013.

Once a mechanism is broken, the security officer must deploy another one, which will eventually be in turn broken, leading the officer to deploy a new mechanism, and so on and so forth [7]. Deploying a defensive mechanism has a cost, for example, the cost of deploying a SPAM filter within a particular organization has been calculated at about fifteen thousand euro for the first year [22]. Furthermore, the security officer must usually work within a given budget constraint, and has therefore a limited number of defense mechanisms to deploy. This raises the question whether we can better plan the release of defensive algorithms, so as to extend the period for which the combined set of algorithms is effective? For instance, could it be useful to break up one defensive algorithm into multiple algorithms, and release them one by one? Or could it be useful to reorder the release of the various algorithms to maximize the overall time taken by the attacker to break all algorithms?

In this paper, we are interested to address the following research question: *"Does the order in which different defensive mechanisms are released impact the time an attacker needs to break each one of them?"* The main reasoning behind considering this question may be answered affirmatively is that the time it takes an attacker to break a defensive algorithms may depend on what the attacker has learned from earlier successful attacks on similar algorithms. If that is true, one may be able to defend better against attacks by impairing the process of learning of attackers. There may be many ways in which one can try to achieve this, but in this paper we consider the most direct implication of this reasoning, namely that the order in which defensive algorithms are released may impact the learning process.

We experimentally test the hypothesis that the release order matters. We conduct an experiment with simplified but representative spam filter algorithms, asking two groups of twenty subjects to break these algorithms. The algorithms are presented in a reversed order to the respective groups. By analyzing these groups, the order of release can have a statistically significance influence in the time required by an attacker to break a mechanism. In other words, there is potential to improve the security of a system by optimizing the order in which the defensive algorithms are released.

The work presented here contributes to the effort captured recently in the term 'science of security', to emphasize scientific and empirical studies for security mechanisms rather than designing a set of best practices. In this regard, an important contribution of this work is the method and protocol used to answer the research question.

In addition, the effect of presentation orders on the learning mechanism is not new. Previous researches in the field of education and psychology provide several insights into the effect of presentation orders [15, 16, 17, 20]. However, to the best of our knowledge, we are the first to address this particular issue of the release order strategy. There exists a considerable amount of related work considering the attack and defense interaction as a game-theoretic problem, but these formulations do not fit exactly with our approach. We refer to Section 6 for a further discussion.

The rest of this paper is organized as follows. Section 2 describes the problem as precise as possible through a detailed system model. Section 3 describes the experimental study, and its results are presented in Section 4. The discussion is presented in Section 5. Section 6 discusses related work. Finally, we conclude with overall discussions and future work in Section 7.

2   Problem Definition

In order to precisely define the problem under consideration, we start by providing an abstract system model of the attack scenario, involving the attacker and the system as shown in Figure 1. It describes a general class of security solutions which include CAPTCHAs, certain spam filters, intrusion tolerance algorithms, etc. This class of mechanisms is characterized by an intelligent defensive algorithm being attacked and eventually broken, and then being replaced by a new intelligent defensive mechanism, etc. Furthermore, this model provides the basis of the experimental study that we present in Section 3.

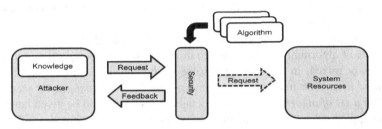

Fig. 1. System Model

System Resources. In the system model, we assume a finite set of resources that can be used, e.g. communication or computation resources. The pool of security algorithms is contained by a security layer deployed to protect the system resources from misuse, e.g. excessively high consumption or consumption for unacceptable purposes. These algorithms classify requests to the system as acceptable or unacceptable based upon a set of rules. If a request is classified as acceptable then the request proceeds and the system resources are consumed. A request that is classified as unacceptable cannot proceed through the security layer, and feedback is provided to the user regarding the failed request.

Attacker. An attacker is an agent (human or computational) that attempts to misuse system resources. The attacker makes requests for the system resources, which pass through the security layer as described above. The attacker has some prior *knowledge* about the rules used to classify request, and attempts to design requests to be classified as acceptable. On each failed attempt, the attacker receives some feedback from the system. This feedback may be a simple Boolean response, or may include reasons for the failure. The attacker can add this feedback to his knowledge, and use this knowledge to inform his subsequent requests. By repeatedly performing this knowledge acquisition process[1], the attacker can derive the rules that are used by algorithms to classify requests. This includes both the parameters used, and the values of these parameters. The attacker can then misuse system resources by sending requests that are structured in such a way that they fulfill the rules of the algorithm in the security layer. In that case, we consider the algorithm 'broken'.

---

[1] In the education context, e.g. [23] stated that the learning is driven by a process of inquiry.

Security Layer. To maintain the security of the system, the security layer must be updated. Within this update, the algorithm used by the security layer is replaced by another algorithm from the pool to encapsulate a different set of rules such that requests that are misusing system resources are no longer permitted to pass through the security layer. The attacker must repeat the process of knowledge acquisition in order to determine the new classification rules, such that he can continue sending requests to misuse system resources. This process of learning takes time and the overall aim of the algorithms is to maximize the time until all are broken.

Algorithms. The selection of algorithm when updating the security layer determines the subsequent security of the system. In particular, a set of algorithms D, $D = \{d_1, d_2, ..., d_n\}$, $n > 1$, $d_n \in D$, represents the security layer of the system. Each of these algorithms has a specific robustness level $dr_i \in DR$. This robustness includes a number of rules $dr_i = \{r_1, r_2, ..., r_n\}$, $n \geq 1$ to protect the system. Based on the rules of an algorithm, a set of algorithm is classified into three types: overlapping rules, not overlapping rules or mixed. In the first type, some of the algorithms are subset from each other $dr_i \subset dr_{i+1}$. The importance of this type can be in *breaking up a secure algorithm into a set of algorithm*, and more details about this would be given latter. In the not overlapping rules type, all the algorithms are independent $dr_i \neq dr_{i+1}$. The importance of this type can be in using *variance algorithms*. The third type is that using mixed overlapping rules and not overlapping rules algorithms $dr_i \subset dr_{i+1}$ and $dr_{i+1} \neq dr_{i+2}$. The importance of this type can be, in addition to the importance of the first and second type, releasing an independent algorithm between dependent algorithms may *impair the attacker's learning process*.

The order in which algorithms are released may thus be important. The longer it takes for the attacker to acquire the necessary knowledge regarding classification, the longer the system is protected from misuse. For instance, in the pool of algorithms that can be selected, there may exist algorithms that have some overlapping or similar rules. The question for the defender then is in what order to release these algorithms so that the time until all algorithms are broken is maximized.

3   Experimental Study

In order to test the hypothesis that the time spent on breaking a set of defensive algorithms depends on the order in which these algorithms are released, we conducted a controlled laboratory experiment in which subjects were asked to break a set of three specifically created spam-filter algorithms. The main hypothesis under test is:

H_1 – The time it takes to break a series of algorithms is dependent on the order in which the algorithms are released

We like to point out that the objective of our experiment is not to say anything definitive about spam filter algorithms. We designed bespoke spam filters that would fit the purposes of our experiment, although we have ventured to create an intuitively appealing experiment that has various elements in common with traditional spam filters. Further, an automated program can be used to break the algorithms. However, a form of understanding of a human learning process can be seen clearly by sending e-mails to evade a spam filter, as automated approaches are abstractions of this human learning process that require encoding by human.

3.1   Experiment Setup

The experiment involves subjects to act as potential attackers carrying out attacks on a test system, within which a number of different security algorithms have been deployed.

Experiment Design. In order to evaluate the time needed to break the algorithms, we decided to use a *between-subjects* design. That is, we have two sets of subjects breaking a series of defensive algorithms where the order is different between the groups. This type of design ensures that the exact same algorithms are used in each experiment condition, and that there is no unnecessary confounding factor biasing the results (at the cost of recruiting relatively many participants). The main independent variable for this experiment is the algorithm order. The time consumed to break each algorithm and the numbers of trials are the dependent variables.

The participants are randomly assigned to one of the following two experimental groups:

- **Group 1:** The order of algorithms for this group was: A1, A2 then A3.
- **Group 2:** The order of algorithms for this group was: A2, A1 then A3.

Specifics about the algorithms will be given in the remainder of this section.

Attackers. A nontrivial problem was to find potential attackers. The aim was attackers that could be considered to be non-specialists. Whilst specialist attackers or security experts could have been recruited, they would give us information mostly about where and how our particular algorithms needed to be improved and less about learning. Forty students were recruited for this experiment (34 male and 6 female, something we did not consider relevant for our experiment). The typical age range of subjects was 24-33 with 4 participants in the group 40+. The subjects of this experiment were 40 master and PhD students from the School of computing science and other schools in Newcastle University. 37 subjects have technical backgrounds (majoring in computer science and engineering), and the remaining 3 subjects nontechnical (in linguistics). It is important to note that because our aim was to recruit non-specialists attackers to observe the learning acquisition, the inconsistency-bias produced by attackers' background is reduced. In addition, as stated in [15, 23] the learning process is achieved regardless the backgrounds.

System. A challenge in designing the experiment is to design a system that can be breached by ordinary people in a matter of minutes. We found that spam filters could offer a very good model for our experimental requirements. Although as mentioned we do not claim or attempt to study and derive results for spam filters themselves, we do believe the simple spam filters we consider have enough similarities with reality to act as an example of the class of systems that we introduced in Section 2.

We developed a web-based system on which to perform the experiment. A Web application was developed, which enables each participant to perform a registration process (e.g. choosing a username, password and educational background), sign a consent form, and read a brief introductory page with necessary information (e.g. description of the experiment, experiment factors, the participant goal, applied method on how to defeat a content-based spam-filter). The participant can then begin the experimental process, interacting with the spam-filter algorithms. The main idea is that the participants try to send e-mails that pass through the spam filters—we describe this in more detail in Section 3.2. The system records all attempts and the time taken by each participant to break each algorithm in each session.

Algorithms. The rationale behind the defensive spam-filter algorithms we constructed is as follows. A simple algorithm A1 acts as base algorithm and a more complicated algorithm A2 extends the rules used by A1. In other words, the rules in A1 are a subset of A2, which we believe is the first case to consider when one wants to test the hypothesis. The third algorithm A3 does not share any rule neither with A1 nor with A2, and acts as a simple independent algorithm. Hence, we challenge our hypothesis H_1 by the two following questions:

Q_1 – Do G1 and G2 break A1 and A2 within a similar amount of time?

Q_2 – Do G1 and G2 break A3 within a similar amount of time?[2]

We will answer in Section 4 negatively to Q_1 and positively to Q_2. We now describe the specific algorithms A1, A2 and A3, as well as pseudo code describing their operation. Modern density-based spam filter [9] forms the base to implement the algorithms. Note that some of the symbol names being used in the pseudo code are given in Table 1.

Table 1. Symbols used in pseudo code and their values in the experiments

Symbol	Meaning	Value
D	Spam threshold	100
N	Number of hash values for each email	100
S_1	Similarity threshold "Algorithm 1&3"	75%
S_2	Similarity threshold "Algorithm 2"	45%

Algorithm 1 (A1). This algorithm is a simple implementation of the proposal of [9] where only the first part of the message is checked for similar hashes. Further, the similarity threshold is 75. The pseudo code of this is shown in Figure 2.

Algorithm 2 (A2). This algorithm is similar to A1 except that before any calculation of the hash values, the message would go through word transformation that

---

[2] We have an additional reason to consider this particular question, namely whether we can justify the use of a Markov decision model with a state space that simply keeps track of which algorithms are broken. The question corresponds to demonstrating the memoryless property of the Markov model with that state space. The Markov decision model itself is outside the scope of this paper, we refer to our work in [10] for more details.

would delete all redundant letters, white spaces, unify letters case, and transform common number shortcuts to their equivalent letters (e.g. 4 would become for). Those transformations would create a harder algorithm since it would detect any attempt of the attacker to trick the spam filter by using those word transformations. Furthermore, the similarity threshold is 45. In other words, this algorithm has more rules to increase the robustness level. The pseudo code of this is shown in Figure 3.

```
Input:  T: Text of Mail
        Var h: Hash value
Output: R: result of detection
New-Hash-DB-Candidate ← Make N Hash values from T
For h in New-Hash-DB-Candidate do
    For each first 25 hash in New-Hash-DB-Candidate do
        If h_i in H1 is similar to h_j in H2
        Then increment similarity, increment j and i=j
            Else increment j
            If H1 and H2 share S_i same hash value
            Then R= detected; Update-Similar-Mail (Mail in Hash-DB pointed by h)
            If No. of Similar Mail > D
            Then Mark Hash-DB as "spam"
            Else R= no similarity // If No Similar Entry exists in Hash DB
                //Store-New-Mail (New-Hash-DB-Candidate)
Return R;
```

Fig. 2. Pseudo code of A1

Algorithm A1 and A2 are the main two algorithms to test our hypothesis. We created a third algorithm A3 that both groups G1 and G2 are tasked to break after breaking A1 and A2. Any difference between the groups in the time to break A3 would be very interesting, because it would suggest that the order in which A1 and A2 were broken in the past determines the success of breaking a future algorithm.

```
Input:  T: Text of Mail
            Var h: Hash value
Output: R: result of detection
// Remove all white spaces; make the whole text  lowercase
T' = Normalise (T)
//Remove triple letters; convert some numbers to letters  (like 4 to for)
New-Hash-DB-Candidate ← Make N Hash values from T
For h in New-Hash-DB-Candidate do
    For each first 25 hash in New-Hash-DB-Candidate do
        If h_i in H1 is similar to h_j in H2
        Then increment similarity, increment j and i=j
        Else increment j
        If H1 and H2 share S_i same hash value
        Then R= detected;
        Update-Similar-Mail (Mail in Hash-DB pointed by h)
        If No. of Similar Mail > D
        Then Mark Hash-DB as "spam"
        Else R= no similarity// If No Similar Entry exists in Hash DB
                //Store-New-Mail (New-Hash-DB-Candidate)
    Return R;
```

Fig. 3. Pseudo code of A2

Algorithm 3 (A3). This algorithm is a simple implementation of the proposal of [9]; however the last part of the message is checked for similar hashes, and the similarity threshold is 75. The pseudo code of this is shown in Figure 4.

It is worthwhile to note that the reason behind using a different threshold is that we empirically found that the similarity threshold can play an important role in terms of determining the difficulty of an algorithm. That is, in A1 and A3, the attacker needs to modify only 25% from the part that the algorithm is checking, while it is 55% in A2.

Briefly, the symbols in Table 1 are explained in the following. As in [9], a hash-based vector representation was used. That is, for each e-mail, hash values of each length 9 substring are calculated[3], and then the first N of them are used as vector representation of the e-mail. To check a single e-mail, in order to find similar previous e-mail which share S% of the same hash values, the algorithm checks the database. As a result, an e-mail transferred more than D times is marked as spam.

```
Input:   T: Text of Mail
         Var h: Hash value
Output: R: result of detection
For read T until the last part
New-Hash-DB-Candidate ← Make N Hash values from the last part of T
For h in New-Hash-DB-Candidate do
    For each first 25 hash in New-Hash-DB-Candidate do
        If h_i in H1 is similar to h_j in H2
        Then increment similarity, increment j and i=j
            Else increment j
            If H1 and H2 share S_i same hash value
            Then R= detected;
                Update-Similar-Mail (Mail in Hash-DB pointed by h)
            If No. of Similar Mail > D
            Then Mark Hash-DB as "spam"
                Else R= no similarity
        // If No Similar Entry exists in Hash DB
        Store-New-Mail (New-Hash-DB-Candidate)
Return R;
```

Fig. 4. Pseudo code of A3

Materials: Stimulus and Rational. The stimulus material provided to participants consisted of some default e-mail text. The subjects were asked to send this text to the server, as if it was a typical e-mail. The e-mail text was chosen to be 512 characters in length. Although real-life spammers may send messages that are shorter than this, the length of messages provides the subjects with sufficient text to utilize a range of different strategies to breach the spam-filter.

The same e-mail text was assigned to all subjects, rather than allowing each subject to write his own e-mail. There were several reasons for this. First, self-written e-mails may be of different lengths, making the measurement and comparison of participant's learning a difficult task. Second, self-written e-mails might be chosen because they are easy to type (or, in perverse cases, particularly hard to type). This would again introduce biases that are difficult to control. Third, the use of the same e-mail template across all subjects means that each subject can be treated as an impostor for all the other subjects, putting testing on a firm foundation. Finally, using the same e-mail for everyone affected experimental control over unanticipated biases.

3.2   Experimental Procedure

In this section, the way we ran the experiment is explained, i.e., instructions to subjects, procedures and the data collected.

---

[3] We use the standard hash function provided in Java library.

Instructions to Subjects. Subjects were instructed to act as attackers whose target is to defeat the spam-filter algorithms by successfully passing the spam filter algorithms for 3 e-mails (where each e-mail is interpreted as a batch of 100). The subjects were instructed that to defeat an algorithm, they should introduce enough changes to the provided message template to trick the spam filter into thinking that the message being sent is genuine. The maximum number of changes they were allowed to introduce at each trial was 80. This makes it impossible for participants to write a completely different message. Moreover, the copy and paste functions were not activated to avoid sending completely different e-mail.

Subjects were instructed that there are a number of candidate attacks that spammers can enact to fool spam filter algorithms. For example [24]: *Random addition*, *Thesaurus substitution*, *Perceptive substitution* and *Aimed addition*. In this way we aimed at creating a level playing field for all participants.

Subjects were told that if they needed a break; they were to do so *after* they had defeated all the algorithms. Subjects were able to gauge their progress by looking at a counter at the right of the screen which showed how many e-mails had been sent successfully so far and how many yet remained. Subjects were admonished to focus on the task and to avoid distractions, such as talking with the experimenter, while the task was in progress.

Procedures. The experiment was conducted in a controlled laboratory environment to avoid any distractions, and collect the desired data without any biases. As we mentioned, each group had an equal number of participants (i.e. 20 participants). Each participant was offered £5 for the participation. To motivate participants to do their best, like real attackers, an additional incentive to increase their motivation was offered. The participant who got the highest score in each group was awarded £40 while the second ranked subject was awarded £20. The highest score is based on the time and number of trials consumed to complete the task.

After every e-mail message send by the participant, the system gives information about the progress made: whether the spam attempt passes or fails, and once the algorithms is considered defeated, a notice that the deployed algorithm of the system has been changed. At the end of the experiment, each participant was informed about the achieved score, the time taken and the number of trials. Finally, the participant was asked to fill a short survey/questionnaire about his or her experience.

Collected Data. The time taken by each participant to defeat the algorithms in each session was recorded by the system. Further, the number of trials and the e-mails sent for each session were recorded as well (for later analysis). Additionally, the questionnaires were collected.

4   Results and Analysis: Does Order Matter?

In the experimental study, all the participants successfully completed their task. We first discuss in Section 4.1 the hypothesis with respect to the ordering of the algorithms A1 and A2. We then discuss in Section 4.2 the hypothesis regarding the insensitivity of the order of A1 and A2 with respect to the time used to defeat A3. Further, the impact of order on defeating all algorithms is presented in Section 4.3.

4.1   Testing Hypothesis If Order Matters

The average time needed to break each algorithm in the two groups is shown in Figure 5. From the totals (the rightmost bar), we see that Group 1 took longer than Group 2. This indicates there are implications to the ordering of the algorithm, but we will discuss this more precisely below. As expected, the 'tougher' algorithm A2 took more time to break than A1. In Group 2 it took on average 16.2 minutes and in Group 1, 14.1 minutes. The time needed to break A1 is far less in Group 2, possibly because learning of the techniques to break A2 first, which is effectively a superset of A1, is enough to break A1. The statistical significance of this will be discussed now.

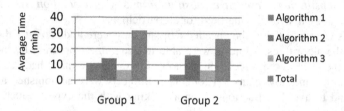

Fig. 5. The average time (in minutes) for 'attackers' in each group to break the algorithms

Table 2. Order matters of two algorithms A1 and A2

Group	Total time				Total trials			
	Avg.	SD	Max	Min	Avg.	SD	Max	Min
1	25.0	10.6	57.1	13.5	33.4	20.1	99.0	14.0
2	20.1	4.3	26.0	10.8	26.1	8.3	40.0	11.0

Table 2 compares the algorithms A1 and A2 in the two groups, with respect to time needed (middle column) as well as trials made (rightmost column). For both, we provide average (Avg.), standard decision (SD) and maximum (Max) and minimum (Min). With respect to average time, we find the following. Time needed for breaking A1 and A2 in Group 1 is 25.0 minutes, while it is 20.1 minutes in Group 2. A t-test yields a result of t=1.89, p<0.1, indicating that the difference between Group 1 and Group 2 is indeed statistically significant.

We can therefore answer negatively to Q_1 by observing that G2 break A1+A2 with significantly less time than G1. This result validates the hypothesis H_1, since we exhibit a case where the order of release has an impact on the time required to break an algorithm.

With respect to the number of trials, we found a less significant difference. The average number of trials is 33.4 trials for Group 1 and 26.1 trials for Group 2. However, this difference is not statistically significant (t=1.55, p=0.139). The discrepancy between time and trials is interesting; we do not believe that this invalidates our claim that order matters but it shows that it is not always apparent (and, of course, as always, possibly not true). We discuss this a bit more at the end of this section.

Table 3. Breaking A1 for each group

Group	Total time A1				Total trials A1			
	Avg.	SD	Max	Min	Avg.	SD	Max	Min
1	10.9	4.7	24.8	5.5	14.8	6.8	31	6
2	3.8	1.3	6.5	0.86	4.3	1.87	8	2

If we then look at A1 and A2 individually, we find that the difference in the total time/trials can be attributed particularly to the time/trials it takes to break A1. Comparing the time and trials to break A1 in the two groups in Table 3, a t-test yields a result of t=6.33, p<0.001, indicating that the time consumed to break A1 in Group 1 is significantly higher than that in Group 2. Also a statistically significant difference is found in the number of trials (t=6.62, p<0.005).

Table 4. Breaking A2 for each group

Group	Total time A2				Total trials A2			
	Avg.	SD	Max	Min	Avg.	SD	Max	Min
1	14.1	6.2	32.3	7.8	18.6	14.7	74	8
2	16.2	3.4	21.3	8.9	21.7	7.2	34	9

Likewise, we compare A2 in the two groups in Table 4. A t-test yields a result of t=-1.32, p=0.196, indicating that the time consumed to break A2 in Group 2 is not significantly higher than that in Group 1. The difference found in number of trials was not found a statistically significant (t=-0.86, p=0.399). In other words, the difference for A2 is less significant than that for A1. This suggests that attackers learn more from A2 than from A1, in terms of how much it speeds them up in attacking the other algorithm.

It is worthwhile to note that previous research assumed, based on psychology studies, that interacting with a limited set of highly similar exemplars leads to more learning than when the instances are distributed and dissimilar [16]. Our order matters results appeared to confirm this assumption. The average time of breaking A1 in Group 2 was 3.8 minutes, and the maximum time was 6.5 compared to 10.9 minutes and the maximum time was 24.8 minutes in Group 1. On the contrary, the average time of breaking A2 in Group 2 was 16.2 minutes instead of 14.1 minutes in Group 1.

4.2   The Influence of Order on Defeating Future Algorithms

The negative answer to Q_1 validates the hypothesis H_1; however we also need to verify that the difference between in G1 and G2 comes indeed from the release order, and not from the fact that G2 contains more naturally talented attackers. To research this question, we added the third algorithm A3 at the end of each experiment. This allows us to check if the order of the previous algorithms has any effect on the time needed to defeat the subsequent algorithm A3.

Table 5. Breaking A3 for each group

Group	Total time A3				Total trials A3			
	Avg.	SD	Max	Min	Avg.	SD	Max	Min
1	6.70	4.93	17	0.97	8.8	10.3	49	2
2	6.5	4.4	16.3	0.56	6.05	4.4	20	2

We compare A3 in the two groups in Table 5. A t-test yields a result of t=0.14, p=0.891, indicating that there is no statistically significant difference between the times needed to break A3 in Group 1 and Group 2, respectively. Also, no statistically significant difference was found in the number of trials (t=1.12, p=0.273). Hence, we can positively answer to Q_2, by observing that G1 and G2 take a similar amount of time to break the independent algorithm A3.

One needs to be careful to generalize this result: we do not claim here that any independent algorithm would require the same amount of time, regardless of the history of the attackers. It may be that if A3 was more closely related to A1 and A2, the results will be different. In addition, one would expect that aspects that influence the working of memory of the attacker may matter, such as the absolute time it takes to break algorithms. After all, it is not unlikely that attackers simply forget more of the knowledge gained from earlier attacks if the attack is longer in the past. So, we look at this experiment as an initial look at this issue.

4.3   The Influence of Order on Defeating All Algorithms

To complete our discussion, we revisit the influence of ordering for the time and effort it takes to break all three algorithms.

Table 6. Breaking all algorithms for each group

Group	Total time				Total trials			
	Avg.	SD	Max	Min	Avg.	SD	Max	Min
1	31.7	10.8	59.4	17.4	42.3	23	112	16
2	26.6	7.36	36.1	12.2	32.1	11	56	13

We compare the effects of all algorithms in the two groups in Table 6. A t-test yields a result of t=1.76, p<0.1, indicating that the time needed to break the series of algorithms in Group 1 is significantly higher than in Group 2. The average number of trials is 42.3 trials in Group 1 compared to 32.1 trials in Group 2 and a t-test yields a result of t=1.78, p<0.1, indicating that the number of trials in Group 1 is statistically significantly higher than in Group 2. This is somewhat surprising, since the time to break A3 differs little between groups, and we showed in Section 4.1 that without algorithm A3 the difference in the total numbers of trials of the two groups is not statistically different. This may suggest that with respect to the number of trials needed the validity of our hypothesis is at the edge of statistical significance.

5   Discussion

Our experimental study provides statistically significant evidence that the release order for a set of algorithms can increase the time needed to break a system's security. In particular, as shown in Table 2, the time required by Group 1 to break the algorithms was significantly higher than Group 2. So, we established the main objective of this paper, namely that 'order matters'.

Since A1 is a simplified version of A2, our experiments also indicate that the success of attacks can be delayed by breaking up an algorithm in parts that are released in sequence. We have to be careful not to generalize that conclusion too quickly, but it is an interesting insight that would imply the intuitive reasoning that by breaking up an algorithm in subsets you 'teach' the attacker how to attack is less valid.

It is important to point out that the value in testing the two conditions (i.e. A1 is deployed before A2 and A2 is deployed before A1) in which the defenses are overlapping was necessary to build our hypothesis on solid grounds before we conduct further experiments. Even though several studies in the psychology and education filed indicated that the learning curves can be considerably increased by interacting with a limited set of highly similar exemplars [e.g. 15, 16], these studies were only focused on the effectiveness of the presentation order on the categorization models. For this reason, in our experiment, even the trivial assumption (i.e. A2 is deployed before A1) is tested to avoid surprises. Hence, the experimental results achieved from these conditions can lead to a further experiment in which the algorithms order is, for instance, subset, independent and superset or other orders, as will be highlighted in the following.

Furthermore, based on the qualitative data, we found that the participants performed the attacking process by strategies using skills gained. Among such wrongful direction is the believing that the algorithm is checking a different part of the e-mail. Interestingly, pervious research assumed, based on empirical results, that the attackers' skills would increase based on the knowledge acquired [5]. Our qualitative data appeared to confirm this assumption.

The concatenation of A3 at the end of both Group 1 and Group 2 yielded an interesting and important result. It showed that despite the knowledge gain at any point of the release chain, injecting a non-subset algorithm would force the attacker back to the learning phase. Accordingly, we investigated in [21] such orders, for examples, A1, A3 and A2 or A2, A3 and A1 that lead to more interesting results. Further, we also note that we used the insight that breaking A3 takes an equal amount of time for both group as a confirmation that a Markov model is an appropriate formalism for the problem at hand, as we shown in [10].

As the results obtained in this paper are very encouraging, optimizing the release order of defensive algorithms is a problem worthwhile to study. The results in this paper are a first step, showing the validity of the problem and providing insights in where to invest future research.

6   Related Work

Attack Modeling. A quantitative analysis of attacker behavior based on empirical data collected from intrusion experiments was presented in [2]. Beside this, Ortalo et al.

described in [6] a technique where the states of the resulting Markov chain denote the enhanced privileges gained by an attacker as a result of series of atomic attacks on a system. Furthermore, generic models have been developed that focus on evaluating security [3, 1]. In relation to the time taken for an attacker to compromise a system and misuse its resources, several studies proposed in [4, 5, 14] a model for estimating the time to compromise a system component that is visible to an attacker. Additionally, McQueen et al. suggested in [4, 5] that the attacker skill levels should be consideration when determining the mean time to compromise a system. With regard to adversarial machine learning, a recent study by Huang et al. explored in [19] that the limits of an adversary's knowledge about the machine learning algorithm and the input data.

Game Theoretic Security Approaches. In traditional network security solutions, one of the first approaches for applying game theory to network security is discussed in [11]. Furthermore, Alpcan and Baser utilized in [12] Min-max Q learning to aid in the gradual improvement of the defender's quality. This work can handle reactive defense actions, while in [13] proposes proactive defense measures. In addition, a study by Jiang et al. [18] focused on active defense using an approach to attack prediction. Furthermore, a game theory approach has been adapted to attack modeling as a means for computing and therefore predicting the expected attacker strategy [8]. Recently, a comprehensive survey has been conducted by Roy et al. [25] concluded that most of the current games theoretic are based on static game, games with perfect information or games with complete information. Indeed, although a number of current models involving dynamic games with incomplete and imperfect information exist, none of them considers learning and/or maximizing the duration of the game as the game's objective.

Effects of Information Order. The idea that the order in which information is received could affect both the learning process and the ultimate knowledge representation is of course commonly studied in the fields such as education or psychology. Most of this literature focused on the similarity-based order. The similarity-based order that maximizes the adjacency of the training examples has investigated by numerous studies [15, 16, 17]. An empirical non-linguistic experiment by Elio and Anderson evaluated in [15] the effects of information order and variance on schema abstraction. This research shown that the low-variance condition group performed better with regards to typicality ratings and accuracy than high-variance condition. Further, this study concluded that the manipulation of presentation orders is a potentially useful tool for studying the mechanisms of learning. Mathy and Feldman recently showed in [20] that a rule-based presentation order (i.e. a small number of rule-learning assumptions) yields superior learning compared to the similarity-based order. Despite these studies provided some insights into presentation orders for investigating categorization processes concept, our study is clearly investigated the effects of presentation order on different concept type.

7   Conclusion and Future Work

This paper reports on experimental validation of the hypothesis that the order in which defensive algorithms are released impacts the success of the attacker. Our work is based on the observation that attackers increase knowledge by learning from their attempted attacks, and on the intuition that the learning experience of attackers can be influenced by the order in which defensive algorithms are released.

Through a between-subjects experiment with simplified but representative spam filter algorithms we were able to show that the order in which defensive algorithms are released indeed influences the time attacks take. This is a very encouraging result for this line of research, indicating that the problem merits study. The experiment also provides an indication that breaking up a defensive algorithm can be a beneficial tool in prolonging the overall attack time, but this issue need to be researched in much more detail before this conclusion can be drawn more widely. Furthermore, the experiment shows that the success in breaking future algorithms does not depend on how that total amount of knowledge was gained.

A number of potential issues for future research follow from our research. Some of the challenges are of technical nature, but the largest challenge may lie in gaining a deeper understanding of the way attackers collect knowledge (i.e., in the way they learn). That would allow us to better estimate the time it takes to break a defensive algorithm under various levels of knowledge gained, and would allow us to determine an optimal strategy without conducting the time-consuming experiments carried out in this paper. Similarly, it will be of interest to investigate deeper if breaking up defensive algorithms in 'subsets' indeed increases the speed at which attackers gain knowledge, as we found in the our experiments.

References

1. Almasizadeh, J., Azgomi, M.A.: Intrusion Process Modeling for Security Quantification. In: 4th the International Conference on Availability, Reliability and Security, pp. 114–121. IEEE Press, Los Alamitos (2009)
2. Jonsson, E., Olovsson, T.: A Quantitative Model of the Security Intrusion Process Based on Attacker Behavior. IEEE Transactions on Software Engineering 23, 235–245 (1997)
3. Madan, B.B., Goseva-Popstojanova, K., Vaidyanathan, K., Trivedi, K.S.: Modeling and Quantification of Security Attributes of Software Systems. In: IEEE International Conference on Dependable Systems and Networks, pp. 505–514. IEEE Press, Los Alamitos (2002)
4. McQueen, M.A., Boyer, W.F., Flynn, M.A., Beitel, G.A.: Time-to-Compromise Model for Cyber Risk Reduction Estimation. In: First Workshop on Quality of Protection, pp. 49–64. Springer, Milan (2005)
5. McQueen, M.A., Boyer, W.F., Flynn, M.A., Beitel, G.: Quantitative Cyber Risk Reduction Estimation Methodology for a Small SCADA Control System. In: 39th Annual Hawaii Conference on System Science, IEEE Press (2006)
6. Ortalo, R., Deswarte, Y., Kaaniche, M.: Experimenting with Quantitative Evaluation Tools for Monitoring Operational Security. IEEE Transactions on Software Engineering 25, 633–650 (1999)
7. Alsuhibany, S.A.: Optimising CAPTCHA Generation. In: 6th International Conference on Availability, Reliability and Security, pp. 740–745. IEEE Press (2011)

8. Sallhammar, K., Knapskog, S.J., Helvik, B.E.: Using Stochastic Game Theory to Compute the Expected Behavior of Attackers. In: International Symposium on Applications and the Internet Workshops (2005)

9. Yoshida, K., Adachi, F., Washio, T., Motoda, H., Homma, T., Nakashima, A., Fujikawa, H., Yamazaki, K.: Density Based Spam Detector. In: ACM SIGKDD International Conference on Knowledge Discovery and Data Mining, pp. 486–493. ACM (2004)

10. Alsuhibany, S.A., Alonizi, A., Morisset, C., van Moorsel, A.: Optimizing the Release Order of Defensive Mechanisms. In: 29th Annual UK Performance Engineering Workshop (to appear)

11. McInerney, J., Tubberud, S., Anwar, S., Hamilton, S.: FRIARS: a Feedback Control System for Information Assurance Using a Markov Decision Process. In: 35th Annual 2001 International Carnahan Conference on Security Technology, pp. 223–228. IEEE Press (2001)

12. Alpcan, T., Baser, T.: An Intrusion Detection Game with Limited Observations. In: 12th International Symposium on Dynamic Games and Applications, France, (2006)

13. Shiva, S., Roy, S., Dasgupta, D.: Game Theory for Cyber Security. In: Sixth Annual Workshop on Cyber Security and Information Intelligence Research (2010)

14. Leversage, D.J., Byres, E.J.: Comparing Electronic Battlefields: Using Mean Time-to-Compromise as a Comparative Security Metric. In: Gorodetsky, V., Kotenko, I., Skormin, V.A. (eds.) MMM-ACNS 2007. CCIS, vol. 1, pp. 213–227. Springer, Heidelberg (2007)

15. Elio, R., Anderson, J.R.: The Effects of Information Order and Learning Mode on Schema Abstraction. Memory and Cognition 12, 20–30 (1984)

16. Sandhofer, C.M., Doumas, L.A.A.: Order of Presentation Effects in Learning Color Categories. Journal of Cognition and Development 9, 194–221 (2008)

17. Medin, D.L., Bettger, J.G.: Presentation Order and Recognition of Categorically Related Examples. Psychonomic Bulletin & Review 1, 250–254 (1994)

18. Jiang, W., Tian, Z., Zhang, H., Song, X.: A Stochastic Game Theoretic Approach to Attack Prediction and Optimal Active Defense Strategy Decision. In: IEEE International Conference on Networking, Sensing and Control, pp. 6–8. IEEE Press (2008)

19. Huang, L., Joseph, A.D., Nelson, B., Rubinstein, B.I.P., Tygar, J.D.: Adversarial Machine Learning. In: 4th ACM workshop on Artificial Intelligence and Security, pp. 43–58 (2011)

20. Mathy, F., Feldman, J.: A Rule-Based Presentation Order Facilitates Category Learning. Psychonomic Bulletin & Review 16, 1050–1057 (2009)

21. Alsuhibany, S.A., van Moorsel, A.: Modelling and Analysis of Release Order of Security Algorithms Using Stochastic Petri Nets. In: 8th International Conference on Availability, Reliability and Security (to appear)

22. Caliendo, M., Clement, M., Papies, D., Scheel-Kopeinig, S.: The Cost Impact of Spam Filters: Measuring the Effect of Information System Technologies in Organizations. Information Systems Research, 1–13 (2012)

23. Kahn, P., O'Rourke, K.: Guide to Curriculum Design: Enquiry-Based Learning. Higher Education Academy, York (2004)

24. Garcia, F.D., Hoepman, J.-H., van Nieuwenhuizen, J.: Spam Filter Analysis. In: 19th IFIP International Information Security Conference, Toulouse, pp. 395–410. Springer (2004)

25. Roy, S., Ellis, C., Shiva, S., Dasgupta, D., Shandilya, V., Wu, Q.: A Survey of Game Theory as Applied to Network Security. In: Hawaii International Conference on System Sciences, pp. 1–10. IEEE Press (2010)

A Multiple-Key Management Scheme
in Wireless Sensor Networks

Jung-Chun Liu[1], Yi-Li Huang[1], Fang-Yie Leu[1,*], Ilsun You[2], Feng-Ching Chiang[1],
Chao-Tung Yang[1], and William Cheng-Chung Chu[1]

[1] Department of Computer Science, TungHai University, Taiwan
{jcliu,yifung,leufy,g01350011,ctyang,cchu}@thu.edu.tw
[2] School of Information Science, Korean Bible University, South Korea
ilsunu@gmail.com

Abstract. In a wireless sensor network (WSN), in order to provide a secure communication environment for all the sensor nodes, we often securely authenticate network nodes and protect all the messages delivered among them. When a sensor node (or simply a node or a sensor) newly joins a WSN, it is required for the Key Distribution Server (KDS) to distribute those generated security keys to this node and all the existing nodes before they can securely communicate with each other. But due to the wireless nature, when a node broadcasts a message M, all its neighbors can receive M. To securely protect this message, a security mechanism is required. Therefore, in this paper we propose a Multiple-key Management Scheme (MMaS for short), in which a sensor N receives two sets of keys from the KDS when the system starts up. The first set, named communication keys, is used by N to securely communicate with its neighbor sensors; the other, called the individual key, is employed to encrypt messages delivered between N and the KDS. When N would like to communicate with another node, e.g., M, they exchange their IDs with each other so as to correctly identify their common keys (CKs), which are used to individually generate a shared key (SK) on both sides for encrypting/decrypting messages transmitted between them. When N leaves the underlying network, the CKs currently related to N can be reused by a newly joining sensor, e.g., M. However, when M joins the network, if no such used ID is available, M will be given a new ID and CKs by the KDS. The KDS will encrypt the CKs, that will be used by an existing node H to communicate with M, with the individual key of H so that only H rather than M can correctly decrypt the CKs, with which to securely communicate with M. The security analysis shows that the proposed system is secure.

Keywords: Multi-key management scheme, Key distribution server, Newly joining node, Shared key, Wireless sensor network, An incrementally constructed system.

1 Introduction

Wireless sensor networks (WSNs) are envisioned to be widely applied to commercial and military applications [1], such as target tracking, health-care [2], environmental

---

* Corresponding author.

A. Cuzzocrea et al. (Eds.): CD-ARES 2013 Workshops, LNCS 8128, pp. 337–344, 2013.

monitoring [3] and homeland security. However, some applications require certain security mechanisms to verify the source of a message and protect the integrity of transmitted data from being maliciously modified. In order to securely authenticate a network entity and deliver messages, a secure communication environment is required. To build a secure sensor network, Wuu et al.[4] proposed a Quorum-based Key Management Scheme. But it has a problem in sensor node addition since the number of sensor nodes (or simply sensors or nodes) must be odd. So each time at least two sensor nodes must be added. Furthermore, when two nodes are newly added to a sensor network, the shared keys (SKs) of some existing sensor nodes are changed. We will show this later. This may crash the normal operation of the whole system.

Generally, an asymmetric cryptographic technique generates many large numbers to encrypt keys and delivered messages. But this is infeasible for WSNs, since sensor nodes are often powered by battery and provided with very limited processing capability. Therefore, to achieve high security and support sensor node addition functionality, by which extra nodes can be easily added to a sensor network, in this study we propose a symmetric cryptographic technique, named the Multi-key Management Scheme (MMaS), based on a $n \times n$ key matrix K, different parts of which are distributed among sensors. Further, due to the fast advancement of hardware technology, memory equipped in sensors is cheaper than before and the size of a WSN grows rapidly in recent years. This further makes MMaS feasible in practical applications.

2   Related Works

Various key pre-distribution schemes used to establish secure channels for wireless sensors have been proposed in literature [4][5].The key pre-distribution scheme of Cheng et al.[5] used a $\sqrt{n} \times \sqrt{n}$ matrix as a key matrix to assign keys to sensors, where n is the total number of sensors in the system.Fig.1 illustrates an example of a key matrix in which the intended network size is n. The scheme has two phases: the key pre-distribution phase and pair-wise key setup phase. At first, the KDS randomly selects n keys from its key pool, in which there are more than 2^{20} distinct keys, and uses the n keys to construct an m x m key matrix K, where $m = \sqrt{n}$. The KDS assigns an element of this matrix, e.g., $K_{i,j}$, as the sensor's ID, and the other entries on the ith row and jth column as the sensor's keys, implying that the matrix is indexed by the IDs of these involved sensors. It also means that this scheme provides the largest maximum supported network size since each element of the matrix represents one sensor node. When a sensor M would like to communicate with another sensor, e.g., N, it identifies the CK indexed by M and N and uses it to encrypt messages.

$K_{1,1}$	$K_{1,2}$	$K_{1,3}$	$K_{1,4}$	$K_{1,5}$
$K_{2,1}$	$K_{2,2}$	$K_{2,3}$	$K_{2,4}$	$K_{2,5}$
$K_{3,1}$	$K_{3,2}$	$K_{3,3}$	$K_{3,4}$	$K_{3,5}$
$K_{4,1}$	$K_{4,2}$	$K_{4,3}$	$K_{4,4}$	$K_{4,5}$
$K_{5,1}$	$K_{5,2}$	$K_{5,3}$	$K_{5,4}$	$K_{5,5}$

Fig. 1. An example of a key matrix

As stated above, Wuu et al.[4] proposed a Quorum-based Key Management Scheme, in which the KDS as shown in Fig. 2generates a$\lfloor n/2 \rfloor \times n$key matrix K and establishes a quorum system S based on K, where each sensor, e.g., j, has the entire column j of matrix K and $\lfloor n/2 \rfloor$other elements, each belonging to one of the $\lfloor n/2 \rfloor$ columns after column j, meaning that each sensor has $n - 1$elements, i.e.,$K_{i,j}, 1 \leq i \leq$ $\lfloor n/2 \rfloor$, and $K_{i,j+i \bmod n}, 1 \leq i \leq \lfloor n/2 \rfloor$, $1 \leq j \leq n$. As shown in Fig. 3,after the deployment of sensors, two arbitrary sensors, e.g., A and B, both can individually identify the CKs assigned to them so that they can mutually authenticate and communicate with each other. In this scheme, node addition is feasible only when some existing IDs that are not in use are available. Also, when two nodes A and B newly join the WSN, as shown in Fig. 4,the SKs of some nodes will be changed. For example, originally the CK of nodes 1 and 5 was $K_{1,1}$. But after sensors A and B join the network, the CK of nodes 1 and 5 becomes $K_{4,5}$. After that, the normal operations of the system will be destroyed.

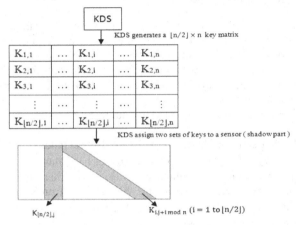

Fig. 2. KDS assigns each sensor node two sets of keys (the shadowed parts)

$K_{1,1}$	$K_{1,2}$	$K_{1,3}$	$K_{1,4}$	$K_{1,5}$	$K_{1,6}$	$K_{1,7}$
$K_{2,1}$	$K_{2,2}$	$K_{2,3}$	$K_{2,4}$	$K_{2,5}$	$K_{2,6}$	$K_{2,7}$
$K_{3,1}$	$K_{3,2}$	$K_{3,3}$	$K_{3,4}$	$K_{3,5}$	$K_{3,6}$	$K_{3,7}$

Fig. 3. Sensors A and B derive a common key

$K_{1,1}$	$K_{1,2}$	$K_{1,3}$	$K_{1,4}$	$K_{1,5}$	$K_{1,6}$	$K_{1,7}$
$K_{2,1}$	$K_{2,2}$	$K_{2,3}$	$K_{2,4}$	$K_{2,5}$	$K_{2,6}$	$K_{2,7}$
$K_{3,1}$	$K_{3,2}$	$K_{3,3}$	$K_{3,4}$	$K_{3,5}$	$K_{3,6}$	$K_{3,7}$

$K_{1,1}$	$K_{1,2}$	$K_{1,3}$	$K_{1,4}$	$K_{1,5}$	$K_{1,6}$	$K_{1,7}$	$K_{1,8}$	$K_{1,9}$
$K_{2,1}$	$K_{2,2}$	$K_{2,3}$	$K_{2,4}$	$K_{2,5}$	$K_{2,6}$	$K_{2,7}$	$K_{2,8}$	$K_{2,9}$
$K_{3,1}$	$K_{3,2}$	$K_{3,3}$	$K_{3,4}$	$K_{3,5}$	$K_{3,6}$	$K_{3,7}$	$K_{3,8}$	$K_{3,9}$
$K_{4,1}$	$K_{4,2}$	$K_{4,3}$	$K_{4,4}$	$K_{4,5}$	$K_{4,6}$	$K_{4,7}$	$K_{4,8}$	$K_{4,9}$

Fig. 4. New sensor nodes A (node 8) and B (node 9) join the network

3   The Proposed Scheme

The MMaS consists of four working phases: the key pre-distribution, shared key establishment, key refreshment, and data transmission phases. In the key pre-distribution phase, the KDS generates a n × nkey matrix, in which the keys are random numbers. After that, the KDS assigns these keys to sensors during the deployment of sensor nodes. Before communicating with each other, each pair of sensors needs to identify the other's CKs and then generates the SK in the shared key establishment phase. When the sensor, e.g., M, joins the network, the KDS broadcasts the ID, i.e., M, and the related CKs, and the system enters its key refreshment phase, in which the receiving sensor accordingly updates its key information. In the data transmission phase, sensors transmit data to their neighbors, and check to see whether a received message is sent by a legal sensor or not.

3.1   Key Pre-Distribution Phase

Each sensor i has two sets of keys. The first set, named communication keys (row i and column i together are called key-cross i), is used to perform one-to-one communication between two sensors by using the computed SK. The other one, called individual key, e.g., $k_{i,i}$, is the key employed by sensor i to communicate with the KDS where$K_{i,i}$ is the ith element along the diagonal of the key matrix. The steps of the key pre-distribution phase are as follows:

Step 1: the KDS generates n^2 random numbers to establish the $n \times n$ key matrix K.

Step 2: the KDS assigns an ID, e.g., i, which is also the index of key $K_{i,i}, 1 \leq i \leq n$, and two common keys $K_{i,j}$ and $K_{j,i}$(see Fig. 5), $1 \leq i, j \leq$ n,to a sensor. After that, sensors i and j can securely communicate with each other by encrypting those messages exchanged between them with the SK derived from$K_{i,j}$and$K_{j,i}$. As stated above, the individual key of sensor i, i.e., $K_{i,i}, 0 < i < n$, is used to encrypt messages delivered between sensor i and the KDS.

$K_{1,1}$	$K_{1,2}$	$K_{1,3}$	$K_{1,4}$	$K_{1,5}$
$K_{2,1}$	$K_{2,2}$	$K_{2,3}$	$K_{2,4}$	$K_{2,5}$
$K_{3,1}$	$K_{3,2}$	$K_{3,3}$	$K_{3,4}$	$K_{3,5}$
$K_{4,1}$	$K_{4,2}$	$K_{4,3}$	$K_{4,4}$	$K_{4,5}$
$K_{5,1}$	$K_{5,2}$	$K_{5,3}$	$K_{5,4}$	$K_{5,5}$

Fig. 5. The KDS generates the n × n key matrix K, in which $\left[K_{1,i}, K_{2,i}, \cdots, K_{i,i}, \cdots, K_{n,i}\right]$and $\left[K_{i,1}, K_{i,2}, \cdots, K_{i,i}, \cdots, K_{i,n}\right]$ are assigned to sensor i

3.2   Dynamic Shared Key Establishing Phase

After the deployment of sensors, when sensor A would like to communicate with sensor B, it sends his own ID, i.e., A, to B. With the two IDs, both side can individually, identify the CKs$K_{A,B}$ and $K_{B,A}, 1 \leq A, B \leq$ n.

Before authenticating node B (node A), node A (node B) generates an authentication message $Auth_A$ ($Auth_B$) which contains the result of a hash function with the concatenation of the CK, i.e., $K_{A,B}$ ($K_{B,A}$), and a random number randA (randB) as its parameter where,

$$AuthA = H(K_{A,B} || randA) \tag{1}$$

and

$$AuthB = H(K_{B,A} || randB) \tag{2}$$

After that, A (B) delivers the message it generates, i.e., AuthA (AuthB), and randA (randB) to B (A). On receiving AuthB and randB, node A retrieves $K_{B,A}$ from its own common keys and invokes Eq. (2) with the concatenation of the retrieved $K_{B,A}$ and the received randB as its parameter to calculate AuthB, denoted by $AuthB_c$, and then checks to see whether the received AuthB, denoted by $AuthB_r$, is equal to $AuthB_c$ or not. If yes, meaning B is a legal one, it retrieves the common keys $K_{A,B}$ and $K_{B,A}$ from its own key array and generates the SK, where

$$SK = K_{A,B} \oplus K_{B,A} \tag{3}$$

In fact, node B does similarly. But the invoked Equation is Eq. (1) and the checked equation is $AuthA_c = AuthA_r$. If they are equal, B generates SK also by invoking Eq. (3).

3.3   Key Refreshment Phase

There are two cases which call for key refreshment. One is when a sensor leaves or joins the network; the other is when CKs of two sensors have been used in communication over a threshold of number.

When a sensor N leaves the network, the KDS broadcasts N to the remaining sensors. On receiving the information, a sensor will no longer communicate with N. In fact, this ID is now available and can be reused. When a sensor, e.g., M, newly joins the network, it faces two situations: with or without an available used ID in the underlying network.

1. If the situation "with an available used ID" occurs, the KDS assigns the ID to M and generates CKs, denoted by $K_{M,N}$ and $K_{N,M}$, used by M and an existing sensor N to communicate with each other, $1 \leq M, N \leq n, M \neq N$.

2. If the situation "without an available used ID" occurs, the KDS will generate a new ID and the corresponding $K_{M,N}$ and $K_{N,M}$. After that, the KDS broadcasts a message containing M's ID and those generated $K_{M,N}$ and $K_{N,M}$, $1 \leq N \leq n$, to all sensors. In this message, the CKs deliverd to sensor N is encrypted by $K_{N,N}$ so that only sensor N can decrypt the CKs sent to it. In our scheme, the addition of M (maybe $M = n + 1$ or $1 \leq M \leq n$) does not change those SKs currently used by existing sensors.

The format of this broadcasted message is shown in Fig. 6, in which a sensor ID, e.g., N, is followed by the common keys, i.e., $K_{M,N}$ and $K_{N,M}$, needed to be updated by sensor N. Upon receiving this message, sensor N sequentially searches the ID field. When ID=N as the head field of sensor N is identified, sensor N decrypts the common keys conveyed in fields following the head field, and accordingly updates its key matrix.

For example, if ID=1, the following two fields are $K_{1,1} \oplus rand_{n+1,1}$ and $K_{1,1} \oplus rand_{1,n+1}$ where $rand_{n+1,1}$ is $K_{n+1,1}$ and $rand_{1,n+1}$ is $K_{1,n+1}$. Only the legal KDS has the right individual key to encrypt the two fields, and only the legal sensor, i.e., sensor 1, which has $K_{1,1}$, is able to decrypt the two fields. Moreover, after obtaining $rand_{n+1,1}$ and $rand_{1,n+1}$, sensor 1 compares the ($rand_{n+1,1} \oplus rand_{1,n+1}$) generated by itself with the fourth field from the head field to see whether they are equal or not. If yes, the message is authenticated.

ID=1	$K_{1,1} \oplus rand_{n+1,1,}$	$K_{1,1} \oplus rand_{1,n+1}$	$rand_{n+1,1} \oplus rand_{1,n+1}$
ID=2	$K_{2,2} \oplus rand_{n+1,2}$	$K_{2,2} \oplus rand_{2,n+1}$	$rand_{n+1,2} \oplus rand_{2,n+1}$

...

| ID=n | $K_{n,n} \oplus rand_{n+1,n}$ | $K_{n,n} \oplus rand_{n,n+1}$ | $rand_{n+1,n} \oplus rand_{n,n+1}$ |

Fig. 6. Format of the message containing sensor IDs, e.g., i, and the common Keys,$rand_{n+1,1,}$ and $rand_{1,n+1}$needed to be updated by sensor i

When the number of communication between sensors A and B is over a predefined threshold, due to security consideration, A and B need to refresh the CK in their upper triangle of K, i.e., $K_{A,B}$ (without changing $K_{B,A}$), by executing the following key refreshment steps under the assumption that $A < B$.

Step 1: Input the CK, i.e., $K_{A,B}$, which is in the upper triangle of the key matrix K, to a predefined hash function to produce a new key, e.g., $K'_{A,B}$, where

$$K'_{A,B} = H(K_{A,B}) \tag{4}$$

Step 2: Compute the new shared key SK' where

$$SK' = K'_{A,B} \oplus K_{B,A} \tag{5}$$

Step 3: Store the SK' as the new shared key in its local variable.

3.4   Data Transmission Phase

After completing the authentication, two sensors can communicate with each other by sending a message, the format of which is shown in Fig. 7.

ID	msg $\oplus$ SK	HMAC

Fig. 7. The format of a data message

When receiving this message, a sensor computes the hash value HMAC = H(ID||msg ⊕ SK, SK) and checks to see whether the value is equal to the one conveyed in the received message or not to ensure data integrity of the message where msg is the data that needs to be sent. Since only a legal sensor has the right SK to produce the correct hash value, if the two values are equal, the message is authenticated, meaning that the sensor sending this message is a legal one.

4 Security Analysis

By using shared keys and the unique individual key, $K_{i,i}$, a sensor node and the KDS, or any two sensor nodes can mutually authenticate each other so as to defend attacks launched by hackers. In this section, we analyze three common attacks, including the eavesdropping, forgery KDS, and forgery sensor node attacks, and show that the MMaS can effectively defend these attacks.

4.1 Eavesdropping Attack

Due to the wireless nature, messages sent by sensor nodes and the KDS can be accessed by a sensor located within the communication area of the sender. As described above, since illegal users cannot decrypt messages protected by the multiple key, i.e., SK and $K_{i,i}$, the messages delivered in the data transmission phase is secure. So the eavesdropping attack does not work.

4.2 Forgery KDS Attack

A forgery KDS may send fake messages intending to cheat sensors that some sensor nodes leave or newly join the network. This kind of attack can be prevented by the unique individual key, $K_{i,i}$, which is only known to the individual sensor and the KDS, and is used to encrypt messages and authenticate the integrity of a message delivered between the node and KDS. Only the legal KDS has the right $K_{i,i}$ and only the corresponding sensors can correctly use it to decrypt the messages issued by the KDS, meaning that the MMaS can effectively defend the forgery KDS attack.

4.3 Forgery Sensor Node Attack

If a hacker, e.g., B', disguising itself as the legal sensor B, sends data messages more than the threshold number in order to falsely trigger CK refreshment between A and B' so as to make the CKs between A and B inconsistent. He/she will be defeated by MMaS, since sensors need to authenticate each other before communication. But the faked node does not have the right CKs. The authentication will fail. Thus B' is incapable of identifying the right SK for further interaction with sensor A. By this SK authentication mechanism, legal sensors will not respond to the faked one's CK refreshment attempt used to falsely alter the keys, and the faked one cannot decrypt messages issued by a legal one because it does not own the right SK.

5 Conclusions and Future Studies

In this paper, we design and analyze a multiple key management scheme, with which to securely protect wireless sensor networks. To increase the resiliency of sensor networks, our scheme supports an efficient sensor-node-addition mechanism to deal with the dilemma in which when a sensor network has no available used IDs, adding extra sensor nodes will change the SKs used by other nodes and may aggravate or even crash the whole system. We also analyze and show that the proposed system can effectively defend three common attacks. The system enhances the security and resiliency of the sensor networks without conducting tremendous amount of computation and complicated asymmetric cryptographic techniques.

In the future, we would like to improve reliability and derive working models for the proposed system. To further enhance performance and reduce the size of a delivered message, we plan to devise an authentication function to substitute for the random number keys and authentication messages. In other words, we only need to invoke a function instead of issuing n authentication messages to authenticate messages. These constitute our future studies.

Acknowledgment. The work was partially supported by TungHai University under the project GREENs and the National Science Council, Taiwan under Grants NSC 101-2221-E-029-003-MY3, and NSC 100-2221-E-029-018.

References

[1] Durisic, M.P., Tafa, Z., Dimic, G., Milutinovic, V.: A Survey of Military Applications of Wireless Sensor Networks. In: Mediterranean Conference on Embedded Computing, pp. 196–199 (June 2012)

[2] Chen, Y.M., Shen, W., Huo, H.W., Xu, Y.Z.: A Smart Gateway for Health Care System Using Wireless Sensor Network. In: International Conference on Sensor Technologies and Applications, pp. 545–550 (July 2010)

[3] Kong, Y.F., Jiang, P.: Development of Data Video Base Station in Water Environment Monitoring Oriented Wireless Sensor Networks. In: International Conference on Embedded Software and Systems Symposia, pp. 281–286 (July 2008)

[4] Wuu, L.C., Hung, C.H., Chang, C.M.: Quorum-based Key Management Scheme in Wireless Sensor Networks. In: International Conference on Ubiquitous Information Management and Communication, vol. 15 (2012)

[5] Cheng, Y., Agrawal, D.P.: Efficient Pairwise Key Establishment and Management in Static Wireless Sensor Networks. In: IEEE International Conference on Mobile Ad hoc and Sensor Systems, pp. 544–550 (2005)

VisSecAnalyzer: A Visual Analytics Tool for Network Security Assessment

Igor Kotenko and Evgenia Novikova

Laboratory of Computer Security Problems
St. Petersburg Institute for Informatics and Automation (SPIIRAS)
39, 14 Liniya, St. Petersburg, Russia
{ivkote,novikova}@comsec.spb.ru

Abstract. Visualization is the essential part of Security Information and Event Management (SIEM) systems. The paper suggests a common framework for SIEM visualization which allows incorporating different visualization technologies and extending easily the application functionality. To illustrate the framework, we developed a SIEM visualization component VisSecAnalyzer. The paper demonstrates its possibilities for the tasks of attack modeling and security assessment. To increase the efficiency of the visualization techniques we applied the principles of the human information perception and interaction.

Keywords: security information visualization, vulnerability analysis and countermeasures, attack graph visualization, information perception and interaction.

1   Introduction

Visual analytics techniques can be efficiently applied when exploring large amounts of data as they can cope with enormous volumes of information and help to extract new knowledge from heterogeneous noisy data. The idea of visual analytics is to combine strengths of human visual system and computational power of automated data processing, making thus possible the development of highly interactive software that allows a user to dive into the data and implement comprehensive analysis in the most promising direction [13].Visual analytics techniques are widely used for security analysis of information systems. However, the most of security visualization tools have been focused largely on active network perimeter monitoring, determining different port scan patterns, detecting anomalies in the "network behavior" of users. Less effort has been done in visualization of the cyber security officer activity, including security assessment, intrusion prevention activity, reasoning and decision support.

In this paper we present visual analytics tool VizSecAnalyzer designed to support the network security level assessment. Its goal is to reveal the most vulnerable nodes of the information system, to form attack patterns, depending on the initial attacker's position and skills, and to adjust countermeasure plan according to the data. It could be used for analyzing software and hardware protection mechanisms used in computer networks and prevention of possible attacks. As the implementation of the preventive measures decreases the risks of security incidents the usage of the tool can increase the

A. Cuzzocrea et al. (Eds.): CD-ARES 2013 Workshops, LNCS 8128, pp. 345–360, 2013.
© IFIP International Federation for Information Processing 2013

overall efficiency of homeland defense activity. The visualization in VizSecAnalyzer consists of interactive graphs, treemaps and pie charts allowing exploration of large-scale networks. Specifically, the contribution of this paper to the field of security visualization is a common framework and the visualization tool that supports security analysis of network "week" places (vulnerabilities, misconfigurations) in context of possible consequences of their exploitation. The paper is organized as follows. *Section 2* analyzes the visualization techniques used for network security assessment. *Section 3* describes the proposed visual models and interaction techniques implemented in the tool. *Section 4* presents case study for network level assessment and countermeasure plan adjustment. Conclusion analyzes the paper results and provides insight into the future research.

2   Related Work

A lot of work has been done on graphic representation of output of security sensors such as IDS, firewalls, etc. [7, 12, 16 - 18, 27, 30]. However, the visualization of complex security events generated by intrusion detection systems that process heterogeneous security information in large-scale architecture, such as presented for example in [6], is not studied extensively. As our tool is purposed to detect potential weaknesses of the network security measures we focus on the tools designed to support preventive activity of the security officer in this section. There has been much research in visualization of security policies and control resource access. Graph-based techniques are usually used to depict and explore control resource access rules [20, 21]. The graph nodes correspond to users, user groups, and resources. The links between nodes reflect user activities or resources the users accessed. The colors are used to highlight user role. Application of graph layouting techniques based on graph semantics can exposure users with similar behaviors, as well as allows detecting incorrect resource access rules or determining an insider threat.

In [1, 2] a graph-based visualization technique is applied for assessing topology based policies used in social networks. They built a graph where the vertexes correspond to the users' profiles and the edges reflect access permissions between users. The color is used to display reachable and unreachable neighborhood regions of the selected user. The visualization tool allows the user to analyze his/her profile from the view point of another user at his/her neighborhood. By clicking on the vertex of the selected user it is possible to get information about resources accessible for this user and a list of primitives that the selected user can initiate against the profile owner.

Heitzmann et al. [10] suggested the visual representation of access control permissions in a standard hierarchical file system in the form of treemaps. The colors are used to display the permissions. For each file or folder the associated node in the treemap is painted green, red, or gray, if the file's permissions are weaker, stronger, or the same as those specified by the baseline which can take one of the values "no access", "read", "read&write", and "full control". The tool draws an orange border around treemap nodes associated with files or folders where inheritance is broken.

Another group of visualization tools purposed for *assessing network security level* visualizes firewall rules in order to enhance understanding and inspecting them. These tools exploit more sophisticated visual models. For example, Tran et al. [31] developed a tool called PolicyVis which maps firewall rules onto the 2D space in form of the rectangles. It uses three different rule fields to build the policy graph, two of which are used to define the vertical and horizontal coordinates of the rectangle and the third field is integrated into the visualization object. The color is used to encode different kinds of traffic (accepted or denied). Since the colors are set transparently, the overlapping rules can be effectively recognized. Overlapping of the rectangles can notify about a potential anomaly.

Original approach for visual analysis of the firewall rules is suggested by Mansmann et al. [19]. It is based on hierarchical sunburst visualization technique [29], which puts a root node as a circle in the middle of the visualization and then recursively maps the elements of each hierarchy level onto ring segments. To be able to represent graphically firewall rules the authors proposed the following hierarchical structure. The first level after the root node for the rules visualization consists of the names of different access lists as shown in Fig. 1.

Fig. 1. Starburst visualization of firewall rules [19]

The second level contains the access privileges ("permit" or "deny"), the 3rd one - the protocol, followed by the source and destination dimensions. To make the exploration process easier the authors established the following color scheme. The fixed colors are used for the most common keywords (e.g. "TCP", "any", "permit", "deny"). Less common keywords and names are assigned repeating colors. Besides, the user can change the depth of the visible graph by establishing the depth level number. To improve the visibility of a node and the readability of its label, the width of a segment can be changed interactively using the mouse wheel.

Vulnerability analysis is a critical component in the evaluation of the network security. Currently, the visualization techniques used to display vulnerability scanner reports are limited to treemaps [9, 20]. For example, Nv tool [9] uses treemaps and linked histograms to allow security analysts and systems administrators to analyze vulnerabilities detected by the Nessus vulnerability scanner [23]. Apart from visualization of the Nessus scans, it supports the analysis of sequential scans by showing which vulnerabilities have been fixed, remain open, or are newly discovered. Nv tool uses a semantic based color scheme where, for example, different colors are used for fixed vulnerabilities, new ones, and open vulnerabilities (Fig. 2).

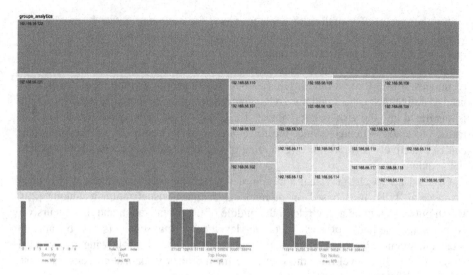

Fig. 2. Using treemaps in the NV tool [9]

Another powerful instrument for security assessment is *attack graph generation*. They are used to determine if designated goal states can be reached by attackers attempting to penetrate computer networks from initial starting states. For this use, they consider the graphs in which the starting node represents an attacker initial position. Other nodes and edges represent actions the attacker takes and changes in the network state caused by these actions. Actions typically involve exploits or exploit steps that take advantage of vulnerabilities in software or protocols.

Natural graphical representation of the attack graphs are graphs themselves [11, 24]. However in the standard exploit dependency representation, the attack graph complexity is $O(scn^2)$, for n machines in the attack graph. Here, s is the average number of exploits against a machine, independent of any particular attacking machine, and factor c is the average number of security conditions per machine.

In order to reduce attack graph complexity several approaches based on attack graph aggregation were suggested. In [25] the graph complexity is achieved through interactive visualization, which includes hierarchical aggregation of graph elements. Aggregation collapses recursively non-overlapping subgraphs of the attack graph to single graph vertices, reducing of attack graph complexity.

In [24, 25] a matrix-based approach is suggested to visualize attack graphs. The attack graph consisting of the n vertices is represented by the $n \times n$ adjacency matrix A, where element a_{ij} of A indicates the presence of an edge from vertex i to vertex j. As in attack graphs, it is possible to have multiple edges between a pair of vertices, for example, multiple exploits between a pair of machines, the authors suggest either to record the actual number of edges, or simply to fix the presence of at least one edge. This visualization technique allows constructing attack patterns by reordering rows and columns of an adjacency matrix as these operations do not affect the structure of the attack graph.

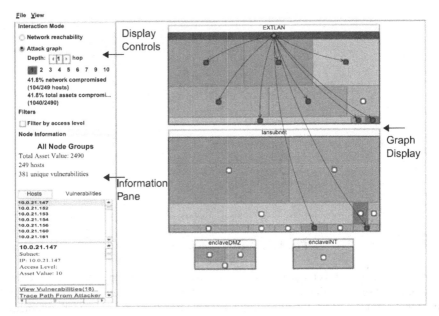

Fig. 3. Attack reachability display [33]

An alternative approach for visualizing the attack graph was proposed in [3,8,32, 33]. It allows mapping the attack graph on the network topology. Separate treemaps are used to represent subnet groups. The inner subgroups are colored according to the selected subnet attribute, and the relative size of each is proportional to the number of hosts it comprises. The attack reachability display is shown in Fig. 3. The user is provided with the possibility to position and resize the subnets to form more intuitive layout. It is also possible to display either incoming or outcoming attack graph edges which are drawn to all nodes that can be reached from the selected node or reach it.

3   VisSecAnalyzer Design

The goal of the VisSecAnalyzer is to provide visual support for cyber security officer when evaluating general network security, analyzing severity of the detected vulnerabilities and assessing efficiency of possible countermeasures such as software update/removal [26].

The VisSecAnalyzer architecture consists of three layers: (1) User interface, (2) Controlling services middleware and (3) Graphical elements. The architecture structure is shown in Fig. 4. The arrows reflect information flows between different architecture elements. The separation of the user interface from the other services allows supporting the development of the front-end user forms of different types, beginning from a simple command line and finishing with the rich multi-window interface including various dashboards. It is supposed that data, which are necessary to visualize, are transferred to the corresponding visualization service which returns the graphical result ready for displaying in application forms.

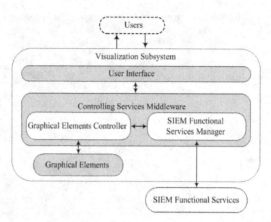

Fig. 4. VisSecAnalyzer architecture

Such abstraction level makes indistinguishable whether input data are received from the user or from the service and who requested visualization – users or SIEM functional services. Thus, the controlling services middleware implements interaction between users and other elements of the model. According to the functional payload of the middleware services they could be divided into two groups – the graphical elements controller and the SIEM functional services manager.

The graphical elements controller is responsible for graphical elements management. It provides the standard interface to visualization pipelines: starts and stops visualization pipelines on the request coming from the user interface level or from the SIEM functional service manager.

The SIEM functional services manager implements a plug-in mechanism for the services realizing functionality of various SIEM components. Such approach allows developing different functional components independently.

The graphical elements level is a library of necessary graphic primitives – graphs, radar charts, histograms, treemaps, geographical maps, etc. Graphical elements implement mapping of the input data to the visualization models, rendering and user interaction with the input data. Interactivity of the graphical items is an important feature of the visualization tool which helps the user with efficient and quick analysis of large data sets. That is why the principle "overview – filter – details on demand" needs to be considered when developing graphic elements. The interaction mechanisms should be used in conjunction with specific clustering algorithms that group data according to their properties and connectivity, thus the reduction of the data dimension can be achieved, and therefore the readability of the generated image is increased. The graphical user interface (GUI) of the tool is designed in such way that it stimulates the exploration process of the user and enhances the understanding of the network "week" places origin and the consequences of their exploitation.

The VisSecAnalyzer visualizes the results of the Attack Modeling and Security Evaluation Component (AMSEC) [15] that produces report on security level of the analyzed network. The AMSEC works as one of the SIEM functional services.

The architecture used allows plugging components for visualization security events generated by different security sensors such as firewalls and intrusion detection systems.

3.1 Data

The main input data for the AMSEC are network topology, host configuration data including software, hardware, user-defined criticality and veracity level, and network alerts. The AMSEC assesses the specified network producing a set of security metrics associated with the network itself and each host in particular. These metrics include, for example, Security Level, Risk Level, and Veracity Level. It also lists a set of vulnerabilities and exposures formed using the host configuration and a vulnerability database, such as NVD [22] or loaded from vulnerability scanner report if available for the specified network. Each vulnerability is described using CVE-code [4], security score [5], brief description and data how it could be patched or mitigated.

Apart from calculated security metrics the AMSEC outputs the attack graph for a given malefactor model [15]. Each node of the graph denotes a specific attack action, and the attack action order reflects the sequence of malefactor actions. The nodes located on one level characterize actions that can be implemented simultaneously or independently from each other, while nodes located on different levels describe actions that are implemented in certain order. The attack action is characterized by its action type, access complexity, mortality, severity, vulnerabilities or exposures used, attacking host and target host.

All this information is used when visualizing reports of the AMSEC as it could provide a clear understanding of the security problem existing in the system.

3.2 Visualization and User Interactions

The VisSecAnalyzer GUI consists of several views designed to efficiently support cyber security analysis process. The main window is divided into subviews (Fig. 5).

The main view 1 shows the topology of the network, while view 2 reflects the structure of the network, depicting domains or specified user network groups.

The user can configure each host and network using the Property View 3. It is possible to specify the predefined properties of the host such as IP address, host type (web server, ftp server, database server, router, firewall, etc.), installed software and hardware, user-defined host criticality. This property view is updated whenever a particular state node is selected. Thus user always has details at hand.

The view 4 shows the security metrics calculated for the network itself: Security level, Risk Level, and Veracity level. Graphical elements corresponding to these security metrics are located on the main tool bar in order to attract user attention immediately. As these metrics can have value from the predefined set of values {Low, Medium, Above Medium, High, Undefined}, they are presented in as a semaphore.

We suppose that such dashboard design gives a general overview about security state of the network and communicate a lot of information in a glance. Thus, the user can analyze calculated host security metrics in the context of initial host configuration; all information is available in different views, but on one dashboard panel.

The graph based techniques are used to represent network topology. Each network object is represented by an icon. The user has the possibility to define icons for each type of the network objects. The background color of the icon is used to encode values of the security metrics calculated for the given host, such as Criticality, Mortality, Risk Level. These metrics are chosen by the user from the predefined list. The brief information about each host is available via a tool tip which appears when the mouse hovers over the network object.

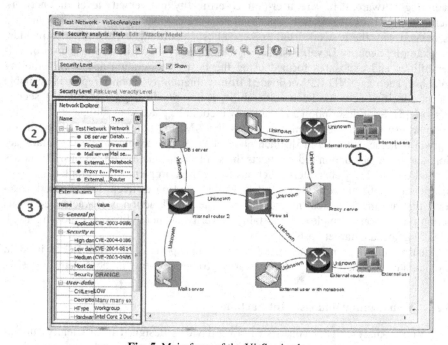

Fig. 5. Main form of the VisSecAnalyzer

In order to display large scale networks a simple geometric zooming and a semantic zooming are used. Using the semantic zooming the nodes can be aggregated according to their properties (belonging to the domain, group, etc.). This aggregation is done interactively - the user can collapse a part of the network or expand aggregated node by choosing corresponding menu item from the context menu of the node.

We use interactive treemaps to present both a vulnerability report and a network security report (Fig. 6). Each nested rectangle displays a network host. The user has an option to choose host attributes (user-defined host criticality, number and severity of detected vulnerabilities and security level) defining rectangle size and color.

By default the size is determined by the user-defined host criticality, and color is defined by security level (Fig. 6a) and vulnerability severity (Fig. 6b). Clicking on the frame of the rectangle denoting the network group (domain or user-defined group) zooms in or zooms out the selected part of the network, while clicking on the rectangle itself updates Property View of the corresponding host.

To display security metrics we use traditional semantic based color scheme, ranging between green and red. When mapping metrics value as green, colors usually notify about normal state, while red ones mean danger. But we avoid using green colors in the reporting about vulnerabilities as they could be confusing to the user. Instead we use yellow color to encode vulnerabilities with low severity level.

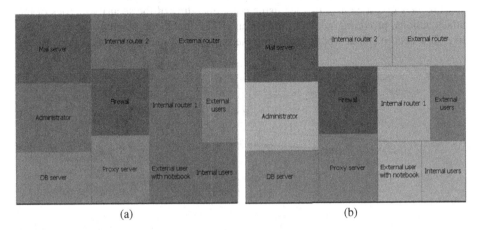

          (a)   (b)

Fig. 6. Security reports in form treemaps: (a) user-defined criticality vs. security level; (b) user-defined criticality vs. vulnerability severity

To depict the attack modeling results, we use graph based attack representation. The notations used to display attack graph are listed in Table 1. We use both color and shape to encode the type of the malefactor action. Such solution allows using color to display different security metrics calculated for each action.

Table 1. Notation used to display elements of attack graph

Notation	Description
	initial location of the malefactor
a	specific atomic attack action
s	scenario which does not exploit vulnerabilities
v	attack action that exploits a vulnerability

Attack graphs help to investigate attack deployment in the analyzed network, following malefactor actions step by step (Fig. 7). We implemented two possible graph layouts: (1) tree layout (Fig. 7a) and (2) radial layout which gives more compact view (Fig. 7b).

But network attack graphs can be both large and exhibit very dense connectivity making their analysis unfeasible task [24].

In order to solve this problem we propose using the following interaction techniques to make the analysis process easier and usage attack modeling techniques for security tasks more efficient.

Geometric zooming. It allows user to focus on a specific part of the attack graph and decrease the graph dense connectivity. The distance between graph nodes can be changed interactively using the mouse wheel.

Layout reconfiguration. We propose using two graph layouts: tree and radial. Radial layout is more compact and allows user to view the whole graph.

This view could be useful when using color encoding of the security metrics of the attack actions, providing general impression on the attack complexity or severity. The tree view is convenient when identifying the sequence of the malefactor actions.

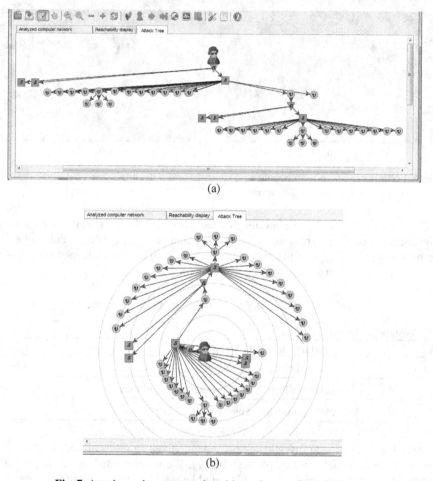

Fig. 7. Attack graph representation: (a) tree layout; (b) radial layout

Semantic zooming (aggregation). We suggest applying semantic based aggregation techniques for reducing the complexity of the graph. Depending on such graph node properties as action type, host or node connectivity the graph vertexes could be replaced by one meta-node. The used aggregation rules are depicted in Fig. 8.

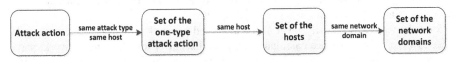

Fig. 8. Attack graph aggregation rules

Details on demand. By clicking on the corresponding graph node the user gets detailed information shown in Property View. This information includes attack type, attacking host and targeted host, user criticality value, vulnerability specific information (metric, CVE code [3] and description), and host metrics if calculated (Mortality, Risk Level). This informational display is updated whenever a particular graph node is selected.

Linking and Brushing. This effect can be applied in order to outline the path of the attack. When switched to this mode the user can select the attack action by clicking on it, this will make all subsequent and precedent nodes linked to the node of his/her interest remain colored while the rest will be drawn in grayscale (Fig. 9).

The graph based attack views are good when studying the sequence of the malefactor actions, but they do not provide an intuitive view on the compromised hosts in the network. We consider using treemaps as they can compactly represent the network. In this case the color of the rectangle reflects the state of the host (red - the host is reached by attacker, green - the attacker cannot get access to the host).

In this case it is possible to use green color as it informs the user that the network hosts are secured and do not need deployment of new protection mechanisms.

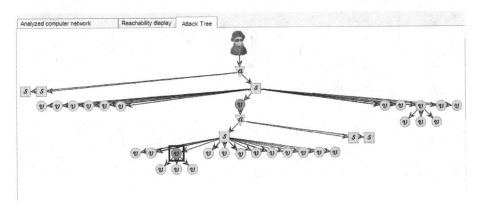

Fig. 9. Effect of linking and brushing

4 Case Study and Usability Evaluation

In order to assess the efficiency of the visualization mechanisms developed we created a test network with typical topology. It consisted of several servers (database server, mail server, internal and external web servers), firewall, IDS and more that 100 workstations (internal users). On all hosts Microsoft SQL Server 3 was installed, DBMS Apache Derby 10.1 was used on database servers, mail server had Microsoft

Exchange Server 7 SP1 installed, while workstations were equipped with mail client Microsoft Outlook 2003 and Microsoft Office 2003.

In order to assess security level of the analyzed network the NVD vulnerability databases were used. Then we calculated integrated security level for the network, and it turned to be a red one (very high criticality). The tool provided a possibility to highlight the security level of nodes in order to determine the most critical ones. In our case the most critical hosts were firewall and mail server.

By clicking on each critical host it was possible to see vulnerabilities grouped according their severity level, thus it is possible to identify the most critical ones at ones.

Thus for the mail server the most dangerous vulnerability turned to be CVE-2007-3898, that allows remote attackers to spoof DNS replies, poison the DNS cache, and facilitate further attack vectors.

Using treemap, the sizes of rectangles of which depend on user-defined criticality level and color is defined by security level, we could see that the mail server should be served in first turn and then firewall in order to increase the security level.

Then we could analyze the consequences of the mail-server compromise. By setting initial location to the mail server and constructing attack graph we could conduct reachability analysis.

Fig. 10 illustrates the compromised and secured hosts presented in the form of treemap. It is clearly seen the malefactor could reach data base server, thus receiving access to the sensitive to organization information.

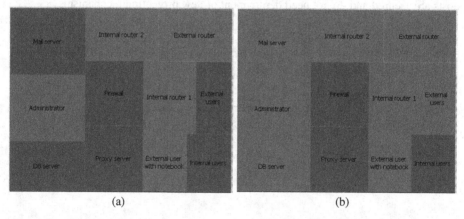

(a)   (b)

Fig. 10. Reachability analysis using treemap: (a) the initial position of the attacker is set to mail server; (b) the initial position of the attacker is set to firewall, the mail server vulnerability is mitigated

In order to mitigate the given problem it is possible to update software and use Microsoft Exchange Server 8 SP1. In this case we could see that the security level of the mail server became green, what corresponds to secured state of the host.

To assess the usability of the designed GUI we used the requirements of the ISO/IEC 9126 standard purposed to evaluate the software quality [14]. When evaluating the GUI usability we mainly focused on metrics used to assess GUI attractiveness as the goal of the developed tool is to enhance the operator efficiency through effective graphical presentation of the data and possibility to investigate them interactively. And it was important for us to receive a feedback about chosen visual models, implemented interaction techniques, color scheme, etc. Additionally, we also included functional metrics describing functionality of the application such as a possibility to create, modify network configuration, detect critical hosts and implement experiments "what-if". Table 2 shows an example of metrics included in questionnaire.

In order to implement GUI usability assessment we invited specialists in information security as well as experts in ergonomics and GUI design. It is worth noticing that we questioned both practitioners and scientific researchers.

First they were given a short introductory course on the VizSecAnalyzer. Afterwards they were given a set of simple tasks such as creation of network model for a given network description or modification of existing configuration, detection of the critical nodes and a questionnaire to get acquainted with the tool and then the experts had to rank the metrics from 0 to 5, where the higher value means better implementation. Additionally they had to assess their own competence in the subject. Later the questionnaires were processed in order to elaborate averaged rank for each metrics.

Table 2. Metrics used in questionnaire

Name	Description
Visual metrics	
Information Architecture and Hierarchy	addresses current screen layout and assesses conceptual structure of the information and its logical layout
Ease of Navigation	superscribes issues of navigation affecting data flow and user orientation, it is used to assess how user can navigate in the system in order to get necessary information
Iconography	evaluates current icon use per available user functions and data presentation (i.e. displaying types of network hosts, attack actions)
Color scheme	outlines current color scheme of text and graphic elements within the user interface to ease navigation, create emphasis, and warn users through the application
Visual models	assesses the use of visual models and interaction techniques associated with them for a given task
Customization of GUI	considers a proportion of the customizable elements in GUI
Functional metrics	
Configuration of the network and its hosts	assesses a possibility to configure network and software properties
Downloading and saving of network configuration from/to file and database	evaluates a possibility to download existing network configuration form database (or file) and save changes in current configurations
Implementation of the experiments "what-if"	assesses a possibility to implement experiments "what-if" by specifying different malefactor models, initial location or applying patches for vulnerable hosts

According to the overall ranking the quality of the tool is good (rank 4 of 5). Most of the experts marked a good choice of visual models. Apart from this some experts gave useful comments on further elaboration of GUI such as a possibility to manage object properties by setting up their visibility in Property Editor View.

We compared the VizSecAnalyzer with the tools described in Section 2 and implement similar functionality: Nv [9], GARNET [33], NAVIGATOR [3]. We left out approach to attack graph visualization suggested in [24] as there is no implementation for it. The rest described tools deal with policy assessment. Nv tool is designed to visualize vulnerability scanner reports thus it implements only a part of the VizSecAnalyser functionality. The GARNET and NAVIGATOR is probably the closest to our approach. These tools are aimed to analyze the attack reachability by presenting network domains using treemaps. The information detailing in these tools is limited to the domain level while in our tool the user can drill down to host level due to implemented interaction techniques. The reachability display of the Navigator is better than in our tool as it shows the attack deployment, but this lack is compensated by graph-based view of the VizSecAnalyzer and aggregation technique that allows aggregating network nodes to the domain level thus hiding excessive information. Though both tools provide a possibility to implement "what-if" experiments, but our tool allows specifying the attacker model and provides more convenient interface for network configuring. Apart from this the VizSecAnalyser visualizes vulnerability reports highlighting the most critical assets. Among commercial tools the Network Vulnerability Manager of RedSeal company [28] exhibit the similar functionality. It also provides treemap-based view of vulnerability reports and allows identifying those vulnerabilities that can be accessed from threat sources to isolate exposure to attacks. However it does not allow implementing "what-if" experiments taking the attacker model into account and does not display calculated security metrics based on attack graph analysis. The visualization of network traffic, e.g. [7, 12, 16-18, 27, 30], systems shows what is happening or has happened, but not the comparatively large set of what could happen.

5   Conclusion

In the paper we analyzed the visualization techniques used for network security assessment, suggested a common framework for SIEM visualization and developed the SIEM visualization component VisSecAnalyzer.

We described the proposed visual models and interaction techniques implemented in the VisSecAnalyzer, and presented case study for network level assessment and countermeasure plan adjustment. VisSecAnalyzer is intended for analyzing general security level, determining the most critical hosts and assessing consequences of exploitation of week places in security mechanisms. These data are used for prioritization of the needed countermeasures. The paper demonstrated the VisSecAnalyzer possibilities for the tasks of attack modeling and security assessment. Usability evaluation of the VisSecAnalyzer showed the quality of the tool is good.

The future research will be devoted to further elaboration and experimental analysis of suggested visualization techniques. We will evaluate the performance of proposed visualization system and assess the usability of the graphical user interfaces.

Acknowledgements. This research is being supported by grant of the Russian Foundation of Basic Research (project #13-01-00843-a), Program of fundamental research of the Department for Nanotechnologies and Informational Technologies of the Russian Academy of Sciences (contract #2.2), State contract #11.519.11.4008 and partly funded by the EU as part of the SecFutur and MASSIF projects.

References

1. Anwar, M., Fong, P.W.L., Yang, X.-D., Hamilton, H.: Visualizing Privacy Implications of Access Control Policies in Social Network Systems. In: Garcia-Alfaro, J., Navarro-Arribas, G., Cuppens-Boulahia, N., Roudier, Y. (eds.) DPM 2009. LNCS, vol. 5939, pp. 106–120. Springer, Heidelberg (2010)
2. Anwar, M., Fong, P.W.L.: P.: A Visualisation Tool for Evaluating Access Control Policies in Facebook-style Social Network Systems. Proc. of the 27th Annual ACM Symposium on Applied Computing (SAC 2012), pp. 1443–1450. ACM, New York (2012)
3. Chu, M., Ingols, K., Lippmann, R., Webster, S., Boyer, S.: Visualizing Attack Graphs, Reachability, and Trust Relationships with NAVIGATOR. In: Proc. of the Seventh International Symposium on Visualization for Cyber Security, Ontario, Canada, pp. 22–33 (2010)
4. Common Vulnerabilities and Exposures, http://cve.mitre.org/
5. Common Vulnerability Scoring System, http://www.first.org/cvss/
6. Ficco, M., Romano, L.: A generic intrusion detection and diagnoser system based on complex event processing. In: Proc. of the 1st International Conference on Data Compression, Communication, and Processing, pp. 275–284 (2011)
7. Fischer, F., Fuchs, J., Mansmann, F.: ClockMap: Enhancing Circular Treemaps with Temporal Glyphs for Time-Series Data. In: Proceedings of the Eurographics Conference on Visualization (EuroVis), pp. 97–101 (2012)
8. O'Hare, S., Noel, S., Prole, K.: A Graph-theoretic Visualization Approach to Network Risk Analysis. In: Goodall, J.R., Conti, G., Ma, K.-L. (eds.) VizSec 2008. LNCS, vol. 5210, pp. 60–67. Springer, Heidelberg (2008)
9. Harrison, L., Spahn, R., Iannacone, M., Downing, E., Goodall, J.R.: NV: Nessus Vulnerability Visualisation for the Web. In: Proc. of the VizSec 2012, Seattle, WA, USA, October 15 (2012)
10. Heitzmann, A., Palazzi, B., Papamanthou, C., Tamassia, R.: Effective Visualization of File System Access-Control. In: Goodall, J.R., Conti, G., Ma, K.-L. (eds.) VizSec 2008. LNCS, vol. 5210, pp. 18–25. Springer, Heidelberg (2008)
11. Homer, J., Varikuti, A., Ou, X., McQueen, M.A.: Improving Attack Graph Visualization through Data Reduction and Attack Grouping. In: Goodall, J.R., Conti, G., Ma, K.-L. (eds.) VizSec 2008. LNCS, vol. 5210, pp. 68–79. Springer, Heidelberg (2008)
12. Inoue, D., Eto, M., Suzuki, K., Suzuki, M., Nakao, K.: DAEDALUS-VIZ: Novel Real-time 3D Visualization for Darknet Monitoring-based Alert System. In: Proc. VizSec 2012, Seattle, WA, USA, October 15 (2012)
13. Keim, D.A., Andrienko, G., Fekete, J.-D., Görg, C., Kohlhammer, J., Melançon, G.: Visual Analytics: Definition, Process, and Challenges. In: Kerren, A., Stasko, J.T., Fekete, J.-D., North, C. (eds.) Information Visualization. LNCS, vol. 4950, pp. 154–175. Springer, Heidelberg (2008)
14. Komiyama, T.: Usability Evaluation Based on International Standards for Software Quality Evaluation. Nec Technical Journal 3(2) (2008)

15. Kotenko, I., Chechulin, A.: Attack Modeling and Security Evaluation in SIEM Systems. International Transactions on Systems Science and Applications 8, 129–147 (2012)
16. Lakkaraju, K., Yurcik, W., Lee, A.J.: NVisionIP: Netflow visualizations of system state for security situational awareness. In: Proc. of the ACM Workshop on Visualization and Data Mining for Computer Security (VizSEC/DMSEC 2004), New York, USA, pp. 65–72 (2004)
17. Lau, S.: The spinning cube of potential doom. Communications of the ACM 47(6), 24–26 (2004)
18. Lee, C.P., Trost, J., Gibbs, N., Beyah, N., Copeland, J.A.: Visual Firewall: Real-time Network Security Monitor. In: Proc. of the IEEE Workshop on Visualization for Computer Security (VizSEC 2005), pp. 129–136 (2005)
19. Mansmann, F., Göbel, T., Cheswick, W.: Visual Analysis of Complex Firewall Configurations. In: Proc. of VizSec 2012, Seattle, WA, USA, October 15 (2012)
20. Marty, R.: Applied Security Visualisation. Addison Wesley Professional, NY (2008)
21. Montemayor, J., Freeman, A., Gersh, J., Llanso, T., Patrone, D.: Information Visualisation for Rule-based Resource Access Control. In: Proc. of International Symposium on Usable Privacy and Security, SOUPS (2006)
22. National Vulnerability Database, http://nvd.nist.gov/
23. Nessus vulnerability scanner website, http://www.tenable.com/
24. Noel, S., Jacobs, M., Kalapa, P., Jajodia, S.: Multiple Coordinated Views for Network Attack Graphs. In: Proc. of the IEEE Workshops on Visualisation for Computer Security, p. 12. IEEE Computer Society (2005)
25. Noel, S., Jajodia, S.: Understanding Complex Network Attack Graphs through Clustered Adjacency Matrices. In: Proc. of the 21st Annual Computer Security Applications Conference, ACSAC 2005, pp. 160–169. IEEE Computer Society (2005)
26. Novikova, E., Kotenko, I.: Analytical Visualization Techniques for Security Information and Event Management. In: Proc. of the 21st Euromicro International Conference on Parallel, Distributed and Network-based Processing (PDP 2013), Belfast, Northern Ireland, Los Alamitos, California, pp. 519–525. IEEE Computer Society (2013)
27. Ohno, K., Koike, H., Koizumi, K.: IP Matrix: an effective visualization framework for cyber threat monitoring. In: Proc. of the 9th International Conference on Information Visualization (IV 2005), pp. 678–685. IEEE Computer Society, Washington, DC (2005)
28. RedSeal Networks Vulnerability & Risk Management Solution, http://www.redsealnetworks.com/solutions/vulnerability/
29. Stasko, J., Catrambone, R., Guzdial, M., McDonald, K.: An Evaluation of Space-filling Information Visualisations for Depicting Hierarchical Structures. International Journal of Human-Computer Studies 53(5), 663–694 (2000)
30. Taylor, T., Brooks, S., Mchugh, J., Brooks, S.: NetBytes Viewer: An Entity-based Netflow Visualization Utility for Identifying Intrusive Behavior. In: VizSEC 2007: Proc. of the 2007 Workshop on Visualization for Computer Security, pp. 101–114 (2008)
31. Tran, T., Al-Shaer, E., Boutaba, R.: PolicyVis: Firewall Security Policy Visualisation and Inspection. In: Proc. of the 21st Conference on Large Installation System Administration Conference (LISA 2007), pp. 1–16. USENIX Association, Berkeley (2007)
32. Williams, L., Lippmann, R., Ingols, K.: An Interactive Attack Graph Cascade and Reachability Display. In: Proc. of the Workshop on Visualisation for Computer Security, Sacramento, California, USA, pp. 221–236. Springer, Heidelberg (2007)
33. Williams, L., Lippmann, R., Ingols, K.: GARNET: A Graphical Attack Graph and Reachability Network Evaluation Tool. In: Goodall, J.R., Conti, G., Ma, K.-L. (eds.) VizSec 2008. LNCS, vol. 5210, pp. 44–59. Springer, Heidelberg (2008)

A Denial of Service Attack to GSM Networks via Attach Procedure

Nicola Gobbo[1], Alessio Merlo[2], and Mauro Migliardi[1]

[1] Università degli Studi di Padova
`gobbonic@dei.unipd.it, mauro.migliardi@unipd.it`
[2] Università degli Studi E-Campus
`alessio.merlo@uniecampus.it`

Abstract. Mobile Network Operators (MNOs) keep a strict control over users accessing the networks by means of the Subscriber Identity Module (SIM). This module grants the user access to the network, by performing the registration and authentication of the user's device. Without a valid Subscribe Identity Module (SIM) module and a successful authentication, mobile devices are not granted access and, hence, they are not allowed to inject any traffic in the mobile infrastructure. Nevertheless, in this paper we describe an attack to the security of a mobile network allowing an unauthenticated malicious mobile device to inject traffic in the mobile operator's infrastructure. We show that even with devices without any SIM module it is possible to inject high levels of signaling traffic in the mobile infrastructure, causing significant service degradation up to a full-fledged Denial of Service (DoS) attack.

Keywords: Mobile Security, GSM, cellular networks security, DoS attack.

1 Introduction

Mobile phones are one of the most pervasively deployed technology in the world and cellular networks have reached worldwide coverage. On one hand, the evolution from early analog networks to recent 4G LTE solutions has allowed operators to offer new services to their customers. On the other hand, the same evolution has pushed new needs into the customers; such needs have evolved from simple phone calls and SMS to internet connections and high speed access to streaming data.

The availability of smartphones with wide touch-screen displays as well as the always-on, high bandwidth IP connectivity have generated a growing set of services and applications ranging from e-mail to remote banking, from e-shopping to music streaming, from video on demand to geo-localized social networks. In turn, the ease of use and the availability of a rich a set of functionalities have instilled into users a growing familiarity and a sense of dependency. This dependency does not exist only for leisurable activities, but has a definite onset also in business and critical tasks. In particular, the last year has seen a significant

A. Cuzzocrea et al. (Eds.): CD-ARES 2013 Workshops, LNCS 8128, pp. 361–376, 2013.

penetration in govern agencies and public bodies. To this aim, we can cite the recent security certification of Android smartphones by the US Department of Defense [29] that allows the deployment of Dell hardware with Froyo (Android OS v2.2) in the Pentagon. A second example is the adoption of tablet PCs (Apple iPad) by the Chicago hospital and the Loyola University Medical Center in Maywood. Finally, several research projects are focusing on the deployment of health-care services onto the tablet PC platform with widely goals from simple access to medical records [14], to reminders for medication intake [30], to decision support systems [22], to automatic recognition of pathological states [25], to systems for memory support [23]. For these reasons, mobile networks security analysis should emphasize availability along with confidentiality and integrity.

However, the introduction of new technologies cannot be decoupled from the support to legacy ones, since i) a high number of older terminals are still active, and ii) some manufactures keep producing 2G-only phones to satisfy low-end market. For these reasons, each new radio access technology has to be deployed alongside existing ones, leading to hybrid architectures where some network components are shared among different technological infrastructures. This condition is driving operators toward single Radio Access Network solutions, causing a cellular site to broadcast signals related to up to 3 different technologies in 5 different frequency bands. Such a composite network architecture co-exists with a design traditionally focused on making mobile networks smarter and smarter, while keeping devices crowding their cells as "dumb" as possible [18,28]. Today's smartphones are far more intelligent and powerful than their predecessors. However, networks still don't profit from their enhanced processing power; on the contrary they assume the lowest possible capability in order to maintain compatibility with older devices. This assumption results in higher signaling traffic levels between network nodes[1] and more complex system management.

The complexity of the network structure may hide both unknown and known vulnerabilities. For an interesting survey on threats undermining the world of mobile telecommunication, the reader can refer to [10]. For the case of known vulnerabilities, the true impact on the mobile phone network may have not been sufficiently assessed in a way that is similar to what happens in mobile OSes [5]. To this aim, in this paper we extend the work by Khan et al. [21] focusing on the *attach phase* of GSM protocol and we show that it is possible to mount a complete attack even without hijacking or controlling a large number of user IDs recognized by the network. To achieve our goal, we study the amount of signalling traffic that a dedicated SIM-less device can inject into an operator's core network, by pushing air interface to its design limit. Such activity may obviously disable the signalling capabilities of the cells under attack, causing a local Denial of Service (DoS) similar to the one that can be achieved with a radio jammer; however, to reach a very critical level of disruption, the generated traffic may be targeted at the Home Location Register (HLR), i.e. the database containing information on mobile subscribers. Since this database is a critical

---

[1] http://connectedplanetonline.com/mss/4g-world/the-lte-signaling-challenge-0919/ (accessed in May 2013).

component of the core network, an outage of its functionality may cause an interruption of other mobile services too, finally resulting in a mobile network DoS. In our study, we leverage the HLR performance measurement conducted by Traynor et al. [27], showing that it is possible to mount an attack without any SIM module.

The remainder of this paper is structured as follow: in Section 2 we provide a description of the architecture of GSM networks; in Section 3 we analyze the state of the art in the field and we discuss the results obtained in previous related works; in section 4 we describe how it is possible to launch a DoS attack with a number of SIMless devices; finally, in section 5, we provide some concluding remarks and we describe the future direction of our study.

2   GSM Network Description

Global System for Mobile Communications (GSM) standard (2G) was initially designed to carry efficiently circuit switched voice communications in full duplex, with a main advantage over previous analog generation: all the processing happens in the digital domain. The standard protocol set expanded over time with addictions that, from Mobile Network Operators (MNOs) point of view, require just a software upgrade on already deployed hardware; consumers, instead, need modern and more powerful devices to experiment newly offered services. The first addiction to GSM has been General Packet Radio Service (GPRS) that introduced data delivery alongside of voice communications, in both circuit switched and —the more efficient— packet switched mode. Apart from calls GPRS permits data connection throughputs roughly ranging in the 9–170$k$bps interval; augmenting this modest numbers has been the main target of the second GSM enhancement: Enhanced Data Rates for GSM Evolution (EDGE). EDGE is a backward-compatible extension to GSM/GPRS network that introduce new coding and transmission techniques thus allowing for data rates up to 470$k$bps.

A typical GSM Public Land Mobile Network (PLMN) consists at least of the infrastructures depicted in figure 1. It is mainly split up in three different portions: i) the Mobile Station (MS) or User Equipment (UE), ii) the GSM/EDGE Radio Access Network (GERAN), iii) the Core Network (CN) or Network Switching Subsystem (NSS) with fully separated packet and circuit switched domains.

The MS may be a mobile phone or a mobile broadband modem with appropriate protocol stack and capabilities as defined by specifications. Nonetheless whichever device is used to connect to the network, there will be a Subscribe Identity Module (SIM) in it. SIMs are smart cards usually referred to as the furthest extension of mobile operator's network; it securely stores user identity, represented by the International Mobile Subscriber Identity (IMSI), and its related secret key, as long as the algorithms needed during the Authentication and Key Agreement (AKA) phase.

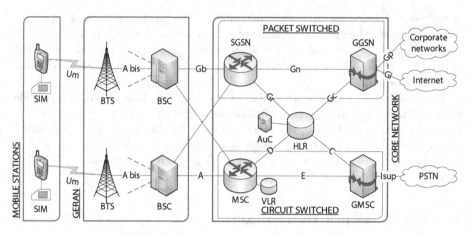

Fig. 1. Representation of the main components of a standard GPRS network

MSs communicate over air interface with the Base Transceiver Station (BTS). This is the first element composing the Radio Access Network (RAN), in GSM it has minimum functionality in the sense that it just consists of a transceiver that controls the physical layer transmission. A typical GSM BTS serves three 120° sectors —also called cells— by means of one or more antennas per sector; antennas are powered by amplifiers that gets their pilot signals from one or more baseband modules which are finally connected to the transceiver. BTS are grouped together in tens or hundreds and connected with Base Station Controllers (BSCs), which are the devices accounting for radio resource management, MSs mobility management functions and encryption of user data prior to transmission over the air interface.

Each BSC has a couple of connections toward the core network: one linking the Serving GPRS Support Node (SGSN) carrying packet switched data, the other linking the Mobile Switching Center (MSC) and transporting circuit switched informations. This division is due to the fact that the data delivery capability of the GPRS has been a posthumous addendum to the NSS, so it has been designed for deployment in environments where GSM core networks have been already running. Both SGSN and MSC act as switching and end point for end-to-end connections in their own domains; they manage hand-overs between different BSCs as well as authentication checking and charging functions. The most valuable operation of these equipments, however, is the mobility management: they keep track of MS movements inside their service area and locate it whenever required. To carry out this operation an auxiliary database called Visitor Location Register (VLR) is used: it contains the user identity at the BSC-level along with an indication of its current location and a pointer to the main user record which is contained in another database called Home Location Register (HLR). The HLR maintains a record for each mobile phone subscriber with details like the telephone number, IMSI and a secret key (i.e. the same contained in the SIM), call blocking and forwarding and a pointer to the most updated VLR the user is known to be roaming on. HLR is a core component for the networks because it has to be queried for phone call and SMS delivery, billing procedures and authentication: this latter function is supported by the Authentication Center (AuC) which calculates challenges and responses that are sent to the MSC/SGSN for actual user validation.

3   Related Works

Cellular networks seem unaffected by the same threats that, almost daily, came up in the newspapers regarding other types of widely spread systems like the Internet. Nonetheless, even if a large security outbreak has not already made its way through the news, mobile operators' network security has been studied in the literature for quite a long time. Initially, most of the attention of researchers was focused on confidentiality and integrity [8], [7], [12], [9] of data travelling over the wireless portion of the system; however, in more recent works, the problem of the actual availability of the services provided by the network, both in the wireless segment and in the core network segment, has gained popularity, becoming the focus of different studies.

The simplest way to prevent a mobile network from offering its services is using a radio jammer. Moving from physical towards upper layers increases both the complexity of the attack and the size of the involved network segment. In order to be able to prove higher layer attacks possible, however, researchers have had to wait for a device with extensible capabilities, a kind of device that made its first market appearance in 2000 but actually had a significant deployment only in 2007: the *smartphone*[2]. Until late 1990s mobile phones had only basic phone features so the user had complete control over what the terminals were doing. This fact, however, has been subverted by the first iPhone release in 2007 and, more specifically, by the introduction of Apple App Store. The iPhone, in fact, as all the smartphones marketed today, ran an operating system over which a series of applications are executed. The advent of this application-enabled phones and centralized software distribution systems attracted the attention both of attackers[3] and of security researchers. In particular, the research community has proved that the open feature set nature of the smartphone makes it the device capable of massive and distribute mobile network attacks [13].

Past Internet security studies prove that in order to mount a DoS attack a botnet is the tool that provides the most suitable characteristics; however, mobile networks have constraints and peculiarities that should be taken into consideration both during the infection phase [16] and in the setup of the command and control mechanism [24] [11]. An attacker capable of controlling a botnet can use infected devices for multiple purposes: spam delivery, sending calls or SMS toward premium price services, spoofing user identity and remote wiretapping become all straightforward for an attacker [18,15]. A malicious entity may also

---

[2] en.wikipedia.org/wiki/Smartphone (accessed in May 2013).

[3] http://arstechnica.com/security/2013/04/family-of-badnews-malware-in-google-play-downloaded-up-to-9-million-times/ (accessed on May 2013).

try to kick mobile network elements out of service. As an example, Guo et al. [18] predicted that a few dozens of subverted smartphones, served by the same base station, can jeopardize its availability by making no-answer calls and thus saturating provisioned voice channels. If phones are not located in the same place, authors outlined that it is still possible to put call aggregation points to a halt by means of a *distributed* denial of service: the number of needed controlled devices is indeed higher than the one needed in the previous case, but, due to the fact that PSTN, cellular switches and call centers are designed for a limited Busy Hour Call Attempts, the attack is still feasible.

Later studies still focusing on DoS attacks show that it is possible to achieve the needed level of service degradation in a more efficient way: instead of consuming traffic (or user-plane) channels, an attacker may try to flood control channels which are usually separated from traffic ones and significantly more limited in terms of available bandwidth. One of the first work in this direction is from Traynor et al. [26]. In a strict sense, the attack described here doesn't use a botnet but, in a broader sense, every mobile phone is an accomplice because what it has to do is just receiving incoming requests. They show how the interconnection between the mobile network and the Internet via, for example, on-line SMS delivery capabilities, may be exploited by an attacker continuously sending text messages to an especially crafted hit-list of telephone numbers. Such a data flood, estimated in roughly 580kbps, is enough to keep a control channel shared by voice and SMS busy, thus unavailable to accept or delivery new voice calls. Another study from Traynor et al. [28] focuses on the GPRS network and characterizes two different types of DoS attacks targeting data connection setup and tear-down mechanisms. Tear-down mechanism affects only the data portion of the network trying to keep reserved all Temporary Flow Identifiers (TFIs) that distinguish different data flows. In the setup attack, instead, authors moves the focus from resource exhaustion to control channel depletion, analysing the Random Access Channel (RACH). They find out that, for the Manhattan borough, 3Mbps of malicious traffic cause a data and voice connection blocking probability of 65% and, along with that, they point out that, this time, attacking data realm affects voice realm too, because of the single shared control channel.

A significant advancement in the analysis of mobile network security has been achieved when researchers found a way to attack core network elements, proving that network-wide service deterioration possible. Khan et al. and Kambourakis et al. [21,20] examine UMTS security architecture finding some protocols flaws that can be used to delete, modify or replay some unauthenticated or not integrity protected messages. This flaws may permit revealing user identities (IMSI), launching DoS attacks against both user phones and network nodes or impersonating the network acting as a man-in-the-middle. These studies, however, do not detail the amount of resources needed to mount a successful DoS attack. An attempt to evaluate the amount of resources needed can be found in the work by Traynor et al. [27]. The first step is a performance characterization of different HLR devices in different network deployments. The authors identify the transaction most suitable to mount an HLR DoS attack, searching for a compromise between resource consumption and execution time. By means of a simulation of the network behaviour they find that about 11750 infected devices submitting an "insert call forwarding" every 4.7 seconds are sufficient to reduce HLR throughput of legitimate traffic by more than 93%.

Concluding this summary of works related to DoS attacks in mobile cellular networks, it is interesting to notice the "big picture" that [18] and [28] try to draw. Currently studied mobile network DoS attacks roots their cause in the fact that this networks were designed to manage traffic with highly predictable properties but, once connected to the Internet, such constraints hold no more. The Internet was designed with architectural assumptions that are in complete opposition from the ones adopted for cellular networks; this creates a disparity in the effort spent to set up and tear down a connection, necessarily leading to a bottle neck. Moreover mobile terminals have been traditionally considered dumb because of their limited battery life and computational power: this second assumption, however, holds no more in the smartphone era and its underestimation both increases network design complexity and forces core elements to early commit far more resources than those needed by an unauthenticated device. In the following sections we show how it is possible to leverage these facts to greatly reduce the amount of resources needed to mount a successful DoS attack against cellular networks.

4   Squeezing Radio Access Protocols

When a mobile phone is switched on, GSM and UMTS protocols define what operations should be performed in order to *attach* to the network. Despite differences between the two technologies that derive from the fact that they use different radio interfaces —GSM uses TDMA while UMTS uses WCDMA— a high level description of these procedures can be described as follows: i) cell discovery, ii) best server synchronization, iii) attachment request, iv) authentication and key agreement (AKA) and v) temporary identity creation. The peculiarity of this procedure is that it cannot leverage previously accrued knowledge as it must accommodate for new devices of which there is no previous information. Moreover the design described in the introduction, i.e. the model of a smart-network and of dumb terminals, requires the whole procedure to be computationally light for the terminals and to delegate to the network most of the operations and resources. Thus, the terminals do not have to commit significant resources but the network does. These two facts are the basis of the vulnerability to DoS that is present in the attach procedure; in fact, during the AKA step, an unauthenticated device may force the core network to carry on computations that are more resource consuming than the request itself. As described by Khan et al. work [21], the way an attack could be mounted is straightforward: in a preliminary phase an attacker builds a database of valid IMSIs, then, he floods the network with *attach requests* each one carrying a different IMSI chosen from said database. The cellular network forwards the requests to HLR/AuC where each IMSI is validated and, being authentic, triggers the calculation of authentication information that are sent to SGSN that, in turn, must submit the challenge back

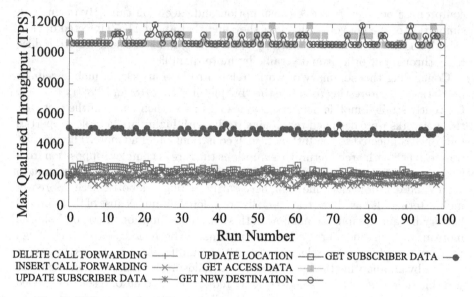

Fig. 2. HLR throughput for each transaction type with 500k subscribers [27]

to the mobile station and verify the reply correctness. As the attacker is not in possess of the SIM corresponding to the IMSI used, he doesn't know the correct answer; however, has not need for it, in fact his goal is to exhaust HLR/AuC computing resources thus he is already hitting the target with all the valid *attach requests* he is injecting. Although authors describe this attack with UMTS architecture in mind, it is important to notice that it can be performed, with minimal changes, both to old GSM [19] and new LTE [1] networks.

Khan work, however, does not provide a value for the HLR/AuC performance, thus it does not provide the number of terminals needed by an attacker in order to considerably degrade HLR services, using the attack described above. A partial analysis of this problem comes from Traynor et al. article [27]. In this work they outline an attack targeting HLR, but they adopt a different approach that leverages a botnet of authenticated devices, repeatedly injecting resource-demanding transactions available only to already attached terminals. In order to find the transaction that best suits their needs, the authors measure the average throughput —in transactions per second (TPS)— of an HLR setup, with respect to different transaction types. Their results are presented in figure 2. They choose the *insert call forwarding* procedure as the attack vector because it offers the best trade-off between computational load and execution speed. As the next step, authors simulate the effect of injecting attack traffic on an HLR already serving a typical mix of transactions: doing so they found that injecting 2500TPS the HLR capability to handle legitimate requests —under low-traffic assumptions— is reduced by 93%.

From figure 2 it is possible to determine that the *get access data* procedure is roughly 5 times faster than the *insert call forwarding* one, so, in order to achieve the same level of service degradation, we assume that the attack traffic must be multiplied by 5. This puts our target to 12500TPS, however, for the attacker this is a worst case scenario: in fact Traynor's tests focus only on the HLR, disregarding the computations at the AuC that is needed to calculate authentication information.

4.1   Regular Mobile Phones Are a Limiting Factor

To launch the attack Traynor needs a smartphone botnet for two reasons: first, clients must be authenticated before submitting an *insert call forwarding* request; second, this very kind of procedure is a standard one, so it is possible for an application to ask the underlying operating system to begin its execution. In our scenario, instead, regular phones are a limiting factor. First, from a smartphone's OS there's no way to distinguish among the steps of the GSM authentication procedure once it has been started: OSes control the modem component via a Radio Interface Layer[4] which converts high level actions such "call number" or "send SMS" into AT commands that the modem logic can understand [3]. Both high level actions and AT commands, however, are too abstract for our needs because the only way to force the attach procedure would be switching the radio off and on again. This operation is completely contained inside the GSM protocol stack and operatively hidden inside the baseband module itself, thus the module informs the OS only after the completion or failure of the entire procedure. More in details, in a mobile phone the access to the network can take only one of these three roads: 1) if the device has a valid SIM module, then the attach procedure completes unless there is a failure on the network side; 2) if the device has an invalid SIM module, then it initiate the attach procedure, but the network rejects it without needing a significant amount of resources; 3) if the device has no SIM module at all, then it does not even initiate the attach procedure. The only way to use a standard phone for performing multiple attach procedures is to equip it with a programmable SIM card and instruct the card to return a different IMSI as well as a random challenge response at each invocation. However, in this case too the solution is definitely sub-optimal because of the phone itself. Built-in mobile protocol stack is implemented strictly following 3GPP specifications which, in turn, are full of transmission wait times, exponential backoffs, maximum re-transmission trials and other artifices [2] designed with the precise purpose to induce a fair use of the network resources. As a proof of this fact Traynor highlights that, during his network behaviour measurements, he was forced to insert a 2s delay between each request: its removal, otherwise, caused extended execution times. The very goal of a DoS attack, on the contrary, is to unfairly squander the network resources in order to prevent legitimate devices to access the service; furthermore

---

[4] RIL specifications are available for Windows Mobile® http://msdn.microsoft.com/ en-us/library/aa920475.aspx (accessed on May 2013) and Android http://www. kandroid.org/online-pdk/guide/telephony.html (accessed on May 2013).

we want to reach the limits of the air interface in order to cut down the number of attacking point. For these reasons we claim that the tool best suited to an attacker needs is a dedicated device capable of accessing the network without needing a valid SIM, and without the timing guards and the strict adherence to the protocol that are normally introduced in components aimed at the consumer market.

4.2   Analysing the Air Interface

We now analyze the peculiarities of GSM air interface protocol to evaluate its limits in terms of number of *attach requests* sent to the base station per second. In this process we suppose to be the only device communicating with the target cell; this hypothesis is unrealistic, but is a direct consequence of the unfairness of the attacking device: while legitimate mobile phones would backoff when facing a traffic problem, our device actively works toward the consumption of all the cell's resources. Thus, most of the time a mobile phone tries to get access, it won't be served because of the high number of requests injected by the attacking device, moreover, as soon as a legitimate request completes, the high number of requests injected by the attacking device generates a high probability that the just freed resources will be grabbed by the attacker and made unavailable to legitimate, well behaved devices.

GSM Protocol. GSM attach procedure involves only three channels as depicted in figure 3: RACH, AGCH and SDCCH.

Channels are logical entities used to carry specific traffic types; they are laid over GSM's frequency and time division multiple access (FDMA / TDMA) texture. For each carrier frequency, the fundamental building block is the TDMA frame that, in turn, is divided into 8 time slots, each during $577\mu s$. Channel are broadcast over the air interface time-multiplexed into the multiframe structure: we focus on control-type multiframes which are dedicated to signalling and are made up of 51 frames, thus are repeating with periodicity $235.38ms$. The standard dictates the available configurations for control-type multiframes: they differ for the number of available SDCCHs and, even if combined, it is possible to have at most 12 SDCCHs. [19]

In order to evaluate the design limits of the GSM protocol, we need to analyse each channel and to find out which one introduces the maximum bottleneck. The RACH —the Random Access Channel— is the uplink channel used to carry mobile phone's access requests; in normal conditions, it is governed by the slotted ALOHA protocol, so, in order to maximize its performances, protocol developer designed RACH messages to fill just a single timeslot. We specified "normal conditions" because, in our scenario, we don't care about contention that may be caused by other devices, thus, differently from the normal scenario, we do not apply any backoff and we aim directly at the full channel consumption. In such a scenario, a 12 SDCCHs configuration provides 27 RACH access slots each multiframe and this means a capacity of:

$$\rho_{RACH} = \frac{27}{235.38ms} \approx 114.7 \text{ requests per second} \tag{1}$$

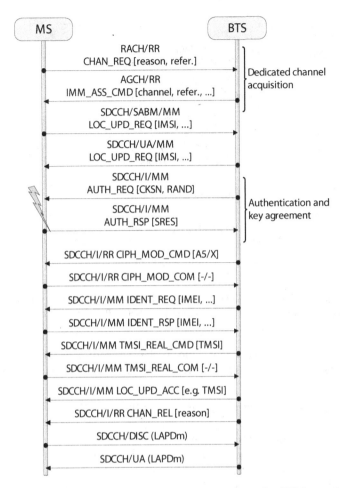

Fig. 3. Messages exchanged between MS and BTS during the GSM attach procedure [19]. The lighting on the left mark the message replaced during the attack.

This result is not fully consistent with the 80TPS calculated by [27] for the slotted ALOHA instance: authors assume a multiframe entirely dedicated to RACH slots, but this is not the case when 12 SDCCHs are deployed [19, page 99].

The Access Grant (AGCH) downlink channel is used to answer incoming random access request; it carries the information needed by the mobile phone to access the dedicated channel used for further communications. Messages over

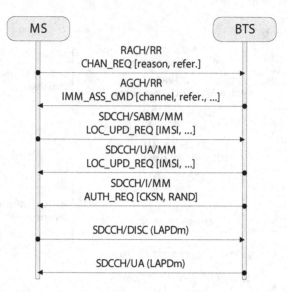

Fig. 4. Messages exchanged between MS and BTS during the attack: our device solicits an early disconnection right after receiving the AUTH_REQ from the network

AGCH fills 4 consecutive time slots due to channel coding and interleaving; this scheme allows the BSS to answer up to 3 RACH requests every multiframe[5]:

$$\rho_{AGCH} = \frac{3}{235.38ms} \approx 12.7 \text{ requests per second} \qquad (2)$$

which represent a tighter limit than RACH.

The main part of the attach procedure is delivered via Standalone Dedicated Control Channel (SDCCH) that is an bidirectional channel assigned to a mobile terminal and is reserved to it until a special *channel release* message is issued by the BSC. As we stated above, in our scenario we assume the presence of 12 SDCCHs; determining their occupation time, however, is quite tricky. Traynor et al. [27] measured an average time of 3s to perform a complete attach where 0.5s are needed by the core network to contact HLR/AuC, calculate the authentication information and receive data back. We prove that the remaining 2.5s are spent to send messages back and forth between the mobile phone and the BTS. A multiframe can carry just one message for each SDCCH in each direction, but, when the BTS requires information to the mobile phone, the latter one can answer in the same multiframe: in fact the GSM protocol states a displacement between downlink and uplink multiframes that allows the MS to compute its reply. Given these two rules and assuming two multiframes needed for the

---

[5] The BSS may use the extended version of the *immediate assignment* command that allow channel assignment to two mobile phones simultaneously, thus doubling AGCH capacity: we will see, however, that also in the more stringent case the AGCH is not the attack bottleneck.

RACH-AGCH exchange, we may conclude that completing the attach procedure requires 11 multiframes, that is $11 \times 235.38ms = 2.6s$ that is almost exactly the time obtained in Traynor's measurements. Thus we say that, during message exchange between the MS and the BTS, the only wait time is related to the HLR/AuC interrogation; this, in turn, allows us to estimate SDCCH utilization time during our attack. Message exchange will be modified just from *authentication response* message on, in the way depicted in figure 4. After receiving the *authentication request* the device answers back with a LAPD$_m$ DISC message that request BTS to terminate the multiple frame operation, releasing its Layer 2 connection [4]. We use this procedure instead of replying with a wrong SRES for two reasons: first, it speeds up the SDCCH release cutting the number of needed messages from 10 to 7; second, the *authentication request* message, containing the challenge, already carries the proof that the HLR/AuC has been consulted.

Using the same rule, we now require 6 multiframes, 4 of which are carried over SDCCH, leading to a channel holding time of $4 \times 235.38ms + 0.5s = 1.44s$, thus a 12 SDCCHs capacity of:

$$\rho_{SDCCHs} = \frac{12}{1.44s} \approx 8.3 \text{ requests per second} \tag{3}$$

Comparing each channel capacity and choosing the lower one, we argue that GSM attacking capabilities are limited by the SDCCH channel at a rate of 8TPS. This result tell us that a GSM-only attack can be mounted with 1563 SIMless devices spread over the same number of cells. Furthermore, we have proved that using SIMless devices is not only possible but, compared with the number of devices required for a botnet based attack, allows reducing the amount of resources of an order of magnitude. Finally, it is important to notice that the devices enrolled in a botnet are still positioned by their rightful owners, independently from the attacker will. Thus, it is possible that an unusual clustering of users (e.g. an event in a theatre or a concert) could produce a concentration of devices that saturates the cell signalling bandwidth and prevents some of the botnets node to fulfil their full attacking potential. On the contrary, the device we envision is not owned by an unknowing user, it can be precisely placed by the attacker and even remotely triggered to start the attack. All of these factors represents a significant increase in the dangerousness of the described attack when compared with the ones described in previous works.

5   Conclusions and Future Works

Cellular networks are one of the infrastructure designated as critical both in the American and the European vision of the homeland security. This has lead to a large number of studies that have analysed the architecture of the networks to identify and possibly mend vulnerabilities that could be exploited to mount attacks.

Each infrastructure has been deeply analysed and many possible sweet spots for an attack have been neutralized; however, two new factors aggravate the complexity in the infrastructure defence. The first of these factors is the appearance of programmable mobile phones; the second aggravating factor is, as it has been already pinpointed in previous works [5] [6] the interplay between different well known components: in this case coexisting different generations of networks. In past works several ways to mount DoS attack leveraging the programmability of modern smartphones have been described, however, these works described methodologies that needed hijacking more than 10.000 smartphones with valid SIM modules in order to mount a successful attack.

In this paper we have described a different approach, we have evaluated the possibility to bypass the strict timings enforced by the cellular network protocols by means of a dedicated radio device. This allowed us to prove that it is possible to inject into the cellular networks signalling traffic without having the control of valid SIM modules. The amount of resources that we can force the infrastructure to squander through the network of a single generation (e.g. 2G, the GSM network) is sufficient to produce a significant degradation of the service although the number of needed devices is still very high. Nonetheless, this result is very significant: first, the usage of a SIMless device allows gathering the resources needed to mount the attack without interfering with users and running the risk of being discovered; second, the usage of devices that are not in possession of unknowing users allows optimal distribution of attacking devices and removes the risk that the attack fails because of an incorrect placement of the botnet nodes. The possibility to hit a single infrastructure component through different generations of network, thus leveraging the interplay between network generations in the cellular infrastructure, would allow reducing the number of attacking devices need. In fact, combining the signalling bandwidth of GSM with the one made available by the 3G (UMTS) let each attacking device to inject more traffic into the network. The combination of this with what we presented in this paper, though, is part of a broader study [17] which has been submitted to the Journal of Ambient Intelligence and Humanized Computing.

References

1. 3GPP: TS 23.401 — General Packet Radio Service (GPRS) enhancements for Evolved Universal Terrestrial Radio Access Network (E-UTRAN) access,
   http://www.3gpp.org/ftp/Specs/html-info/23401.htm
2. 3GPP: TS 25.214 — Physical layer procedures (FDD),
   http://www.3gpp.org/ftp/Specs/html-info/25214.htm
3. 3GPP: TS 27.007 — AT command set for User Equipment (UE),
   http://www.3gpp.org/ftp/Specs/html-info/27007.htm
4. 3GPP: TS 44.006 — Mobile Station - Base Stations System (MS - BSS) interface Data Link (DL) layer specification,
   http://www.3gpp.org/ftp/Specs/html-info/44006.htm
5. Armando, A., Merlo, A., Migliardi, M., Verderame, L.: Would you mind forking this process? A Denial of Service attack on Android (and some countermeasures). In: Gritzalis, D., Furnell, S., Theoharidou, M. (eds.) SEC 2012. IFIP AICT, vol. 376, pp. 13–24. Springer, Heidelberg (2012)
6. Armando, A., Merlo, A., Migliardi, M., Verderame, L.: Breaking and fixing the Android Launching Flow. Computers & Security (2013),
   http://www.sciencedirect.com/science/article/pii/S0167404813000540

7. Castiglione, A., Cattaneo, G., Cembalo, M., De Santis, A., Faruolo, P., Petagna, F., Ferraro Petrillo, U.: Engineering a secure mobile messaging framework. Computers & Security 31(6), 771–781 (2012)

8. Castiglione, A., Cattaneo, G., De Maio, G., Petagna, F.: SECR3T: Secure End-to-End Communication over 3G Telecommunication Networks. In: 2011 Fifth International Conference on Innovative Mobile and Internet Services in Ubiquitous Computing (IMIS), pp. 520–526 (2011)

9. Castiglione, A., Cattaneo, G., De Santis, A., Petagna, F., Ferraro Petrillo, U.: SPEECH: Secure Personal End-to-End Communication with Handheld. In: ISSE 2006, Securing Electronic Busines Processes, pp. 287–297. Vieweg (2006), http://dx.doi.org/10.1007/978-3-8348-9195-2_31

10. Castiglione, A., De Prisco, R., De Santis, A.: Do You Trust Your Phone? In: Di Noia, T., Buccafurri, F. (eds.) EC-Web 2009. LNCS, vol. 5692, pp. 50–61. Springer, Heidelberg (2009), http://dx.doi.org/10.1007/978-3-642-03964-5_6

11. Castiglione, A., De Prisco, R., De Santis, A., Fiore, U., Palmieri, F.: A botnet-based command and control approach relying on swarm intelligence. Journal of Network and Computer Applications (2013), http://dx.doi.org/10.1016/j.jnca.2013.05.002

12. De Santis, A., Castiglione, A., Cattaneo, G., Cembalo, M., Petagna, F., Ferraro Petrillo, U.: An Extensible Framework for Efficient Secure SMS. In: 2010 International Conference on Complex, Intelligent and Software Intensive Systems, pp. 843–850 (2010)

13. Derr, K.: Nightmares with mobile devices are just around the corner? In: IEEE International Conference on Portable Information Devices, PORTABLE 2007, pp. 1–5 (2007)

14. Doukas, C., Pliakas, T., Maglogiannis, I.: Mobile healthcare information management utilizing cloud computing and android os. In: 2010 Annual International Conference of the IEEE Engineering in Medicine and Biology Society (EMBC), pp. 1037–1040. IEEE (2010)

15. Felt, A.P., Finifter, M., Chin, E., Hanna, S., Wagner, D.: A survey of mobile malware in the wild. In: Proceedings of the 1st ACM Workshop on Security and Privacy in Smartphones and Mobile Devices, pp. 3–14. ACM (2011)

16. Fleizach, C., Liljenstam, M., Johansson, P., Voelker, G.M., Mehes, A.: Can you infect me now?: malware propagation in mobile phone networks. In: Proceedings of the 2007 ACM Workshop on Recurring Malcode, pp. 61–68. ACM (2007)

17. Gobbo, N., Merlo, A., Migliardi, M.: Attacking the attach procedure in cellular networks. Journal of Ambient Intelligence and Humanized Computing (2014)

18. Guo, C., Wang, H.J., Zhu, W.: Smart-phone attacks and defenses. In: HotNets III (2004)

19. Heine, G., Horrer, M.: GSM networks: protocols, terminology, and implementation. Artech House, Inc. (1999)

20. Kambourakis, G., Kolias, C., Gritzalis, S., Hyuk-Park, J.: Signaling-oriented DoS attacks in UMTS networks. In: Park, J.H., Chen, H.-H., Atiquzzaman, M., Lee, C., Kim, T.-H., Yeo, S.-S. (eds.) ISA 2009. LNCS, vol. 5576, pp. 280–289. Springer, Heidelberg (2009)

21. Khan, M., Ahmed, A., Cheema, A.R.: Vulnerabilities of umts access domain security architecture. In: Ninth ACIS International Conference on Software Engineering, Artificial Intelligence, Networking, and Parallel/Distributed Computing, SNPD 2008, pp. 350–355. IEEE (2008)

N. Gobbo, A. Merlo, and M. Migliardi

22. Kuntagod, N., Mukherjee, C.: Mobile decision support system for outreach health worker. In: 2011 13th IEEE International Conference on e-Health Networking Applications and Services (Healthcom), pp. 56–59. IEEE (2011)
23. Migliardi, M., Gaudina, M.: Memory Support through Pervasive and Mobile Systems. In: Inter-Cooperative Collective Intelligence: Techniques and Applications. SCI. Springer (2013)
24. Mulliner, C., Seifert, J.P.: Rise of the iBots: Owning a telco network. In: 2010 5th International Conference on Malicious and Unwanted Software (MALWARE), pp. 71–80. IEEE (2010)
25. Tacconi, C., Mellone, S., Chiari, L.: Smartphone-based applications for investigating falls and mobility. In: 2011 5th International Conference on Pervasive Computing Technologies for Healthcare (PervasiveHealth), pp. 258–261. IEEE (2011)
26. Traynor, P., Enck, W., McDaniel, P., La Porta, T.: Mitigating attacks on open functionality in sms-capable cellular networks. In: Proceedings of the 12th Annual International Conference on Mobile Computing and Networking, pp. 182–193. ACM (2006)
27. Traynor, P., Lin, M., Ongtang, M., Rao, V., Jaeger, T., McDaniel, P., La Porta, T.: On cellular botnets: measuring the impact of malicious devices on a cellular network core. In: Proceedings of the 16th ACM Conference on Computer and Communications Security, pp. 223–234. ACM (2009)
28. Traynor, P., McDaniel, P., La Porta, T., et al.: On attack causality in internet-connected cellular networks. In: Proceedings of 16th USENIX Security Symposium on USENIX Security Symposium, pp. 1–16. USENIX Association (2007)
29. U.S. Department of Defense: Security Technical implementation Guide, http://iase.disa.mil/stigs/net_perimeter/wireless/smartphone.html
30. Wang, M.Y., Zao, J.K., Tsai, P., Liu, J.: Wedjat: a mobile phone based medicine in-take reminder and monitor. In: Ninth IEEE International Conference on Bioinformatics and BioEngineering, BIBE 2009, pp. 423–430. IEEE (2009)

PPM: Privacy Policy Manager for Personalized Services

Shinsaku Kiyomoto[1], Toru Nakamura[1], Haruo Takasaki[2],
Ryu Watanabe[1], and Yutaka Miyake[1]

[1] KDDI R & D Laboratories Inc.
2-1-15 Ohara, Fujimino-shi, Saitama, 356-8502, Japan
kiyomoto@kddilabs.jp
[2] KDDI Research Institute Inc.
3-10-10 Iidabashi, Chiyoda-ku, Tokyo, 102-8460, Japan

Abstract. In this paper, we introduce a new architecture for personalized services. The architecture separates access control using a user own privacy policy from data storage for private information, and it supports privacy policy management by users. We design a core module, the Privacy Policy Manager (PPM). The module includes several functionalities: ID management, privacy policy management, control of information flows, and recording the flows.

1 Introduction

Personalized services have been successfully implemented in a variety of services such as targeted advertisements, personalized searches, and location-based services. Privacy breach has been a major concern for users of personalized services, not only online web services but also offline real services. O2O (Online to Offline) is a new direction for commercial services; however, privacy concerns have become serious due to the expansion of service collaborations. Users have been very concerned when diverted to services they were unaware of having any relationship with. In fact, some research results [26,34] have suggested that Internet ads personalized with private data leak users' private information. On the other hand, it has been suggested that the creation of privacy awareness can assist users in dealing with context-aware services without harming their privacy unintentionally [15].

Another issue is the burden of checking on and maintaining privacy policies[33]. Users must check the privacy policies of a service that is presented by a service provider before using the service. Each service provider prepares a privacy policy for each service, so users must often check on many privacy policies. Furthermore, it is troublesome that users cannot determine or customize the privacy policies for themselves. If a user does not agree with the privacy policy of a service, the user cannot use the service.

Solove suggested that the privacy self-management model cannot achieve the goals demanded of it, and it has been pushed beyond its limits, while privacy

A. Cuzzocrea et al. (Eds.): CD-ARES 2013 Workshops, LNCS 8128, pp. 377–392, 2013.

law has been relying too heavily upon the privacy self-management model [43]. In his paper, issues involved in giving consent to a privacy policy are clarified as: (1) developing a coherent approach to consent, one that accounts for social science's discoveries about how humans make decisions about personal data, and (2) developing more substantive privacy rules. An experimental result [1] by Acquisti and Grossklags shows a lack of knowledge about technological and legal forms of privacy protection when confirming privacy policy. Their observations suggest that several difficulties obstruct even concerned and motivated individuals in attempts to protect their own private information. One article [41] also suggested that users were not familiar with technical and legal terms related to privacy. Moreover, it was suggested that users' knowledge about privacy threats and technologies that help to protect their privacy is quite inadequate [30].

The Platform for Privacy Preferences Project (P3P) [44,10] enables websites to express their privacy practices in a standard format that can be retrieved automatically and interpreted easily by user agents. The project provides user agent modules that allow users to be informed of site practices and to automate decision-making based on these practices when appropriate. However, in practice, it is not used by online and offline services [40] due to complex policy definitions, even though some browsers have a module for privacy matching. Furthermore, it is only considered to implement the module on web browsers.

In this paper, we consider an architecture for personalized services, and solutions to privacy problems related to personalized services. The architecture separates data storage from access control based on a privacy policy, and it supports privacy policy management by users. We design a core module named Privacy Policy Manager (PPM) that provides two functionalities: ID management and privacy policy management.

2   Towards Privacy-Preserving Personalized Services

In this section, we introduce the background of our study and clarify issues that arise in designing the architecture.

2.1   Personal Data Service

A personal data vault has been presented as support for a user-transparent architecture that can control information flow [19]. It is a secure container to which only the individual has complete access. It decouples the capture and archiving of personal data streams from the function for sharing that information. The personal data vault would then facilitate the selective sharing of subsets of the information with various services. There are some platforms that manage a personal data vault. An individual can execute functions in the personal data vault: controlled push and informed pull. Each platform is managed by a company, so individuals must trust the service provider of the platform. To solve this problem, the concept of Personal Data Service (PDS) has been presented, and some research projects have provided tools for realizing individual-based management of private information.

The PDS is a platform that allows users to control their own information by themselves. It is used for sharing personal data with friends and organizations that are trusted. The PDS holds an individual's sensitive data such as address, credit card, and employment and gives the user access control functionality. The concept of the PDS is an individual-centric model, meaning that centralized access control by each individual should be provided on their own terminal. Both an access control mechanism and data stage for the sensitive data are implemented in a program (such as a web browser) on the terminal. By using the PDS, users are allowed to securely manage their own information and control data flows of the information. Higgins [21] is a browser extension including modules for PDS, and it supports PDS for browser interactions and web client interactions. The project Danube [13] is another instance of PDS for web services. The VRM project [42] is a research project that aims to provide a platform and tools for realizing a personal data service. The project defines five principles for customers who use privacy preserving services.

- *Customers must enter relationships with vendors as independent actors.*
- *Customers must be the points of integration for their own data.*
- *Customers must have control of data they generate and gather. This means they must be able to share data selectively and voluntarily.*
- *Customers must be able to assert their own terms of engagement.*
- *Customers must be free to express their demands and intentions outside of any one company's control.*

On the other hand, there is a problem in that an individual must manage all functionalities for protecting and controlling his/her private information. Thus, a more user-friendly architecture is required. We will formalize issues for personalized services based on the above principles in the next subsection.

2.2 Issues for Personalized Services

There are some issues in existing services, handling of an individual's private information, when seen as a personal data service. The PDS solves some problems outlined in this subsection, but some issues remain for constructing user-friendly architecture. We should clarify the issues before designing an architecture for personalized services. Four issues are summarized the following:

- *Complexity.* Current service providers issue their own privacy policies for each service. Users must examine and accept a huge amount of information in multiple policies before even beginning to use the services.
- *Flexibility.* Privacy policies are determined at the initiative of service providers. Some conditions of privacy policies (including *opt-out*) may be selected, but there is no guarantee that the conditions fit the user's privacy needs.
- *Availability.* Distribution of private information is restricted. Privacy related information is useful for user-centric (personalized) services such as recommendation services and support services. However, the service provider has

appropriate methods for information distribution without privacy breach. Each service provider presents its own privacy policy, and it only covers the service from the service provider. Users hope to apply a common privacy policy for all services.

– *Assurance.* Users are necessarily concerned about the management of private information by the service provider. How to ensure the integrity of operations and how to improve the credibility of service providers are important issues as services using private information expand.

In this paper, we present an architecture that deals with the above issues.

3   Architecture for Personalized Services

In this section, we introduce an architecture for personalized services under a new personal data service concept. To deal with the issues listed in the previous section, we design an architecture that supports users in their effort to enforce their common privacy policies and that reduces the complexity of operations on the user side. The main features of the architecture are as follows;

– **Separation of Access Control and Policy Management.** We separate the functionality of the personal data service into two parts: data storage and access control. A trusted entity manages the access control portion to support individuals in configuring appropriate privacy policies and controlling information flows based on those privacy policies. The construction of data storage is beyond the scope of this paper; it is assumed that this is managed by each individual or distributed into some domains. Privacy policies are managed in the trusted entity in order to apply common policies to several services.
– **Support for Policy Management.** The architecture provides a mechanism that supports management of user privacy policies. The mechanism helps to create a common privacy policy of each user and optimize it based on user suggestions.
– **Interoperable Architecture.** The architecture provides a function for ID federation, and users delegate ID management for accessing several service providers to the architecture side in conjunction with the common privacy policy management.
– **Log Management.** The architecture has a proxy between users and service providers. All communication is recorded into a trusted area of the architecture. Thus, users can verify flows of private information.

Figure 1 shows the architecture. The main component of the architecture is a Privacy Policy Manager (PPM). The PPM manages an individual's privacy policies and controls flows of private information according to those privacy policies. The PPM is built on a trusted entity in a domain, and each separate domain has at least one PPM. Individuals register their privacy policy with a PPM located in a domain to which the individual belongs, and configure the actions to be taken

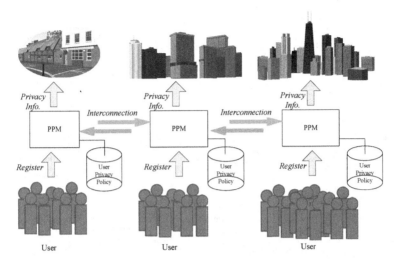

Fig. 1. Architecture for Privacy Policy Management

when a service provider requests private information whose delivery violates the privacy policies. For example, the PPM asks an individual whether the private information should be sent, when the act of sending the information is against the privacy policy of the individual. Inter-communication between PPMs is considered in the architecture. If an individual moves to another area, it is expected that the individual will access a PPM in the other area. In this situation, the new PPM requests the PPM that has the individual's privacy policy to transfer the privacy policy or a notice of a judgment on whether private information can be sent to a service provider.

Concept of Opt-In Domain. The "Opt-In Domain" is a concept for a comprehensive agreement on private information usage. Individuals generally have been concerned about privacy breaches in many situations, because they think that their private information may be used by unknown services or transferred to other service providers. On the other hand, availability is a problem on the service provider's side, as discussed in the previous section. The "Opt-In Domain" concept allows the use of private information not only by a service provider but also by other service providers who are located in a certain area (same domain), such as a local area, shopping mall, amusement park, small town, or university. The use of private information is restricted within a boundary defined in physical or virtual space[1]. In this concept, individuals define a privacy policy for a certain domain and give service providers in the domain-permission to access the individual's private information that is gathered in the domain. Our framework fits this concept because the PPM manages a comprehensive agreement on behalf of service providers.

---

[1] Note that a physical boundary is more acceptable to individuals, because it is an intuitive boundary, and individuals feel more confidence in this. Individual's acceptance of boundaries will be analyzed by an experiment in our future work.

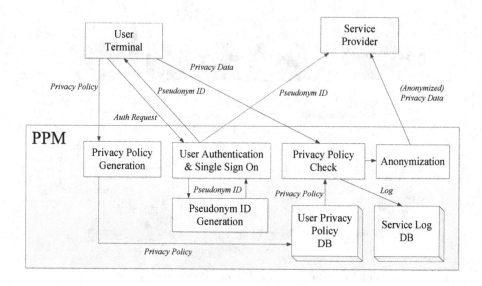

Fig. 2. Privacy Policy Manager

4   Privacy Policy Manager

The Privacy Policy Manager (PPM) is the core model for the architecture. Individuals are users of a PPM on their domain, and an individual's privacy policy is managed in the database of the PPM, and information flow is controlled based on the privacy policies. The main role of the PPM is ID management, including user authentication and privacy policy management. Figure 2 shows an overview of the PPM. The PPM is similar to a proxy service including an access control mechanism, and has the following functions;

- User authentication and ID Federation.
  For user convenience, a single-sign-on scheme should be used. The PPM generates a pseudonym ID for each service provider and registers the pseudonym IDs to service providers. Once a user logs into the PPM, the user uses services provided by the service providers without additional login processes. The PPM automatically translates the user's original ID into the pseudonym ID and notifies the login condition to a service provider, when the user uses the service. The detailed mechanism of ID generation is explained in 4.2.
- Creation and Update of User Privacy Policy.
  The PPM should provide a user-friendly GUI for creating a user's privacy policy. Furthermore, registered privacy policies should frequently be updated based on records of service use. We define two functions f_m and f_w for privacy policy management in later subsections.
- Privacy Policy Checking.
  When a service provider requests that a user send private information, the

PPM should check the user's privacy policy and decide whether to send the private information.

− Storing Records of Service Use.
Visualization of flows transferring private information is an important role of the PPM. All service access goes through the PPM. The PPM should hold all logs of the information flow, and provide them to users. We consider a concept called *user consent log search*, which is explained in 4.5

− Communication with other PPMs.
To support a roaming user who belongs to another PPM, the PPM should have a communication function to ask for a privacy policy or a judgment about privacy control. The protocols are summarized in 4.6.

− Anonymization and Obfuscation (Optional).
It is assumed that private information cannot be sent to a service provider in the original form, but that it is possible to send it after anonymization or obfuscation. For example, a user may allow the sending of approximate location information instead of precise location information such as GPS data. Thus, the PPM should have a function to modify private information in order to satisfy the privacy policy of a user. We can use existing techniques referred in section 5 for anonymization and obfuscation.

4.1 Procedure

The PPM has the role of a proxy that mediates communication between a user and a service provider. A pseudonym ID is also provided by the PPM in order to hide the user's identity and avoid a privacy breach that would make the user's actions traceable across several services. The procedure in a sample case of service use is as follows;

1. A user registers his/her privacy policy with the PPM before using services.
2. When a user registers with a service provider, the user first accesses the PPM and requests a pseudonym ID with an identification of the service provider. The PPM generates the pseudonym ID and sends it to the user.
3. When the user uses the service of the service provider, the user first logs in with the PPM. The user accesses to the service provider using the pseudonym ID. The service provider obtains authentication status from the PPM, then provides the service to the user.
4. During service provision, the service provider requests that the user send private information to the service provider via the PPM. The user sends private information to the service provider via the PPM. The PPM checks the privacy policy of the user and transfers the private information if allowed by the privacy policy.
5. The PPM stores the logs of the transfer of the private information.
6. The PPM updates the privacy policy of the user, if needed.

An offline batch operation to update of a privacy policy may be allowed, when updating would otherwise impose an excessive burden on the PPM.

4.2　Pseudonym ID Generation and ID Management

When the same IDs are used to identify users for all services, there is a privacy breach in that user activities on each service can be linked by their IDs. One simple solution to this problem is to use different IDs for each service. Users' activities then cannot be linked by their IDs even if service providers collude with each other. However, using different IDs on each service means that the PPM manages many IDs. We use a cryptographic technique for user ID generation on the PPM in order to reduce the cost of ID management by the PPM. The IDs that are used by service providers for user identification are generated from the user login ID plus a user secret like his/her password to the PPM, using a cryptographic technique.

A "pseudonym ID (pID)" is generated and used for each service in the architecture. The relationship between the newly generated ID and the user login ID (uID) is hidden in the pID itself. The PPM, which generated the ID, retains a master key K_m and does not have to maintain the relationship itself. An encryption key K_s is generated as $K_s = H(K_m \| user\ secret)$, where $H(*)$ is a cryptographic hash function like SHA-256 and $user\ secret$ is an input by the user during the user authentication process. The symbol $\|$ denotes concatenation of data. Note that the PPM does not hold K_s itself as a security requirement. The ID generation scheme is shown below;

$$pID = E_{K_s}(uID \| S_{info})$$

where S_{info} represents any bit string that is different for each service provider, such as the name of the service provider, and $E_{K_s}(*)$ is a symmetric key encryption algorithm with a secret key K_s. We use AES-256 (Advanced Encryption Standard with a 256-bit key) as the encryption algorithm for ID generation. The PPM dynamically generates the ID for each service provider and sends it to the user. We assume an *offline attacker* who can access local files of the PPM but cannot obtain any information from code that is executing on the PPM or a physical memory of an environment running on the PPM. That means that we assume an attack by a *curious* operator of the PPM. The PPM execution is protected by using software tamper-resistant techniques and memory-protection techniques; however, the *curious* operator (*offline attacker*) still has a chance to examine local files. The pseudonym ID is generated from a *user secret* and the master key K_m securely embedded in the PPM. Thus, the *offline attacker* cannot generate the pseudonym ID, and tracing the actions of a particular user is impossible.

4.3　Privacy Policy Creation and Modification

The PPM has the function of creating and updating user privacy policies. It is an essential task for a user to configure a precise privacy policy before service use. In our architecture, the PPM provides two steps: initial creation of a privacy policy and customization of the privacy policy.

A hierarchical structure is used to define a privacy policy $\mathcal{P}$ in the PPM. Let $P_i \in \mathcal{P}$ $(0 \leq i \leq l_i)$ be the ith item in the policy, and P_i has sub-items P_{ij} $(0 \leq j \leq l_{ij})$. If $P_0 = A$, then all items are allowed. In a similar fashion, P_{ij} has sub-items P_{ijk}. If the parent item is A, then all child items are A. In the initial policy creation, a user defines a policy for each top-level item such as $P_1 = A, P_2 = \neg A, P_3 = \neg A, ...$, where A denotes "allowed to send", and $\neg A$ denotes "not allowed to send". For example, if P_1 is a policy governing location information from the GPS of the user's terminal, the location information can be sent to all service providers. Thus, almost all items in the initial policy are defined as $\neg A$.

When a user uses a location-based service, the PPM receives a request with a permission description D_x (that is the same as a description of privacy policy items) from the service provider, and checks the privacy policy governing location information. For example, the permission description is denoted as "$D_x = P_{1433}$: Brief location information (town level) for a trust level 3 service provider". Let b_x be a feedback from the user for the permission description D_x. If the policy governing location information says that $P_1 = \neg A$, the PPM asks the user whether the permission described is allowed ($b_x = 1$) or not ($b_x = 0$). If the user grants permission, the location information is sent and the privacy policy is updated to add the item P_{1433}. Thus, the policy is modified as $f_m(\mathcal{P}, D_x, b_x) = \{P_1 = \neg A, P_{14} = \neg A, P_{143} = \neg A, P_{1433} = A\}$, where $f_m(*, *, *)$ is a modification function of the privacy policy. Then other items such as P_{1432} are implicitly configured as $\neg A$. For precise and usable privacy policy setting, we need to define groups of service providers. The above example case includes "trust level" as an index for grouping. The trust level should be defined by a trusted entity such as a rating agency selected by the users as trustworthy. Another case is to define two groups: a group of service providers in the same domain and a group of service providers out of the domain. This definition is reflected by "opt-in domain" explained in section 3.

We also consider a policy recommendation, which can be presented during the initial policy creation. The PPM shows an individual an example privacy policy of a user who has a similar profile as the individual, or a typical policy setting. Furthermore, it is possible to recommend modification of the privacy policy based on the privacy policies of similar users. Kelley et al. presented a user-controllable policy learning approach that involves neighborhood users' searches to explore incremental modifications of the user's current policy [31] and applied it to the people-finder [35]. We apply a similar technique to our policy generation and modification to reduce the complexity of operations required of users. Privacy policies should be encrypted by the master key K_m and stored in the user privacy policy database.

4.4   User-Friendly Interface for Privacy Policy

One problem with privacy policy management by the user is the complicated descriptions required in a privacy policy. To realize user-friendly privacy policy management, we should consider two technical issues: (1) the policy should be easy to configure, and (2) the policy should be easy to understand. Issue (1) was discussed in the previous section, so we mainly discuss issue (2) in this subsection.

To realize an easily-understood overview of a policy, a transforming function $f_w(x, y, z)$ from the machine-friendly format to a user-friendly format is needed. We consider the use of a layered view of a privacy policy. The initial view of the privacy policy is the top level, and the relevant part of the second level of the privacy policy is shown when a user clicks a certain top level item. The item that describes exceptions to items should be shown and other common items are displayed as one-paragraph descriptions. Let d be the level of description, and u be a user preference for a view of a privacy policy. The function $f_w(*, *, *)$ outputs a privacy view $\mathcal{P}_{view}$ as $f_w(\mathcal{P}, d, u) = \mathcal{P}_{view}$. For example, $f_w(\mathcal{P}, d_1, u_k) = \{P_0 = A, P_1 = \neg A, P_2 = \neg A, ..., P_{l_i} = \neg A\}$, where d_1 is the top-level of the privacy policy $\mathcal{P}$, and u_k is a preference of a user k. In the example case in the previous subsection, $f_w(\mathcal{P}, d_4 = 143*, u_k = all) = \{P_{1433} = A, others = \neg A\}$, because common items are merged. The policy view is optimized for each user, by using the user preference that is based on requirements and feedbacks input from users.

Another point is the description of each item; user-friendly description should be used to indicate the item. One useful technique is to highlight critical parts or unusual parts of the policy. For example, when items that many other users agree to is also agreed to by the user, the items are indicated with green color, and an item that includes critical private information or where many other users disagree is indicated red when the user agrees to the unusual item. A detailed design for privacy policy visualization is an open issue for our future research.

4.5   Log Management

The PPM stores records of private information flows that include pseudonym ID, date and time, service provider name, and types of private information that have a structure similar to those mentioned in the privacy policy definition, but not include private information itself. The records are written into the service log DB of the PPM. Users can search their own records using retrieval keys: user ID and service provider name, user ID and type of private information, and three keys of user ID, service provider name, and type of private information within a given range of dates and times. The database should be encrypted and protected against external attackers.

User Consent Log Search. The PPM cannot trace or search user logs without the consent of the user. User authentication is required to search the database and a user provides *user secret* to the PPM during the authentication process. The PPM cannot compute a secret key K_s to generate the pseudonym ID without user consent, because the secret key K_s is needed to generate a pseudonym ID. Thus, it is impossible for an *offline attacker* such as a curious operator of the PPM to search a particular user's records. There are some cryptographic techniques for private search, but those schemes requires heavy computational costs; thus ,we design a lightweight user consent log search scheme.

4.6   Interoperability between PPMs

A user accesses a PPM in a domain that the user belongs to, and uses several services in the same domain. For more general use cases, we should consider the case in which the user may access other PPMs in different domains. To build PPMs in different domains, we realize a distributed architecture of PPMs, and a concentration of transaction to a PPM is avoided. The PPM has connections with service providers in the same domain, and privacy policy formats for the service providers, but the PPM may not have access to service providers in different domains and appropriate privacy policy information about the service provider. Therefore, users have to use a separate PPM in each domain. When the user accesses a PPM in a different domain, that PPM has to transfer the user's request to the PPM in the user's home domain. This situation is similar to roaming schemes for user authentication. Protocols should be designed for the interoperability of PPMs. There are four protocols for realizing interoperability.

– A protocol for requesting user authentication from the home PPM.
– A protocol for downloading a user privacy policy from the home PPM.
– A protocol for uploading a modified user privacy policy to the home PPM.
– A protocol for sending logs of service use to the home PPM.

After user authentication is successful, the PPM downloads the user privacy policy from the home PPM of the user. The user privacy policy is modified, where the user privacy policy does not include permission items needed for service use. The PPM asks the user whether the permission items are allowed, and if so, adds the permission items to the user's privacy policy. The modified user privacy policy should be uploaded automatically to the home PPM, and the old user privacy policy is then replaced by the uploaded privacy policy. A public key infrastructure is needed for mutual authentication between PPMs. A private key is securely embedded in the PPM. The general steps of the protocols are as follows;

1. PPMs establish a secure channel to execute an authenticated key exchange protocol including public-key-certificate-based mutual authentication such as the ephemeral DH with RSA certificates mode (DHE-RSA) in TLS 1.2 [16]. Each PPM is endorsed by a trusted entity and holds a valid certificate, so a PPM can authenticate other PPMs to execute the authenticated key exchange protocol.
2. PPMs communicate with other PPMs using the protocols. All transaction data is sent via a secure channel, so all transaction data is securely protected.

5   Related Work

In this section, we introduce related work regarding an architecture for privacy preserving services.

5.1   ID Management for Privacy Protection

The Identity management (IdM) [9] technique is a method to control user information, which was originally developed for intra-net use. The concept of a user-centric IdM [18,2] is also one of the most important features for privacy protection on IdM. Under this concept, users have the right to control their identities, which are shared among ID providers (IDPs) and service providers (SPs). Therefore, IDP requires user permission, if it is to provide user information to SPs. J. Altmann *et al.* have proposed a user centric framework for IdM [2]. The framework provides comprehensive IdM for users and protects user concerns without revealing business interests.

5.2   Privacy Policy Management

The Privacy Bird [11,12]is an extension of a web browser and automatically retrieves the P3P policies of a web site. However, Kolter and Pernul[33] suggested that the available privacy preference settings of the Privacy Bird result in inadequate user acceptance, putting the ultimate goal of real-world use at risk. Thus, they proposed a user-friendly, P3P-based privacy preference generator [33] for service providers, including a configuration wizard and a preference summary.

Yee presented a privacy policy checker [47] for online services. The checker compares user privacy policy with provider privacy policy and then automatically determines whether the service can be used. Biswas presented an algorithm [7] that detects conflicts of privacy settings between user preference and the requirements of an application on a smart phone. Privacy Butler [46] is a personal privacy manager that can monitor a person's online presence and attempt to make corrections based on a privacy policy for user's online presence in a social network. The concept of the Privacy Butler is similar to the concept of our project, but it focuses on modifications to content hosted by social networking services; it monitors whether the modification is a satisfactory match for the privacy policy. Privacy Mirror [8] is a tool that is intended to show users what information about them is available online.

Some languages to describe privacy policies have been presented in [10,14,6]. Backes *et al.* examined some comparisons of enterprise privacy policies using formal abstract syntax and semantics to express the policy contents [4].

The objectives of the VRM project [42] are making individuals the collection centers for their own data and giving them the ability to share data selectively, controlling how their data is used by others, and asserting their own terms of service. The concept is based on Personal Data Service (PDS) and it is essentially similar to our proposal, but their approach is a combined model of access control and data storage.

5.3   Privacy Preserving Techniques

Adnostic [39] is a privacy-aware accounting tool to correctly bill advertisers without leaking the private information identifying which user clicks on what ads.

RePriv [22] provides a verified miner tool through a browser plug-in that allows a user to control how much private information leaves through a browser and to which web site. Guha *et al.* presented a way of disguising the user's identity and obfuscating private information before releasing it [27]. Hardt and Nath proposed a flexible framework [28] for personalizing ad delivery to smart phones. They proposed a differentially-private distributed protocol to compute various statistics required for their framework. Kido *et. al.* proposed a *false dummy method* [32], where a user sends n different locations to a location database server, with only one of them being correct (the rest are "dummies" that mask the true location). Hong and Landay introduced an architecture based on *landmark objects* [29], in which users refer to the location of a significant object (landmark) in their vicinity, rather than sending an exact location. This scheme makes it difficult to control the granularity of location information and thus may not be suitable for some types of location-based services. Recent research [37] has focused on establishing location anonymity in the spatial domain. Gruteser and Grunwald [25] suggested "blurring" the user's location by subdividing space in such a way that each subdivision contains at least $k - 1$ other users. Gedik and Liu [23] adapted this to allow users to be assigned personalized values of the masking parameter k. Mokbel *et. al.* presented a hierarchical partitioning method to improve the efficiency of location perturbation [38]. Selection of optimal subdivision spaces was investigated in [36,5]. In [24] a decentralized approach without an anonymizer was considered in order to realize good load balancing. However, communication between users is required to calculate the anonymized location information. Ardagna *et al.* presented a location obfuscation [3] that provides privacy-preserved location information without relying on trusted entities. Perturbation methods[20,45,17] iare used for adding a random noise as chaff in an interactive setting.

6   Discussion and Conclusion

We have presented an architecture for privacy-preserving services and designed a core module PPM. The PPM supports privacy management by users and acts a proxy that checks flows of private information and records them. Our concept is a delegation of access control and policy management that are inconveniently complex for users to a trusted third party, even though our architecture is based on the concept of PDS. In the architecture, users can verify that private information flows use the service log database. Furthermore, our design of the PPM includes consideration of a potential *offline attacker* in order to ensure the security of the PPM. Availability and flexibility are achieved by the PPM which provides centralized management of common user privacy policies and a policy checking mechanism that refers to the common policies. As suggested in published studies [15], it is expected that users should be able to easily use user-centric services to provide a clear view of information flows and to ensure access control based on their own privacy policies.

We are implementing a prototype system using the PPM and plan to conduct a demonstration experiment using the prototype system in a large shopping area.

Acknowledgment. This work has been supported by the New Energy and Industrial Technology Development Organization (NEDO) funded project, "Development and demonstration of life support services that facilitate movement around stations by utilization urban special information."

References

1. Acquisti, A., Grossklags, J.: Privacy and rationality in individual decision making. IEEE Security Privacy 3(1), 26–33 (2005)
2. Altmann, J., Sampath, R.: Unique: A user-centric framework for network identity management. In: 10th IEEE/IFIP Network Operations and Management Symposium, NOMS 2006, pp. 495–506 (2006)
3. Ardagna, C.A., Cremonini, M., De Capitani di Vimercati, S., Samarati, P.: An obfuscation-based approach for protecting location privacy. IEEE Transactions on Dependable and Secure Computing 8(1), 13–27 (2011)
4. Backes, M., Karjoth, G., Bagga, W., Schunter, M.: Efficient comparison of enterprise privacy policies. In: Proceedings of the 2004 ACM Symposium on Applied Computing, SAC 2004, pp. 375–382 (2004)
5. Bamba, B., Liu, L., Pesti, P., Wang, T.: Supporting anonymous location queries in mobile environments with privacygrid. In: Proc. of 17th International World Wide Web Conference (WWW 2008), pp. 237–246 (2008)
6. Bekara, K., Ben Mustapha, Y., Laurent, M.: Xpacml extensible privacy access control markup language. In: 2010 Second International Conference on Communications and Networking (ComNet), pp. 1–5 (2010)
7. Biswas, D.: Privacy policies change management for smartphones. In: 2012 IEEE International Conference on Pervasive Computing and Communications Workshops (PERCOM Workshops), pp. 70–75 (2012)
8. Bylund, M., Karlgren, J., Olsson, F., Sanches, P., Arvidsson, C.-H.: Mirroring your web presence. In: Proceedings of the 2008 ACM Workshop on Search in Social Media, SSM 2008, pp. 87–90 (2008)
9. Chadwick, D.W.: Federated identity management. In: Foundations of Security Analysis and Design V, pp. 96–120 (2009)
10. Cranor, L.F.: P3p: making privacy policies more useful. IEEE Security Privacy 1(6), 50–55 (2003)
11. Cranor, L.F., Arjula, M., Guduru, P.: Use of a p3p user agent by early adopters. In: Proceedings of the 2002 ACM Workshop on Privacy in the Electronic Society, WPES 2002, pp. 1–10 (2002)
12. Cranor, L.F., Guduru, P., Arjula, M.: User interfaces for privacy agents. ACM Trans. Comput.-Hum. Interact. 13(2), 135–178 (2006)
13. Danube, P.: Danube, identity and communication for political and social innovation. Project Danube Web Page (2010), http://projectdanube.org/
14. Dehghantanha, A., Udzir, N.I., Mahmod, R.: Towards a pervasive formal privacy language. In: 2010 IEEE 24th International Conference on Advanced Information Networking and Applications Workshops (WAINA), pp. 1085–1091 (2010)
15. Deuker, A.: Addressing the privacy paradox by expanded privacy awareness - the example of context-aware services. Privacy and Identity Management for Life 320, 275–283 (2010)

16. Dierks, T., Rescorla, E.: The transport layer security (TLS) protocol version 1.2. Internet Engineering Task Force (IETF), RFC5246 (2008)
17. Dwork, C., McSherry, F., Nissim, K., Smith, A.: Calibrating noise to sensitivity in private data analysis. In: Halevi, S., Rabin, T. (eds.) TCC 2006. LNCS, vol. 3876, pp. 265–284. Springer, Heidelberg (2006)
18. Eap, T., Hatala, M., Gasevic, D.: Enabling user control with personal identity management. In: IEEE International Conference on Services Computing, SCC 2007, pp. 60–67 (2007)
19. Estrin, D.: Participatory sensing: applications and architecture [internet predictions]. IEEE Internet Computing 14(1), 12–42 (2010)
20. Fienberg, S.E., McIntyre, J.: Data swapping: Variations on a theme by dalenius and reiss. In: Domingo-Ferrer, J., Torra, V. (eds.) PSD 2004. LNCS, vol. 3050, pp. 14–29. Springer, Heidelberg (2004)
21. The Eclipse Foundation. Higgins, personal data service. Higgins Home (2009), http://www.eclipse.org/higgins/
22. Fredrikson, M., Livshits, B.: RePriv - re-envisioning in-browser privacy. Microsoft Research Technical Report, MSR-TR-2010-116 (2010)
23. Gedik, M., Liu, L.: A customizable k-anonymity model for protecting location privacy. In: Proc. of the 25th International Conference on Distributed Computing Systems (ICDCS 2005), pp. 620–629 (2005)
24. Ghinita, G., Kalnis, P., Skiadopoulos, S.: PRIVÉ: Anonymous location-based queries in distributed mobile systems. In: Proc. of 16th International World Wide Web Conference (WWW 2007), pp. 371–380 (2007)
25. Gruteser, M., Grunwald, D.: Anonymous usage of location-based services through spatial and temporal cloaking. In: Proc. of the 1st International Conference on Mobile Systems, Applications, and Services (MobiSys 2003), pp. 163–168 (2003)
26. Guha, S., Cheng, B., Francis, P.: Challenges in measuring online advertising systems. In: Proceedings of the 10th ACM SIGCOMM Conference on Internet Measurement, IMC 2010, pp. 81–87 (2010)
27. Guha, S., Reznichenko, A., Tang, K., Haddadi, H., Francis, P.: Serving ads from localhost for performance, privacy, and profit. In: Proc. of the 8th ACM Workshop on Hot Topics in Networks (HotNets-VIII), HOTNETS 2009 (2009)
28. Hardt, M., Nath, S.: Privacy-aware personalization for mobile advertising. In: Proceedings of the 2012 ACM Conference on Computer and Communications Security, CCS 2012, pp. 662–673 (2012)
29. Hong, J.I., Landay, J.A.: An architecture for privacy-sensitive ubiquitous computing. In: Proc. of the 2nd International Conference on Mobile Systems, Applications, and Services (MobiSys 2004), pp. 177–189 (2004)
30. Jensen, C., Potts, C., Jensen, C.: Privacy practices of internet users: self-reports versus observed behavior. Int. J. Hum.-Comput. Stud. 63(1-2), 203–227 (2005)
31. Kelley, P.G., Drielsma, P.H., Sadeh, N., Cranor, L.F.: User-controllable learning of security and privacy policies. In: Proc. of the 1st ACM Workshop on AISec, AISec 2008, pp. 11–18 (2008)
32. Kido, H., Yanagisawa, Y., Satoh, T.: An anonymous communication technique using dummies for location-based services. In: Proc. of IEEE International Conference on Pervasive Services 2005 (ICPS 2005), pp. 88–97 (2005)
33. Kolter, J., Pernul, G.: Generating user-understandable privacy preferences. In: International Conference on Availability, Reliability and Security, ARES 2009., pp. 299–306 (2009)

34. Korolova, A.: Privacy violations using microtargeted ads: A case study. In: Proceedings of the 2010 IEEE International Conference on Data Mining Workshops, ICDMW 2010, pp. 474–482 (2010)
35. Lin, J., Xiang, G., Hong, J.I., Sadeh, N.: Modeling people's place naming preferences in location sharing. In: Proceedings of the 12th ACM International Conference on Ubiquitous Computing, Ubicomp 2010, pp. 75–84 (2010)
36. Mascetti, S., Bettini, C.: A comparison of spatial generalization algorithms for lbs privacy preservation. In: Proc. of the 1st International Workshop on Privacy-Aware Location-Based Mobile Services (PALMS 2007), pp. 258–262 (2007)
37. Mokbel, M.F.: Towards privacy-aware location-based database servers. In: Proc. of the 22nd Internationl Conference on Sata Engineering Workshops (ICDEW 2006), pp. 93–102 (2006)
38. Mokbel, M.F., Chow, C.Y., Aref, W.G.: The new casper: Query processing for location services without compromising privacy. In: Proc. of the 32nd International Conference on Very Large Data Bases (VLDB 2006), pp. 763–774 (2006)
39. Narayanan, A., Thiagarajan, N., Lakhani, M., Hamburg, M., Boneh, D.: Location privacy via private proximity testing. In: Proc. of the Network and Distributed System Security Symposium, NDSS 2011 (2011)
40. Pedersen, A.: P3 - problems, progress, potential. Privacy Laws & Business International Newsletter 2, 20–21 (2003)
41. Pollach, I.: What's wrong with online privacy policies? Commun. ACM 50(9), 103–108 (2007)
42. Searls, D.: Project vrm - vendor relationship management. Project of the Berkman Center for Internet Society at Harvard University (2013)
43. Solove, D.J.: Privacy self-management and the consent paradox. Harvard Law Review 126 (2013)
44. W3C. The platform for privacy preferences 1.0 (P3P1.0) specification. Platform for Privacy Preferences (P3P) Project (2002)
45. Winkler, W.E.: Masking and re-identification methods for public-use microdata: Overview and research problems. In: Domingo-Ferrer, J., Torra, V. (eds.) PSD 2004. LNCS, vol. 3050, pp. 231–246. Springer, Heidelberg (2004)
46. Wishart, R., Corapi, D., Madhavapeddy, A., Sloman, M.: Privacy butler: A personal privacy rights manager for online presence. In: 2010 8th IEEE International Conference on Pervasive Computing and Communications Workshops (PERCOM Workshops), pp. 672–677 (2010)
47. Yee, G.O.M.: An automatic privacy policy agreement checker for e-services. In: International Conference on Availability, Reliability and Security, ARES 2009, pp. 307–315 (2009)

An Attribute Based Private Data Sharing Scheme for People-Centric Sensing Networks

Bo Liu, Baokang Zhao[*], Bo Liu, and Chunqing Wu

School of Computer Science
National University of Defense Technology
Changsha, Hunan, China
liub0yayu@gmail.com, {bkzhao,boliu,chunqingwu}@nudt.edu.cn

Abstract. In recent years, people-centric sensing networks have attracted much research effort. To date, there are still some significant security and privacy challenges in people-centric sensing networks. In this paper, we focus on the private data sharing and protection in people-centric sensing networks. First, we formalize the network model with relay nodes which improves the data forwarding efficiency of networks. Second, we propose a novel Attribute based Private data sharing protocol in People-centric sensing networks (APP). Relying on the technology of ciphertext policy attribute based encryption, our APP protocol can protect the privacy and integrity with efficient approaches of authentication, encryption, transmission and decryption. Also, we propose an associative data indexing scheme to improve the private data sharing performance. Finally, we discuss the performance evaluation of APP protocol in detail and find that it can achieve much better efficiency.

Keywords: people-centric sensing networks; relay nodes; privacy; security.

1 Introduction

In recent years, people-centric sensing networks, such as BikeNet [1], CitySense [2], have been subject to extensive research efforts. Unlike traditional sensor networks where humans are passive data consumers that interact with physically embedded static sensors, people-centric sensing networks allow people to collect, store, process, or share information with friends by carrying mobile sensing devices [3]. Nowadays, with the widely used popular consumer electronics like PDAs and mobile phones, the people-centric sensor networking issues have attracted a lot of research efforts (such as [4], [5]).

In a people-centric sensing network, humans, rather than physical devices, are the focal point of the processed sensor-based information. With the ubiquitous devices, people can gather, analyze, and share targeted information about their daily life patterns and activities like [6].

---

[*] Corresponding author.

A. Cuzzocrea et al. (Eds.): CD-ARES 2013 Workshops, LNCS 8128, pp. 393–407, 2013.

While it brings forth an amazing domain of new applica-tions (such as the Metro-Sense Project [7], the UCLA Urban Sensing Project [8], the CitySense Project [9] and so on), there are still some significant security and privacy challeng-es in people-centric sensing networks[10] [11].

1.1   Secutrity and Privacy Challenges

Since sensor devices carried by people are highly mobile, the topology of the network is not fixed at all. The research about people-centric sensing inspires some new archi-tectures and applications, such as [12], [13]. The private data is gathered and transmit-ted frequently among the sensor nodes and strong cryptographic techniques should be employed [14] [15]. The existing security approaches with fixed topologies cannot be employed in people-centric network at all [16] [17] [18] [19].

- **Privacy**

The people-centric sensing applications entail unrestricted dissemination of consum-ers' sensor data. Users have to control who can access information about their private data. Critical access controlling and cryptography technologies should be employed.

- **Integrity**

Generally, a people-centric sensing system provides anonymity to those nodes that are tasked. It's difficult to guarantee the integrity of information. If a user falsifies data, it's hard to trace the misbehaving. It's always a major challenge to find an approach that balances privacy with data integrity.

In people-centric sensing networks, we can provide the security protections by en-crypting data with different keys when users want to share the private information with others.

- **Symmetric key encryption**

In symmetric key encryption, consumers have to discuss a uniform key before they share private data. In an people-centric sensing network, the sensor devices are not approached to each other all the time. Key distribution and management is really very hard when somebody wants to send messages.

- **Conventional public key encryption**

In conventional public key encryption like RSA, an encryption key and a decryption key are used. One should know the public key before data sharing. The storage of public keys and communication cost both are considerable critical when sensor nodes have to share data with many other nodes. Also, this will lead to similar key manage-ment problems as symmetric key encryption.

- **Identity based encryption**

Identity based encryption (IBE) is a form of asymmetric cryptography [20] [21]. Un-like RSA, IBE has simplified key generation and management approaches. Generally, the public keys are generated from identity strings and only the CA or PKG (private key generator) can create the private keys to decrypt the data. When the sensor node wants to share data with others, it doesn't have to store many public keys [22]. However, when somebody wants to share data with many friends, he has to encrypt the same data for many copies with different public keys.

- **Ciphertext policy attribute based encryption (CP-ABE)**

CP-ABE [23] is type of public-key encryption. In CP-ABE scenario, users' private keys are associated with sets of attributes. A user can encrypt a data with a specific access policy, defining types of receivers who will be able to decrypt the ciphertext. Users post sets of attributes to obtain their corresponding secret keys from the third party, private key generator. The decryption of a ciphertext is possible only if the set of attributes of the secret key satisfies the access policy associated to the ciphertext.

In this paper, we focus on designing a high security and private protection protocol based on CP-ABE to solve the privacy and integrity challenges in people-centric sensing networks.

1.2   Our Contributions

Based on the above observations, in this paper, we propose a novel Attribute based Privacy aware data sharing protocol in People centric sensing networks (APP). Based on CP-ABE, the proposed APP protocol provides outstanding security and privacy protections in people-centric sensing networks. Specifically, the contributions of this paper are threefold.

First, we heuristically propose the people-centric sensing network model with relay nodes. Since data is forwarded in an opportunistic way in people-centric networks, relay nodes can improve the data forwarding efficiency of networks.

Second, we propose the APP protocol, an attribute based privacy aware data sharing protocol in people centric sensing network. With relay nodes, APP protocol can achieve high transmission efficiency. In addition, APP can also resist most existing security threads in people-centric sensing networks, such as data analysis attack, tracing attack and so on.

Third, we give the security analysis and the performance evaluation with commercial ARM experimental platform. The experimental results show that our APP protocol performs reasonable performance.

The rest of the paper is as follows. We give the brief introduction to CP-ABE in Section 2. In section 3, we formalize the people-centric sensing network and thread models and identify our design goal. Then, we present the APP protocol in Section 4. Security analysis is given in Section 5, followed by the experimental results and performance evaluations in Section 6. Conclusion can be found in Section 7.

2   Ciphertext Policy Attribute Based Encryption

Ciphertext Policy Attribute Based Encryption (CP-ABE) was proposed by Bethencourt et al. in 2007 [23]. In CP-ABE, a set of attributes defines a user and access policy defines which ciphertext an authorized user is able to decrypt. Private Key Generator (PKG), a trusted third party handles the issuance of private keys.

CP-ABE uses a Bilinear Map system to achieve its security goals. In this section, we will give the brief introduction to bilinear maps and show the algorithm of CP-ABE scheme.

2.1   Bilinear Maps

In this part, we present a few facts associated to groups with bilinear maps.

Given two multiplicative cyclic groups G_0, G_1 and a generator g for G_1, a Bilinear map e can be defined as $e : G_0 \times G_0 \rightarrow G_1$ [24]. The bilinear map e satisfies two properties:

- Non-degeneracy: $e(g, g) \neq 1$.
- Bilinearity: $e(u^a, v^b) = e(u, v)^{ab}$ for all $u, v \in G_0$ and $a, b \in Z_p$.

If the group operations in G_0 and the bilinear map $e(u^a, v^b) = e(u, v)^{ab}$ are both efficiently computable, G_0 is a bilinear group and e is symmetric since $e(g^a, g^b) = e(g^b, g^a)$.

2.2   The CP-ABE Scheme

The CP-ABE scheme consists of five functions [23] [25].

- **Setup** The Setup function will choose a random bilinear group G_0 of prime order p and generator g. The function will return a master key (β, g^α) and a public key $PK = G_0$, g, $h = g^\beta$, $f = g^{1/\beta}$, $e(g, g)^\alpha$ with two random exponents $\alpha, \beta \in Z_p$.
- **Encrpyt(PK, M, τ)** This function encrypts a message M with the public key PK and the access policy τ.
- **KeyGen(MK, S)** This function generate a user private key with the master key MK and an attribute set S.
- **Decrypt(CT, SK, x)** This function is used to extract the secret message associated with the file CT with a private key SK and a node x which comes from access policy tree τ.
- **Delegate(SK, S')** This function enables a user to delegate some or all privileges to another user with his own private key SK.

3   Models and Design Goal

In this section, we formalize the people-centric sensing network model with relay nodes. Then, we give the threat model and our design goal.

3.1   The People-Centric Network Model With Relay Nodes

With relay nodes, people-centric networks can achieve high transmission efficiency. Such networks are characterized by five kinds of network roles and each kind of which has unique characteristics. The network model is shown in Fig. 1.

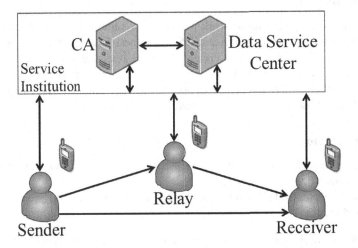

Fig. 1. The people-centric network model with relay nodes

- *Certificate Authority (CA):* Every sensing node must be registered in CA if it's first time to access to the people-centric sensing network. CA publishes the public key which is used to encrypt private data. CA can produce the private key with a set of attribute posted by the requester. In this paper, we assume that all information exchange on the internet between CA and consumers uses conventional protocols such as SSL.
- *Data Service Center (DSC):* DSC is isolated with the CA and there are no users' private keys stored in DSC. All data stored in DSC is encrypted. We assume that the DSC is honest. It will not modify or delete users' data and it will never understand the context of private data.
- *Sender:* Sender is a sensing node that wants to share private data with others. All private data should be encrypted with a self-defined access policy before transferred. If the destination node is nearby, the private data will be sent to it directly. Otherwise, the data will be sent to the DSC when the sender node can connect to the DSC server. If can't, the data will be stored in local and transferred to neighbor nodes when it can connect to.

- *Relay:* Relay is a sensing node that is not the destination node but can forward the encrypted data to other nodes. Similar with a *sender* node, relay will send data to DSC when it can connect to the server. Otherwise, it will gather the encrypted data and transfer it to other nodes when it can connect to.
- *Receiver:* Receiver is the destination of the sender node. In order to gain the private data from sender, receiver posts a query request to the DSC server and gains data from DSC. Receiver tries to decrypt data with its own private key. If receiver gathers data from other nodes is exactly the wishing data, it won't send it to DSC again.

3.2   Assumptions

In our people-centric sensing network model, we assume that only CA can generate private keys used for decrypting data. DSC is honest and won't delete and modify users' data. Sensing nodes cannot create the secret keys needed to decrypt the message. We assume that PK is the public key and SK is the private key. Users can obtain the master public key PK and their own private keys preliminary. The communication between CA and users employs security protocols like SSL.

3.3   Threat Model

In our threat model, CA and DSC are trustable and honest. However, the sensing nodes are honest but may be curious.

In specific, we consider the adversary can perform the following attacks to subvert privacy and security.

- *Eavesdropping Attack:* After eavesdropping a packet, the adversary tries to recover the private data and identify the source node.
- Obfuscation *Attack:* The adversary may swap data from different packets to confuse the receiver nodes.
- *Tracing Attack:* The adversary eavesdrops the transmission of a single packet and tries to trace the source and destination locations.
- *Matching Attack:* The adversary may try to generate many keys and encrypt all possible values using different keys to determine whether there is a match for the packet that he eavesdrops.

3.4   Design Goal

Our design goal in this paper is to develop an attribute based privacy aware data sharing protocol in people centric sensing network. Specifically, we focus on the following two desirable objectives.

- *Resisting privacy-related attacks in people-centric sensing networks.* In people-centric sensing networks, the collected and delivered data is usually associated to users' private information. Therefore, the users' privacy must be protected in order for people-centric sensing networks wide acceptance to the public.

- *Achieving effectively private data sharing performance.* When users want to share private data with friends, we can encrypt data with different keys for each node. This will cost much computational resource and transmission overhead. Therefore, we must improve the private data sharing performance.

4   Proposed APP Protocol

Security and privacy challenges have been discussed in Section 1. In this section, we present our attribute based privacy aware data sharing protocol in people centric sensing network (APP). APP protocol is based on CP-ABE which has been introduced in Section 2. The security assumptions are shown in Section 3.B.

APP protocol consists of the following four phases: First is the initialization phase where the consumer first joins in the network. Second is the data collection phase, which outlines how sensing nodes encrypt the private data. Following is the data delivery phase that describes how a sensing node transfers data to DSC or to a neighbor node. Finally, the data retrieve phase occurs when a receiver node needs to obtain data from DSC. In APP protocol, users should be authenticated with each other first before their communication.

We first describe the authentication approach employed in APP protocol and then delve into the details of our protocol.

Algorithm 1. Authentication between nodes
1.   Each node (Alice and Bob) derives a random number N and string A_u which is part of its own attribute set S.
2.   Alice generates string $m_1 = (N \mid A_{u\text{-}Bob})$ and Bob generates string $m_2 = (N \mid A_{u\text{-}Alice})$.
3.   Alice calculates $c_1 = \text{Encrypt}(m_1, SK_{Alice})$ and sends it to Bob.
4.   Bob calculates $\text{Decrypt}(c_1, A_{u\text{-}Alice})$ to gain N and $A_{u\text{-}Bob}$. If $A_{u\text{-}Bob}$ is incorrect, the authentication will break down. If not, go to step 5.
5.   Bob calculates $c_2 = \text{Encrypt}(m_2, SK_{Bob})$ and sends it to Alice.
6.   Alice calculates $\text{Decrypt}(c_2, A_{u\text{-}Bob})$ to gain N and $A_{u\text{-}Alice}$. If $A_{u\text{-}Alice}$ or N is incorrect, the authentication will break down. If not, authentication accomplished.

4.1   Authentication

The authentication algorithm employs when the sensing nodes (Alice and Bob) need to communicate with each other. When a sensing node accesses to the DSC server, authentication also should be employed.

4.2   Description of the APP Protocol

1)   System Initialization
Based on the system requirements, the following steps should be performed to bootstrap the whole system.

- CA first chooses a random bilinear group G_0 of prime order p and generator g, and two random exponents $\alpha, \beta \in Z_p$. Then CA gains a master key $MK : (\beta, g^\alpha)$ and a public key $PK = G_0$, g, $h = g^\beta$, $f = g^{1/\beta}$, $e(g,g)^\alpha$.
- Each user $u_i \in U = \{u_1, u_2, \cdots\}$ announces the attribute set S_i. The user u_i registers in CA with his attribute set.
- CA generates the private key SK_i with S_i and MK. Then, CA pushes the private and public keys to the registered user back.

2) Data collection

Algorithm 2. Encrypting data by sender nodes

1. Sender node generates a random number N and string A_u which is part of its own attribute set S.
2. Sender node defines access policy τ.
3. Calculate $m_1 = (N \mid A_u)$, $m_2 = (N \mid data)$.
4. Calculate $c_1 = \text{Encrypt}(PK, m_1, \tau)$.
5. Calculate $c_2 = \text{Encrypt}(PK, m_2, \tau)$.

The tuple (c_1, c_2) is then stored in the *sender* node memory. Note that the access policy τ allows the receiver and himself to decrypt the data. Such policy avoids data duplicate delivering in a loop between nodes.

3) Data delivery

In APP scheme, sensing nodes will deliver its data to DSC first when it wants to share data with others. If the node cannot reach to the DSC server, it will deliver its data to neighbor nodes.

4) Data retrieve

Algorithm 3. Data retrieve by receiver nodes

1. Calculate $\text{Decrypt}(c_1, SK)$, get N_1 and A_u.
2. Calculate $\text{Decrypt}(c_2, SK)$, get N_2 and *data*.
3. **if** N_1 equals N_2 **then**
4.   receiver accepts A_u and data
5. **else**
6.   Drop data.
7. **end if**

The sensing node will request data from the DSC periodically when connecting to the DSC server. If the sensing node cannot connect to DSC server, it receives data from *relay* or *sender* nodes.

When the data has been gathered in the *receiver* sensing nodes, the algorithm 3 will be conducted to retrieve data.

Since all private data is encrypted, the DSC cannot return specific encrypted data packets associated with users. The DSC server can return c_is for the *receiver* node first. The sensing node tries to decrypt c_is first and decides whether to accept the private data from users with attribute A_u. Since the length of c_1 is much shorter than that of c_2, this approach can improve efficiency and reduce the communication time. Since the DSC server understands nothing about the context of the tuples, it's unable to index any of tuples. This feature protects the privacy of the sharing data.

4.3   Query Improvement

In APP protocol, the *receiver* node has to query all the encrypted tuples in DSC in order to gain the shared private data. Assuming there are n tuples in DSC, the *receiver* node will cost $O(n)$ time to decrypt the c_is to determine which tuple should be accepted. We define this produce as *Query*.

When there are amounts of tuples in DSC, the APP protocol will achieve poor performance. The poor performance is because the DSC server is unable to index any of the tuples. Since the DSC server learns nothing from the encrypted tuples. For instance, consider that the *sender* node may want to share amounts of private data with *receiver* nodes. The *sender* node will encrypt data with the same access policy. We can achieve reasonable performance if the index is constructed.

In order to improve the query performance, we propose the Associative Data Index and query scheme (ADI). The ADI scheme consists of the following two produces.

1)   Associative data indexing

- Suppose that the *sender* node encrypts amounts of private data with access policy tree τ and gains the tuples $\{(c_1, c_2)_1, (c_1, c_2)_2, ..., (c_1, c_2)_k\}$.
- The *sender* node calculates the message $m_2 = (N \mid p_1 \mid p_2 \mid \cdots \mid p_k)$, where $p_i, (1 \leq i \leq k)$ means the index pointing to $(c_1, c_2)_i$.
- The *sender* node calculates $c_2 = Encrypt(PK, m_3, \tau)$.

2)   Querying

- The *receiver* node query c_is from the DSC server.
- If the *receiver* node decrypts data and gains the index message $(N \mid p_1 \mid p_2 \mid \cdots \mid p_k)$, it will drop all the other tuples which are not associated with the index data.

With ADI scheme, we can reasonably improve the query performance. Since DSC learns nothing about the tuples, ADI improves the query performance and also protects the privacy of users.

5   Security Analysis

In this part, we give the security analysis of our proposed APP protocols. In our security protocol, we assume that CA and DSC are honest. We assume that the private key distribution is security when SSL or other security protocols employed.

- **Resilience to Eavesdropping Attack**

In the proposed APP protocol, the *sender* node has encrypted private data into a tuple (c_1, c_2). The adversary eavesdrops the tuple (c_1, c_2) during the secret message delivering to the DSC server or to neighbor nodes. If the adversary is able to recovery the original data after gathering amounts of tuples, he will be success in his attack. The adversary will learn nothing from the ciphertext without the destination node's private key. Therefore, the proposed APP protocol can resist the eavesdropping attack.

- **Resilience to Obfuscation Attack**

Considering that, a curious *relay* node can gain encrypted tuples from different communication links. It may swap the c_2s from different tuples to confuse the *receiver* node.

Notice that in an encrypted tuple, it embeds the same random number N in both c_1 and c_2. The *receiver* node accepts the data in c_2 only if both random numbers match. Therefore, the proposed APP protocol can resist the obfuscation attack.

- **Resilience to Tracing Attack**

First, the destination node information is encrypted in each tuple with access policy τ. The ciphertext can be decrypted only if the private key SK satisfies τ. The adversary can learn nothing about the destination and can't generate the private keys.

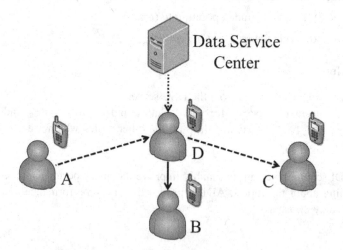

Fig. 2. The nodes play as mixed roles in people-centric sensing network

Second, every sensing node in people-centric sensing network plays the *sender, relay* and *receiver* role at the same time. As it shown in Fig. 2, the sensing node D plays the *relay* role to node A and C, the *sender* role to node B and the *receiver* role to DSC. The adversary can't distinguish where the data really comes from and where is going to.

By summarizing the above, the proposed APP protocol can resist tracing attack.

- **Resilience to Matching Attack**

The adversary may try to generate many public keys and access policies, and encrypt all possible values using different public keys and policies to determine whether there is a match for the tuple (c_1, c_2). Since the sharing private data is various (such as messages and photographs), and every encrypted tuple uses a random number, the tuples will be quite different even using the same public key, same access policy and by the same sender.

Relying on CP-ABE, our proposed APP protocol can protect the privacy and integrity with efficiently authentication, encryption, transmission and decryption approaches.

6   Performance Evaluation

In this section, we study the performance of the proposed APP protocol. The performance evaluation metrics are key generation time, encryption time, data transmission overhead and decryption time. The data transmission overhead is defined as the increased data size after encrypted private data with different access policies. In addition, following the earlier design goal, we analyze the private data sharing performance.

In APP protocol, we employ the CP-ABE toolkit [25] on commercial ARM experimental platforms (S3C6410, 667MHz, ARM 11 Series (1176) [26]).

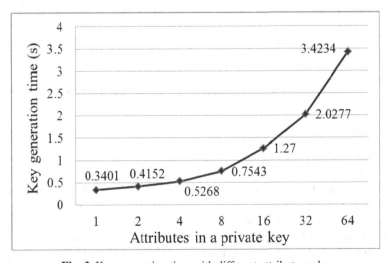

Fig. 3. Key generation time with different attribute scales

6.1   Key Generation Time

All private keys are produced by CA. We use personal computer as CA server (1GB, Intel i5@2.5GHz) and test the private key generation time with different scales of attributes. The result is shown in Fig. 3.

As it shown in Fig. 3, it will cost more time to generate a private key with a larger attribute scale. For example, it costs 0.3401 second to generate the private key with only one attribute while 3.4234 second with sixty-four attributes. The attribute scale should be balanced between security demands and key generation time.

6.2   Encryption Time

Encrypting data with different access policies will lead to different time overhead. In CP-ABE scheme, access policy is a 'AND' and 'OR' tree structure [23]. Leaf nodes are the certain access requirements. We measured the encryption efficiency of CP-ABE with different leaf scales and fixed data size (1KB). As is shown in Fig. 4, critical access policy will lead to much encryption overhead.

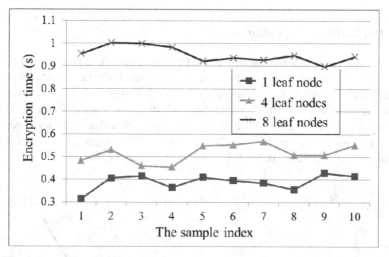

Fig. 4. Encryption time with different access leaf scales and fixed data size (1KB)

6.3   Data Transmission Overhead

In APP, data transmission overhead mainly means the encrypted data size. We conduct experiment with different access policies and different data sizes and find that the increased encrypted size only associated to access policies. The experiment result is shown in Fig. 5. For example, the increased data size is 9532 bytes when we want to share private data with friends with a certain 32 leaf nodes access policy. The increased data size has less relationship with original data size. Therefore, the access policies should be balanced between the increased data size, the encryption time and security demands.

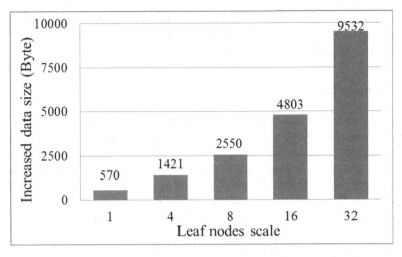

Fig. 5. The increased data size with different leaf nodes scales

6.4   Decryption Time

The decryption phase greatly affects the APP protocol performance. Since the receiver has to query all the encrypted tuples in DSC to gain the shared private data.

We measure decryption time for one receiver node by amount of times and find that it costs about 0.20 second per leaf node to decrypt the private data.

6.5   Query Performance

Assuming that there are amounts of tuples in DSC, and about 5% of the tuples are desired to share with the *receiver* node R. The average query performance is shown in Fig. 6.

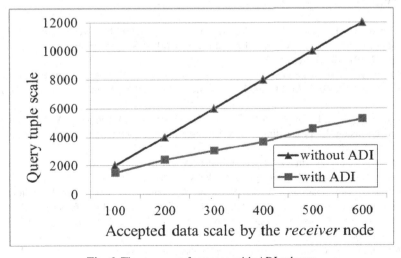

Fig. 6. The query performance with ADI scheme

For example, without ADI scheme, the *receiver* node has to query about 12000 tuples in total. It's only about 5700 tuples will be queried with ADI. The ADI scheme reasonably improves our APP protocol performance.

7   Conclusion

In this paper, we have presented a novel Attribute based Privacy aware data sharing protocol in People centric sensing networks (APP). Relying on the CP-ABE scheme, our APP protocol can protect the privacy and integrity with efficiently authentication, encryption, transmission and decryption approaches. With Associative Data Index and query scheme (ADI), our proposed APP protocol achieves effectively performance for private data sharing. We discussed the performance evaluation of APP protocol in detail and found that it can achieve much better efficiency with well-designed index schemes.

Acknowledgment. The work described in this paper is partially supported by the grants of the National Basic Research Program of China (973 project) under Grant No.2009CB320503, 2012CB315906; the project   of National Science Foundation of China under grant No. 61070199, 61103189, 61103194, 61103182, 61202488, 61272482; the National High Technology Research and Development Program of China (863 Program) No. 2011AA01A103, 2012AA01A506, 2013AA013505, the Research Fund for the Doctoral Program of Higher Education of China under Grant No. 20114307110006, 20124307120032, the program for Changjiang Scholars and Innovative Research Team in University (No.IRT1012), Science and Technology Innovative Research Team in Higher Educational Institutions of Hunan Province("network technology"); and Hunan Province Natural Science Foundation of China (11JJ7003).

References

[1] Eisenman, S.B., et al.: The BikeNet Mobile Sensing System for Cyclist Experience Mapping. In: Proc. 5th ACM Conf. Embedded Networked Sensor Systems (SENSYS 2007), pp. 87–101. ACM Press (2007)
[2] Murty, R., et al.: CitySense: A Vision for an Urban-Scale Wireless Networking Testbed. In: Proc. 2008 IEEE Int'l Conf. Technologies for Homeland Security, pp. 583–588. IEEE Press (2008)
[3] Campbell, A.T., Eisenman, S.B., Lane, N.D., Miluzzo, E., Peterson, R.A.: People-centric urban sensing. In: Proceedings of the Second Annual International Wireless Internet Conference (WICON), pp. 18–31. ACM Press (August 2006)
[4] Oliver, N., Flores-Mangas, F.: Healthgear: A real-time wearable system for monitoring and analyzing physiological signals. In: BSN, pp. 61–64 (2006)
[5] Chen, G., Govindaswamy, P., Li, N., Wang, J.: Continuous camera-based monitoring for assistive environments. In: Proceedings of the 1st International Conference on PErvasive Technologies Related to Assistive Environments, PETRA 2008, pp. 31:1–31:8. ACM, New York (2008)
[6] Milenkovi, A., Otto, C., Jovanov, E.: Wireless sensor networks for personal health monitoring: Issues and an implementation. Comput. Commun. 29, 2521–2533 (2006)

[7] Eisenman, S.B., Lane, N.D., Miluzzo, E., Peterson, R.A., Ahn, G.-S., Campbell, A.T.: MetroSense Project: People-Centric Sensing at Scale. In: Proc. of Workshop on World-Sensor-Web (WSW 2006), Boulder, October 31, pp. 6–11 (2006)

[8] CENS Urban Sensing project (2006), http://research.cens.ucla.edu/projects/2006/Systems/Urban_Sensing/ (website visited January 2013)

[9] Murty, R., et al.: CitySense: A Vision for an Urban-Scale Wireless Networking Testbed. In: Proc. 2008 IEEE Int'l Conf. Technologies for Homeland Security, pp. 583–588. IEEE Press (2008)

[10] Giannetsos, T., Dimitriou, T., Prasad, N.R.: People-Centric Sensing in Assistive Healthcare: Privacy Challenges and Directions. Security Comm. Networks, 1–12 (2010)

[11] Athanasios, G.: Security Threats in Wireless Sensor Networks: Implementation of Attacks & Defense Mechanisms. Aalborg University (2011)

[12] Burke, J., Estrin, D., Hansen, M., Parker, A., Ramanathan, N., Reddy, S., Srivastava, M.B.: Participatory sensing. In: Workshop on World-Sensor-Web (WSW 2006): Mobile Device Centric Sensor Networks and Applications, pp. 117–134 (2006)

[13] Eagle, N., (Sandy) Pentland, A.: Reality mining: sensing complex social systems. Personal Ubiquitous Comput. 10, 255–268 (2006)

[14] Chan, H., Perrig, A., Song, D.: Secure hierarchical in-network aggregation in sensor networks. In: Proceedings of the ACM Conference on Computer and Communications Security (CCS), pp. 278–287. ACM Press (October 2006)

[15] Cornelius, C., Kapadia, A., Kotz, D., Peebles, D., Shin, M., Triandopoulos, N.: Anony-Sense: Privacy-Aware People-Centric Sensing. In: Proc. ACM 6th Int'l Conf. on Mobile Systems, Applications and Services (MOBISYS 2008), Breckenridge (June 2008)

[16] Przydatek, B., Song, D., Perrig, A.: SIA: Secure information aggregation in sensor networks. In: Proceedings of the International Conference on Embedded Networked Sensor Systems (SenSys). ACM Press (2003)

[17] Deng, J., Han, R., Mishra, S.: A performance evaluation of intrusion-tolerant routing in wireless sensor networks. In: Zhao, F., Guibas, L.J. (eds.) IPSN 2003. LNCS, vol. 2634, pp. 349–364. Springer, Heidelberg (2003)

[18] Zhu, S., Setia, S., Jajodia, S.: Leap: efficient security mechanisms for large-scale distributed sensor networks. In: Proceedings of the ACM Conference on Computer and Communications Security (CCS), pp. 62–72. ACM Press (2003)

[19] Yin, C., Huang, S., Su, P., Gao, C.: Secure routing for large-scale wireless sensor networks. In: Proceedings of the International Conference on Communication Technology, ICCT (April 2003)

[20] Boneh, D., Franklin, M.: Identity-based encryption from the Weil pairing. In: Kilian, J. (ed.) CRYPTO 2001. LNCS, vol. 2139, pp. 213–229. Springer, Heidelberg (2001)

[21] Mont, M., Bramhall, P., Harrison, K.: A flexible role-based secure messaging service: Exploiting IBE technology for privacy in health care. In: Proc. Int. Workshop on Database Expert Syst. Appl., pp. 432–437 (2003)

[22] Tan, C.C., Wang, H., Zhong, S., et al.: IBE-lite: a lightweight identity-based cryptography for body sensor networks. IEEE Transactions on Information Technology in Biomedicine 13(6), 926–932 (2009)

[23] Bethencourt, J., Sahai, A., Waters, B.: Ciphertext-policy attribute-based encryption. In: Proceedings of the 2007 IEEE Symposium on Security and Privacy, SP 2007, pp. 321–334. IEEE Computer Society, Washington, DC (2007)

[24] Bilinear map (March 2013), http://en.wikipedia.org/wiki/Bilinear_map

[25] Ciphertext-policy attribute-based encryption (March 2013), http://acsc.cs.utexas.edu/cpabe/

[26] Samsung S3C6410 (March 2013), http://www.samsung.com/global/business/semiconductor/product/application/detail?productId=7115&iaId=835

Intelligent UBMSS Systems
for Strategic Information Management

Lidia Ogiela and Marek R. Ogiela

AGH University of Science and Technology
Al. Mickiewicza 30, PL-30-059 Krakow, Poland
{logiela,mogiela}@agh.edu.pl

Abstract. In this publication will be described the most important features of UBMSS cognitive information systems, as well as security issues connected with these new generation information systems. Such systems are mainly designed to perform an intelligent information management based on semantic analysis of data merit content. In paper will be also presented some possibilities to develop such systems for strategic information management in state or government institution. The paper will describe both UMBSS internal safety features, and external possible application of authentication procedures along with intelligent information management.

Keywords: Strategic information management, security of information systems, cognitive systems in homeland security.

1   Introduction

Intelligent UBMSS (Understanding Based Management Support Systems) systems are one of the modern classes of cognitive information systems. Cognitive analysis processes are characteristic of the intellectual processes running in the human brain, particularly those of analyzing, interpreting, reasoning, and forecasting about specific situations, meanings and the significance of information.

Cognitive reasoning consists in analyzing and understanding the contents and the semantics of the data examined. Such examination may be very important during strategic information management in different companies or institution.

In such systems the semantic analysis is based on a lexical analysis in which the structure of a given word is used to describe it, and to find the meaning of the content of the word. The basis for this analysis is a specific language to which the above element belongs, and the process of understanding results from comparing the previously recorded expectations concerning specific features of data with the features from the input information. The set of expectations concerning the anticipated features of the analyzed elements is produced by analyzing the knowledge of experts whose expectations of the meanings of particular situations are presented in the system database. This set of semantic hypotheses is compared with the stream of input data, and this leads to cognitive resonance [2, 3, 4,5]. This process produces a list of selected

A. Cuzzocrea et al. (Eds.): CD-ARES 2013 Workshops, LNCS 8128, pp. 408–413, 2013.

interpretations which were found to correspond to the analyzed input data – this leads to the stage of understanding the analyzed data.

Presented cognitive resonance functions may be used to guarantee the security and safety features during management of strategic or secret information, both in layered and hierarchical management structures.

2   An Idea of UBMSS Cognitive Systems

The general goal of UBMSS is to support enterprise management and handling in secure manner of strategic information, as well as its distribution for authorized persons or participants of communication protocols. Such systems may also be used for another procedures mostly connected with economical task like focus on the correct choice of the right economic ratios and theirs prediction for near future. These ratios precisely reflect the business activity of a given enterprise, its standing, its financial result, and are also an expression of the record and the generalization of specific economic events.

During our research we could also analyze some security features of such systems and theirs possibility of theirs application for strategic information management in the form of secret information sharing for layered and hierarchical structures.

3   UBMSS Systems for Strategic Information Management

Using UBMSS systems, an information is divided within institutions or organizations regardless of its type or the purpose for which the organization collects it. The significance of information splitting may depend on the method of its splitting, the purpose of splitting it, and the type of information. The significance of information sharing, on the other hand, may depend on its importance and the meaning it contains for the specific organization. If information is important and of great materiality for the organization or for e.g. external organizations, then it makes sense to attempt sharing this information to protect it and secure it from disclosure to unauthorized persons (or organizations). When defining the type of information to undergo the splitting or sharing process, we should consider its 'character' determined by its confidentiality, significance and importance, because only important information justifies applying the method of its division and the effort to do so.

Multi-level information division algorithms are named after the type of division applied. This division can be hierarchical or by layers. The principal difference between the presented types of divisions concerns the method of introducing the division itself. When a division is made within homogenous, uniform groups of layers, then it is a layer division, whereas if the division is made regardless of the homogeneity of the group or layer but by reference to several groups ordered hierarchically, it is a hierarchical division [8].

A layer division is thus a division made relative to a given layer, while a hierarchical division accounts for the hierarchy (dependency) of the structure or more structures relative to one another.

Information can be divided both within the entire structure in which some hierarchical dependency is identified, within a given group, or within any homogenous layer. This is why, depending on the type of information divided, it makes sense to identify correctly selected information dividing algorithms.

The division of information between the members of a given group in which everyone has the same privileges is a layer division.

A hierarchical division is characterized by the ability to make any division of secret information in the way determined by the access rights at individual levels of a hierarchical structure.

4   Types of UBMSS Systems

There are various methods of information protecting from being accessed by persons not authorized to learn it. Based on such different approaches we can define two types of UBMSS systems. The first class may contain the procedures in which the secret information will be secured using some individual personal biometrics, and the second one based on mathematical linguistic formalisms [7].

The first class of UBMSS systems are connected with biometric threshold schemes [10, 11], which particularly use some most important physical and biometric features like the iris, the shape of fingerprints, hand bones or veins [9], anatomical features [1], face, the structure of blood vessels [6] and also the DNA code [10].

The second class of UBMSS systems uses linguistic coding processes, which are based on the use of mathematical linguistic formalisms, particularly grammatical formalisms to record and interpret the meaning of the secured data. Linguistic coding processes are used because of the ability to execute generalised information coding similar to DNA cryptography [10], but in UBMSS systems it is also possible to code longer bit sequences containing more than 2 bits of information. This coding is done using terminal symbols introduced in special grammar.

5   Example of Application UBMSS System for Strategic Information Management

This section presents an example of information splitting using UBMSS system and the distribution of secret parts with the use of the linguistic or biometric threshold schemes. This example represents a simplified model aimed at demonstrating the opportunities offered by UBMSS systems to create and distribute secret information between persons at various management levels or employees at various organisational levels. The UBMSS schemes for information distribution enable generating and distributing parts of the shared information both in layered and hierarchical structures. For this reason, the discussion of the example shown in Fig. 1 will apply to executing precisely these sharing types.

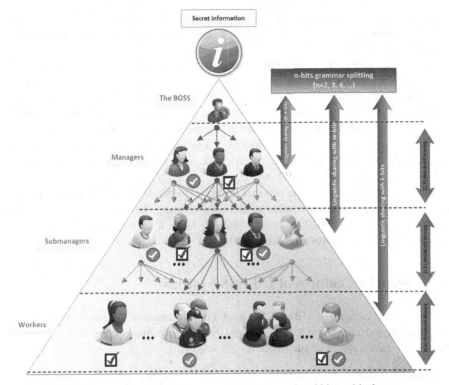

Fig. 1. An example of splitting a secret in the layered and hierarchical way

The first case presented in the example diagram in Fig. 1 concerns the method of sharing and distributing a secret for individual layers in a management pyramid.

These layers may be treated as completely independent, and then the highest authorities will share the secret in various layers independently, but the sharing will be done in various ways using linguistic threshold schemes based on various grammars, i.e. coding the shared input data with bit blocks of different lengths. In Fig. 1 this is marked with vertical red arrows of various lengths. In such layered sharing, employees at a given level are equal and have the same rights to access the secret data, but individual layers stay completely independent, so staff from a given management level cannot cooperate with individuals from other management layers when restoring the secret.

However, as the highest authorities of the enterprise or the arbitrator performing the sharing may also provide lower levels with information about the grammar used (or biometric information) for this sharing, an additional opportunity arises for information to flow between individual management layers, causing a transition from a layered structure to a hierarchical one.

Fig. 1 also demonstrates that hierarchical sharing can be executed in such a way that the secret shares obtained at various levels of the management hierarchy can be shared again using a selected threshold scheme and information about the chosen formal grammar (blue arrows of equal lengths joining individual layers of the management pyramid). In this protocol, every share of the secret generated for a selected employee may be shared at the lower level between a greater number of staff of that lower level.

When we analyse the information sharing procedure in hierarchical structures, the Boss holds important information which can be shared between his/her subordinates observing layer relationships, i.e. employees of a given level are equal and have equal rights to access the secret data under consideration. However, individual layers are not completely separated from one another in information terms and in this regard to not retain their independence, as secret shares at a given management layer can, at subsequent steps, be shared between selected employees of a lower level. This procedure can be repeated for further, still lower layers.

Within such a structure, the original information can be reconstructed in any layer by combining the required number of shadows or using shares coming from different layers. In the second case, a greater number of shares from lower levels is required to reconstruct selected shares from higher layers.

6   Security Features of UBMSS Systems

As was noted before the UBMSS systems could guarantee the security of strategic information and also some safety features during performing secret distribution. The most important features of such systems are following:

- UBMSS systems are suitable for dividing important strategic data and assigning its shares to members of the authorized group;
- UBMSS systems can handle any digital data (text or image) which needs to be intelligently divided among authorized persons and then possible to secretly reconstruct;
- UBMSS systems may be used in different economical management structures e.g. hierarchical, divisional, functional etc.

7   Conclusions

In this paper were presented the cognitive UBMSS systems designed for the secure information management in various management structures. Such systems have the ability to perform a semantic analysis of information which allow to classify it for different semantic categories. Such semantic analysis may further supporting decision-making processes in particular institution or company. Such systems allow also to perform an intelligent information management especially for important, and strategic data. In this paper there were described such possibilities, and also defined two different classes of secure information sharing, especially based on linguistic approach as well as based on some personal biometric features [12]. It seems that in near future such systems will play an increasing role in developing new solutions in areas of very special and strategic information management, especially for government use or homeland security areas.

Acknowledgments. This work has been supported by the National Science Centre, Republic of Poland, under project number 2012/05/B/HS4/03625.

References

1. Bodzioch, S., Ogiela, M.R.: New approach to gallbladder ultrasonic images analysis and lesions recognition. Comput. Med. Imaging Graph. 33, 154–170 (2009)
2. Cohen, H., Lefebvre, C. (eds.): Handbook of Categorization in Cognitive Science. Elsevier, The Netherlands (2005)
3. Meystel, A.M., Albus, J.S.: Intelligent Systems – Architecture, Design, and Control. Wiley & Sons, Inc., Canada (2002)
4. Ogiela, L.: Syntactic Approach to Cognitive Interpretation of Medical Patterns. In: Xiong, C.-H., Liu, H., Huang, Y., Xiong, Y.L. (eds.) ICIRA 2008, Part I. LNCS (LNAI), vol. 5314, pp. 456–462. Springer, Heidelberg (2008)
5. Ogiela, L.: Cognitive systems for medical pattern understanding and diagnosis. In: Lovrek, I., Howlett, R.J., Jain, L.C. (eds.) KES 2008, Part I. LNCS (LNAI), vol. 5177, pp. 394–400. Springer, Heidelberg (2008)
6. Ogiela, L.: UBIAS Systems for Cognitive Interpretation and Analysis of Medical Images. Opto-Electronics Review 17(2), 166–179 (2009)
7. Ogiela, L., Ogiela, M.R.: Cognitive Techniques in Visual Data Interpretation. SCI, vol. 228. Springer, Heidelberg (2009)
8. Ogiela, M.R., Ogiela, U.: The use of mathematical linguistic methods in creating secret sharing threshold algorithms. Computers and Mathematics with Applications 60(2), 267–271 (2010)
9. Ogiela, L., Ogiela, M.R.: Advances in Cognitive Information Systems. COSMOS, vol. 17. Springer, Heidelberg (2012)
10. Ogiela, M.R., Ogiela, U.: DNA-like linguistic secret sharing for strategic information systems. International Journal of Information Management 32, 175–181 (2012)
11. Ogiela, M.R., Ogiela, U.: Linguistic Protocols for Secure Information Management and Sharing. Computers and Mathematics with Applications 63(2), 564–572 (2012)
12. Peters, W.: Representing Humans in System Security Models: An Actor-Network Approach. Journal of Wireless Mobile Networks, Ubiquitous Computing, and Dependable Applications 2(1), 75–92 (2011)

Fully Distributed Secure Video Surveillance Via Portable Device with User Awareness

Arcangelo Castiglione[1,*], Ciriaco D'Ambrosio[1],
Alfredo De Santis[1], and Francesco Palmieri[2]

[1] Dipartimento di Informatica, Università di Salerno
Via Ponte don Melillo, I-84084, Fisciano (SA), Italy
{ads,arccas}@dia.unisa.it, cdambrosio@unisa.it
[2] Dipartimento di Ingegneria Industriale e dell'Informazione
Seconda Università di Napoli
Via Roma 29, Aversa (CE), I-81031, Italy
fpalmier@unina.it

Abstract. Internet-based video surveillance systems are now widespread in the modern e-Society, since they can be used to manage multiple physical security problems in a lot of contexts. Moreover, the growing diffusion of portable device, along with the necessity of keeping specific environments and motion events under control, brought out the need for more flexible and proactive systems, which allow the management of such scenarios. However, most of the state of the art video surveillance systems are known to be unscalable, unreliable, insecure, and do not provide adequate guarantees for user awareness when a determined situation of interest occurs. Furthermore, almost all the currently defined systems, lack in operation flexibility: they are designed for a specific context and can not be easily adapted to the different ones.

In this work, we propose general-purpose video surveillance system, which is fully distributed and accessible through ubiquitous portable devices. Such system, whose architecture is based on a self-organizing overlay network built on top of a mixture of already existing physical network connections, provides an high degree of reliability for the interactions among all its components, and ensures to its users, regardless of where they are located, the ability to receive notifications upon the occurrence of interesting events.

Keywords: P2P Surveillance, Ubiquitous User Awareness, Secure P2P Systems, Mission Critical Systems, Portable Surveillance Monitor, Kademlia.

1 Introduction

The ever-growing need for security in the modern society, led to an increasing demand for surveillance activities in many areas, which may include transportation

---

* Corresponding author.

A. Cuzzocrea et al. (Eds.): CD-ARES 2013 Workshops, LNCS 8128, pp. 414–429, 2013.
© IFIP International Federation for Information Processing 2013

applications, monitoring of public places, remote surveillance of human activities, monitoring for quality control in industrial processes, remote surveillance in forensic applications and military sites [1]. The new generation video surveillance systems, are concerned with the monitoring of permanent and transients objects within a given area or environment, both indoor and outdoor [2], [3], [4], [5] and typically rely on *Computer Vision* techniques [6], [7], [8] [9]. By using such techniques, our system is able to automatically interpret the scene, as well as to understand and predict actions and interactions taking place among the observed objects, based on the information acquired by the involved observation camera(s).

Depending on scenarios in which they operate, that are often mission-critical and require real-time response, such systems must provide, fully or partially, the following basic features: availability, reliability, scalability and security [10]. At the state of the art, many network-based video surveillance solutions have been proposed, each one with its own specific characteristics, strengths and weaknesses. However, most of the widely known systems, are usually designed for a specific context, and can not be easily adapted to the different ones. Nowadays, those systems are typically structured according to the traditional client-server paradigm [11], [12], [13], [14], [15], [16] or are based on complex overlay communication [17], [18] and middleware [19], [10] architectures or, even when claim to be structured according to a resilient and robust *Peer-to-Peer (P2P)* [20] scheme, this is only partially true, because their operations still rely on the presence of a centralized directory service, that can be easily identified as the system's security and performance bottleneck.

Hence, it is easy to note that all the currently available systems, do not provide proper guarantees of availability, scalability and reliability that are, however, the fundamental requirements in a modern and really effective surveillance solution. Moreover, we point out that even if the surveillance systems are mainly used to monitor and improve the security in certain specific scenarios and environments, none of them address the problems of authentication and privacy among the involved parties, as well as the surveillance data integrity ones, except the one presented in [21], [22], which partially addresses the privacy issue among the interacting entities. Furthermore, no distributed video surveillance solution has yet been proposed, allowing a portable device to be efficiently and securely notified, in an ubiquitous manner, about the occurrence of certain interesting situations.

In order to cope with all the above issues, we propose a fully distributed flexible and adaptive video surveillance system, composed by a set of interacting peer nodes within a self-organizing overlay network, each connected with one or more camera(s). To ensure the needed robustness and scalability guarantees, such system is structured according to a completely decentralized and distributed model, based on the use of a P2P implicit communication architecture among its components. In particular, it is based on Kademlia, a *Distributed Hash Table (DHT)* management facility for pure P2P organizations, used by many systems such as *Kad, Overnet, BitTorrent* and *Gnutella*. The system we proposed can be accessed in an ubiquitous manner through the use of any portable device (e.g., smartphones, tablets, laptops, etc.), even when it has limited hardware features. Moreover, it can be instructed to autonomously detect, recognize and classify certain situations of interest that may occur in monitored environments, by using sophisticated Computer Vision techniques. Given the scenarios where our system is able to operate effectively, which can be mission critical, highly risky, and also prone to attack given the potentially sensitive information that it has to manage, we paid particular attention to confidentiality and integrity of the involved surveillance data. In particular, authentication, confidentiality, integrity and non-repudiation are fully guaranteed for all the interactions and data exchange operations that take place among the system components. Ubiquitous surveillance capabilities are granted to any authorized mobile user, who, by using its own remote network access facilities, can arbitrarily choose to monitor his places of interest from everywhere and at any time. Furthermore, when there is a situation of potential interest and the mobile user is not connected to the system, he can be notified in real-time about such events through SMS and e-mail, in order to take the appropriate actions as quickly as possible. We engineered a simple proof ì-of-concept prototype of this system in order to evaluate its performance in terms of scalability, reliability, fault tolerance and security. In particular, we simulated the use of the proposed system in a WAN. The results of the tests we performed, shown that it guarantees good performance with respect to objectives we set out above.

The remainder of the paper is organized as follows: Section 2 provides a description of the basic prerequisite concepts needed to better present the proposed solution. Section 3 gives a general system overview from the architectural point of view together with some implementation details. Section 4 describes the module responsible for the user situation awareness. Section 5 highlights all the security aspects of the system while Section 6 describes the proof-of-concept implementation and the functional tests performed on it. Finally, Section 7 shows some possible future extensions and draws the conclusions.

2   Background

2.1   Peer-to-Peer Overlay Organizations

A P2P overlay is a flexible virtual organization of logical associations between peer entities that is dynamically built and managed on top of existing network connections. The fundamental features of such organization is the ability of each participating entity of searching within the organization for some specific key or attribute and finding all the other networked entities within the overlay organization that are associated to that key/attribute in a very effective way, independently from its physical location and network dependent information. Simply stated, to search a node(s), characterized by some specific attributes a querier does not need to know the IP address of the involved entities, but only attributes characterizing it. Moreover, such organizations are self-organizing, that is, participating peer nodes may dynamically join and leave the overlay in a seamless way without requiring complex reconfiguration operations or affecting the behavior and operations of other nodes in a significant way. From a performance perspective, modern structured P2P overlays support the localization of any resource/peer in a bounded time that scales with the total number of nodes n in the overlay as $O(log(n))$.

2.2   The Kademlia Overlay DHT System

Kademlia is a DHT management infrastructure for decentralized P2P networked systems [23] where each peer component is identified by a unique n-bits identifier (node ID), usually determined by using an hash function on its IP address. Basing its decisions on these identifiers the Kademlia P2P algorithm determines where to store information, and which peers are going to be responsible for it, according to a fully distributed hash table scheme. The distance between two peers is computed as the exclusive OR (XOR) of two node IDs and taking the result as an integer number. This ensures, due to the symmetric nature of the XOR operation, also the symmetry of the associated overlay structure. Each node stores contact information about the other ones in a properly crafted *"routing table"* needed to ensure the mutual reachability among nodes. Nodes are logically managed as leaves into a binary search tree where the position of each node is determined by the shortest unique prefix of its ID. In order to face the problem of stale contacts due to *churn* (departure of peers) [24], Kademlia uses redundancy, i.e., the routing table stores more than one contact (typically k) for a given distance. Every node keeps a list of: IP address, UDP port and node ID, for nodes of distance between 2^i and 2^{i+1} from itself, with $0 \le i \le n$, where n is the number of bits in the node ID. These lists, called k-buckets, have at most k elements. For example, in a network with $k = 20$, each node will have lists containing up to 20 nodes for a particular bit (a particular distance from itself). k-buckets are kept sorted by the time at which the associated contacts were last seen. The routing table is organized as a binary tree whose leaves are k-buckets. Thus, each lookup step has a choice of k different contacts for the next step. When a k-bucket is full and a new node is discovered for that k-bucket, the least recently seen node in the k-bucket is probed through a PING operation. If the node is found to be still alive, the new node is placed in a secondary list, called *replacement cache*, which is used only if a node in the k-bucket stops responding. In other words, new nodes are used only when older ones disappear. Kademlia has four messages, corresponding to remote procedure calls:

- *PING:* probes a peer to check if it is active.
- *STORE:* instructs a peer to store a {*key, value*} pair for later retrieval.
- *FIND_NODE:* takes an ID, and returns {*IP address, UDP port, NodeID*} triples for the k peers it knows that are closest to the target ID.
- *FIND_VALUE:* is similar to FIND_NODE, it returns {*IP address, UDP port, NodeID*} triples, except for the case when a peer received a STORE for the key, it just return the stored value.

A node which would like to join the network must first performs a bootstrap process with another node that is already participating in the Kademlia network. The joining node inserts the bootstrap node into one of its k-buckets and then does a FIND_NODE of its own ID against the bootstrap node. The "*self-lookup*" will populate other nodes' k-buckets with the new node ID, and the joining node's k-buckets with nodes in the path among it and the bootstra node. Afterwards, the joining node refreshes all the k-buckets further away than the k-bucket the bootstrap node falls in. Kademlia uses *iterative routing*, where the client is responsible for the entire lookup process. At each step, the client sends a lookup request to the next-hop peer and waits for a lookup reply. The reply lets the client know what the next hop is. In Kademlia, a peer must locate the k closest peers to some given node ID. This lookup initiator starts by picking α peers (*parallel routing*) from its closest non-empty k-bucket [25], and then sends parallel asynchronous FIND_NODE messages to the α peers it has chosen. If a FIND_NODE operation fails to return a peer that is closer than the closest peers already seen, the initiator resends the FIND_NODE to any of the k closest peers that has not been already queried.

In supporting key-based searches on its own DHT infrastructure, Kademlia does not introduce periodic overhead, but exploits the previous search transactions to stabilize the overlay network connections.

3   The System Overview

The proposed surveillance system is composed by three logical entities: the surveillance node, the portable device needing to access the surveillance data and the P2P overlay communication and search infrastructure, used to implement a fully distributed index for the rapid localization of surveillance nodes associated to specific monitoring environments. The overall system architecture is sketched in Figure 1.

3.1   Basic Architectural Choices

The system is able to support a large number of video monitoring stations, located in different physical places, each one with its own access privileges and private views. These stations are controlled by surveillance nodes, reachable though the Internet or a mix or public and private networks and typically run on generic *Commercial Off-The-Shelf (COTS)* workstation hardware. Each surveillance node, associated to one or more camera(s), is autonomously responsible for all the interactions among controlled cameras and portable devices, involved in the monitoring of certain areas or environments, in order to detect situations of interest.

The surveillance node, also deals with the acquisition of relevant information from camera(s), along with the management of the whole Computer Vision process. These activities are managed by using the user situation awareness module, which issues real-time notifications when a situation of interest subscribed by a portable device occurs.

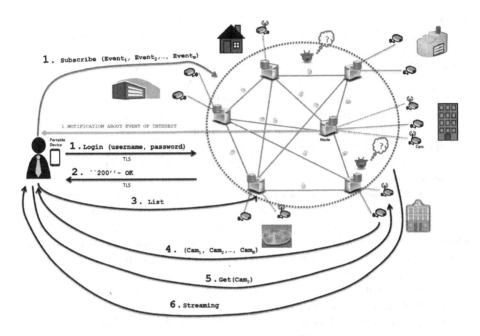

Fig. 1. The overall system architecture and the components interaction

The portable device, instead, represents the system interface for the mobile user, which is interested in monitoring a specific area or environment and wants to have an awareness about the occurrence of specific situations or events.

The P2P overlay communication and search infrastructure is based on Kademlia [23], which, as we have previously seen, is a DHT for decentralized P2P overlay organizations. We made that choice since Kademlia, among the existing similar systems, is the one which minimizes the number of messages sent by each node in order to acquire information about the registered surveillance services and their associated nodes.

We model our system in a fully distributed way, where the whole architecture is organized as a P2P network of nodes, which may be geographically located everywhere on the Internet or connected to any combination of local and wide area IP-based communication infrastructures, and may use completely different kinds of networking and communication technologies, as shown in Figure 1.

We have chosen this architectural scheme since among the similar available, it is the one which best supports our needs of reliability, scalability and availability, by exploiting the self-organization capabilities of the DHT overlay communication infrastructure. In fact, in traditional systems, the surveillance stations are accessible by their users only through a centralized brokering services, imposing severe limits on the scalability and reliability of the whole solution. That is, the system performance, in presence of n client and server nodes, has to scale with $O(n^2)$ due to the $n \cdot (n-1)$ potential relationships among the n involved entities, and this is clearly not acceptable for very large n, for example in systems with many monitoring sites and a huge number of users, such as the publicly accessible ones, usually deployed in the tourism and travel sectors. In other words, the number of hosts that can be monitored at a given time, is limited by the bandwidth and the processing power of the central brokering system, and hence the solution does not scale. Furthermore, once the single central brokering unit fails, the whole system will lose its functionality and the entire set of controlled places will be without any kind of surveillance. Simply stated, any centralized brokering service becomes a single point of failure.

On the contrary, the proposed solution avoids the necessity of any centralized directory or brokering services providing access to surveillance nodes and their managed resources. In particular, by eliminating single points of failure and performance bottlenecks, such solution provides our system with the ability of allowing quick topology changes and easily grow/shrink by adding or removing new nodes or portable devices according to a plug-and-play paradigm, without complex configuration and management tasks. In this way, it is easier to ensure an high degree of scalability and flexibility, and the overall architecture is able to survive to failures or disruptions of any of its components, without stopping its global operations, so that any kind of damage only affects the locally involved nodes.

Moreover, in presence of a very large number of nodes scattered throughout the Internet, the Kademlia-based solution allows the delivery of multiple parallel queries for the same key to different peers. In this way, any delay or timeout on a specific route to destination do not necessarily affect the search process, thus ensuring faster and more reliable searches, also in presence of a large number of nodes continuously joining and leaving the overlay network.

3.2   Implementation Details

The system, is accessible to both the surveillance nodes and mobile monitoring devices through a publicly available hostname, registered on the *Internet Domain Name System* (*DNS*). Such an hostname, is dynamically mapped to one of the nodes in the P2P network, through *Dynamic DNS* [26] techniques. A new node or portable device who want to join our system, must only know such hostname, along with the proper access credentials (username and password, or digital X.509 certificate). The above hostname, must be also used as the Kademlia bootstrap node for all the entities (surveillance nodes and portable devices devices) that need to access the overlay network infrastructure. Surveillance nodes, when joining such network, register their monitoring capabilities, in terms of associated camera(s)/monitored environment(s), by storing on the Kademlia DHT each environment identifier (*key*), together with the serving node IP address (*value*). Portable devices, which want to join the surveillance system, can search the Kademlia overlay for keys corresponding to the environments of interest under monitoring, by obtaining the IP addresses of associated surveillance nodes, in order to connect to them for visualizing the cameras' video materials.

Moreover, a portable device that is not currently joined, can be asynchronously notified about the occurrence of events of interest (motion detection, etc.). It is important to point out that there is no explicit communication among surveillance nodes, which only interact among themselves indirectly, by exposing and sharing their service information (monitored environments) through the overlay DHT facilities. Instead, the communication among portable devices and surveillance nodes takes place according to the traditional client-server paradigm, where each surveillance node assumes the role of server for all the mobile nodes' queries. In particular, the interaction between such two parties, is carried out via (secure) *TCP* socket, by using an ad-hoc *FTP-like* protocol, for the delivery of control messages (queries and results) and video surveillance data. Like in *passive-mode FTP*, such ad-hoc protocol (as defined in [21]) in order to overcome limitations introduced by firewalls or NATs, as well as restrictions and policies imposed by cellular operators, forces the portable device to open two communication channels, one for the sending of control messages and the other for data transfer, by thus avoiding the opening of any connection backwards, from the surveillance node to the mobile one. The messages used for the interaction among a node and a portable device are four: *Login, List, MGet* and *Subscribe*. The *Login* message is used by the portable device for communicating to the node its login credentials, i.e., username, password and optionally its own certificate, in the event that strong mutual authentication among endpoints is needed. The authentication phase, accomplished through the use of such message, can be successful or not. If it has been successfully completed, the node sends to portable device a message which contains the "200" return code, as in the standard *FTP*, and the interaction between these two parts continues normally. In the case of failure, the portable device is notified about that by the node, and it is shown an alert message on its display. Upon a successful authentication, a portable device can use the *List* message for requesting a preview (typically in *JPEG*) of each of the environments monitored by the node to which it is connected. As soon as a node receives such command, it takes a snapshot from each of its camera(s), and send such snapshot(s) to the portable device. When a portable device, based on the snapshot(s) it has received, chooses the particular environment which intends to monitor (identified by an univocal code), at this point it can use the *MGet* command. Once a node receives this command, it creates a data channel with the portable device, and through this mechanism it sends a video streaming to the latter. It is important to point out that a portable device, after its successful connection to a surveillance node, is able to communicate the possible events in which it is interested and for which it wants to receive notifications, by using the *Subscribe* message.

4   The User Awareness Module

If an event of interest for a particular place occurs when the user is not connected to the system, such user has no awareness about what has happened, and therefore has no information about that. Hence, we decided to provide our system with an asynchronous notification facility, that enables the user to have the full control on what happens, even when it is not connected. For this reason, our system allows the user to specify places and scenarios which he/she intends to monitor, as well as the events of interest.

When an event in a place of interest occurs, the user is notified as quickly and reliably as possible in order to appropriately manage such a situation. The notification must reach the user in an ubiquitous way. For this reason, we think that *GSM* network coverage is a fairly realistic assumption, so our system sends to the user a notification message through the SMS system. However, in some particular circumstances, the user may not be connected to the cellular network and may only use a local data network (such as Wi-Fi). Therefore, our system uses as a notification method, at the same time, the one based on SMS and the other based on e-mail. The notification message, includes all the information defining the event, along with any other useful thing to remedy it in the most appropriate and quick way. In order to guarantee the user awareness about the monitored scenarios, we enable our system to semantically interpret detected objects behavior.

The system we propose is autonomously able to identify and learn from events and occurring interactions, that take place in a given monitored environment [1]. In particular, we provide our system with a component dealing with the so-called *Computer Vision*, which allows video processing, real time scene recognition with related data analysis and decision making with respect to them [6], [7], [8], [9], [11]. We implemented the Computer Vision module through the use of the *Open Source Computer Vision (OpenCV)* library [27], [28]. OpenCV is a library of programming functions, mainly aimed at real-time Computer Vision and is released under the BSD license. The Computer Vision, can be considered as a process constituted by a number of phases that may vary, depending on the operating scenario and the specific system application domain. Such phases, can be typically grouped into four main blocks, which are *image preprocessing*, *object recognition* with *motion detection*, *object monitoring* and *reasoning* with *activity recognition* [29], [5], [4], [2].

In the preprocessing phase, the image sequence produced by one or more camera(s), is processed by our Computer Vision module in order to ensure resampling, noise reduction, contrast enhancement and scale space representation. The recognition phase, instead, finds an object within an image or video sequence, also when such object is partially obstructed from view. In particular, in such a phase, image features such as lines, edges and ridges, along with any other localized points at various levels of complexity, are extracted in order to obtain the segmentation of one or multiple image regions which contain a specific object of interest. The motion detection phase, detects a change in position of an object relative to its surroundings or the change in the surroundings relative to an object. Object monitoring (or tracking), instead, locates a moving object (or multiple objects) over time by using one or more camera(s). The main aim of such phase is to associate target objects in consecutive video frames. It is important to point out that the association can be especially difficult when the objects are moving fast relative to the frame rate, or when the tracked object changes orientation over time. In order to manage such situations, our system employs a motion model which describes how the image of the target might change for different possible motions of the object. The last Computer Vision phase

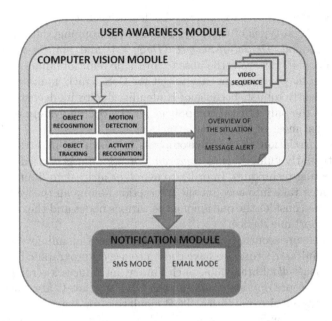

Fig. 2. The user awareness module

implemented by our system is the activity recognition, that is, the process of recognize actions and goals of one or more actors from a series of observations on their actions and environmental conditions. After such phase, if a potential situation of interest for the mobile user is detected, then the system triggers the notification module which takes care of notifying users about the events of interest. Such a component, dealing with the user notification, is composed by two modules, the former takes secure and efficient delivery of SMS messages, while the latter takes care of sending e-mail messages. It is easy to note that the portable device, when it is joining the system must provide one or more e-mail addresses, along with one or more telephone numbers, by which it intends to be notified. In Figure 2, we show the various components which constitute the user situation awareness module, along with its flow of events. Video streaming, acquired from different camera(s) connected to each node of our system, is continuously analyzed by the corresponding module responsible for the Computer Vision process. As soon as such module detects, based on how it has been trained by, the occurrence of a certain situation of interest it provides the user with an overview of the situation that has arisen, through an appropriate alert message, which is sent either by SMS and through e-mail.

5   The Security Services

It can be easily observed that due to its mission critical nature, any surveillance system is particularly exposed to security problems [30], especially because of the scenarios where it has to operate. In detail, such type of system may be subjected to several types of threats, such as eavesdropping, data modification, IP address spoofing, *Denial-of-Service* (*DoS*) [31] and *man-in-the-middle* attacks [32], [33], [34]. However, the absence of single point of failure, and hence of elements which may become an easy target for DoS attack, makes the proposed solution sufficiently robust, because of Kademlia, due to its decentralized architecture that is the only critical component for the overall system operations, is resistant against most of the known attacks.

Moreover, in relation to the environments in which it operates, our system may be particularly vulnerable to *compromised-key attacks* carried out by using social engineering techniques. In order to avoid, or at least to limit such kind of attacks, we must take into account the interaction among all the system parties. In particular we consider the one among the various nodes and the other between a node and a portable device.

In order to ensure security during the access to the Kademlia overlay information exchange infrastructure, we have chosen to use cryptographic functions provided by *maidsafe-dht* library [35]. Such library, introduces a strong encryption layer to ensure secure operations within the DHT overlay. It also ensures to our system *NAT* traversal capabilities, TCP emulation for fault tolerance, routing of queries through low-latency paths as well as use of asynchronous and parallel queries to avoid timeout delays from failed nodes. Furthermore, maidsafe-dht also includes some significant enhancements to the traditional Kademlia implementation, by providing a downlist modification with notification of dead nodes in searches as well as forcing partner bucket to contain the most recent closest nodes, in order to further increase the reliability of the whole DHT system.

Instead, regarding the interaction among a node and a portable device, our system uses the *Transport Layer Security* (*TLS*) protocol, which ensures security and privacy for stream-oriented communications. We also paid particular attention to security concerning user notifications about situations of interest.

In particular, security properties of component which deals with SMS based notification, rely on the *SEESMS* architecture (*Secure Extensible and Efficient SMS*) [36], initially presented in [37].

SEESMS is a framework for the exchange of secure SMS, which aims to be efficient through the support of several cryptosystems by using a modular architecture, as it is shown in Figure 3. In particular, it is important to point out that the SMS notification module of our system is implemented by using the Secure SMS Management Center of SEESMS, while the SEESMS client is included within the portable device. Such framework, represents a tool which uses an SMS based communication mechanism to exchange encrypted, non-repudiable and tamper-proof messages. One of the main advantage of SEESMS over similar systems, is the possibility to choose which combination of cryptosystem/security parameters to use during message exchange. Moreover, one of the two parties (node or portable device), could set a minimum security level to be fulfilled during the communication, giving the other peer the possibility to increase (but not decrease) it. From an architectural point of view, as can be seen from Figure 3,

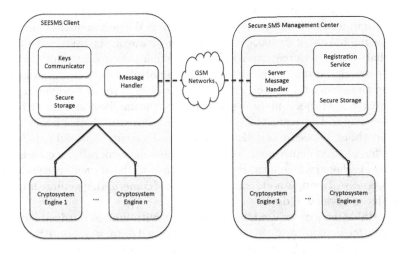

Fig. 3. The SEESMS architecture

the flexibility of SEESMS has been made possible by the adoption of a modular architecture, where the cryptographic functions of the framework are not built into SEESMS, but are delegated to some external pluggable modules.

On the other hand, with respect to the security of e-mail based notification, we chose to rely on the *Secure/Multipurpose Internet Mail Extensions (S/MIME)* standard [38], in order to use X.509 certificate for signing and encrypting each e-mail notification message sent. By doing this, we intend to guarantee identification (authentication), confidentiality, integrity and non-repudiation of all the notification messages sent, in order to avoid fake alerts to be maliciously sent to the monitoring users.

6   Proof-of-Concept and Functional Evaluation

We engineered a very simple proof-of-concept prototype of our system in order to validate its functional behavior and test the effectiveness of the aforementioned surveillance architecture, with an emphasis on the use of currently available COTS devices and open-source components. The testing was carried out on three surveillance nodes connected to the network in a stable way, along with three other ones which dynamically connect and disconnect from it. Each node used for the functional testing operations consists of conventional PCs with different hardware characteristics, each one controlling a single camera, interconnected through a Local Area Network (LAN). We also used several common portable devices (smartphones and tablets), connected to the network in different ways, ranging from *Wi-Fi* LAN connections to *3G/UMTS* ones, provided by traditional cellular Internet service providers.

In general, our preliminary functional tests, shown that, by dynamically varying the number of its parties as well as the amount of data exchanged, our system continues to behave correctly and is essentially not affected from the above events, both in terms of performance and efficiency. We point out that, due to the self-organizing nature of its basic association mechanism, the system tends to be highly reliable. The resources exposed from surveillance nodes dynamically joining the P2P network, become correctly available to portable devices almost immediately after the successful connection and registration of the corresponding information. Search operations on the overlay DHT by the mobile nodes are carried out instantaneously and are resilient to multiple node failures until other nodes are able to respond about a specific key. However, this feature can be useful only in presence of different surveillance nodes controlling the same camera(s), according to an architectural scheme which introduces redundancy at the surveillance node level, since in presence of a single node controlling a set of camera(s), its failure implicitly isolates all the associated devices.

The portable devices we used, including those with limited hardware features, showed for access, monitoring and control of recorded data, a response time in the order of a few milliseconds. Also the notification task appears to be very lightweight and well tolerated by portable devices. For measuring the response time which concerns detection and notification of interesting events, we configured the system in order to make it able to recognize and notify the user about the occurrence of common situations, such as the entrance of people into a given environment or the move of an object. We also empirically evaluated the time elapsed since the detection of an event by a node, until the receipt of a notification by the portable device. Such time, may vary from one to ten minutes, depending on the complexity associated to the detection and understanding of the occurred event. However, the asynchronous notification task, affects that time only by a negligible factor. The security of our system, was assessed by subjecting it to several attacks, carried out through exploits and tools for sniffing (e.g., Wireshark) and man-in-the-middle (e.g., Ettercap) attacks. In addition, we also used a vulnerability scanner (Nessus) to asses the whole testing network where the surveillance nodes have been located. The system has been found to be sufficiently secure with respect to the analysis carried out by using such tools.

7   Conclusions and Future Work

The system we propose ensures to the mobile user a complete awareness about the scenarios under consideration, over the whole P2P-based surveillance organization. The use awareness module combines video analysis, intelligence and ability to cope with real-time events of interest.

Our system guarantees to mobile users real-time monitoring of scenarios and notification about relevant events as soon as they occur, always by paying particular attention to all the security issues that may arise. In the future, we intend to provide our system with a Web-based interface which enables the uniform access to its services, thus avoiding the use of a specific client for that purpose. Furthermore, in order to improve the efficiency of data exchange, we plan to use data compression techniques over the communication channel among the portable device and the surveillance node.

We also plan to take advantage of new features provided by the *"Smart Cameras"*, and in general by the *"Embedded Smart Devices"*, especially to alleviate the computational load that each node must handle, considering the number of performed operations. Our further aim, is also to improve the system security, by involving biometric techniques, smart cards and trusted hardware modules, in order to prevent compromised-key attack and insiders' threats due to social engineering techniques. Moreover, we intend to store some interesting data acquired, and to protect them by using an *Attribute-Based Encryption Scheme*, which permits the fine-grained access control over them [39]. We think that, it would be particularly interesting to provide each node also with different types of sensor(s), such as detectors for smells (to prevent gas leaks), vibrations (for earthquakes) and noises (to help the system in low light conditions).

Finally, it may be useful to use optimization algorithms, for the exact positioning of camera(s) and sensor(s), according to the specific monitored place. By adding such new features, we intend to create an even more intelligent system, which enables the user to have an additional support, concerning not only the monitoring, but also the deployment of camera(s) and sensor(s).

References

1. Valera, M., Velastin, S.: Intelligent distributed surveillance systems: a review. IEE Proceedings Vision, Image and Signal Processing, IET 152(2), 192–204 (2005)
2. Hu, W., Tan, T., Wang, L., Maybank, S.: A survey on visual surveillance of object motion and behaviors. IEEE Transactions on Systems, Man, and Cybernetics, Part C: Applications and Reviews 34(3), 334–352 (2004)
3. Hampapur, A., Brown, L., Connell, J., Ekin, A., Haas, N., Lu, M., Merkl, H., Pankanti, S.: Smart video surveillance: exploring the concept of multiscale spatiotemporal tracking. IEEE Signal Processing Magazine 22(2), 38–51 (2005)
4. Buxton, H., Gong, S.: Visual surveillance in a dynamic and uncertain world. Artificial Intelligence 78(1), 431–459 (1995)
5. Cucchiara, R., Grana, C., Piccardi, M., Prati, A.: Detecting moving objects, ghosts, and shadows in video streams. IEEE Transactions on Pattern Analysis and Machine Intelligence 25(10), 1337–1342 (2003)
6. Hartley, R., Zisserman, A.: Multiple view geometry in computer vision, vol. 2. Cambridge University Press (2000)
7. Forsyth, D.A., Ponce, J.: Computer vision: a modern approach. Prentice Hall Professional Technical Reference (2002)
8. Parker, J.R.: Algorithms for image processing and computer vision. Wiley Publishing (2010)
9. Moeslund, T.B., Granum, E.: A survey of computer vision-based human motion capture. Computer Vision and Image Understanding 81(3), 231–268 (2001)
10. Kornecki, A.: Middleware for distributed video surveillance. IEEE Distributed Systems Online 9(2), 1 (2008)
11. Cucchiara, R., Grana, C., Prati, A., Vezzani, R.: Computer vision techniques for PDA accessibility of in-house video surveillance. In: First ACM SIGMM International Workshop on Video Surveillance, IWVS 2003, pp. 87–97. ACM, New York (2003)

12. Javed, O., Rasheed, Z., Alatas, O., Shah, M.: KNIGHT trade;: a real time surveillance system for multiple and non-overlapping cameras. In: Proceedings of 2003 International Conference on Multimedia and Expo, ICME 2003, vol. 1, pp. 649–652 (July 2003)
13. Comaniciu, D., Berton, F., Ramesh, V.: Adaptive Resolution System for Distributed Surveillance. Real-Time Imaging 8(5), 427–437 (2002)
14. Cucchiara, R., Prati, A., Vezzani, R.: A multi-camera vision system for fall detection and alarm generation. Expert Systems 24(5), 334–345 (2007)
15. Ostheimer, D., Lemay, S., Ghazal, M., Mayisela, D., Amer, A., Dagba, P.F.: A modular distributed video surveillance system over IP. In: Canadian Conference on Electrical and Computer Engineering, CCECE 2006, pp. 518–521. IEEE (2006)
16. Castiglione, A., Cepparulo, M., De Santis, A., Palmieri, F.: Towards a Lawfully Secure and Privacy Preserving Video Surveillance System. In: Buccafurri, F., Semeraro, G. (eds.) E-Commerce and Web Technologies. LNBIP, vol. 61, pp. 73–84. Springer, Heidelberg (2010)
17. Yuan, X., Sun, Z., Varol, Y., Bebis, G.: A distributed visual surveillance system. In: Proceedings of the IEEE Conference on Advanced Video and Signal Based Surveillance, pp. 199–204. IEEE (2003)
18. Dias, H., Rocha, J., Silva, P., Leao, C., Reis, L.P.: Distributed surveillance system. In: Portuguese Conference on Artificial Intelligence, EPIA 2005, pp. 257–261. IEEE (2005)
19. Desurmont, X., Bastide, A., Czyz, J., Parisot, C., Delaigle, J.F., Macq, B.: A general purpose system for distributed surveillance and communication. In: Intelligent Distributed Video Surveillance Systems, pp. 121–156 (2006)
20. Wu, Y.S., Chang, Y.S., Juang, T.Y., Yen, J.S.: An Architecture for Video Surveillance Service Based on P2P and Cloud Computing. In: 2012 9th International Conference on Ubiquitous Intelligence & Computing and 9th International Conference on Autonomic & Trusted Computing (UIC/ATC), pp. 661–666. IEEE (2012)
21. Albano, P., Bruno, A., Carpentieri, B., Castiglione, A., Castiglione, A., Palmieri, F., Pizzolante, R., You, I.: A Secure Distributed Video Surveillance System Based on Portable Devices. In: Quirchmayr, G., Basl, J., You, I., Xu, L., Weippl, E. (eds.) CD-ARES 2012. LNCS, vol. 7465, pp. 403–415. Springer, Heidelberg (2012)
22. Albano, P., Bruno, A., Carpentieri, B., Castiglione, A., Castiglione, A., Palmieri, F., Pizzolante, R., Yim, K., You, I.: Secure and distributed video surveillance via portable devices. Journal of Ambient Intelligence and Humanized Computing, 1–9 (2013)
23. Maymounkov, P., Mazières, D.: Kademlia: A peer-to-peer information system based on the XOR metric. In: Druschel, P., Kaashoek, M.F., Rowstron, A. (eds.) IPTPS 2002. LNCS, vol. 2429, pp. 53–65. Springer, Heidelberg (2002)
24. Rhea, S.C., Geels, D., Roscoe, T., Kubiatowicz, J.: Handling churn in a DHT. Computer Science Division, University of California (2003)
25. Stutzbach, D., Rejaie, R.: Improving lookup performance over a widely-deployed DHT. In: Proc. Infocom, vol. 6 (2006)
26. Vixie, P., Thomson, S., Rekhter, Y., Bound, J.: Dynamic Updates in the Domain Name System (DNS UPDATE). RFC 2136 (Proposed Standard), Updated by RFCs 3007, 4035, 4033, 4034 (April 1997)
27. Bradski, G.: The OpenCV library. Doctor Dobbs Journal 25(11), 120–126 (2000)
28. Bradski, G., Kaehler, A.: Learning OpenCV: Computer vision with the OpenCV library. O'Reilly Media, Incorporated (2008)

29. Wijnhoven, R., Jaspers, E., et al.: Flexible surveillance system architecture for prototyping video content analysis algorithms. In: International Society for Optics and Photonics Electronic Imaging 2006, p. 60730R (2006)
30. Castiglione, A., De Prisco, R., De Santis, A.: Do you trust your phone? In: Di Noia, T., Buccafurri, F. (eds.) EC-Web 2009. LNCS, vol. 5692, pp. 50–61. Springer, Heidelberg (2009)
31. Naoumov, N., Ross, K.: Exploiting P2P systems for DDoS attacks. In: Proceedings of the 1st International Conference on Scalable Information Systems, p. 47. ACM (2006)
32. Wallach, D.S.: A survey of peer-to-peer security issues. In: Okada, M., Babu, C. S., Scedrov, A., Tokuda, H. (eds.) ISSS 2002. LNCS, vol. 2609, pp. 42–57. Springer, Heidelberg (2003)
33. Urdaneta, G., Pierre, G., Steen, M.V.: A survey of DHT security techniques. ACM Computing Surveys (CSUR) 43(2), 8 (2011)
34. Wang, P., Tyra, J., Chan-Tin, E., Malchow, T., Kune, D.F., Hopper, N., Kim, Y.: Attacking the KAD network. In: Proceedings of the 4th International Conference on Security and Privacy in Communication Netowrks, p. 23. ACM (2008)
35. Irvine, D.: Kademlia DHT with NAT traversal, http://code.google.com/p/maidsafe-dht/ (accessed June 16, 2013)
36. Castiglione, A., Cattaneo, G., Cembalo, M., De Santis, A., Faruolo, P., Petagna, F., Ferraro Petrillo, U.: Engineering a secure mobile messaging framework. Computers & Security 31(6), 771–781 (2012)
37. De Santis, A., Castiglione, A., Cattaneo, G., Cembalo, M., Petagna, F., Ferraro Petrillo, U.: An Extensible Framework for Efficient Secure SMS. In: 2010 International Conference on Complex, Intelligent and Software Intensive Systems, pp. 843–850 (2010)
38. Ramsdell, B.: S/MIME version 3 message specification (1999)
39. Goyal, V., Pandey, O., Sahai, A., Waters, B.: Attribute-based encryption for fine-grained access control of encrypted data. In: Proceedings of the 13th ACM Conference on Computer and Communications Security, pp. 89–98. ACM (2006)

Computer Karate Trainer in Tasks of Personal and Homeland Security Defense

Tomasz Hachaj[1] and Marek R. Ogiela[2]

[1] Pedagogical University of Krakow, 2 Podchorazych Ave, 30-084 Krakow, Poland
tomekhachaj@o2.pl
[2] AGH University of Science and Technology, 30 Mickiewicza Ave, 30-059 Krakow, Poland
mogiela@agh.edu.pl

Abstract. In this paper will be presented a new possibility of using GDL (Gesture Description Language) approach for recognition of basic combat techniques from martial arts. The GDL approach allows not only to analyze the several Shorin-Ryu Karate techniques but also to support the training and teaching activities of such arts. Moreover the GDL allow performing the human behavioral analysis, which may be important for recognition of dangerous situations while ensuring the homeland security.

Keywords: GDL, gesture description language, semantic classifier, gestures recognition, karate, self-defense.

1 Introduction

In case of attack of foe who has more physical strength, proper self-defense training might save the life and health of potential victim. The knowledge of defense martial arts is important aspect of personal and social security. In our opinion easy and common access to cheap self-defense courses would highly increase dexterity, confidence and composure in crisis situations of large society group. This is how popularization of personal training program can affect the homeland security. Some aspects of self-defense training require physical contact with human trainer however some exercises can be practiced alone. Those are arduous repetitions of movement sequences that have to be "remembered by body" to be quickly and subconsciously performed if there is only time for rapid reaction. We believe that those exercises can be overseen by computer application which will give advices and motivation to the adept. What is more that kind of application can be run whenever user wants to train. The overseeing computer programs of that type have to recognize specialized movement sequences – gestures of the user. The problem of computer gestures recognition has long history and there are many approaches how to deal with this task. The most popular are:

- Statistical methods [1],
- Neural networks and fuzzy sets [2],
- Optimal path finding [3],
- Semantic methods and finite state machines [4], [5].

A. Cuzzocrea et al. (Eds.): CD-ARES 2013 Workshops, LNCS 8128, pp. 430–441, 2013.

Lately appearance of new relatively cheap multimedia hardware enabled to introduce full body tracking and gestures recognition technology to personal computers and gaming consoles. For example a Kinect controller captures depth data stream which is then processed [6] in order to detect three-dimensional coordinates of 20 body joints (so called skeleton data). This approach has many important advantages:

- It does not require special markers to be placed over tracked body,
- It track skeleton relatively fast (with approximate frequency of 30 Hz),
- It has been proven that it can provide input data applicable for vast range of pattern recognition methods [7], [8].
- The multimedia controller is much cheaper than motion-capture hardware.

It was only matter of time while this technology has been applied to more sophisticated gestures that those that appears in computer games. Work [8] introduces a method for real-time gesture recognition from a noisy skeleton stream, such as the ones extracted from Kinect depth sensors. Each pose is described using a tailored angular representation of the skeleton joints. Those descriptors serve to identify key poses through a multi-class classifier derived from Support Vector learning machines. The gesture is labeled on-the-fly from the key pose sequence through a decision forest that naturally performs the gesture time warping and avoids the requirement for an initial or neutral pose.

The computer – aided training and rehabilitation was a concept of many previously published papers and implemented systems. For many years the application of gestures recognition methods were limited because of specialized motion – capture hardware requirements [9]. Lately the Kinect technology was used in number of sports video game like "My Self Defence Coach", "UFC Personal Trainer" or "Nike+ Kinect Training" [10] however those applications are mainly done for entertainment and should not be treated as reliable computer coaching programs. One of the first well described approach of applying Kinect in personal training systems in presented in [7]. This work aims at automatically recognizing sequences of complex Karate movements and giving a measure of the quality of the movements performed. The proposed system is constituted by four different modules: skeleton representation, pose classification, temporal alignment, and scoring. The proposed system is tested on a set of different punch, kick and defense karate moves executed starting from the simplest case, i.e. fixed static stances up to sequences in which the starting stances is different from the ending one. The skeleton is represented by chosen 14 angles designated by vectors defined by selected skeleton joints. Each gesture is split into keyposes. The classification of key poses is done with a multi-class Support Vector Machine (SVM), which recognizes key poses with a one-versus-all approach. The temporal alignment of sequences is done with classic Dynamic Time Warping approach. The system proposed in that paper has however two very important limitations caused by hardware and applied methodology. It has to be remembered that depth data captured by the Kinect sensor can be visualized as relief – like plate. If particular part of the body is covered by one another it exact position cannot be accurately measured. If this situation happens the tracking software computes the position of "invisible joint" estimating its position basing on known position of neighboring joints. This approach however might be highly insufficient in some real-life situations. The second limitation is pattern recognition method itself. Training of SVM (and other popular classifiers) requires huge data set to obtain high effectiveness. This might be a serious obstacle which limits this methodology only for research centers that manage to gather sufficiently big training dataset. However, it should be remembered that each self-defense trainer exactly knows how the particular movements should be performed and what are the key-poses that have to be present in gestures sequence. In this paper we presents our novel method GDL (Gesture Description Language) for overcoming those hardware and methodology limitations and results of the initial tests of our approach. The GDL allows not only to analyze the several Shorin-Ryu Karate techniques but also to support the training and teaching activities of such arts. Moreover the GDL allow performing the human behavioral analysis, which may be important for recognition of dangerous treats while ensuring the homeland security.

2   Methodology

In this paragraph we will discuss our approach for calibration of multi - Kinect environment that can use standard tracking libraries for skeleton segmentation. In the second part of this paragraph the karate techniques recognition approach will be presented.

2.1   Overcoming Hardware Limitation

In order to acquire real three dimensional skeleton of observed user (not only as relief – like plate projection) more than one capture device has to be used. The most intuitive hardware configuration is presented in Figure 1 – left. Three devices are positioned around object of observation on the vertices of equilateral triangle. This configuration however requires new depth stream processing algorithm. Because of that we propose another hardware configuration (Figure 1 – right). It also uses three sensors, the center one and two additional rotated around y (vertical) axis at the angle of $\frac{\pi}{4}$ and $-\frac{\pi}{4}$ to center one relatively. With this Kinects positioning it is still possible to use standard tracking software. As we have proved in paragraph 3 of this paper filming the same scene from different angles enables to acquire more tracking information. Right parts of the body are better (more efficiently) tracked by right Kinect while left parts are more efficiently tracked by left one. That is because if for example user is performing Mae-geri kick with his right leg, in the end phase of movement the right knee is in the same vertical position as right foot and hip. It cannot be reliably tracked by center (the one that is in front of user) sensor because foot cover the position of two other body joints. In the same time those three joints are not overlapping from perspective of right sensor. The tracking software supplies us with three dimensional coordinates of body joints with information if particular joint position is obtained from direct tracking or it was estimated because that one is not visible. Knowing if joint tracked from central Kinect has exact coordinates or not we can use the coordinates from left or right additional device to make the overall skeleton position more reliable.

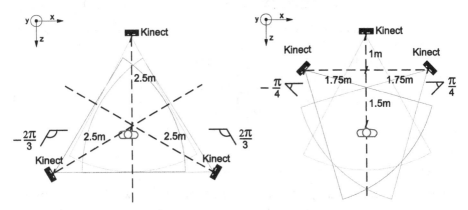

Fig. 1. Example multi Kinect setup, left – three devices are situated around the user, right – three devices are situated in front of user. Detailed description is in text.

Each Kinect measures distance to observed point in its own right-handed Cartesian frame situated relatively to sensor orientation. Because of that same point V has different coordinates $\bar{v}' = [x', y', z', 1]$ and $\bar{v} = [x, y, z, 1]$ relatively to each pair of devices. Our task now is to map all of those points to the same coordinate system. In order to do this we have to find linear transform that is represented by following matrix:

$$\bar{v}' \cdot \begin{bmatrix} a_{11} & a_{12} & a_{13} & 0 \\ a_{21} & a_{22} & a_{23} & 0 \\ a_{31} & a_{32} & a_{33} & 0 \\ t_x & t_y & t_z & 1 \end{bmatrix} = \bar{v} \qquad (1)$$

Where a_{ij} coordinates represents the rotation and t_k translation. To compute unknown values we have to know coordinates of points in both Cartesian frames. Let us assume that a Cartesian frame that represents orientation of each Kinect was translated and rotated around y (vertical) axis relatively to each other frame. That means there are four degrees of freedom (three for translation, one for rotation). Knowing that the linear transformation that maps coordinates of a point represented by vector $\bar{v}'$ in one coordinate system to coordinates $\bar{v}$ in another one has form of following matrix:

$$\bar{v'} \cdot \begin{bmatrix} \cos(\beta) & 0 & -\sin(\beta) & 0 \\ 0 & 1 & 0 & 0 \\ \sin(\beta) & 0 & \cos(\beta) & 0 \\ t_x & t_y & t_z & 1 \end{bmatrix} = \bar{v} \qquad (2)$$

In order to find unknown matrix coefficients following linear system has to be solved:

$$\begin{bmatrix} x_1' & z_1' & 1 & 0 \\ z_1' & -x_1' & 0 & 1 \\ x_2' & z_2' & 1 & 0 \\ z_2' & -x_2' & 0 & 1 \end{bmatrix} \cdot \begin{bmatrix} \cos(\beta) \\ \sin(\beta) \\ t_x \\ t_z \end{bmatrix} = \begin{bmatrix} x_1 \\ z_1 \\ x_2 \\ z_2 \end{bmatrix} \qquad (3)$$

$y' + t_y = y_1$

Where $\bar{v_1} = [x_1, y_1, z_1, 1]$, $\bar{v_2} = [x_2, y_2, z_2, 1]$ are points which coordinates are known in both frames. That matrix has to be solved both for center-left Kinects set and center-right Kinects set.

2.2   GDL Classifier in Task of Shorin-Ryu Karate Recognition

GDL is a semantic classifier that uses syntactic description of gestures to be detected. The preliminary description of GDL architecture has been presented in [11]. In those papers we discussed application of this methodology to recognition basic common life gestures (like waving or clapping). However it is also possible to apply GDL to sophisticated and complex movement sequences like those from Shorin-Ryu Karate. The schema of gestures recognition pipeline with GDL classifier is presented in Figure 2. Movement is separated into key frames. Each key frame is represented by a rule in GDL script that has a conclusion. If a rule is satisfied for actual set of body joints positions (GDL uses forward chaining reasoning schema) its conclusion is memorized. It is possible to check with GDL script if some conclusion was satisfied in given time period. With this mechanism it is possible to generate chains of key frames, which create gestures. Because of space limitation we cannot present detailed description of all possible GDL script productions. Instead of that in Appendix we will show GDL script listings of all tested Karate techniques. The GDL syntax is very intuitive so we believe that short comments in source code will be sufficient for understanding.

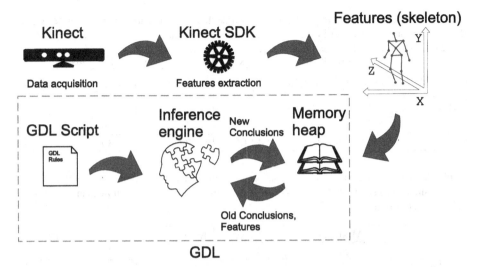

Fig. 2. The schema of gestures recognition pipeline with GDL classifier. The input data is recorded with depth sensor (for example Kinect). Then data is processed with appropriate libraries to extract features - skeleton. The skeleton is an input to GDL classifier. In GDL movement is described by set of rules consisted in GDL script file (GDL script is context – free grammar). Inference engine performs forward chaining reasoning on those rules. The conclusions of satisfied rules are stored in memory heap together with actual and previously captured skeletons and previously satisfied conclusions.

3   Results

In order to check possibilities of using GDL approach for recognition of basic combat techniques from martial arts, together with black belt instructor (3 dan) of Shorin-Ryu Karate we have created GDL script descriptions of one stationary position (Motodachi), one block (Age-uke) and one kick (Mae-geri). Than we recorded the instructor performing those techniques with system presented in Figure 2. Tables 1-2 summarize the classification results of our experiment. The description in first column is the actual technique (or group of techniques) that is present in particular recording. Each technique (or group of techniques) was repeated 50 times. Symbol + means that particular recording consisted of more than one technique. Description in first row is classification results. Last row sums up percentage of correct classifications of particular technique. Summing up, we had 150 recordings of karate techniques. In this experiment we check if it is possible to recognize the considered techniques and if multi sensor system setup increases overall recognition rate.

Table 1. The classification results of our experiment. Data was captured with single Kinect device (central one). Number in each cell is how many recordings belong to the certain class.

	Moto-dachi	Age-uke	Mae-geri	Not classified
Moto-dachi	50	0	0	0
Age-uke + Moto-dachi	49	21	0	1+29=30
Mae-geri	0	0	1	49
%	99.0%	42.0%	2.0%	39.5%

Table 2. The classification results of our experiment. Data was captured with three Kinect devices situated as shown in Figure 1 on the right. Number in each cell is how many recordings belong to the certain class.

	Moto-dachi	Age-uke	Mae-geri	Not classified
Moto-dachi	50	0	0	0
Age-uke + Moto-dachi	49	42	0	1+8=9
Mae-geri	0	0	32	18
%	99.0%	84.0%	64.0%	13.5%

Figure 3 graphically compares results presented in Table 1 and Table 2.

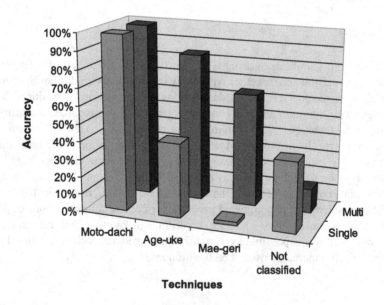

Fig. 3. Plot that graphically compares results presented in Table 1 and Table 2

4   Discussion and Conclusion

As has been shown in our experiment it is possible to overcome limitation of single capturing device by adding more devices of the same type that gather user data at different angles. What is more our approach can be used with standard tracking libraries. Our experiment has also shown that integration of tracking data acquired by several Kinect devices with standard software increases the effectiveness of GDL classifier. This is due the fact that additional sensors that are situated at different angles than central one are capable of tracking body joints that in some situations might be covered by different body parts. This condition is especially visible in case of non-static Karate techniques: Age-uke and Mae-geri. After integrating skeleton data from three sensors as it was presented in paragraph 2 the recognition rate of Age-uke was increased by 42% and Mae-geri by 62%. All recognition errors were caused by inaccurate tracking of users' body joints. We anticipate that we can minimize "not classified" error rate even more by applying device setup that was presented in Figure 1 – left. This sensor positioning will supply the system with "real" three dimensional measurements however the new tacking algorithm has to be generated. The creation of this new algorithm will be our goal for the future research.

Fig. 4. The set of photographs taken during test session of our training system. In top left and top right photo we see hardware set up. It is consisted of three PC computers connected together in local network. Each of them runs single instance of application that implements gesture recognition pipeline from Figure 2. The recordings are synchronized by synchronization server that sends timestamps to each instance by UDP protocol. In bottom left and right photo we can see system performing real-time recognition of defined Karate techniques.

We have created the prototype of our training system which was used to gather data presented in result section and to our novel methodology validation. The photographs taken during this test session are presented in Figure 4. The implementation of system is capable of real time recognition of defined rules. The GDL approach allows not only to analyze the several Shorin-Ryu Karate techniques but also to support the training and teaching activities of such arts. In present form our approach enables karate techniques recognition that indicate to user if he or she made the gesture "enough similar to the pattern" to be classified. The proposed approach has to be expanded by additional module that would give the user the supporting information how well (how similarly to pattern) he made his gesture. In paper [7] authors proposed the scoring methodology to give as output a score representative of the effectiveness and quality of the move performed independently of the move length. The final score is obtained by regression among human judgments and the normalized dynamic time warping distances obtained by each technique. The model fitted is a 5-parameters logistic. This approach can easily be adapted to our solution. In the future we will generate another scoring methodology to make scoring dependent only to similarity of performed movement to GDL script description.

Our future goal will be development of GDL script for recognition of complete set of most popular karate techniques. The completed classifier will be than utilized in self-training multimedia application. We also plan to expand the GDL script syntactic [12] to enable creation rules that describes behavior of more than one tracked user at the same time. With this simple extension GDL will allow to perform the human behavioral and human interaction analysis, which may be important for recognition of dangerous situations while ensuring the homeland security.

Acknowledgments. We kindly acknowledge the support of this study by a Pedagogical University of Krakow Statutory Research Grant.

References

1. Vinayak, S., Murugappan, H.R., Liu, K., Vinayak, Murugappan, S., Liu, H.R., Ramani, K.: Shape-It-Up: Hand gesture based creative expression of 3D shapes using intelligent generalized cylinders. Computer-Aided Design 45, 277–287 (2013)
2. Elakkiya, R., Selvamai, K., Velumadhava Rao, R., Kannan, A.: Fuzzy Hand Gesture Recognition Based Human Computer Interface Intelligent System. UACEE International Journal of Advances in Computer Networks and its Security 2(1), 29–33
3. Augsburg University (2011), Full Body Interaction Framework:
   http://hcm-lab.de/fubi.html
4. Arulkarthick, V.J., Sangeetha, D., Umamaheswari, S.: Sign Language Recognition using K-Means Clustered Haar-Like Features and a Stochastic Context Free Grammar. European Journal of Scientific Research 78(1), 74–84 (2012) ISSN 1450-216X
5. Yeasin, M., Chaudhuri, S.: Visual understanding of dynamic hand gestures. Pattern Recognition 33, 1805–1817 (2000)
6. Shotton, J., Fitzgibbon, A., Cook, M., Sharp, T., Finocchio, M., Moore, R., Kipman, A., Blake, A.: Real-time human pose recognition in parts from single depth images. In: CVPR, vol. 3 (2011)
7. Bianco, S., Tisato, F.: Karate moves recognition from skeletal motion. In: Proc. SPIE 8650, Three-Dimensional Image Processing (3DIP) and Applications 2013, 86500K (March 12, 2013), doi:10.1117/12.2006229

9. Mirabella, O., Raucea, A., Fisichella, F., Gentile, L.: A motion capture system for sport training and rehabilitation. In: 2011 4th International Conference on Human System Interactions (HSI), pp. 52–59 (2011), doi:10.1109/HSI.2011.5937342
10. List of games that utilize Kinect sensor, http://www.xbox.com/pl-PL/Kinect/Games
11. Hachaj, T., Ogiela, M.R.: Semantic Description and Recognition of Human Body Poses and Movement Sequences with Gesture Description Language. In: Kim, T.-h., Kang, J.-J., Grosky, W.I., Arslan, T., Pissinou, N. (eds.) MulGraB, BSBT and IUrC 2012. CCIS, vol. 353, pp. 1–8. Springer, Heidelberg (2012)
12. Ogiela, M.R., Piekarczyk, M.: Random graph languages for distorted and ambiguous patterns: single layer model. In: Proceedings of the Sixth International Conference on Innovative Mobile and Internet Services in Ubiquitous Computing (IMIS 2012), Palermo, Italy, July 4-6, pp. 108–113 (2012)

5   Appendix – GDL Script Bases and Examples

Skeleton is consisted of body joints. There are following possible names of body joints:

```
HipCenter, Spine, ShoulderCenter, Head, ShoulderLeft, El-
bowLeft, WristLeft, HandLeft, ShoulderRight, ElbowRight,
WristRight, HandRight, HipLeft, KneeLeft, AnkleLeft,
FootLeft, HipRight, KneeRight, AnkleRight, FootRight.
```

Each rule starts with RULE keyword, and ends with conclusion name which is preceded by THEN keyword.
Syntax:

```
HipLeft.xyz[0]
```

means that you take three dimensional coordinate of joint HipLeft from the top of memory heap (actual joint position).
Synatx:

```
HipLeft.y[0]
```

means that you take only y-coordinate (vertical). The coordinate frame is right – handed as shown in Figure 1.

```
KneeRight.a[0]
```

is an angle between vectors defined by joint KneeRight and two neighboring joints (HipRight and AnkleRight), the vertex of the angle is in joint KneeRight.

```
angle(HipLeft.xyz[0] - KneeLeft.xyz[0], HipRight.xyz[0]
- KneeRight.xyz[0])
```

is angle between two vectors defined by joints coordinates.

ABS is absolute value of real number.

DISTANCE is an Euclidean distance between vectors.

| is logical "or" operator, & is logical "and" operator.

```
sequenceexists("[MaeMiddleRight,1][MaeStart,1]")
```

is true if conclusion MaeMiddleRight has appeared in memory heap not longer than 1 second ago (this is "1" digit after comma) and MaeStart has appeared in memory heap not longer 1 second ago while MaeMiddleRight has appeared in memory heap.

The following listing is GDL script we defined together with black belt instructor (3 dan) of Shorin-Ryu Karate. Because of space limitation and intuitiveness of description we leave the detailed analysis to the reader.

```
/////////////////////
//Moto-dachi
/////////////////////
RULE angle(HipLeft.xyz[0] - KneeLeft.xyz[0],  Hi-
pRight.xyz[0] - KneeRight.xyz[0]) > 5
& angle(HipLeft.xyz[0] - KneeLeft.xyz[0],  Hi-
pRight.xyz[0] - KneeRight.xyz[0]) < 45
THEN MotoLegsA
RULE HipRight.z[0] < HipLeft.z[0] & KneeRight.z[0] <
KneeLeft.z[0]
& AnkleRight.z[0] < AnkleLeft.z[0]
THEN MotoLegsZRight //right leg is in front of body
RULE HipRight.z[0] > HipLeft.z[0] & KneeRight.z[0] >
KneeLeft.z[0]
& AnkleRight.z[0] > AnkleLeft.z[0]
THEN MotoLegsZLeft //left leg is in fornt of body
RULE ABS(AnkleRight.z[0] - AnkleLeft.z[0]) >
ABS(DISTANCE(HipRight.xyz[0], HipLeft.xyz[0]))
THEN MotoStepFront
RULE KneeRight.a[0] > 150 & KneeLeft.a[0] > 150
THEN MotoKnee
RULE   (MotoStepFront & MotoLegsA & MotoKnee)
& (MotoLegsZRight | MotoLegsZLeft) & StandStill
THEN Moto-dachi

/////////////////////
//Age-uke
/////////////////////
RULE WristRight.y[0] < WristLeft.y[0] THEN AgeUkeRStart
```

```
RULE WristRight.y[0] > WristLeft.y[0] THEN AgeUkeLStart
RULE ElbowRight.a[0] > 80 & Distance(WristRight.xyz[0],
HipRight.xyz[0]) < 200 THEN AgeUkeRightHand
RULE ElbowLeft.a[0] > 80 & Distance(WristLeft.xyz[0],
HipLeft.xyz[0]) < 200 THEN AgeUkeLeftHand
RULE ABS(WristLeft.y[0] - Head.y[0]) < 100 &
ABS(WristLeft.x[0] - Head.x[0]) < 100 & ElbowLeft.a[0] >
90 & ElbowLeft.a[0] < 150
THEN AgeUkeRightHandLeftHandBlock
RULE ABS(WristRight.y[0] - Head.y[0]) < 100 &
ABS(WristRight.x[0] - Head.x[0]) < 100 & ElbowRight.a[0]
> 90 & ElbowRight.a[0] < 150
THEN AgeUkeLeftHandRightHandBlock
RULE (AgeUkeLeftHand & AgeUkeLeftHandRightHandBlock)
THEN AgeUkeRStop
RULE (AgeUkeRightHand & AgeUkeRightHandLeftHandBlock)
THEN AgeUkeLStop
Rule (AgeUkeRStop & sequenceexists("[AgeUkeRStart,1]"))
| (AgeUkeLStop & sequenceexists("[AgeUkeLStart,1]")) &
StandStill
THEN Age-uke

///////////////////
//Mae-geri
///////////////////
RULE ABS(AnkleRight.y[0] - AnkleLeft.y[0]) < 50
THEN MaeStart
RULE (HipRight.y[0] - KneeRight.y[0]) < 100 &
ABS(KneeRight.a[0] - 90) < 30
THEN MaeMiddleRight
RULE (HipRight.y[0] - KneeRight.y[0]) < 200 & Knee-
Right.a[0] > 150
THEN MaeEndRight
RULE (HipLeft.y[0] - KneeLeft.y[0]) < 100 &
ABS(KneeLeft.a[0] - 90) < 30
THEN MaeMiddleLeft
RULE (HipLeft.y[0] - KneeLeft.y[0]) < 200 & KneeLeft.a[0]
> 150
THEN MaeEndLeft
RULE (sequenceexists("[MaeMiddleRight,1][MaeStart,1]") &
MaeEndRight)
| (sequenceexists("[MaeMiddleLeft,1][MaeStart,1]") &
MaeEndLeft)
THEN Mae-geri
```

Trustworthiness Evaluation of Multi-sensor Situation Recognition in Transit Surveillance Scenarios

Francesco Flammini[1], Stefano Marrone[2], Nicola Mazzocca[3], Alfio Pappalardo[1], Concetta Pragliola[1], Valeria Vittorini[3]

[1] Ansaldo STS, Innovation & Competitiveness Unit, Naples, Italy
{francesco.flammini,alfio.pappalardo,
concetta.pragliola}@ansaldo-sts.com
[2] Seconda Università di Napoli, Dip. Di Matematica e Fisica, Caserta, Italy
stefano.marrone@unina2.it
[3] Università "Federico II" di Napoli, Dip. di Ingegneria Elettrica e Tecnologie
dell'Informazione, Naples, Italy
{nicola.mazzocca,valeria.vittorini}@unina.it

Abstract. Physical Security Information Management (PSIM) systems are a recent introduction in the surveillance of critical infrastructures, like those used for mass-transit. In those systems, different sensors are integrated as separate event detection devices, each of them generating independent alarms. In order to lower the rate of false alarms and provide greater situation awareness for surveillance operators, we have developed a framework – namely DETECT – for correlating information coming from multiple heterogeneous sensors. DETECT uses detection models based on (extended) Event Trees in order to generate higher level warnings when a known threat scenario is being detected. In this paper we extend DETECT by adopting probabilistic models for the evaluation of threat detection trustworthiness on reference scenarios. The approach also allows for a quantitative evaluation of model sensitivity to sensor faults. The results of a case-study in the transit system domain demonstrate the increase of trust one could expect when using scenarios characterized in a probabilistic way for the threat detection instead of single-sensor alarms. Furthermore, we show how a model analysis can serve at design time to support decisions about the type and redundancy of detectors.

Keywords: Physical Security, Sensor and Data Analysis, Event Correlation, Trustworthiness, Probabilistic Modelling, Quantitative Evaluation.

1   Introduction

In modern society the assurance of a secure environment is paramount due to the increasing number of threats against critical infrastructures. The number and the diversity of sensors used in modern wide-area surveillance is continuously increasing [1]. The type of sensors includes: (1) Environmental probes measuring temperature, humidity, light, smoke, pressure and acceleration; (2) Intrusion sensors, like magnetic contacts, infrared/microwave/ultrasound motion detectors, etc.; (3) Radio-Frequency

A. Cuzzocrea et al. (Eds.): CD-ARES 2013 Workshops, LNCS 8128, pp. 442–456, 2013.

Identifiers (RFID) and position detectors, via satellite and/or electronic compasses; (4) Smart-cameras and microphones with advanced audio-video analytics capabilities; (5) Chemical Biological Radiological Nuclear explosive (CBRNe) detectors. Different types of sensing units are often integrated in smart-sensors like the so called 'motes' of Wireless Sensor Networks (WSN), featuring on-board 'intelligence' through programmable embedded devices with dedicated operating systems, processors and memory [5].

Such a wide range of sensors provides a large quantity of heterogeneous information which has to be handled properly, in terms of pre-processing, integration and reasoning, in order to effectively support PSIM operators; otherwise, there is the serious risk of overwhelming operators with unnecessary information, warnings or alarms, with the consequence of making them unable to perform their task and possibly underestimate critical situations [3][4].

In such a context, the issue of automatic situation recognition in PSIM is of paramount importance. However, not much work has been done in the research literature to develop frameworks and tools aiding surveillance operators to take advantage of recent developments in sensor technology. In other words, so far researchers seem to ignore the apparent paradox according to which the more and complex the sensors, the more and complex the tasks required for operators to manage and verify their alarms.

We have addressed the issue of automatic situation recognition by developing a framework for model-based event correlation in infrastructure surveillance. The framework – named DETECT – is able to store in its knowledge base any number of threat scenarios described in the form of Event Trees, and then recognize those scenarios in real-time, providing early warnings to PSIM users [6][7].

In this paper we adopt a model-based evaluation approach to quantitatively assess the effectiveness of DETECT in reducing the number of false alarms, thus increasing the overall trustworthiness of the surveillance system. The evaluation is dependent on sensor technologies and scenario descriptions, and it is based on stochastic modelling techniques. To achieve such an objective, some mappings are performed from Event Trees to other formalisms like Fault Trees, Bayesian Networks and Petri Nets (and their extensions). Those formalisms are widespread in dependability modelling and allow engineers to perform several useful analyses, including 'what if' and 'sensitivity', accounting for false alarms and even sensor hardware faults.

Generally speaking, the method used for the analysis, which is the main original contribution of this paper, allows to:

- Support design choices in terms of type and reliability of detectors, redundancy configurations, scenario descriptions.

- Demonstrate the effectiveness of the overall approach in practical surveillance scenarios, in terms of the increase of trustworthiness in threat detection with respect to single sensors.

In order to demonstrate the application of the methodology, a threat scenario of a terrorist attack in a metro railway station is considered.

The rest of this paper is structured as follows. Section 2 provides an overview of the related literature on DETECT and for trustworthiness evaluation of surveillance systems and it introduces the basic concepts of the event description language. Section 3 describes the process used for the analysis customizing it to the Bayesian Networks formalism in Section 4. Section 5 presents the case-study application using a metro-railway threat scenario. Finally, Section 6 provides the conclusions and hints for future improvements.

2   Background

The first concept of DETECT has been described in [6], where the overall architecture of the framework is presented, including the composite event specification language (EDL, Event Description Language), the modules for the management of detection models and the scenario repository. In [7], an overall system including a middleware for the integration of heterogeneous sensor networks is described and applied to railway surveillance case-studies. Reference [14] discusses the integration of DETECT in the PSIM system developed by AnsaldoSTS, namely RailSentry [2], presenting the reference scenario which will be also used in this paper. In order to detect redundancies while updating the scenario repository (off-line issue) and to increase the robustness of DETECT with respect to imperfect modelling and/or missed detections (on-line issue), distance metrics between Event Trees are introduced in [15].

A survey of state-of-the-art in physical security technologies and advanced surveillance paradigms, including a section on PSIM systems, is provided in [16]. Contemporary remote surveillance systems for public safety are also discussed in [17]. Technology and market-oriented considerations on PSIM can be also found in [18] and [21].

In [8] the authors address the issue of providing fault-tolerant solutions for WSN, using event specification languages and voting schemes; however, no model-based performance evaluation approach is provided. A similar issue is addressed in [9], where the discussion focuses on different levels of information/decision fusion on WSN event detection using appropriate classifiers and reaching a consensus among them in order to enhance trustworthiness. Reference [13] describes a method for evaluating the reliability of WSN using the Fault Tree modelling formalism, but the analysis is limited to hardware faults (quantified by the Mean Time Between Failures, MTBF) and homogenous devices (i.e. the WSN motes). Performance evaluation aspects of distributed heterogeneous surveillance systems are instead addressed in [11], which only lists the general issues and some pointers to the related literature. Reference [10] about the trustworthiness analysis of sensor networks in cyber-physical system is apparently one of the most related to the topics of this paper, since it focuses on the reduction of false alarms by clustering sensors according to their locations and by building appropriate object-alarm graphs; however, the approach is quite different from the one of DETECT and furthermore it applies to homogenous detectors. Another general discussion on the importance of the evaluation of performance metrics and human factors in distributed surveillance systems can be found in [12]; however, no hints are provided in that paper about how to perform such an evaluation on real systems.

Regarding the dependability modelling approach used in this paper, it is based on the results of the comparison among formalisms (i.e. Fault Trees, Bayesian Networks and Stochastic Petri Nets) in terms of modelling power and solving efficiency that has been reported in [20] and also applied in [19] to a different case-study using an approach known as 'multi-formalism'.

2.1   Event Description Language

Threat scenarios are described in DETECT using a specific Event Description Language (EDL) and stored in a Scenario Repository. In this way we are able to permanently store all scenario features in an interoperable format (i.e. XML). A high level architecture of the framework is depicted in Fig. 1.

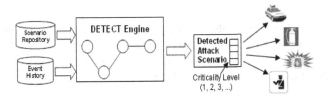

Fig. 1. The DETECT framework

A threat scenario expressed by EDL consists of a set of basic events detected by the sensing devices. An event is a happening that occurs at some locations and at some points in time. In this context, events are related to sensor data (i.e. temperature higher than a threshold). Events are classified as *primitive events* and *composite events*. A primitive event is a condition on a specific sensor which is associated with some parameters (i.e. event identifier, time of occurrence, etc...). A composite event is a combination of primitive events by means of proper operators. Each event is denoted by an *event expression*, whose complexity grows with the number of involved events. Given the expressions $E_1, E_2, ..., E_n$, every applicaann on them through any operator is still an expression. Event expressions are represented by *Event Trees*, where primitive events are at the leaves and internal nodes represent EDL operators.

DETECT is able to support the composition of complex events in EDL through a *Scenario GUI* (Graphical User Interface), used to draw threat scenarios by means of a user-friendly interface. Furthermore, in the operational phase, a model manager macro-module has the responsibility of performing queries on the Event History database for the real-time feeding of detection models corresponding to threat scenarios, according to predetermined policies. Those policies, namely *parameter contexts*, are used to set a specific consumption mode of the occurrences of the events collected in the database. The EDL is based on the Snoop event algebra [24], considering the following operators: OR, AND, ANY, SEQ. For sake of space and due to their simplicity, the operators are not presented and further details are present in the literature.

3   Trustworthiness Modelling Process

The advantage of the modelling and analysis activity is twofold. On one hand it can be used during the design phase since it allows to quantitatively evaluate different design options for sensing and decision mechanisms allowing cost/effective trade-offs in protection systems design. In fact, the sensing strategies can differ in the number of sensors, in their reliability and/or in their efficiency in event detection; decision options are related to the logics that can be applied for correlating primitive events. On the other hand, the model can be used at run-time due to the possibility of tuning the models using data collected during the operational phase (i.e. event history log files merged with operator feedback about false negative/positive), allowing incremental refinement of detection models.

Fig. 2 shows how the aforementioned objectives can be achieved in an integrated process, in which both the monitored and monitoring systems are represented using probabilistic modelling formalisms. Quantitative model evaluation enables two possibilities:

- When used at design-time, the analyses can be used to compute the probability of having an alarm and its confusion matrix (i.e. the false positive and false negative probabilities). Such information can be used in order to improve the system by using more accurate or redundant sensors.

- When used at run-time, the detected events can be used as the evidence in the models. In such a way, the probability that the configuration of the primitive events is actually representative of the composite event (i.e. the threat scenario) can be dynamically adapted. Consequently, alarms can be generated only when the confidence in the detection is greater than a certain threshold.

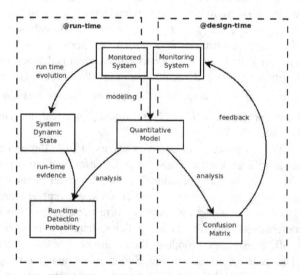
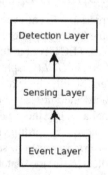

Fig. 2. The modelling and analysis process

Fig. 3. Surveillance model layers

Focusing on the design-time analysis, it is essential to develop an appropriate modelling methodology. In the context of surveillance systems trustworthiness evaluation, models of interest can be structured in three layers as depicted in

Fig. 3. These layers are:

- *Event layer*: this layer is devoted to modelling the actual cause-consequence relations in real environments. It determines how complex situations can be broken down into basic events (e.g. sneaking into a room by the window implies the breaking of the glass). It is usually the output of physical security surveys and risk assessment. In its most trivial form, it is constituted by the sequence of basic events associated to a threat scenario.

- *Sensing layer*: this layer models the sensors as objects with their characteristics (e.g. event detection capabilities, hardware reliability, detection performance) and the basic sensing actions with respect to the events identified in the lower layer.

- *Decision layer*: this layer addresses the (probabilistic) combination of simple events by means of EDL operators. It is important to note that this layer is built on top of the Sensing layer instead of the Event layer, since it does not deal with events actually occurring in the reality but with the ones generated by the sensing system, which can be different according to sensor types, deployment granularity, and detection performance.

In the following of this paper we mainly concentrate on the upper layer; however, the outputs of detection model evaluation can be used as inputs to refine threat modelling and better define sensor design parameters in order to meet the requirements of specific applications.

4   Application of the Modelling Process

In this Section we instantiate the process schema shown in Fig. 2 using the Bayesian Networks (BN) reference formalism, which features several advantages when employed in situation recognition. Fault Tree (FT) and Petri Net (PN) based processes can be equally derived from the general process schema. A complete comparison of these formalisms against their modelling power and efficiency is reported in [21]. In brief, FTs are very easy to build and analyse, but they have a limited modelling power. On the other hand, PNs feature a great expressive power but they are limited by the well-known state space explosion problem. BNs represent a good trade-off between those two extremes.

The operators used to build the Event Trees according to the event correlation approach implemented by DETECT have been briefly described in Section 2.2. Bayesian Networks fit the need to extend decision mechanisms adding the capability to handle probabilistic aspects. In fact features such as sensor hardware reliability and detection performance (i.e. false positive and false negative probabilities) rather than uncertainty in event modelling can be dealt with by appropriate BN subnets.

The process presented in Section 3 can be customized in the case of the BN formalism considering the specific types of analysis that can be conducted on a BN model [23]. Let: A be the set of alarms associated with threat scenarios; E be the set of events that can occur in the real environment; S be the set of states of the sensors. If we suppose $a \in A$, $e \in E$, $s \in S$, these three different indexes can be computed by solving the BN model:

- *Prior probability*, $P(a)$, that is the likelihood of occurrence of an alarm before any evidence relevant to the alarm has been observed. This index is the probability that an alarm is raised and it may be used at the design time of a PSIM system to predict the expected alarm rate, provided that the rate of primitive events is known a-priori.

- *Posterior probability*, $P(a \mid e, s)$, that is the conditional probability that an alarm is raised after some evidence is given. This index represents the probability of having an alarm in specific conditions, e.g. when some events happen (e.g. intrusion) and some others are generated by the surveillance system (e.g. sensor failure). It is useful at both design and run times. When used at design time it can be used to evaluate the performance of the detection system (i.e. the confusion matrix[1]). In addition, the Posterior probability may be used to perform a 'what-if' analysis in order to evaluate the performance degradation in case of sensor failures. When used at run-time, a posterior analysis on the model fed with real evidence of events and/or sensor failures may provide a surveillance operator with alerts if probabilities are higher than a certain threshold.

- *Likelihood*, $P(e \mid a, s)$, that is the probability of observing an element of E (real threat scenario) given evidence in A and S. In practice, it can be used to determine the probability that the alarm is trustworthy given that it has been generated. This kind of analysis is useful at run-time since it can support the decision making of the operators.

The layered model presented in Section 3 is substituted by a Bayesian Network where the BN nodes modelling the elements of the Event Layer are at the bottom, the ones representing the Sensing Layer are in the middle, the ones translating EDL operators at the Detection Layer are on the top. Specifically, we focus on the definition of a BN pattern that models the Sensing Layer and on the translation of EDL operators into BN elements. The BN pattern depicted in Fig. 4 shows how sensing can be modelled by means of three variables:

- **ev:** binary independent variable that models the occurrence of primitive events. The possible values of the variable are *{true, false}*;

- **sens:** binary independent variable representing sensor operation that can be *{ok, down}*;

---

[1] In this case of event detection, the confusion matrix accounts for binary events which can be *true* (i.e. occurred) or *false*. In DETECT, the false positive probability is given by $P(a =$ true $\mid e =$ false$)$ while the false negative probability is $P(a =$ false$\mid e =$ true$)$.

- **det**: binary variable modelling event detection by the sensor. This is a *{true, false, unknown}* dependent variable whose Conditional Probability Table (CPT) is reported in Tab. 1. The CPT is built considering the two probabilities: false-positive (*sfp*) and false-negative (*sfn*).

All the elements on the left side of Tab. 1 are translated into BN variables. The diverse operators are differentiated by CPTs.

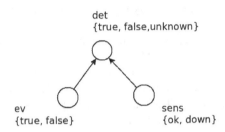

Fig. 4. BN pattern for the Sensing Layer

Please note that, as combinatorial formalisms, Fault Trees and Bayesian Networks cannot precisely model the SEQ operator since they do not allow taking into account state and time dependant properties. In order to overcome such a limitation, more powerful formalisms are needed, like Dynamic Bayesian Networks or Petri Nets. However, it is possible to approximate a SEQ operator by an AND. In fact, since the SEQ requires the occurrence of events in a certain order, the set of cases in which e.g. *SEQ (E1, E2)* is true is a subset of the set in which *AND (E1, E2)* is true. Thus, by substituting the SEQ with AND in the trustworthiness model, we are overestimating the false positive rate for the specific scenario.

Table 1. CPT of the Sensing Layer pattern

		det		
c	**sens**	true	false	unknown
false	down	0	0	1
false	ok	sfp	1-sfp	0
true	down	0	0	1
true	ok	1-sfn	sfn	0

5   Modelling Trustworthiness in a Specific Scenario

The effectiveness of the modelling approach, described in the previous section, is demonstrated using a case-study in the mass transit domain, whose assets are vulnerable to several threats, including terrorist attacks. Therefore, surveillance systems for mass transit feature a growing number of heterogeneous sensing devices. In such a context, the quantitative evaluation of model trustworthiness and sensitivity to sensor faults is very important to design robust surveillance systems and to reduce the number of unnecessary alerts. In particular, at design time the results of model analysis provide valuable information to assess the level of redundancy and diversity required for the sensors, in order to find the appropriate configuration to comply with performance targets, perhaps given by the requirements specification of the end-user. Feedbacks from model evaluation can suggest changes about sensor dislocation and technologies. An estimation of detection model trustworthiness is essential also in real-time, whether using statically or dynamically updated data, in order to define confidence thresholds for triggering high level warnings and even automatic response actions.

Let us consider a threat scenario similar to the chemical attack with Sarin agent occurred in the Tokyo subway on March 20, 1995, which caused 12 fatalities and 5500 injured [22]. The available technologies to early detect and assess the threat include intelligent cameras, audio sensors and specific standoff CWA (Chemical Warfare Agents) detectors, which feature a limited alarm trustworthiness. By means of the DETECT framework, the events detected by these sensors could be correlated as well as reported in the threat scenario representation in the reference [14]. The main CWA detection technologies include Ion Mobility Spectroscopy (IMS), Surface Acoustic Wave (SAW), Infrared Radiation (IR), etc. They are employed in ad-hoc standoff detectors, characterized by different performances. One of the most accurate devices, the automatic passive IR sensor, can recognize a vapor cloud from several kilometres with a 87% detection rate. Obviously, it is possible to combine heterogeneous detectors (e.g. IMS/SAW and IR) and to correlate their alarms according to different criteria (e.g. logic, temporal, and spatial), in order to increase the CWA detection reliability. The same considerations apply to the alarms detected by the other sensing devices.

The threat scenario consists of a simultaneous drop of CWA in subway platforms. Let us assume the following likely set of events:

1. attackers stay on the platforms, ready to drop the CWA;

2. contaminated persons fall down on the floor;

3. people around the contaminated area run away and/or scream;

4. CWA spreads in the platform level and possibly reaches higher levels.

In each subway site, it is possible to use two smart-cameras positioned at platform end walls, a microphone in the middle and two CWA standoff detectors positioned on the platform and on the escalators. The scenario can be formally described by means of the notation "sensor description (sensor ID) :: event description (event ID)":

- *Intelligent Camera (S1) :: Fall of person (E1)*

- *Intelligent Camera (S1) :: Abnormal running (E2)*

- *Intelligent Camera (S2) :: Fall of person (E1)*

- *Intelligent Camera (S2) :: Abnormal running (E2)*

- *Audio sensor (S3) :: Scream (E3)*

- *IMS/SAW detector (S4) :: CWA detection (E4)*

- *IR detector (S5) :: CWA detection (E4)*

The Event Tree model of the CWA threat scenario is depicted in Fig. 5.

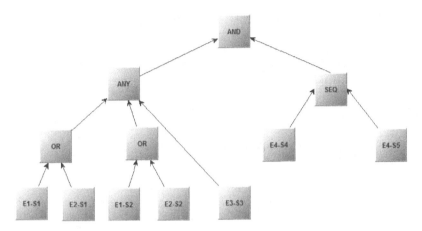

Fig. 5. Event tree associated to the CWA threat scenario

The OR operators correlate the events "person falling" and "person running", detectable by the two redundant intelligent cameras monitoring the platform. The other child node (E3-S3) of the ANY operator represents the event "person screaming", detectable by the intelligent microphone. When 2 out of these 3 events are detected in a certain (limited) time frame, the situation can reasonably be considered abnormal, so that a warning to the operator can be issued. The SEQ operator represents the upward CWA spread, detectable by the two redundant CWA sensors, installed at different levels. Finally the AND operator at the top of the tree represents the composite event associated with the whole CWA threat scenario.

As described in the previous section, each occurrence of an event can be *true* with a probability *p*, or *false* with a probability 1-*p*. Each sensor can be available, i.e. *ok*, with a probability *q*, or unavailable, i.e. *down*, with a probability *1-q*. Finally, each single event detected by a sensor can be *true, false,* or *unknown* according to the occurrence of the event condition and to the availability of the sensor at that time. Moreover, each sensor, for each detectable event, is characterized by the values: *sfn* and *sfp*, which are the sensor false positive and false negative probabilities. The BN model of the event tree is built and analysed according to the modelling schema and methodology described in the previous sections and it is represented in Fig. 6.

The Event Layer is constituted by a node *E* that represents the actual CWA attack, while *E1, E2, E3* and *E4* are the primitive events that can be detected by the sensors. The interface between Event Layer and Sensor Layer is the set of *E1, E2, E3* and *E4* nodes. In the Sensor Layer, there are five nodes (*S1, S2, S3, S4* and *S5*) representing sensors and seven nodes (*E1-S1, E2-S1, E1-S2, E2-S2, E3-S3, E4-S4* and *E4-S5*) representing the sensed events. These seven event nodes constitute the interface between the Sensing Layer and the Detection Layers. Such an interface is built according to the mapping between EDL operators and BNs. As already stated, the SEQ operator has been substituted by the AND operator, introducing a modelling error.

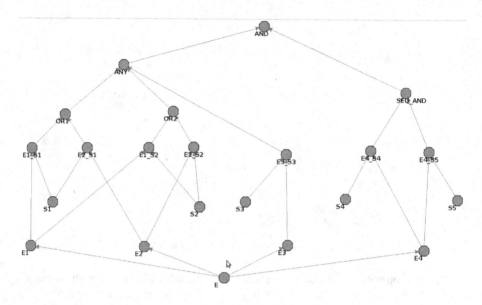

Fig. 6. BN model of the CWA threat scenario

The model has been evaluated on the basis of the parameters summarized in Tab. 2, where (non conditional) probabilities refer to a standard time frame of 1 hour. The parameters have been valued considering realistic pseudo-data, since exact values depend on risk assessment results, specific sensor technology as well as operational reports in the real environment.

For the sake of brevity, we report only the posterior probability analysis that has been performed in order to evaluate the confusion matrix (see Tab. 3). The left column represents the evidence, that can be *true* (CWA threat is actually happening) or *false*. The other columns represent the probability of CWA threat alarm is generated ('Alarm on', which can be a true positive, *tp*, or false positive, *fp*, depending whether the evidence is true or false, respectively) or not ('Alarm off', which can be a *tn* or a *fn*, depending whether the evidence is false or true, respectively), or being inactive due to the unavailability of essential sensors. The results show that the rate of alarms, and in particular the *fp* and *fn* probabilities, is largely acceptable, according to recent ergonomics studies [4]. Furthermore, the value of *fp* is much less than false positives generated by single sensors. The evaluation of those parameters is essential to ensure system effectiveness and usability in real environments.

Table 2. BN model parameters

Name	Description	Node	Value
attackProb	Probability of having a CWA attack	E	10^{-6}
running	Probability of a running man in normal conditions (not related to an attack)	E1	$4*10^{-1}$
falling	Probability of a falling man in normal conditions (not related to an attack)	E2	10^{-3}
screaming	Probability of a scream in normal conditions (not related to an attack)	E3	$5*10^{-3}$
U_1	Unavailability of sensor 1	S1	$2*10^{-4}$
U_2	Unavailability of sensor 2	S2	$2*10^{-4}$
U_3	Unavailability of sensor 3	S3	10^{-4}
U_4	Unavailability of sensor 4	S4	$2*10^{-5}$
U_5	Unavailability of sensor 5	S5	10^{-5}
Sfp_{11} Sfp_{12}	Sensor false positive probability of sensor 1 (resp. 2) when sensing event 1	E1-S1	$3*10^{-2}$
Sfn_{11} Sfn_{12}	Sensor false negative probability of sensor 2 (resp. 2) when sensing event 1	E1-S2	$2*10^{-2}$
Sfp_{21} Sfp_{22}	Sensor false positive probability of sensor 1 (resp. 2) when sensing event 2	E2-S1	$2*10^{-2}$
Sfn_{21} Sfn_{22}	Sensor false negative probability of sensor 2 (resp. 2) when sensing event 2	E2-S2	$3*10^{-2}$
Sfp_{33}	Sensor false positive probability of sensor 3 when sensing event 3	E3-S3	$2*10^{-2}$
Sfn_{33}	Sensor false negative probability of sensor 3 when sensing event 3		$1.2*10^{-2}$
Sfp_{44}	Sensor false positive probability of sensor 4 when sensing event 4	E4-S4	$0.8*10^{-2}$
Sfn_{44}	Sensor false negative probability of sensor 4 when sensing event 4		$0.2*10^{-2}$
Sfp_{55}	Sensor false positive probability of sensor 5 when sensing event 5	E5-S5	$0.7*10^{-2}$
Sfn_{55}	Sensor false negative probability of sensor 5 when sensing event 5		$0.3*10^{-2}$

Table 3. Confusion matrix of the CWA threat scenario

Evidence	Alarm on	Alarm off
True	0.995 (*tp*)	$0.22*10^{-4}$ (*fn*)
False	$0.5*10^{-2}$ (*fp*)	0.999978 (*tn*)

6   Conclusions and Future Work

Trustworthiness evaluation of models employed in situation assessment has a great practical importance in several applications of critical infrastructure surveillance. In those domains, quantitative evaluation is essential since the output of detection models is used to support decisions of the operators. Trustworthiness models allow to evaluate the robustness of PSIM systems also with respect to human errors and/or sensor faults, and to demonstrate compliance to performance and ergonomic requirements. In this paper, we have provided a structured trustworthiness modelling approach especially suited to surveillance systems featuring situation recognition capabilities based on Event Trees, which is the threat specification formalism used in the DETECT framework.

The effectiveness of the approach described in this paper is twofold. At design time, the results of the analysis provide a guide to support the choice and dislocation of sensors with respect to specific threats. At run-time, trustworthiness indices can be associated with detection models and hence to alarms reported to the operators, taking into account sensor performance and dependability parameters. Furthermore, at run-time:

- Sensor status (e.g. events detected, hardware failures, etc.) can be used to update trustworthiness indices in real-time

- The feedback of the operators over a significant time period can be used to fine-tune trustworthiness parameters (e.g. the *fp* probability can be estimated by counting the average number of false alerts generated by single sensors or even by DETECT, and by normalizing that number according to the reference time frame).

We have shown that among the probabilistic modelling formalisms, BNs are the most suited to this kind of application, allowing a very good trade-off between ease of modelling and expressive power.

The results achieved by model evaluation demonstrate the effectiveness of the DETECT event correlation approach to reduce the number of unnecessary alerts, warning and alarms, thus improving PSIM ergonomics and usability. Model evaluation also allows to perform 'what-if' predictions and sensitivity analyses with respect to changes in detection model structure and parameters, enabling and supporting design optimisation at several levels.

Future developments will address the following: evaluation results are going to be extended using further models and simulation campaigns; data coming from on-the-field experimentations and long term observations is going to be integrated with the models and used to validate them. The aforementioned automatic update of trustworthiness parameters is being implemented in DETECT using appropriate modules and exploiting the integration of DETECT in the PSIM system developed by AnsaldoSTS.

References

1. Garcia, M.L.: The Design and Evaluation of Physical Protection Systems. Butterworth-Heinemann (2001)
2. Bocchetti, G., Flammini, F., Pragliola, C., Pappalardo, A.: Dependable integrated surveillance systems for the physical security of metro railways. In: IEEE Procs. of the Third ACM/IEEE International Conference on Distributed Smart Cameras (ICDSC 2009), pp. 1–7 (2009)
3. Zhu, Z., Huang, T.S.: Multimodal Surveillance: Sensors, Algorithms and Systems. Artech House Publisher (2007)
4. Wickens, C., Dixon, S.: The benefits of imperfect diagnostic automation: a synthesis of the literature. Theoretical Issues in Ergonomics Science 8(3), 201–212 (2007)
5. Flammini, F., Gaglione, A., Mazzocca, N., Moscato, V., Pragliola, C.: Wireless Sensor Data Fusion for Critical Infrastructure Security. In: Corchado, E., Zunino, R., Gastaldo, P., Herrero, Á. (eds.) CISIS 2008. AISC, vol. 53, pp. 92–99. Springer, Heidelberg (2009)
6. Flammini, F., Gaglione, A., Mazzocca, N., Pragliola, C.: DETECT: a novel framework for the detection of attacks to critical infrastructures. In: Martorell, et al. (eds.) Safety, Reliability and Risk Analysis: Theory, Methods and Applications, Procs of ESREL 2008, pp. 105–112 (2008)
7. Flammini, F., Gaglione, A., Mazzocca, N., Moscato, V., Pragliola, C.: On-line integration and reasoning of multi-sensor data to enhance infrastructure surveillance. Journal of Information Assurance and Security (JIAS) 4(2), 183–191 (2009)
8. Ortmann, S., Langendoerfer, P.: Enhancing reliability of sensor networks by fine tuning their event observation behavior. In: Proc. 2008 International Symposium on a World of Wireless, Mobile and Multimedia Networks (WOWMOM 2008), pp. 1–6. IEEE Computer Society, Washington, DC (2008)
9. Bahrepour, M., Meratnia, N., Havinga, P.J.M.: Sensor Fusion-based Event Detection in Wireless Sensor Networks. In: 6th Annual International Conference on Mobile and Ubiquitous Systems: Networking and Services, MobiQuitous 2009, Toronto, Canada, July 13-16 (2009)
10. Tang, L.-A., Yu, X., Kim, S., Han, J., Hung, C.-C., Peng, W.-C.: Tru-Alarm: Trustworthiness Analysis of Sensor Networks in Cyber-Physical Systems. In: Proceedings of the 2010 IEEE International Conference on Data Mining (ICDM 2010). IEEE Computer Society, Washington, DC (2010)
11. Legg, J.A.: Distributed Multisensor Fusion System Specification and Evaluation Issues. Defence Science and Technology Organisation, Edinburgh, South Australia 5111, Australia (October 2005)
12. Karimaa, A.: Efficient Video Surveillance: Performance Evaluation in Distributed Video Surveillance Systems. In: Lin, W. (ed.) Video Surveillance. InTech (2011) ISBN: 978-953-307-436-8
13. Silva, I., Guedes, L.A., Portugal, P., Vasques, F.: Reliability and Availability Evaluation of Wireless Sensor Networks for Industrial Applications. Sensors 12(1), 806–838 (2012)
14. Flammini, F., Mazzocca, N., Pappalardo, A., Pragliola, C., Vittorini, V.: Augmenting surveillance system capabilities by exploiting event correlation and distributed attack detection. In: Tjoa, A.M., Quirchmayr, G., You, I., Xu, L. (eds.) ARES 2011. LNCS, vol. 6908, pp. 191–204. Springer, Heidelberg (2011)
15. Flammini, F., Pappalardo, A., Pragliola, C., Vittorini, V.: A robust approach for on-line and off-line threat detection based on event tree similarity analysis. In: Proc. Workshop on Multimedia Systems for Surveillance (MMSS) in Conjunction with 8th IEEE International Conference on Advanced Video and Signal-Based Surveillance, Klagenfurt, Austria, August 29-30, pp. 414–419 (2011)

16. Flammini, F., Pappalardo, A., Vittorini, V.: Challenges and emerging paradigms for augmented surveillance. In: Effective Surveillance for Homeland Security: Combining Technology and Social Issues. Taylor & Francis/CRC Press (to appear, 2013)

17. Räty, T.D.: Survey on contemporary remote surveillance systems for public safety. IEEE Trans. Sys. Man Cyber. Part C 5(40), 493–515 (2010)

18. Hunt, S.: Physical security information management (PSIM): The basics,
    http://www.csoonline.com/article/622321/
    physical-security-information-management-psim-the-basics

19. Flammini, F., Marrone, S., Mazzocca, N., Vittorini, V.: A new modelling approach to the safety evaluation of N-modular redundant computer systems in presence of imperfect maintenance. Reliability Engineering & System Safety 94(9), 1422–1432 (2009)

20. Bobbio, A., Ciancamerla, E., Franceschinis, G., Gaeta, R., Minichino, M., Portinale, L.: Sequential application of heterogeneous models for the safety analysis of a control system: a case study. Reliability Engineering & System Safety Journal, RESS 81(3), 269–280 (2003)

21. Frost & Sullivan: Analysis of the Worldwide Physical Security Information Management Market (November 2010), http://www.cnlsoftware.com/media/reports/
    Analysis_Worldwide_Physical_Security_Information_Management_
    Market.pdf

22. National Consortium for the Study of Terrorism and Responses to Terrorism (START), Global Terrorism Database [199503200014] (2012),
    http://www.start.umd.edu/gtd (retrieved)

23. Charniak, E.: Bayesian Networks without Tears. AI Magazine (1991)

24. Chakravarthy, S., Mishra, D.: Snoop, An expressive event specification language for active databases. Data Knowl. Eng., 14(1), 1–26 (1994)

25. Codetta-Raiteri, D.: The Conversion of Dynamic Fault Trees to Stochastic Petri Nets, as a case of Graph Transformation. Electronic Notes in Theoretical Computer Science 127(2), 45–60 (2005)

A New Approach to Develop a Dependable Security Case by Combining Real Life Security Experiences (Lessons Learned) with D-Case Development Process

Vaise Patu and Shuichiro Yamamoto

Nagoya University, Furo-cho Chikusa-ku, Nagoya City 〒464-8601, Japan
{dr.vpatu,yamamotosui}@icts.nagoya-u.ac.jp

Abstract. Modern information and distributed systems runs for extensive periods of time and are being constantly improved in service objectives under evolving technologies and changing regulations and standards. These systems have become extremely complex and therefore, it is very important that they are to be dependable in order for them to execute their functionalities and purposes correctly or to an acceptable level of services. However, due to the ever-growing complexity of information and distributed systems, it is very difficult to achieve dependability by relying only on conventional technologies such as development processes and formal methods. And therefore the idea of Assurance Case or D-Case (dependability case) has become more and more a popular notion. Recently, D-Case which is an extension form of Assurance Case, is more commonly associated with the safely aspect of dependability. And because of this regard, safety cases are more well known in comparison to other aspects of dependability such as availability, integrity and confidentiality witch are all related to the security domain. In this paper, we introduce our new approach to the development of a dependable security case.

1 Introduction

It is very difficult to define what exactly a secure system means, because the concerns in the security domain are too diverse. For example, some secure systems are more concerned with unauthorized access to information, while some are more concerned with denial-of-service attacks and so on. In this paper, we discussed how we developed a dependable security case for our e-learning distributed system by utilizing the knowledge we gained from previous occurred attacks as a mechanism to build solutions that counters any more future attacks of the same kind. As we all know, it is common for network systems to contain security vulnerabilities that allow unauthorized personnel to compromise the systems, steal intellectual property, or disclosure sensitive data. To combat these vulnerabilities, a proactive approach to building secure network systems and strong evident based security case is necessary.

A. Cuzzocrea et al. (Eds.): CD-ARES 2013 Workshops, LNCS 8128, pp. 457–464, 2013.

There are many well-written documents on how to write safety cases and reliability cases but very few on security cases. The reason for this is not the concern of this paper but to propose our method on how we developed our security case by complying with previous systems risks and attacks and the lessons we learned from it.

2   Our New Approach to the Development of a Dependable Security Case

How we decide on the aspect of the system to be assured using an assurance case, is directly derives from the system under review risk analysis results and its set of requirements. However in our approach, we also added in our experience (lessons learned) gained from the attacks our system faced in the past as shown in figure 1. Since we are building a security case, it was close to impossible for us to predict the vulnerabilities and the security risks that reside in our system architecture when our distributed e-learning system starts its operation. But as we continued our operation for almost 6 years now, we gradually improved our system performance and security by building counter measures to any severe exploitation we faced in the past. As an example in Table 1, we have listed down some of the most common security vulnerabilities that are most popularly delt with in the domain of security especially when dealing with information and network systems. From the this known list of security vulnerabilities / claims, we build from it a coreponding list of solutions or evidence that comes in handy when we go through the process of creating of our security case.

Fig. 1. To achieve the goal of system dependability, we proposed the addition of a 3rd requirement, which are the reports of previous encountered system risks and attacks

The solution column is a result of our discussion, on how we should change our system configurations in order to minimize the effects of these attacks if we encountered if we encounter them in the future. We developed our 4-step process to register new attacks once we discover them.

    A)   Identifying the type of attack
    B)   Describe the nature of the attack
    C)   Build a counter strategy for the attack via discussions
    D)   Store the completed report to our system repository for future reference

Table 1. Our completed table of the known list of the most common security vulnerabilities traced back to the risk initiated network component and the solutions we have to limit the risk causal factors

Network Component at Risk	Security Vulnerabilities (- Claims)	Proposed Solution / Evidence
Boarder Router	Inadequate router access control: Misconfigured router ACLs can allow information leakage through ICMP, IP, NetBIOS and lead to unauthorized access to services on your DMZ servers.	All Router ACLs configurations should be checked and monitored constantly for accuracy
Remote Access Server	Unmonitored remote access points provide one of the easiest means of access to your corporate network. Telecommuters often connect to the Internet with little protection, exposing sensitive files to attack.	(i) Limit the number of Remote Access Servers within the system. (ii) All Remote Access Servers should be under monitoring continuously
Firewall	Misconfigured firewall ACLs can allow access to internal systems directly or once a DMZ server is compromised.	(i) Firewall ACLs configurations should be checked and monitored constantly for accuracy. (ii) Backup the completed configurations into a secure separate location.
Internet / DMZ Server	Information leakage can provide the attacker with operating system and application versions, users, groups, shares, DNS information via zone transfers and running services like SNMP, finger, SMTP, telnet, rusers, rpcinfo, NetBIOS.	\<Undeveloped\>
	Hosts running unnecessary services such as RPC, FTP, DNS, SMTP are easily compromised.	Limit the using of services such as RPD, FTP, DNS and SMTP
	Misconfigured Internet servers, especially CGI and ASP scripts on web servers, anonymous FTP with world-writable directories and XSS vulnerabilities	(i) All CGI and ASP scripts should be double checked by a second party for accuracy before the system is deployed (ii) Forbid the use of FTP with anonymous accounts and passwords on the system
	Inadequate logging, monitoring and detection capabilities at the network and host level	Boost continuous monitoring of the full system log-files in a daily or weekly bases to up the security threats early detection capability of the system
Branch Office	Excessive trust relationships such as Windows Domain Trusts, UNIX rhosts, and SSH files can provide attackers with unauthorized access to sensitive systems	\<Undeveloped\>
Workstation	Weak, easy to guess passwords at the workstation level can compromise your company's server	\<Undeveloped\>
	Unauthenticated services like X Windows allow users to capture remote keystrokes or workstation keystrokes after software is installed	\<Undeveloped\>
Internal LAN Server	Excessive file and directory access controls (Windows shares and UNIX NFS exports)	\<Undeveloped\>
	Software that is unpatched, outdated or left in default configurations, especially web servers are vulnerable to attacks	\<Undeveloped\>

3   Building of the Security D-Case

Our new approach of creating a dependable security case was first introduced and tested as an experiment to provide assurance to the security aspect of our distributed e-learning system. However, more experiment and tests (trail and error) is still needed in order to take much of the work into the next stage. The good news is, security is no stranger to network and information systems. These systems have been associated with security for as long as networking and information systems existed. What is really new here is the urge to associate network systems with assurance case to give some kind of confidence to the system stakeholders that the system they are getting will behave as predicted and function well at a certain level when it faced by security risks and attacks in the future.

3.1   Phase 1 of the Development Process - Set a Top Goal

Depending on the aspect of dependability we are writing the assurance case for, we could easily identify the most upper goal or the top goal for your D-Case diagram. In our example, since we are building a security case, therefore our top goal also known as the main claim should be: "System is reasonably secure".

In support of the top goal or top claim, we need some input documents into the context nodes. These documents provide the environment information about the system. This includes any sort of attachment that helps to make the main argument truthful or convincing. For example, documents like the system requirements, which tells of what kind of security requirements that the system has in order to secure the system from unwanted attacks, or any kinds of security design architecture diagram if any, and so forth. Figure 2 is to provide a visualized view of what this paragraph is trying explain. Figure 1 shows only the top most part of our security case diagram.

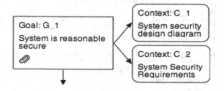

Fig. 2. The top part of the security case tree diagram

3.2   Phase 2 of the Development Process - Set an Argument Strategy to Decompose the Main Goal to Sub-goals

After the top goal is set with all the necessary contexts. What follows is the decomposition step or stage of the main argument or the 'main goal' into two or more sub-goals. However, prior to the decomposition stage, where the 'sub-goal nodes' comes into the picture, the node called 'strategy' is inserted between the main goal and the sub-goals. The strategy node should explain or give a sense of justification or reasoning to why the security case builders decided to decompose the main goal into such and such number of sub-goals. In figure 3, the strategy links us to some of the identified security vulnerabilities displayed in table 1. In this example, we took 6 identified security vulnerabilities as sub-goals. And the strategy is to argue over each of the 6 identified security vulnerabilities.

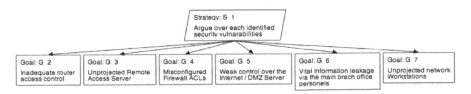

Fig. 3. This figure shows the decomposition process from the top goal into sub-goals with the strategy node in between

No matter what the assurance case is, whether it is a safety case, reliability case or a security case, they all follow a kind of pattern. For example, security case patterns are claims-argument-evidence structures that can be reused in many different security cases. The security case method offers the opportunity for security and domain experts to organize security knowledge and mitigation strategies in the form of security case patterns. Such patterns can then be shared among the security community and other stakeholder communities and continually built upon, refined, and improved. A growing repository of security case patterns is a huge possibility for a variety of domains and operational contexts that not only would provide greater opportunities for reuse and standardization of assurance arguments, but also could allow the security community to associate an historical record of security performance and return on investment with particular security case patterns.

In the last measure to our security case, we would see that some of the sub-goals got themselves a straight forward evident or solution that satisfy the final objective in supporting of the main goal, while in some sub-goals, they have to be expanded more widely in order to get to the heart of where the evident truly exist. Figure 4 shows how sub-goals one, two and three are decomposed until the evident that satisfy all the objectives of the security case main goal.

And finally as shown in Figure 5, we decomposed sub-goal 4 into four more sub-goals of sub-goal 4.1, sub-goal 4.2, sub-goal 4.3 and sub-goal 4.4. Note that for sub-goal 4.1, we added one property of GSN called undeveloped which is truly meant that this sub-goal 4.1 is not yet completed within the security case. Many factors could contribute to be the reason why a sub-goal is labeled undeveloped. For example, one of the factors could be that the evident or evidence provided to satisfy the objective of sub-goal 4.1 is not well defined by both the networking engineers and the security case builders.

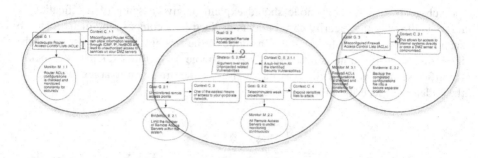

Fig. 4. This part of the Security Case shows how sub-goals 1,2 and 3 are being decomposed right down to the evident nodes

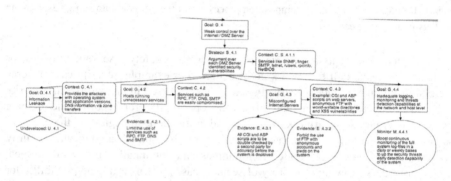

Fig. 5. This figure shows how sub-goal 4 is decomposed into 4 more sub-goals of 4.1, 4.2, 4.3 and 4.4

4   Evaluations and Conclusion

The nature of network system attacks are consequently unpredictable. Therefore relying solely on risk assessment and analysis results may not be sufficient enough to argue the security case of your system to its stakeholders. We definitely need to collect previous attacks reports (lessons learned) from systems with similar functions and design with your system. Because of this, the **"Time factor"** that took for developing our security case reduces significantly. Another benefit is **Cost**. Developing Assurance Cases at the moment can cost a lot according to a report from Carnegie Mellon University. Then **Simplicity**. Building a dependability case can be a major challenge to those who just entered the field of Assurance Cases. However, our approach has proven to be very straightforward and therefore easy to absorb by the newbies.

We proposed the combination of security engineering knowledge and experiences with D-Case to develop strong and valid assessment security cases. This is done by integrating past experience of security breach and system development, in fact turning the security assurance cases into a system development tool. In this methodology, requirements and system goals become high-level goals in the security case tree, which is subsequently extended in a way that reflects each stage of development, later stages corresponding to lower level claims in the security case tree. Strategies for deriving sub-goals from parent goals can be based on the strategies for deriving more concrete views and models of the system under development, and should include an extensive vulnerability and risk analysis of the system view at hand. The sub-goals produced in this way at one stage of development should be regarded as requirements for the subsequent stages. For reuse, patterns of decomposition of goals/claims into sub-goals for different types of systems and security requirements might turn out to be a useful by-product.

We conducted an experiment to prove our evaluation. 4 graduate students and 3 undergraduate students of Nagoya University carried out the experiment, plus 3 network engineers whom are looking after the KISSEL system. At the end of our experiment, we find out that more than 95% of the participants agreed that our new method was very straight forward and very easy to follow in creating their own security case diagram. 90% agreed that depending on the length of the teams' discussions, the new method takes very few hours to complete once the solutions are final from the discussions. Then about the cost of the work, 99% of the participant felt that the cost of the new method if applied to all the factors shown in the experiment, should be much less than predicted before the experiment was carried out.

It's very difficult to collect previous attack reports from other similar systems. We find this quite a challenging task. On one occasion, we got a reply back from one of the system administrator we collaborated with saying that his University refuse to assist us with our request to use their network reports due to confidentiality reasons. However, some big companies like IBM for one are quite open about these kinds of reports. They even share them for free online via white papers. Also, we found out that our security cases diagram contains very sensitive information about our system. Therefore another new issue that arose after completing our work was to decide whether to save the assurance case diagrams via our system database or to store them as paper file documents.

In this paper we proposed a new approach for developing security cases. The ideas mentioned were (1) how we derived our security case diagram from complying with previous attacks reports and risk (lessons learned). (2) We shared our experiment of using our approach by applying it to our server distributed e-learning system called KISSEL. (3) Our new approach gives us the benefits in Time Efficiency, Low Cost and Simplicity. We have shown an experiment of using our method by non-experts on a web-server demo system. Currently we have preparing the feasibility experiments of our method on a few cases targeting university students and engineers. In the experiments we plan to do comparison evaluation with/without our method. Furthermore, applying our method to cyber-security issue is one of our important next goals. We would like to present the results in near future.

References

1. Ankrum, T.S., Kromholz, A.H.: Structured assurance cases: three common standards. In: Proceedings of the Ninth IEEE International Symposium on High-Assurance Systems Engineering (HASE 2005), pp. 99–108 (2005)
2. Avizienis, A., Laprie, J.-C., Randell, B.: Fundamental Concepts of Dependability. In: Proceedings of the Third Information Survivability Workshop, ISW 2000 (2000)
3. Bloomfield, R., Littlewood, B.: Multi-legged Arguments: The Impact of Diversity Upon Confidence in Dependability Arguments. In: Proceedings of 2003 International Conference on Dependable Systems and Networks, San Francisco, California. IEEE Computer Society Press (2003)
4. Jackson, D., Thomas, M., Millett, L.I. (eds.): Software for Dependable Systems: Sufficient Evidence? Committee on Certifiably Dependable Software Systems, Computer Science and Telecommunications Board, National Research Council. National Academies Press, ISBN:0-309-66738-0, http://www.nap.edu/catalog/11923.html
5. Kelly, T.P.: Arguing Safety—A Systematic Approach to Safety Case Management. DPhil Thesis, York University, Department of Computer Science Report YCST (May 1999)
6. DoD. Ministry of Defence, Defence Standard 00-56, Issue 4 (Publication Date June 01, 2007)
7. Howell, C.: Workshop on Assurance Cases: Best Practices, Possible Obstacles, and Future Opportunities. In: DSN 2004 (2004)
8. http://www.adelard.com/web/hnav/ASCE/choosingasce/cae.html
9. Bishop, P., Bloomfield, R.: A Methodology for Safety Case Development. In: Proc. of the 6th Safety-critical Systems Symposium, Birmingham, UK (February 1998)
10. Toulmin, S.: The Use of Argument. Cambridge University Press (1958)
11. Besnard, P., Hunter, A.: Elements of Argumentation. The MIT Press (2008)
12. Leveson, N.: The Use of Safety Cases in Certification and Requlation. ESD Working Paper Series. MIT, Boston (2011)
13. Kelly, T., Weaver, R.: The Goal Structuring Notation – a safety argument notation. In: Proc. of DSN 2004, Workshop on Assurance Cases (2004)
14. Jackson, D., Thomas, M., Milett, L.: Software for Dependable Systems: Sufficient evidence? National Academic Press (2007)
15. D-Case Editor (2011), http://www.dependable-os.net/tech/D-CaseEditor/
16. Matsuno, Y., Takamura, H., Ishikawa, Y.: A Dependability Case Editor with Pattern Library. In: Proc. IEEE HASE, pp. 170–171 (2010)
17. Despotou, G.: Managing the Evolution of Dependability Cases for Systems of Systems. PhD Thesis, YCST-2007-16, High Integrity Research Group, Department of Computer Science, University of York, United Kindgom (2007)
18. Weinstock, C.B., Goodenough, J.B., Hudak, J.J.: Dependability Cases. Technical Note CMU/SEI-2004-TN-016, SEI, Carnegie Mellon University (2004)

Author Index